ANNUAL PROGRESS IN CHILD PSYCHIATRY AND CHILD DEVELOPMENT

ANNUAL PROGRESS IN CHILD PSYCHIATRY AND CHILD DEVELOPMENT 1999

Edited by

MARGARET E. HERTZIG, M.D.

Professor of Psychiatry
Cornell University Medical College

and

ELLEN A. FARBER, Ph.D.

Clinical Assistant Professor of Psychology in Psychiatry
Cornell University Medical College

Psychology Press
Taylor & Francis Group

New York   London

First published by BRUNNER-MAZEL Philadelphia and London

First issued in paperback 2012

This edition published 2012 by **Psychology Press**

Psychology Press	Psychology Press
Taylor & Francis Group	Taylor & Francis Group
711 Third Avenue	27 Church Road, Hove
New York, NY 10017	East Sussex BN3 2FA

Psychology Press is an imprint of Taylor & Francis, an informa group company

ANNUAL PROGRESS IN CHILD PSYCHIATRY AND CHILD DEVELOPMENT 1999

Printed by Sheridan Books–Braun-Brunfield, Ann Arbor, MI, 2001

A CIP catalog record for this book is available from the British Library.

Library of Congress Cataloging-in-Publication Data

Available from the publisher.

ISBN: 1-58391-046-8 (Case)
ISBN 978-0-415-64586-7 (Paperback)

CONTENTS

I. DEVELOPMENTAL STUDIES 1

   1. Physical Activity Play: The Nature and Function of a
       Neglected Aspect of Play 5
      A. D. Pellegrini and Peter K. Smith

   2. Child Development and Emergent Literacy..................... 37
      Grover J. Whitehurst and Christopher J. Lonigan

   3. How Shall We Speak of Children's Personalities in Middle
       Childhood? A Preliminary Taxonomy 77
      Rebecca L. Shiner

   4. Worry in Normal Children 127
      Peter Muris, Cor Meesters, Harald Merckelbach,
      Ann Sermon, and Sandra Zwakhalen

   5. Children's Recollections of Traumatic and Nontraumatic Events .. 141
      Robyn Fivush

II. SOCIAL AND CROSS-CULTURAL ISSUES...................... 165

   6. Child-Rearing Attitudes and Behavioral Inhibition in Chinese and
       Canadian Toddlers: A Cross-Cultural Study 167
      Xinyin Chen, Kenneth H. Rubin, Guozhen Cen, Paul D. Hastings,
      Huichang Chen, and Shannon L. Stewart

   7. A Cross-National Study of Self-Evaluations and Attributions in
       Parenting: Argentina, Belgium, France, Israel, Italy,
       Japan, and the United States 187
      Marc H. Bornstein, O. Maurice Haynes, Hiroshi Azuma,
      Celia Galperin, Sharone Maital, Misako Ogino,
      Kathleen Painter, Liliana Pascual, Marie-Germaine Pechuex,
      Charles Rahn, Sueko Toda, Paola Venuti, André Vyt,
      and Barbara Wright

   8. Relationship Between Hunger and Psychosocial Functioning in
       Low-Income American Children 215
      J. Michael Murphy, Cheryl A. Wehler, Maria E. Pagano,
      Michelle Little, Ronald E. Kleinman, and Michael S. Jellinek

9. What Matters? What Does Not? Five Perspectives on the Association
Between Marital Transitions and Children's Adjustment . .   229
*E. Mavis Hetherington, Margaret Bridges, and
Glendessa M. Insabelle*

III. PEDIATRICS AND CHILD PSYCHIATRY   263
10. Attachment and Feeding Problems: A Reexamination of Nonorganic
Failure to Thrive and Attachment Insecurity   267
*Irene Chatoor, Jody Ganiban, Virginia Colin, Nancy Plummer,
and Robert J. Harmon*
11. Psychiatric Illness and Family Support in Children and Adolescents
With Diabetic Ketoacidosis: A Controlled Study   281
*Deanna S. Liss, David A. Waller, Betsy D. Kennard,
Donald McIntire, Patricia Capra, and Jacqualene Stephens*
12. Headaches and Psychopathology in Children and Adolescents   295
Helen Link Egger, Adrian Angold, and E. Jane Costello

IV. CLINICAL ISSUES   309
13. Course of Tic Severity in Tourette Syndrome: The First Two Decades   313
*James F. Leckman, Heping Zhang, Amy Vitale, Fatima Lahnin,
Kimberly Lynch, Colin Bondi, Young-Shin Kim, and
Bradley S. Peterson*
14. "Multidimensionally Impaired Disorder": Is It a Variant of
Very Early-Onset Schizophrenia?   327
*Sanjiv Kumra, Leslie K. Jacobsen, Marge Lenane,
Theodore P. Zahn, Edythe Wiggs, Javad Alaghband-Rad,
F. Xavier Castellanos, Jean A. Frazier, Kathleen McKenna,
Charles T. Gordon, Amy Smith, Susan Hamburger, and
Judith L. Rapoport*
15. A Prospective Longitudinal Study of Attachment Disorganization/
Disorientation   343
Elizabeth A. Carlson
16. Interaction of Temperamental Resistance to Control and Restrictive
Parenting in the Development of Externalizing Behavior .   377
*John E. Bates, Kenneth A. Dodge, Gregory S. Pettit and
Beth Ridge*

V. CLINICAL ISSUES: FOLLOW-THROUGH STUDIES   403
17. Longitudinal Study of Co-occurring Psychiatric Disorders and
Substance Use   407
Judith S. Brook, Patricia Cohen, and David W. Brook

18. What Happens to "Bad" Girls? A Review of the Adult Outcomes of
Antisocial Adolescent Girls 421
Kathleen A. Pajer

19. IQ Decline During Childhood and Adult Psychotic Symptoms in a
Community Sample: A 19-Year Longitudinal Study 439
William S. Kremen, Stephen L. Buka, Larry J. Seidman,
Jill M. Goldstein, Danny Koren, and Ming T. Tsuang

VI. TREATMENT ISSUES 451

20. Practitioner Review: Psychological and Educational
Treatments for Autism 453
Patricia Howlin

21. Cognitive-Behavioral Treatment of School Phobia 483
Cynthia G. Last, Cheri Hansen, and Nathalie Franco

Part I

DEVELOPMENTAL STUDIES

This section includes five papers on diverse topics in child development. The first paper is a summary of a rarely discussed topic, "Physical activity play: the nature and function of a neglected aspect of play." Most studies of play have focused on pretend play. The authors define physical activity play as "purposeless" and enjoyable, moderate to vigorous physical activity. It may be social or solitary and it may involve games with rules or symbolic activity. Although they define play as purposeless to the player, the authors contend physical activity play serves an important developmental function. They go on to describe age and gender trends in physical activity play. The paper also outlines types of physical training including rhythmic stereotypies seen in infants and exercise play seen in older children.

One type of physical activity play that has been studied more extensively than others is rough and tumble play. The functions and variations of rough and tumble play are described such as the differences between play chasing and play fighting. The authors note the overlap between symbolic and physical activity play. For example, when children chase and wrestle in the context of playing "superheroes."

The authors use ethological (observational) studies to propose functions for each of the three types of physical activity play discussed. Rhythmic stereotypies were hypothesized to improve control of motor patterns and exercise play was hypothesized to improve strength. In contrast, rough and tumble play was hypothesized to serve a more social function, namely the establishment of dominance.

The second paper by Whitehurst and Lonigan is a review of "emergent literacy." Emergent literacy is defined as "the skills, knowledge and attitudes that are developmental precursors to reading and writing." The authors distinguish emergent literacy as more developmental and continuous in nature than the reading readiness approach. The paper is worthwhile in its laying out the specific skills that are precursors to decoding and to comprehension. The two overarching categories are inside-out and outside-in skills. The inside-out skills are more important when the child is first beginning to read. The outside-in skills are more important when moving beyond the beginning reader stage to fluency and comprehension.

The **outside-in** processes include language skills, knowledge of narrative and conventions of print. The **inside-out** processes include knowledge of graphemes (letters) and phonological (sounds) and grammatical awareness. Other factors important for reading are mentioned including phonological or short-term memory. The skills from the three areas are presented along with sample measures.

The paper also describes observational and intervention studies that explored how children learn to read. Of particular interest are their descriptions of "emergent literacy environments." They describe features of both home and school that have been successful in promoting specific aspects of emerging literacy. The authors note inherent differences among socioeconomic groups in preparing children for reading. They go beyond the factors that can not be changed to describing successful interventions such as dialogic reading. This is a comprehensive paper on literacy—a critical life skill.

The third paper, by Shiner, is noteworthy for its exploration of personality development in middle childhood. Personality development research seems to skip from infancy and preschool to adolescence and adulthood. The early childhood theories typically discuss individual differences as temperament while individual differences in adults are called personality. Middle childhood (ages six to twelve) is actually the time of consolidation of personality characteristics and may be an important predictor of adult adjustment.

Shiner critiques the five major temperament and personality theories and discusses their applicability to personality development in middle childhood. In her critique of the temperament models, Shiner notes that many of the concepts applicable to infants, such as regularity of biological functions, have to be reconceptualized for older children.

Using concepts from the five most prominent childhood models as well as the adult personality literature, Shiner presents a preliminary taxonomy of personality traits for middle childhood. She proposes four higher-order factors: 1) positive emotionality-extroversion, 2) negative emotionality-neuroticism, 3) aggressiveness/prosocial tendencies and 4) constraint-conscientiousness. Multiple lower-order factors are described within these categories. This preliminary taxonomy lays the groundwork for future research to study individual differences in these traits. This paper represents a thoughtful summary of individual development in middle childhood and personality theories in general.

The fourth paper in this section by Muris and his colleagues investigates worry in middle childhood. They present normative data for 193 8- to 13-year old children from public schools in the Netherlands and Belgium. The authors provide data on the content and severity of worrying and the association between worry, trait anxiety, and depression in a non-clinical sample. The measures included the Trait Anxiety scale of the State-Trait Anxiety Scale and the Depression Questionnaire for children developed by De Wit. A Worry Scale for Children, developed by the authors, asked about specific fears. The Overanxious Disorder section of the DISC, standardized diagnostics interview, and worry interviews (asking about the content of their main intense worry) were used.

Results in this study indicated that 31% of the children reported that they never worried. Of those children who worried, at least occasionally, the most frequent worries had to do with school performance, dying and health and social contacts. There were significant associations between the worry, anxiety and depression questionnaires. Approximately six percent of the sample met clinical criteria for overanxious disorder or generalized anxiety disorder. The authors conclude that although "worry" is a fairly common phenomenon, only a small minority of children suffers from overanxious or generalized anxiety disorders. The latter are significant disorders that are fairly easy to screen for. In concluding the authors note measures that might be useful for screening school children for anxiety disorders. They also refer to the cognitive behavioral treatments that have been found most helpful.

The last paper in this section, "Children's recollections of traumatic and nontraumatic events" is relevant to the developmental and clinical literature. It provides an excellent discussion of children's memories for trauma. Approximately 25% of people are believed to experience trauma as a child. Trauma is viewed as "threats to physical and emotional integrity." Fivush describes the development of event memory. She then describes case studies of severely traumatized children. Next she reviews the experimental research on children's memories for stressful experiences. She concludes by summarizing the critical issues in the study of trauma memory.

The studies indicated that by about age three years, children could provide coherent accounts of past experiences. There were individual differences in the ability to recall and discuss events. There were also individual differences in the type of assistance adults provided in helping children to form coherent memories.

1

Physical Activity Play: The Nature and Function of a Neglected Aspect of Play

A. D. Pellegrini and Peter K. Smith

In this review, we consider the nature and possible developmental functions of physical activity play, defined as a playful context combined with a dimension of physical vigor. We distinguish 3 kinds of physical activity play, with consecutive age peaks: rhythmic stereotypies peaking in infancy, exercise play peaking during the preschool years, and rough-and-tumble play peaking in middle childhood. Gender differences (greater prevalence in males) characterize the latter 2 forms. Function is considered in terms of beneficial immediate and deferred consequences in physical, cognitive, and social domains. Whereas most theories assume that children's play has deferred benefits, we suggest that forms of physical activity play serve primarily immediate developmental functions. Rhythmic stereotypies in infancy are hypothesized to improve control of specific motor patterns. Exercise play is hypothesized to function primarily for strength and endurance training; less clear evidence exists for possible benefits for fat reduction and thermoregulation. In addition, there may be cognitive benefits of exercise play that we hypothesize to be largely incidental to its playful or physical nature. Rough-and-tumble play has a distinctive social component; we hypothesize that it serves primarily dominance functions; evidence for benefits to fighting skills or to emotional coding are more equivocal. Further research is indicated, given the potentially important implications for children's education, health, and development.

INTRODUCTION

Over the past 30 years, the study of children's play has been a popular topic of scientific inquiry (see the chapter on play in the fourth edition of the *Manual of Child Psychology*; Rubin, Fein, & Vandenberg, 1983). Pretend play is the aspect of children's play most thoroughly studied (see Fein, 1981). Indeed, the paradigmatic study of young children's play has probably been the study of children's symbolic use of play objects in a developmental progression (e.g., McCune, 1995).

Yet these analyses ignore some of the most common forms of play, as well as some basic theoretical assumptions regarding the functions of play. Children's play often has a vigorous physical component, and thus it may variously be called physical activity play, locomotor play, or exercise play. Much of children's physical activity can be seen as playful in the sense that it is minimally constrained by adult demands. Adults, however, often show some ambivalence toward children's high levels of physical activity. This ambivalence may also be reflected in the relative paucity of research on children's physical activity generally (Pellegrini & Smith, 1993; Welsh & Labbé, 1994), and on physical activity play and rough-and-tumble play in particular (Humphreys & Smith, 1984). Yet physical activity levels may be important, not only for physical development, but also perhaps for cognitive performance subsequent to physical activity, and even for aspects of social organization and social skills. Physical activity play may, in some senses, matter psychologically.

In this review, we discuss the definition of physical activity play, and age and gender trends; we then consider the evidence regarding its functional benefits.

WHAT IS PHYSICAL ACTIVITY PLAY?
GENERAL DEFINITIONAL ISSUES

Both child developmentalists and animal ethologists agree that play behavior is enjoyable, and that players, typically children or juveniles, are concerned with means over ends, and that the activity appears to be "purposeless," or to occur for its own sake (Martin & Caro, 1985; Rubin et al., 1983; Smith & Vollstedt, 1985). Physical activity play, specifically, may involve symbolic activity or games with rules; the activity may be social or solitary, but the distinguishing behavioral features are a playful context, combined with what Simons-Morton et al. (1990) describe as moderate to vigorous physical activity, such that metabolic activity is well above resting metabolic rate. Paradigm examples of physical activity play include running, climbing, chasing, and play fighting, the latter being a component of rough-and-tumble play (R & T).

The criterion of purposelessness in the definition of play seems to present a logical problem when play is also considered to be functional (Martin & Caro, 1985). How can play simultaneously serve no purpose and serve a developmental function? One way to resolve this problem is to consider play as serving minimal immediate functions during childhood, with benefits deferred until maturity. Alternatively, play may serve immediate functions about which players and others are unaware. We will hypothesize about such functions. We first consider age and gender trends, because these may indicate different types of physical activity play that may have different functional significance (Byers & Walker, 1995).

AGE AND GENDER TRENDS IN PHYSICAL ACTIVITY PLAY

Studies relevant to age and gender trends for physical activity play are presented in Table A1 of the Appendix.

Age Trends

Play generally follows an inverted-U developmental course: It begins in early infancy, peaks during childhood, then declines during adolescence, and all but disappears by adulthood (Byers & Walker, 1995; Fagen, 1981; Rubin et al., 1983). However, the trends in physical activity play in humans appear to show three successive peaks, reflecting three types of play, probably with different functions. We designate these as (1) rhythmic stereotypies, (2) exercise play, and (3) R & T. We discuss each in turn.

Rhythmic stereotypies. Although most studies in the infancy literature relate to the ontogeny of symbolic play with parents (e.g., Bornstein & Tamis-LeMonda, 1995) and sensori-motor exploration/play (e.g., Ruff & Saltarelli, 1993), there is limited evidence documenting infants' physical activity play. Thelen's (1979, 1980) longitudinal study of infants' "rhythmical stereotypies" during the first year of life provides basic and important descriptive information. Rhythmical stereotypic behaviors are similar to our definition of physical activity play to the extent that they are gross motor movements, "and it is difficult to ascribe goal or purpose to those movements" (Thelen, 1979, p. 699); examples include body rocking and foot kicking. The onset of these behaviors is probably controlled by general neuromuscular maturation.

Stereotypic behaviors tend to peak during the midpoint of the first year of life; at 6 months, some infants spend as much as 40% of a 1 hr observational period in stereotypic behavior (Thelen, 1980). After this point, the behaviors gradually disappear from normal children's behavioral repertoires (Thelen, 1979). Across the first year of life, infants spend 5.2% of their time in stereotypic behaviors (Thelen, 1980). Some early parent-infant interactions probably provide other physical play opportunities. For example, Roopnarine, Hooper, Ahmeduzzaman, and Pollack's (1993) examination of play between parents and 1-year-old infants in India suggests that play, such as tossing the infant in the air and bouncing on the knee (but also including R & T), accounted for 13% of all play, whereas object play accounted for 80%. Similarly low rates of American parent-infant physical play (or vestibular stimulation) were reported by Thelen (1980).

Exercise play. By exercise play we mean gross locomotor movements in the context of play. The distinguishing feature of this play is its physical vigor; it may or may not be social, but the distinctively specialized social form of R & T is discussed later.

Exercise play in this sense can start at the end of the first year. It can be solitary or with parents or peers. In fact, much of the research on parent-infant play does not distinguish between exercise play and R & T, but appears to be describing "rough physical play" (Carson, Burks, & Parke, 1993; Roopnarine et al., 1993), which we consider under R & T later. Low rates of American parent-infant physical play have been reported by MacDonald and Parke (1986), with rates peaking at around 4 years of age. A few cases of infant exercise play without parents have been reported. Konner (1972), for example, observed that a Botswana foraging group encouraged infants to chase after and catch large insects.

As we move to the preschool period, greater incidences of exercise play are reported. As was the case in infancy, most of the peer play literature for this period focuses on pretend play, not physical activity play. Where the latter is reported, it is often in the form of R & T, which tends to co-occur with pretend during this period (Pellegrini & Perlmutter, 1987; Smith, 1973; Smith & Connolly, 1980). In a few studies, "gross motor" play other than R & T is reported, sometimes occurring alone, sometimes with peers (rather than with parents).

Exercise play seems to increase from the toddler to preschool period and then declines during the primary school years, with a likely peak at around 4 to 5 years (Eaton & Yu, 1989; Routh, Schroeder, & O'Tuama, 1974). Specifically, for 2-year-olds, Rosenthal (1994) reports that it accounts for about 7% of behavior observed in day-care settings. For children 2 to 4 years of age, Field (1994) reports physical activity play accounting for 10% of all day-care behavior. Similarly, Bloch's (1989) observational study in Senegal found that gross motor activities accounted for 11% and 13% of children's play in the home at 2 to 4 years of age and 5 to 6 years of age, respectively.

In two ethological studies in British nursery schools, using a variety of samples, McGrew (1972) and Smith and Connolly (1980) observed children's behavior at a micro-analytical level. In McGrew's sample, with a mean age of 49.2 months, approximately 20% of children's activity was physically vigorous, such as run, flee, wrestle, chase, jump, push and pull, lift, and climb. Similarly, in Smith and Connolly's (1980) sample, with a mean age of 43.3 months, vigorous activities, such as run, chase, and climb (but also including R & T), accounted for 21% of their behavior.

As children move into primary school, a decline in physical activity is witnessed. For children aged 6 to 10 years, "exercise play" accounted for only 13% of all outdoor behavior observed during school recess periods (Pellegrini, 1990). This relative decrease in play might be underestimated, however, because the primary school observations occurred on school playgrounds, rather than in classrooms, unlike most studies of preschoolers; the relative spatial density of classrooms, compared to playgrounds, inhibits gross motor activity (Smith & Connolly, 1980).

It will be important for our later argument to demonstrate that during the preschool/ primary school years children engage in substantial amounts of exercise play. Blatchford (1996) described the general levels of English primary school children's activity on the school playground and found that most (60% of the children) are engaged in some form of physically active play or games during their daily break times, which lasted between 65 and 75 min.

What about physical activity outside the school context? Simons-Morton and colleagues (1990) studied children aged 9 and 10 years, using children's self-reported frequency of moderate to vigorous physical activity (MVPA) over 3 days. Major sources of MVPA were running, walking fast, games and sports, and cycling. MVPAs generally were slightly more common before or after school (2.3/day) than during school (1.6/day). Throughout the whole day, most children engaged in one or two long (>10 min) MVPAs/day.

In general, then, exercise play is quite common in early/middle childhood, and appears to peak in the preschool and early primary grades, although more evidence is certainly needed to clarify exactly when the age peak occurs.

Rough-and-tumble play. Rough-and-tumble play refers to vigorous behaviors such as wrestling, grappling, kicking, and tumbling that would appear to be aggressive except for the playful context; chasing is sometimes included within this definition, but here we restrict it to the former contact behaviors. Whereas exercise play may or may not be social, R & T is necessarily so.

The earliest cases of children's R & T play are supported by a parent, often the father in the case of rough physical play (Carson et al., 1993; Roopnarine et al., 1993). As reviewed earlier, rates of such play are low. At around 4 years of age, R & T accounts for about 8% of observed parent-child behavior (Jacklin, DiPietro, & Maccoby, 1984).

Rough-and-tumble play with peers is more thoroughly documented; its frequency follows an inverted-U developmental curve. For preschool children, it accounts for approximately

3%–5% of play behavior (Pellegrini, 1984); at 6 to 10 years, it accounts for 7%–8% of recess behavior (Boulton, 1992; Pellegrini, 1988); and during the period from 7 to 11 years, for about 10% (Humphreys & Smith, 1987). At 11 to 13 years it falls to 5% (Boulton, 1992; Pellegrini, 1995a), and there is a further decrease to only 3% at 14 years (Pellegrini, 1995b).

These studies used similar definitions and methodologies, so that this age curve can be advanced with reasonable confidence. Rough-and-tumble play appears to increase through the preschool and primary years and peak in the later primary years, around 8 to 10 years, just prior to early adolescence; this appears to be a distinctively later peak than that for exercise play, provisionally described as being at 4–5 years.

Summary of age trends. In summary, forms of physical activity play are quite common in childhood. In primary schools, most children engage in active play during their daily break times; further, levels of physical activity play are moderate for most children when they are out of school. An analysis of age trends suggests three successive inverted-U curves describing three different forms of physical activity play. Rhythmic stereotypies peak in infancy, at around 6 months of age; exercise play peaks during the preschool years, accounting for up to 20% of observed school recess behavior, and declines during the primary school years, accounting for about 13% of observed behavior. Rough-and-tumble increases during the late preschool and early primary school years, accounting for about 5% of observed recess behavior, peaks in later primary years at around 10%, and then declines during early adolescence, accounting for less than 5% of play. We postulate that these successive age peaks reflect different forms of play with different functions.

Gender Differences

Rhythmic stereotypies. No sex differences are reported in the incidence of rhythmic stereo-typies. Thelen (1980) compared rates for 10 male and 10 female infants; these averaged 35.1 and 34.4 bouts per hour, respectively, a very small and nonsignificant difference.

Exercise play. Males tend to engage in exercise play at higher rates than females. Eaton and Enns's (1986) meta-analysis of 90 studies of gender differences in motor activity level reported a significant difference in favor of males, with the effect size tending to increase from infancy to mid-adolescence. Part of this gender difference may be due to differential maturation rates. Eaton and Yu (1989) found that relative maturity (percent of estimated adult height attained) interacted with gender, being negatively related to activity level, with girls being both less active and more physically mature than boys.

In these studies, R & T was probably included with exercise play; although R & T takes up a smaller percentage of time through the early primary years (see discussion of age trends), some of the gender difference in exercise play may be attributable to the well-documented gender difference in R & T (next section); it will be important for future research to delineate gender differences with an unconfounded measure of exercise play.

Rough-and-tumble play. Males exceed females in frequency of R & T in virtually all cultures that have been examined (DiPietro, 1981; Humphreys & Smith, 1984) and also among many other mammalian species (Meaney, Stewart, & Beatty, 1985; Smith, 1982). This is true for parent-child rough play (Carson et al., 1993; Roopnarine et al., 1993) and for peer play (Humphreys & Smith, 1984; Pellegrini, 1989a); this gender difference is more marked for contact R & T than for play chasing (Smith & Connolly, 1980).

Differences in boys' and girls' initiation of and response to R & T may be implicated in these gender differences. Both the animal and child literatures often show males' higher rates of initiation of R & T bouts and females' higher withdrawal from bouts (Fabes, 1994; Meaney et al., 1985; Pellis, Field, Smith, & Pellis, 1996). Females may withdraw from R & T initiations as they react differently from males to tactile stimulation of the sort that characterizes R & T (Meaney et al., 1985; Pellis et al., 1996). The physical vigor and roughness typical of boys' play groups seem to be important factors for girls segregating themselves from boys' play groups (Fabes, 1994; Maccoby, 1986).

Causal factors in gender differences. Gender differences appear to be absent in rhythmical stereotypies, but appreciable for both exercise play and R & T. Hypotheses about the functions of play must take account of such gender differences and the causation of such differences.

Hormonal influences on play have been implicated in gender differences in R & T. Hormonal influences typically center around the effects of endogenous and exogenous androgens on neural organization and behavior (Meaney et al., 1985). Normal exposure to androgens during fetal development predisposes boys, compared to girls, toward physical activity and R & T. Excessive amounts of these male hormones are hypothesized to "masculinize" females' play (Collaer & Hines, 1995). The experimental literature involving mice, rats, hamsters, and monkeys supports the androgenization hypothesis (Collaer & Hines, 1995; Quadagno, Briscoe, & Quadagno, 1977). For obvious ethical reasons, the effects of androgens on human behavior can only be studied through natural experiments, where fetuses receive abnormally high levels of these male hormones because of genetic defects (e.g., Congenital Adrenal Hyperplasia [CAH]) or difficulties during pregnancy (e.g., where mothers take synthetic progestins).

Most human studies of CAH support the androgenization hypothesis. These studies typically have used questionnaire methodology to ask parents or children about their preferences for various activities, including physically active sports and R & T. The frequently cited research of Money and colleagues (e.g., Money & Ehrhardt, 1972) has shown that androgenized girls are more "tomboyish": They prefer male activities more than do nonandrogenized girls. Using observations of toy preferences in CAH children compared to controls, Berenbaum and Snyder (1995) found that CAH girls showed greater preference for boys' toys and activities.

Although Hines and Kaufman (1994) found no increase of R & T in CAH girls, the children were observed for only one 12 min session in an experimental room of undisclosed size—conditions that may have inhibited children's exhibition of normal behavior, including R & T.

Socialization interacts with hormonal events to affect gender differences (Ehrhardt, 1984; Fabes, 1994; Maccoby, 1986; Meaney et al., 1985; Quadagno et al., 1977). Beginning with interactions with their parents, boys and girls are socialized into different, and often segregated, worlds that tend to reinforce these gender differences (Maccoby, 1986; Meaney et al., 1985). For example, fathers spend more time with their sons than with their daughters (Parke & Suomi, 1981), and when with their sons, they engage in physically vigorous play (Carson et al., 1993; MacDonald, 1993; MacDonald & Parke, 1986). That girls are more closely supervised by parents and teachers (Fagot, 1974, 1994) may further inhibit their physically vigorous behavior (Maccoby, 1986).

FUNCTIONS OF PHYSICAL ACTIVITY PLAY

In his discussion of ways in which behavior can be explained, Tinbergen (1963) described the "Four Whys" of behavior as being immediate causation, developmental history, immediate function, and ultimate function in terms of evolutionary history. For the purposes of this article, we do not consider function in its "ultimate" sense (Hinde, 1980, p. 102), that is, in terms of survival or reproductive success over succeeding generations. To directly address ultimate function, a more wide-ranging analysis would be necessary, to an extent that would necessarily be very speculative given the limited evidence available. Instead, we consider function in terms of the "beneficial consequences" of the behavior to the individual (Hinde, 1980). These consequences can be either immediate or deferred.

For almost a century, the dominant view in child development (Groos, 1998, 1901) has been that play has deferred benefits. That is, during the period of extended childhood, children engage in play to learn and practice those skills necessary to be functioning adult members of society. This assumption is based on the long-held emphasis among child developmentalists on developmental continuity (Bateson, 1981; Gomendio, 1988; Kagan, 1971). Bateson's (1976) metaphor for the deferred-benefit view of play is "scaffolding": Play functions in skill assembly, and then is disassembled when the skill is mastered.

Alternatively, play may be viewed not as an incomplete or imperfect version of adult behavior, but as having immediate benefits during childhood. This "metamorphic" (Bateson, 1976) view posits that play and its consequences are unique to the niche of childhood, and that later benefits are not necessary for its explanation (Bjorklund & Green, 1992; Gomendio, 1988; Pellegrini, Horvat, & Huberty, 1998). This view is consistent with recent discussions suggesting that play occurs at specific periods during which development may be modified (Byers & Walker, 1995; Thelen, 1979). Accordingly, the previously discussed age distribution of physical activity play may be useful in evaluating functional hypotheses.

Different forms and dimensions of physical activity play may serve specific developmental functions (Gomendio, 1988; Smith, 1982). We discuss the function(s) of physical activity play, considering the age trends and gender differences summarized above. We also consider both the dimension of physical activity itself and the dimension of social participation that distinguishes exercise play from R & T. Although some authors list up to 30 possible functions for play (Baldwin & Baldwin, 1977), certain functions (physical training, cognitive, and social) are most commonly advanced. Appendix Table A2 summarizes the extant studies, by function.

As a first step in establishing the functional importance of physical activity play during childhood, we present evidence from a small number of play-deprivation studies, either natural or experimental. These suggest that a lack of opportunity to engage in physical activity play leads to compensation later, concluding that play is of functional benefit.

In Thelen's (1980) study of rhythmic stereotypies in the first year of life, infants who engaged in a lot of these spontaneous physical activities when given the opportunity were those observed to receive less vestibular stimulation from caregivers and those who were more often restricted in natural movements (e.g., placed in infant seats). Thelen (1980, p. 148) concluded that "deprivation of active as well as passive movement may . . . promote stereotypy."

Three sets of field experiments have looked at deprivation of physical activity play during childhood; in these, although exercise play was the primary outcome variable, R & T would also have been included.

Smith and Hagan (1980) studied English preschool children (3–4 years) who were deprived of vigorous exercise by varying the amount of time they remained in their classrooms engaged in sedentary seatwork. After deprivation periods, they played outdoors. On the long, compared to short, deprivation days, children's play was more vigorous in the immediate postdeprivation period.

Utilizing a similar deprivation paradigm with American primary school children (5–9 years), Pellegrini and colleagues (Pellegrini & Davis, 1993; Pellegrini, Huberty, & Jones, 1995) replicated Smith and Hagan's results: Long, compared to short, deprivation periods resulted in higher levels of physical activity. Deprivation, however, interacted with gender of the child; boys, compared to girls, were especially active after long deprivation.

These results support the following generalization: If children are deprived of opportunities for physical activity play, they will, when given the opportunity to play, engage in more intense and sustained bouts of physical activity play than they would have done if not so deprived. This generalization, in turn, suggests that physical activity play is serving some developmental function(s) such that a lack of it leads to compensation.

In the remainder of this section, we first consider physical training (and related) functions of rhythmical stereotypies and of exercise play. We then examine possible cognitive functions of exercise play. We assume that any physical training functions and cognitive functions of exercise play would also apply to R & T, which has some of the same physical components. We then examine different hypotheses for social functions for R & T only, because this is the form of physical activity play that is characteristically and necessarily social.

Physical Training

Both rhythmic stereotypies and exercise play seem to have physical training benefits. *Rhythmic stereotypies.* Activities such as waving the arms and kicking peak at around 6 months of age. The onset of these actions is probably controlled by general maturational processes, which correspond to neuromuscular maturation (Field, Ting, & Shuman, 1979). Thelen (1979), in her naturalistic longitudinal study of infants' rhythmic stereotypies, suggests that this is a sensitive period in neuromuscular development, similar to the argument of Byers and Walker (1995). Her functional inferences about physical activities are based on the systematic onset of specific behaviors and their co-occurrence with milestones of motor development. Thelen found that the individual behaviors appeared during a restricted period; onset was not randomly distributed. This pattern, she argued, is indicative of neuromuscular maturation. To support this claim further, she presented significant correlations between the age of onset of stereotypic groups (e.g., legs, arms, hands and knees) and the age of passing items from the Bayley Scales of Infant Development reflecting neuromuscular, not cognitive, development. Rhythmic movements of given body systems appear to increase just before the infant achieves voluntary control of that system.

We postulate that infants' rhythmic stereotypies are primarily functional for the immediate benefits of improving control of specific motor patterns. The correspondence between the ages at which these movements occur and cerebral development suggests that, initially, rhythmic stereotypies may be manifestations of immature sensorimotor integration. Play may modify or eliminate irrelevant synapse formations; with maturation, these patterns are used in more goal-directed ways (Byers & Walker, 1995; Thelen, 1979). Such a hypothesis is consistent with the lack of gender differences in these behaviors, because there is no reason to suppose that control of motor patterns at this very basic level of generality is more important for boys than for girls.

Exercise play. With the onset of locomotion, another developmental course may begin, as evidenced by the correspondence between exercise play and muscle differentiation, strength, and endurance. Brownlee (1954) was the first to propose that animal play was related to juvenile muscle development. Fagen (1976) extended this argument by proposing deferred benefits of exercise play for motor training, specifically, muscle strength, general cardiopulmonary functioning, and metabolic capacity. He suggested that the forms of exercise play, often involving varied, interrupted, and repeated use of muscle groups, as well as whole-body activities, would be well suited to these deferred benefits. Byers and Walker (1995), in a thorough review of the animal play and motor training literatures, evaluated the issue of immediate or deferred benefits of exercise play for three aspects of motor training: endurance, strength, and skill and economy of movement. They suggest that exercise play may improve skill and economy of movement due to the effects of exercise on muscle fiber differentiation and cerebellar synaptogenesis. They present developmental data from house mice, rats, cats, and giraffes and conclude that physical activity in the juvenile period, beginning in the early postnatal period and declining at mid-lactation, is a sensitive period in the development of these functions. Exercise play during this period has a lasting effect on subsequent economy and skill of movement.

In human children, exercise play may help shape the muscle fibers used in later physically vigorous activities. This could improve the economy and skill of movement along the lines suggested by Byers and Walker in other species, although we know of no direct evidence for this. However, the evidence suggests that endurance and strength may be developed through sustained exercise bouts. The age course of exercise play also corresponds to the growth of arm and leg muscles and bones during the preschool period (Tanner, 1970). Exercise play during the school years and beyond might continue to benefit muscle and bone remodeling and strength and endurance training; physiological effects have been observed into adulthood in numerous species (Byers & Walker, 1995).

Byers and Walker (1995, p. 29) were skeptical that exercise play functions to support strength or endurance. They concluded that "in many species, it is unlikely that play is a form of endurance or strength training because play bouts are too brief to prompt such benefits of exercise." They suggested that children would need to engage in daily bouts of exercise play, lasting 1 hr, 4 to 5 days per week, to increase endurance significantly. However, based on previous data from research on preschool and primary school children's playtime and activities out of school, we postulate that children at these ages may well engage in exercise play at levels meeting these criteria. Ethological preschool studies discussed above show that 20% of children's behavior during free-play periods, usually lasting the whole morning, was classified as vigorous (McGrew, 1972; Smith & Connolly, 1980). Although some primary school children's play opportunities may be more limited, due to school regimens, their recess periods, typically accounting for 20–60 min/day in American schools and 65–75 min/day in English primary schools (Blatchford, 1996), are also characterized by exercise play (Blatchford, 1996; Pellegrini, 1990). These activities are supplemented by activities in other contexts, as children usually engage in more than two physically vigorous activities daily outside of school (Simons-Morton et al., 1990).

Additional evidence for the role of physical activity play and endurance training comes from comparisons of athletes and nonathletes. Although we recognize the limitations of these comparisons for making functional inferences, they do provide some evidence in a very restricted literature. This evidence supports the hypothesis that children who habitually engage in vigorous games and sports show immediate benefits in terms of being fitter than children who do not. Smoll and Schutz (1985) studied 3,000 students in British Columbia aged 9, 13, and 17 years. Athletes emerged as significantly fitter than nonathletes on all physical fitness tests. This was true for both boys and girls. Differences between athletes and nonathletes were small at 9 years, but increased substantially by 13 and 17 years. This would be consistent with physical training effects of such participation, although other explanations—such as selective participation and dropout—are also possible.

Relatedly, Lussier and Buskirk (1977) examined the effects of a 12 week endurance training program (distance running) on 8- to 12-year-old boys and girls. Training decreased heart rate during submaximal workloads and increased maximum oxygen uptake. Other studies of endurance training have had positive immediate results, and reviews (e.g., Rowland, 1985; Simons-Morton, O'Hara, Simons-Morton, & Parcel, 1987) concur in concluding that regular, high-intensity training can improve cardiorespiratory functioning.

The evidence presented thus far suggests that children are given opportunities for exercise play that are probably adequate for endurance training; but before firm conclusions are made, even for the preschool and primary school periods, more research is needed to document the intensity and duration of exercise play. Further, we do not know, beyond the preschool period, the extent to which vigorous physical activities are playful, per se, or not. This remains an important task for future research.

In summary, exercise play, in the preschool years especially, seems sufficiently frequent that it can serve an immediate function for endurance and strength training. It may also improve skill and economy of movement, although specific evidence for this is lacking. This hypothesized set of functions is consistent with the age curve for exercise play (Tanner, 1970). More intriguing is its relation to the gender difference observed. Strength training at least would be more important for males in the "environment of evolutionary adaptedness" for fighting and hunting skills (e.g., Boulton & Smith, 1992); however, it could also be argued that endurance training is equally or more important for females (for gathering activities). Although very speculative at present, such hypotheses could lead to more differentiated predictions concerning gender differences in types of exercise play, analogous to Silverman and Eals's (1992) differentiation of types of spatial ability in relation to gender differences.

Two other functional hypotheses regarding the physical component of exercise play can be taken from the animal literature; these are the fat-reduction hypothesis and the thermoregulation hypothesis.

Initial studies of physical activity play in children were theoretically framed in variants of Spencer's (1898) Surplus Energy theory, in which such play was seen as a way of dissipating energy surplus to bodily requirements. Although little logical or empirical support currently exists for this theory (Burghardt, 1984, 1988; Smith, 1982; Smith & Hagan, 1980), Barber (1991) develops a variant of the argument. He suggests that energy is not usually in short supply for young mammals, and that play prevents obesity by ensuring that "surplus" energy is not stored as unnecessary fat. In particular, some young animals may need to consume large amounts of food to get enough protein, and play can "burn off" the excess requirements. In addition, play, by generating heat, may provide defense against cold exposure.

These postulated functions could be applied to human children as well as to other young mammals. The childhood period, which involves high rates and levels of physical activity play, also corresponds negatively to gains in fat (Tanner, 1970, p. 86). That is, after 9 months of age, when play involving locomotion is increasing, fat gain has a negative velocity until 6 to 8 years of age. Although these age trends are consistent with Barber's hypothesis applied to human children, gender differences are not; there seems no reason to suppose that fat reduction should be more important for boys in the preschool years.

The vigorous dimension of exercise play may also serve an immediate function in relation to thermoregulation—the ability of individuals to regulate their body temperatures (Burghardt, 1988). According to this hypothesis, children would engage in exercise play, which expends stored caloric energy, to raise their body temperature when the ambient temperature is low (Barber, 1991). The empirical record provides some support for this claim. Studies of outdoor play have found that exercise play is increased by cool ambient temperatures for preschool (Smith & Hagan, 1980) and primary school children (Pellegrini et al., 1995), and low levels of exercise play are observed in tropical climates (Cullumbine, 1950). Whereas exercise play might be used by children to raise body temperature, nonplayful physical activity is another way in which human beings of all ages (and other mammals; Barber, 1991) can raise their body temperatures in cold climates. Therefore, these benefits are not limited to childhood. In addition, this hypothesis does not explain the specific age course of exercise play, nor does it explain the gender difference found. We hypothesize that thermoregulation is an incidental benefit of exercise play, and that thermoregulation, when important, can also be achieved by other means so far as humans are concerned.

In summary, we postulate that exercise play functions primarily to develop physical strength, endurance, and economy of movement; there is some evidence to support the fat-reduction theory; and thermoregulation is postulated to be an incidental benefit of exercise play. We next examine possible cognitive functions for exercise play.

Cognitive Performance and Exercise Play

Less obvious than the likely benefits of exercise play for physical development are possible effects on psychological, and especially cognitive, factors. Here we review whether engaging in exercise play has proximal consequences for cognitive performance. Effects on cognitive tasks might be expected from several theoretical viewpoints; however, these theories link any cognitive benefits to outcomes one step removed from exercise play per se, namely, arousal, breaks from cognitive tasks, and sense of mastery or well-being.

First, exercise play can lead to heightened arousal, which might influence performance following the inverted-U hypothesis (Tomporowski & Ellis, 1986). That is, moderate levels of arousal lead to better performance than do higher or lower levels. Alternatively, increased arousal may lead to a narrowing of attention to core task components (Easterbrook, 1959).

Second, exercise play might, by breaking up cognitive tasks, provide spaced or distributed practice rather than massed practice. In another version of this approach, stemming from the cognitive immaturity hypothesis, the specifically playful nature of the break could be considered important. Relatedly, effects on performance, possibly mediated by breaks and enhanced attention, might be dependent upon enhanced feelings of mastery, or of well-being, after exercise play.

Unfortunately, much of the available research on exercise and cognitive performance is on adults. Tomporowski and Ellis (1986) provided a comprehensive review of 27 such studies directly linking exercise intervention—only some of which can be defined as exercise play— to cognitive performance. They considered effects of different types of exercise (short or long duration; anaerobic or aerobic) on cognitive tasks given during and/or after the exercise.

The pattern of findings is conflicting. The only consistent trends emerged from studies of brief, high-intensity anaerobic exercise (hand dynamometer, or weight-pulling); here, moderate levels of muscular exertion usually improved cognitive task performance assessed during the exercise (e.g., participants would grip a hand dynamometer in each hand and recall nonsense syllables). This generally inconclusive pattern of findings may be due both to inconsistencies across studies and to confounding factors, such as different levels of participants' motivation to participate or different initial levels of physical fitness.

Although information on children is limited, a large-scale study of the benefits of guided physical activity (physical education classes) on children's school performance was conducted by Shephard and colleagues (1983; Vollé et al., 1982). As part of the Trois Rivieres project in Canada, entire primary school classrooms (grades 2–6) received an additional 5 hr of physical education per week; control classrooms received no physical education. Teachers apparently were aware of children's condition assignments, but the influence of teacher bias was minimized by the administration of independent, province-wide examinations. The academic performance of children in the experimental group was superior to that of the control children. The authors suggest that the benefits shown in this project may have been due either to arousal caused by the enhanced exercise or by shortening of class work time (and hence "spaced practice") by inserting physical education classes (Shephard, 1983).

The latter interpretation is consistent with Stevenson and Lee's interpretation (1990) of achievement in Japanese, Taiwanese, and American schools. They suggested that the frequent breaks between periods of intense work in Japanese schools (usually 10 min every hour) maximize children's cognitive performance. That children's task vigilance increases when the time spent on the task is distributed, rather than massed, is a consistent finding in the animal and human learning literatures (Dempster, 1988). The massed versus distributed practice literature consistently shows few differences across age from preschool to old age (Dempster, 1988). Individual differences in children, such as "distractibility" or "activity" levels, may mediate the effectiveness of distributed practice regimens, however, and should be addressed in future research.

It thus remains questionable whether it is exercise play per se, rather than just a break from sustained classroom work, that is responsible for any increased cognitive performance. In a series of experiments with primary school children, Pellegrini and colleagues (1995) examined the relation between the level of physical activity in exercise play on the school playground during recess and subsequent attention to standardized classroom tasks. They found no relation between post-recess attention and levels of physical activity in recess exercise play, as measured behaviorally by an indicator of caloric expenditure ranging from a resting state to a highly vigorous state. Attention to standardized tasks after recess, however, was higher than before recess. They concluded that the break between tasks, not physical activity in exercise play per se, was responsible for the increased attention. From this viewpoint, any break that provided an activity different from the classroom activities could serve this function.

The Cognitive Immaturity Hypothesis

An adaptation of the cognitive immaturity hypothesis (Bjorklund & Green, 1992; Pellegrini & Bjorklund, 1997) would suggest that not only is spaced or distributed practice important for attention and cognitive performance, but that the nature of the intervening break period is crucial; and, specifically, that activity of a playful nature might be important. This hypothesis holds that immaturity is not just something to overcome, but that children's immature nervous systems may be adapted to deal effectively with the cognitive demands they face in their daily lives at those particular developmental periods. Specifically, young children have difficulty keeping extraneous information from entering short-term memory store. As a result, their working memories are often cluttered with irrelevant information, leaving less mental capacity for task-relevant information or for the execution of cognitive strategies. Younger children may require a greater change in activity or stimulus materials before they experience a release from interference (Bjorklund, 1978); hence, a shorter attention span in childhood, and an inclination to play, may have adaptive value.

From this perspective, there would be a general increase in interference when children perform a series of cognitive tasks, regardless of the nature of those tasks. Although one would predict, from a massed versus distributed practice perspective, that changing from one type of cognitive activity to another would yield some attentional benefit, children, especially young children, may experience a continued buildup of interference with repeated performance of even very different cognitive/academic tasks, all of which require concentration; thus, children may experience greater benefit from a drastic change in activity, such as is afforded by exercise play at recess.

Exercise play could be beneficial in this way, both because it is nonacademic and also because it is self-motivated, playful, and associated with enjoyment, self-efficacy, and mastery. The cognitive immaturity hypothesis (Bjorklund, in press; Bjorklund & Green, 1992), as well as other theories of play (Pellis & Pellis, in press; Piaget, 1962; Vygotsky, 1978), postulate that children's play is associated with a sense of mastery and well-being, and that this has cognitive implications.

On this viewpoint, the playful nature of exercise play would be important for its attentional benefits in providing a break in academic, teacher-led cognitive tasks; especially for preschool and young elementary school children, such a function is consistent with the age distribution of exercise play. Once again, however, a gender difference would not be predicted.

In summary, evidence for the direct role of exercise play in cognitive performance is incomplete. It does not seem likely that any such benefits are a primary function of exercise play. They do not explain the gender difference observed. In addition, the organized massed cognitive practice of schooling is a recent cultural invention, and therefore the complementary benefits of spaced practice provided by exercise play—even if specifically related to its playful nature, as the cognitive immaturity hypothesis predicts—would also be recent in human history. We hypothesize that the cognitive benefits associated with exercise play are in fact incidental or serendipitous, due to the fact that it provides a playful break from demanding tasks.

Thus far we have considered the benefits of the physical component of exercise play, irrespective of its social nature. However, children often engage in physical activity play with partners; and rough-and-tumble play (play fighting, wrestling) is a specialized form of physical activity play with a distinctive age curve, suggesting that it has its own functions. We propose that such functions will be primarily social, because purely physical or cognitive functions of the kind reviewed earlier could be provided by exercise play generally and may not require the specific forms of R & T observed. We also recognize, as noted above, the possibility that R & T may have motor training benefits.

Social Functions and Rough-and-Tumble Play

The distinct functional significance of R & T is suggested by two arguments. The first is the relative and peak frequencies with which it is observed during childhood. Rough-and-tumble play peaks later than exercise play, during the middle childhood period, when it accounts for about 10% of free-play behavior; it then declines in adolescence, accounting for less than 5%. This peak period co-occurs with children's establishing social status in peer groups (Waters & Sroufe, 1983).

The second is an argument by design. Rough-and-tumble play is a distinctive form of behavior. It is superficially similar to real fighting; however, it is different in many respects and should be regarded as a separate construct (Pellis & Pellis, in press). A number of distinguishing criteria have been identified by observational and ethological research (Smith, 1989); in addition, young children from a variety of nations also consider then to be distinct (Boulton, 1993; Costabile et al., 1991; Pellegrini, 1989b). That R & T and aggression are independent systems during childhood also has support from behavioral observations of children from numerous cultures showing that R & T, at least before adolescence, is not correlated with, and does not escalate to, aggression for most children (Blurton Jones, 1972; Fry, 1987; Pellegrini, 1988). Finally, the endocrinological and neural controls for fighting and for R & T appear to be different in many mammalian species (Meaney et al., 1985). We review here evidence relating R & T to fighting skills, to dominance functions, and to skills of emotional encoding and decoding.

R & T and fighting skills. The most traditional view in the animal and human literature (Smith, 1982; Symons, 1978) is that R & T functions to provide safe practice for fighting (and possibly hunting) skills that will be useful in later life. This hypothesis would be consistent with the strong gender difference observed, if one assumes that fighting and hunting skills were and are more characteristically male activities (Boulton & Smith, 1992). It does not, however, predict the age curve for R & T, because "safe" practice of such skills might be especially important in adolescence, when R & T declines. Also, there is little or no direct evidence linking R & T to fighting or hunting skills, in either the animal or human literature. Finally, this hypothesis does not predict the age changes in "cheating" observed in human R & T. Players "cheat" when they violate the rules of play by manipulating the nonserious tenor of the activity for their own, exploitive ends. We do not dismiss this argument—indeed, we suspect that it may be a phylogenetically prior function with some remaining relevance for younger children. However, we turn to the argument for dominance functions of R & T, which have not received the same attention but which may yield new insights in the case of human R & T.

R & T and dominance relationships. Dominance is defined as a dyadic, affiliative relationship between individuals, not in terms of one's aggressiveness (Hinde, 1974). Dominance hierarchies are generally unique to specific groups and ecologies, the implication being that individuals might have different dominance status in different groups and ecologies (deWaal, 1985; Hartup, 1983; Strayer, 1980). Although explicable in terms of advantage to dominant individuals, dominance hierarchies also mediate group members' access to valued resources and reduce intragroup aggression in many situations (Dunbar, 1988).

We postulate that R & T may serve a social function in peer groups, for boys especially, by assisting in the establishing and maintaining of dominance relationships. The idea that R & T is related to establishing and maintaining dominance status is consistent with arguments from design. Males often use quasi-agonistic displays (e.g., soft or no-contact kicks and punches, light pushes) in the service of dominance. Very similar behaviors are also displayed in R & T (Blurton Jones, 1972), but these behaviors are embedded in a nonserious context: Kicks and punches do not make contact, and if they do they are soft; players are smiling; and they often handicap themselves (e.g., let the player on the bottom of a pile get on top).

Because self-handicapping seems to occur in the R & T of both nonhuman primates and children, Symons (1978) was critical of the hypothesis that R & T is related to dominance. However, subsequent findings counter this argument in two ways. First, children can often evaluate the strength of others from R & T bouts, despite self-handicapping and restraint. Second, in some youngsters, especially by adolescence, it now appears that subtle or not so subtle forms of "cheating" may occur, demonstrating clearly to opponents and to onlookers that one participant is in fact stronger (Neill, 1976; Pellegrini, 1995b; Smith & Boulton, 1990). In fewer cases, youngsters initiating R & T turn it into aggression (Pellegrini, 1988, 1995b).

A dominance function is also consistent with the gender differences in R & T. Children establish and maintain dominance in different ways. Girls use primarily verbal rather than physical means to gain and keep resources (Charlesworth & Dzur, 1987). Boys, on the other hand, use a variety of skills, some of which are related to physical prowess, to regulate access to resources (e.g., struggling over access to a toy). Physical prowess, or toughness, when used in conjunction with more affiliative skills is an important dimension of boys' peer group status (Strayer, 1980), popularity (Pellegrini, 1995b; Vaughn & Waters, 1981), and social leadership (Hartup, 1983).

Age trends in R & T are also consistent with a dominance function if we consider that the immediate preadolescent period is one in which it is important to establish peer group dominance. At this age, youngsters experience rapid change in body size, along with changes in environment, as they move from primary to secondary school. The argument that males use R& T to establish dominance as they move into adolescence is also consistent with theory and research in the animal literature (Dunbar, 1988; Fagen, 1981).

Data from observations and interviews suggest that R & T may be involved in dominance in two ways, each of which is age-related. The first is indirect; R & T may provide a way of assessing the strength of others so as to decide one's strategy vis-à-vis dominance competition—a form of "ritualized aggression," as described in other mammalian species, which leads to real fighting in only certain circumstances. Observations by Paquette (1994) support the idea that young chimpanzees can use R & T to learn the strengths and weaknesses of others in planning challenges for dominance, suggesting that R & T is more useful for this than real fights because of the lesser chance of injury or intervention by a third party.

Similarly, children's R & T occurs in symmetrical groups, or with children of similar dominance status, and many children say they can determine their own as well as peers' strength from these encounters (Smith, Hunter, Carvalho, & Costabile, 1992). R & T tends to occur between friends (Humphreys & Smith, 1987; Smith & Lewis, 1985) and in groups of three to four children (Pellegrini, 1993); these findings indicate that it is a safe and relatively visible venue to test and exhibit physical strength. Thus, through R & T, children can, in an indirect way, assess their own strength and that of others; in this way they prepare for dominance encounters through the primary school period.

The second way in which R & T may provide the context for establishing or maintaining dominance is more direct. Participants may use an R & T bout to get their partners in a position where they can actually display their superior strength or assert dominance, for example, by pinning or intimidating a playmate. Participants doing this may have lulled their partners into a false sense of security by using the predominantly playful nature of R & T, or may have used the self-handicapping and reversal criteria of R & T to get themselves into a "winning" position. This could be called a "cheating" use of R & T for dominance purposes.

For preadolescents, in contrast to adolescents, R & T is not correlated with peer-nominated dominance, and it occurs with partners of similar dominance status (Humphreys & Smith, 1987; Pellegrini, 1993); also, in most cases, R & T is not exploited for immediate aggressive ends (Pellegrini, 1988). This suggests that R & T may not be used to establish dominance in this second direct way before adolescence.

Rough-and-tumble play and actual fighting remain separate for most children during the primary school years; there are cases, however, involving sociometrically rejected children especially (Pellegrini, 1988), where R & T and fighting are linked. The ethnographic record also provides illustrations. Sluckin's (1981) in-depth study of British 5- to 9-year-old children's behavior and perceptions of their lives in the school playground provides examples of R & T being used to deceive and manipulate peers. Similarly, the work of Oswald and colleagues (Oswald, Krappmann, Chowduri, & Salisch, 1987) in Germany with children aged 6 to 10 years found instances of hurtfulness in the play of the older children in this age range.

However, a different picture emerges in early adolescence. Neill (1976, p. 219) was the first to suggest that adolescent boys' R & T might be used to establish dominance. His factor-analytic study of 12- to 13-year-old boys' playground behavior found that R & T and aggression often co-occurred. Neill stated that R & T might be a "means of asserting or maintaining dominance; once a weaker boy has registered distress the bond can be maintained by the fight taking a more playful form, but if he does not do so at the start of the fight, the stronger boy may increase the intensity of the fight until he does."

This age change in the function of R & T received some support from Humphreys and Smith (1987). They found that at 11 years, but not at 7 and 9 years, dominance was a factor in partner choice in R & T. When the younger children engaged in R & T, they did so in symmetrical groups, or with peers of similar dominance status; for the older children, dominant youngsters initiated R & T with less dominant youngsters, or in asymmetrical groups.

This finding would be consistent with stronger children using R & T to exhibit dominance with weaker children. Results from a study by Pellegrini (1995b) shed further light on this age trend. In a longitudinal study of adolescent boys, he found that asymmetrical choices for R & T were observed during the first year of middle school (12 years), but not the second (13 years). He also found that during the first year of middle school, boys' R & T was correlated with peer-nominated dominance; only with sociometrically rejected boys, not popular or average boys, did R & T lead to and relate to aggression, however. During the second year of middle school, R & T continued to relate to dominance status, but it did not lead or relate to aggression. These results suggest that R & T is used to establish dominance in early adolescence; once established, the hierarchy reduces aggression, and R & T declines.

R & T and emotional coding skills. An important dimension of social skill is the ability to encode and decode social signals. Successful encoding and decoding of messages, such as "This is play," is necessary if play is to be initiated and maintained (Bateson, 1972; Bekoff, 1995). Behaviors that send the message "This is play" are typically exaggerated, compared to more functional counterparts (Biben & Suomi, 1993); for example, play fighting, compared to real fighting, might be characterized by an open mouth, hunched shoulders, and rhythmic movement of the hands.

Research by Parke and colleagues indicates that the ability to encode and decode play signals can originate in vigorous play between parents (primarily fathers) and their children (primarily sons) beginning in infancy and continuing throughout childhood (Carson et al., 1993; Parke, Cassidy, Burks, Carson, & Boyum, 1992). They found the amount of time spent in vigorous play bouts to be positively related to preschool children's ability to decode emotional expressions, such as happy, sad, angry, scared, and neutral (Parke et al., 1992). Further, children's expression of emotional states was also related positively to bout length (Parke et al., 1992). Involvement in R & T with peers, expressed in terms of proportion of total behavioral output, has also been found to relate to primary school children's ability to decode play signals (Pellegrini, 1988). It may thus be the case that parent-child play provides the groundwork for children's ability to encode and decode emotions, with this ability later being used in physical activity play with peers.

However, there are difficulties with this hypothesis. First, these correlational studies do not establish cause and effect; it is equally plausible that the causal relation is such that those children less able to encode/decode emotions are less willing to engage in R & T. Second, and more conclusively, these hypotheses are inconsistent with observed gender differences; encoding and decoding of emotions should be just as important for girls as for boys, and they certainly are no worse at it than boys. Yet the gender difference in R & T is a well established finding.

In summary, we hypothesize that the primary function of R & T through the primary years is to provide a way in which boys assess the strength of others for dominance purposes; it may also provide practice in fighting skills, but little direct evidence exists to support this. There is good evidence that in early adolescence (and perhaps earlier for rejected children) R & T can function to actually establish dominance status in boys' peer groups. The contemporaneous correlations between R & T and dominance and R & T and popularity for adolescent boys suggest that R & T is only one behavioral strategy used by boys to gain and maintain status. Finally, we hypothesize that any benefits for emotional encoding or decoding are incidental benefits of R & T, achievable in other ways, rather than functions.

SUGGESTIONS FOR FUTURE RESEARCH

In light of the relative paucity of research in the area of physical activity play, we suggest directions for future research on the nature of such play and its hypothesized benefits in physical, cognitive, and social domains.

The Need for Naturalistic Data on Forms and Amounts of Physical Activity Play

There is a need for more descriptive data on the forms of physical activity play and their age trends through childhood and adolescence. The review by Byers and Walker (1995) and our own analyses here show the importance of age trends in examining functional hypotheses. Yet, for exercise play especially, data are scanty. Although we can be reasonably confident of the inverted-U curve with age, we cannot be confident that the peak is at 4–5 years as we have assumed. Also, different types of exercise play may peak at different ages, and the developmental course may be different for boys and girls. The difference in age peaks between exercise play and R & T, together with other differences, has led us to separate them for functional consideration. Similarly, different aspects of exercise play and R & T may relate to somewhat different, if related, functions of strength training, endurance training, and skill and economy of movement.

Related to this, we need more data on gender differences in exercise play, unconfounded by R & T. We can be confident of the gender differences in R & T, and they fit readily with the predominant functional hypothesis for R & T—social dominance. Gender differences in exercise play are more intriguing with respect to functional hypotheses. Conceivably, these differences may be more complex and differentiated than previously thought, as Silverman and Eals (1992) found in the domain of spatial ability; for example, gender differences might be different for aspects of exercise play relevant to strength as opposed to those relevant to endurance.

Functions of Exercise Play for Strength, Endurance, and Economy and Skill of Movement

The benefits of exercise play for two dimensions of motor training—strength and endurance—should be immediate and occur across the life span. By immediate we mean that strength and endurance will result from repeated activity bouts, usually across the span of a number of weeks (Byers & Walker, 1995). However, we need more information on duration, frequency, and intensity of physical exercise of both the playful and nonplayful variety from infancy through adulthood, and the correspondence between these data and measures of immediate and sustained fitness. To test the hypothesis that exercise play relates to bone remodeling and physical endurance and strength, as measured by decreased heart rate during exercise or VO_2Max (the maximum rate of oxygen uptake during exercise), we need to measure the separate contributions of nonplayful and playful vigorous activity to physiological measures of endurance and strength.

Function of Exercise Play for Cognitive Performance

The beneficial consequences of exercise play for children's cognitive functioning are not firmly established. Although exercise play breaks are related to children's attention to classroom tasks (Pellegrini & Davis, 1993; Pellegrini et al., 1995), alternative explanations abound. Future research should examine the extent to which cognitive performance—for example, task attention measured by gaze and heart-rate variability and possibly vagal tone (Obrist, Howard, Sutterer, Hennis, & Murrell, 1973; Porges, 1992) for children of different ages—is increased as a function of "breaks" during cognitive tasks.

Determining the character of the breaks—how playful, how physically vigorous, or how academic—is crucial for explaining extant and future findings. Distributed practice theory predicts that any break in the duration of cognitive tasks, whether it be playful or nonplayful, should increase performance on the criterion task. The cognitive immaturity hypothesis predicts, on the other hand, that playful breaks between demanding tasks where close attention is expected, such as computing mathematics problems, are necessary to reduce cognitive interference and facilitate preschool children's performance. However, the theory does not make a prediction related to the physically vigorous dimension of play.

Age of the participant is an important factor in testing these theories. Distributed practice affects cognitive performance across the life span (e.g., Dempster, 1988), whereas the effects of play, following the cognitive immaturity hypothesis, should be limited to the niche of childhood. According to the cognitive immaturity hypothesis only, the playful nature of the break should become less crucial with increasing age.

The cognitive immaturity hypothesis also posits cognitive benefits associated with increased feelings of self-efficacy. Young children should overestimate their competence in cognitive and social domains; this orientation should then lead to increased self-efficacy, which should, in turn, encourage children to explore new arenas and to persist at difficult tasks (Bjorklund, in press). That preschool children overestimate their own social and cognitive performance on a number of social and cognitive tasks, and that these estimates become more realistic by the late elementary school years, is well established (Stipek & Maclver, 1989). Thus, the increase in children's self-efficacy attributed to play may result from this more general orientation to overestimate their own performance. At the simplest level, this hypothesis could be tested by examining the correlations between the frequency with which children engage in R & T and the degree to which they overestimate their own toughness, after more general levels of overestimation are controlled.

Functions of R & T. More naturalistic data are needed for R & T in the preschool and primary school periods, and especially at the transition into adolescence. Even during the preschool and primary school period, R & T is not sufficiently well understood. Most studies of preschoolers' play, following Piagetian (1962) theory, have been concerned primarily with pretend play, with some attention given to functional and constructive play (Rubin et al., 1983). Given the co-occurrence of R & T and pretend and the theoretical bias toward studying pretend, it may have been the case that the occurrence of R & T during the preschool period has been underreported. For example, children's play following a "Star Wars" theme is usually coded as social pretend, not R & T (as reported in Rubin et al., 1983, p. 723). Future research should reevaluate the place of R & T during the preschool period by considering its pretend and nonpretend dimensions, as well as the play fighting and chase dimensions.

For a number of reasons, the distinction between play fighting and play chasing is an important one for future work. First, most young children enjoy chasing, but fewer, mostly boys, enjoy play fighting (Smith et al., 1992). Second, chasing and play fighting are statistically independent of each other and have different consequences (Pellegrini, 1993). Further, for older and rejected youngsters, play fighting relates to dominance status, whereas chasing does not (Pellegrini, 1995b).

Related to this, we need to know more about the ways in which R & T is used by boys to establish and maintain social leadership and dominance in their peer groups. We hypothesize that R & T is used primarily to assess the strength of others in the peer group. This hypothesis is based on several untested assumptions. First, those boys who engage in more R & T should have more accurate knowledge of relative strength or "toughness" in the peer group (see Sluckin & Smith, 1977). Second, particular choices of R & T partners should relate to particular knowledge of relative strength vis-à-vis those partners. It would be particularly relevant to engage in R & T with a boy joining the peer group, whose strength was not known. Relatedly, R & T would be an important predictor of peer leadership, including dominance, especially as boys enter new social institutions, such as a new school.

We posit that an alternative pathway for boys to use R & T for dominance purposes is directly via "cheating." However, "cheating" is a double-edged tool; public display of dominance in this way both enhances the success of that particular bout for dominance assertion, but also starts to get the boy who cheated a particular reputation in this respect. Thus, children should not cheat repeatedly at R & T. Where cheating does occur, it may be in the presence of a crowd who can witness their exhibition. It may also be the case that boys initially cheat at R & T by inflicting pain and thereby gaining public notice of their "toughness," then apologize (under the guise of an "honest mistake") and resume another form of play or social interaction.

An uninvestigated topic in this context is children's ability to detect cheating in R & T. Ability to detect cheating could be measured by children's responses to filmed play and real fighting bouts. Alternatively, naturalistic data could be gathered on children's actual responses (either as participants or onlookers) to cheating in R & T bouts. Such direct observations would be difficult to collect given the relative infrequency of cheating in R & T, so use of hypothetical situations, although less ecologically valid, may be more practical.

There may also be cognitive implications of children's ability to detect cheating in social interactions (i.e., accepting the benefits of a social contract without paying the accepted cost). Ethological theory (e.g., Humphrey, 1976) and recent evidence (Cosmides, 1989) suggest that detection of cheating may be an important component in the evolution of "social intelligence." There may be a relation between engaging in R & T and the ability to later detect cheating or violations, not only in the specific context of R & T, as just described, but also on socially framed conditional logic problems as used by Cosmides (i.e., do people test hypotheses by searching for evidence that could falsify them).

Gender differences in R & T also warrant future research. Specifically, direct observations should distinguish initiation of R & T bouts, and response to such initiations. For example, do boys and girls respond differently to R & T initiations? Gender differences in the preference for R & T may be related to differential responses to physical stimulation generally (Meaney et al., 1985).

But it also may be the case that there are individual differences, associated with factors such as CAH and temperament, within each gender. Longitudinal observations could be made of CAH and non-CAH girls' and boys' sensitivity to tactile stimulation, as well as their R & T with parents and then peers. Early observations of tactile sensitivity and subsequent play with parents should provide information on the specific and interactive contributions of each factor to children's engagement in R & T with peers.

Testing Functional Hypotheses with Cost-Benefit Analyses

We have made functional inferences based on the co-occurrence of physical activity play and beneficial consequences in physical training, cognitive performance, and social dominance skills. A complementary approach to the study of function, cost-benefit analysis, has been advanced by behavioral ecologists (e.g., Krebs & Davies, 1993) and applied to animal and children's play with generally supportive results (e.g., Caro, 1995; Pellegrini et al., 1998). From an evolutionary perspective, costs associated with play should have corresponding benefits for the individuals of the species in which the play behavior is typically observed. If this were not the case, play would not have been naturally selected for and maintained across generations.

Costs associated with physical activity play can be expressed in terms of time spent playing, calories, or energy expended during play, and in terms of survivorship where death or injury result from play (Martin & Caro, 1985). High costs should be associated with high benefits, and low costs should more likely be associated with low benefits. Benefits for play need not be absolutely high, but merely greater than associated costs (Caro, 1995).

Application of a cost-benefit analysis to children's play would be useful on a number of fronts. First, it would empirically test the widely held assumption that play during childhood consumes a substantial portion of children's time and energy budgets. Second, a description of the time and energy expenditure on physical activity play across childhood would complement the information provided in this review and that provided by Byers and Walker (1995). Functional hypotheses could be evaluated by relating different measures of cost to measures of motor training, cognitive performance, and social dominance during childhood and into adulthood.

CONCLUSION

We have undertaken a functional analysis of a neglected aspect of play, physical activity play. It has not been extensively studied in the child development literature, yet the ethological literature suggests that of all forms of play, it is among the best candidates for serving developmental function(s) (Fagen, 1981).

In the literature reviewed here, certain functions emerge as being better supported than others. We relate these functions to three main forms of physical activity play, distinguished by successive age peaks in incidence. We postulate that rhythmic stereotypies function primarily for establishing voluntary motor control.

Exercise play peaks in the preschool years. The vigorous physical component of exercise play has immediate beneficial consequences for children in motor training. This is consistent with ethological/evolutionary reasoning as well as with the evidence, and might be hypothesized to be the earliest ultimate function for exercise play in mammals. There may be additional benefits of fat reduction and thermoregulation, which we hypothesize to be incidental. The physical component of exercise play also may have benefits for cognitive performance. We view the evidence here as more tenuous; cognitive benefits attributed to physically vigorous dimensions of play may be epiphenomenal to breaks from work, which need not necessarily be physically vigorous, or even playful.

Rough-and-tumble is a form of play with a strong gender difference, which peaks later, in middle childhood. The predominant hypothesis has been that R & T may provide training for fighting/hunting skills, especially in males (Smith, 1982; Symons, 1978). We do not dismiss this hypothesis; it may, in fact, have been an originating or ultimate function for R & T as a social form of physical play found in certain species, but direct support for this hypothesis is minimal. Instead, we develop the hypothesis that, in human children especially, R & T can function to develop and maintain leadership and dominance in the peer group, especially for adolescents. These trajectories interact with sociometric status in complex ways still to be fully explored. Less well supported is the hypothesis that parent-infant rough play and R & T may function to improve skills of encoding and decoding emotional signals.

In summary, we believe that physical activity play deserves greater attention from psychologists and educators. In general, our conclusions have been strongly tempered by the insufficiency of available evidence. What evidence there is has not infrequently come from areas such as sports science, rather than psychology, with a consequent neglect of psychological variables. There is scope for considerable conceptual rethinking in the area; in particular, the usual stress on deferred rather than immediate benefits of play deserves reevaluation.

Even if benefits of physical activity play are more immediate than deferred, they may still be important. There are public health implications for the role of physical activity play for the physical fitness of children growing up in a modern industrial society. Children have limited opportunities for physical activity, due to shortage of play spaces, dangerous neighborhoods, and the increased demands of formal schooling. That children seem to "need" physical activity is supported by the rebound effects observed in deprivation studies. The evidence suggests that if children are deprived of physical activity play for long periods of time, their health, in terms of cardiovascular and physical fitness, may suffer. There may also be social consequences of R & T, a common form of physical activity play that may be necessary in the normal developmental sequence of boys' peer groups. We hope that future research efforts can be directed both to the theoretical issues of function and to the practical implications affecting children's health and development.

ACKNOWLEDGMENTS

We acknowledge the comments of G. M. Burghardt and L. Galda, as well as beneficial discussions with D. J. Bjorklund, P. Blatchford, T. M. Caro, R. Dishman, R. Fagen, C. Hamilton, and B. Sutton-Smith. This work was partially supported by grants to the first author from the W. T. Grant Foundation and the School of Education, University of Wales, Cardiff.

ADDRESSES AND AFFILIATIONS

Corresponding author: A. D. Pellegrini, Department of Educational Psychology, Burton Hall, University of Minnesota, Minneapolis, MN 55455. P. K. Smith is at Goldsmiths College, the University of London.

APPENDIX

TABLE A1
Empirical Studies of Age and Gender Trends

Authors	Date	N	Age	Method	Activity
Bloch	1989	54	0–6 years	Observations	Physical activity, Other play
Boulton	1992	86	11 and 12 years	Observations	Playground behavior, Peer group
Eaton & Keats	1982	69	4 years	Observations, Actometer	Physical activity
Eaton & Yu	1989	83	6.6 years	Adult rating	Physical activity
Field	1994	36	25–60 months	Observations	Physical activity, Other play
Hovell et al.	1978	300	9–12 years	Observations	Physical activity
Humphreys & Smith	1987	94	7–11 years	Observations, Peer nominations	R & T, Friendship, Dominance
Konner	1972	36	newborn–5 years	Observations, Tests	Movement, Subsistence play
McGrew	1972	62	36–58 months	Observation	R & T, Vigorous play, Social behavior
Pellegrini	1984	20	3–4 years	Observations	Play, R & T
Pellegrini	1988	32	5–12 years	Observations, Sociometry	R & T, Games, Aggression
Pellegrini	1989a, 1989b	94	5–12 years	Observations	R & T, Games, Aggression
Pellegrini	1990	94	5–12 years	Observations	Vigorous play, R & T
Pellegrini	1995a, 1995b	82	12–13 years	Observations, Sociometry, Dominance	R & T, Aggression
Roopnarine et al.	1993	34	1 year	Observations	R & T, Physical play
Rosenthal	1994	82	2 years	Observations	Object play, Motor play, Peer play
Routh et al.	1974	140	3–9 years	Observations, Parent ratings	Physical activity
Simons-Morton et al.	1990	870	9–11 years	Self-report	Physical activity
Smith & Connolly	1980	142	28–56 months	Observations	R & T, Vigorous play, Social behavior
Thelen	1979	20	28–52 weeks	Observations	Rhythmic stereotypies
Thelen	1980	20	28–52 weeks	Observations, Motor tests, IQ	Rhythmic stereotypies

TABLE A2
Studies of Function

Authors	Date	N	Age	Method	Activity
				Thermoregulative Functions	
Cullumbine	1950	225	Adults	Douglas bag expenditure, Ambient temp.	Energy
Pellegrini et al.	1995	62	5–9 years	Observations	Physical activity, Attention
		45	7–9 years	Observations	Physical activity, Attention
		44	9 years	Observations	Physical activity, Attention
Smith & Hagan	1980	36	2–4 years	Observations	Exercise play
			Strength, Endurance, and Economy of Movement Function		
Cummings et al.	1969	89	11–14 years	Aerobic capacity	PE programs
Lussier & Buskirk	1977	26	8–12 years	Aerobic capacity	PE programs
Pellegrini & Davis	1993	23	9 years	Observations	Physical activity
Pellegrini et al.[a]	1995	62	5–9 years	Observations	Physical activity, Attention
		45	7–9 years	Observations	Physical activity, Attention
		44	9 years	Observations	Physical activity, Attention
Smith & Hagan[a]	1980	36	2–4 years	Observations	Exercise play
Smoll & Schutz	1985	2,000	17 years	Strength, Endurance	Athlete/Nonathlete
Thelen[a]	1979	20	28–52 weeks	Observations	Rhythmic stereotypies
			Dominance and Emotional Encoding		
Blurton Jones	1972	13	2–4 years	Observations	Social behavior, R & T, Aggression
Boulton	1991	89	9–11 years	Observations, Interviews	R & T
Boulton	1993	89	8–11 years	Observations, Interviews	R & T, Aggression
Carson et al.	1993		7 months–10 years	Interviews, Observations	Physical Play
Costabile et al.	1991	256	8 and 11 years	Interviews	R & T, Aggression
DiPietro	1981	52	4 years	Observations	R & T, Physical activity, Playmates
Fry	1987	24	3–8 years	Observations	R & T, Aggression
Humphreys & Smith[a]	1987	94	7–11 years	Observations, Peer nominations	R & T, Friendship, Dominance
MacDonald	1987	36	3–5 years	Observations, Sociometry	R & T, Parent roles

Author	Year	N	Method	Focus
MacDonald & Parke	1984	27	Observations, Sociometry, Teacher ratings	R & T, Parent roles, Affect displays
MacDonald & Parke	1986	746	Survey	Physical play
Neill	1976	34	Observations	R & T, Aggression
Oswald et al.	1987	52	Ethnography: Observations, Interview	Social behavior, R & T, Fighting
Parke et al.	1992	158	Observations, Sociometry	Physical play, Parental role
Pellegrini[a]	1988	32	Observations, Sociometry	R & T, Games, Aggression
Pellegrini[a]	1989a, 1989b	94	Observations	R & T, Games, Aggression
Pellegrini	1993	42	Observations, Play partners, Interview	R & T, Dominance
Pellegrini	1994	54	Observations, Play partners, Sociometry, Interview	R & T, Dominance, Aggression
Pellegrini[a]	1995a, 1995b	82	Observations, Sociometry	R & T, Aggression, Dominance
Sluckin	1981	100	Ethnography: Observations, Interviews, Play partners	Playground behavior, Aggression
Smith	1973	29	Observations	Social behavior, R & T, Aggression
Smith & Lewis	1985	26	Observations, Sociometry, Interview, Play partners	R & T, Aggression
Cognitive Performance Function				
Pellegrini & Davis[a]	1993	23	Observations	Physical activity
Pellegrini et al.[a]	1995	62	Observations	Physical activity, Attention
		45	Observations	Physical activity, Attention
		44	Observations	Physical activity, Attention
Stevenson & Lee	1990	480	Questionnaires, Achievement	Break periods
Volle et al.	1982	546	PE training, Achievement, Teacher attitude, Observations, Student diaries	PE programs

[a]Indicates that the entry has appeared before.

REFERENCES

Baldwin, J. D., & Baldwin, J. I. (1977). The role of learning phenomena in the ontogeny of exploration and play. In S. Chevalier-Skolinikoff & F. E. Poirer (Eds.), *Primate biosocial development* (pp. 343–406). New York: Garland.

Barber, N. (1991). Play and energy regulation in mammals. *Quarterly Review of Biology, 66*, 129–147.

Bateson, G. (1972). *Steps to an ecology of mind.* San Francisco: Chandler.

Bateson, P. P. G. (1976). Rules and reciprocity in behavioural development. In P. P. G. Bateson & R. Hinde (Eds.), *Growing points in ethology* (pp. 401–421). Cambridge: Cambridge University Press.

Bateson, P. P. G. (1981). Discontinuities in development and changes in the organization of play in cats. In K. Immelmann, G. Barlow, L. Petrinovich, & M. Main (Eds.), *Behavioral development* (pp. 281–295). New York: Cambridge University Press.

Bekoff, M. (1995). Play signals as punctuation: The structure of social play in canids. *Behaviour, 132*, 419–429.

Berenbaum, S. A., & Snyder, E. (1995). Early hormonal influences on childhood sex-typed activity and playmate preferences: Implications for the development of sexual orientation. *Developmental Psychology, 31*, 31–42.

Biben, M., & Suomi, S. J. (1993). Lessons from primate play. In K. MacDonald (Ed.), *Parent-child play* (pp. 185–196). Albany: State University of New York Press.

Bjorklund, D. J. (1978). Negative transfer in children's recall of categorized material. *Journal of Experimental Child Psychology, 26*, 299–307.

Bjorklund, D. J. (in press). The role of immaturity in human development. *Psychological Bulletin.*

Bjorklund, D., & Green, B. (1992). The adaptive nature of cognitive immaturity. *American Psychologist, 47*, 46–54.

Blatchford, P. (1996, October). *A national survey of break time in English schools.* Paper presented at the annual meetings of the British Educational Research Association, Lancaster.

Bloch, M. N. (1989). Young boys' and girls' play in the home and in the community: A cultural ecological framework. In M. N. Bloch & A. D. Pellegrini (Eds.), *The ecological context of children's play* (pp. 120–154). Norwood, NJ: Ablex.

Blurton Jones, N. G. (1972). Categories of child interaction. In N. G. Blurton Jones (Ed.), *Ethological studies of child behaviour* (pp. 97–129). London: Cambridge University Press.

Bornstein, M. H., & Tamis-LeMonda, C. S. (1995). Parent-child symbolic play: Three theories in search of an effect. *Developmental Review, 15*, 382–400.

Boulton, M. J. (1991). Partner preference in middle school children's playful fighting and chasing. *Ethology and Sociobiology, 12*, 177–193.

Boulton, M. J. (1992). Participation in playground activities at middle school. *Educational Research, 34*, 167–182.

Boulton, M. J. (1993). Children's ability to distinguish between playful and aggressive fighting: A developmental perspective. *British Journal of Developmental Psychology, 11*, 249–263.

Boulton, M. J., & Smith, P. K. (1990). Affective bias in children's perceptions of dominance relationships. *Child Development, 61*, 221–229.

Boulton, M. J., & Smith, P. K. (1992). The social nature of play-fighting and play chasing: Mechanisms and strategies underlying cooperation and compromise. In J. H. Barkow, L. Cosmides, & J. Tooby (Eds.), *The adapted mind* (pp. 429–444). New York and Oxford: Oxford University Press.

Brownlee, A. (1954). Play in domestic cattle: An investigation into its nature. *British Veterinary Journal, 110*, 48–68.

Burghardt, G. (1984). On the origins of play. In P. K. Smith (Ed.), *Play in animals and humans* (pp. 5–42). Oxford: Blackwell.

Burghardt, G. (1988). Precocity, play, and the ectotherm-endotherm transition. In E. M. Blass (Ed.), *Handbook of behavioral neurobiology* (Vol. 9, pp. 102–148). New York: Plenum.

Byers, J. A., & Walker, C. (1995). Refining the motor training hypothesis for the evolution of play. *American Naturalist, 146*, 25–40.

Caro, T. M. (1995). Short-term costs and correlates of play in cheetahs. *Animal Behaviour, 49*, 333–345.

Carson, J., Burks, V., & Parke, R. (1993). Parent-child physical play: Determinants and consequences. In K. MacDonald (Ed.), *Parent-child play* (pp. 197–220). Albany: State University of New York Press.

Charlesworth, W. R., & Dzur, C. (1987). Gender comparisons of preschoolers' behavior and resource utilization in group problem solving. *Child Development, 58*, 191–200.

Collaer, M. L., & Hines, M. (1995). Human behavioral sex differences: A role for gonadal hormones during early development. *Psychological Bulletin, 118*, 55–107.

Cosmides, L. (1989). The logic of social exchange: Has natural selection shaped how humans reason? *Cognition, 31*, 187–276.

Costabile, A., Smith, P. K., Matheson, L., Aston, J., Hunter, T., & Boulton, M. J. (1991). A cross-national comparison of how children distinguish serious and playful fighting. *Developmental Psychology, 27*, 881–887.

Cullumbine, H. (1950). Heat production and energy requirements of tropical people. *Journal of Applied Physiology, 2*, 201–210.

Cummings, C. R., Goulding, D., & Bagley, G. (1969). *Canadian Medical Association Journal, 101*, 69–73.

Dempster, F. (1988). The spacing effect. *American Psychologist, 43*, 627–634.

deWaal, F. B. M. (1985). The integration of dominance and social bonding in primates. *Quarterly Review of Biology, 61*, 459–479.

DiPietro, J. A. (1981). Rough-and-tumble play: A function of gender. *Developmental Psychology, 17*, 50–58.

Dunbar, R. I. M. (1988). *Primate social systems*. Ithaca, NY: Cornell University Press.

Easterbrook, J. A. (1959). The effect of emotion on cue utilization and the organization of behavior. *Psychological Review, 66*, 183–201.

Eaton, W. C., & Enns, L. R. (1986). Sex differences in human motor activity level. *Psychological Bulletin, 100*, 19–28.

Eaton, W. C., & Keats, J. G. (1982). Peer presence, stress, and sex differences in motor activity of preschoolers. *Developmental Psychology, 18*, 534–540.

Eaton, W. C., & Yu, A. P. (1989). Are sex differences in child motor activity level a function of sex differences in maturational status? *Child Development, 60*, 1005–1011.

Ehrhardt, A. A. (1984). Gender differences: A biosocial perspective. In A. Sondergegger (Ed.), *Nebraska symposium on motivation* (pp. 33–50). Lincoln: University of Nebraska Press.

Fabes, R. A. (1994). Physiological, emotional, and behavioral correlates of gender segregation. In C. Leaper (Ed.), *Childhood gender segregation: Causes and consequences* (pp. 19–34). San Francisco: Jossey-Bass.

Fagen, R. (1976). Exercise, play, and physical training in mammals. In P. P. G. Bateson & P. H. Klopfer (Eds.), *Perspectives in ethology* (Vol. 2, pp. 189–219). London: Plenum.

Fagen, R. (1981). *Animal play behavior.* New York: Oxford.

Fagot, B. I. (1974). Sex differences in toddlers' behavior and parental reaction. *Developmental Psychology, 10,* 554–558.

Fagot, B. I. (1994). Peer relations and the development of competence in boys and girls. In C. Leaper (Ed.), *Childhood gender segregations: Causes and consequences* (pp. 53–66). San Francisco: Jossey-Bass.

Fein, G. (1981). Pretend play: An integrative review. *Child Development, 52,* 1095–118.

Field, T. M. (1994). Infant day care facilitates later social behavior and school performance. In E. V. Jacobs & H. Goelman (Eds.), *Children's play in child care settings* (pp. 69–84). Albany: State University of New York Press.

Field, T. M., Ting, G., & Shuman, H. H. (1979). The onset of rhythmic activities in normal and high-risk infants. *Developmental Psychobiology, 12,* 97–100.

Fry, D. P. (1987). Difference between play fighting and serious fighting among Zapotec children. *Ethology and Sociobiology, 8,* 285–306.

Gomendio, M. (1988). The development of different types of play in gazelles: Implications for the nature and functions of play. *Animal Behaviour, 36,* 825–836.

Groos, K. (1898). *The play of animals.* New York: Appleton.

Groos, K. (1901). *The play of man.* New York: Appleton.

Hartup, W. W. (1983). Peer relations. In E. M. Hetherington (Ed.), P. H. Mussen (Series Ed.), *Handbook of child psychology: Vol. 4. Socialization, personality, and social development* (pp. 103–196). New York: Wiley.

Hinde, R. A. (1974). *Biological basis of human social behavior.* New York: Academic Press.

Hinde, R. A. (1980). *Ethology.* London: Fontana.

Hines, M., & Kaufman, F. R. (1994). Androgen and the development of human sex-typical behavior: Rough-and-tumble play and sex of preferred playmates in children with Congenital Adrenal Hyperplasia (CAH). *Child Development, 65,* 1042–1053.

Hovell, M. F., Bursick, J. H., Shockley, R., & McClure, J. (1976). An evaluation of elementary students' voluntary physical activity during recess. *Research Quarterly in Exercise Sports, 49,* 460–474.

Humphreys, A. P., & Smith, P. K. (1984). Rough-and-tumble play in preschool and playground. In P. K. Smith (Ed.), *Play in animals and humans* (pp. 241–270). Oxford: Blackwell.

Humphreys, A. P., & Smith, P. K. (1987). Rough-and-tumble play, friendship, and dominance in school children: Evidence for continuity and change with age. *Child Development, 58,* 201–212.

Humphrey, N. (1976). The social function of intellect. In P. P. G. Bateson & R. A. Hinde (Eds.), *Growing points in ethology* (pp. 303–317). Cambridge: Cambridge University Press.

Jacklin, C. N., DiPietro, J. A., & Maccoby, E. E. (1984). Sex-typing behavior and sex-typing pressure in child/parent interaction. *Archives of Sexual Behavior, 13,* 413–425.

Kagan, J. (1971). *Continuity and change in infancy.* New York: Wiley.

Konner, M. J. (1972). Aspects of the developmental ethology of a foraging people. In N. Blurton Jones (Ed.), *Ethological studies of child behaviour* (pp. 285–304). London: Cambridge University Press.

Krebs, J. R., & Davies, N. B. (1993). *An introduction to behavioural ecology.* Oxford: Blackwell.

Lussier, L., & Buskirk, E. R. (1977). Effects of an endurance training regimen on assessment of work capacity in prepubertal children. *Annals of the New York Academy of Sciences, 301*, 734–747.

Maccoby, E. E. (1986). Social groupings in childhood: Their relationship to prosocial and antisocial behavior in boys and girls. In D. Olweus, J. Block, & M. Radke-Yarrow (Eds.), *Development of antisocial and prosocial behavior: Research, theory, and issues* (pp. 263–280). New York: Academic Press.

MacDonald, K. (1987). Parent-child physical play with rejected, neglected, and popular boys. *Developmental Psychology, 23*, 705–711.

MacDonald, K. (1993). Parent-child play: An evolutionary perspective. In K. MacDonald (Ed.), *Parent-child play* (pp. 113–143). Albany: State University of New York Press.

MacDonald, K., & Parke, R. D. (1984). Bridging the gap: Parent-child play interactions and peer interactive competence. *Child Development, 55*, 1265–1277.

MacDonald, K., & Parke, R. D. (1986). Parent-child physical play: The effects of sex and age of children. *Sex Roles, 15*, 367–378.

Martin, P., & Caro, T. (1985). On the function of play and its role in behavioral development. In J. Rosenblatt, C. Beer, M. Bushnel, & P. Slater (Eds.), *Advances in the study of behavior* (Vol 15, pp. 59–103). New York: Academic Press.

McCune, L. (1995). A normative study of representational play and the transition to language. *Developmental Psychology, 31*, 198–206.

McGrew, W. C. (1972). *An ecological study of children's behaviour*. London: Academic Press.

Meaney, M. J., Stewart, J., & Beatty, W. W. (1985). Sex differences in social play. In J. Rosenblatt, C. Beer, M. C. Bushnel, & P. Slater (Eds.), *Advances in the study of behavior* (Vol. 15, pp. 2–58). New York: Academic Press.

Money, J., & Ehrhardt, A. A. (1972). *Man and woman: Boy and girl*. Baltimore, MD: Johns Hopkins University Press.

Neill, S. R. StJ. (1976). Aggressive and non-aggressive fighting in twelve-to-thirteen year old pre-adolescent boys. *Journal of Child Psychology and Psychiatry, 17*, 213–220.

Obrist, P., Howard, J., Sutterer, J., Hennis, R., & Murrell, D. (1973). Cardiac-somatic changes during a simple reaction time study. *Journal of Experimental Child Psychology, 16*, 346–362.

Oswald, H., Krappmann, L., Chowduri, F., & Salisch, M. (1987). Gaps and bridges: Interactions between girls and boys in elementary schools. *Sociological Studies of Child Development, 2*, 205–223.

Paquette, D. (1994). Fighting and play fighting in captive adolescent chimpanzees. *Aggressive Behaviour, 20*, 49–65.

Parke, R. D., Cassidy, J., Burks, Carson, J., & Boyum, L. (1992). Familial contributions to peer competence among young children: The role of interactive and affective processes. In R. D. Parke & G. Ladd (Eds.), *Family-peer relationships* (pp. 107–134). Hillsdale, NJ: Erlbaum.

Parke, R. D., & Suomi, S. J. (1981). Adult male infant relationships: Human and nonhuman primate evidence. In K. Immelman, G. W. Barlow, L. Petronovitch, & M. Main (Eds.), *Behavioral development* (pp. 700–725). New York: Cambridge University Press.

Pellegrini, A. D. (1984). The social cognitive ecology of preschool classrooms. *International Journal of Behavioral Development, 7*, 321–332.

Pellegrini, A. D. (1988). Elementary school children's rough-and-tumble play and social competence. *Developmental Psychology, 24*, 802–806.

Pellegrini, A. D. (1989a). Elementary school children's rough-and-tumble play. *Early Childhood Research Quarterly, 4,* 245–260.

Pellegrini, A. D. (1989b). What is a category? The case of rough-and-tumble play. *Ethology and Sociobiology, 10,* 331–341.

Pellegrini, A. D. (1990). Elementary school children's playground behavior: Implications for social cognitive development. *Children's Environment Quarterly, 7,* 8–16.

Pellegrini, A. D. (1993). Boys' rough-and-tumble play, social competence, and group composition. *British Journal of Developmental Psychology, 11,* 237–248.

Pellegrini, A. D. (1994). The rough play of adolescent boys of differing sociometric status. *International Journal of Behavioral Development, 17,* 525–540.

Pellegrini, A. D. (1995a). *School recess and playground behavior.* Albany: State University of New York Press.

Pellegrini, A. D. (1995b). A longitudinal study of boys' rough-and-tumble play and dominance during early adolescence. *Journal of Applied Developmental Psychology, 16,* 77–93.

Pellegrini, A. D., & Bjorklund, D. F. (1997). The role of recess in children's cognitive performance. *Educational Psycholgist, 37,* 35–40.

Pellegrini, A. D., & Davis, P. (1993). Relations between children's playground and classroom behaviour. *British Journal of Educational Psychology, 63,* 86–95.

Pellegrini, A. D., Horvat, M., & Huberty, P. D. (1998). The relative cost of children's physical activity play. *Animal Behaviour, 55.*

Pellegrini, A. D., Huberty, P. D., & Jones, I. (1995). The effects of recess timing on children's classroom and playground behavior. *American Educational Research Journal, 32,* 845–864.

Pellegrini, A. D., & Perlmutter, J. C. (1987). A re-examination of the Smilansky-Parten matrix of play behavior. *Journal of Research in Childhood Education, 2,* 89–96.

Pellegrini, A. D., & Smith, P. K. (1993). School recess: Implications for education and development. *Review of Educational Research, 63,* 51–67.

Pellis, S. M., Field, E. F., Smith, L. K., & Pellis, V. C. (1996). Multiple differences in the play fighting of male and female rats. *Neuroscience and Biobehavioral Reviews, 21,* 105–120.

Pellis, S. M., & Pellis, V. C. (in press). The structure-function interface in the analysis of play fighting. In M. Bekoff & J. A. Byers (Eds.), *Play behavior: Comparative, evolutionary, and ethological aspects.* New York: Cambridge University Press.

Piaget, J. (1962). *Play, dreams, and imitation in childhood.* New York: Norton.

Porges, S. W. (1992). Autonomic regulation and attention. In B. A. Campbell, H. Hayne, R. Richardson (Eds.), *Attention and information processing in infants and adults* (pp. 201–223). Hillsdale, NJ: Erlbaum.

Quadagno, D. M., Briscoe, R., & Quadagno, J. S. (1977). Effects of perinatal gonadal hormones on selected nonsexual behavior patterns: A critical assessment of the nonhuman and human literature. *Psychological Bulletin, 84,* 62–82.

Roopnarine, J. L., Hooper, F., Ahmeduzzaman, A., & Pollack, B. (1993). Gentle play partners: Mother-child and father-child play in New Delhi, India. In K. MacDonald (Ed.), *Parent-child play* (pp. 287–304). Albany: State University of New York Press.

Rosenthal, M. K. (1994). Social and non-social play of infants and toddlers in family day care. In E. V. Jacobs & H. Goelman (Eds.), *Children's play in child care settings* (pp. 163–192). Albany: State University of New York Press.

Routh, D. K., Schroeder, C. S., & O'Tuama, L. A. (1974). Development of activity level in children. *Developmental Psychology, 10*, 163–168.

Rowland, T. W. (1985). Aerobic response to endurance training in prepubescent children: A critical analysis. *Medicine and Science in Sports and Exercise, 17*, 493–497.

Rubin, K. H., Fein, G., & Vandenberg, B. (1983). Play. In E. M. Hetherington (Ed.), P. H. Mussen (Series Ed.), *Handbook of child psychology: Vol. 4. Socialization, personality, and social development* (pp. 693–774). New York: Wiley.

Ruff, H. A., & Saltarelli, L. M. (1993). Exploratory play with objects: Basic cognitive processes and individual differences. In M. Bornstein & A. W. O'Reilly (Eds.), *The role of play in the development of thought* (pp. 5–15). San Francisco: Jossey-Bass.

Shephard, R. J. (1983). Physical activity and the healthy mind. *Canadian Medical Association Journal, 128*, 525–530.

Silverman, I., & Eals, M. (1992). Sex differences in spatial ability: Evolutionary theory and data. In J. Barkow, L. Cosmides, & J. Tooby (Eds.), *The adapted mind* (pp. 533–549). New York: Oxford University Press.

Simons-Morton, B. G., O'Hara, N. M., Parcel, G. S., Huang, I. W., Baranowski, T., & Wilson, B. (1990). Children's frequency of participation in moderate to vigorous physical activities. *Research Quarterly for Exercise and Sport, 61*, 307–314.

Simons-Morton, B. G., O'Hara, N. M., Simons-Morton, D. G., & Parcel, G. S. (1987). Children and fitness: A public health perspective. *Research Quarterly for Exercise and Sport, 58*, 293–302.

Sluckin, A. M. (1981). *Growing up in the playground: The social development of children.* London: Routledge & Kegan Paul.

Sluckin, A. M., & Smith, P. K. (1977). Two approaches to the concept of dominance in preschool children. *Child Development, 48*, 917–923.

Smith, P. K. (1973). Temporal clusters and individual differences in the behaviour of preschool children. In R. Michael & J. Crook (Eds.), *Comparative ecology and behaviour of primates* (pp. 752–798). London: Academic Press.

Smith, P. K. (1982). Does play matter? Functional and evolutionary aspects of animal and human play. *Behavioral and Brain Sciences, 5*, 139–184.

Smith, P. K. (1989). The role of rough-and-tumble play in the development of social competence: Theoretical perspectives and empirical evidence. In B. H. Schneider, G. Attili, J. Nadel, & R. P. Weissman (Eds.), *Social competence in developmental perspective* (pp. 239–255). Dordrecht: Kluwer.

Smith, P. K., & Boulton, M. J. (1990). Rough-and-tumble play, aggression and dominance: Perception and behavior in children's encounters. *Human Development, 33*, 271–282.

Smith, P. K., & Connolly, K. (1980). *The ecology of preschool behaviour.* Cambridge: Cambridge University Press.

Smith, P. K., & Hagan, T. (1980). Effects of deprivation on exercise play in nursery school children. *Animal Behaviour, 28*, 922–928.

Smith, P. K., Hunter, T., Carvalho, A., & Costabile, A. (1992). Children's perceptions of play-fighting, play-chasing and real fighting: A cross-national interview study. *Social Development, 1*, 211–229.

Smith, P. K., & Lewis, K. (1985). Rough-and-tumble play, fighting, and chasing in nursery school children. *Ethology and Sociobiology, 6*, 175–181.

Smith, P. K., & Vollstedt, R. (1985). On defining play. *Child Development, 56,* 1042–1050.

Smoll, F. L., & Schutz, R. W. (1985). Physical fitness differences between athletes and nonathletes: Do changes occur as a function of age and sex? *Human Movement Science, 4,* 189–202.

Spencer, H. (1898). *The principles of psychology: Vol. 2.* New York: Appleton.

Stevenson, H. W., & Lee, S. Y. (1990). Contexts of achievement. *Monographs for the Society for Research in Child Development, 55* (1–2, Serial No. 221).

Stipek, D., & MacIver, D. (1989). Developmental changes in children's assessment of intellectual competence. *Child Development, 60,* 521–538.

Strayer, F. F. (1980). Social ecology of the preschool peer group. In W. A. Collins (Ed.), *The Minnesota symposia on child development: Vol. 13. Development of cognition, affect, and social relations* (pp. 165–196). Hillsdale, NJ: Erlbaum.

Symons, D. (1978). *Play and aggression: A study of rhesus monkeys.* New York: Columbia University Press.

Tanner, J. M. (1970). Physical growth. In P. H. Mussen (Ed.), *Manual of child psychology* (Vol. *1,* pp. 77–156). New York: Wiley.

Thelen, E. (1979). Rhythmical stereotypies in normal human infants. *Animal Behaviour, 27,* 699–715.

Thelen, E. (1980). Determinants of amounts of stereotyped behavior in normal human infants. *Ethology and Sociobiology, 1,* 141–150.

Tinbergen, N. (1963). On the aims and methods of ethology. *Zeitschrift fur Tierpsychologie, 20,* 410–433.

Tomporowski, P. D., & Ellis, N. R. (1986). Effects of exercise on cognitive processes: A review. *Psychological Bulletin, 99,* 338–346.

Vaughn, B. E., & Waters, E. (1981). Attention structure, sociometric status, and dominance: Interrelations, behavioral correlates, and relationships to social competence. *Developmental Psychology, 17,* 275–288.

Vollé, M., Shephard, R. J., Lavalle, H., LaBarre, R., Jequier, J. C., & Rajic, M. (1982). Influence of a program of required physical activity upon academic performance. In H. Lavalle & R. J. Shephard (Eds.), *Croissance et développement de l'enfant* (pp. 91–109). Trois Rivières: Universite de Quebec.

Vygotsky, L. (1978). *Mind in society.* Cambridge, MA. Harvard University Press.

Waters, E., & Sroufe, L. A. (1983). Social competence as a developmental construct. *Developmental Review, 3,* 79–97.

Welsh, M. C., & Labbé, E. F. (1994). Children and aerobic exercise: A review of cognitive and behavioral effects. *Journal of Experimental Child Psychology, 58,* 405–417.

2

Child Development and Emergent Literacy

Grover J. Whitehurst and Christopher J. Lonigan

Emergent literacy consists of the skills, knowledge, and attitudes that are developmental precursors to reading and writing. This article offers a preliminary typology of children's emergent literacy skills, a review of the evidence that relates emergent literacy to reading, and a review of the evidence for linkage between children's emergent literacy environments and the development of emergent literacy skills. We propose that emergent literacy consists of at least two distinct domains: inside-out skills (e.g., phonological awareness, letter knowledge) and outside-in skills (e.g., language, conceptual knowledge). These different domains are not the product of the same experiences and appear to be influential at different points in time during reading acquisition. Whereas outside-in skills are associated with those aspects of children's literacy environments typically measured, little is known about the origins of inside-out skills. Evidence from interventions to enhance emergent literacy suggests that relatively intensive and multifaceted interventions are needed to improve reading achievement maximally. A number of successful preschool interventions for outside-in skills exist, and computer-based tasks designed to teach children inside-out skills seem promising. Future research directions include more sophisticated multidimensional examination of emergent literacy skills and environments, better integration with reading research, and longer-term evaluation of preschool interventions. Policy implications for emergent literacy intervention and reading education are discussed.

INTRODUCTION

There are few more attractive cultural icons in late twentieth-century America than the image of a parent sharing a picture book with a child. Of the competition, apple pie can make you fat; the flag can lead to war; and even motherhood, with which shared reading is associated, often draws forth complex, ruffled images. Shared book reading, however, speaks of love, the importance of the family unit, and parental commitment to a child's future. Shared reading embraces goals of educational advancement, cultural uplift, and literate discourse. It is, to use a phrase of Kagan's (1996), "a pleasing idea."

This pleasing idea is part of a topic of inquiry known as *emergent literacy*. Our aim here is to survey emergent literacy with a particular emphasis on applied issues, at a level that may be useful to psychologists and educators whose focal interests lie elsewhere. We first catalog the component skills, knowledge, and attitudes that constitute the domain of emergent literacy, and then review evidence on links between those components and conventional literacy. Next we review research on how variation in natural environments supports or impedes the development of emergent literacy, followed by a survey of interventions to enhance emergent literacy, emphasizing programs that aim to promote emergent literacy in children from low-income backgrounds. Finally, we summarize the state of this field, its social policy implications, and needed directions for future research. The "pleasing idea" will not emerge unscathed. Few if any conceptions look the same in the light of empirical scrutiny as they do in a romantic prism. We conclude, however, that there is substantial educational and social value in work that has already been done on emergent literacy, and there is promise of more to come.

WHAT IS EMERGENT LITERACY?

The term "emergent literacy" is used to denote the idea that the acquisition of literacy is best conceptualized as a developmental continuum, with its origins early in the life of a child, rather than an all-or-none phenomenon that begins when children start school. This conceptualization departs from other perspectives on reading acquisition in suggesting that there is no clear demarcation between reading and pre-reading. For instance, the "reading readiness" approach, which preceded an emergent literacy perspective and is still dominant in many educational arenas, has as its focus the question of what skills children need to have mastered before they can profit from formal reading instruction. Such perspectives create a boundary between the "prereading" behaviors of children, and the "real" reading that children are taught in educational settings. In contrast, an emergent literacy perspective views literacy-related behaviors occurring in the preschool period as legitimate and important aspects of literacy. A second distinction between an emergent literacy perspective and other perspectives on literacy is the assumption that reading, writing, and oral language develop concurrently and interdependently from an early age from children's exposure to interactions in the social contexts in which literacy is a component, and in the absence of formal instruction. More traditional approaches often treat writing as secondary to reading and focus on the formal instruction required for children to be able to read and write.

Although investigators have examined the literacy-related behaviors of preschool-aged children for some time (e.g., Durkin, 1966), the term "emergent literacy" is typically attributed to Clay (1966). A more formal introduction of the term and field of inquiry was heralded by Teale and Sulzby's (1986) book, *Emergent Literacy: Writing and Reading*. Current inquiry into emergent literacy represents a broad field with multiple perspectives and a wide range of research methodologies. This avenue of inquiry is complicated by changing conceptualizations of what constitutes literacy. For instance, recent years have seen an almost unbounded definition of literacy that is often extended to any situation in which an individual negotiates or interacts with the environment through the use of a symbolic system (i.e., maps, bus schedules, store coupons). We restrict our focus to more conventional forms of literacy (i.e., the reading or writing of alphabetic texts). The majority of research on emergent literacy has been conducted with English-speaking children learning an alphabetic writing system. Consequently, the extent to which these concepts of emergent literacy extend to children learning other writing systems or languages other than English is not clear.

A Definition

Emergent literacy consists of the skills, knowledge, and attitudes that are presumed to be developmental precursors to conventional forms of reading and writing (Sulzby, 1989; Sulzby & Teale, 1991; Teale & Sulzby, 1986) and the environments that support these developments (e.g., shared book reading; Lonigan, 1994; Whitehurst et al., 1988). In addition, the term has been used to refer to a point of view about the importance of social interactions in literacy-rich environments for prereaders (Fitzgerald, Schuele, & Roberts, 1992) and to advocacy for related social and educational policies (Bush, 1990; Copperman, 1986). We distinguish these three uses with the terms *emergent literacy* (characteristics of prereaders that may relate to later reading and writing), *emergent literacy environments* (experiences that may affect the development of emergent literacy), and the *emergent literacy movement* (advocacy of practices that increase social interactions in a literate environment for prereaders).

Components of Emergent Literacy

Two strands of research provide information about the components of emergent literacy. One research perspective, which consists of mainly quantitative studies, has examined the relation between emergent literacy and the acquisition of conventional literacy. The other research perspective, which tends to consist of qualitative studies, has examined the development of behaviors of preschool-aged children in response to literacy materials and tasks. Emergent literacy comes in many forms, and the typology we offer has some empirical support, but is preliminary (see Table 1 for a brief summary and list of common measures).

Language. Several aspects of children's language skills are important at different points in the process of literacy acquisition. Initially, vocabulary is important. Reading is a process of translating visual codes into meaningful language. In the earliest stages, reading in an alphabetic system involves decoding letters into corresponding sounds and linking those sounds to single words. For instance, a child just learning to read conventionally might approach the word "bats" by sounding out /b/. . ./æ/. . ./t/. . ./s/. Not infrequently, one can hear a beginning reader get that far and be stumped, even though all the letters have been sounded out correctly. A teacher or parent might encourage the child to blend the sounds together by reducing the delays between the sounds for each letter by saying the letter sounds more rapidly. Whereas adults would understand this phonological rendering, beginning readers can get this far and still not recognize that they are saying "bats." To them these are still four isolated sounds. Sometimes there is a pause while the child takes the next step and links the phonological representation to a meaningful word, or the link is provided by an adult, who, sensing that the child doesn't know what he has said, will help by saying something like, "Yes, /b/ . /æ/ . /t/ . /s/, 'bats.' You read it." In either case, one frequently

TABLE 1
Components of Emergent Literacy, Measures, and Their Relation to Reading Skills

Component	Brief Definition	Sample Measure	Effects[a]
Outside-in processes:			
Language	Semantic, syntactic, and conceptual knowledge	PPVT-R[b] (Dunn & Dunn, 1981); EOWPVT-R[b] (Gardner, 1990); Reynell Developmental Language Scales (Reynell, 1985); CELF-Preschool (Wiig, Secord, & Semel, 1992)	R, EL
Narrative	Understanding and producing narrative	The Renfrew Bus Story (Glasgow & Cowley, 1994); experimenter generated[c]	R
Conventions of print	Knowledge of standard print format (e.g., left-to-right, front-to-back orientation)	Concepts about Print Test (Clay, 1979b); DSC[b] print concepts subscale (CTB, 1990)	R
Emergent reading	Pretending to read	Environmental print[d]	N
Inside-out processes:			
Knowledge of graphemes	Letter-name knowledge	Letter identification (Woodcock, 1987); DSC[b] memory subscale (CTB, 1990)	R, EL
Phonological awareness	Detection of rhyme; manipulation of syllables; manipulation of individual phonemes (e.g., count, delete)	Oddity tasks (MacLean et al., 1987); blending/deletion of syllables (e.g., Wagner et al., 1987); phoneme counting;[e] phoneme deletion;[e] DSC[b] auditory subscale (CTB, 1990)	R
Syntactic awareness	Repair grammatical errors	Word-order violations (e.g., Tunmer et al., 1988); CELF-Preschool (Wiig et al., 1992)	R
Phoneme-grapheme correspondence	Letter-sound knowledge; pseudoword decoding	Word attack (Woodcock, 1987); DSC[b] memory subscale (CTB, 1990)	R, EL
Emergent writing	Phonetic spelling	Invented spelling[f]	R, EL
Other factors:			
Phonological memory	Short-term memory for phonologically coded information (e.g., numbers, nonwords, sentences)	Digit span (WISC-R; Wechsler, 1974); Nonword repetition (e.g., Gathercole et al., 1991); memory for sentences (Woodcock & Johnson, 1977)	R
Rapid naming	Rapid naming of serial lists of letters, numbers, or colors	Rapid naming tests (e.g., McBride-Chang & Manis, 1996)	R
Print motivation	Interest in print shared reading	Requests for shared-reading[g]	R, EL

[a] Effects of individual differences in emergent literacy components: N = no effect demonstrated; EL = effect on other emergent literacy components (e.g., effect of language on narrative); R = effect of emergent literacy component on reading in elementary school.

[b] PPVT-R = Peabody Picture Vocabulary Test—Revised; EOWPVT-R = Expressive One-Word Picture Vocabulary Test—Revised; DSC = Developing Skills Checklist.

[c] See, e.g., Teale & Sulzby (1986).

[d] Standardized measures of environmental print do not exist; the assessment procedure commonly employed involves showing children product labels or pictures of familiar signs (e.g., McDonalds).

[e] See Yopp (1988) and Stanovich, Cunningham, and Cramer (1984) for examples of tasks.

[f] No standardized test of invented spelling is available (see Teale & Sulzby, 1986).

[g] A variety of observational and questionnaire methods of assessing print motivation have been used by researchers (e.g., Crain-Thoresen & Dale, 1992; Scarborough & Dobrich, 1994).

sees the look of pleasure or relief on the child's face at this resolution, which makes sense of the letters and corresponding sounds.

Reading, even in its earliest stages, is a process that is motivated by the extraction of meaning. Imagine the scenario above with a child who has never seen a bat and does not know what the word means. In this case the adult's attempt to help is useless because the child has no semantic representation to which the phonological code can be mapped. Consistent with this logical connection between reading and language, several studies have demonstrated a longitudinal relation between the extent of oral language and later reading proficiency within typically developing, reading-delayed, and language-delayed children (e.g., Bishop & Adams, 1990; Butler, Marsh, Sheppard, & Sheppard, 1985; Pikulski & Tobin, 1989; Scarborough, 1989; Share, Jorm, MacLean, & Mathews, 1984). Other research (see below) indicates that a child's semantic and syntactic abilities assume greater importance later in the sequence of learning to read, when the child is reading for meaning, than early in the sequence, when the child is learning to sound out single words (see Mason, 1992; Snow, Barnes, Chandler, Hemphill, & Goodman, 1991; Whitehurst, 1996a).

In addition to the influence of vocabulary knowledge and the ability to understand and produce increasingly complex syntactic constructions on children's literacy skills, Snow and colleagues (e.g., Dickinson & Snow, 1987; Dickinson & Tabors, 1991; Snow, 1983) have proposed that children's understanding of text and story narratives is facilitated by the acquisition of decontextualized language. Decontextualized language refers to language, such as that used in story narratives and other written forms of communication, that is used to convey novel information to audiences who may share only limited background knowledge with the speaker or who may be physically removed from the things or events described. In contrast, contextualized uses of language rely on shared physical context, knowledge, and immediate feedback. Children's decontextualized language skills are related to conventional literacy skills such as decoding, understanding story narratives, and print production (e.g., Dickinson & Snow, 1987).

Conventions of print. Books are constructed according to a set of conventions that can be understood without being able to read (Clay, 1979a). In English, these include the left-to-right and top-to-bottom direction of print on each page, the sequence and direction in which the print progresses from front to back across pages, the difference between the covers and the pages of the book, the difference between pictures and print on a page, and the meaning of elements of punctuation, including spaces between words and periods at the ends of sentences. Knowing these conventions aids in the process of learning to read (e.g., Clay, 1979b; Tunmer, Herriman, & Nesdale, 1988). For example, Tunmer et al. found that scores on Clay's (1979b) *Concepts about Print Test* at the beginning of first grade predicted children's reading comprehension and decoding abilities at the end of second grade even after controlling for differences in vocabulary and metalinguistic awareness.

Knowledge of letters. In alphabetic writing systems, decoding printed words involves the translation of units of print to units of sound, and writing involves translating units of sound into units of print. At the most basic level, this task requires knowing the names of letters. A beginning reader who does not know the letters of the alphabet cannot learn to which sounds those letters relate (Bond & Dykstra, 1967; Chall, 1967; Mason, 1980). In some cases, this task is facilitated by the fact that some letter names provide clues to their sounds. Knowledge of the alphabet at entry into school is one of the strongest single predictors of short- and long-term literacy success (Stevenson & Newman, 1986); however, interventions that teach children letter names do not seem to produce large effects on reading acquisition (Adams, 1990). Because of this finding, Adams (1990) suggested that higher levels of letter knowledge may reflect a greater underlying knowledge of and familiarity with print or other literacy-related processes. Consequently, whereas teaching letter names may increase surface letter knowledge, it may not affect other underlying literacy-related processes, such as print familiarity. A number of recent studies, however, have indicated that letter knowledge significantly influences the acquisition of some phonological sensitivity skills (e.g., Bowey, 1994; Johnston, Anderson, & Holligan, 1996; Stahl & Murray, 1994) as defined below.

Linguistic awareness. Just as children must be able to discriminate units of print (e.g., letters, words, sentences), so too must they be able to discriminate units of language (e.g., phonemes, words, propositions) to read successfully. Normally developing children in the late preschool period can discriminate among and within these units of language. Linguistic discrimination, however, is not the same as linguistic awareness. Linguistic awareness is metalinguistic. It involves the ability to take language as a cognitive object and to possess information about the manner in which language is constructed and used. A child might well be able to discriminate the difference between two words as evidenced by auditory evoked responses (Molfese, 1990; Molfese, Morris, & Romski, 1990) or by simply being able to respond appropriately to linguistic units incorporating these distinctions (e.g., "Show me the *hat*. Now touch the *bat*"). However, the same child might have no awareness that "hat" and "bat" are units of language called words that are constructed from units of sound that share two phonemes and differ on a third.

Linguistic awareness is not an all-or-none phenomenon. A child may be aware of some portion of the way language is organized (e.g., that propositions are formed from words) without being aware of other aspects of linguistic organization (e.g., that words are formed from phonemes). Evidence suggests a developmental hierarchy of children's sensitivity to linguistic units (e.g., measured by the ability to segment a spoken sentence or word). For example, children seem to achieve syllabic sensitivity earlier than they achieve sensitivity to phonemes (e.g., Fox & Routh, 1975; Liberman, Shankweiler, Fischer, & Carter, 1974), and children's sensitivity to intrasyllabic units and rhyme normally precedes their sensitivity to phonemes (e.g., MacLean, Bryant, & Bradley, 1987; Treiman, 1992). The operationalization of the construct of linguistic awareness is further complicated by the fact that tasks used in assessment vary considerably in the cognitive and linguistic demands they place on children within particular levels of language. For example, phoneme isolation (e.g., "What is the first sound in *fish*?") is substantially easier for kindergartners than phoneme deletion (e.g., "What would *fish* sound like if you took away the /f/ sound?"; Stahl & Murray, 1994; Stanovich, Cunningham, & Cramer, 1984), even though both are measures of phonological sensitivity that appear to call on the same phonological insights.

A growing body of research indicates that individual differences in phonological sensitivity are causally related to the rate of acquisition of reading skills (Bradley & Bryant, 1983, 1985; Mann & Liberman, 1984; Share et al., 1984; Stanovich, Cunningham, & Freeman, 1984; Wagner & Torgesen, 1987). Children who are better at detecting syllables, rhymes, or phonemes are quicker to learn to read (i.e., decode words), and this relation is present even after variability in reading skill due to intelligence, receptive vocabulary, memory skills, and social class is partialed out (e.g., Bryant, MacLean, Bradley, & Crossland, 1990; MacLean et al., 1987; Wagner, Torgesen, & Rashotte, 1994). Moreover the relation appears to be reciprocal. That is, phonological sensitivity is critical to learning to read, and learning to read increases phonological sensitivity (e.g., Perfetti, Beck, Bell, & Hughes, 1987; Wagner et al., 1994). Phonological sensitivity is also related to children's spelling abilities (e.g., Bryant et al., 1990).

Nearly all research on linguistic awareness in emergent literacy has focused on phonological sensitivity (i.e., that words are constructed from sounds) rather than higher levels of linguistic awareness (e.g., that propositions are formed from words). It is possible that awareness of other levels of linguistic structure (e.g., words as constituents of propositions, events as components of narratives or stories; Bruner, 1986; Mandler & Johnson, 1977; Nelson, 1996) assumes greater importance when the child is reading for understanding rather than reading to decode. For instance, syntactic awareness and pragmatic awareness (i.e., comprehension monitoring) appear to play a role in reading comprehension and a lesser role in word identification (Chaney, 1992; Tunmer & Hoover, 1992; Tunmer et al., 1988; Tunmer, Nesdale, & Wright, 1987).

Phoneme-grapheme correspondence. Understanding the links between phonemes and alphabet letters is either the most advanced of the emergent literacy skills or the least advanced of the conventional literacy skills a child must acquire, depending on where one draws the boundary between conventional literacy and emergent literacy. Knowledge of phoneme-grapheme correspondence requires knowledge of both the sounds of individual letters and combinations of letters (e.g., the /f/ sound in the graphemes f, and ph). It is assessed, for example, by showing the child letters and asking, "What sounds do these letters make?" At later stages, it is assessed by phonological recoding tasks (i.e., reading pseudowords), which also involve the ability to blend the individual phonemes. Children who have better phonological recoding ability have higher levels of reading achievement (Gough & Walsh, 1991; Hoover & Gough, 1990; Jorm, Share, MacLean, & Mathews, 1984; Juel, 1988; Tunmer et al., 1988).

Emergent reading. Pretending to read and reading environmental print are examples of emergent reading (Teale & Sulzby, 1986). Before children can read words, they are often able to recognize labels, signs, and other forms of environmental print. Advocates within the emergent literacy movement (e.g., Goodman, 1986) have suggested that this skill demonstrates children's ability to derive the meaning of text within context. However, studies have not generally supported a direct causal link between the ability to read environmental print and later word identification skills (Gough, 1993; Masonheimer, Drum, & Ehri, 1984; Stahl & Murray, 1993). Purcell-Gates (1996; Purcell-Gates & Dahl, 1991) has assessed a factor that she terms "intentionality" by asking children what printed words on a page might signify. Children who indicate that they understand the functions of print (e.g., that the print tells a story or gives directions) have high levels of print intentionality. In contrast, children who have low levels of print intentionality do not indicate that they understand that print is a symbol system with linguistic meaning (e.g., they may simply name letters when asked what words might signify). Purcell-Gates (1996) found that children's understanding of the functions of print (i.e., intentionality) was related to children's print concepts, understanding of the alphabetic principle, and concepts of writing (i.e., use of letter-like symbols).

A number of qualitative studies have examined how preschool-aged children behave in situations in which reading is typically required in order to uncover the knowledge and beliefs that children may have concerning reading. For example, Ferreiro and Teberosky (1982) conducted an extensive study of 4- to 6-year-old children in Argentina and described what appeared to be an orderly developmental progression of children's understanding of print. For instance, 4-year-old children recognized the distinction between "just letters" and "something to read" (typically three or more letters). Ferreiro and Teberosky (1982) also reported that children pass through stages where they believe that print is a nonlinguistic representation of an object, for example, a picture or icon, to believing that print codes only parts of the linguistic stream (e.g., the nouns), to understanding that there is a one-to-one correspondence between the print and the language that results from reading.

Sulzby and others (e.g., Pappas & Brown, 1988; Purcell-Gates, 1988; Sulzby, 1985, 1988) have used children's emergent readings of books to develop an understanding of children's acquisition of the written language register (i.e., the language common to text) and sense of story. For example, in a longitudinal study Sulzby (1985) asked 24 4- to 6-year-old children to "read" one of their favorite storybooks at the beginning and end of kindergarten. At the beginning of kindergarten, she found that most children produced story-like readings that were governed primarily by the pictures, and approximately half of these story-like readings had oral language form (e.g., labeling of pictures) rather than written language form. At the end of kindergarten, although children had retained their relative rank of story reading complexity, most had advanced to a more complex level of emergent reading (e.g., readings governed by pictures but using written language form). Sulzby (1985) provided additional data from a cross-sectional study showing a developmental pattern of increasingly sophisticated emergent reading in 2- to 5-year-old children.

Emergent writing. Behaviors such as pretending to write and learning to write letters are examples of emergent writing. Many adults have had the experience of seeing a young child scribble some indecipherable marks on paper and then ask an adult to read what it says. The child is indicating that he or she knows print has meaning without yet knowing how to write. There have been a number of descriptive studies of children's emergent writing (e.g., Ferreiro & Teberosky, 1982; Harste, Woodward, & Burke, 1984; Sulzby, 1986). Most of these studies converge on a common developmental pattern of children's emergent writing. It appears that very young children treat writing in a pictographic sense that includes using drawing as writing or using scribble-like markings with meaning only to the child. Later, children begin to use different letters, numbers, and letter-like forms to represent the different things being written about. In this phase, children may reorder relatively few symbols to stand for the different words. Often in this phase, characteristics of the thing written are encoded into the word (e.g., a bear is bigger than a duck, therefore, the word "bear" has to be bigger than the word "duck"). For many children in the late preschool period, letters come to stand for the different syllables in words, and from this stage children finally begin to use letters to represent the individual sounds (e.g., phonemes) in words.

Even when children use letters to represent individual sounds, they often do so in an idiosyncratic way (e.g., representing only the first and last sounds of a word as in the spelling

"BK" for the word "bike"). This type of writing has been termed "invented spelling," which consists of writing words following a more or less phonological, rather than orthographic, strategy. Some evidence suggests that invented spelling is a good vehicle for bringing about phonological sensitivity and knowledge of grapheme-phoneme correspondence (e.g., Clarke, 1988; Ehri, 1988). Whereas there is evidence of age-graded emergence of these writing patterns, children often move between levels of writing depending on the writing task (e.g., invented spelling for short familiar words, idiosyncratic use of letters for sentences) but tend to show stability within task (Ferreiro & Teberosky, 1982; Sulzby, Barnhardt, & Hieshima, 1989). Interestingly, children do not always employ phonetic decoding to reread their text even when it was apparently encoded phonetically (i.e., using invented spelling). For instance, when asked to reread their writing children may not track the print or may locate words in different places across rereadings (e.g., Ferreiro & Teberosky, 1982).

Other cognitive factors. A number of more general cognitive factors have also been implicated in the acquisition of emergent and conventional literacy skills. Phonological memory (i.e., the ability to immediately recall nonwords or digit series of increasing length presented orally) appears to be related to children's rate of vocabulary acquisition (Gathercole, Willis, Emslie, & Baddeley, 1992) and reading acquisition (Gathercole, Willis, & Baddeley, 1991; Rohl & Pratt, 1995; Wagner et al., 1994). Rapid naming (i.e., naming arrays of digits, letters, colors, or objects as quickly as possible) taps phonological access to long-term memory (e.g., Wagner & Torgeson, 1987), and recent data suggest that poor performance on rapid naming tasks may discriminate poor readers from good readers independently of phonological sensitivity (McBride-Chang & Manis, 1996). Whereas both phonological memory and rapid naming are related to phonological sensitivity, evidence indicates that they are distinct processes, particularly in older children (e.g., Wagner et al., 1994).

Print motivation. Print motivation refers to children's relative interest in reading and writing activities. Many advocates of emergent literacy argue that children are interested in literacy and, therefore, make active attempts to develop an understanding of print. Several studies have attempted to assess children's interest in literacy using a variety of methods such as parent-report of child interest, parent-report of the frequency of requests for shared reading, examining the proportion of time children spend in literacy-related activities relative to nonliteracy activities (e.g., Lomax, 1977; Thomas, 1984), or by examining degree of engagement during shared reading (Crain-Thoresen & Dale, 1992). Some evidence suggests that these early manifestations of print motivation are associated with emergent literacy skills and later reading achievement (e.g., Crain-Thoreson & Dale, 1992; Payne, Whitehurst, & Angell, 1994; Scarborough & Dobrich, 1994; Thomas, 1984). A child who is interested in literacy is more likely to facilitate shared reading interactions, notice print in the environment, ask questions about the meaning of print, and spend more time reading once he or she is able. During the early school years, print motivation may lead children to do more reading on their own, and print exposure is also a predictor of growth in reading achievement for school-aged children (e.g., Cunningham & Stanovich, 1991; Stanovich & West, 1989; West, Stanovich, & Mitchell, 1993).

Summary. From an emergent literacy perspective, children learn much about reading and writing prior to formal schooling. In the narrow sense, children acquire knowledge of vocabulary, syntax, narrative structure, metalinguistic aspects of language, letters, and text that directly relate to the acquisition of conventional reading (i.e., decoding and/or comprehension) and writing. These components of emergent literacy are the beginnings of the skills that a child needs to acquire in order to become literate in the conventional sense. In a broader sense, children acquire knowledge on the functions, uses, conventions, and significance of text. This knowledge may be reflected in activities such as emergent reading and emergent writing, reading environmental print, and general print motivation. These activities may not reflect component skills in the sense that they are connected to decoding, encoding, or comprehension skills directly. Rather, this knowledge may reflect a child's developing conceptualization of reading and writing and may interact with both formal and informal learning opportunities to advance a child's acquisition of conventional literacy.

These different areas of literacy knowledge have usually been examined by two different research traditions. The component skills area has focused on relating emergent literacy to conventional reading and writing outcomes but has generally not attended to the development of these skills. This approach has often been eschewed by advocates of emergent literacy because it focuses on the narrow aspects of literacy from an adult perspective. In contrast, the focus on children's development of broader literacy knowledge has provided rich descriptions of the ways children interact with literacy materials but generally has neither examined the convergent and independent properties of this knowledge nor demonstrated a causal relation between the development of this knowledge and the development of conventional literacy. Information from both approaches has much to add to an understanding of emergent literacy, and an empirical and theoretical synthesis is both required and possible.

Two Domains of Emergent Literacy

Specification of a complete model of how these different components of emergent literacy develop, influence each other, and influence the development of conventional forms of reading and writing in the context of other skills is not possible given current research. However, a broad division is possible. The model we propose is that emergent and conventional literacy consists of two interdependent sets of skills and processes: *outside-in* and *inside-out*, as represented in Figure 1 (see Gough, 1991, for a related distinction between decoding and comprehension).

The outside-in units in Figure 1 represent children's understanding of the context in which the writing they are trying to read (or write) occurs. The inside-out units represent children's knowledge of the rules for translating the particular writing they are trying to read into sounds (or sounds into print for writing; see Table 1 for a classification of emergent literacy skills following this framework). Imagine a child trying to read the sentence, "She sent off to the very best seed house for five bushels of lupine seed" (Cooney, 1982, p. 21). The ability to decode the letters in this sentence into correct phonological representations (i.e., being able to say the sentence) depends on knowing letters, sounds, links between letters and sounds, punctuation, sentence grammar, and cognitive processes, such as being able to remember and organize these elements into a production sequence. These are inside-out processes, which is to say that they are based on and keyed to the elements of

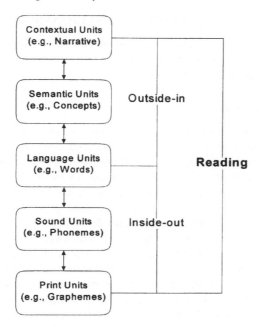

Figure 1. Fluent reading involves a number of component skills and processes. A reader must decode units of print into units of sound and units of sound into units of language. This is an inside-out process. However, being able to say a written word or series of written words is only a part of reading. The fluent reader must understand those auditory derivations, which involves placing them in the correct conceptual and contextual framework. This is an outside-in process. The bidirectional arrows in the figure illustrate that there is cross talk between different components of reading. For example, the sentence context affects the phonological rendering of the italicized letters in these two phases: "a *lea*d balloon," "*lea*d me there."

the sentence itself. However, a child could have the requisite *inside-out* skills to read the sentence aloud and still not read it successfully. What does the sentence mean? Comprehension of all but the simplest of writing depends on knowledge that cannot be found in the word or sentence itself. Who is the "she" referred to in the sentence above? Why is she sending away for seed? Why does she need five bushels? What is lupine? In short what is the narrative, conceptual, and semantic context in which this sentence is found, and how does the sentence make sense within that context? Answering these questions depends on *outside-in* processes, which is to say that the child must bring to bear knowledge of the world, semantic knowledge, and knowledge of the written context in which this particular sentence occurred. A child who cannot translate a sequence of graphemes into sounds cannot understand a written sentence, but neither can a child who does not understand anything about the concepts and context in which the sentence occurs. Outside-in and inside-out processes are both essential to reading and work simultaneously in readers who are reading well.

EMERGENT LITERACY ENVIRONMENTS

Robust relations exist between several components of emergent literacy and conventional literacy. What aspects of emergent literacy environments support the development of these and other components of emergent literacy?

Home Literacy Environment

Significant correlations exist between the home literacy environment and preschool children's language abilities (e.g., Beals, DeTemple, & Dickinson, 1994; Crain-Thoreson & Dale, 1992; Mason, 1980; Mason & Dunning, 1986; Rowe, 1991; Snow et al., 1991; Wells, 1985; Wells, Barnes, & Wells, 1984; and see recent review by Bus, van IJzendoorn, & Pellegrini, 1995). It has also been suggested that the home literacy environment is associated with the development of other components of emergent literacy (e.g., Anderson & Stokes, 1984; Purcell-Gates, 1996; Purcell-Gates & Dahl, 1991; Teale, 1986); however, there has been less quantitative work that has focused on these components.

Language outcomes. The prototypical and iconic aspect of home literacy, shared book reading, provides an extremely rich source of information and opportunity for children to learn language in a developmentally sensitive context (e.g., DeLoache & DeMendoza, 1987; Ninio, 1980; Pellegrini, Brody, & Sigel, 1985; Sénéchal, Cornell, & Broda, 1995; Wheeler, 1983). For instance, Wells (1985) found that approximately 5% of the daily speech of 24-month-old children occurred in the context of storytime. Ninio and Bruner (1978) reported that the most frequent context for maternal labeling of objects was during shared reading. Shared reading and print exposure foster vocabulary development in preschool children (e.g., Cornell, Sénéchal, & Broda, 1988; Elley, 1989; Jenkins, Stein, & Wysocki, 1984; Sénéchal & Cornell, 1993; Sénéchal, LeFevre, Hudson, & Lawson, 1996; Sénéchal, Thomas, & Monker, 1995). Print exposure also has substantial effects on the development of reading skills at older ages when children are already reading (e.g., Allen, Cipielewski, & Stanovich, 1992; Anderson & Freebody, 1981; Cunningham & Stanovich, 1991; Echols, West, Stanovich, & Zehr, 1996; Nagy, Anderson, & Herman, 1987).

Sénéchal et al. (1996) reported that other aspects of the home literacy environment (e.g., number of books in the home, library visits, parents' own print exposure) were related to children's vocabulary skills; however, only the frequency of library visits was related to children's vocabulary after controlling for the effects of children's print exposure. Payne et al. (1994) found that adult literacy activities (e.g., the amount of time a parent spends reading for pleasure) were not significantly related to children's language, which was best predicted by activities that directly involved the child (i.e., frequency of shared reading, number of children's books in the home, frequency of library visits with child). Other aspects of adult-child verbal interactions have also been implicated in the acquisition of some emergent literacy skills. For example, Dickinson and Tabors (1991; see also Beals et al., 1994) reported that features of conversations among parents and children during meals and other conversational interactions (e.g., the proportion of narrative and explanatory talk) contributed to the development of children's decontextualized language skills.

Nonlanguage outcomes. Compared to research examining the relation between home literacy environments and children's oral language skills, there has been relatively little quantitative research concerning home literacy environments and other emergent literacy skills. Both Wells (1985) and Crain-Thoreson and Dale (1992) found that the frequency of shared reading was related to concepts of print measures. Purcell-Gates (1996), in a study of 24 4- to 6-year-old children from low-income families, reported that families in which there were more higher-level literacy events occurring in the home (i.e., reading and writing texts at the level of connected discourse) had children with a higher level of knowledge about the uses and functions of written language, more knowledge of the written language register, and more conventional concepts about print. Mason (1992) reported that shared reading and children's reading and writing at home were associated with children's abilities to label environmental print. Print motivation may also be the product of early experiences with shared reading (e.g., Lomax, 1977; Lonigan, 1994).

Existing studies do not support a direct link between shared reading and growth in phonological skills (e.g., Lonigan, Dyer, & Anthony, 1996; Raz & Bryant, 1990; Whitehurst, 1996a). For example, Lonigan et al. found that growth in preschool phonological sensitivity was related to parental involvement in literacy activities in the home but growth in phonological sensitivity was not associated with shared reading frequency. Recently, Sénéchal, LeFevre, Thomas, and Daley (in press) reported that kindergarten and first-grade children's written language knowledge (i.e., print concepts, letter knowledge, invented spelling, word identification) was associated with parental attempts to teach their children about print but not exposure to storybooks. In contrast, children's oral language skills were associated with storybook exposure but not parents' attempts to teach print.

Rhyming skills. Children's early knowledge of and/or experience with rhyme may play a role in the development of phonological sensitivity (e.g., MacLean et al., 1987). Preschool-aged children are able to detect rhyme even when other phonological sensitivity measures are too difficult (e.g., Bradley & Bryant, 1983; Kirtley, Bryant, MacLean, & Bradley, 1989; Lenel & Cantor, 1981; Stanovich, Cunningham, & Freeman, 1984), and this ability predicts subsequent word identification (MacLean et al., 1987; Bryant et al., 1990). The exact nature of the relation between the ability to detect rhyme, phonological awareness, and reading is still the subject of debate (e.g., Cardoso-Martins, 1994). Rhyming may be an early form of phonological sensitivity (Bryant et al., 1990), and/or rhyming may enable children to begin to learn orthographic patterns via analogy (i.e., recognizing common spelling patterns between words that rhyme; Goswami & Bryant, 1992; Walton, 1995). Experiences that teach children about rhyme sensitize them to the sound structure of words (e.g., Bradley & Bryant, 1983); however, a specific connection between such experiences in the home and rhyming ability has yet to be demonstrated.

Preschool and Teacher Effects

Children's day-care and preschool environments can have positive effects on children's emergent literacy (Bryant, Burchinal, Lau, & Sparling, 1994; Scarr & McCartney, 1988; Schliecker, White, & Jacobs, 1991). The most commonly used measure of day-care quality is the Early Childhood Environmental Rating Scale (ECERS; Harms & Clifford, 1980), a rating scale that provides an assessment of aspects of the curriculum, the environment, teacher-child interactions, and teaching practices within the classroom. Bryant et al. (1994) measured the quality of 32 Head Start classrooms in North Carolina using the ECERS, and the cognitive ability and achievement of children from these classes. Quality of home environment was measured using the Home Screening Questionnaire (Frankenberg & Coons, 1986), which includes questions about the language stimulation in the environment, schedule and organization at home, use of punishment by parents, and family activities, and was completed during an interview with the parent. When home environment was controlled statistically, ECERS scores still predicted children's cognitive and achievement scores.

Whereas the ECERS focuses on very broad classroom and center variables, Crone (1996) found that dimensions of teacher behavior during shared reading (e.g., dramatic quality, warmth, attempts to engage individual children) related to children's active involvement in shared reading and individual differences in children's phonological processing ability on the Developing Skills Checklist (CTB, 1990). Dickinson and Smith (1994) also examined the effects of preschool teachers' interactional styles during shared reading on the vocabulary and story comprehension abilities of 25 4-year-old children in 25 different preschool classrooms. They found that the proportion of teacher and child talk during reading that included analysis of characters or events, predictions of coming events, and discussion of vocabulary (e.g., definitions, comments about sounds or functions of words) was significantly associated with a higher level of children's vocabulary and story comprehension even when controlling for the total amount of teacher and child speech. Other research has also found that characteristics of preschool settings such as opportunities to engage in shared reading, writing activities, and teachers' child-direct speech is associated with higher levels of vocabulary, print concepts, and story comprehension (e.g., Dickinson & Tabors, 1991).

Causal Modeling

There have been relatively few studies examining relations between the multidimensional aspects of emergent literacy, emergent literacy environments, and reading and writing development over time (but see Mason, 1992). Such work is important because of the tangled web of correlations among emergent literacy environments, emergent literacy skills, and conventional literacy skills. Bivariate or cross-sectional studies are likely to generate an incomplete and distorted picture of the causal pathways to conventional literacy. Whitehurst (1996a) developed a structural equation model to explain how children's emergent literacy skills evolve over time and how children's literacy environments relate to these skills and reading acquisition for a group of 200 4-year-old Head Start children followed until they were 7 years old. A simplified version of this model is shown in Figure 2.

A number of important conclusions can be derived from the model. First inside-out emergent literacy skills, including phonological sensitivity, are as critical to reading acquisition for a low-income population as they are for the socioeconomically heterogeneous samples that have been studied previously (e.g., Share et al., 1984). The variable reflecting insideout skills (i.e., letter knowledge, phonological sensitivity, emergent writing) is the strongest predictor of reading at the end of first grade. Second, there is strong continuity

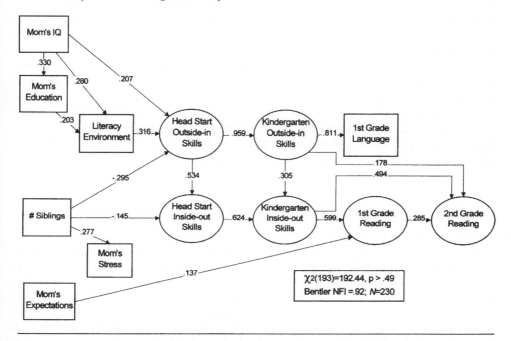

Figure 2. This structural equation model is derived from longitudinal data on children who were initially assessed when they were in Head Start at age 4 and who were followed until the end of the second grade at age 7. To simplify the schematic, neither measurement variables that served as indicators of latent variables (the ovals in the figure) nor error variances are represented. The outside-in latent variable was measured using standardized tests of receptive and expressive vocabulary. The inside-out latent variable was indexed with measures of linguistic awareness, letter knowledge, and emergent writing. All of the arrows in the figure represent statistically significant paths of influence; the numbers associated with each arrow can be interpreted as standardized regression beta weights. Note the strong continuity from outside-in to outside-in latent variables and from inside-out to inside-out latent variables across age as well as the independence of the outside-in latent variable and reading in first grade. Reading in the first and second grade is strongly determined by individual differences in inside-out skills at the end of kindergarten.

between outside-in emergent literacy skills (i.e., receptive and expressive language) from preschool into the early school years and similarly strong continuity between inside-out emergent literacy skills and measures of conventional literacy (i.e., word decoding, spelling, comprehension) during the same period. Third, outside-in and inside-out emergent literacy skills become increasingly independent from preschool to first grade when reading involves mainly learning to decode words. Language skills (outside-in skills), however, again play a significant role in reading in the second grade as the focus shifts from decoding to reading comprehension. Fourth, the main effects of the literacy environment on children's emergent literacy skills are indirect through their effects on children's language skills. Finally, the model identifies only number of siblings in the home as a developmental precursor of inside-out emergent literacy skills. Perhaps children need to engage in a lot of conversation with adults to develop phonological sensitivity, and perhaps these experiences are compromised in families in which adult time has to be shared among many children.

Clearly this is an incomplete model of the development of emergent literacy skills and conventional literacy skills in children from low-income families, limited as it is to home variables, and providing much more information with regard to origins of outside-in emergent literacy than origins of inside-out emergent literacy. However, these results indicate that the experiences that lead to the development of inside-out skills are not the same as those that lead to the development of outside-in skills (i.e., language), and that early differences in these areas are relatively stable across time, a conclusion supported in other populations (Byrne, Freebody, & Gates, 1992; Wagner et al., 1994).

SOCIAL CLASS DIFFERENCES IN EMERGENT LITERACY

According to the 1991 Carnegie Foundation report, *Ready to Learn: A Mandate for the Nation,* 35% of children in the United States enter public schools with such low levels of the skills and motivation that are needed as starting points in our current educational system that they are at substantial risk of early academic difficulties. Although one might quarrel with definitions and causes, there seems to be little doubt that there is a significant mismatch between what many children bring to their first school experience and what schools expect of them if they are to succeed. This problem, often called school readiness, is strongly linked to family income. When schools are ranked by the median socioeconomic status of their students' families, SES correlates .68 with academic achievement (White, 1982). The National Assessment of Educational Progress (1991) has documented substantial differences in the reading and writing ability of children as a function of the economic level of their parents. Socioeconomic status is also one of the strongest predictors of performance differences in children at the beginning of first grade (Entwisle & Alexander, cited in Alexander & Entwisle, 1988, p. 99). These performance differences have been reported in reading achievement and a number of the emergent literacy skills outlined previously.

The relation between the skills with which children enter school and their later academic performance is strikingly stable (Baydar, Brooks-Gunn, & Furstenberg, 1993; Stevenson & Newman, 1986; Tramontana, Hooper, & Selzer, 1988). For instance, juel (1988) reported that the probability that a child would remain a poor reader at the end of the fourth grade if he or she was a poor reader at the end of the first grade was .88. Moreover, as noted by Stanovich (e.g., 1986), deficits in reading skills initially may be relatively specific, but this specificity breaks down as the reciprocal relation between reading and achievement in other areas increases.

Emergent Literacy Skills

Children from low-income families are at risk for reading difficulties (e.g., Dubow & Ippolito, 1994; Juel, Griffith, & Gough, 1986; Smith & Dixon, 1995) and are also more likely to be slow in the development of language skills (e.g., Juel et al., 1986; Lonigan & Whitehurst, in press; Whitehurst, 1996b). In addition, there are SES differences in children's letter knowledge and phonological sensitivity prior to school entry (Bowey, 1995; Lonigan, Burgess, Anthony, & Barker, in press; MacLean et al., 1987; Raz & Bryant, 1990), and these differences in phonological sensitivity relate to later differences in word decoding skills (Raz & Bryant, 1990).

Emergent Literacy Experiences

There are large social class differences in children's exposure to experiences that might support the development of emergent literacy skills. Ninio (1980) found that mothers from lower-SES groups engaged in fewer teaching behaviors during shared reading than mothers from middle-class groups. Numerous studies have documented differences in the pattern of book ownership and frequency of shared reading between lower- versus higher-SES families (e.g., Anderson & Stokes, 1984; Feitelson & Goldstein, 1986; Heath, 1982; Raz & Bryant, 1990; Teale, 1986). For instance, McCormick and Mason (1986) reported that 47% of their sample of public-aid parents reported no alphabet books in the home, whereas only 3% of their sample of professional parents reported the absence of such books. Adams (1990, p. 85) estimated that the typical middle-class child enters first grade with 1,000–1,700 hours of one-on-one picture book reading, whereas a child from a low-income family averages just 25 hours.

INTERVENTIONS TO ENHANCE EMERGENT LITERACY

On the assumption that enhancing emergent literacy skills will increase subsequent reading achievement, interventions have been developed to improve one or more components of emergent literacy. These studies have potential implications for the theory of emergent literacy and the development of conventional literacy as well as for creating cost-effective programs for low-income and other children that produce substantial and lasting benefits for children's literacy.

Dialogic Reading

Whitehurst and colleagues have demonstrated that a program of shared-reading, called *dialogic reading*, can produce substantial changes in preschool children's language skills. Dialogic reading involves several changes in the way adults typically read books to children. Central to these changes is a shift in roles. During typical shared-reading, the adult reads and the child listens, but in dialogic reading the child learns to become the storyteller. The adult assumes the role of an active listener, asking questions, adding information, and prompting the child to increase the sophistication of descriptions of the material in the picture book. A child's responses to the book are encouraged through praise and repetition, and more sophisticated responses are encouraged by expansions of the child's utterances and by more challenging questions from the adult reading partner. For 2- and 3-year-olds, questions from adults focus on individual pages in a book, asking the child to describe objects, actions, and events on the page (e.g., "What is this? What color is the duck? What is the duck doing?"). For 4- and 5-year-olds questions increasingly focus on the narrative as a whole or on relations between the book and the child's life (e.g., "Have you ever seen a duck swimming? What did it look like?").

Dialogic reading has been shown to produce larger effects on the language skills of children from middle- to upper-income families than a similar amount of typical picture book reading (Arnold, Lonigan, Whitehurst, & Epstein, 1994; Whitehurst et al., 1988). Studies conducted with children from low-income families attending child care demonstrate that both child-care teachers and parents using a 6-week small-group center-based or home dialogic reading intervention can produce substantial positive changes in the development of children's language as measured by standardized and naturalistic measures (Lonigan & Whitehurst, in press; Valdez-Menchaca & Whitehurst, 1992; Whitehurst, Arnold, et al., 1994) that are maintained 6 months following the intervention (Whitehurst, Arnold, et al., 1994).

Whitehurst evaluated the combination of dialogic reading and a center-based phonological sensitivity training program adapted from Byrne and Fielding-Barnsley's (1991a) *Sound Foundations* with a group of 357 4-year-olds attending eight different Head Start centers (Whitehurst, 1997a). Children in control classrooms received the regular Head Start curriculum, and children in the intervention condition were involved in small-group dialogic reading several times each week in intervention classrooms over the course of the school year. These same children brought home the book that was being used in the classroom each week for use with their primary caregivers. Results at the end of the Head Start year showed large and educationally significant effects of the intervention on a writing factor and a concepts of print factor but no significant effects on a linguistic awareness factor; effects on language were mediated by the degree to which parents were involved in the at-home component of the shared reading program. Effects on language, writing, and print knowledge favoring children in the intervention condition were still significant a year later at the end of kindergarten, with effect sizes in these three domains ranging from ⅓ to ½ a standard deviation (Whitehurst, 1997a). Consistent with other research reported above, shared reading interventions do not appear to result in significant growth in phonological sensitivity (Lonigan, Anthony, Dyer, & Collins, 1995; Whitehurst, Epstein, et al., 1994), demonstrating the relative independence between language and shared reading, on the one hand, and phonological sensitivity, on the other.

It is difficult to implement and maintain an intensive program of shared reading in child care settings. Substantial variability in center compliance with the dialogic reading program schedule, which significantly moderates the program's effects, is typical (Lonigan & Whitehurst, in press; Whitehurst, Arnold, et al., 1994), and centers tend not to continue the necessary small-group reading outside of the experimental context (Whitehurst, Arnold, et al., 1994). Successful alternatives to child care intervention include outreach from pediatric outpatient settings (e.g., Needlman, Fried, Morley, Taylor, & Zuckerman, 1991), library outreach programs (e.g., Morisset, 1993), and the use of community volunteers (e.g., Lonigan et al., 1995).

Little Books

Even simple emergent literacy interventions can be effective if they are sufficiently intensive. McCormick and Mason (1986) conducted two quasi-experimental studies evaluating the efficacy of providing their "Little Books" to prereaders from low- and middle-income families. Little Books are small, easy-to-read books that contain simple words, simple illustrations, and repetitive text. Intervention group children in the first study were given a Little Book to keep, their parents were provided additional Little Books and a printed guideline for their use, and more Little Books were mailed to the child's home during the summer and fall. The intervention group of the second study received only the first packet of Little Books. Emergent literacy skills were assessed at the beginning and end of the following school year. In the first study, the intervention group scored higher than the control group on several composite measures, including word knowledge, spelling knowledge, and number of words read from the Little Books. In the second study, the intervention group read more words from the Little Books but did not differ on any other measure.

Changes in Preschool Emergent Literacy Environments

Changes in children's preschool environments can have an impact on children's emergent literacy skills. For example, Neuman and Roskos (1993) examined the effects of creating literacy-rich play settings in Head Start centers. They randomly assigned eight different Head Start classrooms to either a no-treatment control group, an office play setting with adult monitor group, or an office play setting with adult interaction group. The office play settings were structured to provide children with opportunities to interact with print and writing in the form of signs and labels, functional print items (e.g., calendar, telephone book), and writing materials. In the adult interaction group, a volunteer parent was instructed to assist children in their literacy play (e.g., by modeling literacy behavior like "taking an order" or writing a list). In the adult monitor group, a volunteer adult was instructed to simply observe children in their play and take notes on the quality of the children's play behavior. Prior to the intervention, all of the classrooms had little literacy materials available to the children. For instance, each classroom had approximately 10 books in a library corner but no writing materials freely available to the children. Across the intervention, children had access to these literacy-play settings 3 days each week for 5 months. Observations across the intervention period indicated that the proportion of literacy behaviors increased in the classrooms with the office-play settings. At the end of the 5 months, 138 children were administered three measures of emergent literacy. Children in both intervention conditions scored higher on an environmental print task than children in the control classrooms, and children in the adult interaction classrooms scored higher than children in the adult monitor classrooms on this measure. Children in both intervention classrooms also scored higher than children in the control classrooms on a measure of labeling functional print items (e.g., a calendar, a typed business letter) but not on a measure of describing the functions of the print items.

Intergenerational Family Literacy

Intergenerational literacy programs focus intervention efforts on the family, rather than on the child or caregiver separately, based on the hypothesis that maximal effects will be achieved by combining the positive effects of early childhood intervention with a facilitative effect of better early parenting, improvement in family income, increased adult literacy, and enhanced parental support for children's school-related functioning (St. Pierre, Layzer, & Barnes, 1995). Most programs integrate early childhood intervention, parenting skills education, and other parent education (e.g., literacy, job skills, vocational training), but they differ substantially in the intensity and mode of delivery of services.

Minimal effects have been observed on children's short-term cognitive, behavioral, or health-related outcomes in evaluation studies. For instance, in a randomized experimental design, children participating in the U.S. Department of Education's national family literacy initiative, Even Start, gained no more than children in the control condition on language or school readiness skills. In a study of a larger Even Start sample, a medium effect was reported on school readiness skills; however, this difference was not maintained once children entered school, and it was found in a nonexperimental design in which gains were estimated against projected normative growth rates rather than against a control or comparison group (St. Pierre et al., 1995).

In contrast to the weak effects found on child outcomes, intergenerational literacy programs typically produce positive effects on parent attitudes or behaviors related to literacy or learning (e.g., parent-child interaction, literacy materials in the home) and generate increases in obtaining GED certificates by adults. However, little or no effects are found on formal measures of adult literacy or on family income (St. Pierre et al., 1995).

Phonological Sensitivity Training

As noted above, children's phonological sensitivity is one of the strongest predictors of later reading achievement. Experimental studies of programs designed to teach children phonological sensitivity show positive effects on children's reading and spelling skills (e.g., Ball & Blachman, 1988; Bradley & Bryant, 1985; Lundberg, Frost, & Petersen, 1988; Torgesen, Morgan, & Davis, 1992; Uhry & Shepherd, 1993), and programs that include letter-sound training (e.g., Ball & Blachman, 1988; Bradley & Bryant, 1985) produce larger results (Wagner, 1996). The majority of these programs teach children how to categorize objects on the basis of certain sounds (e.g., initial phonemes). Other programs explicitly teach children phonemic analysis and synthesis skills. Torgesen et al. (1992) compared the effects of training synthesis skills only to training both analysis and synthesis skills. During a 7 week program, groups of three to five children in the combined training group worked with an adult to learn how to identify and pronounce the initial, final, or middle sounds in two- and three-phoneme words (analysis). These children were then taught how to pronounce words after hearing their phonemes in isolation. Children in the synthesis condition received only the blending training. A control group listened to stories, engaged in discussions about the stories, and answered comprehension questions. Results indicated that both training groups experienced increases in synthesis skills, whereas only the combined group increased in their analysis skills and scored higher than the other two groups on a reading analogue task.

Whereas most phonological sensitivity training studies have been conducted with children at the beginning stages of learning to read (i.e., kindergarten or first grade), Byrne and Fielding-Barnsley (1991b) found that preschool children (*M* age = 55 months) exposed to 12 weeks of their *Sound Foundations* program demonstrated greater increases in phonological sensitivity than a group of control children exposed to storybook reading and a semantic categorization program. This intervention program consisted of teaching children six phonemes in the initial and final positions of words by drawing attention to the sound in words, discussing how the sound is made by the mouth, reciting rhymes with the phoneme in the appropriate position, and encouraging children to find objects in a poster that had the sound in the initial (or final) position. Worksheets in which children identified and colored items with the phoneme in the correct position were used, and the letter for the phoneme was displayed. A final stage of training introduced children to two card games that required matching objects on the basis of initial or final phonemes. Some of the gains children in Byrne and Fielding-Barnsley (1991b) made were maintained through the first and second grades (Byrne & Fielding-Barnsley, 1993, 1995). However, an uncontrolled trial using regular preschool teachers and classrooms found substantially smaller effects and a large degree of variability in the fidelity of program implementation (Byrne & Fielding Barnsley, 1995), findings which call into question the potential success of a staff-implemented phonological training program under nonexperimental conditions in children's preschool environments.

Whole Language Instruction

The whole language approach to beginning reading can be considered an extension of an emergent literacy philosophy to reading instruction. Whole language instruction involves an increased emphasis on the outside-in components of reading compared with the inside-out components (e.g., see Adams, 1991; Adams & Bruck, 1995). Whole language adherents believe that there are strong parallels between the acquisition of reading and the acquisition of oral language, and they therefore argue that reading acquisition would occur as easily and naturally as language acquisition if the meaning and purpose of text were emphasized. However, Liberman and Liberman (1992; see also Perfetti, 1991) note many differences between oral language and text that suggest that the parallel between language and reading acquisition does not stand up to careful scrutiny. Additionally, studies concerning skilled reading clearly disconfirm a core assumption of whole language, that skilled reading involves a "psycholinguistic guessing game" (Goodman, 1967) in which the reader deduces unfamiliar words from their context. Skilled readers process each individual word when reading text (Carpenter & Just, 1981; Just & Carpenter, 1987; Paterson & Coltheart, 1987) and are unable to guess a word correctly from context more than 25% of the time (e.g., Gough, Alford, & Holley-Wilcox, 1981; Perfetti, Goldman, & Hogaboam, 1979). Contrary to the whole language position, it is only for individuals whose word identification skills are poor that contextual cues contribute to the accuracy and speed of word identification (e.g., Bruck, 1990; Perfetti et al., 1979; Simons & Leu, 1987; Stanovich, 1981).

As contentious as the debate between advocates of whole language and code-based instruction (e.g., emphasis on phonics and other inside-out units) has often been, it is important to recognize that there are significant points of overlap. Indeed, our conceptual model in Figure 1 indicates that skilled reading and writing inseparably involve both inside-out and outside-in processes and skills. Components of phonological sensitivity or phonics instruction can be successfully incorporated into an instructional program in which the functions, meanings, and value of text are emphasized (Castle, Riach, & Nicholson, 1994; Foorman, Francis, Novy, & Liberman, 1991; Hatcher, Hulme, & Ellis, 1994; McGuinness,

McGuinness, & Donohue, 1995; Stanovich & Stanovich, 1995; Vellutino, 1991). Results of a meta-analysis by Stahl, McKenna, and Pagnucco (1994) indicate that instructional programs that include both whole language (outside-in) and skills-based (inside-out) components produce positive effects on both achievement and attitudes toward reading.

That does not mean, however, that an empirically guided instructional strategy for beginning reading allows free choice of instructional components. A large research literature consistently demonstrates that skills-based instruction (e.g., phonics) produces superior results in reading skills in comparison to reading instruction that does not include a skills emphasis (Adams & Bruck, 1993, 1995; Stanovich & Stanovich, 1995; Vellutino, 1991). This result is obtained with children from middle- and upper-income families as well as with children from lower-income families (Stanovich & Stanovich, 1995). In the context of this research, whole language is the useful handmaiden to code-based instruction; it is not a successful stand-alone approach for many children. Although most children will learn to read regardless of the instructional strategy to which they are exposed, a substantial number of children will have difficulty. Recent data indicate that those children who benefit least from typical "extra-help" remediation are those with phonological sensitivity deficits (Vellutino et al., 1996), a finding that highlights the importance of skills-based instruction for the at-risk reader.

A LOOK TO THE FUTURE

Similar to its subject matter, the study of emergent literacy is in the early stages of development. Although the current state of the area provides evidence of a number of paths through which children's acquisition of reading and writing can be understood, there are many questions without answers. It seems clear that well-developed language skills, letter knowledge, and some form of phonological sensitivity are necessary for reading and writing, and that the origins of these components of emergent literacy are found during the preschool years. Preschool measures of these components predict subsequent reading achievement (see Table 1 and Figure 2). However, the interactions between, or relative independence of, various emergent literacy skills are not clear. Consequently, a well-elaborated developmental model of emergent literacy is not yet possible. It is clear that aspects of the home literacy environment, such as shared reading, benefit children's language development, and that there are a number of interventions that can be used to enhance both language and phonological sensitivity during the preschool period. This brief review suggests a number of research and social policy initiatives that will expand knowledge of emergent literacy and incorporate what is already known into current practices. Several of these points are expanded below.

Directions for Future Research
Different domains of emergent literacy. Most research has not distinguished between different forms of emergent literacy experience and different forms of emergent literacy skills. Typically one finds studies involving a single measure of emergent literacy experience (e.g., frequency of shared reading) and a single measure of emergent literacy outcome (e.g., preschool language use). The predominance of such univariate approaches, coupled

with methodological weaknesses in terms of sample size and statistical treatment, may be the reason one recent review of the literature found relatively weak empirical support for the connection between shared reading and the development of emergent literacy skills (Scarborough & Dobrich, 1994; see critiques by Bus et al., 1995; Lonigan, 1994). A number of studies indicate clearly the need to separate different types of emergent literacy skill and to question whether each of those types of skill arises from the same matrix of experience (e.g., Sénéchal et al., in press; Whitehurst, 1996a).

The two domains of emergent literacy (i.e., inside-out and outside-in skills) appear to be most strongly related to reading development at different points in the reading acquisition process. Inside-out emergent literacy skills are critically important in the earliest stage of learning to read when the focus is on decoding text. This is as true in children who are at risk of reading difficulties because of variables that correlate with low-income family background as it is in children who are at risk because of a specific deficit in phonological sensitivity. Outside-in emergent literacy skills are also critical to learning to read, but may play a greater role at the stage at which children begin to read more complex text for meaning and pleasure than in the initial stage of learning to decode (e.g., Snow et al., 1991; Whitehurst, 1996a).

Inside-out and outside-in components of emergent literacy are not the product of the same experiences. Most aspects of children's emergent literacy environments that are typically measured, including print exposure, are associated with the outside-in skills. Extant data shed little light on the environmental correlates of the inside-out skills. The literature does suggest a number of possible candidates, however. One of these is the opportunity to engage in conversation with adults (Whitehurst, 1996a). For instance, Caravolas and Bruck (1993) reported that development of phonological sensitivity is shaped by frequency and form of phonological input (see also Caravolas, 1993). Similarly, Murray, Stahl, and Ivey (1996) demonstrated that exposure to alphabet books that included letter-sound information resulted in more gains in phonological sensitivity than exposure to alphabet books without letter-sound information, or exposure to storybooks. Regardless of the specific mechanism for these effects, children in low-income groups receive little exposure to these situations (e.g., Heath, 1989; McCormick & Mason, 1986).

Better integration of research. For some aspects of emergent literacy (e.g., emergent writing, emergent reading), we know how the skills develop and where they come from but little about their function or utility. For other components (e.g., linguistic awareness), we know what the skills are good for but little about how they develop and their origins. Progress will require an understanding of what aspects of emergent literacy are related to what aspects of reading and writing, and what features of emergent literacy environments are related to what aspects of emergent literacy. Localization of these effects is likely to change as the demands of literacy acquisition change (i.e., from primarily decoding to comprehension). Progress in this domain will be advanced by a synthesis of the two research traditions that have examined emergent literacy. Whereas the qualitative approach has provided rich descriptions of children's emergent literacy, demonstrations of the significance and independence of the observed behaviors is required. The more quantitative-oriented approach has provided important information concerning the emergent literacy skills critical for the transition to conventional literacy; however, questions concerning the origins of these skills need to be addressed. A causal modeling approach may be an effective means of answering some of these questions, and answers to these questions will allow refinement of interventions for emergent literacy and conventional literacy (i.e., reading and writing).

Longer-term outcomes of interventions. Short-term results of emergent literacy interventions are promising enough to both warrant and require long-term outcome studies. Given the evidence that the outside-in skills of emergent literacy significantly relate to learning to read, it is not unreasonable to expect that effects of interventions shown to improve these skills (e.g., Lonigan & Whitehurst, in press; Whitehurst, Arnold et al., 1994) will affect children's reading and writing outcomes. However, because most of the evidence linking outside-in skills and reading comes from correlational studies, there is little unambiguous evidence that improving outside-in skills through shared reading or other activities will improve later literacy acquisition (e.g., Lonigan, 1994; Scarborough & Dobrich, 1994). Moreover, given that language skills may not have their most significant role in reading achievement until second or third grade (Whitehurst, 1996a), researchers interested in demonstrating long-term effects of early shared reading experiences must be persistent and patient. The interventions themselves must also represent a sufficient dosage in the sense that a few months or a year of increased print exposure in the preschool period may not be enough to sustain language gains through the early elementary school years. Similarly, results of programs to teach the inside-out skills of emergent literacy provide a promising avenue by which children's early reading and writing can be improved. However, questions remain concerning whether these effects generalize to fluent reading in context for meaning, and how to effectively deliver training in real preschool and kindergarten classrooms.

Implications for Public Policy

Despite these limitations in current knowledge concerning emergent literacy, we believe that existing data support a number of public policy directions concerning both interventions for promoting emergent literacy skills and educational practices concerning the teaching of conventional literacy.

Multifaceted interventions. Because both outside-in and inside-out components are required for eventual reading success, interventions need to target both areas. Interventions that focus on increasing children's experience with picture books and other literacy materials and the frequency of their verbal interactions with adults around emergent-literacy materials, such as dialogic reading, have their primary effect on the outside-in skills of emergent literacy. Interventions focused on improving phonological processing skills in children have effects on the inside-out skills of emergent literacy. Acquisition of the inside-out skills of emergent literacy requires more explicit teaching than many children receive before they enter school, particularly children from backgrounds of poverty, who are much less likely than their middle-class counterparts to have been exposed to activities such as alphabet boards, learning to print their names, or playing rhyming games.

Developmentally appropriate interventions. Although the evidence indicates that the inside-out skills of emergent literacy can be taught to prereaders and that this training transfers to reading-related tasks, a practical intervention will have to be much more developmentally appropriate in technique and much broader in content than the laboratory-like methods that have been employed to date. A primary criterion for developmentally appropriate practice at the preschool level is that children be allowed to learn through active exploration and interaction (Bredecamp, 1986). Even if one could overcome the practical barriers of training teachers to implement a curriculum for inside-out emergent skills and design teaching materials that would sustain children's interest over an extended period, it would be impossible to have teacher-to-child ratios that would allow children to proceed individually at their own pace. Moreover, teacher-led instruction to groups of children would simply require too much sitting still, too much attending to the teacher, and too much feedback of right and wrong to be considered developmentally appropriate for preschoolers.

Computer-based interventions. We believe that computer-based technology is the most promising method for dealing with these limitations and effectively teaching inside-out emergent literacy skills in preschool and kindergarten settings. There is now a large literature demonstrating that preschoolers can interact successfully with computers both in terms of sustained interest and substantive gains in knowledge (e.g., Lepper & Gurtner, 1989). Well-designed software allows children to learn through active exploration and interaction. Preliminary evidence points to the potential effectiveness of software designed to teach phonological sensitivity skills to children (Barker & Torgesen, 1995; Foster, Erickson, Foster, Brinkman, & Torgesen, 1994).

Foster et al. (1994) conducted two experiments in which preschool and kindergarten children were randomly assigned to receive either their standard school curriculum or between 5 and 8 hours of exposure to *DaisyQuest* (Erickson, Foster, Foster, Torgesen, & Packer, 1992), a computer program designed to teach phonological sensitivity in the context of an interactive adventure game. Children in the experimental group in both studies demonstrated significant and large gains in phonological skills compared to the children in the no-treatment control group. The obtained effect sizes of 1.05 standard deviation units on tests of phonological sensitivity compared favorably to longer teacher-led programs with older children (e.g., Torgesen et al., 1992). In a second study, Barker and Torgesen (1995) examined the effectiveness of the *DaisyQuest* program with a group of 54 at-risk first-grade children who were randomly assigned to either an experimental or control group. Children in the experimental group received approximately 8 hours of exposure to the program, and children in the control group received an equal amount of exposure to computer programs designed to teach early math skills or other reading skills. Exposure to the *DaisyQuest* program produced significant and large improvements in children's phonological sensitivity and word identification skills compared to the control groups (i.e., an effect size of 1.1 standard deviation units was obtained on the measure of phoneme segmentation).

Dangers of a critical period model. One of the dangers of the assumption in the whole language movement that learning to read is similar to learning to talk is the implication that there is a "critical period" for learning to read and write as there may be for learning to talk. Under this scenario, children who are at risk for problems in learning to read must receive intervention early if they are to become literate. In this context, deficiencies in children's emergent literacy experience of the types evidenced by many children from low-income backgrounds are thought to doom them to reading failure in elementary school. Although we have documented strong correlations between emergent literacy skills and later reading achievement, these findings are descriptive, not prescriptive.

This point is illustrated by data from Whitehurst (1997b) on the differential course of development of two groups of children who started and ended Head Start within programs run in the same suburban county by the same Head Start agency, but in two different locations approximately 15 miles apart. The children entered and exited Head Start at very similar and relatively low levels of development on language and other emergent literacy skills and then, depending on the location of their Head Start center, transitioned into either school district P or school district C. District P was a demographically mixed and stable district serving free lunch (an index of poverty) to 34% of its students, while district C was a district in demographic flux as it served increasing numbers of children of recent non-English-speaking immigrants from central America; district C served free lunch to 58% of its children.

Figure 3 plots Peabody Picture Vocabulary Test (PPVT) (Dunn & Dunn, 1981) scores on four occasions, starting with entry into Head Start, again on exit from Head Start, again on exit from kindergarten, and again on exit from first grade. The final data points are scores on the Wide Range Achievement Test Word Reading subscale (WRAT) (Jastak & Wilkinson, 1984) on exit from first grade. Note that for children in district C, growth is a smoothly decelerating function and that WRAT scores at the end of first grade are exactly

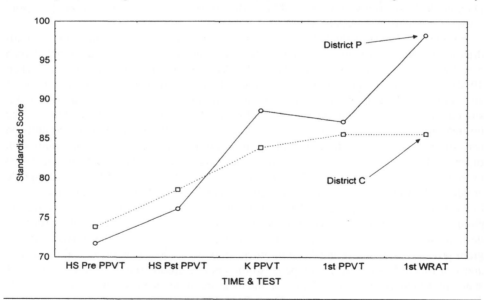

Figure 3. These longitudinal data represent receptive language scores (PPVT) and reading scores (WRAT) for two groups of children from low-income families who entered and exited Head Start with similar levels of language and other emergent literacy skills. Children then transitioned into either school district C ($N = 48$ children) or P ($N = 24$ children), with district C serving a much more economically depressed community than district P. Children in district P are close to the national mean on word reading at the end of first grade and are performing a standard deviation higher on reading than their peers in district C. Both groups of children had low levels of emergent literacy skills at entry into public school and would have been viewed as at high risk for developing reading problems. Deficiencies in emergent literacy skills influence but do not foredoom later reading success.

at the same level as PPVT scores. In contrast, children in district P show a bigger jump in PPVT scores from Head Start to kindergarten than do their peers in district C. Further, and here is the important point, their word-reading skills at the end of first grade are nearly a whole standard deviation higher than their PPVT scores and nearly a whole standard deviation higher than the reading scores of their peers in district C. Children in district P, who started Head Start nearly two standard deviations below the mean in language abilities and thus could be considered at very high risk of reading failure, are close to the mean of the population on reading ability at the end of first grade. In contrast, their peers in district C, who were indistinguishable from the district P children on skill measures taken during Head Start and on measures of family demographics, are failing at reading at the end of first grade. Presumably, the differences between the reading outcomes of these two groups of children are due to differences in the effectiveness of instruction across the two school districts. The striking contrast between the academic fates of these two groups of children should serve as a warning against the view that deficiencies in emergent literacy skills necessarily prevent effective reading instruction.

Literacy is a relatively late development in the history of the human species. It is not a spontaneous achievement as evidenced by the fact that even in industrialized societies such as the United States the number of adults who are not functionally literate hovers around 20% (e.g., National Center for Educational Statistics, 1996). Conventional literacy consists of a set of skills that must be taught and learned. Learning to play the piano would be a more appropriate model for learning to read and write than would learning to talk. Clearly, the more piano lessons a person has and the more that person practices, the better that person will play the piano, but the person who starts taking piano lessons at age 10 and continues until age 16 is not necessarily at a disadvantage compared to the person who starts at age 6 and continues until age 12 (e.g., Ericsson, Krampe, & Tesch-Romer, 1993). Switching from playing the piano to reading, the worldwide success of adult literacy programs provides clear evidence that one can be taught to read at any age from late preschool through adulthood. In addition, there is little if any evidence that the underlying inside-out components of literacy are age-graded. For example, Morais, Content, Bertelson, and Cary (1988) found that Portuguese illiterate adults could quickly learn to perform a pseudoword phoneme deletion task when provided with corrective feedback and instructions.

The reason that emergent literacy skills are important for children entering elementary school is not that children with low levels of those skills cannot succeed in the task of learning to read. Rather, the reason is that schools provide an age-graded rather than skills-graded curriculum in which early delays are magnified at each additional step as the gap increases between what children bring to the curriculum and what the curriculum demands. To return to the model of piano playing, it would be as if the person who started lessons at age 10 were given as the first lesson the fingering exercises for the Beethoven sonata being worked on by the 10-year-old who started lessons at age 6. The developmental function for learning to read is cultural and exogenous, not biological and endogenous.

Although we have presented compelling evidence that learning to read is easier for children with higher levels of emergent literacy skills and that interventions can enhance emergent literacy skills, literacy is too important to a child's life-long prospects for our schools to give up on children who are not prepared for the typical reading curriculum. We can help children at risk for developing reading problems by enhancing their emergent literacy skills through the use of preschool emergent literacy interventions and/or skills-based reading instruction, but we can also hurt their chances irrevocably if we allow deficiencies in emergent literacy to serve as an excuse not to teach reading effectively to children who arrive at school unprepared.

ACKNOWLEDGMENTS

Preparation of this manuscript was supported by grants to the first author from the Pew Charitable Trusts (91-01249-000) and the Administration for Children and Families (90-CD-0957) (90-YD-0026). Views expressed herein are those of the authors and have not been cleared by the grantors.

ADDRESSES AND AFFILIATIONS

Corresponding author: Grover J. Whitehurst, Department of Psychology, SUNY, Stony Brook, NY 11794-2500; e-mail: gwhitehurst@ccmail.sunysb.edu.Christopher J. Lonigan is at Florida State University.

REFERENCES

Adams, M. J. (1990). *Learning to read: Thinking and learning about print.* Cambridge, MA: MIT Press.

Adams, M. J. (1991). Why not phonics and whole language? In W. Ellis (Ed.), *All language and the creation of literacy* (pp. 40–52). Baltimore, MD: Orton Dyslexia Society.

Adams, M. J., & Bruck, M. (1993). Word recognition: The interface of educational policies and scientific research. *Reading and Writing: An Interdisciplinary Journal, 5,* 113–139.

Adams, M. J., & Bruck, M. (1995). Resolving the debate. *American Educator, 19,* 7–20.

Alexander, K. L., & Entwisle, D. R. (1988). Achievement in the first two years of school: Patterns and processes. *Monographs of the Society for Research in Child Development, 53*(2, Serial No. 218).

Allen, L., Cipielewski, J., & Stanovich, K. E. (1992). Multiple indicators of children's reading habits and attitudes: Construct validity and cognitive correlates. *Journal of Educational Psychology, 84,* 489–503.

Anderson, A. B., & Stokes, S. J. (1984). Social and institutional influences on the development and practice of literacy. In H. Goelman, A. Oberg, & F. Smith (Eds.), *Awakening to literacy.* Exeter, NH: Heinemann.

Anderson, R. C., & Freebody, P. (1981). Vocabulary knowledge. In J. Guthrie (Ed.), *Comprehension and teaching: Research reviews* (pp. 77–117). Newark, DE: International Reading Association.

Arnold, D. H., Lonigan, C. J., Whitehurst, G. J., & Epstein, J. N. (1994). Accelerating language development through picture book reading: Replication and extension to a videotape training format. *Journal of Educational Psychology, 86,* 235–243.

Ball, E. W., & Blachman, B. A. (1988). Phoneme segmentation training: Effect on reading readiness. *Annals of Dyslexia, 38,* 208–225.

Barker, T. A., & Torgesen, J. K. (1995). An evaluation of computer-assisted instruction in phonological awareness with below average readers. *Journal of Educational Computing Research, 13,* 89–103.

Baydar, N., Brooks-Gunn, J., & Furstenberg, F. F. (1993). Early warning signs of functional illiteracy: Predictors in childhood and adolescence. *Child Development, 64,* 815–829.

Beals, D. E., DeTemple, J. M., & Dickinson, D. K. (1994). Talking and listening that support early literacy development of children from low-income families. In D. K. Dickinson (Ed.), *Bridges to literacy: Children, families, and schools,* Cambridge, MA: Blackwell.

Bishop, D. V. M., & Adams, C. (1990). A prospective study of the relationship between specific language impairment, phonological disorders and reading retardation. *Journal of Child Psychology and Psychiatry and Allied Disciplines, 31,* 1027–1050.

Bond, G. L., & Dykstra, R. (1967). The cooperative research program in first-grade reading instruction. *Reading Research Quarterly, 2,* 5–142.

Bowey, J. A. (1994). Phonological sensitivity in novice readers and nonreaders. *Journal of Experimental Child Psychology, 58,* 134–159.

Bowey, J. A. (1995). Socioeconomic status differences in preschool phonological sensitivity and first-grade reading achievement. *Journal of Educational Psychology, 87,* 476–487.

Bradley, L., & Bryant, P. E. (1983). Categorizing sounds and learning to read: A causal connection. *Nature, 301,* 419–421.

Bradley, L., & Bryant, P. (1985). *Rhyme and reason in reading and spelling.* Ann Arbor: University of Michigan Press.

Bredekamp. S. (Ed.). (1986). *Developmentally appropriate practice.* Washington, DC: National Association for the Education of Young Children.

Bruck, M. (1990). Word recognition skins of adults with childhood diagnoses of dyslexia. *Developmental Psychology, 26,* 439–454.

Bruner, J. S. (1986). *Actual minds, possible worlds.* Cambridge, MA: Harvard University Press.

Bryant, D. M., Burchinal, M., Lau, L. B., & Sparling, J. J. (1994). Family and classroom correlates of Head Start children's developmental outcomes. *Early Childhood Research Quarterly, 9,* 289–304.

Bryant, P. E., MacLean, M., Bradley, L. L., & Crossland, J. (1990). Rhyme and alliteration, phoneme detection, and learning to read. *Developmental Psychology, 26,* 429–438.

Bus, A. G., van IJzendoorn, M. H., & Pellegrini, A. (1995). Joint book reading makes for success in learning to read: A meta-analysis on intergenerational transmission of literacy. *Review of Educational Research, 65,* 1–21.

Bush, B. (1990). Parenting's best-kept secret; Reading to your children. *Reader's Digest, 137,* 67–70.

Butler, S. R., Marsh, H. W., Sheppard, M. J., & Sheppard, J. L. (1985). Seven-year longitudinal study of the early prediction of reading achievement. *Journal of Educational Psychology, 77,* 349–361.

Byrne, B., & Fielding-Barnsley, R. F. (1991a). *Sound foundations.* Artarmon, New South Wales, Australia: Leyden Educational Publishers.

Byrne, B., & Fielding-Barnsley, R. F. (1991b). Evaluation of a program to teach phonemic awareness to young children. *Journal of Educational Psychology, 82,* 805–812.

Byrne, B., & Fielding-Barnsley, R. F. (1993). Evaluation of a program to teach phonemic awareness to young children: A one year follow-up. *Journal of Educational Psychology, 85,* 104–111.

Byrne, B., & Fielding-Barnsley, R. (1995). Evaluation of a program to teach phonemic awareness to young children: A 2- and 3-year follow-up and a new preschool trial. *Journal of Educational Psychology, 87*, 488–503.

Byrne, B., Freebody, P., & Gates, A. (1992). Longitudinal data on the relations of word-reading strategies to comprehension, reading time, and phonemic awareness. *Reading Research Quarterly, 27*, 141–151.

Caravolas, M. (1993). Language specific influences of phonology and orthography on emergent literacy. In J. Altarriba (Ed.), *Cognition and culture: A cross-cultural approach to cognitive psychology* (pp. 177–175). Amsterdam: North-Holland.

Caravolas, M., & Bruck, M. (1993). The effect of oral and written language input on children's phonological awareness: A cross-linguistic study. *Journal of Experimental Child Psychology, 55*, 1–30.

Cardoso-Martins, C. (1994). Rhyme perception: Global or analytical? *Journal of Experimental Child Psychology, 57*, 26–41.

Carpenter, P. A., & Just, M. A. (1981). Cognitive processes in reading: Models based on readers' eye fixations. In A. M. Lesgold & C. A. Perfetti (Eds.), *Interactive processes in reading* (pp. 177–213). Hillsdale, NJ: Erlbaum.

Castle, J. M., Riach, J., & Nicholson, T. (1994). Getting off to a better start in reading and spelling: The effects of phonemic awareness instruction within a whole language program. *Journal of Educational Psychology, 86*, 350–359.

Chall, J. S. (1967). *Learning to read: The great debate.* New York: McGraw-Hill.

Chaney, C. (1992). Language development, metalinguistic skills, and print awareness in 3-year-old children. *Applied Psycholinguistics, 13*, 485–514.

Clay, M. M. (1966). *Emergent reading behavior.* Unpublished doctoral dissertation, University of Auckland, New Zealand.

Clay, M. M. (1979a). *Reading: The patterning of complex behavior.* Auckland: Heinemann.

Clay, M. M. (1979b). *The early detection of reading difficulties* (3d ed.). Portsmouth, NH: Heinemann.

Cooney, B. (1982). *Miss Rumphius.* New York: Puffin.

Copperman, P. (1986). *Taking books to heart: How to develop a love of reading in your child.* Reading, MA: Addison-Wesley.

Cornell, E. H., Sénéchal, M., & Broda, L. S. (1988). Recall of picture books by 3-year-old children: Testing and repetition effects in joint reading activities. *Journal of Educational Psychology, 80*, 537–542.

Crain-Thoreson, C., & Dale, P. S. (1992). Do early talkers become early readers? Linguistic precocity, preschool language, and emergent literacy. *Developmental Psychology, 28*, 421–429.

Crone, D. (1996). *Teacher's reading style and Head Start children's engagement in shared reading.* Paper presented at the Head Start's Third National Research Conference, Washington, DC.

CTB. (1990). *Developing Skills Checklist.* Monterey, CA: McGraw-Hill.

Cunningham, A. E., & Stanovich, K. E. (1991). Tracking the unique effects of print exposure in children: Associations with vocabulary, general knowledge, and spelling. *Journal of Educational Psychology, 83*, 264–274.

DeLoache, J. S., & DeMendoza, O. A. P. (1987). Joint picturebook interactions of mothers and one-year-old children. *British Journal of Developmental Psychology, 5*, 111–123.

Dickinson, D. K., & Smith, M. W. (1994). Long-term effects of preschool teachers' book readings on low-income children's vocabulary and story comprehension. *Reading Research Quarterly, 29,* 105–121.

Dickinson, D. K., & Snow, C. E. (1987). Interrelationships among prereading and oral language skills in kindergartners from two social classes. *Early Childhood Research Quarterly, 2,* 1–25.

Dickinson, D. K., & Tabors, P. O. (1991). Early literacy: Linkages between home, school, and literacy achievement at age five. *Journal of Research in Childhood Education, 6,* 30–46.

Dubow, E. F., & Ippolito, M. F. (1994). Effects of poverty and quality of the home environment on changes in the academic and behavioral adjustment of elementary school-age children. *Journal of Clinical Child Psychology, 23,* 401–412.

Dunn, L. M., & Dunn, L. M. (1981). *Peabody Picture Vocabulary Test—Revised.* Circle Pines, NM: American Guidance Service.

Durkin, D. (1966). *Children who read early.* New York: Teachers College Press.

Echols, L. D., West, R. F., Stanovich, K. E., & Zehr, K. S. (1996). Using children's literacy activities to predict growth in verbal cognitive skills: A longitudinal investigation. *Journal of Educational Psychology, 88,* 296–304.

Ehri, L. C. (1988). Movement in word reading and spelling: How spelling contributes to reading. In J. Mason (Ed.), *Reading and writing connections.* Newton, MA: Allyn & Bacon.

Elley, W. B. (1989). Vocabulary acquisition from listening to stories. *Reading Research Quarterly, 24,* 174–187.

Ericsson, K. A., Krampe, R. T., & Tesch-Romer, C. (1993). The role of deliberate practice in the acquisition of expert performance. *Psychological Review, 100,* 363–406.

Erickson, G. C., Foster, K. C., Foster, D. F., Torgesen, J. K., & Packer, S. (1992). *DaisyQuest.* Scotts Valley, CA: Great Wave Software.

Feitelson, D., & Goldstein, Z. (1986). Patterns of book ownership and reading to young children in Israeli school-oriented and nonschool-oriented families. *Reading Teacher, 39,* 924–930.

Ferreiro, E., & Teberosky, A. (1982). *Literacy before schooling.* Exeter, NH: Heinemann.

Fitzgerald, J., Schuele, C. M., & Roberts, J. E. (1992). Emergent literacy: What is it and what does the teacher of children with learning disabilities need to know about it? *Reading and Writing Quarterly, 8,* 71–85.

Foorman, B. R., Francis, D. J., Novy, D. M., & Liberman, D. (1991). How letter-sound instruction mediates progress in first-grade reading and spelling. *Journal of Educational Psychology, 83,* 456–469.

Foster, K. C., Erickson, G. C., Foster, D. F., Brinkman, D., & Torgesen, J. K. (1994). Computer administered instruction in phonological awareness: Evaluation of the DaisyQuest Program. *Journal of Research and Development in Education, 27,* 126–137.

Fox, B., & Routh, D. K. (1975). Analyzing spoken language into words, syllables, and phonemes: A developmental study. *Journal of Psycholinguistic Research, 4,* 331–342.

Frankenberg, W. K., & Coons, C. E. (1986). Home Screening Questionnaire: Its validity in assessing home environment. *Journal of Pediatrics, 108,* 624–626.

Gardner, M. F. (1990). *Expressive One-Word Picture Vocabulary Test—Revised.* Novato, CA: Academic Therapy.

Gathercole, S. E., Willis, C. S., & Baddeley, A. D. (1991). Differentiating phonological memory and awareness of rhyme. Reading and vocabulary development in children. *British Journal of Psychology, 82*, 387–406.

Gathercole, S. E., Willis, C. S., Emslie, H., & Baddeley, A. D. (1992). Phonological memory and vocabulary development during the early school years: A longitudinal study. *Developmental Psychology, 28*, 887–898.

Glasgow, C., & Cowley, J. (1994). *The Renfrew bus story—American edition.* Centreville, DE: Centreville School.

Goodman, K. S. (1967). Reading: A psycholinguistic guessing game. *Journal of the Reading Specialist, 6*, 126–135.

Goodman, K. S. (1986). *What's whole in whole language?* Portsmouth, NY: Heinemann.

Goswami, U., & Bryant, P. (1992). Rhyme, analogy, and children's reading. In P. B. Gough, L. C. Ehri, & R. Treiman (Eds.), *Reading acquisition* (pp. 49–64). Hillsdale. NJ: Erlbaum.

Gough, P. B. (1991). The complexity of reading. In R. R. Hoffman & D. S. Palermo (Eds.), *Cognition and the symbolic processes* (pp. 141–149). Hillsdale, NJ: Erlbaum.

Gough, P. B. (1993). The beginning of decoding. *Reading and Writing: An Interdisciplinary Journal, 5*, 181–192.

Gough, P. B., Alford, J. A., & Holley-Wilcox, P. (1981). Words and contexts. In O. J. L. Tzeng & H. Singer (Eds.), *Perception of print: Reading research in experimental psychology* (pp. 85–102). Hillsdale, NJ: Erlbaum.

Gough, P. B., & Walsh, M. (1991). Chinese, Phoenicians, and the orthographic cypher of English. In S. Brady & D. Shankweiler (Eds.), *Phonological processes in literacy: A tribute to Isabelle Y. Liberman.* Hillsdale, NJ: Erlbaum.

Harms, T., & Clifford, R. M. (1980). *Early Childhood Environment Rating Scale:* New York: Teachers College Press.

Harste, J. E., Woodward, V. A., & Burke, C. L. (1984). *Language stories and literacy lessons.* Portsmouth, NH: Heinemann.

Hatcher, P. J., Hulme, C., & Ellis, A. W. (1994). Ameliorating early reading failure by integrating the teaching of reading and phonological skills: The phonological linkage hypothesis. *Child Development, 65*, 41–57.

Heath, S. B. (1982). What no bedtime story means: Narrative skills at home and school. *Language in Society, 11*, 49–76.

Heath, S. B. (1989). Oral and literate traditions among Black Americans living in poverty: Children and their development: Knowledge base, research agenda, and social policy application [Special issue]. *American Psychologist, 44*, 367–373.

Hoover, W., & Gough, P. B. (1990). The simple view of reading. *Reading and Writing, 2*, 127–160.

Jastak, S., & Wilkinson, G. S. (1984). *Wide Range Achievement Test—Revised.* Wilmington, DE: Jastak Associates.

Jenkins, J. R., Stein, M. L., & Wysocki, K. (1984). Learning vocabulary through reading. *American Educational Research Journal, 21*, 767–787.

Johnston, R. S., Anderson, M., & Holligan, C. (1996). Knowledge of the alphabet and explicit awareness of phonemes in prereaders: The nature of the relationship. *Reading and Writing: An Interdisciplinary Journal, 8*, 217–234.

Jorm, A. F., Share, D. L., MacLean, R., & Matthews, R. (1984). Phonological recoding skills and learning to read: A longitudinal study. *Applied Psycholinguistics, 5*, 201–207.

Juel, C. (1988). Learning to read and write: A longitudinal study of 54 children from first through fourth grades. *Journal of Educational Psychology, 80*, 437–447.

Juel, C., Griffith, P. L., & Gough, P. B. (1986). Acquisition of literacy: A longitudinal study of children in first and second grade. *Journal of Educational Psychology, 78*, 243–255.

Just, M. A., & Carpenter, P. A. (1987). *The psychology of reading and language comprehension.* Boston: Allyn & Bacon.

Kagan, J. (1996). Three pleasing ideas. *American Psychologist, 51*, 901–908.

Kirtley, C., Bryant, P., MacLean, M., & Bradley, L. (1989). Rhyme, rime, and the onset of reading. *Journal of Experimental Child Psychology, 48*, 224–245.

Lenel, J. C., & Cantor, J. H. (1981). Rhyme recognition and phonemic perception in young children. *Journal of Psycholinguistic Research, 10*, 57–67.

Lepper, M. R., & Gurtner, J. (1989). Children and computers: Approaching the 21st century. *American Psychologist, 89*, 170–178.

Liberman, I. Y., & Liberman, A. M. (1992). Whole language versus code emphasis: Underlying assumptions and their implications for reading instruction. In P. B. Gough, L. C. Ehri, & R. Treiman (Eds.), *Reading acquisition* (pp. 343–366). Hillsdale, NJ: Erlbaum.

Liberman, I. Y., Shankweiler, D., Fischer, F. W., & Carter, B. (1974). Explicit syllable and phoneme segmentation in young children. *Journal of Experimental Child Psychology, 18*, 201–212.

Lomax, C. M. (1977). Interest in books and stories at nursery school. *Educational Research, 19*, 100–112.

Lonigan, C. J. (1994). Reading to preschoolers exposed: Is the emperor really naked? *Developmental Review, 14*, 303–323.

Lonigan, C. J., Anthony, J. L., Dyer, S. M., & Collins, K. (1995). Evaluation of a language enrichment program for preschool-aged children from low-income backgrounds. *Association for the Advancement of Behavior Therapy Abstracts, 2*, 365.

Lonigan, C. J., Burgess, S. R., Anthony, J. L., & Barker, T. A. (in press). Development of phonological awareness in two- to five-year-old children. *Journal of Educational Psychology.*

Lonigan, C. J., Dyer, S. M., & Anthony, J. L. (1996, April). *The influence of the home literacy environment on the development of literacy skills in children from diverse racial and economic backgrounds.* Paper presented at the annual convention of the American Educational Research Association, New York.

Lonigan, C. J., & Whitehurst, G. J. (in press). Examination of the relative efficacy of parent and teacher involvement in a shared-reading intervention for preschool children from low-income backgrounds. *Early Childhood Research Quarterly.*

Lundberg, I., Frost, J., & Petersen, O. (1988). Effects of an extensive program for stimulating phonological awareness in preschool children. *Reading Research Quarterly, 23*, 263–284.

MacLean, M., Bryant, P., & Bradley, L. (1987). Rhymes, nursery rhymes, and reading in early childhood. *Merrill-Palmer Quarterly, 33*, 255–282.

Mandler, J. M., & Johnson, N. S. (1977). Remembrance of things parse: Story structure and recall. *Cognitive Psychology, 9*, 111–151.

Mann, V. A., & Liberman, I. Y. (1984). Phonological awareness and short-term memory. *Journal of Learning Disabilities, 17,* 592–599.

Mason, J. M. (1980). When children do begin to read: An exploration of four year old children's letter and word reading competencies. *Reading Research Quarterly, 15,* 203–227.

Mason, J. M. (1992). Reading stories to preliterate children: A proposed connection to reading. In P. B. Gough, L. C. Ehri, & R. Treiman (Eds.), *Reading acquisition* (pp. 215–243). Hillsdale, NJ: Erlbaum.

Mason, J. M., & Dunning, D. (1986). *Toward a model relating home literacy with beginning reading.* Paper presented to the American Educational Research Association, San Francisco.

Masonheimer, P. E., Drum, P. A., & Ehri, L. C. (1984). Does environmental print identification lead children into word reading? *Journal of Reading Behavior, 16,* 257–271.

McBride-Chang, C., & Manis, F. R. (1996). Structural invariance in the associations of naming speed, phonological awareness, and verbal reasoning in good and poor readers: A test of the double deficit hypothesis. *Reading and Writing, 8,* 323–339.

McCormick, C. E., & Mason, J. M. (1986). Intervention procedures for increasing preschool children's interest in and knowledge about reading. In W. H. Teale & E. Sulzby (Eds.), *Emergent literacy: Writing and reading* (pp. 90–115). Norwood, NJ: Ablex.

McGuinness, D., McGuinness, C., & Donohue, J. (1995). Phonological training and the alphabet principle: Evidence for reciprocal causality. *Reading Research Quarterly, 30,* 830–852.

Molfese, D. L. (1990). Auditory evoked responses recorded from 16-month-old human infants to words they did and did not know. *Brain and Language, 38,* 345–363.

Molfese, D. L., Morris, R. D., & Romski, M. A. (1990). Semantic discrimination in nonspeaking youngsters with moderate or severe retardation: Electrophysiological correlates. *Brain and Language, 38,* 61–74.

Morais, J., Content, A., Bertelson, P., & Cary, L. (1988). Is there a critical period for the acquisition of segmental analysis? *Cognitive Neuropsychology, 5,* 347–352.

Morisset, C. E. (1993). SPARK: Seattle's parents are reading to kids. *Society for Research in Child Development Abstracts, 9,* 219.

Murray, B. A., Stahl, S. A., & Ivey, M. G. (1996). Developing phoneme awareness through alphabet books. *Reading and Writing, 8,* 307–322.

Nagy, W. E., Anderson, R. C., & Herman, P. A. (1987). Learning word meanings from context during normal reading. *American Educational Research Journal, 24,* 237–270.

National Assessment of Educational Progress. (1991). *The 1989–90 National assessment of reading and literature.* Denver: Author.

National Center for Education Statistics. (1996). *International comparisons of adult literacy.* Washington, DC: Author.

Needlman, R., Fried, I., Morley, D., Taylor, S., & Zuckerman, B. (1991). Clinic-based interventions to promote literacy. *American Journal of Diseases of Children, 145,* 881–884.

Nelson, K. (1996). *Language in cognitive development.* Cambridge: Cambridge University Press.

Neuman, S. B., & Roskos, K. (1993). Access to print for children of poverty: Differential effects of adult mediation and literacy-enriched play settings on environmental and functional print tasks. *American Educational Research Journal, 30,* 95–122.

Ninio, A. (1980). Picture book reading in mother-infant dyads belonging to two subgroups in Israel. *Child Development, 51,* 587–590.

Ninio, A., & Bruner, J. S. (1978). The achievement and antecedents of labeling. *Journal of Child Language*, *5*, 1–15.

Pappas, C. C., & Brown, E. (1988). The development of children's sense of the written story language register: An analysis of the texture of "pretend reading." *Linguistics and Education*, *1*, 45–79.

Patterson, K. E., & Coltheart, V. (1987). Phonological processes in reading: A tutorial review. In M. Coltheart (Ed.), *Attention and performance: Vol. 12. The psychology of reading* (pp. 421–447). Hove, England: Erlbaum.

Payne, A. C., Whitehurst, G. J., & Angell, A. L. (1994). The role of literacy environment in the language development of children from low-income families. *Early Childhood Research Quarterly*, *9*, 427–440.

Pellegrini, A. D., Brody, G. H., & Sigel, I. E. (1985). Parent's book-reading habits with their children. *Journal of Educational Psychology*, *77*, 332–340.

Perfetti, C. A. (1991). The psychology, pedagogy, and politics of reading. *Psychological Science*, *2*, 70–76.

Perfetti, C. A., Beck, I., Bell, L. C., & Hughes, C. (1987). Phonemic knowledge and learning to read are reciprocal: A longitudinal study of first grade children. *Merrill-Palmer Quarterly*, *33*, 283–319.

Perfetti, C. A., Goldman, S. R., & Hogaboam, T. W. (1979). Reading skill and the identification of words in discourse context. *Memory and Cognition*, *7*, 273–282.

Pikulski, J. J., & Tobin, A. W. (1989). Factors associated with long-term reading achievement of early readers. In S. McCormick, J. Zutell, P. Scharer, & P. O'Keefe (Eds.), *Cognitive and social perspectives for literacy research and instruction.* Chicago: National Reading Conference.

Purcell-Gates, V. (1988). Lexical and syntactic knowledge of written narrative held by well-read-to kindergartners and second graders. *Research in the Teaching of English*, *22*, 128–160.

Purcell-Gates, V. (1996). Stories, coupons, and the TV Guide: Relationships between home literacy experiences and emergent literacy knowledge. *Reading Research Quarterly*, *31*, 406–428.

Purcell-Gates, V., & Dahl, K. L. (1991). Low-SES children's success and failure at early literacy learning in skills-based classrooms. *Journal of Reading Behavior*, *23*, 1–34.

Raz, I. S., & Bryant, P. (1990). Social background, phonological awareness and children's reading. *British Journal of Developmental Psychology*, *8*, 209–225.

Reynell, J. K. (1985). *Reynell developmental language scales second revision.* Windsor, England: NFER-Nelson.

Rohl, M., & Pratt, C. (1995). Phonological awareness, verbal working memory and the acquisition of literacy. *Reading and Writing*, *7*, 327–360.

Rowe, K. J. (1991). The influence of reading activity at home on students, attitudes towards reading, classroom attentiveness and reading achievement: An application of structural equation modelling. *British Journal of Educational Psychology*, *61*, 19–35.

Scarborough, H. S. (1989). Prediction of reading dysfunction from familial and individual differences. *Journal of Educational Psychology*, *81*, 101–108.

Scarborough, H. S., & Dobrich, W. (1994). On the efficacy of reading to preschoolers. *Developmental Review*, *14*, 245–230.

Scarr, S., & McCartney, K. (1988). Far from home: An experimental evaluation of the Mother-Child Home Program in Bermuda. *Child Development*, *59*, 531–543.

Schliecker, E., White, D. R., & Jacobs, E. (1991). The role of day care quality in the prediction of children's vocabulary. *Canadian Journal of Behavioural Science*, *23*, 12–24.

Sénéchal, M., & Cornell, E. H. (1993). Vocabulary acquisition through shared reading experiences. *Reading Research Quarterly*, *28*, 360–375.

Sénéchal, M., Cornell, E. H., & Broda, L. S. (1995). Age-related differences in the organization of parent-infant interactions during picture-book reading. *Early Childhood Research Quarterly*, *10*, 317–337.

Sénéchal, M., LeFevre, J., Hudson, E., & Lawson, E. P. (1996). Knowledge of storybooks as a predictor of young children's vocabulary. *Journal of Educational Psychology*, *88*, 520–536.

Sénéchal, M., LeFevre, J., Thomas, E. M., & Daley, K. E. (in press). Differential effects of home literacy experiences on the development of oral and written language. *Reading Research Quarterly*.

Sénéchal, M., Thomas, E. H., & Monker, J. A. (1995). Individual differences in 4-year-old children's acquisition of vocabulary during storybook reading. *Journal of Educational Psychology*, *87*, 218–229.

Share, D. L., Jorm, A. F., MacLean, R., & Mathews, R. (1984). Sources of individual differences in reading acquisition. *Journal of Educational Psychology*, *76*, 1309–1324.

Simons, H. D., & Leu, D. J. (1987). The use of contextual and graphic information in word recognition by second-, fourth-, and sixth-grade readers. *Journal of Reading Behavior*, *19*, 33–47.

Smith, S. S., & Dixon, R. G. (1995). Literacy concepts of low- and middle-class four-year-olds entering preschool. *Journal of Educational Research*, *88*, 243–253.

Snow, C. E. (1983). Literacy and language: Relationships during the preschool years. *Harvard educational Review*, *53*, 165–189.

Snow, C. E., Barnes, W. S., Chandler, J. Hemphill, L., & Goodman, I. F. (1991). *Unfulfilled expectations: Home and school influences on literacy*. Cambridge, MA: Harvard University Press.

Stahl, S. A., McKenna, M. C., & Pagnucco, J. R. (1995). The effects of whole-language instruction: An update and a reappraisal. *Educational Psychologist*, *29*, 175–185.

Stahl, S. A., & Murray, B. A. (1993). Environmental print, phonemic awareness, letter recognition, and word recognition. *National Reading Conference Yearbook*, *42*, 227–233.

Stahl, S. A., & Murray, B. A. (1994). Defining phonological awareness and its relationship to early reading. *Journal of Educational Psychology*, *86*, 221–234.

Stanovich, K. E. (1981). Attentional and automatic context effects in reading. In A. Lesgold & C. Perfetti (Eds.), *Interactive processes in reading* (pp. 241–263). Hillsdale, NJ: Erlbaum.

Stanovich, K. E. (1986). Matthew effects in reading: Some consequences of individual differences in the acquisition of literacy. *Reading Research Quarterly*, *21*, 360–407.

Stanovich, K. E., Cunningham, A. E., & Cramer, B. B. (1984). Assessing phonological awareness in kindergarten children: Issues of task comparability. *Journal of Experimental Child Psychology*, *38*, 175–190.

Stanovich, K. E., Cunningham, A. E., & Freeman, D. J. (1984). Intelligence, cognitive skills, and early reading progress. *Reading Research Quarterly*, *19*, 270–303.

Stanovich, K. E., & Stanovich, P. J. (1995). How research might inform the debate about early reading acquisition. *Journal of Research in Reading*, *18*, 87–105.

Stanovich, K. E., & West, R. F. (1989). Exposure to print and orthographic processing. *Reading Research Quarterly*, *24*, 402–433.

Stevenson, H. W., & Newman, R. S. (1986). Long-term prediction of achievement and attitudes in mathematics and reading. *Child Development, 57,* 646–659.

St. Pierre, R. G., Layzer, J. I., & Barnes, H. V. (1995). Two-generation programs: Design, cost, and short-term effectiveness. *Future of Children, 5,* 76–93.

Sulzby, E. (1985). Children's emergent reading of favorite storybooks: A developmental study. *Reading Research Quarterly, 20,* 458–481.

Sulzby, E. (1986). Writing and reading: Signs of oral and written language organization in the young child. In W. H. Teale & E. Sulzby (Eds.), *Emergent literacy: Reading and writing* (pp. 50–87). Norwood, NJ: Ablex.

Sulzby, E. (1989). Assessment of writing and of children's language while writing. In L. Morrow & J. Smith (Eds.), *The role of assessment and measurement in early literacy instruction* (pp. 83–109). Englewood Cliffs, NJ: Prentice-Hall.

Sulzby, E., Barnhart, J., & Hieshima, J. (1989). Forms of writing and rereading from writing: A preliminary report. In J. Mason (Ed.), *Reading and writing connections* (pp. 31–63). Needham Heights, MA: Allyn & Bacon.

Sulzby, E., & Teale, W. (1991). Emergent literacy. In R. Barr, M. Kamil, P. Mosenthal, & P. D. Pearson (Eds.), *Handbook of reading research* (Vol. 2, pp. 727–758). New York: Longman.

Teale, W. H. (1986). Home background and young children's literacy development. In W. H. Teale & E. Sulzby (Eds.), *Emergent literacy: Writing and reading.* Norwood, NJ: Ablex.

Teale, W. H., & Sulzby, E. (Eds.), (1986). *Emergent literacy: Writing and reading.* Norwood, NJ: Ablex.

Thomas, B. (1984). Early toy preferences of four-year-old readers and nonreaders. *Child Development, 55,* 424–430.

Torgesen, J. K., Morgan, S., & Davis, C. (1992). Effects of two types of phonological awareness training on word learning in kindergarten children. *Journal of Educational Psychology, 84,* 364–370.

Tramontana, M. G., Hooper, S., & Selzer, S. C. (1988). Research on preschool prediction of later academic achievement: A review. *Developmental Review, 8,* 89–146.

Treiman, R. (1992). The role of intrasyllabic units in learning to read and spell. In P. B. Gough, L. C. Ehri, & R. Treiman (Eds.), *Reading acquisition* (pp. 107–143). Hillsdale, NJ: Erlbaum.

Tunmer, W. E., Herriman, M. L., & Nesdale, A. R. (1988). Metalinguistic abilities and beginning reading. *Reading Research Quarterly, 23,* 134–158.

Tunmer, W. E., & Hoover, W. A. (1992). Cognitive and linguistic factors in learning to read. In P. B. Gough, L. C. Ehri, & R. Treiman (Eds.), *Reading acquisition.* Hillsdale, NJ: Erlbaum.

Tunmer, W. E., Nesdale, A. R., & Wright, A. D. (1987). Syntactic awareness and reading acquisition. *British Journal of Developmental Psychology, 5,* 25–34.

Uhry, J. K., & Shepherd, M. J. (1993). Segmentation/spelling instruction as part of a first-grade reading program: Effects on several measures of reading. *Reading Research Quarterly, 28,* 218–233.

Valdez-Menchaca, M. C., & Whitehurst, G. J. (1992). Accelerating language development through picture book reading: A systematic extension to Mexican day-care. *Developmental Psychology, 28,* 1106–1114.

Vellutino, F. R. (1991). Introduction to three studies on reading acquisition: Convergent findings on theoretical foundations of code-oriented versus whole-language approaches to reading instruction. *Journal of Educational Psychology, 83,* 437–443.

Vellutino, F. R., Scanlon, D. M., Sipay, E. R., Small, S. G., Pratt. A., Chen, R., & Denckla, M. B. (1996). Cognitive profiles of difficult-to-remediate and readily remediated poor readers: Early intervention as a vehicle for distinguishing between cognitive and experiential deficits as basic causes of specific reading disability. *Journal of Educational Psychology, 88,* 601–638.

Wagner, R. K. (1996, April). *Metaanalysis of the effects of phonological awareness training with children.* Paper presented at the annual convention of the American Educational Research Association, New York.

Wagner, R. K., Balthazor, M., Hurley, S., Morgan, S., Rashotte, C., Shaner, R., Simmons, K., & Stage, S. (1987). The nature of prereaders' phonological processing abilities. *Cognitive Development, 2,* 355–373.

Wagner, R. K., & Torgesen, J. K. (1987). The nature of phonological processing and its causal role in the acquisition of reading skills. *Psychological Bulletin, 101,* 192–212.

Wagner, R. K., Torgesen, J. K., & Rashotte, C. A. (1994). Development of reading-related phonological processing abilities: New evidence of bidirectional causality from a latent variable longitudinal study. *Developmental Psychology, 30,* 73–87.

Walton, P. D. (1995). Rhyming ability, phoneme identity, letter-sound knowledge, and the use of orthographic analogy by prereaders. *Journal of Educational Psychology, 87,* 587–597.

Wechsler, D. (1974). *Manual for the Wechsler Intelligence Scales for Children—Revised.* New York: Psychological Corp.

Wells, G. (1985). *Language development in the preschool years.* New York: Cambridge University Press.

Wells, G., Barnes, S., & Wells, J. (1984). *Linguistic influences on educational attainment.* Final report to the Department of Education and Science.

West, R. F., Stanovich, K. E., & Mitchell, H. R. (1993). Reading in the real world and its correlates. *Reading Research Quarterly, 28,* 34–51.

Wheeler, M. P. (1983). Context-related age changes in mother's speech: Joint book reading. *Journal of Child Language, 10,* 259–263.

White, K. (1982). The relation between socioeconomic status and academic achievement. *Psychological Bulletin, 91,* 461–481.

Whitehurst, G. J. (1996a, April). *A structural equation model of the role of home literacy environment in the development of emergent literacy skills in children from low-income backgrounds.* Paper presented at the annual convention of the American Educational Research Association, New York.

Whitehurst, G. J. (1996b). Language processes in context: Language learning in children reared in poverty. In L. B. Adamson & M. A. Romski (Eds.), *Research on communication and language disorders: Contribution to theories of language development.* Baltimore: Brookes.

Whitehurst, G. J. (April, 1997a). *Long-term effects of an emergent literacy intervention in Head Start.* Presented as part of a symposium, Child and Family Literacy in the Context of Intervention Programs, at the 1997 meeting of the Society for Research in Child Development, Washington, DC.

Whitehurst, G. J. (April, 1997b). *Continuities and discontinuities in the move from emergent literacy to reading.* Presented as part of a symposium. Developmental Psychologists Contribute to Early Childhood Education, at the 1997 meeting of the Society for Research in Child Development, Washington, DC.

Whitehurst, G. J., Arnold, D. H., Epstein, J. N., Angell, A. L., Smith, M., & Fischel, J. E. (1994). A picture book reading intervention in daycare and home for children from low-income families. *Developmental Psychology, 30,* 679–689.

Whitehurst, G. J., Epstein, J. N., Angell, A. C., Payne, A. C., Crone, D. A., & Fischel, J. E. (1994). Outcomes of an emergent literacy intervention in Head Start. *Journal of Educational Psychology, 86,* 542–555.

Whitehurst, G. J., Falco, F., Lonigan, C. J., Fischel, J. E., DeBaryshe, B. D., Valdez-Menchaca, M. C., & Caulfield, M. (1988). Accelerating language development through picture-book reading. *Developmental Psychology, 24,* 552–558.

Wiig, E. H., Secord, W., & Semel, E. (1992). *CELF-Preschool: Clinical Evaluation of Language Fundamentals—Preschool.* New York: Psychological Corp.

Woodcock, R. W. (1987). *Woodcock Reading Mastery Tests—Revised.* Circles Pines, MN: American Guidance Service.

Woodcock, R. W., & Johnson, M. B. (1977). *Woodcock-Johnson Psycho-Educational Battery.* Allen, TX: DLM Teacher Resources.

Yopp, H. K. (1988). The validity and reliability of phonemic awareness tests. *Reading Research Quarterly, 23,* 159–177.

3

How Shall We Speak of Children's Personalities in Middle Childhood? A Preliminary Taxonomy

Rebecca L. Shiner

University of Minnesota, Twin Cities Campus

Developmental researchers have neglected the study of personality traits in middle childhood, thus leaving unanswered many questions about childhood personality structure. This article presents a developmental framework for understanding personality in middle childhood and critically reviews 5 models of temperament and personality structure in this age range: the models of A. Thomas and S. Chess, A. H. Buss and R. Plomin, M. K. Rothbart, J. Block and J. H. Block, and the Big Five. A number of robust personality dimensions common to these models and the broader developmental and adult personality literatures are then discussed: sociability, social inhibition, dominance, negative emotionality, aggressiveness, prosocial disposition, persistence/attention, mastery motivation, inhibitory control, and activity level. These dimensions represent a preliminary taxonomy of personality traits for exploring questions of individual development in childhood.

A quick glance at elementary school children playing at recess, studying at school, and interacting with family and friends at home reveals striking differences among them. Particular children may be expressive, inquisitive, kind, irritable, impetuous, or quick to withdraw under stress. Individual differences like these would be labeled as *personality traits* if they were found in adults; yet, despite some notable exceptions (e.g., J. Block, 1971; Bronson, 1966; Cattell & Coan, 1957; Digman, 1963; Kagan & Moss, 1962), researchers investigating middle childhood have tended to disregard the study of personality traits until fairly recently.

This article is adapted from an orals paper submitted to the Department of Psychology, University of Minnesota, Twin Cities Campus. The work was supported by the Eva O. Miller and Dissertation fellowships granted by the graduate school of the University of Minnesota, Twin Cities Campus. I would like to thank my advisors Auke Tellegen and Ann Masten for their reviews of this article.

Correspondence concerning this article should be addressed to Rebecca L. Shiner, Department of Psychology, University of Minnesota, Twin Cities Campus, 75 East River Road, Elliott Hall, Minneapolis, Minnesota 55455. Electronic mail may be sent to hundreddollardog@yahoo.com.

The gap in research on individual differences in middle childhood is particularly striking, given the vast amount of research on temperament in early childhood and on personality in late adolescence and adulthood. Until fairly recently, temperament research has focused almost exclusively on infants, toddlers, and preschoolers, thereby leaving out samples of older children. Although individual traits, such as impulsivity, activity level, aggression, and social inhibition have been studied in isolation in older children, a more full range of personality traits has not been investigated as often. Because of the relative paucity of research in this area, the domains of individual differences and personality structure have been described as *empty sets* in the study of child development (Halverson, Kohnstamm, & Martin, 1994, p. 368).

The neglect of the study of personality traits in middle childhood is especially notable in light of common claims that important foundations of personality structure are manifest by this period. Sigmund Freud (1966) argued that, by the beginning of the latency period (approximately ages 6 to 12), both the structures of personality—the id, ego, and superego—and the relations among these structures are already significantly determined. Anna Freud, echoing the claims of her father, spoke of middle childhood as "the time when a child's character is built and consolidated, or isn't," (Coles, 1997, p. 98). Similarly, Collins (1984) in summarizing the work of a panel focusing on middle childhood concluded, "It is not surprising, then, that development in middle childhood appears to have considerable significance for behavioral orientations, success, and adjustment in adolescence and adulthood" (p. 400). Thus, it has been suggested that the personality functioning of children during this period of development is well established and portends later functioning.

Within recent years, the number of studies exploring personality structure in middle childhood has increased substantially. Some of these studies are the fruit of longitudinal investigations of temperament or personality that have been extended from early childhood into later childhood. Other research represents the downward extension of adult personality structure into childhood. Because of these studies, there is no need to start from scratch in developing a taxonomy of personality for this age range; however, none of the current models of childhood personality can be heralded as a comprehensive taxonomy for middle childhood, because these models were not designed to measure the full range of personality traits in this period.

At the present time, there is a great need to reflect critically on the current research on temperament and personality structure in middle childhood, with the goal of delineating robust personality traits that can be measured during this important developmental period. This article provides such a review in three major sections. First, I describe a developmental framework for exploring temperament and personality in this age range. Second, I survey and critique five of the most important contemporary models of temperament and personality; these five models were chosen because of their prominent use in research on children. Third, I synthesize that which is solidly useful from each of these models with what is known from other developmental and adult personality research in order to generate a more comprehensive taxonomy of personality traits for middle childhood. It is to be hoped that such a synthesis lays the groundwork for further research on the emergence and developmental significance of childhood personality.

A DEVELOPMENTAL PERSPECTIVE ON PERSONALITY
IN OLDER CHILDREN

Definitional Concerns: Temperament and Personality

Although researchers do not share a consensual definition of temperament (Goldsmith et al., 1987), in the developmental literature, temperamental traits are usually conceived of as individual differences in behavior that appear early in life. Traits with strong emotional underpinnings have been salient in most models of temperament (Hartup & van Lieshout, 1995). Allport considered temperament to be simply "the characteristic phenomena of an individual's emotional nature" (Allport, 1961, p. 34). Many other researchers, however, include other individual differences, such as attentional self-regulation (Rothbart & Derryberry, 1981). Although most developmental researchers do not require genetic origins for a trait to be considered temperamental, they generally emphasize the constitutional or biological nature of temperament dimensions (Bates & Wachs, 1994; Goldsmith et al., 1987; Prior, 1992). Conceptions of adult temperament do not always require the early emergence of traits, but these models similarly presume the neurobiological basis of temperament (e.g., Gray, 1987; Strelau, 1987). Thus, most developmental models of temperament have emphasized behavioral consistencies that appear early in life, that are frequently but not exclusively emotional in nature, and that have a presumed neurobiological basis.

It is important to stress that the developmental study of temperament originated in research on infants and very young children (e.g., Thomas & Chess, 1977). Thomas and Chess, in fact, originally called temperament dimensions *primary reaction patterns* to highlight the early appearance of such traits. This original interest in very early-appearing individual differences has restricted the domain of temperament dimensions studied at later ages. Traits that fit many of the criteria for being temperamental have generally been excluded if they cannot be identified in infants (e.g., aggressiveness). Traits that are more salient and meaningful in infants (e.g., regularity of biological functions or the capacity to be distracted by something when distressed) have had to be reconceptualized when measured in older children. Because most studies of individual differences in school-age children have used a temperament model rather than a broader personality model, the domain of individual differences studied has often remained significantly restricted to traits that may be found in very young children.

Although temperamental traits are typically considered all of personality in infancy, many researchers consider temperament to be only one subset of personality in later childhood and adulthood. Allport's classic definition of personality captures the broad purview of this domain: "Personality is the dynamic organization within the individual of those psychophysical systems that determine his unique adjustments to his environment" (1937, p. 48). Researchers have studied a very wide range of "psychophysical systems," including individuals' motives, values, styles of relating to others, attachment patterns, and life stories, in addition to more frequently studied traits such as extroversion and neuroticism (McAdams, 1996). Personality also encompasses various aspects of the self, such as self-esteem, conscious and unconscious self-representations, self-presentation, and identity (Westen, 1995, p. 509).

Allport's definition of personality highlights the importance of understanding the organization of personality systems within the individual. Murray (1938) similarly emphasized the integration of various facets of personality within the whole organism. Pervin (1996) has suggested that this perspective on personality "lends itself to an interest in how parts fit together as well as to individual units, that is, to an interest in questions of pattern, organization, and coherence" (p. 314). *Idiographic* research is the name given to the research that explores such questions through the intensive study of patterns within individuals. Despite these high aspirations for understanding the whole person, adult personality researchers more often have examined individual differences in the levels of personality traits across individuals; this research is termed *nomothetic*. Developmental researchers likewise have tended to measure individuals' relative standing on single traits, although a number of researchers have studied groups of individuals who share patterns of personality traits (e.g., J. Block, 1971; Caspi & Silva, 1995; Robins, John, Caspi, Moffitt, & Stouthamer-Loeber, 1996). Both the idiographic and nomothetic perspectives are valuable, because each yields different information about personality functioning (Runyan, 1983). Nomothetic research potentially may inform the study of the whole person, because it may help identify the crucial units of study, Allport's "psychophysical systems."

How Does Earlier Temperament Become Later Personality?

The assumption that early childhood temperament is the substrate from which personality develops (e.g., Hartup & van Lieshout, 1995; Rothbart & Ahadi, 1994) raises important questions about how early temperament is transformed into personality in later childhood and adulthood. Empirical research on this topic is relatively limited, because there are few studies that have traced children's personalities from early childhood into their later years. It is possible, however, to delineate some of the processes through which such transformations may occur.

Because of developmental changes within children, it is likely that the units of personality become increasingly differentiated from infancy through later childhood and adolescence (Buss & Finn, 1987; Rothbart, 1989a). In other words, children's maturation permits the development and expression of new personality traits. The development of motor skills, language, cognition, self-awareness, self-concept, and empathy all impact the personality characteristics that children can display. For example, aggression cannot be measured in infants. Although infants may differ in temperamental differences that are likely to be related to later aggression (e.g., irritable distress; Thomas, Chess, & Birch, 1968), infants cannot exhibit differences in aggression until they develop the motor and language skills necessary to direct aggressive actions toward others. Similarly, children cannot vary along a dimension of dominance until they have developed the skills necessary to interact with peers. Thus, the structure of personality is likely to change over the course of childhood because of children's increasing capacities. This perspective is consonant with the numerous general models of development that posit increasingly differentiated and complex behavioral patterns over development (Ford, 1987; Werner, 1957).

As the dimensions of personality become differentiated over the early years of life, it is possible that these emerging individual differences become increasingly integrated with one another. Numerous theorists have suggested that development proceeds through the simultaneous differentiation and hierarchical integration of biological and behavioral systems (Cicchetti & Tucker, 1994; Ford, 1987; Werner, 1957); such hierarchical integration seems likely within the domain of personality as well. With each developmental transition, then, new personality traits may emerge, and the internal patterning of personality may also change for each individual. For example, a preschool girl with strong approach tendencies may have some difficulty inhibiting herself when she faces situations that promise great rewards; however, if the girl develops greater inhibitory control during the transition to middle childhood, she may learn to channel those approach tendencies in largely positive directions. In this example, the approach and control systems have become increasingly integrated. It may be particularly important to study children's emerging personalities during periods of transition in order to understand whether personality traits become reorganized with each developmental shift.

Caspi (1998) has outlined six processes through which children's original temperaments may become elaborated into later more differentiated personality traits through transactions with the environment. First, temperament is likely to influence the processes through which children learn starting early in childhood. For example, certain individuals are more susceptible to positive and negative reinforcement and punishment than others; children also differ strikingly in their persistence and attention, temperamental traits that are likely to influence learning. Second, starting in infancy and continuing into adulthood, the reactions that are elicited from important others, including parents, teachers, and friends, differ among individuals. Numerous theorists have emphasized the crucial role children play in evoking differential responses from others (Bell, 1968; Belsky, 1981). Parents respond differently to their infants depending on their levels of attention and irritability (Saudino & Plomin, 1997; van den Boom & Hoeksma, 1994). In later years, aggressive boys provoke aversive reactions from their parents, in turn evoking even greater aggression in the child (Patterson, 1976, 1982). Evocative personality influences of these sorts are likely to be highly important in the development of personality.

Caspi (1998) suggested that the other processes of temperament–environment transaction become operative later in childhood than the previous two. The third process is environmental construal; children's subjective perceptions of the environment influence their experience of events and other people. Relatively few studies have explored the relationship between children's personalities and their subjective experiences of the world around them; however, there is evidence for distinctive social information processing styles associated with both aggression and depression (Crick & Dodge, 1994). Fourth, children's temperaments are likely to influence the comparisons they make between themselves and others or between themselves at an earlier time and themselves at a later time. Such comparisons likely are key determinants of children's self-concepts and self-esteem. Children do begin comparing themselves to peers by middle childhood (Harter, 1996, 1998), but little is known about how personality may shape such comparisons.

Fifth, over the course of development, children have increasing control over the environments and experiences they face; their emerging personalities shape the environments they select, whether consciously or unconsciously. For example, aspects of children's personalities (e.g., excitement seeking or behavioral inhibition) may help determine their circle of friends (MacDonald, 1996), the activities in which they participate, and the ways they choose to spend their free time. Similarly, children with externalizing behaviors experience a greater number of controllable negative life events, perhaps in part because they generate such negative events (Masten, Neemann, & Andenas, 1994). By adulthood, environmental selection may be one of the most important ways that personality shapes life experiences, because personality potentially informs the selection of both marital partners and work environments. Sixth and finally, children's personalities are likely to influence the ways in which they manipulate their environments, including their attempts to change others' behavior. These processes may become particularly important as children become more skilled in regulating their own behavior and more insightful into the causes of others' behavior.

Developmental Shifts in Personality Functioning in Middle Childhood

Children's increasing capacities at the start of middle childhood shape their personality functioning. Children's cognitive and emotional capacities undergo a significant transition during the years from age 5 to age 8, at least in many western cultures. S. H. White (1965) highlighted this transitional period in an important article on the "5 to 7 year shift." More recent research has suggested that many of the changes in this period can be understood in quantitative rather than qualitative terms; however, it is still recognized that most children undergo important changes during this transitional period (Sameroff & Haith, 1996). Specifically, children's thought becomes more flexible and integrative and therefore more closely resembles adult thought (Sameroff & Haith, 1996). Relatedly, children's self-understanding changes: Children can increasingly describe themselves using trait labels, see themselves as possessing attributes that are opposite in valence (e.g., smart and dumb), evaluate themselves in both positive and negative terms, and compare themselves with peers (Harter, 1996, 1998). Children's own self-representations are likely to become much more important determinants of their personality functioning during middle childhood, because school-age children can reflect on themselves in a more nuanced, differentiated manner than preschool-age children.

A second crucial change in the early years of middle childhood involves the development of more sophisticated self-regulatory capacities. Throughout middle childhood, children develop (a) better skills in carrying out organized, planned behavior and (b) greater self-monitoring abilities. There is evidence that significant development in the frontal lobes occurs during the years from age 5 to age 8. Researchers have suggested that children's improved executive functioning in middle childhood may be related to the increasing myelination of the frontal lobes and the greater coordination of the electrical activity in the frontal lobes with other parts of the brain (Janowsky & Carper, 1995; Thatcher, 1994).

At the behavioral level, changes in executive functioning or self-regulation are well documented. School-age children are more capable of generating strategies for handling emotionally arousing situations and social conflicts than are younger children (Altshuler & Ruble, 1989; Rubin & Krasnor, 1985). They also show improvement in devising means of resisting temptation and delaying gratification, in contrast with preschoolers, who are more dependent on adults for help in generating strategies (Toner & Smith, 1977). As children's self-regulation becomes more sophisticated, their skills in exercising self-control are likely to moderate the expression of other personality traits. For example, Asendorpf (1994) obtained evidence that, during ages 4 to 10, more intelligent or more socially competent children showed decreases in inhibition toward strangers and school peers, relative to less competent children; these children may have had greater self-regulatory skills that increasingly enabled them to cope with challenging social situations. Clearly, in studying personality in middle childhood, it will be particularly important to understand the role of personality traits involving self-regulation.

The developmental changes that occur during the years from 5 to 8 do not involve merely maturational changes within children; rather, one of the most striking changes in this period is the restructuring of children's environments. In an early report, Rogoff and colleagues documented that in 50 communities around the world children are accorded greater responsibilities and are considered more truly teachable after the years from 5 to 7 (Rogoff, Sellers, Pirrotta, Fox, & White, 1975). In many nonwestern cultures, these greater responsibilities include taking care of younger children and carrying out domestic duties (Weisner, 1996). In western cultures (and increasingly in non-western cultures), children begin formal schooling at the start of middle childhood. Even for children with preschool experience, formal schooling represents a significant environmental shift. Once in school, children are expected to participate in more structured activities with a heavy cognitive focus, are evaluated with more stringent standards, and are expected to adapt to having fewer adults available (Ladd, 1996). Furthermore, children spend significantly more time with peers, both at school and at home, and they have more opportunities to play or work alone (Cole & Cole, 1996).

This environmental shift has important implications for the measurement of personality in middle childhood. The wider range of contexts may permit clearer expression of certain personality traits. For example, as children have increasing freedom to choose whether to spend time with others or alone, differences in their levels of sociability may become apparent. Similarly, children's increased opportunities to interact with peers under less adult supervision may make individual differences in dominance easier to measure. Although individual differences in traits such as sociability or dominance may be apparent earlier in life, children's increasing freedom to select their environments may make these personality traits more salient and therefore easier to measure later in childhood. In contrast, other personality traits may become more difficult to measure at this age. As children's self-regulatory capacities grow in middle childhood, one way children cope with potentially threatening situations may be to select environments that minimize stress. For example, a shy child may choose to avoid interactions with new peers, and a irritable child may choose to stay away from provocative situations; in these cases, an observer may have some difficulty accurately estimating the child's shyness or irritability. Thus, children's changing environments may differentially impact their personality functioning during this developmental period.

CONTEMPORARY MODELS OF TEMPERAMENT AND PERSONALITY IN MIDDLE CHILDHOOD

The Evaluation of Temperament and Personality Models

Before the discussion turns to specific models of temperament and personality in middle childhood, it is important to note briefly the criteria by which they can be evaluated. The models to be discussed were not developed to be comprehensive personality taxonomies. Rather, in most cases the psychologists and psychiatrists who developed these models were attempting to answer specific questions about development, and the individual difference dimensions they measured reflect those concerns. For example, Thomas and Chess were interested in the links between early temperament and the development of psychopathology (Thomas et al., 1968). They were also attuned to what temperament dimensions might be important to parents and pediatricians (Thomas, Chess, Birch, Hertzig, & Korn, 1963). These concerns focused their temperament assessment on behaviors with potential clinical relevance. Because the other models similarly were not designed to measure the full range of personality traits in middle childhood and adolescence, it is not reasonable to evaluate these models on the basis of their comprehensiveness.

As noted at the beginning of this article, although the models to be discussed are not necessarily comprehensive, they do highlight important dimensions of personality functioning in middle childhood and adolescence. Some of the researchers who developed these models attended to theoretical concerns in generating personality dimensions. Others delineated dimensions on the basis of intuition, experience, and conceptual concerns, although they lacked a formal guiding theory. Still other researchers used empirical methods such as factor analysis to differentiate various personality dimensions. In short, the resulting models vary widely in terms of theoretical development and empirical evidence. Thus, the personality dimensions in each model can be evaluated on the basis of a combination of their theoretical significance and empirical support (Burisch, 1984).

Studies Deriving From the Work of Thomas and Chess

The early work of Alexander Thomas and Stella Chess generated great interest in the study of temperament in infants and young children. Although other researchers had studied individual differences in infancy (e.g., Escalona, 1968), it was Thomas and Chess's work that brought issues of temperament to the attention of many clinicians and developmental researchers. Thomas and Chess (Goldsmith et al., 1987) defined temperament as follows: "We conceptualize temperament as the stylistic component of behavior—that is, the *how* of behavior as differentiated from motivation, the *why* of behavior, and abilities, the *what* of behavior" (p. 508). Even though Thomas and Chess intended to exclude the content or *what* of behavior, some of their temperament dimensions actually did include the content of behavior (e.g., quality of mood). Although this early definition was not entirely accurate, it powerfully sparked interest in individual differences in children's behavioral styles within the fields of child psychology, psychiatry, and pediatrics.

On the basis of this temperament conception, Thomas and Chess initiated a study of 141 infants and their parents in 1956, the now well-known New York Longitudinal Study (NYLS). They submitted the first 22 parent interviews to what they have described as an *inductive content analysis* to determine which categories of behavior both appeared in all children and seemed to have potential significance for psychological development (Goldsmith et al., 1987; Thomas & Chess, 1977; Thomas et al., 1963). They chose the following nine categories of behavior: (a) activity level; (b) rhythmicity of biological functions; (c) initial approach or withdrawal from any new stimulus; (d) adaptability to new situations after the initial response; (e) threshold of responsiveness to external stimulation; (f) intensity of reaction regardless of its quality; (g) general mood, ranging from positive to negative; (h) distractibility, or capacity to have behavior changed by external stimulation; and (i) attention span and persistence in the face of obstacles impeding current activity. Thomas and Chess's formulation of infant temperament dimensions profoundly shaped later work deriving from their model and spurred the development of parent and teacher questionnaire measures of the nine NYLS dimensions in early and middle childhood (Hegvik, McDevitt, & Carey, 1982; Keogh, Pullis, & Cadwell, 1982; martin, 1988; McDevitt & Carey, 1978; Windle & Lerner, 1986).

A number of researchers have raised questions about the conceptual distinctiveness of the nine NYLS dimensions because of the scales' low internal consistencies and high interscale correlations (McClowry, Hegvik, & Teglasi, 1993; Windle, 1988). These concerns led researchers to conduct factor analyses of the questionnaires as a way of achieving greater clarity about the underlying dimensions. Presley and Martin (1994) and Martin, Wisenbaker, and Huttunen (1994) summarized the results of many of these studies, including several published studies carried out with children between the ages of 6 and 12 (Baker & Velicer, 1982; Keogh et al., 1982; Lerner, Palermo, Spiro, & Nesselroad, 1982; McClowry et al., 1993; Presley & Martin, 1994; Windle, Iwawaki, & Lerner, 1987; Windle & Lerner, 1986). Since the writing of the two cited reviews, at least one other factor-analytic study of a NYLS-related questionnaire has been published (Sanson, Smart, Prior, Oberklaid, & Pedlow, 1994), with generally comparable results.

Presley and Martin (1994) and Martin, Wisenbaker, et al. (1994) suggested that across studies there is evidence for seven factors, although some of these temperament dimensions are more robust than others. Five of the dimensions are conceptually similar to the original NYLS dimensions. First, an activity-level factor tapping gross motor activity is clear in many of the studies, at least from preschool through adulthood in parental and self-ratings. It does not clearly emerge in teacher reports, because it seems to merge with teachers' perceptions of children's task persistence. Second, a task-persistence factor emerges from parent, teacher, and self-ratings at all ages. In preschool, this factor includes items measuring the ability to remain seated and focused and the ability to persist in a task even if it is frustrating. In later childhood, attentional capabilities come to the fore. Third, a social-inhibition factor measures inhibition in encounters with new people and new situations; this dimension is comparable to the original approach–withdrawal dimension. Social responsiveness to known others is not included in this factor. Fourth, a dimension tapping biological rhythmicity appears in a small number of studies of preschoolers and adolescents.

Fifth, in some studies, a threshold factor taps children's differential sensitivity and responsiveness to sensory stimuli. In other studies, the threshold items sometimes load on a negative emotionality–inflexibility factor. Rothbart and Bates (1998) have argued that threshold and susceptibility to distress are linked in the developmental literature, perhaps because both relate to the sensitivity or reactivity of a child's nervous system. It is possible that threshold becomes subsumed under a broader negative emotionality dimension over time.

Two other temperament dimensions identified through the factor analytic studies relate in a more complicated way to the original NYLS dimensions. From infancy through adulthood, there is a robust dimension that includes elements of the original mood, intensity, and adaptability dimensions. Presley and Martin (1994) call this dimension *negative emotionality*, although the negative emotions tapped by this factor are usually limited to forms of irritable distress, often in response to external stressors like disapproval from others or changes in plans or activities. Other negative emotions like sadness, anxiety, and fear are generally not included. The negative-emotionality factor resembles the *difficult-temperament* type that has been studied so frequently; studies examining the relation between these two constructs could help to clarify the differences between the two.

A second factor relating in a more complicated manner to the original NYLS scales seems to measure adaptability or manageability. Although the content of this factor varies somewhat from one study to the next, it generally taps a child's ability to adjust quickly in the face of a changing environment and to cooperate with unpleasant occurrences. Martin, Wisenbaker, et al. (1994) acknowledged that they were "less convinced of the uniformity of this cluster of factors than any other cluster considered here" (p. 166). The adaptability factor overlaps considerably with the negative emotionality factor in that many negative emotionality items explicitly include negative reactions in the face of change. Sanson et al. (1994) actually obtained a factor they labeled *negative reactivity*, which encompassed both negative emotionality and adaptability. The adaptability factor has been found less often in reports of older children and adolescents and in teacher reports. Perhaps negative emotionality and inflexibility in the face of environmental stressors become increasingly interrelated with age. It is also possible, however, that if more items tapping positive emotions are measured in conjunction with adaptability, a more robust positive-adaptability factor will emerge.

Thomas and Chess's keen clinical insights provided the foundation for measuring temperamental individuality among children. They succeeded in their goal of identifying early behavioral tendencies with important clinical ramifications: Numerous studies have linked the NYLS dimensions with later internalizing and externalizing disorders (summarized in Rothbart & Bates, 1998). Thomas and Chess's conceptual approach to generating temperament dimensions has been refined by the more recent factor-analytic studies. This empirical work has added greater conceptual clarity to the previous NYLS model of temperament by carving up the underlying temperamental dimensions in a more parsimonious manner. Additional research is now needed to examine the developmental significance of these dimensions. Several of these temperament traits, such as biological rhythmicity and threshold, may not be as important for older children as for infants; however, as described hereafter, many of the other traits identified by the NYLS studies appear to have significant ramifications for older children's functioning.

The EASI Model of Temperament as Personality Traits

A number of alternative developmental models of temperament have been introduced since the initial NYLS formulation of temperament. One of these models, the emotionality–activity–sociability–impulsivity (EASI) model developed by Buss and Plomin (1975, 1984), provides an interesting contrast to the NYLS conceptualization of temperament. The two models differ strikingly with respect to both their rationales for choosing temperament dimensions and their methods of measuring these dimensions.

Buss and Plomin (1975, 1984; Goldsmith et al., 1987) specify a number of features they require for a trait to be considered a temperament dimension. Most important, evidence of substantial heritability is required. Another essential feature of temperament dimensions is appearance within the first year of life. Buss and Plomin suggest that temperamental traits should be relatively stable during childhood and should be conceptualized in fairly broad terms. Finally, Buss and Plomin (1984) are interested in traits that are likely to have an enduring impact on personality development; for this reason, they selected their temperament dimensions "with an eye to personality development and the later appearance of these traits" (p. 85). They attended particularly to personality traits emphasized in the adult personality literature. This attention to adult personality contrasts significantly with the NYLS study's emphasis on choosing individual differences that are most salient in infancy.

Buss and Plomin (1975, 1984) originally chose four temperament traits represented in the acronym *EASI*. Emotionality describes the extent to which a person is aroused emotionally and the intensity of that person's emotional response. The emotions referred to here are in effect only negative ones, because only a handful of negative emotions produce the high levels of arousal implicit in Buss and Plomin's definition; thus, this dimension could be more accurately characterized as negative emotionality. Buss and Plomin have suggested that emotionality manifests itself as general distress in infants and later differentiates into fear and anger. It is striking that Buss and Plomin did not measure positive affect (smiling and laughter), given that this trait does appear to emerge early. Activity refers to the tempo and vigor of a person's energy output in both motor movements and speech. Buss and Plomin (1975) described sociability as "seeking other persons, preferring their presence, and responding to them" (p. 88). The more sociable a person is, the more that person finds the responsivity and attention of others to be rewarding. In Buss and Plomin's later formulation of temperament, they distinguished sociability from shyness, which they saw as behavioral inhibition and feelings of distress in interactions with strangers. Their construct of sociability consequently differs from the social inhibition dimension found in the factor analyses of NYLS questionnaires. For each of these traits, Buss and Plomin have provided a compelling case, on the basis of data concerning genetic underpinnings and developmental course, that it meets their criteria for being a temperament trait.

The fourth original temperament was impulsivity, which was seen as the ability to inhibit or control behavior but also included decision time, persistence, and excitement seeking. In their subsequent revision of the EASI theory, Buss and Plomin (1984) dropped impulsivity from the list of temperament traits, because they found that the various facets of impulsivity did not cohere when questionnaire measures of impulsivity were factor analyzed. Others have obtained similar results regarding the EASI impulsivity dimension (e.g., Braithwaite, Duncan-Jones, Bosly-Craft, & Goodchild, 1984). Only the excitement-seeking component seemed to be cohesive, but because prior to 1984 there was little evidence for genetic underpinnings of this trait, impulsivity was dropped from the model. Buss (1995) has since concluded that the most recent evidence suggests that impulsivity is, in fact, substantially heritable, and he has redefined impulsivity to include three components: emotional and behavioral control, discipline and persistence, and mental reflection and planfulness.

Buss and Plomin attended to psychometric considerations in developing the EASI questionnaire. Two early studies of the childhood temperament questionnaire established its factor structure in samples of children ages 1 to 9. In the first study, Buss and Plomin (1975) essentially obtained four factors that closely resembled the proposed temperament constructs. The dimensions were fairly distinct, except for a high correlation between activity and impulsivity. In a later study of both the EASI and NYLS temperament dimensions, Rowe and Plomin (1977) found six underlying factors: sociability–shyness, negative emotionality, activity, task persistence, reaction to food, and soothability.

The two parent-report studies establishing the factor structure of the EASI primarily included participants age 6 or younger. This leaves unanswered the question of whether emotionality, sociability, and activity can be measured by use of the EASI during middle childhood and early adolescence. Boer and Westenberg (1994) recently reported that a factor analysis of ratings of elementary school children had yielded separate shyness, activity, and emotionality factors. The sociability items merged with the shyness dimension in the youngest children and with activity in the oldest. Because the most recent form of the EASI (Buss & Plomin, 1984) includes separate scales for sociability and shyness, it would be helpful to know whether factor analyses of data from other samples would indicate that these two dimensions are distinguishable in middle childhood.

There is some evidence for the predictive or concurrent validity of the EASI dimensions around the middle childhood years. First-grade children appear to be more susceptible to the negative effect of high stress on externalizing behavior if they are more emotional, more active, or less sociable (Rende & Plomin, 1992). Emotionality also predicts internalizing difficulties in the form of major depression among adolescents ages 11 to 16 (Goodyer, Ashby, Altham, Vize, & Cooper, 1993). Observations of 4-year-old children's reluctance to join other children are related to teacher ratings of sociability-shyness (Coplan, Rubin, Fox, Calkins, & Stewart, 1994). Although these initial findings are promising, the EASI model has been used relatively rarely by researchers studying older children, so there is still little available information concerning the predictive validity of these dimensions, as measured by the EASI questionnaire.

Several questions about the EASI model still need to be resolved. One important issue is whether the four EASI dimensions are, in fact, any more heritable than any other personality traits. Most of the research on the heritability of temperament in young children has been conducted by use of some form of the EASI. Although twin studies of young children have found evidence of genetic influences on the four EASI traits, the dizygotic (DZ) twin correlations in all of the studies have been near zero or even negative (Pedersen, 1993). These DZ correlations are a problem, because DZ twins should resemble each other to some extent because they share half of their genes. Goldsmith, Buss, and Lemery (1997) recently summarized the results of the small number of twin studies that examined other temperament traits in early childhood, including the NYLS traits and dimensions measured by Rothbart and colleagues' *Children's Behavior Questionnaire* (CBQ; Rothbart, Ahadi, Hershey, & Fisher, 1996) and Goldsmith's (1996) *Toddler Behavior Assessment Questionnaire*. Essentially, all of the traits measured showed evidence of heritability, except for rhythmicity and pleasure (a measure of positive emotions). Similarly, the research on heritability of personality in adults gives no evidence that certain personality traits are more heritable than others (Caspi, 1998). For example, in a study of adult twins who had either been reared apart or together (Tellegen et al., 1988), dimensions similar to several of the

EASI traits were measured: social closeness (sociability), stress reaction (emotionality), and constraint (reversed impulsivity). The heritabilities for these three dimensions fell in the range of .40 to .53, the same general range as the other personality traits measured. The four EASI traits thus may not be distinctive in the extent to which they are heritable.

As mentioned previously, the EASI questionnaire needs to be validated with samples of older children and adolescents to determine how well the four traits can be measured in these age groups and whether the traits become differentiated in the ways Buss and Plomin have suggested (e.g., emotionality splitting into fear and anger). It would be particularly helpful to explore whether impulsivity, as Buss (1995) has recently reconceptualized it, coheres as a single dimension. Despite these remaining questions, there is much to commend this model. The EASI model combines carefully articulated theories for each of its dimensions with psychometric evidence for at least three of the traits. Thus, there is good evidence that traits of negative emotionality, activity, and sociability–social inhibition can be measured by the start of middle childhood.

Rothbart's Psychobiological Model of Temperament

Rothbart and colleagues have elaborated a theoretical and empirical model of temperament that is tied closely to presumed neurobiological functioning (Derryberry & Rothbart, 1988; Rothbart, 1989b; Rothbart & Derryberry, 1981). In this model, temperamental traits are defined as "constitutional differences in reactivity and self-regulation, with 'constitutional' seen as the relatively enduring biological makeup of the organism influenced over time by heredity, maturation, and experience" (Rothbart & Derryberry, 1981, p. 37). *Reactivity* refers to the arousability of an individual's behavioral, emotional, and biological responses. *Self-regulation* refers to the processes that modulate an individual's reactivity, including individual differences in "attention, approach and withdrawal, attack, behavioral inhibition, and self-soothing" (Ahadi, Rothbart, & Ye, 1993, p. 360). The processes of reactivity and self-regulation are seen as developing over time. For example, in early infancy a child may engage in self-regulation by looking away from something that is too intensely stimulating, whereas later the child may inhibit a response to unfamiliar or intense stimuli or use verbal self-regulation (Rothbart, 1989a; Rothbart & Posner, 1985).

Rothbart and colleagues have recently constructed a parent-rating temperament measure for use with children ages 4 to 7 (the CBQ; Rothbart et al., 1996). Fifteen scales were created to measure components of reactivity and self-regulation. In developing these scales, Rothbart and colleagues considered other childhood temperament models (the NYLS and EASI models), adult temperament and personality models, and research on basic emotions (Izard, 1977). The fifteen scales are as follows: activity level, anger–frustration, approach (positive excitement when anticipating pleasurable activities), attentional focusing (similar to persistence in the NYLS model), discomfort (negative emotions resulting from sensory stimuli), fear, high-intensity pleasure (pleasure in highly stimulating situations), impulsivity (speed of response initiation), inhibitory control (ability to inhibit inappropriate approach tendencies), low-intensity pleasure (pleasure in situations with low levels of stimulation), perceptual sensitivity (similar to threshold in the NYLS model), sadness (lowered mood in the face of some negative happening), shyness (social inhibition in novel situations), smiling and laughter, soothability, and falling reactivity. Notable on this list is the inclusion of several scales tapping aspects of positive emotionality.

Mothers of 6- and 7-year-old children in the United States and in the People's Republic of China (PRC) completed the questionnaire (Ahadi et al., 1993; Rothbart et al., 1996).[1] The 15 scale scores (not the individual item scores) were obliquely factored separately for the U.S. and PRC samples. Similar but not invariant factor structures were found for both samples. Three factors were observed, which, as the authors noted, resemble Tellegen's adult higher order dimensions of positive emotionality, negative emotionality, and constraint (Tellegen, 1985; Tellegen & Waller, in press). In naming these factors, the researchers drew from both Tellegen's work and other adult-personality research. First, a factor that could be labeled *surgency, positive emotionality*, or *extroversion* was obtained. In the Chinese sample, approach, high-intensity pleasure, smiling, activity level, and impulsivity loaded positively on this factor, and shyness loaded negatively. The results for the American sample were similar, except that approach and smiling loaded only moderately on this factor. Ahadi and Rothbart (1994) interpreted the first factor as an approach system, which includes an individual's tendencies both to be receptive to reward signals from the environment and to be involved vigorously with the environment. This factor appears to have tapped positive emotionality more strongly in the Chinese sample.

Second, a negative-emotionality or neuroticism factor emerged; on this factor, discomfort, fear, anger, sadness, and shyness loaded positively, and soothability loaded negatively for the Chinese and American samples. In the U.S. sample, approach also loaded moderately on this factor. Ahadi and Rothbart suggested that this second factor taps an underlying anxiety system, comparable to Gray's (1987) behavioral inhibition system. They described this system as encompassing an individual's propensities toward experiencing negative emotions in response to signals of threat.

The third factor appeared to measure elements of behavioral constraint; here inhibitory control, attentional focusing, low-intensity pleasure, and perceptual sensitivity all loaded positively in the Chinese and American samples. In addition, smiling loaded highly on this factor in the American sample. Ahadi and Rothbart (1994) suggested that this factor taps *effortful control* or the "superordinate self-regulatory systems that can assert control over the reactive and self-regulatory processes of other temperament systems, so that an analogy to 'effort' or 'will' is appropriate" (p. 196). The self-regulatory processes are presumed to modulate the experience and expression of the approach and anxiety systems.

There is some evidence that the three higher order factors relate meaningfully to both earlier temperament and concurrent social behavior. Rothbart, Ahadi, and Hershey (1994) administered a measure of social behavior to the mothers of 6–7-year-old American children and found that the three higher order factors related in theoretically predictable ways to the scales tapping individual differences in aggression, empathy, guilt–shame, help seeking, and negativity in response to new situations. For example, negative affect moderately

---

[1] Both Ahadi et al. (1993) and Rothbart et al. (1996) presented results for factor analyses of the CBQ with samples of 6- and 7-year-old children from the United States. I describe the results from the Rothbart et al. paper, because this sample is significantly larger and subsumes the sample included in the published paper by Ahadi et al.

predicted both shame–guilt and negativity, and effortful control predicted both empathy and guilt–shame. Ahadi and Rothbart (1994) have also found in a small subsample of the American children that the 6–7-year-olds' temperament dimensions were significantly predicted by laboratory assessments of these same children as infants. For example, infant time to approach laboratory objects positively predicted approach and impulsivity and negatively predicted inhibitory control and attentional focusing at the later age. Despite the small sample size, these longitudinal results provide some theoretically interesting indications of how temperament might develop over time.

Rothbart and colleagues' psychobiological model of temperament appears to show promise for capturing important differences in middle childhood. Because the CBQ is a new instrument, additional psychometric data are needed to assess whether the 15 subscales tap important, internally consistent, and valid dimensions of temperament at ages 4 to 7. In particular, the internal structure of the battery warrants further examination and possibly clarification; factor analysis of the CBQ items (as opposed to factor analysis of the 15 scale scores) could help determine whether the 15 individual scales represent distinguishable dimensions of temperament. Although some of the CBQ dimensions may not be broad enough to be considered general childhood personality traits (e.g., discomfort, low-intensity pleasure), they may turn out to be components of broader personality dimensions. The CBQ model is a particularly helpful addition to the temperament literature, because it includes positive emotions and aspects of self-control, dimensions which have often been left out of other temperament systems. The CBQ is therefore a more comprehensive instrument than some other temperament measures. The three higher order factors also need to be replicated. Finally, this model is to be commended for its emphasis on the processes underlying temperamental functioning.

Having explored several temperament models that have been extended into later childhood, I turn now to two models of individual differences that are typically labeled *personality* approaches.

Ego Resiliency and Ego Control

J. Block and J. H. Block have introduced two higher order personality constructs to account for broad aspects of individual functioning from young childhood (J. H. Block & Block, 1980) through adulthood (J. Block, 1965, 1971): *ego resiliency* and *ego control*. More so than most of the other temperament or personality constructs surveyed here, ego resiliency and ego control have theoretical roots (J. Block, 1981; J. Block & Kremen, 1996; J. H. Block & Block, 1980). They were originally developed from a theoretical integration of psychoanalytic concepts of the ego and Lewinian concepts of boundaries among psychological needs. According to the psychoanalytic model of personality development adopted by J. Block and J. H. Block, infants and young children must learn how to negotiate the difficult gap between their internal drives and the realities of the outside environment. Children therefore face the challenge of regulating their impulses in order to both maximally satisfy their own drives and prevent environmental danger; in other words, "the human goal is to be as undercontrolled as possible and as overcontrolled as necessary" (J. Block & Kremen, 1996, p. 351). J. Block and J. H. Block posited that the structures of ego resiliency and ego control develop to enable individuals to carry out this difficult task.

Ego control is understood as "the threshold or operating characteristics of an individual with regard to the expression or containment of impulses, feelings, and desires" (J. H. Block & Block, 1980, p. 43). At one end of the ego-control continuum, individuals are undercontrolled; these individuals do not readily contain their impulses and feelings, which become expressed quite directly and spontaneously. These individuals also tend to be distracted by external stimulation and to have difficulty delaying gratification. At the opposite end of the continuum are the overcontrollers, who tend to inhibit impulse expression or to express impulses only indirectly. They delay gratification too long or too often and may focus on and pursue external information with excessively dogged persistence. J. Block and J. H. Block therefore see both extremes of the ego-control continuum as potentially maladaptive. Ego control differs in this respect from other constructs of behavioral control that typically frame high levels of behavioral control in a positive light. In contrast, according to this model very high levels of ego control are likely to prevent an individual from achieving true impulse satisfaction.

Ego resiliency represents a person's flexibility in modulating his or her typical level of ego control to best meet environmental challenges. Ego resiliency thus enables the "complementary coupling of external affordances and constraints with the internal motivations and needs of the individual" (J. Block & Kremen, 1996). A person low in ego resiliency is termed *ego brittle*; such a person has only a limited repertoire of responses to environmental variations and therefore becomes perseverative or "stuck" in the face of stress. In contrast, the person high on ego resiliency is seen as nimbly negotiating the adaptive challenges presented. This person can tighten or loosen ego control, depending on the particular combination of external circumstances and internal needs. One can never be too ego resilient in this model; therefore, ego resiliency and ego control differ in the adaptiveness of their high extremes.

J. H. Block and Block (1980) measured ego resiliency and ego control in a longitudinal study of children beginning at the age of 3. In this study, ego resiliency and ego control were measured through a variety of methods, including various observers' personality ratings (usually in the form of Q sorts), self-report questionnaires at later ages, and laboratory or test data. At the ages of 3, 4, 5, and 7, the two ego constructs were operationalized by (a) composites of the laboratory–test data and (b) composities of Q-sort items. The Q-sort items and laboratory tasks chosen to measure the two dimensions were selected rationally, that is on primarily theoretical grounds. At ages 3 and 4, children low on the laboratory measures of ego control were seen by their teachers as more active, aggressive, and outgoing and less compliant and orderly than children scoring high on this same measure (p. 68). Children who obtained high ego-resiliency scores were described by their teachers as empathic, able to cope with stress, and competent and less anxious and seeking of reassurance than children low on ego resiliency (pp. 68–70). This early report provided preliminary external validation for both ego control and ego resiliency during ages 3 to 4 and more limited validation at age 7.

A number of other studies have adduced evidence of concurrent and predictive validity of measures of ego control and ego resiliency in middle childhood and early adolescence. Ego resiliency relates positively to school achievement, peer ratings of being liked rather than disliked, general intelligence, and higher levels of within-person consistency over time (Asendorpf & van Aken, 1991; van Aken, 1992). Ego resiliency is negatively related to Piaget's Level I egocentrism, or the inability to perceive objects from a number of perspectives (Gjerde, Block, & Block, 1986). There is also evidence that children with a history of secure attachment tend to be more ego resilient in middle childhood than those children with a history of insecure attachment (Arend, Gove, & Sroufe, 1979; Urban, Carlson, Egeland, & Sroufe, 1991). Longitudinal research has linked lower ego control (for boys and girls) and lower ego resiliency (for girls only) in preschool with adolescent drug usage (J. Block, Block, & Keyes, 1988). Both dimensions relate positively to children's ability to delay gratification concurrently and across time (Funder & Block, 1989; Krueger, Caspi, Moffitt, White, & Stouthamer-Loeber, 1996). Thus, there is substantial evidence that measures of ego resiliency and ego control predict important aspects of children's functioning, both concurrently and across time.

There is also some evidence for the theoretically predicted nonlinear relationship between ego resiliency and ego control. Eisenberg, Guthrie, et al. (1997) obtained teachers' and parents' Q-sort ratings of ego resiliency and ego control in children from kindergarten through third grade. For both teachers' and parents' ratings, there was a quadratic relationship between ego control and ego resiliency. For teachers, ego resiliency was greatest at the middle levels of ego control. For parents, ego resiliency was greater at high and middle levels of ego control than at low levels; in addition, there was a linear relationship between the two constructs. In other words, for both teachers' and parents' reports, children low in ego control evidenced low levels of ego resiliency. The teachers' ratings provided some evidence for J. Block and J. H. Block's contention that excessive ego control may at times be detrimental to children's functioning.

As noted, the ego-control and ego-resiliency constructs reflect a strongly theoretical orientation. Although these constructs are well elaborated and external correlates have been demonstrated, the empirical evidence for the internal structural validity of the dimensions is still limited. J. Block and J. H. Block's earlier work used both laboratory and Q-sort measures of the two traits. More recent studies exploring the correlates of these two dimensions in children and adolescents have typically measured ego control and ego resiliency by comparing children's scores on the California Child Q-Set (J. Block & Block, 1969/1980) with theoretically derived prototypes of ego-control and ego-resiliency. Factor analyses of both the California Child Q-Set and the California Adult Q-Set (J. Block, 1961/1978) have yielded five or more factors, which do not conform to the ego-control or ego-resilience constructs (John, Caspi, Robins, Moffitt, & Stouthamer-Loeber, 1994; Lanning, 1994; van Lieshout & Haselager, 1994). Thus, factor analyses of the key instruments used for measuring ego control and ego resiliency do not appear to confirm the theoretically postulated internal structure of the two dimensions.

The psychologically complex ego-control and ego-resiliency constructs appear to overlap conceptually with a number of seemingly more "elemental" temperament constructs. Theoretically motivated empirical work could help clarify the shared and distinctive features of ego control and ego resiliency and related constructs by exploring them in the same study. From a discriminant-validity point-of-view, the conceptual core of ego resiliency particularly warrants demarcation, because ego resiliency as currently measured typically correlates with virtually all positive child behaviors and traits (see, e.g., Robins, John, & Caspi, 1994). In part, this may be due to the current operationalization of ego resiliency within the California Child Q-Set. Some of the items measuring this construct describe the positive socioemotional outcomes of resiliency rather than resiliency per se (the same is true for the current operationaliation of ego control). The very breadth of the ego-resiliency construct may further complicate attempts to link it confirmably to identifiable psychological and psychobiological mechanisms. The "adaptability" dimension uncovered in some NYLS-related studies may represent a similar but perhaps more narrowly delineated ability to adjust quickly in the face of a changing environment.

A recent study distinguishing IQ and ego resiliency in a sample of young adults provides one example of how construct elucidation for ego control and ego resiliency could be carried out (J. Block & Kremen, 1996). In this study, measures of "pure" IQ and ego resiliency were created by use of partial correlations; these "pure" measures had clearly different personality correlates. Further research of this sort could more effectively position these two theoretically rich, dynamic constructs within the larger context of the developmental and adult personality literatures.

The Big Five in Children and Adolescents

In adult personality research, an approach called the *Big Five* has increasingly garnered adherents who argue that five higher order factors encompass the domain of personality descriptions (Digman, 1990; Digman & Takemoto-Chock, 1981; Goldberg, 1993; McCrae & John, 1992). The five factors and sample descriptors are as follows: (a) Extroversion—*active, assertive, energetic, enthusiastic, outgoing, surgent*, and *talkative* versus *silent, passive*, and *reserved*; (b) Agreeableness—*appreciative, forgiving, generous, kind, sympathetic*, and *trusting* versus *hostile, selfish, unsympathetic, uncooperative, rude*, and *mistrustful*; (c) Conscientiousness—*efficient, organized, planful, reliable, responsible, thorough, able to delay gratification*, and *has high aspirations* versus *careless, negligent*, and *unreliable*; (d) Neuroticism—*anxious, self-pitying, tense, touchy, unstable, worrying*, and *moody*; and (e) Openness to Experience or Intellect—*artistic, curious, imaginative, creative, has wide interests*, and *insightful* versus *shallow* and *imperceptive* (Goldberg, 1993, p. 27; McCrae & Costa, 1987, pp. 86–89; McCrae & John, 1992, pp. 178–179).

Support for the Big Five structure of personality in adults derives from two primary sources. First, research conducted in the *lexical tradition* is based on the assumption that the individual differences that are the most important in human functioning will be encoded in the natural language. Sets of trait-descriptive adjectives have been selected from the dictionary to elicit self-ratings and ratings of others. The factor structures of these ratings have been examined to determine their implicit dimensional structure. Such research has yielded the above-described five factors (Goldberg, 1990; Peabody & Goldberg, 1989). The lexical Big Five research has recently come under criticism for relying on a restricted sample of trait descriptors; the constricted range of traits included is the result of unexamined assumptions about what words constitute "true" personality descriptors (see, e.g., Benet & Waller, 1995, and Tellegen, 1993). In particular, many evaluative adjectives (e.g., *odd*) and emotional-responsiveness terms, which are potentially important for the assessment of temperament, have been excluded. The lexical hypothesis itself has come under criticism. For example, J. Block (1995) has argued that single-word descriptors are inadequate to capture all the important dimensions of human personality and that potentially important dimensions may not have a large number of descriptors.

A second source of evidence for the Big Five includes factor analyses of broad-spectrum personality measures as varied as the Jackson Personality Research Form (Costa & McCrae, 1988; Jackson, 1974) and the adult California Q-Sort (J. Block, 1961/1978; McCrae, Costa, & Busch, 1986). Five-factor advocates have interpreted the findings from these studies as providing diverse support for the five-factor model, leading McCrae and John (1992) to claim boldly, "We believe that its long history, cross-cultural replication, and empirical validation across many methods and instruments make the five-factor model a basic discovery of personality psychology—core knowledge upon which other findings can be built" (p. 207). J. Block (1995) and others have contested these conclusions and have argued a strongly dissenting viewpoint.

In recent years, researchers have become increasingly interested in applying the five-factor model to children and adolescents. Some early personality research conducted by Digman helped spur such interest. Digman and colleagues (Digman & Inouye, 1986; Digman & Takemoto-Chock, 1981) reported results of two studies in which first-grade and sixth-grade elementary school children were rated by teachers on a number of personality-trait terms. In both studies, factor analyses of the teachers' ratings resulted in five factors that are comparable to those obtained in the adult Big Five studies, with some slight differences: Agreeableness included descriptors suggesting submissiveness both to other children and to adults; and Openness primarily included aspects of intellect, not openness. In a later work, Digman (1994) presented reanalyses of teachers' ratings of two other groups of students using a different list of personality adjectives; again, factor analyses of the two data sets yielded very similar results, essentially a Big Five factor structure. Digman's work provided early evidence that the Big Five could be measured effectively in children by use of lists of adjectives similar to those used in the adult lexical studies.

Other studies have tended to corroborate Digman's findings. Victor (1994) administered Digman's adjective rating lists to teachers of fifth- and sixth-grade students. Again, the Big Five emerged, and the factor loadings mirrored Digman's findings quite well. Graziano and Ward (1992) similarly obtained teachers' ratings of a sample of sixth and seventh graders using Digman's trait lists. Factor analysis resulted in the Big Five factors, but item loadings on the factors were not reported. Mervielde, Buyst, and De Fruyt (1995) obtained teachers' ratings on a different list of adjectives for children in kindergarten and in Grades 1–2, 3–4, and 5–6. Extroversion, Agreeableness, and Neuroticism emerged as independent factors across all grade groups. Although a Conscientiousness factor appeared in all groups, this factor also included several Openness items in kindergarten and Grades 5–6. Taken as a group, these studies provide evidence that something akin to the Big Five factor structure emerges from teachers' ratings of children on relatively short lists of trait descriptors.

As in the adult research, the Big Five factors in children have been uncovered in a measure not created to tap those dimensions: the California Child Q-Set (J. Block & Block, 1969/1980). Van Lieshout and Haselager (1993, 1994) used a Dutch version of the Q set in six studies of children ranging in age from 3 to 17 with a variety of respondents, including parents, teachers, best friends, and the participants themselves (in two samples in which the children were of age 11 or older). When the results of the six studies were combined and factor analyzed, seven factors emerged: the Big Five and two others, motor activity and dependency. A third "extra" factor appeared in certain subsamples: A factor indicating irritability and immaturity appeared for preschool-and school-age children and for the overall sample of girls.

Agreeableness and Neuroticism appeared as robust factors across ages and respondents, but the content of the Extroversion and Conscientiousness factors was more variable by subsample. Openness varied the most from sample to sample and tended to include a broad range of items (such as attractiveness and motor activity) in the overall sample of girls and the sample of children ages 3 to 7. The results for children ages 3 to 7 less closely approximated the Big Five structure than did the results for older children and adolescents. Teachers' ratings provided the clearest factor structure, followed in structural clarity by parents' ratings. The early adolescents themselves and their best friends produced ratings that less clearly approximated the five-factor model.

In a similar study, John et al. (1994; also presented in Robins et al., 1994) factor analyzed the results of a maternal California Q sort for 12–13-year-old boys. Here again, seven factors were obtained; this time, the Big Five factors emerged along with factors tapping positive aspects of high activity–approach and irritability–immaturity. Overall, the scales showed moderate congruence with the factors obtained in adult Q sort studies; the congruence was somewhat lesser for the Neuroticism and Openness factors. On the basis of the small number of currently available studies, it appears that the Big Five factors can be obtained in analyses of adjective lists similar to Digman's list of traits, whereas more than five factors can be extracted from the California Child Q-Set.

There are some preliminary external-validity data available for the Big Five in child-hood and early adolescence. For example, less agreeable adolescents report higher levels of day-to-day conflicts and greater acceptance of destructive conflict tactics than do more agreeable adolescents; they also have poorer relationships with peers and teachers (Graziano, Jensen-Campbell, & Finch, 1997; Jensen-Campbell, 1995; Jensen-Campbell, Graziano, & Hair, 1996). Openness and Conscientiousness predict children's academic achievement, Agreeableness relates negatively to conduct disorder and positively to good classroom be-havior, and Conscientiousness relates negatively to attention problems (Graziano et al., 1997; Mervielde et al., 1995; Victor, 1994). Graziano et al. (1997) have obtained evidence that aspects of adolescents' self-esteem mediate the relationship between their Extrover-sion, Neuroticism, and Openness and their adjustment in specific domains. Digman (1989) found high levels of stability for the five factors in a sample of students studied longitu-dinally over a period of 4 years. Digman also reported that a composite measure of child-hood Conscientiousness correlated .70 with GPA at graduation from high school and .51 with occupational status in the mid-20s. Low conscientiousness in boys relates to juvenile delinquency, externalizing disorders, and internalizing disorders (John et al., 1994). This preliminary validation for the Big Five dimensions appears promising, but there is a great need for more comparisons between Big Five ratings and conceptually similar personality or temperament measures to provide construct validation.

The Big Five studies have provided evidence for the five-factor model in ratings of children and adolescents older than age 7. The Big Five factor structure appears to be most robust in teacher ratings. The evidence for Openness as a dimension is not as strong as that obtained for the other dimensions: Openness typically is not measured with as much internal consistency, and the Openness factor does not emerge as clearly in the factor analytic studies. It is possible that the traits tapped by Openness may not be well developed in children. It should be emphasized, though, that the Openness to Experience trait is not well defined in adults either (DeRaad, 1994). The relative weakness of this factor in children may simply perpetuate the conceptual ambiguity of its adult prototype.

The emergence of three extra factors in the studies with the California Q sort raises the intriguing possibility that more than five factors could be obtained in adjective ratings of children as well, if more items were included. The adjective-ratings studies of children completed thus far have used fairly short lists of traits (generally around 45 items). As with the adult lexical studies, these trait lists are fairly restricted in the range of content represented and have resulted in undue "prestructuring" of the findings (Block, 1995). It is quite possible that longer trait lists may produce greater numbers of factors or even different types of factors. There is evidence that, when less restrictive pools of adjectives are used in studies of adults, more than five dimensions are uncovered, and the Big Five–like dimensions that do emerge demarcate meaningfully differing content domains (Benet & Waller, 1995; Tellegen, 1993; Waller, in press). Thus, it still cannot be concluded that factor analyses of representative natural language descriptors will yield the Big Five factors in studies with children.

The results of the Big Five studies in adults and children indicate that adults view both children and adults in terms of roughly comparable underlying dimensions of personality. As Tellegen (1993) has suggested, these Big Five dimensions may represent "folk concepts" (p. 126) or common-sense notions adults share about how personality traits tend to cluster together. As folk conceptions, these dimensions are likely to relate meaningfully to children's psychosocial functioning: Parents' and teachers' perceptions of children's personalities are likely to influence their behavior toward these children and thus the children's own development. The children's own emerging perceptions of self and others can likewise be expected to play a formative role. It is interesting to note that, in some of the few childhood personality studies to include child raters (van Lieshout & Haselager, 1994), the results are more equivocal in terms of the Big Five factor structure. To understand these apparent age differences more clearly, a more explicitly developmental perspective may be needed on natural-language personality factors as emerging person–perceptual structures.

The Big Five dimensions differ from the temperament and personality dimensions examined thus far in that psychological theory was not used to guide the selection of trait dimensions to be measured, other than in the selection of trait terms to be analyzed. Even in the case of the NYLS model, which was not derived from any formal theory, the temperament dimensions were delineated on a conceptual basis. In contrast, the Big Five dimensions in adults and children were derived solely from the application of factor analysis to adjective lists and personality inventories made up of descriptors intended to be representative of the natural-language personality-descriptive domain. Although the empirical basis of the Big Five is a strength, the absence as yet of a strong theoretical perspective is not. It should be noted, though, that some thoughtful post hoc theoretical interpretations of these dimensions have been proposed (e.g., Graziano, 1994; Graziano & Eisenberg, 1997; MacDonald, 1995).

Because the development of the Big Five model was not guided by theoretical considerations, the Big Five dimensions may obscure underlying, more narrow lower order trait distinctions. For example, depending in part on the particular Big Five version, the dimension of Extroversion encompasses aspects of both dominance and sociability; components of sociability and dominance may also be included in the Agreeableness dimension. Similarly, anger proneness sometimes appears as an aspect of Neuroticism and at other times merges with the Agreeableness factor. The atheoretical nature of the Big Five provides no conceptual framework for resolving questions about the placement of lower order traits within the higher order structure. Furthermore, because each of the Big Five dimensions appears to encompass fundamentally distinctive facets or lower order traits, the differential contributions of these underlying traits to children's functioning may be obscured when only the higher order Big Five dimensions are used. This problem may be especially acute in samples of children, in that the content of the Big Five appears to be particularly heterogeneous in the California Q-sort studies. Careful work in measuring lower level traits more validly and reliably may yield evidence for other higher order dimensions.

Nevertheless, the Big Five represents one potentially viable model for higher order personality traits in children and adolescents. The research on the Big Five in children has considerably broadened the purview of personality research in children beyond the confines of typical temperament research by including measures of traits that appear after the first couple years of life. This model awaits further confirmation of its validity and of its comprehensiveness in measuring personality in children, however, and should not be taken as the last word on higher order personality structure in children at this early stage in research on this topic.

The Five Childhood Temperament and Personality Models: Divergence in Methodologies, Convergence in Findings

The five models of temperament and personality examined here—the models of Thomas and Chess, Buss and Plomin, Rothbart, J. Block and J. H. Block, and the Big Five—highlight a broad array of robust personality traits in middle childhood and early adolescence. The models notably differ in terms of how the structure of personality is established. For the most part, the creators of the temperament models chose to focus on those traits that are most salient in very young children, with only a couple of exceptions (e.g., the inhibitory-control dimension measured on the CBQ develops somewhat later in childhood than the other dimensions). In contrast, the two personality models surveyed include some traits that emerge more fully in the preschool years, such as the prosocial tendencies encompassed by the Agreeableness dimension.

As noted previously, the creators of some of these models emphasized theoretical considerations in the delineation of personality dimensions. Although J. Block and J. H. Block's ego-control and ego-resiliency model is the most striking example of such an approach because of its psychodynamic roots, conceptual or theoretical concerns significantly shaped the creation of all the models, with the exception of the Big Five approach. The theoretical concerns central to each model differed, however. For example, Thomas and Chess developed their dimensions on the basis of what temperamental traits may have clinical import for parents of infants or for clinicians. In contrast, the models developed by Buss and Plomin and by Rothbart and colleagues incorporated temperament dimensions highlighted in the adult literature on personality. These two models are also strongly characterized by their emphasis on the genetic or biological bases of temperament. The five models also were derived by or refined through empirical methods. The Big Five model typifies an approach in which empirical results (specifically factor analytic results) determined the personality dimensions; however, factor analysis was likewise used to understand the underlying dimensions in the NYLS, EASI, and CBQ models. For all five models, there is accompanying evidence of correlations of the personality dimensions with real-world criteria, although such evidence is scantier than one might like.

Despite the varying theoretical concerns and empirical methods undergirding each model, there is some convergence of findings across models. For example, all the models encompass dimensions of behavioral control, albeit in numerous forms. Similarly, virtually all of the models include a dimension of social inhibition. It is to these consistencies across the models that I now turn.

WHAT PERSONALITY TRAITS CAN BE MEASURED IN MIDDLE CHILDHOOD?

The Task of Constructing a Taxonomy of Personality Traits

Despite the relative neglect of the study of personality within the field of child development, the foundations of a childhood personality taxonomy already exist within the child development literature. Although none of the contemporary models was designed to describe personality comprehensively, taken together they can provide richer coverage of potential personality traits measurable in middle childhood. The dimensions highlighted by the above-described personality models converge with a number of personality traits studied by developmental researchers. Thus, we can profitably integrate what is known from the temperament and personality models surveyed here with the childhood traits described in the broader developmental and personality literatures in order to generate a preliminary taxonomy of childhood personality dimensions. I have chosen to focus on lower order traits rather than on broader, higher order ones. Lower order traits describe a narrower range of behavior (e.g., sociability), whereas higher order traits encompass a wider range of behaviors (e.g., extroversion). I selected this focus on lower order traits, because the research on higher order factors in children is in its very early stages. Aside from the studies of ego resiliency and ego control, Rothbart's work on the CBQ, and the more recent Big Five studies in children, the vast majority of research on childhood personality has examined lower order traits. There is therefore a great need to bring order to this vast array of studies of single lower level traits.

In the following section, the lower order traits are grouped under the rubric of several higher order traits, including positive emotionality–extroversion, negative emotionality–neuroticism, and constraint–conscientiousness. These higher order traits have been identified in a number of programs of adult personality research: the Big Five work in adults (Digman, 1990); Tellegen's Multidimensional Personality Questionnaire (Tellegen & Waller, in press), and Zuckerman's Alternative Big Five (Zuckerman, Kuhlman, Joireman, Teta, & Kraft, 1993; Zuckerman, Kuhlman, Thornquist, & Kiers, 1991). H. J. Eysenck's (1952) P-E-N personality model also includes extroversion and neuroticism factors. Significant differences remain among these models, and the lower order factors included in each superfactor vary from one system to the next; however, much of the core content for each superfactor is shared across models. Rothbart and Bates (1998) argued that three similar temperamental systems emerge in research on older children (they included agreeableness as another higher order ·dimension found in children, but they acknowledge that the evidence for this dimension in children is relatively thin). In the following section, I assign the lower order factors to these broad superfactors on the basis of current research relating lower and higher order factors in children and adults and on the basis of conceptually coherent links between the two.

Positive Emotionality–Extroversion

Individual differences in aspects of positive emotionality–extroversion clearly manifest themselves by middle childhood. Rothbart and Bates (1998) have suggested that these traits relate to children's tendencies to be receptive to reward signals from the environment. These traits also measure children's various tendencies to be vigorously, actively, and positively involved with the world around them.

By early childhood, variations in sociability–social inhibition emerge. As noted previously, Buss and Plomin (1984) distinguished between shyness or social inhibition (i.e., reluctance to act and feelings of discomfort in encounters with strangers or possibly other groups of people) and sociability (i.e., the preference to be with others rather than alone and social responsiveness with known others). There is clear evidence supporting the first of these traits, *social inhibition with strangers*, from early childhood through middle childhood and into adulthood; this trait appears to be moderately stable by early childhood (Asendorpf, 1993a; Gest, 1997). Social inhibition with strangers consistently appears as a factor in the NYLS-related studies, and it is measured by the shyness scale on the CBQ. It has proven to be a robust dimension of temperament in Asendorpf's research on behavioral inhibition and shyness (1990, 1991, 1993b) and in Kagan and colleagues' studies of behavioral inhibition to the unfamiliar (Kagan, Reznick, Clarke, Snidman, & Garcia-Coll, 1984; Kagan, Reznick, & Snidman, 1987), although Kagan's construct is broader than social inhibition in that it also encompasses inhibition with novel nonsocial stimuli.

Over time inhibition with strangers appears to become differentiated from *shyness with known others*. Although the two types of social withdrawal are modestly to moderately correlated in preschool- and school-age children, the relationship between the two decreases over time (Asendorpf, 1990; Gersten, 1989). Furthermore, the two types of withdrawal relate differently to children's functioning. In a longitudinal study of children from preschool through first grade, children's shyness with known peers related to their being rebuffed when they tried to initiate contact with other children, whereas stranger wariness had no such detrimental correlates (Asendorpf, 1990). In addition, shyness with peers predicted later poor social self-esteem, whereas stranger wariness did not (Asendorpf & van Aken,

1994). Gest (1997) similarly found that stranger wariness did not correlate with acceptance by classmates or emotional distress in an elementary school sample. There is some evidence, however, that shyness with known peers is not consistently associated with social neglect or rejection until later in elementary school (Harrist, Zaia, Bates, Dodge, & Pettit, 1997; Younger & Boyko, 1987).

Stranger wariness may become elaborated into shyness with familiar people for some children, including those with poorer intellectual or social competence (Asendorpf, 1994). In middle childhood, children's growing capacity to reflect on themselves and to see themselves through others' eyes (Markus & Nurius, 1984) may pave the way for the development of the self-consciousness later associated with shyness in adults (Asendorpf, 1989). The developmental pathway from social inhibition with strangers to shyness with familiar people needs to be explored further to determine the extent to which these two constructs represent distinctive personality traits by middle childhood. Although social inhibition with strangers has been studied more frequently in children, shyness with known others may well prove to have greater significance for children's functioning by middle childhood.

The narrow-band construct of *sociability* (social responsiveness and the preference to be with others) has been studied far less often in children than social inhibition or shyness. A number of studies have examined sociability as part of a larger social responsiveness dimension that includes shyness (e.g., Bronson, 1966; Caspi, Elder, & Bem, 1988; Kagan & Moss, 1962). In the Big Five factor structure, elements of sociability (e.g., *keeps thoughts and feelings to self* [reversed] and *likes to be by self* [reversed]) are combined with elements of shyness (e.g., *shy and reserved*) to form the Extroversion factor (van Lieshout & Haselager, 1993, 1994). Similarly, items tapping sociability and shyness loaded on the same factor in three studies examining the EASI questionnaire in samples of young children (Boer & Westenberg, 1994; Buss & Plomin, 1975; Rowe & Plomin, 1977).

Although it may be difficult to distinguish shyness and sociability in young children, the two traits may become more distinct by middle childhood (see, e.g., Boer & Westenberg, 1994). In middle childhood, shyness may be difficult to distinguish from low sociability in children's behavioral reactions to unfamiliar peers, because over time both types of children tend to retreat from social play (Asendorpf, 1991). Asendorpf and Meier (1993) provided evidence, however, that these two traits can be distinguished behaviorally in second graders by the way they choose to spend their free time. These researchers found that during the afternoon (a time when children can exert greater freedom of choice in selecting their activities), unsociable children opt to spend more time at home and away from social interactions than do more sociable children; in contrast, shy children do not differ from nonshy children in these respects. More recently, Harrist et al. (1997) used cluster analysis to identify distinct groups of shy, socially anxious children and unsociable children in a sample of socially withdrawn kindergartners. According to a recent report by Larson (1997), by seventh-to-ninth grade, youth report even greater voluntary control over the amount of time spent alone at home than do older children. Because children have greater opportunities to choose patterns of social interaction in middle childhood and adolescence, it seems likely that individual differences in sociability become a more important determinant of children's social behavior during this period; consequently, it may become easier to distinguish children's sociability and their shyness.

By middle childhood, sociability and shyness most likely represent two different behavioral systems. Sociability may primarily tap elements of approach and positive emotionality, as it does in adults (Church, 1994; Tellegen & Waller, in press). In contrast, shyness is likely to be a more multidimensional trait combining elements of low approach, high negative emotionality, and high behavioral avoidance (Asendorpf, 1990, 1993a; Eisenberg, Fabes, & Murphy, 1995; Rothbart & Bates, 1998). The causes of shyness may, in fact, be quite heterogeneous; low levels of approach or high levels of fear–behavioral inhibition may each predominate in different individuals. By adulthood, sociability and shyness are clearly distinct. In a college sample, shyness and sociability were found to correlate only modestly and to relate differently to related constructs, such as fears and self-esteem (Cheek & Buss, 1981).[2] Further research exploring the correlates of high and low sociability in children could help differentiate this construct from shyness. Closer examination of children's motivations for their social behavior may also help to distinguish the two traits.

Dominance appears to be another dimension of extroversion that can be measured by middle childhood. Dominance represents the extent to which a child exerts an influence on others' (particularly other children's) behavior, in part through organizing their behavior. This dimension also encompasses a child's ability to act cooperatively and competitively to procure desirable resources (Charlesworth & Dzur, 1987). In adults, this aspect of extroversion also includes an individual's tendency to capture others' attention in social situations and to enjoy such attention (Tellegen & Waller, in press; Watson & Clark, 1997).

Aspects of dominance emerge in the Big Five Extroversion factor in items such as *outspoken, self-minimizing* (reversed), and *tends to yield and give in* (reversed), (Digman, 1989; van Lieshout & Haselager, 1993, 1994). Although a dominance dimension does not seem to be well represented in the studies reviewed above, it emerges as an important individual difference in other developmental research. As early as preschool age, children can be ranked along a dominance dimension and evidence stable rankings over a short period of time (Charlesworth & Dzur, 1987; Charlesworth & la Freniere, 1983; la Freniere & Charlesworth, 1983). Furthermore, children's dominance is related to their access to desired resources. In elementary school children's peer ratings, dominance emerges as one part of a sociability–leadership factor (Morison & Masten, 1991). Many items from this factor, such as *good leader, everyone listens to, can get things going*, appear to tap a child's influence over other children. In the now-classic "Robbers Cave" experiment (Sherif, Harvey, White, Hood, & Sherif, 1961), the boys who went on to become leaders evidenced skill in organizing activities and games. Not surprising, children's dominance has significant implications for their peer functioning; it also appears to relate to their levels of prosocial behavior (Eisenberg & Fabes, 1998). It is not yet clear what other domains are affected by children's relative standing on this personality dimension, but this trait may be important for an understanding of children's emerging capacities for leadership.

A final possible aspect of positive emotionality–approach in middle childhood is more speculative: Children may differ along a dimension of a generally positive emotional

---

[2]Interestingly, this distinction between sociability and shyness in adults is mirrored in the current psychiatric distinction between schizoid personality disorder, an extreme form of low sociability, and social phobia, an extreme form of high shyness (American Psychiatric Association, 1994).

orientation, or *well-being*. Even in infancy, children differ along a dimension of general positive emotionality, including their tendencies toward smiling and laughter and their cooperativeness with caregivers (Rothbart & Mauro, 1990). Goldsmith (1996) has documented that a dimension labeled *pleasure* can be measured in toddlers; this dimension taps children's smiling, laughter, and general enjoyment in familiar settings. The pleasure dimension relates positively to parental reports of children's empathy and negatively to their reported aggression and "difficultness." Among slightly older children, the smiling and laughter scale on the CBQ (Rothbart et al., 1996) may tap aspects of a generally positive sense of well-being. This dimension appears worthy of study in samples of older children; it is not clear whether such a dimension of positive well-being could be distinguished from other dimensions of positive emotionality, such as sociability and dominance. Although the dimension of positive well-being is more speculative, because it has rarely been studied in older children, there appears to be good evidence supporting the other two positive emotionality dimensions of sociability and dominance and the complex dimension of social inhibition.

Negative Emotionality–Neuroticism

Negative emotionality is a robust facet of personality functioning in middle childhood: Dimensions tapping negative emotions emerge in virtually all temperament and personality models. The inclusion of negative emotionality in all models of temperament and personality indicates that developmental researchers have considered children's propensities toward fear, sadness, anger, and general distress to be extremely important aspects of their personality functioning. Factor analyses of the NYLS scales result in a factor that taps negative emotionality, particularly those negative emotions that emerge in the face of external stressors. Negative emotional reactivity appears as a coherent dimension in infants, young children, and adults in the EASI model. Factor analyses of the CBQ scales also result in a clear negative-emotionality dimension that incorporates the scales of discomfort, fear, anger, sadness, shyness, and soothability (loading negatively; Ahadi et al., 1993). These findings parallel those obtained in adult research by Tellegen (Tellegen, 1985; Tellegen & Waller, in press) and by Watson and Clark (1984). In these studies, a higher order negative emotionality factor emerges that taps an individual's propensity toward experiencing negative emotions, such as anxiety, resentment, and anger, in a wide variety of situations and toward having negatively charged relationships; this factor also includes a person's vulnerabilities toward the adverse effects of stress.

Several programs of research have explored the significance of children's negative emotionality. Rothbart and Bates (1998), summarizing the literature linking temperament and adjustment, noted that negative emotionality appears to be associated with both externalizing and internalizing difficulties in middle childhood. Eisenberg and colleagues have examined the relationship between negative emotionality and social functioning in preschoolers and elementary school children. In a series of studies, these researchers have found that children's negative emotionality relates negatively to their social skills and popularity (for boys), socially appropriate behavior (i.e., low levels of aggression and disruptive behavior and good social skills), and a composite measure of prosocial behavior, social insecurity (reversed), and popularity (Eisenberg et al., 1993; Eisenberg, Fabes, Murphy, Maszk, et al., 1995). Children's negative emotionality predicts their social functioning both concurrently and across time. In fact, children who experience a decline in social functioning differ from other children in their high levels of negative emotionality (Eisenberg, Fabes, et al., 1997). Negative emotionality also relates negatively to children's sympathy for others, particularly among boys, perhaps because children who are distressed have more difficulty focusing on others' experiences (Eisenberg et al., 1996). Children who tend to experience high levels of negative emotions appear to be at risk for poor social development in a variety of arenas.

As noted previously, Buss and Plomin (1975, 1984) have suggested that infants' negative emotionality is initially expressed as general distress and later differentiates into fear and anger. Buss and Plomin (1984) have obtained evidence for separate fear and anger dimensions in adults. More recently, Rothbart and Bates (1998) have provided compelling evidence that two similar traits, *fearful distress* and *irritable distress*, are measurable in both infancy and childhood. Fearful distress primarily taps a child's tendency to withdraw fearfully from new situations; this construct is similar to behavioral inhibition to the unfamiliar. In contrast, irritable distress taps a child's propensity toward irritability and anger–frustration, particularly in the face of external limitations. The Neuroticism factor obtained in the Big Five studies in middle childhood and adolescence appears to measure only the first of these traits. Negative emotions, such as fear, anxiety, low confidence, tension, and guilt, form the core of the Neuroticism dimension in these studies; emotions such as anger and hostility are not included. John et al. (1994) actually obtained separate factors for neuroticism and irritability in their Big Five study. Taken together, these studies suggest that over time two distinct but still related negative-emotionality traits may develop; one that taps emotions such as fear, distress, worry, and guilt and one that taps anger and irritability. Future research should explore the possible differential impact of these two personality traits on children's adaptation.

Aggressiveness and Prosocial Tendencies

Individual differences in negative emotionality generally and anger specifically are related to another dimension of personality in middle childhood: *aggressiveness*. In adults, aggressiveness appears to be a complex personality dimension involving high negative emotionality and low behavioral constraint (Tellegen & Waller, in press). Among children, according to a recent study of 4–6-year-olds, those who cope with feelings of anger by engaging in physical retaliation and venting of emotions indeed tend to be poor in behavioral regulation and high in *emotional intensity* (Eisenberg, Fabes, Nyman, Bernzweig, & Pinuelas, 1994). Thus, many aggressive children may be those whose strong feelings of anger and frustration are not tempered by good self-control. Because aggression seems to involve poorly socialized anger, it may prove useful to measure aggressiveness as a personality trait that is distinct from the anger–irritability dimension described above. Conceptually, the two traits seem distinct: It is possible for children to experience frequent feelings of anger, irritability, and frustration without directing those feelings toward others and behaving in a hostile manner.

Aggressiveness is not measured in temperament scales, despite its early appearance in children (e.g., Kingston & Prior, 1995); perhaps its exclusion reflects a belief that aggressiveness is strongly influenced by socialization (rather than by temperament) or that it cannot be measured in infants. Aggression does emerge, however, as a salient component of Agreeableness in the Big Five research with children. Furthermore, there is abundant evidence that after early childhood, children differ significantly in their levels of overt aggression (Dodge & Frame, 1983; Hartup & van Lieshout, 1995; Kingston & Prior, 1995; Patterson, 1976). Individual differences in aggressiveness, as one part of a pattern of general antisocial tendencies, are markedly stable by middle childhood (Coie & Dodge, 1998; Masten et al., 1995). Boys show particularly high stability of aggressive behavior from preschool to elementary school, and such early aggression relates significantly to peer rejection in the new school context (Ladd, 1996). Although boys consistently have been found to show higher levels of aggression, there is recent evidence that girls may engage in a different sort of aggression, *relational aggression*, which includes gossiping and social exclusion (Crick & Grotpeter, 1995). The nature of aggressive behavior changes over middle childhood: There is a shift toward increasingly hostile, person-focused acts and away from overt aggression (Coie & Dodge, 1998). Consequently, it may prove useful to measure a more broad unsocialized interpersonal hostility dimension later in childhood. Although aggression has been left out of most temperament models, it clearly emerges as an important personality dimension in childhood and adolescence.

On the flip side of aggression, prosocial tendencies also appear to be a component of Agreeableness in the Big Five studies. These *prosocial dispositions* are described by items such as, *is considerate of other children, is helpful and cooperative, tends to give, lend, and share, protective of others*, and *recognizes the feelings of others* (van Lieshout & Haselager, 1993, 1994). Graziano and Eisenberg (1997) have suggested that Agreeableness encompasses empathy and altruism, both of which are components of prosocial behavior. Prosocial behavior develops in the 2nd year of life (Hartup & van Lieshout, 1995), and individual differences in prosocial behavior have been found to be modestly to moderately stable during the preschool- and school-age years (Eisenberg et al., 1987; Graziano & Eisenberg, 1997). Older children and adolescents evidence significant consistency in prosocial behavior across situations as well (Eisenberg & Fabes, 1998). There is also evidence that children can be meaningfully differentiated on a dimension of dispositional empathy by the age of 6 (Eisenberg et al., 1996; Eisenberg, Fabes, Schaller, Carlo, & Miller, 1991; Fabes, Eisenberg, Karbon, Troyer, & Switzer, 1994).

Children's prosocial dispositions are clearly linked with their social functioning. A variety of prosocial traits are associated with greater popularity, having friends, and social competence (Eisenberg & Fabes, 1998). In several studies of preschool-age boys, prosocial traits were linked with moderate levels of aggression, perhaps because these boys were more assertive and outgoing (Eisenberg & Mussen, 1989). By middle childhood, however, prosocial children tend to be less aggressive (Eisenberg & Fabes, 1998). As Graziano and Eisenberg (1997) have commented, aggressiveness and prosocial tendencies may eventually prove not to be opposite ends of a single dimension, although they may tend to covary negatively. Their inclusion in the single dimension of Agreeableness in the Big Five model may well obscure their basic distinctiveness.

Constraint–Conscientiousness

All of the temperament and personality models surveyed encompass aspects of control or constraint. Within the broader developmental literature, constructs of self-control are similarly salient. J. Block (1996) recently pointed out that, "with different terminology and with different orientation and intentions, there long has been recognition in developmental psychology and in personality psychology of the crucial importance of behavior monitoring and behavior modulation" (p. 28). Emotion regulation has emerged as an important construct for explaining how children modulate their responses to the environment (Campos, Campos, & Barrett, 1989; Campos, Mumme, Kermoian, & Campos, 1994; Eisenberg et al., 1993; Eisenberg et al., 1996). Children's differential abilities in coping with stress have also been studied (Compas, 1987; Compas, Malcarne, & Fondacaro, 1988), as have their skills in delaying gratification (Mischel, Shoda, & Peake, 1988). Although it is clear that constraint is a vital aspect of children's functioning, it is not as clear how best to parse the underlying dimensions.

One aspect of control that appears in a number of temperament models is *task persistence–focused attention*. In the NYLS studies, this dimension assesses a child's ability to focus on and persist at a task, particularly in the face of external distractions. On the CBQ, the attention scale measures skills in attention regulation, specifically the capacity to shift and focus attention. A similar dimension has been uncovered in several studies attempting to differentiate the facets of impulsivity. For example, J. L. White et al. (1994) conducted a factor analysis of questionnaire and task-performance measures of impulsivity in a sample of boys ages 10 to 13. They obtained a factor they termed *cognitive impulsivity*; this factor tapped the boys' capacities to exercise mental control in cognitive tasks requiring a high level of focus and persistence, such as the Trail Making Test. This factor also tapped the boys' capacity to shift mental sets effectively. A dimension of persistence–attention versus cognitive impulsivity has been obtained in other factor analyses as well (Kindlon, Mezzacappa, & Earls, 1995; Visser, Das-Smaal, & Feji, 1993). There is diverse support for a dimension capturing children's capacity to regulate attention by shifting mental sets, focusing attention, and persisting at a task in the face of distractions.

The negative end of the persistence–attention dimension resembles the inattention cluster of symptoms in Attention-Deficit–Hyperacitivity Disorder (ADHD): for example, "often has difficulty sustaining attention in tasks or play activities," and "often avoids, dislikes, or is reluctant to engage in tasks that require sustained mental effort" (in *Diagnostic and Statistical Manual of Mental Disorders, 4th Edition [DSM–IV]*. American Psychiatric Association, 1994, pp. 83–84). Because deficits in persistence–attention have serious implications for children's academic achievement and conduct, a great deal of research has focused on the negative end of this personality dimension. Although low levels of persistence-attention are clearly linked with poor academic achievement (Barkley, 1997), this dimension is only weakly linked with delinquency and antisocial behavior in children and adolescents (Luengo, Carrillo-de-la-Pena, Otero, & Romero, 1994; J. L. White et al., 1994).

Somewhat less is known about the positive end of the persistence–attention dimension. The task persistence factor shows highly significant relationships with academic achievement, both concurrently and across time (Martin, 1989). In fact, a study with LISREL modeling found that distractibility, persistence, and activity level, when measured in combination in first grade, better jointly predicted academic achievement 4 years later than did academic ability measured in first grade (Martin, Olejnik, & Gaddis, 1994). Persistence–attention appears likely to add to the prediction of academic achievement beyond the prediction afforded by measures of IQ. Children's standing on this dimension also shapes teachers' perceptions of them (Keogh, 1989).

A personality dimension that may be related to persistence is *mastery motivation* or achievement motivation. Children who are high on this personality dimension are motivated by curiosity or interest, take great pleasure in mastering their environments, and prefer challenging tasks to easy ones (Harter, 1978, 1981; Pearlman, 1984). Higher mastery motivation in children relates to greater academic achievement, a stronger sense of individual control, and adaptive coping with failure (Eccles, Wigfield, & Schiefele, 1998; Harter, 1981). In personality studies with adults, a similar achievement trait has been identified that taps a person's tendency to enjoy working hard and to strive toward high standards (e.g., Jackson, 1974; Tellegen & Waller, in press). Tellegen has identified it as an effectance–motivational aspect of a higher level positive emotionality system, tapping a person's tendency to approach situations and tasks with enthusiasm and zest. From this perspective, achievement is distinguished from behavioral control and discipline (Watson & Clark, 1992). It is not yet known whether the task-persistence dimension identified in children encompasses both the effectance and discipline aspects of achievement motivation. Persistence and mastery motivation may represent two distinctive but related personality dimensions, with persistence primarily tapping behavioral control and mastery motivation primarily tapping positive emotionality.

A second lower order dimension of constraint in children encompasses the constructs of *inhibitory control* and *behavioral impulsivity*. Developmental researchers have become increasingly interested in these constructs in recent years because of their putative links to moral and social development (Kochanska, Murray, & Coy, 1997; Kochanska, Murray, Jacques, Koenig, & Vandegeest, 1996; Rothbart & Bates, 1998). There is emerging evidence for an inhibitory-control–behavioral-impulsivity dimension that ranges from the tendency to be planful, cautious, and controlling of one's behavior to the tendency to be incautious and undercontrolled. Researchers who have obtained a factor measuring behavioral impulsivity in children and adolescents have found that it includes children's tendency to approach something quickly without thinking, to have difficulty waiting turns and sitting still, and to speak out when they are expected to be quiet (S. B. G. Eysenck, Easting, & Pearson, 1984; Visser et al., 1993; J. L. White et al., 1994). In defining the positive end of this dimension, Rothbart has emphasized the active, effortful quality of behavioral constraint (Rothbart, 1989a, 1989b) and defines it in terms of a child's capacity to inhibit inappropriate approach tendencies (Rothbart et al., 1996).

Research on both normal and pathological development is providing increasing evidence for the adaptive significance of inhibitory control. Deficits in behavioral inhibitory control are implicated in all of the childhood externalizing disorders: ADHD, Oppositional Defiant Disorder, and Conduct Disorder (in *DSM–IV*, American Psychiatric Association, 1994). Among older children and adolescents, deficits in inhibitory control have been linked to childhood psychopathy, to antisocial and delinquent behavior, and to increases in such troubling behavior over time (Luengo et al., 1994; Lynam, 1997; J. L. White et al., 1994). Poor inhibitory control also appears to be related to attention deficit disorder in children (Barkley, 1997; Douglas, 1983; Schachar & Logan, 1990). In both preschool- and school-age children, inhibitory control relates to conscience development (Kochanska et al., 1996, 1997). Preschool-age children's abilities to delay gratification relate to their social competence, academic achievement, and coping in adolescence (Mischel et al., 1988) and to a number of other positive personality traits in adolescence (Funder, Block, & Block, 1983).

It is important to distinguish behavioral impulsivity reflecting poor self-regulation from seemingly impulsive behavior reflecting energetic, surgent engagement with the environment. As described previously, Rothbart and colleagues identified two separate factors tapping different types of behavioral constraint in two studies of the CBQ. Scales measuring high activity level, approach toward and pleasure in highly stimulating situations, and quick speed of response initiation loaded on an approach or extroversion factor, whereas persistence–attention and inhibitory control loaded on a separate constraint factor (Ahadi et al., 1993; Rothbart et al., 1994; Rothbart et al., 1996). Similarly, S. B. G. Eysenck et al. (1984) uncovered two separate "impulsiveness" dimensions in a factor analysis of a self-report questionnaire for children and adolescents. One dimension measured the children's *excitement-seeking* tendencies, that is, the extent to which they enjoyed risky, exciting activities such as water skiing and their willingness to engage in actions they knew were risky. A second dimension tapped poor behavioral control and the tendency to act without thinking or planning. It appears that there are two related but still distinct types of behavioral control in children. Some surgent, stimulus-seeking children may appear unrestrained, because they are motivated to approach and engage the environment, whereas other children may evidence low levels of constraint, because they have trouble regulating their behavior. Although an approach-related excitement-seeking dimension has been studied infrequently in children, it appears worthy of further study, because it may strongly shape the experiences children seek out (Kafry, 1982).

Finally, it should be noted that there is some debate about how to conceptualize the high end of the inhibitory-control dimension. From the perspective of J. H. Block and Block (1980), it is possible to manifest too much constraint, because exerting too great a degree of control prevents a child from having his or her needs met in the environment. From another perspective, the extreme end could be understood as representing excellent self-regulatory capacities. It is possible that the adaptive significance of high behavioral control may vary from one setting to the next and may depend on an individual's other personality traits. For example, the combination of high control and high fearfulness may have negative results on a child's social functioning; in that case, the child's behavioral control may be due to an inability to act spontaneously rather than to voluntary self-restraint. It is also possible that the inhibitory-control–behavioral-impulsivity dimension is a more unidimensional construct, whereas ego control is a higher order dimension combining inhibitory control and the above-described surgent, approach dimension (Robins et al., 1994). From this perspective, a child exhibiting too high a level of ego control may be low in positive approach and high in inhibitory control. Eisenberg, Guthrie, et al. (1997) have suggested that it may be difficult to detect the hypothesized link between overcontrol and poor social functioning in a normative sample, because the numbers of highly inhibited children may be small in such a population. Future research on inhibitory control–behavioral impulsivity could explicitly test these competing models for understanding the adaptive significance of the high end of this personality dimension.

Further work is much needed to untangle the primary traits underlying behavioral control in children. In particular, there is a need for studies relating the disparate conceptions of behavioral control—emotional regulation, coping, ego control, delay of gratification, persistence, sensation seeking, and inhibitory control—to one another. Studies establishing discriminant and convergent validity for the dimensions would be especially useful.

Traits That Are Particularly Salient Among Children

Two lower order personality dimensions may be more salient in children than in adults. First, motor *activity level* appears to be a robust personality dimension in children from infancy at least through early adolescence. An activity-level dimension appears in the NYLS factor analytic studies, the EASI model, the CBQ, and the Big Five studies with the California Q sort. The vast quantity of research on ADHD similarly speaks for the importance of activity as a dimension in children. It is not clear whether activity level ceases to be a distinct dimension of personality in adults. Because children are much more motorically active than adults, activity level may be more salient in children and therefore may be more easily distinguished from related personality dimensions such as sociability. Eaton (1994) has argued persuasively that activity level may become one aspect of extroversion in adulthood and that the motor activity of children may become transformed into greater talkativeness with age.

In addition, the factor analytic studies of the California Child Q-Sort identified one other trait that may be particularly important in describing children: *dependency*. Children's dependency on adults may be a behavioral tendency that is particularly salient to adults who interact with children. Because this trait was identified only in the studies using one particular instrument, further work will need to determine whether this dimension is robust using other measures. For both activity and dependency, longitudinal research tracing links with later adult personality dimensions would be helpful.

Summary

A variety of lower order personality dimensions have been suggested as providing the building blocks of personality in middle childhood and early adolescence. The preliminary taxonomy for this age range includes the following dimensions: sociability, social inhibition, dominance, negative emotionality (differentiated into two traits, one tapping fear, distress, worry, and guilt and the other tapping anger and irritability), aggressiveness, prosocial disposition, persistence–attention, mastery motivation, inhibitory control–behavioral impulsivity, and activity level. Four more speculative dimensions noted are shyness with known others, well-being, excitement seeking, and dependency. All of these dimensions, with the exceptions of dominance and mastery motivation, are identified as either temperament or personality traits in at least one of the models previously described, and many of the dimensions appear in more than one model. Some of these personality dimensions are so robust across models or across the broader developmental literature that their status as cohesive dimensions in this age range is well established. In particular, inhibition, negative emotionality, aggressiveness, and activity level appear to be well defined, sturdy dimensions. Other traits require clearer demarcation, particularly those dimensions tapping behavioral constraint.

DIRECTIONS FOR FUTURE RESEARCH

Measurement Issues in Assessing Personality in Middle Childhood

There clearly remains much to be learned about the structure of both lower order and higher order personality traits in childhood, and work still needs to be done at both levels of analysis. As noted previously, our understanding of higher level personality systems in childhood in particular is weak, because so little work has been done in this area. In order to examine continuity and change between childhood and adult personality, however, it will be especially helpful to have an enhanced understanding of higher order personality traits in childhood; these early higher order traits can be linked with higher order traits in adulthood, the "developmental targets." Vigorous debate has raged among researchers attempting to elucidate a higher order structure of adult personality. Despite the similar challenges facing developmental researchers, the goal of delineating higher order personality systems in childhood remains an important one. It will also be useful for researchers to examine the relationship between lower order and higher order traits in childhood, in order to clarify the conceptual core of each. Ideally, research on childhood personality will proceed at both levels of analysis, because each level may afford a different type of predictive power. Lower order traits may successfully predict children's functioning in more specific domains (i.e., these traits have greater "fidelity"), whereas broad superfactors may often prove useful in predicting a wide range of outcomes (i.e., these traits have greater "bandwidth").

In creating future measures of personality in childhood, it will be important to attend closely to psychometric issues. In particular, an iterative process of instrument development may produce childhood personality measures with greater reliability and validity (see, e.g., Tellegen & Waller, in press). In this type of iterative process, the researcher begins with a theoretical or conceptual perspective on a particular personality trait (or a number of traits), creates a measure of that trait, and then refines the measurement through data collection. The results of the data collection can then sharpen and deepen the conceptual understanding of that trait, which in turn can lead to improvements in measurement. From this perspective on personality measurement, conceptual elaboration of traits and careful empirical work should mutually influence each other. Many of the temperament and personality measures surveyed here were the result of only one round of test administration, which leaves such measures vulnerable to chance effects and sample idiosyncrasies. Goldsmith (1996) recently demonstrated the benefits of careful conceptualization, repeated instrument administration, and revision through the development of the Toddler Behavior Assessment Questionnaire. Such an iterative process in creating childhood personality measures would yield greater understanding of the underlying personality dimensions themselves and could be applied to the development of both questionnaires and behavioral measures.

Much of the research on childhood personality has focused on single temperamental or personality traits at a time. As Caspi (1998) recently pointed out, "The trait domains most frequently studied by developmentalists . . . have not been related to each other in a coherent taxonomic framework" (p. 316), with the result being "a research discipline filled with many studies of convergent validity and few studies of discriminant validity" (p. 317). Thus, it would be particularly helpful for future studies of childhood personality to measure more than one personality dimension at a time, in part with the goal of establishing discriminant validity for childhood personality dimensions. Measuring more than one dimension at a time would also permit the use of factor analysis to determine whether particular dimensions actually represent distinct and coherent underlying traits. Greater understanding of currently used measures could also be obtained by jointly administering several instruments to establish empirical relationships between related personality constructs.

A final measurement issue concerns the sources of information on children's personalities. J. Block (1977) distinguished among several types of personality data: (a) R data, which are ratings based on observers' evaluations of individuals; (b) S data, which are self-observations; and (c) T data, which are data derived from tests or laboratory tasks. The bulk of the research on childhood temperament and personality incorporates only one of these types of data, typically either R data from parent or teacher ratings or T data from laboratory tasks. The use of a wider variety of types of data would enhance the quality of research in this domain. Because children increasingly understand themselves in terms of traits and can form more realistic views of themselves in middle childhood (Harter, 1996, 1998), it may be possible to use self-ratings as one source of information, at least by the end the middle childhood years. Children's self-perceptions of their personalities may be important determinants of their functioning, even if their perceptions are not consonant with others' views. Peer ratings of personality could also be obtained, perhaps through a class-play method in which children nominate classmates for roles in a hypothetical class play (Morison & Masten, 1991). More extensive use of laboratory data could help to uncover links between personality traits and related biological processes. Future work on childhood personality would clearly benefit from the inclusion of more than one source of data.

The Course of Personality Development in Childhood

A more complete taxonomy of personality in middle childhood will be important in attempts to link earlier temperament with adult personality functioning. At the present time, there is a particular need for improved longitudinal studies examining the course of personality development from early childhood into middle childhood and then into later years (Caspi. 1998). Such studies could examine a wider range of personality traits than has been be typical for previous longitudinal temperament research. A careful examination of children's maturing capacities (e.g., language, cognition, self-awareness, and empathy) could inform decisions about which personality dimensions could be measured in each age range. In particular, it would be helpful to study closely the development of children's personalities in the transition from preschool age into middle childhood. As noted previously, greater differentiation of personality structure is likely to occur with this developmental shift, and reorganization of personality traits within individuals may also take place. Personality functioning in middle childhood has often been considered a much better predictor of later adaptation than personality functioning in the preschool years; thus, it will be important to answer questions about how personality is transformed during this transitional period into patterns with potentially long-lasting import.

As noted earlier, an ultimate goal of personality research is a deeper understanding of the dynamic organization of traits within individuals. One way to study such internal organization is to look at configurations of traits within individuals, that is, multidimensional patterns defined by individuals' standings on several distinctive traits. Developmentalists have been interested in a number of such personality configurations. The difficult temperament described by Thomas and Chess (Thomas & Chess, 1977; Thomas et al., 1963) should perhaps be viewed as a trait configuration, which includes intense and frequent negative moods, withdrawal from new situations, and slow adaptability. Some temperament researchers have argued that the label *difficult* is inappropriate, given that varied temperamental traits may be difficult for caregivers, depending on the context (Goldsmith et al., 1987). The question remains, however, whether there is a pattern of traits that proves particularly challenging for many caregivers. It may be possible to examine empirically whether knowing a child's standing on a pattern of traits is more helpful than knowing the child's standing on individual traits only. Some other childhood personality dimensions described previously may also turn out to be multidimensional traits, such as mastery motivation, excitement seeking, and shyness.

Another striking example of how patterns of traits may operate involves the configuration of high negative emotionality and low behavioral constraint; these traits in combination appear to be particularly detrimental to preschool- and elementary school-age children's social functioning (Eisenberg, Fabes, Murphy, Maszk, et al., 1995; Eisenberg, Fabes, Shepard, et al., 1997). Children with both high negative emotionality and poor regulation may represent a high-risk group. In fact, there is some evidence that men who commit violent offenses exhibit this configuration of traits as children (Henry, Caspi, Moffitt, & Silva, 1996) and that adolescents who are involved in delinquent activities are high in negative emotionality and low in behavioral constraint (Caspi et al., 1994). As is the case with negative emotionality and behavioral constraint, our ability to predict children's outcomes would be enhanced by a more complex approach as to how personality systems may be working in combination. Because traits tapping self-regulation are extremely important as children move into middle childhood, it would be particularly helpful to understand how these self-regulatory systems interact with other facets of personality. The longitudinal assessment of more than one personality dimension would be helpful in determining how individual patterning of traits may shape children's outcomes.

Finally, it should be acknowledged that structural models of personality at times create the false impression that personality functioning is static when, in fact, personality is dynamic. By its very nature, a developmental perspective on personality lends itself to an emphasis on processes. Structural models of childhood personality will be most useful when personality traits can be linked with underlying psychological processes. Children's personalities can be understood in terms of how they influence children's experience of the world and the wide-ranging goals that different children pursue (Dweck, 1996). Thus, knowledge of personality structure in childhood is not an end in itself; rather, a more sophisticated perspective on personality structure will ultimately prove fruitful if it furthers our understanding of the processes through which personality is transformed over the course of development.

REFERENCES

Ahadi, S. A., & Rothbart, M. K. (1994). Temperament, development, and the Big Five. In C. F. Halverson, G. A. Kohnstamm, & R. P. Martin (Eds.), *The developing structure of temperament and personality from infancy to adulthood* (pp. 189–207). Hillsdale, NJ: Erlbaum.

Ahadi, S. A., Rothbart, M. K., & Ye, R. M. (1993). Children's temperament in the US and China: Similarities and differences. *European Journal of Personality, 7*, 359–377.

Allport, G. W. (1937). *Personality: A psychological interpretation.* New York: Holt.

Allport, G. W. (1961). *Pattern and growth in personality.* London: Holt, Rinehart & Winston.

Altshuler, J. L., & Ruble, D. N. (1989). Developmental changes in children's awareness of strategies for coping with uncontrollable stress. *Child Development, 60*, 1337–1349.

American Psychiatric Association. (1994). *Diagnostic and statistical manual of mental disorders* (4th ed.). Washington, DC: Author.

Arend, R., Gove, F. L., & Sroufe, L. A. (1979). Continuity of individual adaptation from infancy to kindergarten: A predictive study of egoresiliency and curiosity in preschoolers. *Child Development, 50*, 950–959.

Asendorpf, J. B. (1989). Shyness as a final common pathway for two different kinds of inhibition. *Journal of Personality and Social Psychology, 57*, 481–492.

Asendorpf, J. B. (1990). Development of inhibition during childhood: Evidence for situational specificity and a two-factor model. *Developmental Psychology, 26*, 721–730.

Asendorpf, J. B. (1991). Development of inhibited children's coping with unfamiliarity. *Child Development, 62*, 1460–1474.

Asendorpf, J. B. (1993a). Abnormal shyness in children. *Journal of Child Psychology and Psychiatry, 34*, 1069–1081.

Asendorpf, J. B. (1993b). Beyond temperament: A two-factorial coping model of the development of inhibition during childhood. In K. H. Rubin & J. B. Asendorpf (Eds.), *Social withdrawal, inhibition, and shyness in childhood* (pp. 265–289). Hillsdale, NJ: Erlbaum.

Asendorpf, J. B. (1994). The malleability of behavior inhibition: A study of individual developmental functions. *Developmental Psychology, 30*, 912–919.

Asendorpf, J. B., & Meier, G. H. (1993). Personality effects on children's speech in everyday life: Sociability-mediated exposure and shyness-mediated reactivity to social situations. *Journal of Personality and Social Psychology, 64*, 1072–1083.

Asendorpf, J. B., & van Aken, M. A. G. (1991). Correlates of the temporal consistency of personality patterns in childhood. *Journal of Personality, 59*, 688–703.

Asendorpf, J. B., & van Aken, M. A. G. (1994). Traits and relationship status: Stranger versus peer group inhibition and test intelligence versus peer group competence as early predictors of later self-esteem. *Child Development, 65*, 1786–1798.

Baker, E. H., & Velicer, W. F. (1982). The structure and reliability of the Teacher Temperament Questionnaire. *Journal of Abnormal Child Psychology, 10,* 531–546.

Barkley, R. A. (1997). Behavioral inhibition, sustained attention, and executive functions: Constructing a unifying theory of ADHD. *Psychological Bulletin, 121,* 65–94.

Bates, J. E., & Wachs, T. D. (Eds.). (1994). *Temperament: Individual differences at the interface of biology and behavior.* Washington, DC: American Psychological Association.

Bell, R. Q. (1968). A reinterpretation of the direction of effects in studies of socialization. *Psychological Review, 75,* 81–85.

Belsky, J. (1981). Early human experience: A family perspective. *Developmental Psychology, 17,* 3–33.

Benet, V., & Waller, N. G. (1995). The Big Seven factor model of personality description: Evidence for its cross-cultural generality in a Spanish sample. *Journal of Personality and Social Psychology, 69,* 701–718.

Block, J. (1965). *The challenge of response sets.* New York: Appleton-Century-Crofts.

Block, J. (1971). *Lives through time.* Berkeley, CA: Bancroft Books.

Block, J. (1977). Advancing the psychology of personality: Paradigmatic shift or improving the quality of research. In D. Magnusson & N. S. Endler (Eds.), *Personality at the crossroads: Current issues in interactional psychology* (pp. 37–63). New York: Wiley.

Block, J. (1978). *The Q-sort method in personality assessment and psychiatric research.* Springfield, IL: Thomas. (Original work published 1961)

Block, J. (1981). Some enduring and consequential structures of personality. In A. I. Rabin, J. Aronoff, A. M. Barclay, & R. A. Zucker (Eds.), *Further explorations in personality* (pp. 27–43). New York: Wiley.

Block, J. (1995). A contrarian view of the Five-Factor approach to personality description. *Psychological Bulletin, 117,* 187–215.

Block, J. (1996). Some jangly remarks on Baumeister & Heatherton. *Psychological Inquiry, 7,* 28–32.

Block, J., & Block, J. H. (1980). *The California Child Q-set.* Palo Alto, CA: Consulting Psychologists Press. (Original work published 1969)

Block, J., Block, J. H., & Keyes, S. (1988). Longitudinally foretelling drug use in adolescence: Early childhood personality and environmental precursors. *Child Development, 59,* 336–355.

Block, J., & Kremen, A. M. (1996). IQ and ego resiliency: Conceptual and empirical connections and separateness. *Journal of Personality and Social Psychology, 70,* 349–361.

Block, J. H., & Block, J. (1980). The role of ego-control and ego-resiliency in the organization of behavior. In W. A. Collins (Ed.), *The Minnesota symposium on child psychology* (Vol. 13, pp. 39–101). Hillsdale, NJ: Erlbaum.

Boer, F., & Westenberg, P. M. (1994). The factor structure of the Buss and Plomin EAS Temperament Survey (parental ratings) in a Dutch sample of elementary school children. *Journal of Personality Assessment, 62,* 537–551.

Braithwaite, V., Duncan-Jones, P., Bosly-Craft, R., & Goodchild, M. (1984). A psychometric investigation of the usefulness of the EASI-III Temperament Survey in the Australian general population. *Australian Journal of Psychology, 36,* 85–95.

Bronson, W. C. (1966). Central orientations: A study of behavior organization from childhood to adolescence. *Child Development, 37,* 125–155.

Burisch, M. (1984). Approaches to personality inventory construction: A comparison of merits. *American Psychologist, 39,* 214–227.

Buss, A. H. (1995). *Personality: Temperament, social behavior, and the self.* Boston: Allyn & Bacon.

Buss, A. H., & Finn, S. E. (1987). Classification of personality traits. *Journal of Personality and Social Psychology, 52,* 432–444.

Buss, A. H., & Plomin, R. (1975). *A temperament theory of personality development.* New York: Wiley.

Buss, A. H., & Plomin, R. (1984). *Temperament: Early developing personality traits.* Hillsdale, NJ: Erlbaum.

Campos, J. J., Campos, R. G., & Barrett, K. C. (1989). Emergent themes in the study of emotional development and emotion regulation. *Developmental Psychology, 25,* 394–402.

Campos, J. J., Mumme, D. L., Kermoian, R., & Campos, R. G. (1994). A functionalist perspective on the nature of emotion. *Monographs of the Society for Research in Child Development, 59* (2–3, Serial No. 240, pp. 284–303).

Caspi, A. (1998). Personality development across the life course. In W. Damon (Series Ed.) & N. Eisenberg (Vol. Ed.), *Handbook of child psychology: Vol. 3. Social, emotional, and personality development* (5th ed., pp. 311–388). New York: Wiley.

Caspi, A., Elder, G. H., Jr., & Bem, D. J. (1988). Moving away from the world: Life-course patterns of shy children. *Developmental Psychology, 24,* 824–831.

Caspi, A., Moffitt, T. E., Silva, P. A., Stouthamer-Loeber, M., Krueger, R. F., & Schmutte, P. S. (1994). Are some people crime-prone? Replications of the personality-crime relationship across countries, genders, races, and methods. *Criminology, 32,* 163–195.

Caspi, A., & Silva, P. A. (1995). Temperamental qualities at age 3 predict personality traits in young adulthood: Longitudinal evidence from a birth cohort. *Child Development, 66,* 486–498.

Cattell, R. B., & Coan, R. A. (1957). Child personality structure as revealed in teachers' ratings. *Journal of Clinical Psychology, 13,* 315–327.

Charlesworth, W. R., & Dzur, C. (1987). Gender comparisons of preschoolers' behavior and resource utilization in group problem solving. *Child Development, 58,* 191–200.

Charlesworth, W. R., & la Freniere, P. (1983). Dominance, friendship, and resource utilization in preschool children's groups. *Ethology and Sociobiology, 4,* 175–186.

Cheek, J. M., & Buss, A. H. (1981). Shyness and sociability. *Journal of Personality and Social Psychology, 41,* 330–339.

Church, T. A. (1994). Relating the Tellegen and five-factor models of personality structure. *Journal of Personality and Social Psychology, 67,* 898–909.

Cicchetti, D., & Tucker, D. (1994). Development and self-regulatory structures of the mind. *Development and Psychopathology, 6,* 533–549.

Coie, J. D., & Dodge, K. A. (1998). Aggression and antisocial behavior. In W. Damon (Series Ed.) & N. Eisenberg (Vol. Ed.), *Handbook of child psychology: Vol. 3. Social, emotional, and personality development* (5th ed.). New York: Wiley.

Cole, M., & Cole, S. R. (1996). *The development of children* (3rd ed.). New York: Freeman.

Coles, R. (1997). *The moral intelligence of children.* New York: Random House.

Collins, W. A. (Ed.). (1984). *Development during middle childhood: The years from six to twelve.* Washington, DC: National Academy Press.

Compas, B. E. (1987). Coping with stress during childhood and adolescence. *Psychological Bulletin*, *101*, 393–403.

Compas, B. E., Malcarne, V. L., & Fondacaro, K. M. (1988). Coping with stressful events in older children and young adolescents. *Journal of Consulting and Clinical Psychology*, *56*, 405–411.

Coplan, R. J., Rubin, K. H., Fox, N. A., Calkins, S. D., & Stewart, S. L. (1994). Being alone, playing alone, and acting alone: Distinguishing among reticence and passive and active solitude in young children. *Child Development*, *65*, 129–137.

Costa, P. T., & McCrae, R. R. (1988). From catalog to classification: Murray's needs and the Five-Factor Model. *Journal of Personality and Social Psychology*, *55*, 258–265.

Crick, N. R., & Dodge, K. A. (1994). A review and reformulation of social information-processing mechanisms in children's social adjustment. *Psychological Bulletin*, *115*, 74–101.

Crick, N. R., & Grotpeter, J. K. (1995). Relational aggression, gender, and social-psychological adjustment. *Child Development*, *66*, 710–722.

De Raad, B. (1994). An expedition in search of a fifth universal factor: Key issues in the lexical approach. *European Journal of Personality*, *8*, 229–250.

Derryberry, D., & Rothbart, M. K. (1988). Arousal, affect, and attention as components of temperament. *Journal of Personality and Social Psychology*: *55*, 958–966.

Digman, J. M. (1963). Principal dimensions of child personality as inferred from teachers' judgments. *Child Development*, *34*, 43–60.

Digman, J. M. (1989). Five robust trait dimensions: Development, stability, and utility. *Journal of Personality*, *57*, 195–214.

Digman, J. M. (1990). Personality structure: Emergence of the Five-Factor Model. *Annual Review of Psychology*, *41*, 417–440.

Digman, J. M. (1994). Child personality and temperament: Does the Five-Factor Model embrace both domains? In C. F. Halverson, G. A. Kohnstamm, & R. P. Martin (Eds.), *The developing structure of temperament and personality from infancy to adulthood* (pp. 323–338). Hillsdale, NJ: Erlbaum.

Digman, J. M., & Inouye, J. (1986). Further specification of the five robust factors of personality. *Journal of Personality and Social Psychology*, *50*, 116–123.

Digman, J. M., & Takemoto-Chock, N. K. (1981). Factors in the natural language of personality: Re-analysis, comparison, and interpretation of six major studies. *Multivariate Behavioral Research*, *16*, 149–170.

Dodge, K. A., & Frame, C. L. (1983). Social cognitive biases and deficits in aggressive boys. *Child Development*, *53*, 620–635.

Douglas, V. I. (1983). Attentional and cognitive problems. In M. Rutter (Ed.), *Developmental neuropsychiatry* (pp. 280–329). New York: Guilford Press.

Dweck, C. S. (1996). Capturing the dynamic nature of personality. *Journal of Research in Personality*, *30*, 348–362.

Eaton, W. O. (1994). Temperament, development, and the Five-Factor model: Lessons from activity level. In C. F. Halverson, G. A. Kohnstamm, & R. P. Martin (Eds.), *The developing structure of temperament and personality from infancy to adulthood* (pp. 173–187). Hillsdale, NJ: Erlbaum.

Eccles, J. S., Wigfield, A., & Schiefele, U. (1998). Motivation to succeed. In W. Damon (Series Ed.) & N. Eisenberg (Vol. Ed.), *Handbook of child psychology: Vol. 3. Social, emotional, and personality development* (5th ed., pp. 1017–1095). New York: Wiley.

Eisenberg, N., & Fabes, R. A. (1998). Prosocial development. In W. Damon (Series Ed.) & N. Eisenberg (Vol. Ed.), *Handbook of child psychology: Vol. 3. Social, emotional, and personality development* (5th ed.). New York: Wiley.

Eisenberg, N., Fabes, R. A., Bernzweig, J., Karbon, M., Poulin, R., & Hanish, L. (1993). The relations of emotionality and regulation to preschoolers' social skills and sociometric status. *Child Development, 64,* 1418–1438.

Eisenberg, N., Fabes, R. A., & Murphy, B. C. (1995). Relations of shyness and low sociability to regulation and emotionality. *Journal of Personality and Social Psychology, 68,* 505–517.

Eisenberg, N., Fabes, R. A., Murphy, B., Karbon, M., Smith, M., & Maszk, P. (1996). The relations of children's dispositional empathy-related responding to their emotionality, regulation, and social functioning. *Developmental Psychology, 32,* 195–209.

Eisenberg, N., Fabes, R. A., Murphy, B., Maszk, P., Smith, M., & Karbon, M. (1995). The role of emotionality and regulation in children's social functioning: A longitudinal study. *Child Development, 66,* 1360–1384.

Eisenberg, N., Fabes, R. A., Nyman, M., Bernzweig, J., & Pinuelas, A. (1994). The relations of emotionality and regulation to children's anger-related reactions. *Child Development, 65,* 109–128.

Eisenberg, N., Fabes, R. A., Schaller, M., Carlo, G., & Miller, P. A. (1991). The relations of parental characteristics and practices to children's vicarious emotional responding. *Child Development, 62,* 1393–1408.

Eisenberg, N., Fabes, R. A., Shepard, S. A., Murphy, B. C., Guthrie, I. K., Jones, S., Friedman, J., Poulin, R., & Maszk, P. (1997). Contemporaneous and longitudinal prediction of children's social functioning from regulation and emotionality. *Child Development, 68,* 642–664.

Eisenberg, N., Guthrie, I. K., Fabes, R. A., Reiser, M., Murphy, B. C., Holgren, R., Maszk, P., & Losoya, S. (1997). The relations of regulation and emotionality to resiliency and competent social functioning in elementary school children. *Child Development, 68,* 295–311.

Eisenberg, N., & Mussen, P. H. (1989). *The roots of prosocial behavior in children.* New York: Cambridge University Press.

Eisenberg, N., Shell, R., Pasternack, J., Lennon, R., Beller, R., & Mathy, R. M. (1987). Prosocial development during middle childhood: A longitudinal study. *Developmental Psychology, 23,* 712–718.

Escalona, S. K. (1968). *The roots of individuality: Normal patterns of development in infancy.* Chicago: Aldine.

Eysenck, H. J. (1952). *The scientific study of personality.* London: Routledge & Kegan Paul.

Eysenck, S. B. G., Easting, G., & Pearson, P. R. (1984). Age norms for impulsiveness, venturesomeness and empathy in children. *Personality and Individual Differences, 5,* 315–321.

Fabes, R. A., Eisenberg, N., Karbon, M., Troyer, D., & Switzer, G. (1994). The relations of children's emotion regulation to their vicarious emotional responses and comforting behaviors. *Child Development, 65,* 1678–1693.

Ford, D. H. (1987). *Humans as self-constructing living systems: A developmental perspective on behavior and personality.* Hillsdale, NJ: Erlbaum.

Freud, S. (1966). *Introductory lectures on psychoanalysis.* New York: Norton.

Funder, D. C., & Block, J. (1989). The role of ego-control, ego-resiliency, and IQ in delay of gratification in adolescence. *Journal of Personality and Social Psychology, 57,* 1041–1050.

Funder, D. C., Block, J. H., & Block, J. (1983). Delay of gratification: Some longitudinal personality correlates. *Journal of Personality and Social Psychology, 44,* 1198–1213.

Gersten, M. (1989). Behavioral inhibition in the classroom. In J. S. Reznick (Ed.), *Perspectives on behavioral inhibition* (pp. 71–91). Chicago: University of Chicago Press.

Gest, S. D. (1997). Behavioral inhibition: Stability and associations with adaptation from childhood to early adulthood. *Journal of Personality and Social Psychology, 72,* 467–475.

Gjerde, P. F., Block, J., & Block, J. H. (1986). Egocentrism and egoresiliency: Personality characteristics associated with perspective-taking from early childhood to adolescence. *Journal of Personality and Social Psychology, 51,* 423–434.

Goldberg, L. R. (1990). An alternative "Description of personality": The Big Five factor structure. *Journal of Personality and Social Psychology, 59,* 1216–1229.

Goldberg, L. R. (1993). The structure of phenotypic personality traits. *American Psychologist, 48,* 26–34.

Goldsmith, H. H. (1996). Studying temperament via construction of the Toddler Temperament Behavior Assessment Questionnaire. *Child Development, 67,* 218–235.

Goldsmith, H. H., Buss, A., Plomin, R., Rothbart, M. K., Thomas, A., Chess, S., Hinde, R. A., & McCall, R. B. (1987). Roundtable: What is temperament? *Child Development, 58,* 505–529.

Goldsmith, H. H., Buss, K. A., & Lemery, K. S. (1997). Toddler and childhood temperament: Expanded content, stronger genetic evidence, new evidence for the importance of the environment. *Developmental Psychology, 33,* 891–905.

Goodyer, I. M., Ashby, L., Altham, P. M. E., Vize, C., & Cooper, P. J. (1993). Temperament and major depression in 11 to 16 year olds. *Journal of Child Psychology and Psychiatry, 34,* 1409–1423.

Gray, J. A. (1987). *The psychology of fear and stress.* New York: Cambridge University Press.

Graziano, W. G. (1994). The development of agreebleness as a dimension of personality. In C. F. Halverson, G. A. Kohnstamm, & R. P. Martin (Eds.), *The developing structure of temperament and personality from infancy to adulthood* (pp. 339–354). Hillsdale, NJ: Erlbaum.

Graziano, W. G., & Eisenberg, N. (1997). Agreebleness: A dimension of personality. In R. Hogan, J. Johnson, & S. Briggs (Eds.), *Handbook of personality psychology* (pp. 795–824). San Diego, CA: Academic Press.

Graziano, W. G., Jensen-Campbell, L. A., & Finch, J. F. (1997). The self as a mediator between personality and adjustment. *Journal of Personality and Social Psychology, 73,* 392–404.

Graziano. W. G., & Ward, D. (1992). Probing the Big Five in adolescence: Personality and adjustment during a developmental transition. *Journal of Personality, 60,* 425–439.

Halverson, C. F., Kohnstamm, G. A., & Martin, R. P. (Eds.), (1994). *The developing structure of temperament and personality from infancy to adulthood.* Hillsdale, NJ: Erlbaum.

Harrist, A. W., Zaia, A. F., Bates, J. E., Dodge, K. A., & Pettit, G. S. (1997). Subtypes of social withdrawal in early childhood: Sociometric status and social–cognitive differences across four years. *Child Development, 68,* 278–294.

Harter, S. (1978). Effectance motivation reconsidered: Toward a developmental model. *Human Development, 21,* 34–64.

Harter, S. (1981). A new self-report scale of intrinsic versus extrinsic orientation in the classroom: Motivational and information components. *Developmental Psychology, 17,* 300–312.

Harter, S. (1996). Developmental changes in self-understanding. In A. J. Sameroff & M. M. Haith (Eds.), *The five to seven year shift* (pp. 207–236). Chicago: University of Chicago Press.

Harter, S. (1998). The development of self-representations. In W. Damon (Series Ed.) & N. Eisenberg (Vol. Ed.), *Handbook of child psychology: Vol. 3. Social, emotional, and personality development* (5th ed., pp. 553–617). New York: Wiley.

Hartup, W. W., & van Lieshout, C. F. M. (1995). Personality development in social context. *Annual Review of Psychology, 46*, 655–687.

Hegvik, R. L., McDevitt, S. C., & Carey, W. B. (1982). The Middle Childhood Temperament Questionnaire, *Developmental and Behavioral Pediatrics, 3*, 197–200.

Henry, B., Caspi, A., Moffitt, T. E., & Silva, P. A. (1996). Temperamental and familial predictors of violent and nonviolent criminal convictions: Age 3 to 18. *Developmental Psychology, 32*, 614–623.

Izard, C. E. (1977). *Human emotions*, New York: Plenum.

Jackson, D. N. (1974). *Personality Research Form Manual* (Rev. ed.). Port Huron, MI: Research Psychologists Press.

Janowsky, J. S., & Carper, R. (1995). A neural basis for cognitive transitions in school-age children. In M. Haith & A. Sameroff (Eds.), *Reason and responsibility: The passage through childhood*. Chicago: University of Chicago Press.

Jensen-Campbell, L. A. (1995). *Perceptions of interpersonal conflict during early adolescence*. Unpublished doctoral dissertation, Texas A & M University, College Station, TX.

Jensen-Campbell, L. A., Graziano, W. G., & Hair, E. C. (1996). Personality and relationships as moderators of interpersonal conflict in adolescence. *Merrill-Palmer Quarterly, 42*, 148–164.

John, O. P., Caspi, A., Robins, R. W., Moffitt, T. E., & Stouthamer-Loeber, M. (1994). The "Little Five": Exploring the nomological network of the Five-Factor model of personality in adolescent boys. *Child Development, 65*, 160–178.

Kafry, D. (1982). Sensation seeking of young children. *Personality and Individual Differences, 3*, 161–166.

Kagan, J., & Moss, H. A. (1962). *Birth to maturity: A study in psychological development*. New York: Wiley.

Kagan, J., Reznick, J. S., Clarke, C., Snidman, N., & Garcia-Coll, C. (1984). Behavioral inhibition to the unfamiliar. *Child Development, 55*, 2212–2225.

Kagan, J., Reznick, J. S., & Snidman, N. (1987). The physiology and psychology of behavioral inhibition in children. *Child Development, 58*, 1459–1473.

Keogh, B. K. (1989). Applying temperament research to school. In G. A. Kohnstamm, J. E. Bates, & M. K. Rothbart (Eds.), *Temperament in childhood* (pp. 437–450). Chichester, England: Wiley.

Keogh, B. K., Pullis, M. E., & Cadwell, J. (1982). A short form of the Teacher Temperament Questionnaire. *Journal of Educational Measurement, 19*, 323–329.

Kindlon, D., Mezzacappa, E., & Earls, F. (1995). Psychometric properties of impulsivity measures: Temporal stability, validity and factor structure. *Journal of Child Psychology and Psychiatry, 36*, 645–661.

Kingston, L., & Prior, M. (1995). The development of patterns of stable, transient, and school-age onset aggressive behavior in young children. *Journal of the American Academy of Child and Adolescent Psychiatry, 34*, 348–358.

Kochanska, G., Murray, K., & Coy, K. C. (1997). Inhibitory control as a contributor to conscience in childhood: From toddler to early school age. *Child Development, 68,* 263–277.

Kochanska, G., Murray, K., Jacques, T. Y., Koenig, A. L., & Vandegeest, K. A. (1996). Inhibitory control in young children and its role in emerging internalization. *Child Development, 67,* 490–507.

Krueger, R. F., Caspi, A., Moffitt, T. E., White, J., & Stouthamer-Loeber, M. (1996). Delay of gratification, psychopathology, and personality: Is low self-control specific to externalizing problems? *Journal of Personality, 64,* 107–129.

Ladd, G. W. (1996). Shifting ecologies during the 5 to 7 year period: Predicting children's adjustment during the transition to grade school. In A. J. Sameroff & M. M. Haith (Eds.), *The five to seven year shift* (pp. 363–386). Chicago: University of Chicago Press.

la Freniere, P., & Charlesworth, W. R. (1983). Dominance, attention, and affiliation in a preschool group: A nine-month longitudinal study. *Ethology and Sociobiology, 4,* 55–67.

Lanning, K. (1994). Dimensionality of observer ratings on the California Adult Q-set. *Journal of Personality and Social Psychology, 67,* 151–160.

Larson, R. W. (1997). The emergence of solitude as a constructive domain of experience in early adolescence. *Child Development, 68,* 80–93.

Lerner, R. M., Palermo, M., Spiro, A., & Nesselroad, J. R. (1982). Assessing the dimensions of temperamental individuality across the life span: The Dimensions of Temperament Survey (DOTS). *Child Development, 53,* 149–159.

Luengo, M. A., Carrillo-de-la-Pena, M. T., Otero, J. M., & Romero, E. (1994). A short-term longitudinal study of impulsivity and antisocial behavior. *Journal of Personality and Social Psychology, 66,* 542–548.

Lynam, D. R. (1997). Pursuing the psychopath: Capturing the fledgling psychopath in a nomological net. *Journal of Abnormal Psychology, 106,* 425–428.

MacDonald, K. (1995). Evolution, the Five-Factor model, and levels of personality. *Journal of Personality, 63,* 525–567.

MacDonald, K. (1996). What do children want? A conceptualization of evolutionary influences on children's motivation in the peer group. *International Journal of Behavioral Development, 19,* 53–73.

Markus, H. J., & Nurius, P. S. (1984). Self-understanding and self-regulation in middle childhood. In W. A. Collins (Ed.), *Development during middle childhood: The years from six to twelve* (pp. 147–183). Washington, DC: National Academy Press.

Martin, R. P. (1988). *The Temperament Assessment Battery for Children,* Brandon, VT: Clinical Psychology Publishing.

Martin, R. P. (1989). Activity level, distractibility, and persistence: Critical characteristics in early schooling. In G. A. Kohnstamm, J. E. Bates, & M. K. Rothbart (Eds.), *Temperament in childhood* (pp. 451–461). Chichester, England: Wiley.

Martin, R. P., Olejnik, S., & Gaddis, L. (1994). Is temperament an important contributor to schooling outcomes in elementary school? Modeling effects of temperament and scholastic ability on academic achievement. In W. B. Carey & S. C. McDevitt (Eds.), *Prevention and early intervention: Individual differences as risk factors for the mental health of children: A Festschrift for Stella Chess and Alexander Thomas* (pp. 59–68). New York: Brunner/Mazel.

Martin, R. P., Wisenbaker, J., & Huttunen, M. (1994). Review of factor analytic studies of temperament measures based on the Thomas-Chess structural model: Implications for the Big Five. In C. F. Halverson, G. A. Kohnstamm, & R. P. Martin (Eds.), *The developing structure of temperament and personality from infancy to adulthood* (pp. 157–172). Hillsdale, NJ: Erlbaum.

Masten, A. S., Coatsworth, J. D., Neeman, J., Gest, S. D., Tellegen, A., & Garmezy, N. (1995). The structure and coherence of competence from childhood through adolescence. *Child Development, 66,* 1635–1659.

Masten, A. S., Neemann, J., & Andenas, S. (1994). Life events and adjustment in adolescents: The significance of event independence, desirability, and chronicity. *Journal of Research on Adolescence, 4,* 71–97.

McAdams, D. P. (1996). Alternative futures for the study of human individuality. *Journal of Research in Personality, 30,* 374–388.

McClowry, S. G., Hegvik, R. L., & Teglasi, H. (1993). An examination of the construct validity of the Middle Childhood Temperament Questionnaire. *Merrill-Palmer Quarterly, 39,* 279–293.

McCrae, R. R., & Costa, P. T. (1987). Validation of the Five-Factor model of personality across instruments and observers. *Journal of Personality and Social Psychology, 52,* 81–90.

McCrae, R. R., Costa, P. T., & Busch, C. M. (1986). Evaluating comprehensiveness in personality systems. The California Q-Set and the Five-Factor model. *Journal of Personality, 54,* 430–446.

McCrae, R. R., & John, O. P. (1992). An introduction to the Five-Factor model and its applications. *Journal of Personality, 60,* 175–215.

McDevitt, S. C., & Carey, W. B. (1978). The measurement of temperament in 3–7 year old children. *Journal of Child Psychology and Psychiatry, 19,* 245–253.

Mervielde, I., Buyst, V., & De Fruyt, F. (1995). The validity of the Big-Five as a model for teachers' ratings of individual differences among children aged 4–12 years. *Personality and Individual Differences, 18,* 525–534.

Mischel, W., Shoda, Y., & Peake, P. K. (1988). The nature of adolescent competencies predicted by preschool delay of gratification. *Journal of Personality and Social Psychology, 54,* 687–696.

Morison, P., & Masten, A. S. (1991). Peer reputation in middle childhood as a predictor of adaptation in adolescence: A seven-year follow-up. *Child Development, 62,* 991–1007.

Murray, H. A. (1938). *Explorations in personality.* New York: Oxford University Press.

Patterson, G. R. (1976). The aggressive child: Victim and architect of a coercive system. In L. Hammerlyck, E. Marsh, & L. Handy (Eds.), *Behavior modification and families* (pp. 267–316). New York: Brunner/Mazel.

Patterson, G. R. (1982). *Coercive family process.* Eugene, OR: Castilia Press.

Peabody, D., & Goldberg, L. R. (1989). Some determinants of factor structures from personality-trait descriptors. *Journal of Personality and Social Psychology, 57,* 552–567.

Pearlman, C. (1984). The effects of level of effectance motivation, IQ, and a penalty/reward contingency on the choice of problem difficulty. *Child Development, 55,* 537–542.

Pedersen, N. L. (1993). Genetic and environmental continuity and change in personality. In T. J. Bouchard, Jr. & P. Propping (Eds.), *Twins as a tool of behavior genetics* (pp. 147–162). New York: Wiley.

Pervin, L. A. (1996). Personality: A view of the future based on a look at the past. *Journal of Research in Personality, 30,* 309–318.

Presley, R., & Martin, R. P. (1994). Toward a structure of preschool temperament: Factor structure of the Temperament Assessment Battery for Children. *Journal of Personality, 62*, 415–448.

Prior, M. (1992). Childhood temperament. *Journal of Child Psychology and Psychiatry, 33*, 249–279.

Rende, R. D., & Plomin, R. (1992). Relations between first-grade stress, temperament, and behavior problems. *Journal of Applied Developmental Psychology, 13*, 435–446.

Robins, R. W., John, O. P., & Caspi, A. (1994). Major dimensions of personality in early adolescence: The Big Five and beyond. In C. F. Halverson, G. A. Kohnstamm, & R. P. Martin (Eds.), *The developing structure of temperament and personality from infancy to adulthood* (pp. 267–291). Hillsdale, NJ: Erlbaum.

Robins, R. W., John, O. P., Caspi, A., Moffitt, T. E., & Stouthamer-Loeber, M. (1996). Resilient, over-controlled, and undercontrolled boys: Three replicable personality types. *Journal of Personality and Social Psychology, 70*, 157–171.

Rogoff, B., Sellers, M. J., Pirrotta, S., Fox, N., & White, S. H. (1975). Age of assignment of roles and responsibilities to children. *Human Development, 18*, 353–369.

Rothbart, M. K. (1989a). Temperament and development. In G. A. Kohnstamm, J. E. Bates, & M. K. Rothbart (Eds.), *Temperament in childhood* (pp. 187–247). Chichester, England: Wiley.

Rothbart, M. K. (1989b). Temperament in childhood: A framework. In G. A. Kohnstamm, J. E. Bates, & M. K. Rothbart (Eds.), *Temperament in childhood* (pp. 59–75). Chichester, England: Wiley.

Rothbart, M. K., & Ahadi, S. A. (1994). Temperament and the development of personality. *Journal of Abnormal Psychology, 103*, 55–66.

Rothbart, M. K., Ahadi, S. A., & Hershey, K. L. (1994). Temperament and social behavior in childhood. *Merrill-Palmer Quarterly, 40*, 21–39.

Rothbart, M. K., Ahadi, S. A., Hershey, K. L., & Fisher, P. (1996). *Temperament in children 4–7 years as assessed in the Children's Behavior Questionnaire.* Manuscript submitted for publication.

Rothbart, M. K., & Bates, J. E. (1998). Temperament. In W. Damon (Series Ed.) & N. Eisenberg (vol. Ed.), *Handbook of child psychology: Vol. 3. Social, emotional and personality development* (5th ed., pp. 105–176). New York: Wiley.

Rothbart, M. K., & Derryberry, D. (1981). Development of individual differences in temperament. In M. E. Lamb & A. L. Brown (Eds.), *Advances in developmental psychology* (Vol. 1, pp. 37–86). Hillsdale, NJ: Erlbaum.

Rothbart, M. K., & Mauro, J. A. (1990). Questionnaire approaches to the study of infant temperament. In J. W. Fagen & J. Colombo (Eds.), *Individual differences in infancy: Reliability, stability, and prediction* (pp. 411–429). Hillsdale, NJ: Erlbaum.

Rothbart, M. K., & Posner, M. (1985). Temperament and the development of self-regulation. In L. C. Hartlage, & C. F. Telzrow (Eds.), *The neuropsychology of individual differences: a developmental perspective* (pp. 93–123). New York: Plenum.

Rowe, D. C., & Plomin, R. (1977). Temperament in early chilhood. *Journal of Personality Assessement, 41*, 150–156.

Rubin, K. H., & Krasnor, L. R. (1985). Social–cognitive and social behavioral perspectives on problem solving. In M. Perlmutter (Ed.), *Minnesota Symposium on Child Psychology* (Vol. 18, pp. 1–68). Hillsdale, NJ: Erlbaum.

Runyan, W. M. (1983). Idiographic goals and methods in the study of lives. *Journal of Personality, 51*, 411–437.

Sameroff, A. J., & Haith, M. M. (1996). *The five to seven year shift*. Chicago: University of Chicago Press.

Sanson, A. V., Smart, D. F., Prior, M., Oberklaid, F., & Pedlow, R. (1994). The structure of temperament from age 3 to 7 years: Age, sex, and sociodemographic influences. *Merrill-Palmer Quarterly, 40*, 233–252.

Saudino, K. J., & Plomin, R. (1997). Cognitive and temperamental mediators of genetic contributions to the home environment during infancy. *Merrill-Palmer Quarterly, 43*, 1–23.

Schachar, R., & Logan, G. D. (1990). Impulsivity and inhibitory control in normal development and childhood psychopathology. *Developmental Psychology, 26*, 710–720.

Sherif, M., Harvey, O., White, B. J., Hood, W. R., & Sherif, C. (1961). *Intergroup conflict and cooperation: The robbers' cave experiment*. Norman, OK: University of Oklahoma Press.

Strelau, J. (1987). The concept of temperament in personality research. *European Journal of Personality, 1*, 107–117.

Tellegen, A. (1985). Structure of mood and personality and their relevance to assessing anxiety, with an emphasis on self-report. In A. H. Tuma & J. D. Maser (Eds.), *Anxiety and the anxiety disorders* (pp. 681–706). Hillsdale, NJ: Erlbaum.

Tellegen, A. (1993). Folk concepts and psychological concepts of personality and personality disorder. *Psychological Inquiry, 4*, 122–130.

Tellegen, A., Lykken, D. T., Bouchard, T. J., Jr., Wilcox, K. J., Segal, E. L., & Rich, S. (1988). Personality similarity in twins reared apart and together. *Journal of Personality and Social Psychology, 54*, 1031–1039.

Tellegen, A., & Waller, N. G. (in press). Exploring personality through test construction: Development of the Multi-Dimensional Personality Questionnaire. In S. R. Briggs & J. M. Cheek (Eds.), *Personality measures: Development and evaluation, Vol. 1*. Greenwich, CN: JAI Press.

Thatcher, R. W. (1994). Cyclic cortical organization. In G. Dawson & K. W. Fischer (Eds.), *Human behavior and the developing brain*. New York: Guilford.

Thomas, A., & Chess, S. (1977). *Temperament and development*. New York: Brunner/Mazel.

Thomas, A., Chess, S., & Birch, H. (1968). *Temperament and behavior disorders in children*. New York: New York University Press.

Thomas. A., Chess, S., Birch, H., Hertzig, M., & Korn, S. (1963). *Behavioral individuality in early childhood*. New York: New York University Press.

Toner, I. J., & Smith, R. A. (1977). Age and overt verbalization in delay maintenance behavior in children. *Journal of Experimental Child Psychology, 24*, 123–128.

Urban, J., Carlson, E., Egeland, B., & Sroufe, L. A. (1991). Patterns of individual adaptation across childhood. *Development and Psychopathology, 3*, 445–460.

van Aken, M. A. G. (1992). The development of general competence and domain-specific competencies. *European Journal of Personality, 6*, 267–282.

van den Boom, D. C., & Hoeksma, J. B. (1994). The effect of infant irritability on mother-infant interaction: A growth-curve analysis. *Developmental Psychology, 30*, 581–590.

van Lieshout, C. F. M., & Haselager, G. J. T. (1993). *The Big Five personality factors in the Nijmegen California Child Q-Set (NCCQ)*. Unpublished manuscript, University of Nijmegen, Nijmegen, the Netherlands.

van Lieshout, C. F. M., & Haselager, G. J. T. (1994). The Big Five personality factors in Q-sort description of children and adolescents. In C. F. Halverson, G. A. Kohnstamm, & R. P. Martin

(Eds.), *The developing structure of temperament and personality from infancy to adulthood* (pp. 293–318). Hillsdale, NJ: Erlbaum.

Victor, J. B. (1994). The five-factor model applied to individual differences in school behavior. In C. F. Halverson, G. A. Kohnstamm, & R. P. Martin (Eds.), *The developing structure of temperament and personality from infancy to adulthood* (pp. 335–370). Hillsdale, NJ: Erlbaum.

Visser, M. R. M., Das-Smaal, E. A., & Feji, J. A. (1993). Impulsivity in the eye of the beholder: An analysis of teachers' concepts of impulsive and reflective behavior. *European Journal of Personality, 7,* 47–63.

Waller, N. G. (in press). Evaluating the structure of personality. In C. R. Cloninger (Ed.), *Personality and psychopathology.* Washington, DC: American Psychiatric Press.

Watson, D., & Clark, L. A. (1984). Negative affectivity: The disposition to experience aversive emotional states. *Psychological Bulletin, 96,* 465–490.

Watson, D., & Clark, L. A. (1992). On traits and temperament: General and specific factors of emotional experience and their relation to the Five-Factor model. *Journal of Personality, 60,* 441–476.

Watson, D., & Clark, L. A. (1997). Extraversion and its positive emotional core. In R. Hogan, J. Johnson, & S. Briggs (Eds.), *Handbook of personality psychology* (pp. 767–793). San Diego, CA: Academic Press.

Weisner, T. S. (1996). The 5 to 7 transition as an ecocultural project. In A. J. Sameroff & M. M. Haith (Eds.), *The five to seven year shift* (pp. 295–326). Chicago: University of Chicago Press.

Werner, H. (1957). The concept of development from a comparative and organismic point of view. In D. B. Harris (Ed.), *The concept of development* (pp. 125–148). Minneapolis, MN: University of Minnesota Press.

Westen, D. (1995). A clinical-empirical model of personality: Life after the Mischelian ice age and the NEO-lithic era. *Journal of Personality, 63,* 495–524.

White, J. L., Moffitt, T. E., Caspi, A., Bartusch, D. J., Needles, D. J., & Stouthamer-Loeber, M. (1994). Measuring impulsivity and examining its relationship to delinquency. *Journal of Abnormal Psychology, 103,* 192–205.

White, S. H. (1965). Evidence for a hierachical arrangement of learning processes. In L. P. Lipsitt & C. C. Spiker (Eds.), *Advances in child development and behavior* (pp. 187–220). New York: Academic Press.

Windle, M. (1988). Psychometric strategies of measures of temperament: A methodological critique. *International Journal of Behavioral Development, 11,* 171–201.

Windle, M., Iawawaki, S., & Lerner, R. M. (1987). Cross-cultural comparability of temperament among Japanese and American early and late adolescents. *Journal of Adolescent Research, 2,* 423–446.

Windle, M., & Lerner, R. M. (1986). Reassessing the dimensions of temperamental individuality across the life span: The Revised Dimensions of Temperament Survey (DOTS–R). *Journal of Adolescent Research, 1,* 213–230.

Younger, A. J., & Boyko, K. A. (1987). Aggression and withdrawal as social schemas underlying children's peer perceptions. *Child Development, 58,* 1094–1100.

Zuckerman, M., Khulman, D. M., Joireman, J., Teta, P., & Kraft, M., (1993). A comparison of three structural models for personality: The Big Three, the Big Five, and the Alternative Five. *Journal of Personality and Social Psychology, 65,* 757–768.

Zuckerman, M., Kuhlman, D. M., Thornquist, M., & Kiers, H. (1991). Five (or three): Robust questionnaire scale factors of personality without culture. *Personality and Individual Differences, 12,* 929–941.

Received June 16, 1997
Revision received May 5, 1998
Accepted May 6, 1998

PART I: DEVELOPMENTAL STUDIES

4

Worry in Normal Children

Peter Muris, Ph.d., Cor Meesters, Ph.d., Harald Merckelbach, Ph.d.,
Ann Sermon, M.Sc., and Sandra Zwakhalen, M.Sc.

Objective: *To investigate worry in a nonclinical sample of children aged 8 to 13 years (N = 193).* **Method:** *Children were interviewed about the content, characteristics, origins, and severity of their main intense worry. Furthermore, children completed questionnaires to study the relationship between worry, trait anxiety, and depression.* **Results:** *Almost 70% of the children reported that they worried every now and then. The content of these worries predominantly pertained to school performance, dying and health, and social contacts. An examination of the characteristics of children's main intense worries revealed that these worries occurred on average 2 to 3 days per week, were accompanied by modest levels of interference and anxiety, elicited relatively high levels of resistance, and were rather difficult to control. A minority of the children were found to exhibit symptoms of worry in the pathological range: the percentages of children who met the* DSM-III-R *criteria of overanxious disorder and generalized anxiety disorder were 4.7% and 6.2%, respectively. Finally, worry, anxiety, and depression seemed to be strongly related.* **Conclusion:** *Worry seems to be a common phenomenon in normal children aged between 8 and 13 years.* J. Am. Acad. Child Adolesc. Psychiatry, *1998, 37(7):703–710.* **Key Words:** *worry, overanxious disorder, generalized anxiety disorder, normal children.*

In the past decade, considerable progress has been achieved in understanding the phenomenon of worry in adults (e.g., Borkovec et al., 1983; Eysenck, 1992). Meanwhile, good empirical work on worry in children is scarce. The few studies that have been carried out indicate that worry is a common phenomenon among children. For example, Orton (1982)

Accepted February 6, 1998.

Drs. Muris and Merckelbach are with the Department of Psychology and Dr. Meesters, Ms. Sermon, and Ms. Zwakhalen are with the Department of Experimental Abnormal Psychology, Maastricht University, The Netherlands.

The teachers and staff of primary schools Pastoor de Klerk in Velten-Beisem, Belgium, Op 't Hwagveld in Meerssen, and De Bundeling in Bunde, The Netherlands, are acknowledged for their participation in this study.

Reprint requests to Dr. Muris, Department of Psychology, Maastricht University, PO. Box 616, 6200 MD Maastricht, The Netherlands.

0890-8567/98/3707–0703/$03.00/0©1998 by the American Academy of Child and Adolescent Psychiatry.

found that more than 70% of a group of primary school children reported 10 or more things about which they worried. Likewise, in a study examining the prevalence of symptoms of anxiety disorders among normal children aged 5 to 19 years, Bell-Dolan et al. (1990) found that up to 30% of the children exhibited subclinical levels of excessive worry.

As in adult worry (e.g., see Borkovec et al., 1986), worry in childhood is predominantly self-referent. That is, children usually worry about threats to their own well-being (e.g., see Silverman et al., 1995). Furthermore, there is evidence to suggest that the content of children's worries is closely linked to their level of development (Vasey and Daleiden, 1994). For instance, in preschool children, worry about imaginary and supernatural threats can be readily observed, but this type of worry declines as children grow older (e.g., see Bauer, 1976). Vasey et al. (1994) examined the content of worries in children aged 5 to 6, 8 to 9, and 11 to 12 years. These authors reported that worries about threats to physical well-being predominated among 5- to 6-year-olds. In addition, this study found that these worries decreased significantly with increasing age. Among 8- to 9- and 11- to 12-year-olds, worries about behavioral competence, social evaluation, and psychological well-being became increasingly prominent. Furthermore, Vasey and colleagues showed that children in the two older age groups generated a significantly greater variety of worries than 5- to 6-year-olds. Vasey (1993) argues that from the age of 8 years, worry becomes increasingly complex because as they develop, children's ability to reason about future possibilities, to consider multiple threatening outcomes, and to elaborate potential negative consequences dramatically increases.

Although it is clear that level of development plays a significant role in childhood worry, it would be interesting to study other factors that might contribute to the origins of worries in children. Vasey and Daleiden (1994) suggest that aversive experiences may play a role in this context. In their words: ". . . a child might remember a threatening event and consider its possible recurrence in the near future" (p. 192).

Another point that warrants further study are the links between childhood worry, anxiety, and depression. It is clear that worry and trait anxiety are related concepts, and this seems to be true for both adult (e.g., Eysenck, 1992) and child (Silverman et al., 1995) populations. So far, few studies have directly examined the connection between worry and depression in children. The studies that have been done have found a positive association between these phenomena (e.g., see Chorpita et al., 1997). A related issue is the actual severity of worry in children. While it is known that many children worry and that levels of worry are positively related to psychopathological indices of anxiety and, possibly, depression, there is little information available on the proportion of children that suffer from pathological variants of worry, i.e., overanxious disorder (OAD) and generalized anxiety disorder (GAD). Two recent studies estimated the prevalence of OAD and GAD in children and youths to be in the order of 2% (Costello et al., 1996; Verhulst et al., 1997).

The purpose of this study was to examine worry in middle childhood in more detail. To begin with, the connection between worry, trait anxiety, and depression was investigated. Second, the content, characteristics, and origins of children's main intense worry were studied. Finally, an attempt was made to evaluate the severity of children's worries. This was done by administering the child version of the Diagnostic Interview Schedule for

Children (DISC) (National Institute of Mental Health, 1992). In this way, it was possible to detect severe worriers, i.e., children who fulfill the *DSM-III-R* (American Psychiatric Association, 1987) criteria for OAD or GAD.

METHOD

Participants

A total of 202 children (94 girls and 108 boys) were recruited from three regular primary schools in Maastricht, The Netherlands, and Velten-Beisem, Belgium. Nine children refused or were not given permission by their parents to participate in the study, leaving 193 children (89 girls and 104 boys; 95.5%) in the final sample. The mean age of these children was 10.8 years (SD = 1.0, range 8–13 years). The percentages of children with low, middle, and upper socioeconomic background (classified by using the occupational levels of both parents, with the guidelines provided by the Dutch Central Bureau of Statistics) were 24.9%, 46.6%, and 28.5%, respectively.

Assessment

Questionnaires. Three questionnaires were used in this study: the trait version of the State-Trait Anxiety Inventory for Children (STAIC) (Spielberger, 1973), the short version of the Depression Questionnaire for Children (DQC) (De Wit, 1987), and the Worry Scale for Children (WSC), which was designed for the purpose of this study.

The STAIC contains two 20-item scales. The State Anxiety scale measures current symptoms of anxiety by asking the child to indicate on a 3-point scale the degree to which he/she is currently experiencing a particular symptom (e.g., "I feel____." 1 = not scared, 2 = scared, or 3 = very scared). The Trait Anxiety scale that was used in the current study measures chronic symptoms of anxiety by asking the child to rate the frequency with which he/she experiences anxiety symptoms (1 = almost never, 2 = sometimes, or 3 = often). Examples of Trait Anxiety scale items are "I am scared," "I feel troubled," "I worry too much," and "I get a funny feeling in my stomach." STAIC Trait Anxiety scores range between 20 and 60, with higher scores reflecting higher levels of anxiety.

The DQC consists of nine items such as "I feel depressed lately" and "I often think that other children don't like me." Children have to indicate whether items are "true" or "not true" for them. Scores vary between 0 (no depression symptoms) and 9 (all depression symptoms present).

The STAIC and the DQC are well-researched instruments and have been found to possess good reliability (in terms of both internal consistency and test-retest reliability) and acceptable validity (Evers et al., 1992).

The WSC was designed for the purpose of this study. The scale was derived from the list of specific worries that was reported by Silverman et al. (1995; p. 678). The WSC consists of 40 items such as "I worry about my performance in school," "I worry about falling ill," "I worry about my parents arguing," and "I worry about what I look like."

Each item is checked on a 3-point scale: 1 = almost never, 2 = sometimes, or 3 = often. WSC scores range between 40 and 120, with higher scores reflecting higher levels of worry.

Diagnostic Interview. The child version of the DISC (version 2.3) is a highly structured, lay-administered interview instrument designed to assess the more common *DSM-III-R* (American Psychiatric Association, 1987) diagnoses found in children and adolescents. Previous research has shown that the instrument possesses adequate test-retest stability (Schwab-Stone et al., 1993), sufficient interrater reliability (Shaffer et al., 1993), and acceptable validity (Piacentini et al., 1993). The DISC was used to get a picture of the severity of children's worries. This was done by administering the Overanxious Disorder section. This section interviews children on three symptom clusters: (1) the presence of worries or unrealistic concerns and an excessive need for reassurance about these concerns during the past 6 months, (2) somatic complaints for which no physical basis can be found, and (3) symptoms of tension, autonomic hyperactivity, and vigilance. On the basis of the interview data obtained with this section, children can be screened for OAD as well as GAD.

Worry Interview. The interview began by giving the children a definition of worry: "Worry is thinking about aversive, negative things that can happen but probably will not happen. These thoughts occur repetitively despite the fact that you don't want to think about these things" (Vasey and Daleiden, 1994). After this instruction, children were asked two questions: "Do you worry every now and then?" and "About what do you worry most?" Next, they were interviewed about the content, characteristics, and origins of their main intense worry. More specifically, they were asked to provide details about the frequency ("How often do you worry about ___?" [1 = 1 day per week, 2 = 2–3 days per week, 3 = 4–5 days per week, 4 = 6–7 days per week]), level of interference ("How much does your worry about ___ disrupt your daily activities?" [1 = not at all; 4 = very much]), resistance ("Do you want to dismiss worries about ___?" [1 = not at all; 4 = very much]), and control-lability ("How often can you stop worrying about ___?" [1 = always; 4 = never]) of their main intense worry. Children were also asked whether their worry provoked anxiety ("How much fear do you feel when you worry about ___?" [1 = no fear at all; 4 = very much fear]). Furthermore, children were questioned about the (mental) control strategies that they used to stop their worry. In addition, children had to indicate when their main intense worry had started and whether they had any idea why they worried about this particular topic. Special attention was given to onset events ("Did an aversive, threatening experience cause you to worry about ___?" "Did you already worry about ___ before this aversive, threatening experience happened?"). Finally, children were asked whether their worry had any positive features.

Procedure

First, children and their parents signed informed consent forms. Hereafter, children completed the STAIC, DQC, and WSC in their classrooms. About 1 week later, children were interviewed individually by a trained research assistant in a private room. Children were first administered the DISC and then the Worry Interview. Children were told that their responses would remain confidential.

Data Analysis

Means and standard deviations of the pertinent measures were calculated. Relevant associations were investigated with Pearson product-moment correlations. Internal consistency of the questionnaires was indexed by means of Cronbach α values. Sex and group differences were evaluated by using t and χ^2 tests.

For the most part, data from all the above-mentioned analyses showed similar results for boys and girls. Therefore, with few exceptions, only the results for the total group are shown.

RESULTS

Worry, Anxiety, and Depression

Table 1 presents general statistics on the WSC, STAIC, and DQC as well as correlations between the three questionnaires. As can be seen, all questionnaires were reliable in internal consistency: Cronbach α values were .91 for the WSC, .88 for the STAIC, and .74 for the DQC. Furthermore, girls had significantly higher WSC ($t_{191} = 2.2$, $p < .05$), STAIC ($t_{191} = 3.1$, $p < .005$), and DQC ($t_{191} = 2.7$, $p < .01$) scores than boys. In other words, girls worried more frequently and were more anxious and depressed than boys.

Correlations between the three questionnaires were all found to be positive and significant (Table 1). Most importantly, worry was related to both trait anxiety ($r_{193} = 0.82$, $p < .001$) and depression ($r_{193} = 0.69$, $p < .001$). Thus, the more children worried, the more anxious and depressed they were.

Because six STAIC items (e.g., "I worry too much"; "I worry about school") directly pertain to worry, a corrected STAIC score was computed in which these items were excluded. The correlation between WSC and corrected STAIC was still positive and significant ($r_{193} = 0.75$, $p < .001$).

Content of Main Intense Worries

The Worry Interview revealed that 133 (64 boys and 69 girls) of the 193 children (68.9%) worried every now and then. The content of what these children reported as their main intense

TABLE 1
Main Statistics on WSC, STAIC, and DQC and Correlations Among These Measures

	α	Total Group		Boys		Girls		WSC	STAIC
		Mean	(SD)	Mean	(SD)	Mean	(SD)		
WSC	.91	57.5	(11.5)	55.8	(10.9)	59.4	(11.9)		
STAIC	.88	31.1	(7.5)	29.6	(7.1)	32.9	(7.6)	0.82*	
DQC	.74	2.3	(2.2)	1.8	(2.1)	2.8	(2.2)	0.69*	0.79*

Note: $N = 193$. WSC = Worry Scale for Children; STAIC = Trait Anxiety scale of the State-Trait Anxiety Inventory for Children; DQC = Depression Questionnaire for Children.
*$p < .001$.

TABLE 2
Rank Order of Main Intense Worries Reported by the Children

Worry About ...	Total Group ($N = 133$)	Boys ($n = 64$)	Girls ($n = 69$)
1. School performance	28	14	14
2. Dying or illness of others	21	13	8
3. Getting sick	16	7	9
4. Being teased	11	6	5
5. Making mistakes	9	5	4
6. Appearance	9	3	6
7. Specific future events (e.g., party)	7	2	5
8. Parents divorcing	6	3	3
9. Whether other children like me	6	2	4
10. Pets	4	1	3
11. Performance in sports	3	1	2
12. Getting friends	3	2	1
13. Moving to a new house	3	1	2
14. Being kidnapped	2	1	1
15. Starting a new school	1	0	1
16. Getting into trouble	1	1	0
17. Not being able to sleep	1	1	0
18. An airplane crashing on our house	1	0	1
19. That my parents discover that I smoke	1	1	0

Note: Sixty children reported that they never worried.

worry is shown in Table 2. The most frequent main intense worries had to do with school performance, dying and health, and social contacts.

Characteristics of Main Intense Worries

The left-hand side of Table 3 presents the characteristics of children's main intense worries and the correlations among these variables. The mean frequency of the main intense worry was 2.1 (SD = 1.1), which corresponds with a frequency of approximately 2 to 3 days per week. Furthermore, mean level of interference and anxiety elicited by the main intense worry were 1.8 (SD = 1.0) and 1.7 (SD = 1.0), respectively. Children reported that their main worry elicited considerable resistance (mean = 3.0, SD = 1.0) but that their worrisome thoughts were rather difficult to stop (mean = 2.9, SD = 1.0). Note further that the correlations among these variables produced the expected pattern (see left-hand side of Table 3). For example, the more frequent the worry, the higher its level of interference, the more resistance it elicited, and so on.

Correlations between WSC, STAIC, and DQC scores, on the one hand, and characteristics of the main intense worry, on the other hand, were also computed. As expected, WSC (being an index of "how often children worry") was most strongly associated with the frequency of the main intense worry, whereas the STAIC was most strongly linked with anxiety elicited

TABLE 3

Characteristics of Children's Main Intense Worry, Correlations Among These Variables,
and Correlations Between WSC, STAIC, DQC, and Characteristics

	Score[a]		1	2	3	4	WSC	STAIC	DQC
	Mean	(SD)	1	2	3	4	WSC	STAIC	DQC
1. Frequency	2.1	(1.1)					0.34**	0.28**	0.30**
2. Level of interference	1.8	(1.0)	0.43**				0.33**	0.42**	0.31**
3. Anxiety	1.7	(1.0)	0.37**	0.43**			0.35**	0.44**	0.38**
4. Resistance	3.0	(1.0)	0.09	0.24*	0.43**		0.20*	0.33**	0.24*
5. Controllability	2.9	(1.0)	0.26*	0.38**	0.38**	0.30**	0.22*	0.38**	0.35**

Note: $N = 133$. WSC = Worry Scale for Children; STAIC = Trait Anxiety scale of the State-Trait Anxiety Inventory for Children; DQC = Depression Questionnaire for Children.
[a]Characteristics were scored on a 4-point scale with higher scores reflecting higher levels of frequency, interference, anxiety, and resistance and lower levels of controllability.
*$p < .05$; **$p < .01$.

by the main worry. Note also that depression (DQC) scores were significantly related to worry characteristics.

Children seemed to use the following strategies to control their main worry: 55.6% ($n = 74$) engaged in some activity that distracted them from their worrisome thoughts, 37.6% ($n = 50$) tried to think about other more pleasant things, and 8.3% ($n = 11$) discussed their worry with other people.

Origins of Main Intense Worry

The questions about the presence of threatening, aversive experiences in relation to the onset of main intense worries revealed that most children (70.7%; $n = 94$) were not able to recall such an event. Nevertheless, a substantial minority of the children (29.3%; $n = 39$) did report that their worry became worse after having experienced an aversive, threatening event or was even caused by such an event (percentages were 12.8% [$n = 17$] and 16.5% [$n = 22$], respectively).

Positive Features of Worry

Some children (i.e., 27.8%; $n = 37$) reported that their worry also had some positive features: it allowed them to cope with a difficult, future event (e.g., test, death of a parent) in a more effective way.

Severity of Children's Worries

The results of the DISC interview are summarized in Table 4. The percentages of children who met the general symptoms of OAD/GAD (i.e., "Are you a person who always worries about something?" and "Are you a person who is often very tense and who is not able to relax?") were 18.7% (i.e., 36 children) and 13.0% (i.e., 25 children), respectively.

TABLE 4
Main Results of the DISC Interview: Percentages of Children Who Fulfilled the (Separate)
Criteria of Overanxious Disorder and Generalized Anxiety Disorder

	DISC Criterion	Total Group ($N = 193$)	Boys ($n = 104$)	Girls ($n = 89$)
General symptoms				
Are you a person who always worries about something?	119	18.7	16.3	21.3
Are you a person who is often very tense and who is not able to relax?	120	13.0	12.5	13.5
Specific worries				
Worry about specific future events	108	6.7	4.8	9.0
Worry about performance at school	109	16.6	15.4	18.0
Worry about performance in sports	110	4.1	1.0*	7.9
Worry about making mistakes	112	9.3	6.7	12.4
Worry about money	113	1.0	1.0	1.1
Worry about making a fool of oneself	114	4.1	1.9	6.7
Worry about appearance	115	6.2	2.9*	10.1
Worry about whether others like you	116	6.2	4.8	7.9
Worry about illness and health	117	11.4	8.7	14.6
Socially oversensitive	118	18.1	17.3	19.1
Somatic/physical symptoms				
Headaches	103	5.7	2.9	9.0
Stomachaches	104	4.7	1.0*	9.0
Other aches	105	5.2	3.8	6.7
Six or more symptoms of tension, autonomic hyperactivity, and vigilance	106	8.3	4.8	12.4
OAD[a]		4.7	1.9*	9.0
GAD[b]		6.2	3.8	9.0
OAD or GAD		6.7	3.8	10.1
OAD and GAD		4.1	1.9	6.7

Note: DISC = Diagnostic Interview Schedule for Children.
[a]The diagnosis overanxious disorder (OAD) was made when children met at least four of the following: 108; 112; 109 or 110 or 114 or 116; 103 or 104 or 105; 115 or 118; 120.
[b]The diagnosis generalized anxiety disorder (GAD) was made when children met 119; and at least two of the following: 108, 109, 110, 112, 113, 114, 116, 117, and 106.
*Difference between boys and girls significant at $p = .05$.

The prevalence of specific worries varied between 1.0% (worry about money) and 16.6% (worry about performance at school). A considerable percentage of children (18.1%) seemed to be socially oversensitive. Furthermore, it was found that 8.3% of the children reported six or more symptoms of tension, autonomic hyperactivity, and vigilance, whereas the percentages of children who reported somatic complaints for which no physical basis could be found varied between 4.7% (stomachaches) and 5.7% (headaches).

A number of sex differences in the prevalence of OAD/GAD symptoms emerged. First, on the whole, girls reported more specific worries than boys, means being 1.1 (SD = 1.5) and 0.6 (SD = 1.0), respectively ($t_{143.88}$ = 2.4, p < .05, separate variance estimate). Worry about performance in sports (χ^2_1 = 5.8, p < .05) and worry about appearance (χ^2_1 = 4.3, p < .05) were reported more often by girls than by boys (Table 4). Second, compared with boys, girls more frequently met the criteria for physical or somatic symptoms of OAD/GAD: mean number of symptoms was 0.1 (SD = 0.5) versus 0.4 (SD = 0.9) ($t_{132.97}$ = 2.2, p < .05, separate variance estimate). In particular, stomachaches were more frequently reported by girls than by boys (χ^2_1 = 7.0, p < .05) (Table 4).

The 6-month prevalence of OAD and GAD in our sample was 4.7% and 6.2%, respectively. The total prevalence of either one of the disorders was 6.7%, while 4.1% of the children met the criteria for both disorders. The prevalence rates for girls were higher than those for boys, although only significant for OAD (χ^2_1 = 3.8, p < .05).

Comparison of OAD/GAD Children and Control Children

As can be seen in Table 5, children who met DISC criteria of either OAD or GAD (i.e., OAD/GAD children) had significantly higher scores on WSC (t_{191} = 5.2, p < .001),

TABLE 5

Comparison of Children Who Met the DISC Criteria of Overanxious Disorder or Generalized Anxiety Disorder and Children Who Did Not Fulfill These Criteria (Control Children) on a Number of Worry Measures

	OAD/GAD Children (n = 13)		Control Children (n = 180/120)[a]	
	Mean	(SD)	Mean	(SD)
Questionnaires				
WSC	72.5	(14.3)**	56.4	(10.5)
STAIC	42.1	(9.1)**	30.3	(6.8)
DQC	4.9	(2.1)**	2.1	(2.1)
Diagnostic Interview				
No. of worries	5.8	(2.9)**	0.6	(1.1)
Worry Interview[b]				
Frequency	3.2	(0.8)**	2.0	(1.1)
Level of interference	2.5	(0.9)*	1.6	(1.0)
Anxiety	2.8	(1.3)*	1.6	(0.9)
Resistance	3.2	(0.9)	3.0	(1.1)
Controllability	3.6	(0.7)*	2.8	(1.0)

Note: DISC = Diagnostic Interview Schedule for Children; OAD = overanxious disorder; GAD = generalized anxiety disorder; WSC = Worry Scale for Children; STAIC = Trait Anxiety scale of the State-Trait Anxiety Inventory for Children; DQC = Depression Questionnaire for Children.
[a]The Worry Interview was administered to only 120 control children.
[b]Characteristics were scored on a 4-point scale with higher scores reflecting higher levels of frequency, interference, anxiety, and resistance and lower levels of controllability.
*p < .005; **p < .001.

STAIC (t_{191} = 5.9, $p < .001$), and DQC (t_{191} = 4.8, $p < .001$) than children who did not fulfill these criteria (i.e., control children). Table 5 also shows that OAD/GAD children reported on the average approximately six specific worries, whereas control children had only one topic about which they worried. OAD/GAD children reported a higher frequency of their main worry (t_{131} = 3.7, $p < .001$), a stronger interference with daily activities (t_{131} = 3.3, $p < .005$), more anxiety linked to worry (t_{131} = 3.4, $p < .005$), and more difficulty controlling their worry (t_{131} = 2.9, $p < .005$) than did control children. None of the OAD/GAD children reported that their worry had positive features. In contrast, 30.8% (n = 37) of the control children said that their worry had some positive aspects (χ^2_1 = 5.6, $p < .05$). Furthermore, OAD/GAD children less frequently engaged in activities that distracted them from their worrisome thoughts (χ^2_1 = 6.2, $p < .05$) and more frequently discussed their worry with other people (χ^2_1 = 4.2, $p < .05$) than did control children. There were no significant differences between the two groups with regard to the origins of their main worry.

DISCUSSION

This study investigated worry in a nonclinical sample of children aged between 8 and 13 years. The main results can be cataloged as follows. To begin with, worry was found to be a common phenomenon among the children (cf. Bell-Dolan et al., 1990). Almost 70% reported that they worried every now and then. Second, in line with the previous study of Silverman et al. (1995), the content of these worries predominantly pertained to school performance, dying and health, and social contacts. Third, examination of the characteristics of children's main intense worries revealed that these worries occurred on average 2 to 3 days per week, were accompanied by modest levels of interference and anxiety, elicited relatively high levels of resistance, and were rather difficult to control. Fourth, a minority of the children exhibited symptoms of worry in the pathological range: the percentages of children who met the DISC (i.e., *DSM-III-R*) criteria of OAD and GAD were 4.7% and 6.2%, respectively. Fifth, worry, anxiety, and depression were found to be strongly related to each other.

The 6-month prevalence of OAD/GAD in the current study was higher than that found in previous studies (Costello et al., 1996; Verhulst et al., 1997). For example, Verhulst et al. (1997) who also used the DISC, found prevalence rates of 1.8% for OAD and 0.6% for GAD. Note, however, that Verhulst et al. screened children aged between 13 and 18, whereas our study's sample was considerably younger. Little is known about the exact prevalence rates of OAD and GAD in children of different age groups. This point clearly warrants future research.

In the literature, childhood fears and worries are often bracketed together (see, for a discussion of this point, Vasey and Daleiden, 1994). However, at least at the theoretical and phenomenological level, fear and worry are clearly distinct concepts. Whereas fear is primarily concerned with anxiety that is elicited by the actual confrontation with a phobogenic stimulus (Marks, 1987), worry involves anxious thoughts about the possible occurrence of a negative future event (Borkovec et al., 1983). It is not surprising that the list of main intense worries found in this study is quite different from the list of main intense fears found by Muris et al. (1997) in a sample of children of comparable age and socioeconomic status. For example, none of the children in the current study reported that they worried about animals such as spiders and snakes, whereas in the Muris et al. study these seemed to be frequently feared stimuli.

The direction of sex differences was consistent with previous research in both clinical and nonclinical samples (e.g., Bell-Dolan et al., 1990; Bernstein and Borchardt, 1991). That is, girls exhibit higher levels of symptomatology than boys: they not only scored higher on anxiety, worry, and depression questionnaires, but they also reported more symptoms of OAD or GAD.

Approximately one fourth of the children reported that their main worry served some positive goal. That is, it prepared them to handle a difficult future event. Although a certain level of concern is normal and even necessary as a cue for anticipating and adapting to possible negative events, worry is thought to undermine anticipation and preparation (e.g., Borkovec et al., 1991). In line with this, none of the OAD/GAD children in this study reported that their main worry had a positive feature.

As to the origins of childhood worries, no evidence was obtained for the idea that these worries and concerns were linked to threatening, aversive events. Although a substantial minority of the children in this study reported that their main worry was related to such an event, the comparison of OAD/GAD children and control children suggests that this factor does not play a critical role in the development of worrying. That is, only 7.7% of the OAD/GAD children recalled such an experience compared with 17.5% of the control children. It remains to be seen what factors do play a role in the etiology of childhood worry, OAD, and GAD. It is generally assumed that high levels of trait anxiety predispose to pathological manifestations of worry (e.g., Eysenck, 1992). The current study provides some support for this idea. First, a strong, positive correlation was found between trait anxiety as indexed by the STAIC and frequency of worry as measured by the WSC (even when STAIC "worry" items were excluded). Second, OAD/GAD children clearly exhibited higher scores on the STAIC than control children. However, the best way to examine the assumption that trait anxiety is a risk factor contributing to pathological worry would be a prospective study in which children who subsequently suffer from OAD/GAD are compared with control children in terms of their initial levels of trait anxiety.

The high correlations found between trait anxiety and worry, on the one hand, and depression, on the other hand, fit well with results from earlier studies. A number of analog studies have found significant associations between worry, anxiety, and depression questionnaires (Chorpita et al., 1997; Ollendick et al., 1991). In a similar vein, clinical studies have demonstrated comorbidity between childhood anxiety and depressive disorders (e.g, Strauss et al., 1988). These studies show that a substantial proportion of the children with a diagnosis of major depression also carry a diagnosis of a major anxiety disorder (i.e., separation anxiety disorder or GAD).

Clinical Implications

In conclusion, then, worry seems to be a common phenomenon in normal children aged 8 to 13 years. In agreement with Bell-Dolan et al. (1990), the current data indicate that a considerable minority of children exhibit excessive worry and even suffer from OAD/GAD.

With regard to these findings, two additional remarks are in order. First, OAD/GAD is a serious disorder that undermines normal development (e.g., Silverman and Ginsburg, 1995). Second, OAD/GAD is probably the anxiety disorder with the lowest spontaneous recovery rate (Bernstein and Borchardt, 1991). Therefore, easy-to-administer instruments for detecting OAD/GAD in children would be highly relevant. The recently developed Screen for Child Anxiety Related Emotional Disorders (SCARED) (Birmaher et al., 1997) might be a useful tool for this purpose. This questionnaire taps symptomatology of *DSM-*defined anxiety disorders. A recent study of Muris and colleagues (unpublished) showed that the GAD scale of the SCARED possesses sufficient sensitivity and specificity to detect GAD in nonreferred children. While the development of effective treatment programs for OAD/GAD in children is equally important, controlled research on this topic is sparse. As things stand, the cognitive-behavioral treatment (CBT) program designed by Kendall and associates (e.g., Kendall and Gosch, 1994) is the best candidate. This program teaches children to recognize when they are worrying and to approach such thoughts with more realistic and adaptive self-talk. Kendall (1994; see also Kendall et al., 1997) has found evidence to suggest that CBT is effective in children with OAD. Other treatments that have been suggested for OAD/GAD are exposure and relaxation training (e.g., Eisen and Silverman, 1993), but so far no controlled study has evaluated their effectiveness in children with OAD/GAD. Thus, for future studies, early detection of and effective interventions for children with OAD/GAD seem to be important priorities.

REFERENCES

American Psychiatric Association (1987), *Diagnostic and Statistical Manual of Mental Disorders, 3rd edition-revised (DSM-III-R)*. Washington, DC: American Psychiatric Association

Bauer DH (1976), An exploratory study of developmental changes in children's fears. *J Child Psychol Psychiatry* 17:69–74

Bell-Dolan DJ, Last CG, Strauss CD (1990), Symptoms of anxiety disorders in normal children. *J Am Acad Child Adolesc Psychiatry* 29:759–765

Bernstein GA, Borchardt CM (1991), Anxiety disorders of childhood and adolescence: a critical review. *J Am Acad Child Adolesc Psychiatry* 30:519–532

Birmaher B, Khetarpal S, Brent D et al. (1997), The Screen for Child Anxiety Related Emotional Disorders (SCARED): scale construction and psychometric characteristics. *J Am Acad Child Adolesc Psychiatry* 36:545–553

Borkovec TD, Metzger RL, Pruzinsky T (1986), Anxiety, worry, and the self. In: *Perception of Self in Emotional Disorders and Psychotherapy*, Hartman L, Blankstein KR, eds. New York: Plenum

Borkovec TD, Robinson E, Pruzinsky T, De Pree JA (1983), Preliminary exploration of worry: some characteristics and processes. *Behav Res Ther* 21:9–16

Borkovec TD, Shadick R, Hopkins M (1991), The nature of normal worry and pathological worry. In: *Chronic Anxiety: Generalized Anxiety Disorder and Mixed Anxiety-Depression*, Rapee RM, Barlow DH, eds. New York: Guilford

Chorpita BF, Tracey SA, Brown TA, Collica TJ, Barlow DH (1997), Assessment of worry in children and adolescents: an adaptation of the Penn State Worry Questionnaire. *Behav Res Ther* 35:569–581

Costello EJ, Angold A, Burns BJ et al. (1996), The Great Smoky Mountains Study of Youth: goals, design, methods, and the prevalence of *DSM-III-R disorders. Arch Gen Psychiatry* 53:1129–1136

De Wit CAM (1987), *Depressie-vragenlijst voor kinderen* [Depression Questionnaire for Children]. Amersfoort, The Netherlands: Acco

Eisen AR, Silverman WK (1993), Should I relax or change my thoughts? A preliminary examination of cognitive therapy, relaxation training, and their combination with overanxious children. *J Cognit Psychother* 7:265–280

Evers A, Van Vliet-Mulder JC, Ter Laak J (1992), *Documentatie van tests en testresearch in Nederland* [Documentation of Tests and Test Research in The Netherlands]. Assen, The Netherlands: Van Gorcum

Eysenck MW (1992), *Anxiety: The Cognitive Perspective.* Hove, England: Erlbaum

Kendall PC (1994), Treating anxiety disorders in children: results of a randomized clinical trail. *J Consult Clin Psychol* 62:100–110

Kendall PC, Flannery-Schroeder E, Panichelli-Mindel SM, Southam-Gerow M, Henin A, Warman M (1997), Therapy for youths with anxiety disorders: a second randomized clinical trial. *J Consult Clin Psychol* 65:366–380

Kendall PC, Gosch EA (1994), Cognitive-behavioral interventions. In: *International Handbook of Phobic and Anxiety Disorders in Children and Adolescents*, Ollendick TH, King NJ, Yule W, eds. New York: Plenum

Marks IM (1987), *Fears, Phobias, and Rituals: Panic, Anxiety, and Their Disorders.* New York: Oxford University Press

Muris P, Merckelbach H, Collaris R (1997), Common childhood fears and their origins. *Behav Res Ther* 35:929–937

National Institute of Mental Health (1992), *Diagnostic Interview Schedule for Children (DISC), Version 2.3.* New York: New York State Psychiatric Institute, Division of Child and Adolescent Psychiatry

Ollendick TH, Yule W, Ollier K (1991), Fears in British children and their relationship to manifest anxiety and depression. *J Child Psychol Psychiatry* 32:321–331

Orton GL (1982), A comparative study of children's worries. *J Psychol* 110:153–162

Piacentini J, Shaffer D, Fisher P, Schwab-Stone M, Davies M, Gioia P (1993), The Diagnostic Interview Schedule for Children-revised version (DISC-R), III: concurrent criterion validity. *J Am Acad Child Adolesc Psychiatry* 32:658–665

Schwab-Stone M, Fisher P, Piacentini J, Shaffer D, Davies M, Briggs M (1993), The Diagnositic Interview Schedule for Children-revised version (DISC-R), II: test-retest reliability. *J Am Acad Child Adolesc Psychiatry* 32:651–657

Shaffer D, Schwab-Stone M, Fisher P et al. (1993), the Diagnostic Interview Schedule for Children-revised version (DISC-R), I: preparation, field testing, interrater reliability, and acceptability. *J Am Acad Child Adolesc Psychiatry* 32:643–650

Silverman WK, Ginsburg GS (1995), Specific phobia and generalized anxiety disorder. In: *Anxiety Disorders in Children and Adolescents*, March JS, ed. New York: Guilford

Silverman WK, La Greca AM, Wasserstein S (1995), What do children worry about? Worries and their relationship to anxiety. *Child Dev* 66:671–686

Spielberger C (1973), *Manual for the State-Trait Anxiety Inventory for Children.* Palo, Alto, CA: Consulting Psychologists Press

Strauss CG, Last CG, Hersen M, Kazdin AE (1988), Association between anxiety and depression in children and adolescents with anxiety disorders. *J Abnorm Child Psychol* 16:57–68

Vasey MW (1993), Development and cognition in childhood anxiety: the example of worry. In: *Advances in Clinical Child Psychology*, Ollendick TH, Prinz JR, eds. New York: Plenum

Vasey MW, Crnic KA, Carter WG (1994), Worry in childhood: a developmental perspective. *Cognit Ther Res* 18:529–549

Vasey MW, Daleiden EL (1994), Worry in children. In: *Worrying: Perspectives on Theory, Assessment, and Treatment*, Davey GCL, Tallis F, eds. Chichester, England: Wiley

Verhulst FC, Van der Ende J, Ferdinand RF, Kasius MC (1997), The prevalence of *DSM-III-R* diagnoses in a national sample of Dutch adolescents. *Arch Gen Psychiatry* 54:329–336

5

Children's Recollections of Traumatic and Nontraumatic Events

Robyn Fivush
Emory University

Whereas the social and emotional consequences of childhood trauma are well documented, less is known about how young children understand, represent, and remember traumatic experiences. A review of the literature indicates striking similarities in the development of young children's ability to recall traumatic and nontraumatic events. More specifically, events experienced before the age of about 18 months do not seem to be verbally accessible; events experienced between about 18 months and 2.5–3 years are reported in fragmentary fashion and seem to be prone to increasing error over time. From about age 3 years on, children can give reasonably coherent accounts of their past experiences and can retain these memories over long durations. The ways in which children are able to participate in conversations about events as they are occurring and in retrospect seems to play a critical role in their developing event memories. Implications of the empirical data for understanding trauma memory in childhood are discussed.

Statistics from both clinical and community samples indicate that one out of four individuals in our culture experience trauma as a child (Brewin, Andrews, & Gotlieb, 1993; Elliot, 1996). Given these epidemic proportions, surprisingly little developmental research has focused on how children understand traumatic experiences. Although there is considerable evidence that severe trauma often leads to socioemotional difficulties (Beitchmen, Zucker, Hood, daCosta, Ackman, & Cassavia, 1992; Briere & Elliot, 1994), the processes by which some children are able to cope with even quite severe trauma are mostly unknown. In this review, I will argue that a critical piece of this puzzle relies on the ways in which young children are able to make sense out of their traumatic experiences, and this process, in turn, relies on how children come to represent, interpret and remember trauma.

Address correspondence and reprint requests to: Robyn Fivush, Department of Psychology, Emory University, Atlanta, GA 30322; E-mail: psyrf@emory.edu

In the first section of this paper, I review the literature on the development of event memory. Although this research focuses on children's developing memories of everyday and/or positively valenced events, it provides a framework for understanding the development of memory in general, within which memory for trauma must be placed. I then turn to the clinical literature describing case studies of severely traumatized children. This research provides the richest information on memory of trauma, but obviously lacks certain experimental controls. In the third section, I turn to the small but growing body of experimental research on children's memories for stressful experiences. In trying to integrate findings across these three areas, several issues emerge as critical in the study of trauma memory, and I draw these out in the final section, along with recommendations for future research. Throughout, developmental differences are highlighted, and, in particular, the ways in which developing language skills interact with the development of event memory are discussed.

Before beginning, it is necessary to point out that, although I use the term "trauma" throughout this paper, there is no agreed upon definition of trauma or stress in the literature. The DSM-IV provides a definition of trauma that focuses on threat of death or injury, or the witnessing of death or severe injury (American Psychiatric Association, 1994), but this definition is only loosely used in the clinical literature and is not referred to at all in the experimental literature. Moreover, many of the "stressful" experiences studied in the experimental literature are quite mild (e.g., an inoculation, a broken bone) compared to the extreme stress children are too often exposed to in their everyday lives (e.g., witnessing the brutal murder of a parent, being repeatedly raped by one's father). Further, the DSM-IV definition highlights threat to one's physical integrity, rather than emotional integrity. As several theorists have argued, emotional betrayal may be at the core of traumatic experience (Freyd, 1996; Shay, 1996).

Related to this idea is the issue of the causal explanation of the traumatic experience. Whereas natural disasters may cause a great deal of stress, they are understood in very different ways than are events perpetrated by human agents, such as abuse, rape and torture. Natural disasters will not be as prone to lead the victim to self-blame, nor do natural disasters lead to shame, guilt, and secrecy to the same extent as traumas perpetrated by others. Even within traumas perpetrated by others, the relationship between the victim and the perpetrator plays an important role. Witnessing violence committed by strangers in the community may be different than witnessing domestic violence within one's own home (see Cicchetti, Toth, & Lynch, 1997, for a full theoretical discussion of how different types of traumas may lead to different child outcomes). While it is obviously beyond the scope of this review to provide a viable definition of either trauma or stress, this remains a thorny issue in the field and often makes it difficult to compare across the clinical and experimental literatures.

Finally, I want to emphasize that, because this review focuses on the ways in which children represent and recollect trauma, I am focusing on *verbal* recall of experience. Although experiences may leave many markers, including changes in behavior and personality, the ability to report an experience is the clearest evidence of a specific, conscious, accessible memory of an experience. This raises the difficult but intriguing question of the developing relations between language and memory. I will argue that language allows for a different kind of representation than is available without language and that trauma experienced during the preverbal period is therefore represented in fundamentally different ways than is trauma experienced as children become more verbally sophisticated (see Fivush, Pipe, Murachver, & Reese, 1997; Fivush & Haden, 1997; and Nelson, 1993, 1996, for full theoretical arguments). Moreover, I focus here on verbal recall in the absence of misleading or suggestive questioning. There is no doubt that children, and especially preschoolers, are susceptible to suggestion (see Ceci & Bruck, 1993, for a review), although the conditions under which children are more or less likely to succumb to suggestion are still somewhat controversial (e.g., Goodman & Bottoms, 1993; Goodman, Rudy, Bottoms, & Aman, 1990; Steward, 1993). However, there is general consensus in the field that free recall, even in quite young children, is very accurate. Again, because my focus here is on memory for trauma, and not on forensic interviewing, the issue of suggestibility is not addressed directly.

THE DEVELOPMENT OF EVENT MEMORY

Over the last two decades it has become abundantly clear that even quite young children have well-organized, accurate memories of their past experiences. In 1981 Nelson and Greundel published a seminal study examining preschooler's verbal reports about routine and familiar events, such as going grocery shopping or to McDonald's. In contrast to then prevailing views about the early memory system, children as young as 3 years of age were easily able to give coherent reports of these kinds of events. Although older children generally report more about familiar events than do younger children, younger children's reports are just as well organized as are older children's. More specifically, children's reports are generalized and temporally structured. From age 3 years on, children report what commonly occurs across specific experiences of an event (e.g., "You get a happy meal and you eat it and go home" when reporting going to McDonald's rather than specifying what happened during one specific experience at McDonald's) and children report events in the timeless present tense, indicating a general routine rather than a specific occurrence. Further, children virtually always report the component actions of events in their correct temporal order. The form of children's verbal reports conform to a "script" model, in which events are organized as spatially temporally organized frameworks that specify which actions are most and least likely to occur during any given experience of a recurring event (Schank & Abelson, 1977; see Fivush, 1997, and Nelson, 1986, for reviews of the developmental research).

That even quite young children report familiar events as scripts indicates that they are able to abstract commonalities across their experiences. But how well can young children recall one specific experience? Novel events, events that occur only once and remain relatively distinctive in a child's experience, seem to be quite well recalled by preschoolers. By age 3, children are able to give accurate detailed reports of specific events such as visits to museums, amusements parks, airplane rides, etc., that they have experienced only once (Fivush, Gray, & Fromhoff, 1987; Hamond & Fivush, 1990; Hudson & Nelson, 1986; Todd & Perlmutter, 1980; see Fivush, 1993, for a review). Most impressive, children's event memories endure over long periods of time. For example, children who went to Disney World when they were between the ages of 2.5 and 4.5 years were still able to give extremely accurate and detailed accounts of their experiences 18 months later (Hamond & Fivush). And Fivush and Schwarzmueller (1998) found that children interviewed about novel events at age 3 were still able to recall these events accurately 5 years later when they were 8 years old.

Obviously there is forgetting over time, and there is also some indication of increased error with increasing retention intervals (Hudson & Fivush, 1991; Poole & White, 1993), but the data indicate remarkable abilities to remember distinctive events across the preschool years.

However, a different pattern emerges when we examine a preschooler's ability to recall a single episode of a repeated event. As do adults (Graesser, Woll, Kowalski, & Smith, 1980), children have great difficulty recalling one time that they went to McDonald's, or what happened on a specific day at school (Fivush, 1984; Hudson & Nelson, 1983; see Hudson, Fivush, & Kuebli, 1992, for a review). Unless the particular episode deviates in a substantial way from what usually happens, children have great difficulty reporting a specific instance (Davidson & Hoe, 1993; Hudson, 1990a). Moreover, preschoolers seem to have more difficulty separating specific instances of a repeated event than do older children and adults. Three- and 4-year-old children are especially likely to confuse details among repeated experiences (Farrar & Goodman, 1990). In fact, after experiencing a particular event just a few times, 3- and 4-year-old children are quite likely to report only those actions that occur across occurrences and to omit any actions that occurred during only one occurrence of the event (Bauer & Fivush, 1992; Hudson, 1990a; Hudson & Nelson, 1983; Kuebli & Fivush, 1994).

These patterns indicate that young children may be better able to report the details of a single distinctive experience than a single episode of a repeated event. An event that remains distinctive in the child's experience also remains memorable; children are able to recall these kinds of events in surprising detail even after long delays. But when recalling a repeated event children's reports are more general, focusing on what usually happens. Details of specific experiences are omitted or confused among episodes. It is in this sense that memory is reconstructive; when children (and adults) have multiple experiences that are similar, the memory representation becomes more generalized, and what happened during any specific occurrence is reconstructed from this more general knowledge. Although these script reports are still accurate, in the sense that they describe what usually happens when this event occurs, they are lacking in detail, and may not be completely accurate to any one instance of the event.

Thus, by 3 years of age children are able to report verbally both repeated experiences and distinctive experiences, although these reports differ in their specificity. What about children younger than age 3 years? How do children report events as they are just becoming able to talk about the past, and, most intriguing, are children able to verbally recall events that occurred before they could talk at all?

The Development of Verbal Recall

Children begin to refer to past events linguistically at about 20 months of age (Eisenberg, 1985; Sachs, 1983), although their references are quite attenuated. Virtually all past references at this early age are to just completed or very recent events, and are most often in direct response to an adult's comments. Frequently, children at this age simply confirm or repeat an adult's recollection, or give a one word response to a direct question. Within a few months, children's abilities to refer to the past develop dramatically, and between the ages of about 2.5 and 3 years children become able to give reasonably coherent verbal accounts of past experiences (Eisenberg, 1985; Fivush et al., 1987). However, young children are still dependent on adults to help them structure their recall; they provide information in response to direct questions about what occurred. Over the course of the preschool years, children become less and less dependent on adults' questions to help them recall (see Pillemer & White, 1989, for a review). Essentially, children become more competent narrators about their past experiences, becoming better able to provide a full account of what occurred without specific prompts to do so. However, although younger children need more cues and prompts in order to provide information and even with prompts usually provide less information than older children, what young children do recall is quite accurate, at least in the absence of suggestive or misleading questions.

There is also evidence that children are able to recall events from this period of time even as they grow older. Fivush et al. (1987) demonstrated that children not quite 3 years old were able to report accurately details of experiences that occurred up to 10 months in the past, and Todd and Perlmutter (1980) report that 3-year-olds could accurately recall events that occurred well before their third birthday. However, there does seem to be a lower limit beyond which children do not seem able to recall verbally. Boyer, Barron, and Farrar (1994) found that children who experienced a specific play event when they were 20 months of age were able to reenact the event when they returned to the laboratory playroom more than a year later, but there was little evidence of verbal recall of the event. Similarly, Myers, Perris, and Speaker (1994) followed children over several years to assess their memory for a single experience that occurred at 10 or 14 months of age. Although there was some evidence of behavioral memory of the event, in that children who had experienced the original event showed more interest in the objects used than did children who had not experienced the event, there was virtually no evidence of explicit recall of the event, either through reenacting what had occurred or through verbal report.

In the most comprehensive study of this issue, Bauer and Wewerka (1997) examined children's memory for a series of specific action sequences learned when they were 20 months of age. Memory was assessed after a 1-year delay both behaviorally, in the form of reenactment of the sequences, and verbally. Overall, children recalled the sequences in action. But only those children who were linguistically more sophisticated at the time of the initial experience were subsequently able to recall the event verbally. The patterns suggest that the ability to recall an event verbally may depend on the ability to verbally describe the event at time of experience. Events which occur before sufficient verbal skills develop may not become available for verbal recall even as children develop the language skills necessary for describing that event. Further, 20 to 24 months of age seems to be the average age at which children are able to describe events as they are occurring, as well as the average age at which children begin to refer to very recent past events in language. Of course, given the wide individual differences in language skills, this average age must be interpreted with great caution. As Bauer and Wewerka have demonstrated, it is the language skills that predict subsequent verbal recall and not the age of the child.

It is important to point out that even well before the development of language skills, children are able to retain fairly explicit memories of specific events. Bauer and her colleagues (see Bauer, 1996, 1997, for reviews) have demonstrated that 12- to 13-month-olds can easily learn a sequence of actions performed on a set of novel objects, and, more impressive, when these children return to the laboratory many months later, they still show evidence of recalling the previously learned event sequences. However, these children do not seem to be able to describe these events verbally as they get older. Thus the argument is that there is something special about being able to describe an event verbally as it is occurring that allows for a different kind of representation, one that remains verbally accessible over time.

The Role of Language in Event Memory

What is it about being able to verbally describe an event as it is occurring, even in a limited way, that allows for later verbal recall? Memories of experienced events must be encoded in multiple modalities, including sensory and visual images, but these memories do not seem to be "translatable" into language if they occurred in the first 1.5–2 years of life. At the simplest level, it may be that events must be encoded linguistically in order to be recalled in language. But this only leads to the question of how language changes the memory representation. Following from Vygotskian theory (1978), language can be conceptualized as a tool that allows children to organize experiences in a new way. Most important, language allows children to share their memories with others in a way that is not possible outside of language. Once children have even rudimentary language skills to describe their experiences, they are able to communicate with others about those experiences, even it they can only provide bits and pieces of memory. Essentially, it is discussing experiences with others that leads to more coherently organized memories which remain accessible and verbalizable over time (see Fivush, Haden, & Reese, 1996; and Nelson, 1993, 1996, for related arguments).

Two lines of a evidence support this theoretical speculation. First, the way in which events are talked about as they are occurring has a profound influence on the way in which children subsequently recall that event. Tessler and Nelson (1994) found that when recalling a visit to a museum, or a photo-taking excursion, 4-year-old children recalled those aspects of the event that were mutually discussed by mother and child during the event. Information commented on only by the mother, or even only by the child, tended not to be recalled. So it is not simply what is noticed, or even what is labeled during the event that is critical; rather it is what is jointly constructed through conversations that the child recalls. Recent research by Haden, Didow, Ornstein, and Eckerman (1997) demonstrated the same effect with 2.5-year-olds.

When jointly discussing aspects of an event, the mother and child are essentially creating an extended narrative about what is happening, and this may be what helps organize the event for the child. In an innovative study, Pipe, Dean, Canning, and Murachver (1996) asked 5-year-old children to play "pirate." Half of the children experienced the event with full narration (e.g., "Now we are going to make the magic treasure map. First we have to mix these colors . . . ," etc.) and half the children experienced exactly the same event but with "empty" language (e.g., "Now we're going to do this"). Children's memories for the experience were assessed both through reenactment and verbal recall. Not surprisingly, children experiencing full narration during the event subsequently reported the experience more accurately, more fully, and in a more organized way than did children who experienced only empty language. But intriguingly these same effects held for reenactment of the event, suggesting that the presence of narration helped children form a more organized representation of the experience.

It is not just how an event is talked about as it is occurring that is important; the way in which an event is talked about in retrospect also has an effect. Certainly, young children need a great deal of support from adults, in the form of questions and cues, in order to verbally report their past experiences. The more structure an adult can provide for the young child, the more the child is able to report. Moreover, parents who discuss past events with their preschool children in more detailed and narratively coherent ways have children who come to report their experiences in more detailed and narratively coherent ways (Fivush, 1991; Haden, Haine, & Fivush, 1997; McCabe & Peterson, 1991; Reese, Haden, & Fivush, 1993), indicating that children are learning how to recall their experiences through participating in adult-guided conversations about past events. Interstingly, in the Pipe et al. (1996) study described above, some children experienced the event without narration, but after the experience, they were read a story about playing pirate that essentially provided the missing narrative. Children in this condition recalled the event in the same way as children who participated in the narrated event, indicating that children were able to use the subsequent narration to help them organize the experience after it occurred.[1]

As children engage in narratively organized conversations about events, both as they are occurring and in retrospect, they come to represent their experiences in more coherent ways. Young children seem to be at least somewhat dependent on adults to help them organize their experiences in these ways, but it is children's developing language skills that allows them to engage in these conversations in the first place. The argument, then, is not that language per se leads to a different kind of memory representation, but rather that language provides a new tool allowing children to engage with others in a new way, and this, in turn, allows children to take advantage of the structure provided by adults to help them understand and organize their experiences more coherently. Events that occur before children develop this ability may be remembered in behavior, but the ability to provide a verbal account of an event seems to depend on at least a rudimentary ability to engage in these kinds of conversations when the event is first experienced.

In summary, it is clear that preschool children have accurate, detailed memories of specific experiences and that they can retain these memories over extended periods of time. However, as events are repeated, the representations become more general and details are lost or confused among episodes. Two-year-olds also seem to have accurate memories of past experiences, although their verbal reports are much sparser than older children's. Most provocative, it seems that events occurring before the age of about 20 months may never become accessible for verbal report. As children develop the language skills for engaging in conversations about events as they are occurring and in retrospect, they seem to be developing new ways of representing events that allow for subsequent verbal recall. The question of central interest for this review, of course, is whether memory for traumatic experiences follows this same developmental trajectory.

---

[1]Note, however, that we also know from the large literature on suggestibility that post-event narration that misconstrues what actually happened may have detrimental effects of children's subsequent recall (see Ceci & Bruck, 1993, for a review). Thus the way in which the event is discussed in retrospect can either help or hinder children's event memory, depending on the information provided by the conversational partner.

CLINICAL STUDIES OF REAL-WORLD TRAUMA MEMORIES

Paradoxically, there are two "common-sense" beliefs about trauma memory. On the one hand, it is argued that trauma is so shocking that it is essentially "burned into the brain." Traumatic experiences are retained in all too vivid detail, never to be forgotten. On the other hand, it is also believed that trauma is so overwhelming that one cannot process it, or cope with it, and therefore, trauma memories are pushed aside (repressed, as it were) remaining difficult to bring to mind. Terr (1991) has integrated these folk theories of trauma, and has argued that there are two types of trauma, Type I and Type II. Type I trauma is a single shocking event. Although it may be extended in time, such as the Chowchilla kidnapping in which children were abducted on their school bus and buried alive overnight, the event is a single occurrence. In contrast, Type II trauma is repeated, or chronic traumatic experiences, such as multiple instances of physical or sexual abuse occurring over a period of weeks or years. Terr argues that Type I trauma leads to vivid, accurate memory, whereas Type II trauma leads to patchy or even non-existent memories. The reasoning is that in order to cope with repeated trauma, children begin to dissociate, or distance themselves from the experience as it is occurring. Dissociation during the experience leads to poorer encoding, and thus poorer memory. But notice that this argument implies that the memories are not "recoverable" as information never initially encoded obviously cannot be retrieved.

Terr brings two types of evidence to bear on this theory, First, the clinical literature is rife with examples of young children displaying vivid recall of single traumatic experiences (which will be discussed in more detail below). Second, there has been an overwhelming number of individuals who, as adults, claim to recall histories of repeated childhood sexual abuse that they had previously repressed or forgotten. The problem with this argument is twofold: first, it is not clear how to interpret "recovered" memories (see recent reviews by Conway, 1997, and Pezdek & Banks, 1996). Second, and more germane to this paper, there is no evidence that children themselves are unable to recall repeated experiences of trauma, as Terr's theory suggests. However, it must also be noted that little research has examined children's memories of repeated stressful experiences. Rather, the clinical literature has focused on children's memories of single instances of trauma.

Virtually all the case studies presented indicate that children, at least those age 3 or older at time of experience, are able to recall a single traumatic experience in vivid detail (Pynoos & Nader, 1989; Malmquist, 1986; Terr, 1983, 1988; see Reviere, 1996, for a review). In a seminal study, Terr (1988) described 20 case studies of children between the ages of 1 and 5 years when they experienced a traumatic event, ranging from a dog bite to an evisceration. All children showed evidence of remembering the trauma in their behaviors, such as expressing specific fears, but children below the age of about 18 months when the trauma occurred were unable to express any verbal memory. Children between 18 and about 28 to 36 months at time of trauma could subsequently give fragmented, "spotty" verbal accounts; only those children older than about 2.5–3 years at time of experience were able to give a complete verbal account of the trauma. This pattern suggests that children's verbal ability at the time of experience is a critical factor in their subsequent ability to recall the experience verbally.

This conclusion is complicated somewhat by case studies reported by Hewitt (1994) and Gaensbauer (1995). Hewitt describes one young girl who experienced a single incident of sexual abuse when she was 2 years 7 months but did not disclose it until she was 4 years old and was then able to describe it in detail. Because the incident was not known to the parents, the child had never been asked to recall this experience before the spontaneous disclosure; given the child's age, it is quite likely that she would have been able to report it verbally even at time of occurrence. What is remarkable is that she was able to retain this memory over this period of time even though she had never discussed it with anyone. The second case study reported by Hewitt is more surprising. This child was sexually abused by her grandfather when she was 2 years 1 month of age. At 2 years 3 months she was referred for therapy and, although she could talk about other past experiences, was unresponsive when questioned about the abuse. When she was 6 years old, she began to display overly aggressive behavior and when referred back for therapy now gave a verbal account of her earlier sexual abuse. However, two things need to be considered in evaluating this case description. First, this child was obviously quite verbal as she was able to describe other past experiences when in therapy at 2 years 3 months, so her lack of verbal report of the abuse experience may have been due to reluctance rather than inability to express it verbally. Second, the parents brought her to therapy because they knew she had been abused, and it is quite possible that they spoke with her about this experience in the intervening years, which obviously makes interpretation of the later verbal report difficult.

The most compelling evidence of a preverbal experience being verbally reported later in development is a case study described by Gaensbauer (1995). This child witnessed her mother being blown to pieces by a letter bomb when she was 12 months of age. When she was 3 years old she described isolated details of what she had seen, albeit in a fragmentary way, to her foster mother. Critically, her foster mother did not know any of these details. Thus it seems that some aspects of preverbal experiences may become accessible for verbal recall, but this translation seems limited to describing unconnected bits and pieces of sensory images. While this case study provides provocative data, the bulk of the evidence from the clinical literature suggests that experiences occurring before the age of about 18 months do not become accessible for verbal recall. Experiences between about 18 months and 2.5–3 years can be verbally recalled but this recall is fragmentary. Children older than 2.5–3 years at time of experience remain able to report their traumatic experience in a reasonably coherent narrative over extended periods of time. Intriguingly, this is the same developmental pattern that emerges from children's memories of everyday events discussed earlier.

It is important to stress that I am not arguing that trauma memories (or any memories for that matter) are totally accurate. All memory is at least partly reconstructive and all memories seem to contain at least some error. However, just because a memory report is partly reconstructed from general knowledge does not mean that it is in error; general event schemas are so powerful exactly because they allow us to remember and to predict so accurately. We use our general knowledge about the world to reconstruct what must have happened during this one experience, either by tagging this experience as typical or atypical. That is, some experiences conform to the way things "usually" happen and thus are remembered in this way, whereas other experiences are remembered as distinct in particular ways, and it is these distinctive aspects that make the specific event particularly memorable.

Either way, the specific event may be recalled quite well as a conglomeration of general and specific event knowledge. Indeed, autobiographical memories are usually highly accurate both in adults (Brewer, 1988; Conway, 1995; Neisser et al., 1996; Wagenaar & Groeneweg, 1990) and children (see Fivush, 1993, for a review).

As are more mundane memories, trauma memories are not completely accurate either. For example Pynoos and Nader (1989) examined children's memories of a sniper attack at their school and found that children seriously misjudged where they were when the attack began. Children close to the line of fire placed themselves further away, while children further away tended to place themselves closer. Pynoos and Nader interpret this as the children's need to place themselves spatially in a place that matched their emotional experience—those too close needed to distance themselves whereas those far away needed to express how close to danger they felt. Similarly, Terr (1983) reports that children kidnapped from their school bus and buried alive overnight were able to recall much of the event in vivid detail 4 years later, but there was evidence of error as well. Some children were confused about the chronology of certain events of the day, and one child misremembered one of the kidnappers as being black, when in reality both kidnappers were white. In reviewing the clinical literature, Pynoos, Steinberg, and Aronson (1997) further argue that children may sometimes include fantasies about resolution in their reports of trauma, which may be a useful coping strategy but obviously compromises the memory report.

The fact that trauma memories do contain some error indicates that traumatic experiences are not "burned into the brain," but that they follow some of the same processes that have been documented for more everyday kinds of memories. The question is whether memories for traumatic and/or stressful events are more or less accurate than non-stressful experiences. From the clinical literature, it is difficult to answer this question, both because children's memories of traumatic experiences are not directly compared to their memories for nontraumatic experiences and because the actual event being recalled is often unknown to the interviewer. More experimentally controlled studies allow a more systematic answer to this question.

EXPERIMENTAL STUDIES OF MEMORY FOR STRESSFUL EVENTS

Within the adult literature, there has been substantial investigation of the role of arousal on memory (see Christianson, 1992, for a review). Following from the Yerkes–Dodson law, it was hypothesized that moderate levels of arousal would lead to increased attention and therefore better memory than low levels of arousal. However, as arousal increased to high levels, it would disrupt the system, leading to poorer attention and encoding and thus poorer memory. Hence, an inverted U-shaped function was predicted. Although some research supported such a memory function, the majority of research suggests that increased arousal leads to increased memorability. But this conclusion must be taken with great caution. Research with adults has focused on participants' memories for video displays of emotionally disturbing events, such as car crashes or scenes from horror movies, viewed in a laboratory setting. Although these presentations may lead to increased levels of arousal, they are certainly not commensurate with the level of arousal that would be experienced in a truly traumatic event. Thus it is possible that at extreme levels of arousal, memory would decline.

Research with children has taken a more ecologically valid form. Early investigations manipulated children's arousal in experimental situations. For example, Peters (1991) had children witness a stranger remove a money box from a laboratory playroom in which the child was waiting. Half of the children were led to believe the stranger was a burglar, while half were led to believe the stranger had permission to take the box. All children were then asked to identify the stranger from a lineup. Children believing the stranger had permission performed better than children believing the stranger was a burglar, suggesting that stress interferes with children's memory. However, it must be emphasized that these studies focused exclusively on face recognition of strangers, and did not assess any other aspects of children's memories, such as the actions and objects comprising the event. In general, children, especially young children, are not very good at recognizing faces of strangers (see Davies, 1993, for an overview). Moreover, it is not clear that witnessing a burglary under these conditions is comparable to the kinds of real world traumatic events to which children are exposed.

More recently, several investigators have taken advantage of naturally occurring stressful experiences to examine children's memories of traumatic events. Most often, this research examines painful and stressful medical procedures. Goodman and her colleagues (Goodman, Hirschman, Hepps, & Rudy, 1991; Goodman et al., 1990) pioneered this type of research, examining young children's memories for inoculations, and for voiding cystourethrograms (VCUGs), an extremely stressful medical procedure involving catheritization, filling the bladder with fluid and voiding while still on the examination table. Overall, the results of these studies indicate highly accurate recall of these procedures. However, there are developmental and individual differences. Preschoolers, while largely accurate, are less accurate than school-aged children. Further, some children are more accurate than their same-age peers. Intriguingly, those children whose parents report talking with them about the VCUG procedure after its occurrence were more accurate than children whose parents avoided discussion of the procedure.

Research by Ornstein and his colleagues (Ornstein, 1995; Ornstein, Gordon, & Laurus, 1992) support these findings. They compared children's reports of a well-doctor visit with their reports of a VCUG experience, and found that children were able to provide a more exhaustive and more accurate report of the VCUG than of a well-doctor visit. Moreover, children maintained a high level of recall for the VCUG experience over several months, whereas memory for the well-doctor visit showed a sharper decline in amount of recall and a higher increase in error over time. Again, there were developmental and individual differences, with older children generally providing more detail; although preschoolers provided less information overall than older children, what they did recall was just as accurate. In addition, children who experienced the VCUG with a technician who explained the procedure to them as it was occurring recalled more information than did children who experienced the event with a technician who did not explain the procedure (Principe, 1996). Thus it seems that children's memories of a stressful medical procedure is quite good, and especially so if adults talk with them about what occurred.

The developmental differences are not surprising, in that preschoolers generally recall less than do school age children (Nelson, 1986; Pressley & Schneider, 1986). However, it does seem that preschoolers recall more about stressful events than about non-stressful events. In addition to the Ornstein finding cited above, Bahrick, Parker, Merritt and Fivush (in press) assessed preschooler's memories for Hurricane Andrew, a devastating storm during which children were in their homes while wind and rain caused extensive damage all around them. Three and 4-year-old children provided a surprising amount of information about their experience, averaging over 100 propositions. Because a comparable interview protocol and coding scheme was used, this can be compared to children's memories of a family trip to Disney World (Hamond & Fivush, 1990), in which preschoolers reported approximately 40 propositions. Interestingly, children who weathered the storm under moderate stress (trees falling, windows breaking, water leaking into the house) recalled more information than children experiencing high stress (roofs caving in, flying glass, etc.). Although children experiencing high stress seemed to show less recall than children experiencing moderate stress, they still recalled substantially more than children seem to report about non-stressful experiences.

What of children younger than 3 years? We have already seen from the research on general event memory, as well as from the clinical descriptions of trauma memories, children 3 years and older are able to organize and retain personal experiences, but younger children may have more difficulty remembering and verbally reporting events. Few studies have systematically investigated stressful experiences in children under the age of 3 years. In the first study of its kind, Howe, Courage, and Peterson (1994) assessed children's memories for emergency room experiences for injuries such as lacerations requiring sutures and severe burns. Children ranging in age from 18 months to 5 years were interviewed at home within a few days of their experience and again 6 months later. There was a general increase in ability to report information with age, and the youngest children in particular had great difficulty verbalizing their experiences. More specifically, children younger than 30 months at time of experience recalled little at either interview. Children 30 months and older were able to report their experiences at time of occurrence and could still recall them in as much detail after 6 months. Similar findings are reported by Baker–Ward and Burgwyn–Bailer (1998), who found that 3- to 7-year-old children experiencing facial lacerations were able to recall their experiences accurately and in as much detail after a 1 year delay.

Following up on this methodology, Peterson and Bell (1996) asked 2-, 3-, 4-, and 5-year-old children to recall injuries and emergency room treatments both immediately and 6 months later. From age 3 years on, children were able to report their experiences accurately and in detail, although older children recalled more than did younger children. Most impressive, there was little decline in memory over the 6 month delay. But 2-year-olds showed a different pattern. Although they were able to recall bits and pieces immediately, their reports included more error than did the older children's (whose reports were virtually error-free). Moreover, over time, these very young children showed increasing error in their verbal reports, suggesting that these early fragmentary memories may be especially prone to reconstructive error over time.

More recently, Peterson and Rideout (1997) have reported on the developmental course of trauma memories in even younger children. Children experiencing injuries and emergency room treatments when they were between 12 and 33 months were studied. Children younger than 18 months at time of injury were unable to report their experiences immediately, and were still unable to report their experiences verbally 18 months after the event. Children between 20 and 25 months also could not give a verbal report at time of experience but some of these children were able to recall their experiences 2 years later, although there was a great deal of error. Children older than 27 months displayed impressive recall immediately and 2 years later. This pattern is similar to Terr's description of the development of trauma memories based on clinical case studies. Moreover, although language ability was not directly assessed, Peterson and Rideout note that it appears that it is the child's ability to verbalize the event at the time of occurrence that is the critical factor in long term verbal memory, not the age per se, a finding concordant with Bauer and Werwerka's (1997) conclusions discussed earlier.

RECOLLECTING TRAUMA: SUMMARY AND IMPLICATIONS

Impressively, the experimental and clinical literatures converge on a similar developmental description of verbal memory. Whether reporting everyday events, such as going to McDonald's, distinctive personal experiences, such as a trip to Disney World, a stressful experience, such as getting sutures, or a severely traumatic event, such as sexual abuse, by the age of 3 years children are able to give detailed accurate accounts of what occurred. Although few studies have directly compared memories for traumatic experiences with memories for nontraumatic experiences, what little evidence exists seems to suggest that memories of trauma are at least as detailed if not more so than memories of more mundane experiences. However, several factors need to be integrated with this overall conclusion.

First, although not discussed in this paper, a significant literature on suggestibility indicates that preschoolers are more suggestible than older children (Ceci & Bruck, 1993; Ceci, Toglia, & Ross, 1987). Thus, although in the absence of misleading and coercive questions, preschoolers are able to maintain accurate memories of past experiences over long periods of time, when exposed to suggestive and especially coercive questioning, preschoolers begin to display substantially more error in their reports than do older children. The conditions under which suggestive questioning may be particularly harmful are still under debate. Children seem to be less suggestible about actions performed by themselves or on their own bodies than about actions performed by other people (Goodman et al., 1990; Rudy & Goodman, 1991; Steward, 1993). Children also seem to be less suggestible under interviewing conditions in which they are explicitly told that the interviewer may not know what happened, and that they can answer "I don't know" when appropriate (see Goodman & Bottoms, 1993, for an overview). On the other hand, children seem to be more susceptible to suggestion when misinformation is presented repeatedly across several interviews (Leichtman & Ceci, 1995). However, simply asking a child to recall an event over and over, in the absence of misleading information does not compromise accuracy of recall (Fivush & Schwarzmueller, 1995; Poole & White, 1995), although yes/no questions lead to extremely high levels of inaccuracy, especially among very young children (Peterson & Rideout, 1997; Schwarzmueller, 1997). Clearly, when evaluating children's memories, especially in a forensic situation, the extent and type of interviewing that has occurred must be considered in determining the credibility of the report.

Second, although 3-year-olds are quite accurate in what they report, their recall is considerably sparser than older children's. Moreover they need more help from adults, in the form of prompts and cues in order to recall than do older children. Here, we need to make a distinction between accuracy of recall and exhaustiveness of recall. Older children recall much more of the event, and especially more details about the event than do younger children; thus older children's recall is more exhaustive than is younger children's. But although more limited in amount, what young children do recall is just as accurate as older children's recall. The fact that young children need more encouragement from adults to produce their recall also raises the question of how to best interview young children in forensic situations. Clearly, we need to strike a balance between providing prompts while at the same time not providing any misinformation. Some promising approaches to forensic interviewing of young children have been discussed in the literature (Goodman & Bottoms, 1993), but this is obviously an area in which a great deal more research is needed.

Third, there are substantial individual differences in children's abilities to report their past experiences.[2] Certainly some of the differences early in development are related to language ability. Because children progress through the language learning years at different rates, it follows that their ability to describe their past experiences will differ as well (e.g., Eisenberg, 1985). There are also individual differences in basic memory skills that play a role (e.g., Pressley & Schneider, 1986). In addition to specific individual differences, there are also gender and cultural differences in autobiographical reports. In general, girls seem to have more detailed and more coherent autobiographical memories than do boys (Fivush, 1998; Haden et al., 1997; Reese, Haden, & Fivush, 1996). And Caucasian children seem to have more elaborated, detailed autobiographical narratives than Asian children (Leichtman, 1997). There is also some indication that African American males incorporate more fantasy elements in their autobiographical narratives than do African American girls or Caucasian children of either gender (Sperry, 1991). Most of these differences can be attributed to differences in the ways in which children are socialized to discuss their past experiences (Fivush, in press; Mullen, 1994; Nelson, 1993), a point returned to below. Implications of these differences for forensic interviewing are clear; the social and cultural guidelines for when and how to talk about one's personal past critically influences the ways in which children will report their past experiences, and must be considered both in interviewing young children and in evaluating the credibility of their reports.

Finally, we need to consider the issue of recalling a single versus a repeated experience. Within the literature on event memory, it is very clear that memories of repeated experiences are quite different than memories of single, distinctive events. With increasing experience with an event, children's reports become more general and less detailed. Extrapolating to trauma memories, it would seem that repeated trauma would come to be represented in a script-like format, focusing on commonalties across experiences with a concomitant loss of detail. Provocatively, this prediction is the same as Terr's (1991) prediction about Type II trauma discussed earlier, although the postulated mechanisms are quite different. For Terr, poor memory of repeated trauma is due to dissociation, whereas from script theory, poor memory for repeated trauma would be due to the development of a more generalized schema for the event.

---

[2]Just as there are individual differences in the accuracy and detail of children's autobiographical accounts, there are also individual differences in susceptibility to suggestion. Relations between accuracy and exhaustiveness of the recall and susceptibility to suggestion are still being determined.

Only one study has examined children's reports of a repeated traumatic experience. Howard, Osborne, and Baker–Ward (1997) asked children who had undergone chemotherapy to recall their experiences two years after treatment ended. Children were extremely accurate in reporting their chemotherapy experiences. However, Howard et al. did not differentiate whether children were recalling a specific instance or whether they were recalling what usually occurred. As discussed earlier, script reports are quite accurate to what typically happens, but the details of specific instances can be lost or confused. Still, this study suggests that Terr's theory may not be completely correct, as children did not display poor memory of a repeated trauma. Clearly, this is a critical issue for future research. Because many traumatized children experience repeated instances of trauma, particularly if the trauma is physical or sexual abuse, we must gather more data on the ways in which children come to represent and report these events with increasing experience.

Perhaps most important are the qualitative changes we see in memory under the age of 3 years. Although 2-year-olds are able to verbally report bits and pieces of their past experiences, they have difficulty giving a coherent account of what occurred. More specifically, events experienced below the age of about 18 months may never become accessible for verbal report, although they may continue to influence behavior. Children may be able to retain fairly explicit nonverbal memories of a specific experience; placed back in the original context or given the specific objects, even very young children may be able to re-enact an event. But these early memories are not translated into language as the child's language skills mature. Moreover, without language, it may not be possible to access or report experiences in the absence of physical cues about the event. That is, it is not clear how a memory could be expressed nonverbally with none of the objects from the original event available in the environment.

However, this does not necessarily mean that later memories, memories of events experienced after 18 months, are represented linguistically. Rather, events are experienced in multiple modalities and may remain accessible in multiple modalities over time. Events that cannot be verbally accessed may still be recalled in action, in images and in sensory characteristics. Language adds yet another dimension to the memory representation. But it is a critical dimension in that once children are able to use language as a modality for representing events, they also become capable of sharing their experiences with others in ways that are not possible outside of language. Children can now refer to past events in conversation with parents and caregivers, and this process of reminiscing fundamentally changes the way in which memories can be understood and represented. More specifically, through discussing events with others, both as they are occurring and in retrospect, children become able to organize events in more coherent ways. Through the narrative conventions of describing the past, children come to organize past experiences in more temporally extended and integrated ways. Moreover, narrative forms provide perspective and interpretation of events (Bruner, 1987; Fivush & Haden, 1997; Labov, 1982). Through narrating our experiences, we come to understand what these experiences mean in relation to other events in our lives, and begin to form a narratively organized life history. This narrative history, in turn, contributes to the developing sense of self in time. As children develop the skills for narrating their past, they are also developing an understanding that their past is a part of themselves.

From this perspective, the ability to discuss past experiences with others is a critical component of the developing ability to recall events to oneself. Indeed, there is growing evidence that children's autobiographical and narrative skills develop in social interaction (Engel, 1986; Haden, et al., 1997; Hudson, 1990b; Fivush, 1991; McCabe & Peterson, 1991; Nelson, 1993; Peterson, 1990; Reese, et al., 1993). In general, children who engage in rich, embellished reminiscing with their caregivers come to discuss their past experiences in more coherent and detailed ways.

With respect to trauma memories, children experiencing stressful medical procedures under conditions in which their parents or medical caregivers discuss the events with them recall the event more accurately than children who do not discuss these events with others. Intriguingly, these children also seem to display less stress about the experience, suggesting that talking about traumatic experiences may help children to understand and cope with them. Yet one of the critical aspects of experiencing trauma is the issue of silence.

THE SILENCING OF TRAUMA

Traumatized individuals often report that they are discouraged by others to discuss their experiences. For example, Shay (1996) describes the experience of Vietnam veterans, who returned with horrendous memories they felt a need to share with others and being silenced by family and friends who could not bear to hear what they had to say. Part of this may stem from a folk belief that if we simply do not talk about or think about bad experiences, they will go away. Parents, in particular, may think that if they don't talk about traumatic experiences with their young children, then their children will simply forget what happened. What are the implications of the silencing of trauma for children's ultimate understanding of these kinds of experiences?

The research reviewed in this paper indicates that young children are at least partly dependent on an adult's guidance to organize their experiences. Children experiencing events in the absence of adult provided narration have a less organized and less accurate representation of what occurred. Because these memories are more fragmented, it seems quite likely that it will be more difficult for children to make sense of them and to integrate them with other events in their lives. Notably, within the clinical literature, there is widespread agreement that treatment for traumatized individuals involves constructing a coherent account of what occurred (Foa, Molnar, & Cashman, 1995; Harber & Pennebaker, 1992). Further, there is now a substantial body of empirical support for the idea that creating a coherent account of stressful and traumatic experiences has long term effects on both emotional and physical well-being (see Pennebaker, 1997, for a review). Past event narratives provide a way of understanding and interpreting events. For traumatic experiences, the narrative form may allow children to place these experiences in an appropriate context, to help them cope with these experiences, and ultimately to provide some closure on the event. In the absence of discussing these experiences with others, children may have particular difficulty understanding and coping with trauma. This argument is obviously quite speculative, although as noted there are a few indications in the research findings that provide preliminary support for this position.

If this argument holds, then it has particular implications for memories of abuse, one of the most wide spread traumas experienced by children. Abusive parents do not provide a coherent verbal framework for understanding what is happening. If anything, abusive parents tend to provide a misleading framework for the child (e.g., in physical abuse, labeling it punishment for misbehavior, or in sexual abuse, calling it a special game). Without the opportunity to discuss these experiences with others, abused children may be unable to integrate their traumatic experiences into their developing understanding of other experiences in the world and how these experiences are related to the self. This would most likely produce a fragmentary and disorganized representation of experience. Notice that this description of event representation is related to aspects of clinical descriptions of dissociation in abused children. Thus in the absence of an organized framework for understanding experience, children will display what appears to be dissociative behaviors—an inability to organize experiences, difficulty integrating experience with self-concept, and a general lack of verbal memories of personally experienced events. Clearly, I am not arguing that the consequences of abuse stem solely from the disruption of memory processing, but I would argue that this is an important part of what is happening developmentally for these children.

CONCLUSIONS

The ability to organize and understand our experiences is a basic part of how we make sense of our world. From a very early age, children are actively constructing how things happen, and forming memories of the events of their lives. From approximately age 3 years on, children's event memories seem qualitatively similar across development. Children are able to form and retain accurate, organized, verbally accessible memories of both traumatic and nontraumatic events. Between the ages of about 2 and 3 years, children are able to give fragmentary verbal reports of their experiences, but these reports do not seem as well organized or as accurate as older children's. Moreover, these very early memories may be more prone to increasing error over time than later memories. Below the age of about 18–20 months, children seem unable to verbally report their experiences at all, and they do not seem to be able to construct a verbal report of these very early experiences as their language skills develop. Importantly, the developmental patterns seem quite similar for traumatic and nontraumatic experiences.

The research on traumatic memories conducted thus far, however, has focused on public events, events which may be painful or stressful, but do not involve secrecy or shame. But many traumas experienced by young children are silenced. The ability to discuss past events with others, and to verbally rehearse these events to oneself may play an instrumental role on children's developing abilities to understand and interpret their experiences. Placing past events in the context of one's ongoing life history allows one to integrate past experiences into a cohesive sense of how the world works and who one is. Children experiencing traumatic experiences who are not given the opportunity to discuss these events with others may not be able to integrate these negative experiences, and thus may be left with recurring fragments of memory that are associated with highly negative affect that cannot be resolved. Moreover, in the absence of adult guidance, young children may not be able to provide themselves with an appropriate framework for understanding traumatic experiences and thus remain unable to understand what has happened to them. Thus, although preschool children seem to recall traumatic and non-traumatic events quite well, a critical issue which is only beginning to be addressed in the research literature is the role of language and silence in children's developing memories of events in general, and trauma in particular. As

Binjamin Wilkomirski (1996) writes in his memoirs of his experiences as a child survivor of the Nazi concentration camps,

> I grew up and became an adult in a time and in a society that didn't want to listen, or perhaps was incapable of listening. "Children have no memories, children forget quickly, you must forget it all, it was just a bad dream." These were the words, endlessly repeated, that were used on me from my school days to erase my past and make me keep quiet . . . I wrote these fragments of memory to explore both myself and my earliest childhood; it may also have been an attempt to set myself free. (pp. 153–155)

As feminist theorists have pointed out, giving voice to events lends them power and credibility (Belenky, Clinchy, Goldberger, & Tarule, 1986; Gilligan, 1982). In contrast, silencing events deprives them of reality and meaningfulness. We must understand children's developing memories of trauma both from what they tell us and from what they cannot say.

REFERENCES

American Psychiatric Association. (1994). *Diagnostic and statistical manual of mental disorders* (4th ed.). Washington, DC: Author

Bahrick, L., Parker, J., Merritt, K., & Fivush, R. (in press). Children's memory for Hurricane Andrew. *Journal of Experimental Psychology: Applied.*

Baker–Ward, L., & Burgwyn–Bailer, E. (1998). One-year follow-up of children interviewed regarding treatment of facial lacerations. Manuscript in preparation.

Bauer, P. (1996). Recalling past events: From infancy to early childhood. *Annals of Child Development, 11,* 25–71.

Bauer, P. (1997). Development of memory in early childhood. In N. Cowan (Ed.), *The development of memory in childhood* (pp. 83–112). Sussex: Psychology Press.

Bauer, P., & Fivush, R. (1992). Constructing event representations: Building on a foundation of variation and enabling relations. *Cognitive Development, 7,* 381–401.

Bauer, P., & Wewerka, S. (1997). Saying is revealing: Verbal expression of event memory in the transition from infancy to early childhood. In P. van den Broek, P. J. Bauer, & T. Bourg (Eds.), *Developmental spans in event comprehension and representation: Bridging fictional and actual events* (pp. 139–168). Hillsdale, NJ: Erlbaum.

Beitchmen, J., Zucker, K., Hood, J., daCosta, G., Ackman, D., & Cassavia, E. (1992). A review of the long term effects of child sexual abuse. *Child Abuse and Neglect, 16,* 101–118.

Belenky, M. F., Clinchy, B. M., Goldberger, N. R., & Tarule, J. M. (1986). *Women's ways of knowing: The development of self, voice and mind.* New York: Basic Books.

Boyer, M. E., Barron, K. L., & Farrar, M. J. (1994). Three-year-olds remember a novel event from 20 months: Evidence for long-term memory in children? *Memory, 2,* 417–446.

Brewin, C., Andrews, B., & Gotlieb, I. (1993). Psychopathology and early experience: A reappraisal of retrospective reports. *Psychological Bulletin, 113,* 82–98.

Brewer, W. (1988). Memory for randomly sampled autobiographical events. In U. Neisser & E. Winograd (Eds.), *Remembering reconsidered: Ecological and traditional approaches to the study of memory* (pp. 21–90). New York: Cambridge University Press.

Briere, J., & Elliot, D. M. (1994). Immediate and long-term impacts of child sexual abuse. *The Future of Children, 4*, 54–69.

Bruner, J. (1987). Life as narrative. *Social Research, 54*, 11–32.

Ceci, S. J., & Bruck, M. (1993). Suggestibility of the child witness: A historical review and synthesis. *Psychological Bulletin, 113*, 403–439.

Ceci, S. J., Toglia, M. P., & Ross, D. F. (1987). *Children's eyewitness memory.* New York: Springer–Verlag.

Christianson, S. A. (1992). Emotional stress and eyewitness memory: A critical review. *Psychological Bulletin, 112*, 284–309.

Cicchetti, D., Toth, S. L., & Lynch, M. (1997). Child maltreatment as an illustration of the effects of war on development. In D. Cicchetti & S. L. Toth (Eds.), *Rochester Symposium on Developmental Psychopathology: Vol. VIII. Developmental perspectives on trauma* (pp. 227–262). Rochester, NY: University of Rochester Press.

Conway, M. (1995). *Flashbulb memories.* Hillsdale, NJ: Erlbaum.

Conway, M. (Ed.). (1997). *Recovered memories and false memories.* Oxford: Oxford University Press.

Davidson, D., & Hoe, S. (1993). Children's recall and recognition memory for typical and atypical actions in script-based stories. *Journal of Experimental Child Psychology, 55*, 104–126.

Davies, G. (1993). Children's memory for other people: An integrative review. In C. A. Nelson (Ed.), *Minnesota Symposium on Child Psychology: Memory and affect in development* (Vol. 26, pp. 123–158). Hillsdale, NJ: Erlbaum.

Eisenberg, A. (1985). Learning to describe past experience in conversation. *Discourse Processes, 8*, 177–204.

Elliot, D. (1996). Reports of childhood trauma. Paper presented at The NATO Conference on Recollections of Trauma, Port de Bourgeney, France.

Engel, S. (1986). *Learning to reminisce: A developmental study of how young children talk about the past.* Unpublished doctoral dissertation, City University of New York.

Farrar, M. J., & Goodman, G. S. (1990). Developmental differences in the relation between scripts and episodic memory: Do they exist? In R. Fivush, & J. Hudson (Eds.), *Knowing and remembering in young children* (pp. 30–64). Cambridge: Cambridge University Press.

Fivush, R. (1984). Learning about school: The development of kindergartners' school scripts. *Child Development, 55*, 1697–1709.

Fivush, R. (1991). The social construction of personal narratives, *Merrill–Palmer Quarterly, 37*, 59–82.

Fivush, R. (1993). Developmental perspectives on autobiographical recall. In G. S. Goodman & B. L. Bottoms (Eds.), *Child victims, child witnesses: Understanding and improving testimony* (pp. 1–24). New York: Guilford.

Fivush, R. (1997). Event memory in childhood. In N. Cowan (Ed.), *The development of memory in childhood* (pp. 139–162). Sussex: Psychology Press.

Fivush, R. (1998). Gendered narratives: Elaboration, structure and emotion in parent-child reminscing across the preschool years. In C. P. Thompson, D. J. Herrmann, D. Bruce, J. D. Read, D. G. Payne, & M. P. Toglia (Eds.), *Autobiographical memory: Theoretical and applied perspectives* (pp. 79–104). Hillsdale, NJ: Erlbaum.

Fivush, R., Gray, J. T., & Fromhoff, F. A. (1987). Two year olds' talk about the past. *Cognitive Development, 2,* 393–409.

Fivush, R., & Haden, C. (1997). Narrating and representing experience: Preschoolers developing autobiographical recounts. In P. van den Broek, P. A. Bauer, & T. Bourg (Eds.), *Developmental spans in event comprehension and representation: Bridging fictional and actual events* (pp. 169–198). Hillsdale, NJ: Erlbaum.

Fivush, R., Haden, C., & Reese, E. (1996). Remembering, recounting and reminiscing: The development of autobiographical memory in social context. In D. Rubin (Ed.), *Reconstructing our past: An overview of autobiographical memory* (pp. 341–359). New York: Cambridge University Press.

Fivush, R., Pipe, M.-E., Murachver, T., & Reese, E. (1997). Events spoken and unspoken: Implications of language and memory development for the recovered memory debate. In M. Conway (Ed.), *True and false memories* (pp. 34–62). Oxford University Press.

Fivush, R., & Schwarzmueller, A. (1995). Say it once again: Effects of repeated questions on children's event recall. *Journal of Traumatic Stress, 8,* 555–580.

Fivush, R., & Schwarzmueller, A. (1998). Children remember childhood: Implications for childhood amnesia. *Applied Cognitive Psychology, 12,* 455–473.

Foa, E. B., Molnar, C., & Cashman, L. (1995). Change in rape narratives during exposure therapy for posttraumatic stress disorder. *Journal of Traumatic Stress, 8,* 675–690.

Freyd, J. (1996). *Betrayal trauma: The logic of forgetting childhood abuse.* Cambridge, MA: Harvard University Press.

Gaensbauer, T. J. (1995). Trauma in the preverbal period: Symptoms, memories, and developmental impact. *Psychoanalytic study of the child, 49,* 412–433.

Gilligan, C. (1982). *In a different voice: Psychological theory and women's development.* Cambridge, MA: Harvard University Press.

Goodman, G., & Bottoms, B. (1993). *Child victims, child witnesses: Understanding and improving testimony.* New York: Guilford Press.

Goodman, G. S., Hirschman, J. E., Hepps, D., & Rudy, L. (1991). Children's memory for stressful events. *Merrill Palmer Quarterly, 37,* 109–158.

Goodman, G. S., Rudy, L., Bottoms, B. L., & Aman, C. (1990). Children's concerns and memory: Issues of ecological validity in the study of children's eyewitness testimony. In R. Fivush & J. A. Hudson (Eds.), *Knowing and remembering in young children* (pp. 249–284). New York: Cambridge University Press.

Graesser, A. C., Woll, S. B., Kowalski, D. J., & Smith, D. A. (1980). Memory for typical and atypical actions in scripted activities. *Journal of Experimental Psychology: Human Learning and Memory, 6,* 503–515.

Haden, C. A., Didow, S. M., Ornstein, P. A. & Eckerman, C. O. (1997, April). Mother–child talk about the here-and-now: Linkages to subsequent remembering. In E. Reese (Chair) *Adult–child reminiscing: Theory and practice.* Symposium paper presented at the meetings of the Society for Research in Child Development, Washington, DC.

Haden, C. A., Haine, R., & Fivush, R. (1997). Developing narrative structure in parent-child conversations about the past. *Developmental Psychology, 33.*

Hamond, N. R., & Fivush, R. (1990). Memories of Mickey Mouse: Young children recount their trip to Disney World. *Cognitive Development, 6,* 433–448.

Harber, K. D., & Pennebaker, J. W. (1992). Overcoming tramatic memories. In S. Christianson (Ed.), *The handbook of emotion and memory: Research and theory* (pp. 151–180). Hillsdale, NJ: Erlbaum.

Hewitt, S. A. (1994). Preverbal sexual abuse: What two children report in later years. *Child Abuse and Neglect, 18*, 821–826.

Howard, A. N., Osborne, H. L., & Baker–Ward, L. (1997, April). *Childhood cancer survivors' memory of their treatment after long delays.* Paper presented at the meetings of the Society for Research in Child Development, Washington, DC.

Howe, M. L., Courage, M. L., & Peterson, C. (1994). How can I remember when "I" wasn't there? Long-term retention of traumatic memories and emergence of the cognitive self. *Consciousness and Cognition, 3*, 327–355.

Hudson, J. A. (1990a). Constructive processes in children's event memory. *Developmental Psychology, 2*, 180–187.

Hudson, J. A. (1990b). The emergence of autobiographic memory in mother–child conversation. In R. Fivush & J. A. Hudson (Eds.), *Knowing and remembering in young children* (pp. 166–196). New York: Cambridge University Press.

Hudson, J. A., & Fivush, R. (1991). As time goes by: Sixth graders recall a kindergarten event. *Applied Cognitive Psychology, 5*, 346–360.

Hudson, J. A., Fivush, R., & Kuebli, J. (1992). Scripts and episodes: The development of event memory. *Applied Cognitive Psychology, 6*, 483–505.

Hudson, J. A., & Nelson, K. (1983). Effects of script structure on children's story recall. *Developmental Psychology, 19*, 625–635.

Hudson, J. A., & Nelson, K. (1986). Repeated encounters of a similar kind: Effects of familiarity on children's autobiographic memory. *Cognitive Development, 1*, 253–271.

Kuebli, J., & Fivush, R. (1994). Children's representation and recall of event alternatives. *Journal of Experimental Child Psychology, 58*, 25–45.

Labov, W. (1982). Speech actions and reaction in personal narrative. In D. Tannen (Ed.), *Analyzing discourse: Text and talk*. Washington, DC: Georgetown University Press.

Leichtman, M. D. (1997, April). Memories in Asian and Caucasian children. In E. Reese (Chair) *Adult–child reminiscing: Theory and practice.* Symposium paper presented at the meetings of the Society for Research in Child Development, Washington, DC.

Leichtman, M. D., & Ceci, S. J. (1995). The effects of stereotypes and suggestions on preschoolers reports. *Developmental Psychology, 31*, 58–578.

Malmquist, C. P. (1986). Children who witness parental murder: Post-traumatic aspects. *Journal of the American Academy of Child Psychiatry, 25*, 320–325.

McCabe, A., & Peterson, C. (1991). Getting the story: A longitudinal study of parental styles in eliciting narratives and developing narrative skills. In A. McCabe & C. Peterson (Eds.), *Developing narrative structure* (pp. 217–253). Hillsdale, NJ: Erlbaum.

Mullen, M. K. (1994). Earliest recollections of childhood: A demographic analysis. *Cognition, 52*, 55–79.

Myers, N. A., Perris, E. E., & Speaker, C. J. (1994). Fifty month of memory: A longitudinal study in early childhood. *Memory, 2*, 383–416.

Neisser, U., Winograd, E., Bergman, E., Schreiber, C. A., Palmer, S., & Weldon, M. (1996). Remembering the earthquake: Direct experience vs. hearing the news. *Memory, 4*, 337–357.

Nelson, K. (1986). *Event knowledge: Structure and function in development.* Hillsdale, NJ: Erlbaum.

Nelson, K. (1993). The psychological and social origins of autobiographical memory. *Psychological Science, 1,* 1–8.

Nelson, K. (1996). *Language in cognitive development: Emergence of the mediated mind.* New York: Cambridge University Press.

Nelson, K., & Gruendel, J. M. (1981). Generalized event representations: Basic building blocks of cognitive development. In M. E. Lamb & A. L. Brown (Eds.), *Advances in development psychology* (Vol. 1, pp. 131–158). Hillsdale, NJ: Erlbaum.

Ornstein, P. A. (1995). Children's long-term retention of salient personal experiences. *Journal of Traumatic Stress, 8,* 581–606.

Ornstein, P. A., Gordon, B., & Laurus, D. (1992). Children's memory for a personally experienced event: Implications for testimony. *Applied Cognitive Psychology, 6,* 49–60.

Pennebaker, J. W. (1997). *Opening up.* New York: Guilford.

Peters, D. (1991). The influence of stress and arousal on the child witness. In J. L. Doris (Ed.), *The suggestibility of children's recollections* (pp. 60–76). Washington, DC: American Psychological Association.

Peterson, C. (1990). The who, when and where of early narratives. *Journal of Child Language, 17,* 433–455.

Peterson, C., & Bell, M. (1996). Children's memory for traumatic injury. *Child Development, 67,* 3045–3070.

Peterson, C., & Rideout, V. (1997, April). And I was very very crying: Children's memories of minor medical emergencies. In P. Bauer & M.-E. Pipe (Chairs), *Long-term memory in childhood.* Symposium conducted at the meetings of the Society for Research in Child Development, Washington, DC.

Pezdek, K., & Banks, W. (1996). *The recovered memory debate.* New York: Academic Press.

Pillemer, D., & White, S. H. (1989). Childhood events recalled by children and adults. In H. W. Reese (Ed.), *Advances in child development and behavior* (Vol. 22, pp. 297–346). New York: Academic.

Pipe, M.-E., Dean, J., Canning, J., & Murachver, T. (1996, July). *Narrating events and telling stories.* Paper presented at the second International Conference on Memory, Abano, Italy.

Poole, D. A., & White, L. T. (1993). Two years later: Effects of question repetition and retention interval on the eyewitness testimony of children and adults. *Developmental Psychology, 29,* 844–853.

Poole, D. A., & White, L. T. (1995). Tell me again and again: Stability and change in the repeated testimonies of children and adults. In M. S. Zaragozza, J. R. Graham, G. C. N. Hall, R. Hirschman, & Y. S. Ben–Porath (Eds.), *Memory and testimony in the child witness children's and adults' eyewitness testimony* (pp. 24–43). Thousand Oaks, CA: Sage.

Pressley, M., & Schneider, W. (1986). *Memory development between 2 and 20.* Springer–Verlag.

Principe, G. (1996, March). *Children's memory for a stressful medical procedure.* Paper presented at the Conference on Human Development, Birmingham, AL.

Pynoos, R. S., & Nader, K. (1989). Children's memory and proximity to violence. *Journal of the American Academy of Child and Adolescent Psychiatry, 28,* 236–241.

Pynoos, R. S., Steinberg, A. M., & Aronson, L. (1997). Traumatic experiences: The early organization of memory in school-age children and adolescents. In P. S. Applebaum, L. A. Uyehara, &

M. R. Elin (Eds.), *Trauma and memory: Clinical and legal controversies* (pp. 272–289). New York: Oxford University Press.

Reese, E., Haden, C. A., & Fivush, R. (1993). Mother–child conversations about the past: Relationships of style and memory over time. *Cognitive Development, 8*, 403–430.

Reese, E., Haden, C., & Fivush, R. (1996). Mothers, father, daughters, sons: Gender differences in reminiscing. *Research on Language and Social Interaction, 29*, 27–56.

Reviere, S. (1996). *Memory of childhood trauma.* New York: Guilford.

Rudy, L., & Goodman, G. S. (1991). Effects of participation on children's reports: Implications for children's testimony. *Developmental Psychology, 27*, 527–538.

Sachs, J. (1983). Talking about the there and then: The emergence of displaced reference in parent–child discourse. In K. Nelson (Ed.), *Children's language* (Vol. 4, pp. 1–28). Hillsdale, NJ: Erlbaum.

Schank, R., & Abelson, A. (1977). *Scripts, plans, goals, and understanding.* Hillsdale, NJ: Erlbaum.

Shay, J. (1996). *Achilles in Vietnam: Combat trauma and the undoing of character.* New York: McMillan.

Schwarzmueller, A. (1997). The effects of repeated questions on children's event recall. Unpublished doctoral dissertation, Emory University, Atlanta, GA.

Sperry, L. (1991). *The emergence and development of narrative competence in African-American toddlers from a rural Alabama community.* Unpublished doctoral dissertation, University of Chicago.

Steward, M. (1993). Understanding children's memories of medical procedures: "He didn't touch me and it didn't hurt." In C. A. Nelson (Ed.), *Minnesota Symposium on Child Psychology: Vol. 26. Memory and affect in development* (pp. 171–226). Hillsdale, NJ: Erlbaum.

Terr, L. C. (1983). Chowchilla revisited: The effects of psychic trauma four years after a school-bus kidnapping. *American Journal of Psychiatry, 140*, 1543–1550.

Terr, L. C. (1988). What happens to early memories of trauma? A study of twenty children under age five at the time of documented traumatic events. *Journal of the American Academy of Child and Adolescent Psychiatry, 27*, 96–104.

Terr, L. (1991). Childhood traumas: An outline and overview. *American Journal of Psychiatry, 148*, 10–20.

Tessler, M., & Nelson, K. (1994). Making memories: The influence of joint encoding on later recall by young children. *Consciousness and Cognition, 3*, 307–326.

Todd, C., & Perlmutter, M. (1980). Reality recalled by preschool children. In M. Perlmutter (Ed.), *New directions for child development: No. 10. Children's memory* (pp. 69–86). San Francisco: Jossey–Bass.

Vygotsky, L. S. (1978). *Mind in society: The development of higher psychological processes.* Cambridge, MA: Harvard University Press.

Wagenaar, W. A., & Groeneweg, J. (1990). The memory of concentration camp survivors. *Applied Cognitive Psychology, 4*, 77–87.

Wilkomirski, B. (1996). *Fragments: Memories of a wartime childhood.* New York: Schocken.

Part II

SOCIAL AND CROSS-CULTURAL ISSUES

The next section includes papers on social and cross-cultural issues in child development. There are two papers on parenting in a variety of countries. The other two papers deal with psychosocial issues, the effects of hunger and divorce on child adjustment.

The paper by Chen and colleagues is titled, "Child-rearing attitudes and behavioral inhibition in Chinese and Canadian toddlers: A cross-cultural study." This paper presents intriguing evidence that the construct of behavioral inhibition is not strictly inherited and that it engenders different reactions among Canadian and Chinese mothers. Culturally mediated socialization beliefs and parenting practices account for part of the variation in behavioral inhibition. Chinese children were more inhibited than Canadian children were and girls were more inhibited than boys were. In North America, inhibited children are often viewed as immature and their mothers are not accepting of this behavior. In China, their mothers and peers accepted inhibited children. This was only a correlational study. A longitudinal design would be necessary to demonstrate an interaction between parenting style and child inhibition.

The second cross-cultural study was entitled, "A cross-national study of self-evaluations and attributions in parenting: Argentina, Belgium, France, Israel, Italy, Japan, and the United States." Bornstein and his colleagues had parents of toddlers complete three questionnaires, The Self-Perceptions of the Parental Role, the Parent Attributions Questionnaire and the Social Desirability Scale. The number of mothers selected from each country ranged from 20 to 38 comprising a total sample of 214.

The authors compared self-evaluations of the parental role, and attributions for success and failure in parenting for mothers from the seven countries. The results are fairly complex given all of the possible comparisons. Of note, there were few cross-cultural similarities. There were interesting findings regarding cultural expectations and parents perceptions of their competence and their attributions for parenting failures.

The third paper in this section is the "Relationship between hunger and psychosocial functioning in low-income American children" by Murphy and colleagues. This paper draws on data from a large scale survey called the Community Childhood Hunger Identification Project. Approximately 8% of American children (younger than 12) experience hunger each year. To suggest that hunger has a negative impact on functioning seems intuitive. Yet we need empirical data to support arguments for funding social programs such as the National School Breakfast and Lunch Program. Opponents of these types of programs might argue that hunger is just a reflection of the broader social ills of the inner-city life. For this study 204 school-age children and their parents were assessed at time one using parent, teacher and clinician report measures. At time two, 96 children and their parents were reinterviewed.

Among low-income children, children who experienced hunger or "food insufficiency" were rated as more impaired on both parent and self-reports. Teacher reports indicated higher levels of hyperactivity, absenteeism and tardiness among hungry children compared to non-hungry children.

In the last paper in this section, Hetherington, Bridges and Isabella present an excellent literature review on the impact of divorce and remarriage on children's adjustment. Studies have found a twofold increase in adjustment problems for children from divorced families compared to children in non-divorced families. The authors present five complementary hypotheses that may account for this increase in adjustment problems. The five theoretical perspectives reviewed are as follows: 1) Adjustment difficulties result from individual risk and vulnerability. Persons with negative characteristics are attracted to others with similar problems. These characteristics, in turn, increase one's likelihood of divorce. 2) The family composition theory emphasizes that a two biological parent family is the optimal environment for children. 3) Marital transitions lead to stress and socioeconomic disadvantage. 4) The stress of divorce leads to parental distress and psychological problems such as anxiety and depression. 5) Family process variables, such as problem-solving and the expression of affect, differ in families with stable and non-stable marriages.

It is not surprising that after reviewing studies in support of each of the above risk factors, the authors conclude that all of the factors are likely intertwined. The best understanding of the effects of divorce on children will take into account adult personality characteristics and family functioning prior to divorce as well as the transient psychological problems and socioeconomic circumstances that result from divorce.

6

Child-Rearing Attitudes and Behavioral Inhibition in Chinese and Canadian Toddlers: A Cross-Cultural Study

Xinyin Chen
University of Western Ontario

Kenneth H. Rubin
University of Maryland College Park

Guozhen Cen
Shanghai Teachers' University

Paul D. Hastings
National Institute of Mental Health

Huichang Chen
Beijing Normal University

Shannon L. Stewart
University of Waterloo

Behavioral inhibition data were collected from samples of 2-year-olds from the People's Republic of China and Canada. Information on child-rearing

Guest Editor's Note. Gary Ladd served as action editor for this article.—KHR

Xinyin Chen, Department of Psychology, University of Western Ontario, London, Ontario, Canada; Paul D. Hastings, Section on Developmental Psychopathology. National Institute of Mental Health, Rockville, Maryland; Kenneth H. Rubin, Department of Human Development, University of Maryland College Park; Huichang Chen, Institute of Developmental Psychology, Beijing Normal University, Beijing, People's Republic of China; Guozhen Cen, Department of Educational Administration, Shanghai Teachers' University, Shanghai, People's Republic of China; Shannon L. Stewart, Department of Psychology, University of Waterloo, Waterloo, Ontario, Canada.

The research described herein was supported by grants from the Social Sciences and Humanities Research Council of Canada and the National Institute of Mental Health. We are grateful to the children and mothers for their participation and to the following individuals who aided in the collection and coding of data: Lan-zhi Liang, Yue-bo Zhang, and Li Wang at Beijing Normal University; Bo-shu Li, Dan Li, Zhen-yun Li, and Mowei Liu at Shanghai Teachers' University; and Loretta Lapa, Kelly Lemon, Jo-Anne McKinnon, Amy Rubin, Alice Rushing, and Cherami Wischman at the University of Waterloo.

Correspondence concerning this article should be addressed to Xinyin Chen, Department of Psychology, University of Western Ontario, London, Ontario, Canada N6A 5C2. Electronic mail may be sent to xchen@julian.uwo.ca *attitudes and beliefs was obtained from mothers of the children. Chinese toddlers were significantly more inhibited than their Canadian counterparts. Inhibition was associated positively with mothers' punishment orientation and negatively with mothers' acceptance and encouragement of achievement in the Canadian sample. However, the directions of the relations were opposite in the Chinese sample; child inhibition was associated positively with mothers' warm and accepting attitudes and negatively with rejection and punishment orientation. The results indicated different adaptational meanings of behavioral inhibition across cultures.*

Developmental researchers have reported dramatic individual differences in behavioral reactions to novel social and nonsocial situations during infancy and toddlerhood (e.g., Kagan, Reznick, Clarke, Snidman, & Garcia-Coll, 1984; Rubin, Hastings. Stewart, Henderson, & Chen, 1997). For example, some infants and toddlers are relaxed and spontaneous and display minimal distress in unfamiliar situations. In contrast, children who are identified as behaviorally inhibited and vigilant tend to show high anxiety in novel social situations; they often refuse to engage in play behavior with unfamiliar peers and adults, and they stay in close proximity to their mothers (Fox & Calkins, 1993; Kagan, Reznick, Snidman, Gibbons, & Johnson, 1988; Rubin et al., 1997). It has been found that behavioral inhibition is associated with indexes of social wariness during the preschool years (Kochanska & Radke-Yarrow, 1992; Rubin, Coplan, Fox, & Calkins, 1995). Further, researchers have argued that inhibition and social wariness may serve as dispositional bases for the display of shy and socially reticent behaviors in the child and adolescent peer group (Kagan, 1989; Rubin & Asendorpf, 1993). As such, it may be safe to conclude that behavioral inhibition may play a critical role in social and emotional development.

Behavioral patterns that reflect the construct of inhibition and wariness in novel situations have been found in many cultures, such as England, Germany, Japan, and Sweden (e.g., Asendorpf, 1991; Broberg, Lamb, & Hwang, 1990; Hayashi, Toyama, & Quay, 1976; Stevenson-Hinde & Shouldice, 1993). However, the extent to which inhibited behavior is displayed appears to vary across culture. For example, it has been reported that Chinese, Indonesian, Thai, and Korean children produce more anxious, sensitive, passive, reticent, and socially restrained behaviors in novel situations than do their North American counterparts (Chan & Eysenck, 1981; Farver & Howes, 1988; Kagan, Kearsley & Zelazo, 1978; Tieszen, 1979; Weisz, Suwanlert, Chaiyasit, & Walter, 1987). Given these differences, it seems important to examine whether behavioral inhibition carries with it psychological "meanings" that vary across culture and how culture is involved in the development of behavioral inhibition.

Initial support for cross-cultural variability in the "meanings" of wary, inhibited behavior derives from recent research on caregiver–infant attachment relationships. In these studies, a high frequency of socially wary behavior in the Strange Situation has been considered adaptive in some cultures yet maladaptive in others (e.g., Grossman & Grossman, 1981; Mizuta, Zahn-Waxler, Cole, & Hiruma, 1996). Acknowledgement of differences in the adaptational meanings of inhibited behavior is consistent with the perspective that cultural norms and conventions may affect the perceptions and evaluations of social behaviors (e.g., Benedict, 1934; Gresham, 1986).

The cross-cultural literature has suggested that child-rearing beliefs and practices are important factors that may mediate cultural influences on child development (e.g., Super & Harkness, 1986; Whiting & Edwards, 1988). Parental behaviors and beliefs are guided by general cultural norms and value systems. At the same time, parents interpret and respond to child behavior in accordance with culturally prescribed expectations and socialization goals. Parental attitudes and responses constitute important social conditions that, in turn, maintain and modify the processes, pathways, and outcomes of behavioral development. Thus, the primary purpose of the present study was to examine, from a cross-cultural perspective, the relations between parental attitudes and practices in child-rearing and children's behavioral inhibition.

In Western individualistic cultures, children are encouraged to be assertive and independent in challenging situations. Acquiring self-reliance, autonomy, and assertive social skills are important socialization goals. In contrast, behavioral inhibition, which reflects anxiety, an inability to express one's self, and a lack of confidence, is generally regarded as socially immature, incompetent, and psychologically maladaptive (Rubin & Asendorpf, 1993). Social perceptions and evaluations of children's behaviors may depend, in part, on context (e.g., inhibition may serve as a protective factor that buffers misbehavior under certain circumstances) and personal characteristics, such as age or developmental stage (e.g., inhibited behavior may be regarded as less maladaptive in the early years than in later childhood). However, during development, children are generally expected and socialized to be increasingly assertive and self-reliant rather than reserved and inhibited. Consistently, Western researchers have found that the early production of behavioral inhibition is predictive of shy, withdrawn behavior in childhood (Asendorpf, 1991; Broberg et al., 1990; Fox & Calkins, 1993; Kochanska & Radke-Yarrow, 1992; Reznick et al., 1986; Schwartz, 1997); in turn, shyness and social withdrawal are associated with peer rejection and isolation (e.g., Rubin, Chen, McDougall, Bowker, & McKinnon, 1995). Further, researchers have found that as children begin to acknowledge their difficulties in social interactions and peer relationships, they develop negative perceptions of their social competencies and general self-worth as well as other problems of an internalizing nature (Boivin, Hymel, & Bukowski, 1995; Rubin, Chen, & Hymel, 1993; Rubin, Chen, et al., 1995).

Achieving and maintaining social order and interpersonal harmony are the primary concerns in both traditional and contemporary collectivistic Chinese societies. Individuals are encouraged to restrain personal desires for the benefits and interests of the collective. For example, in both Confucian and Taoist philosophies, behavioral inhibition and self-restraint are considered indexes of social maturity, accomplishment, and mastery (Feng, 1962; King & Bond, 1985). The expression of individuals' needs or striving for autonomous behaviors is considered selfish and socially unacceptable (Ho, 1986). Consistently, it has been found that whereas assertive and independent behaviors are valued in Western individualistic cultures, shy and inhibited behaviors are valued and encouraged in Chinese culture (e.g., Chen, in press; Chen, Rubin, & Sun, 1992; Ho, 1986). Children who are sensitive, wary, cautious, and behaviorally restrained are called "Guai Hai Zi" in Mandarin, which may be translated as meaning "good" or "well-behaved." Unlike their Western counterparts, shy-anxious children in China are regarded as socially competent and understanding; they are accepted by peers and adjust well to their social environments (e.g., Chen et al., 1992; Chen, Rubin, & B. Li, 1995).

The social behaviors valued by a culture may be reflected by parental goals, beliefs, expectations, and behaviors. For example, compared with Western parents, Chinese parents are more controlling and protective in child rearing (Kriger & Kroes, 1972; Lin & Fu, 1990). Chinese parents emphasize behavioral control and obedience. Parents often encourage their young children to stay close to and to be dependent on them (Ho, 1986). Indeed, most Chinese infants and toddlers sleep in the same bed or in the same room as their parents.

Given the aforementioned cultural differences, it is not unreasonable to expect that the patterns of relations between children's expressions of behavioral inhibition and parental attitudes and practices would vary in Chinese and North American cultures. For example, in North America, researchers have reported that preschoolers' wary and inhibited behavior is associated with such parental emotional reactions as concern, disappointment, guilt, and embarrassment (Mills & Rubin, 1990). Moreover, it has been found that mothers of inhibited and withdrawn children are inclined to blame this behavior on traits in their child (Rubin & Mills, 1990). Such dispositional attributions for undesirable behavior have been linked to punitive and ineffective parenting practices (Crockenberg, 1986; Miller, 1995; Peters-Martin & Wachs, 1984). Although researchers have found that mothers of inhibited children may sometimes display highly warm and affectionate behavior, these mothers are generally unresponsive to their children's cues and needs (Rubin et al., 1997). Parental unresponsiveness and insensitivity, which may partially result from children's inhibited behavior, may facilitate the continuation and development of the behavior. Consistent with these findings are data derived from attachment research that have indicated that insecure, resistant babies ("C" babies) who typically display anxious, fearful, and inhibited behavior in the Strange Situation, as well as at home, tend to have parents who are unresponsive, unreliable, and inconsistent in parenting (e.g., Ainsworth, Blehar, Waters, & Wall, 1978; Pederson & Moran, 1995). Unlike mothers of avoidant babies ("A" babies), mothers of anxious, resistant babies may not be hostile or rejecting of their children (Ainsworth et al., 1978).

Inhibited children may experience a different social and emotional family environment in China. Because inhibited behavior is positively valued and considered adaptive, behaviorally inhibited children may not be recipients of negative parental emotions and behaviors. Indeed, in the present study, we expected that inhibited children would be accepted and supported by their parents. Further, parental acceptance, endorsement, and encouragement of inhibited behavior may reinforce the display of restrained and inhibited behavior. Thus, first, we hypothesized that behavioral inhibition would be associated positively with maternal acceptance and negatively with maternal rejection and punishment in Chinese children. In contrast, we predicted that inhibition would be associated negatively with maternal acceptance among Canadian children. Given that mothers of anxious, inhibited children are generally not hostile toward or rejecting of the child, inhibited behavior was not predicted to be associated with maternal rejection in Canadian toddlers.

In both Chinese and North American cultures, parents emphasize and encourage achievement in child rearing. However, the goals and specific tasks that children are encouraged to achieve may be defined and prescribed by what is valued in the culture. In other words, parental encouragement of achievement may indicate cultural values. To further examine cultural meanings of behavioral inhibition, we sought to investigate how inhibition was associated with maternal encouragement of achievement. Given that behavioral inhibition is regarded as maladaptive in North American cultures, we posited that inhibition would be negatively associated with maternal encouragement of achievement. However, because inhibition is consistent with socialization goals and thus positively evaluated in China, we expected that inhibited behavior would be positively associated with maternal encouragement of achievement.

Researchers have reported that Chinese parents are more protective and controlling and less encouraging of independence and exploration than are North American parents (e.g., Ekblad, 1986; Lin & Fu, 1990). It has also been noted that children of highly protective, oversolicitous Western parents tend to display more wary and reserved behavior in unfamiliar situations (e.g., Eisenberg, 1958; Kagan & Moss, 1962; Parker, 1983; Rubin et al., 1997; Rubin & Mills, 1990). Indeed, highly protective and directive parents tend to be "overly" involved and dominant in parent–child interactions; they are less likely to encourage their children to explore independently in novel environments (Parker, 1983). It may be true that highly protective and directive behavior represents a good "fit" with the authoritarian culture of China but is viewed as maladaptive in Western cultures (Chao, 1994). Nevertheless, given the restrictive nature of this parenting behavior, we expected that it would be positively associated with child behavioral inhibition in both Chinese and Canadian children. Consistently, we hypothesized that regardless of the culture, maternal encouragement of independence and autonomy would be negatively related to behavioral inhibition in children.

Finally, according to the "suppression-facilitation" model (Weisz et al., 1987), cultural environments may affect the occurrence and prevalence of social behaviors in a direct fashion. Given that the Chinese cultural milieu is conducive for the development of behavioral inhibition and that inhibition is discouraged in the West, we predicted that consistent with Kagan et al.'s (1978) findings, Chinese toddlers would display more inhibited and wary behavior in novel social situations than Canadian toddlers.

METHOD

Participants

One hundred and fifty Chinese children in two cities of the People's Republic of China and 108 Canadian children in a regional municipality of approximately 250,000 people in southwestern Ontario participated in this study. The mean age was 24.64 months ($SD = 1.99$) for the Chinese and 24.99 months ($SD = 1.08$) for the Canadian children. Mothers were, on average, 30 years 11 months old ($SD = 4$ years 3 months; range $= 24$–39) and fathers were 32 years old ($SD = 3$ years 2 months; range $= 26$–48) in the Chinese sample. The mean age was 31 years 1 month ($SD = 4$ years 1 month; range $= 23$–41) for mothers and 32 years 6 months ($SD = 3$ years 11 months; range $= 24$–43) for fathers in the Canadian sample. The participants were randomly selected by newspaper birth announcements and recruited through telephone solicitation in Canada and local birth registration offices in

China. Ninety-seven percent of the Canadian toddlers were Caucasian, and all participants in China were Chinese.

In the Chinese sample, 44% of the children were from families in which parents were workers or peasants whose educational levels were high school or below high school; 56% of the children were from families in which one or both of the parents were teachers, doctors, or officials whose educational levels ranged mainly from college to university graduate. Canadian children were mainly from middle-class families. Eighty-one percent of the Canadian toddlers had one or more siblings. However, because of the "one-child-per-family" policy that was implemented in the late 1970s, 96% of the Chinese toddlers were only children; the "only" child phenomenon has been an integral part of the family and sociocultural background for child development in contemporary China. Thirty-three percent of the Chinese children and 24% of the Canadian children had out-of-home day-care experience. Nonsignificant differences were found between children with different day-care experiences in each sample on behavioral inhibition and parental child-rearing attitudes. The two samples were representative of the urban population of toddlers in each country. Complete child-rearing data were obtained from mothers of 118 Chinese (64 boys and 54 girls) and 82 Canadian (43 boys and 39 girls) toddlers. The mothers of other children filled the child-rearing measure either incompletely or incorrectly.

Procedure

Mothers and toddlers were invited to visit the university laboratory within 3 months of each toddler's 2nd birthday. During the visit, each toddler–mother dyad experienced an adapted version of the Behavioral Inhibition Paradigm (e.g., Garcia-Coll, Kagan, & Reznick, 1984; Kochanska, 1991). First, each dyad entered an unfamiliar room comprising one large and one small chair and a low table. The child was allowed to play with an assortment of attractive toys for 10 min while the mother sat in the large chair and filled out a questionaire (free play). The experimenter, whom the child had already met, entered with a basket, asked the child to tidy up the toys, and left (cleanup); afterward, the experimenter removed the toys. Next, an unfamiliar woman entered the room with a toy dump truck and some blocks. She sat quietly for 1 min, played with the truck for 1 min, then (if the toddler had not yet approached), encouraged the child to join her in play. After the 3rd min, she left, returning with a toy robot that moved and made noises. The adult did not say anything for 30 s, then invited the child to play with the robot for 1 min. The toy truck and robot were identical in all laboratories. These toys were all made in China and were purchased in a Canadian store. The children in both cultures were familiar with toy trucks. However, according to product description, the black, noisy, and "smoking" toy robot was recommended for children aged 4 years and up; thus, it was unlikely to be familiar to the toddlers in the two samples. Therefore, the procedure was viewed as equally novel–familiar to the Chinese and Canadian children. Toddlers in each sample continued to experience other sessions, including crawling through an inflatable tunnel, interacting with a clown (or a person wearing a tiger mask in China), and a second free-play session. Because there were slight variations between the samples with regard to these latter laboratory sessions, data were not examined comparatively for the present article.

The administration of the laboratory sessions was conducted by Xinyin Chen et al. as well as by graduate and senior undergraduate students in China and Canada. The researchers in China were trained by Xinyin Chen. All laboratory sessions were videotaped through a oneway mirror and were coded in Canada. Written consent was obtained from parents of all participants in Canada and in China.

Inhibition Coding

Following procedures that were described in Garcia-Coll et al. (1984) and Rubin et al. (1997), behavioral inhibition was coded on the basis of the amount of time the toddler spent in physical contact with his or her mother during the free-play, truck and robot episodes, and the child's latency to approach the stranger and to touch the toys. Four data points were obtained for the truck episode; during the 1st and 2nd min, the duration of contact with the mother and the latency to spontaneously approach the unfamiliar adult were recorded. During the 3rd min, the duration of contact with the mother and the latency to approach the unfamiliar adult were recorded after an invitation to approach was given (for children who approached the stranger spontaneously in the 1st and 2nd min, latency was scored as zero). Two data points were obtained for the subsequent robot episode: duration of contact with the mother and latency to touch the robot. Four inhibition scores were computed: (a) duration of contact with the mother in free play, (b) duration of contact with the mother in track and robot episodes, (c) latency to approach the stranger, and (d) latency to touch robot. Following the procedures described by Rubin et al. (1997), the inhibition scores were standardized and aggregated and were used in all statistical analyses.

The data for Chinese toddlers were coded by two Chinese students in the Psychology Department of a Canadian university who were fluent in both English and Chinese languages. The data for the Canadian sample were coded by two English-speaking students. All coders were trained following the same procedures. Reliability, using percentage of agreement, was computed for 10% of each sample. As suggested by other researchers (e.g., Garcia-Coll et al., 1984), intercoder agreement for duration of contact with the mother and latency to approach the unfamiliar adult or toys were calculated through dividing the amount of time of agreement by the total amount of time of agreement and disagreement in seconds. The intercoder reliability for the inhibition behaviors was 96%, ranging from 93% (contact with mother in the robot episode) to 100% (contact with mother in free play) in the Chinese sample, and 90%, ranging from 80% (contact with mother in free play) to 97% (contact with mother in the truck episode) in the Canadian sample.

Child-Rearing Attitudes

Each mother completed the Child-Rearing Practices Report Q-Sort (CRPR; Block, 1981). The CRPR includes 91 items describing child-rearing attitudes, values, beliefs, and behaviors, written on individual cards. Mothers sorted the cards into seven piles (13 cards each), from "least descriptive" to "most descriptive." Consequently, item scores ranged from 1 (*least descriptive*) to 7 (*most descriptive*). The Chinese version of the CRPR was translated and back-translated by the research team. The procedure has established reliability and validity in Western and in some other cultures (e.g., Zahn-Waxler, Friedman, Cole, Mizuta, & Hiruma, 1996). The CRPR has been used and has been proven reliable, valid, and appropriate in Chinese samples (Chen, Dong, & Zhou, 1997; Lin & Fu, 1990). In the present study, indexes of acceptance (e.g., "My child and I have warm, intimate times together."), rejection (e.g., "I often feel angry with my child."), encouragement of achievement (e.g., "I think a child should be encouraged to do things better than others."), encouragement of independence (e.g., "If my child gets into trouble, I expect him or her to handle the problem mostly by himself or herself."), punishment orientation (e.g., "I believe physical punishment to be the best way of disciplining."), and protection and concern (e.g., "I try to stop my child from playing rough games or doing things where he or she might get hurt.") were formed based both on previously published research (e.g., Block, 1981; Lin & Fu, 1990) and on iterative processes of discussion in our collaborative Canadian–Chinese reserch group. The score of each child-rearing variables was computed through dividing the total item score by the number of items in the category. Correlations among child-rearing variables were generally low ($rs < .30$) in the Canadian sample. However, there were moderate to high correlations among maternal acceptance, encouragement of achievement, and encouragement of independence and between maternal rejection and punishment orientation ($rs = .60s$ to $.70s$) in the Chinese sample. This might indicate relatively lower discriminant construct validity of the measure in the Chinese sample.

RESULTS

Toddler Inhibition

The means and standard deviation of inhibition scores for each sample are presented in Table 1. The results indicated that Chinese toddlers spent significantly more time than the Canadian toddlers in direct physical contact with their mothers during the free-play episode. Moreover, Chinese toddlers had significantly higher scores on latency to approach the stranger and to touch the robot. In addition, the percentage of toddlers who made contact with their mothers in the free-play and truck and robot episodes in the Chinese sample was significantly greater than that in the Canadian sample. There were significantly more children in the Chinese sample than in the Canadian sample who did not approach the stranger or touch the robot. Percentages of children in each sample who contacted the mother, did not approach the stranger, or touch the robot are presented in Table 2.

TABLE 1
Means and Standard Deviations of Inhibition Scores

Variable	China		Canada		
	M	*SD*	*M*	*SD*	*t*
Contact with mother in free play	20.20	40.50	8.90	28.00	2.67**
Contact with mother in truck/robot	38.76	60.08	28.78	58.36	1.31
Latency to approach stranger	29.09	17.84	20.68	16.12	3.89***
Latency to touch robot	29.68	15.94	17.41	11.60	7.07***

**$p < .01$. ***$p < .001$.

TABLE 2
Percentage of Children Who Contacted Mother or Did Not
Approach Stranger

Variable	China	Canada	χ^2
Contacted mother in free play	41.06	21.91	10.56***
Contacted mother in truck/robot	60.96	37.26	13.63***
Did not approach stranger	21.09	5.90	12.21***
Did not touch robot	43.24	11.77	30.76***

*** $p < .001$.

There were nonsignificant sex differences in inhibition scores in both samples. The mean scores for boys and girls were as follows: (a) contact with mother in free play: 20.99 and 19.63 ($SDs = 45.46$ and 35.74) in the Chinese sample and 10.00 and 7.74 ($SDs = 31.25$ and 24.55) in the Canadian sample; (b) contact with mother in truck–robot: 36.62 and 40.59 ($SDs = 58.68$ and 61.55) in the Chinese sample and 34.35 and 23.20 ($SDs = 62.43$ and 54.02) in the Canadian sample; (c) latency to approach stranger: 29.64 and 28.62 ($SDs = 18.92$ and 16.95) in the Chinese sample and 19.97 and 21.40 ($SDs = 16.87$ and 15.47) in the Canadian sample; and (d) latency to touch robot: 29.25 and 30.06 ($SD = 16.41$ and 15.61) in the Chinese sample and 17.14 and 17.68 ($SD = 11.74$ and 11.56) in the Canadian sample, respectively.

Child-Rearing Attitudes

The means and standard deviations for the child-rearing variables are presented in Table 3. A multivariate analysis of variance (MANOVA) revealed significant overall effects for culture groups (between factor), $F(1, 196) = 51.06$, $p < .001$, childrearing attitudes (within factor), $F(5, 192) = 85.05$, $p < .001$, and the Culture Group × Child-Rearing (within-factor) interaction, $F(5, 192) = 41.91$, $p < .001$. The results of follow-up t tests indicated that Chinese mothers had significantly lower scores on Acceptance than the Canadian mothers. Chinese mothers had significantly higher scores on Rejection, Encouragement of Achievement. Punishment Orientation, and Protection and Concern than Canadian mothers. Post hoc analyses of the within-factor effect in each sample, using the Tukey honestly

TABLE 3
Means and Standard Deviations of Parenting Scores

Variable	China		Canada		
	M	SD	M	SD	t
Acceptance	4.56	0.78	5.00	0.44	−5.17***
Rejection	3.13	1.13	2.44	0.61	5.68***
Encouragement of achievement	5.13	1.45	4.17	0.65	6.42***
Encouragement of independence	5.10	1.45	5.17	0.73	−0.48
Punishment orientation	3.26	1.03	2.98	0.63	2.42**
Protection and concern	4.10	0.71	3.91	0.53	2.23*

* $p < .05$. ** $p < .01$. *** $p < .001$.

TABLE 4

Correlations Between Child-Rearing Attitudes and Inhibition

Child-Rearing Variable	China $(n = 118)$	Canada $(n = 82)$	Z
Acceptance	.17*	−.22*	2.73**
Rejection	−.18*	.10	−2.00*
Encouragement of achievement	.18*	−.21*	2.72**
Encouragement of independence	.18*	.12	.04
Punishment orientation	−.15*	.21*	−2.52*
Protection and concern	.03	.22*	−1.34

*$p < .05$. **$p < .01$.

significant difference (HSD) approach, revealed that scores of Encouragement of Achievement and Encouragement of Independence were significantly higher than those of Acceptance and Protection, which, in turn, were higher than those of Rejection and Punishment Orientation in the Chinese sample. In the Canadian sample, scores of Acceptance and Encouragement of Independence were significantly higher than those of Encouragement of Achievement and Protection. These scores were significantly higher than those of Punishment and Rejection.

Relations Between Toddler Inhibition and Child-Rearing Attitudes

A series of regression analyses were first conducted to examine the effects of sex on the relations between toddler inhibition and child-rearing variables. Nonsignificant sex effects were found. Thus, the data were combined across sex for all analyses. Correlations between toddler inhibition and child-rearing variables were computed for each sample and compared with the Fisher transformation. The results are presented in Table 4. Toddler inhibition was significantly and positively correlated with maternal acceptance and encouragement of achievement in the Chinese sample but significantly and negatively correlated with these same child-rearing variables in the Canadian sample. The differences between the corresponding correlations in the two samples were significant. Inhibition was significantly and negatively correlated with punishment orientation in the Chinese sample but significantly and positively correlated with punishment orientation in the Canadian sample. The two correlations were significantly different. Inhibition was significantly and negatively correlated with maternal rejection in the Chinese sample; this correlation was nonsignificant in the Canadian sample. The difference between the two correlations was significant. Inhibition was significantly and positively correlated with encouragement of independence in the Chinese sample; this correlation was nonsignificant in the Canadian sample. Finally, child inhibition was significantly and positively correlated with mother's protection and concern in the Canadian sample; this correlation was nonsignificant in the Chinese sample.[1]

---

[1] We identified, in each sample, groups of highly inhibited (top 15%), highly uninhibited (bottom 15%), and average (middle 70%) children and compared them on mothers' child-rearing practices. The results were consistent with those in the correlational analyses.

DISCUSSION

Behavioral inhibition, as one of the fundamental dimensions of human social functioning, may have pervasive and prolonged effects on adaptive and maladaptive development (e.g., Caspi, Elder, & Bem, 1988; Kagan, 1989; Kerr, Lambert, & Bem, 1996). Individual differences in behavioral inhibition have been observed in many cultures (e.g., Asendorpf, 1994; Broberg et al., 1990; Kagan et al., 1978), thereby suggesting that it may be a universal phenomenon. Nevertheless, human inhibitory behavioral systems operate within social and cultural contexts (Buck, 1993; Rickman & Davidson, 1994). Culture imparts meanings to the behavior; determines how individuals, including parents and peers, perceive, evaluate, and react to the behavior; and eventually regulates and directs the developmental processes of the behavior. It was our intention, in the present study, to explore the possibility of differences in the expression of behavioral inhibition among Chinese and Canadian toddlers and to examine the relations between inhibition and mother's child-rearing philosophies and practices. The results of the study indicated that (a) Chinese toddlers were more inhibited than their Canadian age-mates; (b) Chinese and Canadian mothers differed in their socialization values and parenting practices; and (c) child inhibition was associated with mothers' positive attitudes toward the child, including acceptance, lack of punitiveness, and encouragement of achievement among Chinese participants and with punishment and overprotectiveness among Canadian participants.

It has long been argued that parents in different cultures may have different beliefs about and use different practices in child rearing (Super & Harkness, 1986; Whiting & Edwards, 1988). Consistent with this notion, we found that Chinese mothers were (a) more likely to encourage children to achieve, (b) more protective of and concerned about their children, (c) more rejecting and less accepting of their children, and (d) more punishment oriented than Canadian mothers. These results were largely consistent with previous reports (Chao, 1994; Kriger & Kroes, 1972; Lin & Fu, 1990; Steinberg, Dornbusch, & Brown, 1992; Stevenson et al., 1990).

According to the Confucian doctrine of filial piety, children must pledge absolute obedience and reverence to parents. In turn, parents are responsible for "governing" (i.e., teaching and disciplining) their children and are held accountable for their children's failure. The principle of filial piety stipulates (a) parental authority in using coercive parenting strategies, including power-assertion and physical punishment, and, at the same time, (b) parental responsibility to protect the child and to encourage the child to achieve. In China, child achievement is not just an issue for the individual; rather, it is viewed as a reflection of family reputation. It has been reported that Chinese children are pressured heavily by parents to perform optimally in preschool, kindergarten, and school (Stevenson et al., 1990); children who fail to achieve the adults' standards are often regarded as problematic and receive severe punishment (Wu & Tseng, 1985). The results of our study suggest that Chinese parents might be concerned about achievement when their children are very young. Relatively high levels of punitiveness and protectiveness in Chinese mothers might reflect a desire for maintaining their authority while simultaneously wishing to ensure a safe and appropriate milieu for their children.

In contrast, it appeared that Canadian mothers were somewhat less concerned with encouraging their toddlers to achieve. The lower levels of punishment and protectiveness among Canadian mothers might reflect a Western perspective that early behaviors may not have an enduring impact on later development (Rubin & Mills, 1992). These results might also indicate the general disapproval of intrusive and power-assertive strategies in North American cultures.

Consistent with the result concerning punishment orientation, Chinese mothers were found to be less accepting and more rejecting of their children. The differences in mothers' attitudes toward the child might reflect different cultural values on affective involvement in child rearing, as acceptance included warmth and rejection captured elements of coldness and anger. Because of the high emphasis on parental control and directiveness in Chinese culture, Chinese parents may be less likely than Western parents to perceive the importance of positive affect for child social and cognitive development. As a result, children and adults engage in few overt emotional and affective interchanges in China and in other Asian countries (Lin & Fu, 1990; Mizuta et al., 1996). Indeed, Asian cultures strongly value the need for behavioral and emotional control and the restriction of emotional expression during interpersonal interactions, highly expressive individuals are often regarded as poorly regulated and socially immature (Ho, 1986). The control of emotional and affective reactions in parent–child interactions and relationships may also be due to the requirement of maintaining parental authority. The Chinese family is often hierarchical in structure and authoritarian in organization; as authority figures, parents may find it difficult to engage in intimate communication and to express affection explicitly to their children. Parental power assertion with little affective involvement may lead to a low level of parental warmth and eventually be manifested as parental rejection (Rohner, 1986). Recent research has indicated that, in spite of differences on the average level of parental power assertion and warmth, these parenting attitudes and practices have similar meanings in child development in Chinese and Western cultures (Chen, Dong, & Zhou, 1997; Chen, Rubin, & Li, 1997; Rohner, 1986). Obviously, it is important to investigate this issue further.

Given the cultural emphasis on independence in Western individualistic cultures, it would be reasonable to expect that Canadian mothers have higher scores than Chinese mothers on encouragement of independence. However, a nonsignificant difference was found between the two samples on this variable. Similar results were reported in a previous study (e.g., Lin & Fu, 1990). According to Lin and Fu, encouragement of independence is believed by many Chinese parents to be important for the development of social competence and achievement. Further, it has been argued that, like Western mothers, Chinese mothers may realize that to adjust to the changing demands of contemporary society, one needs to be independent and adaptable (Lin & Fu, 1990). This may be the case particularly in urban China today, as the recent "economic reforms" in the country may lead to increasing westernization of parental child-rearing attitudes (Liu et al., 1996).

It should be noted that although there were cross-cultural differences on the average level of specific child-rearing dimensions, the general patterns of the ranking order of these dimensions were highly similar in the two samples. Both Chinese and Canadian mothers scored highest on encouragement of independence, encouragement of achievement, and acceptance and scored lowest on punishment and rejection. The cross-cultural similarities in child-rearing beliefs and behaviors may indicate important common experiences of socialization in human beings (Chen & Kaspar, in press; LeVine, 1988). Of course, the cross-cultural differences and similarities were based mainly on the child-rearing dimensions included in this study. Conclusions concerning cross-cultural socialization patterns beyond these dimensions should be drawn with caution.

In summary, although Chinese and Canadian mothers differed in specific parenting styles, there were cross-cultural similarities in the general patterns of the organization and the integration of child-rearing beliefs and practices. Such group-level cultural differences and similarities provided valuable information concerning the cultural environments in which children live, behave, and develop. Nevertheless, it is also important to examine the relations between parenting styles and child behavior at the intracultural level. Within-culture analyses in the present study revealed that the patterns of the associations between maternal child-rearing attitudes and practices and toddler inhibition were significantly different in the Chinese and Canadian samples. In the Canadian sample, it was found that inhibition was associated positively with mothers' punishment orientation and negatively with mothers' acceptance and encouragement of achievement. However, the directions of the relations were opposite in the Chinese sample; child inhibition was associated positively with acceptance and encouragement of achievement and negatively with rejection and punishment orientation. The correlations were weak in magnitude within each sample. However, the differences in the nature and the directions of the relations were rather remarkable.

As indicated in the Western literature (e.g., Jones & Carpenter, 1986; Rubin & Asendorpf, 1993), inhibited children in North America are regarded as incompetent and immature and appear to require direction and protection. Mothers may not approve of their toddler's inhibited behavior, and they may express their dissatisfaction and disappointment through the demonstration of low acceptance and high punishment. These reactions were evident in the findings of this study; mothers of inhibited toddlers in the Canadian sample were generally less accepting of their children and more likely to endorse the use of punishment in child rearing than mothers of less inhibited toddlers.

Unlike their Canadian counterparts, inhibited children in China tended to be accepted by their mothers. These results were consistent with the earlier findings concerning the relations between shy-inhibited behavior and peer acceptance in Chinese and Canadian children and adolescents (Chen et al., 1992; Chen, Rubin, & B. Li, 1995; Chen, Rubin, & Z. Li, 1995). Earlier studies reported, for example, that whereas shyness and inhibition were associated with peer rejection and social adjustment difficulties in North America, shyness and inhibition, as expressed frequently in China, were correlated with peer and teacher acceptance as well as with markers of psychological adjustment during childhood and adolescence (e.g., Chen, Rubin, & B. Li, 1995; Chen, Rubin, & Z. Li, 1995). Together, cumulative evidence indicates that behavioral inhibition is a culturally bound construct and thus may have different adaptational "meanings" across cultures.

As has been noted in other studies (Eisenberg, 1958; Kagan & Moss, 1962; Parker, 1983), Western mothers who are highly protective tend to have inhibited children. Researchers have argued that these mothers are extremely concerned for their children's well-being and, to meet their goals of child protection, they restrict their children's activities to the point at which the children do not enjoy adequate opportunities to develop comfort, confidence and skills in novel situations (Rubin & Mills, 1992; Rubin et al., 1997). Protective mothers may see their children as particularly vulnerable and thus tend to shield their children from perceived dangers. Thus, children's high levels of inhibition may be either a cause or a consequence, or both, of mothers' heightened protectiveness. Because inhibited behavior is acceptable and encouraged in China, it may be understandable that it did not correlate with maternal concern and protection, despite our initial expectations.

We hypothesized that maternal encouragement of independence would be negatively associated with toddler inhibition in both samples. This hypothesis was not supported in the study. The results indicated that maternal encouragement of independence was non-significantly correlated with inhibition in Canadian children and positively correlated with inhibition in Chinese children. It has been found that Chinese parents believe encouragement of independence is important for child development (Lin & Fu, 1990; Liu et al., 1996). If independence is indeed considered an index of adaptation in China today, as argued by Lin and Fu, it is conceivable that children whose mothers emphasized independence would display the behavior that is encouraged by Chinese mothers. Further investigation is clearly needed on this issue.

It was found that there was a higher overlap among the CRPR dimensions in the Chinese sample than in the Canadian sample. This suggested that the measure might have relatively lower discriminant validity in the Chinese sample. Similar findings have been reported in previous studies (e.g., Zahn-Waxler et al., 1996). Thus, it may be appropriate to understand our results in terms of the general patterns, that is, the associations of inhibited behavior with maternal positive parenting attitudes in China and maternal concern and power assertion in Canada.

The results of the present study indicated that Chinese toddlers were more inhibited than Canadian toddlers. Although dispositional factors may account for part of the cross-cultural variability in early inhibition (Kagan et al., 1978), our study reveals the importance of recognizing the role of culturally mediated socialization beliefs and practices in the development of inhibition. The interactions between parental beliefs and attitudes and children's inhibited behavior may indicate goodness-of-fit processes at the cultural level.

Behavioral inhibition to novelty is considered a dispositional characteristic that may be biologically rooted (Kagan, 1989). It is unclear at this time how the cross-cultural differences in inhibition are reflected at the biological or physiological level. Some initial evidence has indicated that Chinese and European American children differ in autonomic nervous system, such as heart rate variability in novel situations (Kagan et al., 1978). However, it is unknown whether there are differences in regulatory processes, such as frontal brain activities (Fox et al., 1995), which may be particularly relevant to socialization experiences.

In both Chinese and Western cultures, girls have been found to be more shy and inhibited than boys in middle and late childhood and adolescence (e.g., Chen, Rubin, & B. Li, 1995). It is interesting that nonsignificant sex differences were found on behavioral inhibition in both the Chinese and the Canadian toddlers in the present study. Nonsignificant sex differences in inhibition during toddlerhood and early childhood have also been found in previous studies (Broberg et al., 1990; Kochanska, 1991). These findings suggest that socialization may play an important role in the emergence of sex differences in shyness in later childhood. Thus, future research would do well to examine how socialization factors differentially influence the display of shy behavior in girls and boys within and across cultures.

Like many other countries in the world, China is undergoing dramatic changes. Western values and ideologies have been introduced to the country along with advanced technology. In addition, Chinese family structure and organization have changed (Chen, in press). Thus, in the future years, it will be important to investigate how societal and family changes may influence socialization patterns and children's behaviors.

Finally, it should be noted that an interactional model concerning parenting and child inhibition was applied as a conceptual framework for this study. Nevertheless, the data presented herein were correlational, thereby precluding any statements about causality. To better understand how child-rearing beliefs, attitudes, and practices and child inhibition may interact in a cultural context, longitudinal data are necessary. Further, it remains important to investigate, intra- and cross-culturally, how early inhibition and socialization contribute independently and interactively to developmental outcomes.

REFERENCES

Ainsworth, M. D. S., Blehar, M. C., Waters, E., & Wall, S. (1978). *Patterns of attachment: A psychological study of the Strange Situation.* Hillsdale. NJ: Erlbaum.

Asendorpf, J. (1990). Beyond social withdrawal: Shyness, unsociability, and peer avoidance. *Human Development, 33,* 250–259.

Asendorpf, J. (1991). Development of inhibited children's coping with unfamiliarity. *Child Development, 62,* 1460–1474.

Asendorpf, J. (1994, July). *Classmates, friends, and siblings: Differential peer relations of preadolescents and social self-esteem.* Paper presented at the 13th Biennial Meetings of the International Society for the Behavioural Development, Amsterdam. The Netherlands.

Benedict, R. F. (1934). Anthropology and the abnormal. *Journal of General Psychology, 10,* 59–80.

Block, J. H. (1981). *The Child-Rearing Practices Report (CRPR): A set of Q items for the description of parental socialization attitudes and values.* Berkeley: University of California, Institute of Human Development.

Boivin, M., Hymel, S., & Bukowski, W. M. (1995). The roles of social withdrawal, peer rejection, and victimization by peers in predicting loneliness and depressed mood in childhood. *Development and Psychopathology, 7,* 765–785.

Broberg, A., Lamb, M. E., & Hwang, P. (1990). Inhibition: Its stability and correlates in 16- to 40-month-old children. *Child Development, 61,* 1153–1163.

Buck, R. (1993). Emotional communication, emotional competence, and physical illness: A developmental-interactionist view. In H. C. Traue & J. W. Pennebaker (Eds.), *Emotion inhibition and health* (pp. 32–56). Seattle, WA: Hogrefe & Huber Publishers.

Caspi, A., Elder, G. H., Jr., & Bem, D. J. (1988). Moving away from the world: Life-course patterns of shy children. *Developmental Psychology, 24,* 824–831.

Chan, J., & Eysenck, S. B. G. (1981, August). *National differences in personality: Hong Kong and England.* Paper presented at the joint International Association of Cross-Cultural Psychology–International Council of Psychologists Asian Regional Meeting, National Taiwan University, Taipei.

Chao, R. K. (1994). Beyond parental control and authoritarian parenting styles: Understanding Chinese parenting through the cultural notion of training. *Child Development, 65,* 1111–1119.

Chen, X. (in press). The changing Chinese family: Resources, parenting practices, and children's socio-emotional problems. In U. P. Gielen & A. L. Comunian (Eds.), *Family and family therapy in international perspective*. Milan, Italy: Marinelli Editrice.

Chen, X., Dong, Q., & Zhou, H. (1997). Authoritative and authoritarian parenting practices and social and school adjustment in Chinese children: A cross-cultural perspective. *International Journal of Behavioural Development, 20,* 855–873.

Chen, X., & Kaspar, V. (in press). Cross-cultural research on childhood. In U. P. Gielen & A. L. Conmunian (Eds.), *Cross-cultural and international dimensions of psychology*. Trieste, Italy: Edinzioni Lint Trieste.

Chen, X., Rubin, K. H., & Li, B. (1995). Depressed mood in Chinese children: Relations with school performance and family environment. *Journal of Consulting and Clinical Psychology, 63,* 938–947.

Chen, X., Rubin, K. H., & Li, B. (1997). Maternal acceptance and social and school adjustment in Chinese children: A four-year longitudinal study. *Merrill-Palmer Quarterly, 43,* 663–681.

Chen, X., Rubin, K. H., & Li, Z. (1995). Social functioning and adjustment in Chinese children: A longitudinal study. *Developmental Psychology, 1,* 531–539.

Chen, X., Rubin, K. H., & Sun, Y. (1992). Social reputation and peer relationships in Chinese and Canadian children: A cross-cultural study. *Child Development, 63,* 1336–1343.

Crockenberg, S. (1986). Are temperamental differences in babies associated with predictable differences in caregiving? In J. V. Lerner & R. M. Lerner (Eds.), *Temperament and social interaction in infancy and childhood* (pp. 53–72). San Francisco: Jossey-Bass.

Eisenberg, L. (1958). School phobia: A study in the communication of anxiety. *American Journal of Psychiatry, 114,* 712–718.

Ekblad, S. (1986). Relationships between child-rearing practices and primary school children's functional adjustment in the People's Republic of China. *Scandinavian Journal of Psychology, 27,* 220–230.

Farver, J. M., & Howes, C. (1988). Cultural differences in social interaction: A comparison of American and Indonesian children. *Journal of Cross-Cultural Psychology, 19,* 203–215.

Feng, Y. L. (1962). *The spirit of Chinese philosophy*. (E. R. Hughes, Trans.). London: Routledge & Kegan Paul.

Fox. N., & Calkins, S. (1993). Relations between temperament, attachment, and behavioral inhibition: Two possible pathways to extroversion and social withdrawal. In K. H. Rubin & J. Asendorpf (Eds.), *Social withdrawal, inhibition, and shyness in childhood* (pp. 81–100). Chicago: University of Chicago Press.

Fox, N., Rubin, K. H., Calkins, S., Marshall, T. R., Coplan, R. J., Porges, S. W., Long, J. M., & Stewart, S. (1995). Frontal activation asymmetry and social competence at four years of age. *Child Development, 66,* 1770–1784.

Garcia-Coll, C., Kagan, J., & Reznick, J. S. (1984). Behavioral inhibition in young children. *Child Development, 55,* 1005–1019.

Gresham, F. M. (1986). Conceptual issues in the assessment of social competence in children. In P. S. Strain, M. J. Guralnick, & H. M. Walker (Eds.), *Children's social behavior: Development, assessment, and modification* (pp. 143–179). New York: Academic Press.

Grossman, K. E., & Grossman, K. (1981). Parent–infant attachment relationships in Bielefield. In K. Immelmann, B. Barlow, L. Petrovich, M. Main (Eds.), *Behavioral development: The Bielefield interdisciplinary project* (pp. 694–699). New York: Cambridge University Press.

Hayashi, K., Toyama, B., & Quay, H. C. (1976). A cross-cultural study concerned with differential behavioral classification. I. The Behavior checklist. *Japanese Journal of Criminal Psychology*, *2*, 21–28.

Ho, D. Y. F. (1986). Chinese pattern of socialization: A critical review. In M. H. Bond (Ed.), *The psychology of the Chinese people* (pp. 1–37). New York: Oxford University Press.

Jones, W. H., & Carpenter, B. N. (1986). Shyness, social behavior, and relationships. In W. H. Jones, J. M. Cheek, & S. R. Briggs (Eds.), *Shyness: Perspectives on research and treatment* (pp. 227–238). New York: Plenum Press.

Kagan, J. (1989). Temperamental contributions to social behavior. *American Psychologist*, *44*, 668–674.

Kagan, J., Kearsley, R. B., & Zelazo, P. R. (1978). *Infancy: Its place in human development*. Cambridge, MA: Harvard University Press.

Kagan, J., & Moss, H. A. (1962). *Birth to maturity: A study in psychological development*. New York: Wiley.

Kagan, J., Reznick, J. S., Clarke, C., Snidman, N., & Garcia-Coll, C. (1984). Behavioral inhibition to the unfamiliar. *Child Development*, *55*, 2212–2225.

Kagan, J., Reznick, J. S., Snidman, Gibbons, J., & Johnson, M. O. (1988). Childhood derivatives of inhibition and lack of inhibition to the unfamiliar. *Child Development*, *59*, 1580–1589.

Kerr, M., Lambert, W. W., & Bem, D. J. (1996). Life course sequelae of childhood shyness in Sweden: Comparison with the United States. *Developmental Psychology*, *32*, 1100–1105.

King, A. Y. C., & Bond, M. H. (1985). The Confucian paradigm of man: A sociological view. In W. S. Tseng & D. Y. H. Wu (Eds.), *Chinese culture and mental health* (pp. 29–45). San Diego, CA: Academic Press.

Kochanska, G. (1991). Patterns of inhibition to the unfamiliar in children of normal and affectively ill mothers. *Child Development*, *62*, 250–263.

Kochanska, G., & Radke-Yarrow, M. (1992). Early childhood inhibition and the dynamics of the child's interaction with an unfamiliar peer at age five. *Child Development*, *63*, 325–335.

Kriger, S. F., & Kroes, W. H. (1972). Child-rearing attitudes of Chinese, Jewish, and Protestant mothers. *Journal of Social Psychology*, *86*, 205–210.

LeVine, R. A. (1988). Human parental care: Universal goals, cultural strategies, individual behavior. In R. A. LeVine, P. M. Miller, & M. M. West (Eds.), *Parental behavior in diverse societies* (pp. 3–12). San Francisco: Jossey-Bass.

Lin, C. C., & Fu, V. R. (1990). A comparison of child-rearing practices among Chinese, immigrant Chinese, and Caucasian-American parents. *Child Development*, *61*, 429–433.

Liu, J., Li, A., Cao, Z., Fan, Y., Hu, H., Gao, F., & Yuan, J. (1996). A study of the criteria for good parents in Shanghai. *Psychological Development and Education*, *12*, 43–48.

Miller, S. A. (1995). Parents' attributions for their children's behavior. *Child Development*, *66*, 1557–1584.

Mills, R. S. L., & Rubin, K. H. (1990). Parental beliefs about problematic social behaviours in early childhood. *Child Development*, *61*, 25–39.

Mizuta, I., Zahn-Waxler, C., Cole, P. M., & Hiruma, N. (1996). A cross-cultural study of preschoolers' attachment: Security and sensitivity in Japanese and US dyads: *International Journal of Behavioral Development*, *19*, 141–159.

Parker, G. (1983), *Parental overprotection: A risk factor in psychosocial development.* New York: Grune & Stratton.

Pederson, D. R., & Moran, G. (1995). A categorical description of infant–mother relationships in the home and its relation to Q-sort measures of infant–mother interaction. In E. Waters, B. E. Vaughn, G. Poseda, & K. Kondo-Ikemura (Eds.), Caregiving, cultural, and cognitive perspectives on secure-base behavior and working models: New growing points of attachment theory and research. *Monographs of the Society for Research in Child Development, 60,* (2–3, Serial No. 244), 111–132.

Peters-Martin, P., & Wachs, T. D. (1984). A longitudinal study of temperament and its correlates in the first 12 months. *Infant Behavior and Development, 7,* 285–298.

Reznick, J. S., Kagan, J., Snidman, N., Gersten, M., Baak, K., & Rosenberg, A. (1986). Inhibited and uninhibited children: A follow-up study. *Child Development, 57,* 660–680.

Rickman, M. D., & Davidson, R. J. (1994). Personality and behavior in parents of temperamentally inhibited and uninhibited children. *Developmental Psychology, 30,* 346–354.

Rohner, R. P. (1986). *The warmth dimension: Foundation of parental acceptance–rejection theory.* Newbury Park, CA: Sage.

Rubin, K. H., & Asendorpf, J. (1993). *Social withdrawal, inhibition, and shyness in childhood.* Hillsdale, NJ: Erlbaum.

Rubin, K. H., Chen, X., & Hymel, S. (1993). Socio-emotional characteristics of aggressive and withdrawn children. *Merrill-Palmer Quarterly, 39,* 518–534.

Rubin, K. H., Chen, X., McDougall, P., Bowker, A., & McKinnon (1995). The Waterloo Longitudinal Project: Predicting internalizing and externalizing problems in adolescence. *Development and Psychopathology, 7,* 751–764.

Rubin, K. H., Coplan, R. J., Fox, N. A., & Calkins, S. D. (1995). Emotionality, emotion regulation, and preschoolers' social adaptation. *Development and Psychopathology, 7,* 49–62.

Rubin, K. H., Hastings, P. D., Stewart, S., Henderson, H. A., & Chen, X. (1997). The consistency and concomitants of inhibition: Some of the children, all of the time. *Child Development, 68,* 467–483.

Rubin, K. H., & Mills, R. S. L. (1990). Maternal beliefs about adaptive and maladaptive social behaviors in normal, aggressive, and withdrawn preschoolers. *Journal of Abnormal Child Psychology, 18,* 419–435.

Rubin, K. H., & Mills, R. S. L. (1992). Parent's thoughts about children's socially adaptive and maladaptive behaviors: Stability, change and individual differences. In I. Sigel, J. Goodnow, & A. McGilli-cuddy-deLisi (Eds.), *Parental belief systems* (pp. 41–68). Hillsdale, NJ: Erlbaum.

Schwartz, C. E. (1997, April). *Inhibited and uninhibited infants "grown-up" at adolescence. Fears and behavior.* Paper presented at the biennial meeting of the Society for Research in Child Development, Washington, DC.

Steinberg, L., Dornbusch, S., & Brown, B. B. (1992). Ethnic differences in adolescent achievement: A ecological perspective. *American Psychologist, 47,* 723–729.

Stevenson, H. W., Lee, S., Chen, C., Stigler, J. W., Hsu, C., & Kitamura, S. (1990). Contexts of achievement. *Monographs of the Society for Research in Child Development, 55,* (1–2, Serial No. 221).

Stevenson-Hinde, J., & Shouldice, A. (1993). Wariness to strangers: A behavior systems perspective revisited. In K. H. Rubin & J. Asendorpf (Eds.), *Social withdrawal, inhibition, and shyness in childhood* (pp. 101–116). Hillsdale, NJ: Erlbaum.

Super, C. M., & Harkness, S. (1986). The developmental niche: A conceptualization at the interface of child and culture. *International Journal of Behavioral Development, 9*, 545–569.

Tieszen, H. R. (1979). Children's social behavior in a Korean preschool. *Journal of Korean Home Economics Association, 17*, 71–84.

Weisz, J. R., Suwanlert, S., Chaiyasit, W., & Walter, B. R. (1987). Over- and undercontrolled referral problems among Thai and American children and adolescents: The *wat* and *wai* of cultural differences. *Journal of Consulting and Clinical Psychology, 55*, 719–726.

Whiting, B. B., & Edwards, C. P. (1988). *Children of different worlds*. Cambridge, MA: Harvard University Press.

Wu, D. Y. H., & Tseng, W. (1985). Introduction: The characteristics of Chinese culture. In W. Tseng & D. Y. H. Wu (Eds.), *Chinese culture and mental health* (pp. 3–13), San Diego, CA: Academic Press.

Zahn-Waxler, C., Friedman, R. J., Cole, P. M., Mizuta, I., & Hiruma, N. (1996). Japanese and United States preschool children's responses to conflict and distress. *Child Development, 67*, 2462–2477.

7

A Cross-National Study of Self-Evaluations and Attributions in Parenting: Argentina, Belgium, France, Israel, Italy, Japan, and the United States

Marc H. Bornstein, O. Maurice Haynes, Hiroshi Azuma, Celia Galperín, Sharone Maital, Misako Ogino, Kathleen Painter, Liliana Pascual, Marie-Germaine Pêcheux, Charles Rahn, Sueko Toda, Paola Venuti, André Vyt, and Barbara Wright
National Institute of Child Health and Human Development

This study investigated and compared ideas about parenting in Argentine, Belgian, French, Israeli, Italian, Japanese, and U.S. mothers of 20-month-olds. Mothers evaluated their competence, satisfaction, investment, and role balance in parenting and rated attributions of successes and failures in 7 parenting tasks to their own ability, effort, or mood, to difficulty of the task, or to child behavior. Few cross-cultural similarities emerged; rather, systematic culture effects for both self-evaluations and attributions were common, such as varying degrees of competence and satisfaction in parenting, and these effects are interpreted in terms of specific cultural proclivities and emphases. Child gender was not an influential factor. Parents' self-evaluations and attributions help to explain how and why parents parent and provide further insight into the broader cultural contexts of children's development.

In the burgeoning study of parenting, what and how parents think about their own parenting have both descriptive and explanatory values. Two salient aspects of parental

Marc H. Bornstein, O. Maurice Haynes, Hiroshi Azuma, Celia Galperín, Sharone Maital, Misako Ogino, Kathleen Painter, Liliana Pascual, Marie-Germaine Pêcheux. Charles Rahn, Sueko Toda, Paola Venuti. André Vyt, and Barbara Wright, Child and Family Research, National Institute of Child Health and Human Development, National Institutes of Health, Bethesda, Maryland.

We thank members of the ESTUDIO I.P.M. Investigaciones en Psicologia y Medicina, H. Bornstein, S. Galperín, J. Genevro, G. Jaimsky, V. Lewis, J, Ruel, M. I. Sárate, K. Schulthess, J.T.D. Suwalsky, K. M. Tanner, K. Trivisonno, and F. Vander Linden for assistance.

Correspondence concerning this article should be addressed to Marc H. Bornstein, Child and Family Research, Laboratory of Comparative Ethology, National Institute of Child Health and Human Development, National Institutes of Health, Building 31—Room B2B15, 9000 Rockville Pike, Bethesda, Maryland 20892-2030. Electronic mail may be sent to Marc_H_Bornstein@nih.gov.

thought are self-evaluations of parenting and attributions of parental successes and failures. In this study, we obtained information about mothers' self-evaluations of their competence, satisfaction, investment, and role balance in parenting and about mothers' attributions for their successes and failures in diverse parenting tasks; we compared these self-evaluations and attributions among mothers in seven nations, including Argentina, Belgium, France, Israel, Italy, Japan, and the United States.

Parents' ideas about their own parenting may not only shape parents' sense of self but also influence parenting behaviors or mediate the effectiveness of those behaviors and ultimately affect child development (see Goodnow & Collins, 1990; Harkness & Super, 1996; Holden, 1995; McGillicuddy-DeLisi & Sigel, 1995; Miller, 1988). Self-evaluations and attributions might anticipate parenting practices in the same way that Darling and Steinberg (1993) construed parenting goals and values do; Parenting practices fall causally between self-evaluations and attributions, on the one hand, and child outcomes, on the other hand. Of course, children engender parenting beliefs and provoke parenting practices; child rearing is a transactional process. Nonetheless, self-evaluations and attributions exert direct effects on parenting practices, influence the relative effectiveness of parenting practices, and constitute important "emotional climate" variables with respect to parenting practices, any of which influence child growth. How might these parenting beliefs link to parenting behaviors or child outcomes? Regarding self-evaluations, according to the self-efficacy theory (Bandura, 1986), mothers who feel more competent in their role as parent, for example, can be expected to act with their children in more optimal and effective (warm, sensitive, and responsive) ways (e.g., Baldwin, Cole, & Baldwin, 1982; Johnston & Mash, 1989; Peterson & Seligman, 1984). Greater satisfaction with the maternal role is associated with more favorable adjustment to motherhood (e.g., Owen & Cox, 1988). This is similar with attributions. Mothers who attribute child-rearing failures to their own abilities versus their children's behavior, for example, behave in different ways toward their children (e.g., Dix, 1991). More generally, self-evaluations and attributions can be expected to mediate or moderate parents' behaviors (e.g., McGillicuddy-DeLisi & Singel, 1995; Weiner, 1985). As mediators, self-evaluations and attributions convey the effects of events (like child behaviors) on parenting responses (like interactions). As moderators, self-evaluations and attributions may qualify the effects of events on parenting responses. Studying parents' self-evaluations and attributions also contributes to understanding the full social ecology of child development, including the settings in which the child lives, the customs of child care and child rearing, and the psychology of the child's caregivers, as Super and Harkness (1986) theorized in developing the concept of the child's "developmental niche."

Ideas about parenting are multifaceted and are doubtlessly influenced by many factors, including (at least) parents' personality, experiences in parenting, social comparison, and cultural dictates. Insofar as parental self-evaluations and attributions derive, in part, from culture (Goodnow, 1995; Okagaki & Divecha, 1993), they also contribute to the "continuity of culture" by helping to define cultural patterns and by transmitting cultural information across generations (Benedict, 1938; Bornstein & Lamb, 1992; Darling & Steinberg, 1993; Maccoby & Martin, 1983; Murphey, 1992; Rubin & Mills, 1992). In reviewing the literature on parental beliefs in general, Miller (1988) pointed to the need to broaden the scope of contemporary studies of parenting ideas to include diverse cultures as well as a more extensive network of ideas. The parenting constructs of self-evaluation and attribution have been frequent foci of investigation in at-risk families in which either children present internalizing or externalizing problems (e.g., Johnston & Mash, 1989; Mouton & Tuma, 1988) or parents are identified as neglectful or abusive (e.g., Azar, Robinson, Hekimian, & Twentyman, 1984; Newberger & Cook, 1983; see also Bugental, 1992; Bugental & Shennum, 1984). As a consequence, there is also need for normative as well as worldwide information on self-evaluations and attributions in parenting. The cultural significance of such ideas should not be underestimated: Shweder (1991) has argued persuasively that cultural ideas constitute lenses through which reality is not only seen but also interpreted and perhaps constructed. Cognitions deemed to be normative in one culture could be deviant in another; those deemed to have one sort of outcome in one society might well have other outcomes in other societies (Bornstein, 1995). Specifically, self-evaluations and attributions can vary with culture in both connotation and consequence. The cross-cultural investigation of ideas about parenting is, therefore, requisite to a comprehensive understanding of variations in parenting, child-rearing activities, parent–child relationships, and their cultural consequences for child development (Bornstein, 1991, 1995; LeVine, Miller, & West, 1988; Harkness & Super, 1996; Whiting & Whiting, 1975).

The present cross-national study of parenting self-perceptions and attributions arises from a multivariate longitudinal investigation of multicultural pathways to child development and parenting. In the present article, samples from Argentina, Belgium, France, Israel, Italy, Japan, and the United States were selected with certain conventions in mind: In particular, they were matched on several key sociodemographic variables so that patterns of self-evaluations and attributions systematically associated with particular cultures could be isolated. In each sample, the mother is normally the primary caregiver, and the family organization is typically nuclear. All study participants lived in comparable modern suburban-to-urban settings; in each sample, participants came from a cross-section of socioeconomic classes (excluding the very poor or wealthy). Mothers in the seven samples were also all primiparous, and each had a 20-month-old child.

Beyond these similarities, however, variations in cultural background are reflected in differences in conceptions of parenting norms and in modes of implementing parenting practices. Every culture has its own needs and has evolved its own developmental agendum. Evidence from past comparative and ethnographic research suggests that the societies we studied differ in how they conceive of parenting as well as how they actually parent. The study of parenting ideas is relatively new (Goodnow, 1995; Holden, 1995; Smetana, 1994; Harkness & Super, 1996). and cross-cultural studies of parenting are unusually underdeveloped so that we can provide only a thumbnail sketch of each society's child-rearing orientation to help set parents' tasks appropriately. As natives and inhabitants of these societies and as trained professionals, we have formulated informed speculations in the absence of extensive or systematic literatures. Indeed, it is toward the construction and the elaboration of a science of parenting that this effort is organized.

In contemporary middle-class Argentine society, parenting is characterized by a degree of insecurity because there are no clear rules about how to behave as a parent. In recent history, the country has been troubled economically and politically, and social services have been demeaned or discounted. If anything, familial relationships in Argentina have an authoritarian cast, and parents often appeal to this mode in rearing children. In contrast, Belgian parents tend to be comfortable and secure in their parenting philosophy. High levels of social support prepare mothers for parenting, and extended leave provides ample opportunity for new mothers and their babies to become familiar. Belgian mothers hold relatively high academic and behavioral expectations of themselves and of their children. In France, mothers reportedly rely more on their intuitions in parenting—on what comes naturally and spontaneously. Consonantly, they perceive children and child development as transpiring more independent of, than dependent on, parenting. For example, French mothers frequently use the third person (impersonal *on*) in speech to their babies. In Israel, mothers believe that their efforts in child rearing are both an obligation to society and a means to self-fulfillment. A widely held Israeli tenet is that child-rearing responsibilities are to be shared with extended family and others in the community. Within this framework, both attitude surveys and behavioral observations indicate that Israeli mothers are relatively authoritarian and that they expect their children to show independence from an early age. In Italy, the child is sheltered by maternal affect, and mothers perceive child protection and warmth, folding the child into the family (*la famiglia*) as a principal parenting task. In the traditional view, parenting per se is not thought to exert direct effects on child growth and development, mothers actively discourage early self-actualization skills, and mothers hold later expectations for children's developmental accomplishment. Japan is commonly acknowledged to be an inward, traditional society in which people are largely devoted to collectivity and to the harmony of group identity. Japanese mothers expect mastery of emotional maturity, self-control, and social courtesy in their young children; they are indulgent in the early years, and patience, persistence, and group accommodation are the childhood virtues that they promote. In contrast, U.S. child rearing is individualistic, and mothers tend to rely on their own abilities. American mothers are competitive, they want the best for their children, and they feel that the best way to achieve this goal is to prepare themselves to be good parents. (For reviews and empirical support for these views, see Aguinis, 1988; Azuma, 1986; Bellah, Madsen, Sullivan, Swindler, & Tipton, 1985; Bornstein, 1989; Bornstein, Maital, Tal, & Baras, 1995; Bornstein et al., 1992; Bornstein, Tal, & Tamis-LeMonda, 1991; Carugati, Emiliani, & Molinari, 1989; Doi, 1973; Donati, 1985, 1993; Edwards, Gandini, & Giovaninni, 1996; Emiliani & Molinari, 1995; Fillol, 1991; Fogel, Stevenson, & Messinger, 1992; Izraeli, 1992; Kojima, 1986; Maital, 1983; Markus & Kitayama, 1991; Molinari, 1991; New & Richman, 1996; Pascual, 1991; Pascual, Shulthess, Galperín, & Bornstein, 1995; Pêcheux & Labrell, 1994; Peres & Katz, 1981, 1991; Rabain-Jamin & Sabeau-Jouannet, 1997; Rosenthal, 1992; Rosenthal & Zilkha, 1987; Ryback, Saders, Lorentz, & Koestenblatt, 1980; Sabatier, 1994; Sagi & KorenKarie, 1993; Shamgar-Handelman, 1990; Shanan, 1975; Shwalb, Shwalb, & Shoji, 1996; Vonèche, 1987; Whiting & Child, 1953; Zeldin, 1983.)

To illustrate the differential significance of cultural considerations in parenting self-evaluations and attributions, one should consider the following specific predictions from cultures in which parenting ideas are not wholly "terra incognita": Insights into family dynamics gained by New and her colleagues (e.g., New, 1988, 1994; Welles-Nyström, New, & Richman, 1994) in Italy suggest that mothers see development in children as being natural and inevitable and as not requiring adult intervention. As a consequence, we might expect Italian mothers to be less concerned with competence or investment in parenting and to attribute parenting successes and failures not to ability or effort but to child behavior. In Japan, success in child development is attributable to effort rather than to ability, as documented in extensive and comprehensive studies conducted by Stevenson and his colleagues (e.g., Azuma, 1986; Stevenson, Azuma, & Hakuta, 1986; Stevenson & Lee, 1990). As a consequence, we might expect mothers to prize competence and investment and to attribute parenting successes and failures to their own effort and to child behavior rather than to ability. In the United States, in which individualism and self-actualization are valued (e.g., Bellah et al., 1985; Whiting & Child, 1953), competence at parenting might be esteemed, and parenting successes and failures attributed relatively more to ability than to effort on the part of the parent. Thus, the cultures we studied contrast with each other in specific types of competencies that parents wish to promote in children, in paths that parents follow to instill in children the desire for achieving those goals, in developmental timetables that parents wish their children to meet, and in beliefs that parents have about their role in achieving those ends. On these grounds, Argentina, Belgium, France, Israel, Italy, Japan, and the United States constitute an appealing cross-national comparative set in which to investigate culturally common as well as culturally specific aspects of adults' self-evaluations and attributions about parenting.

METHOD

Participants

In this study, 214 mothers of 20-month-old children from Argentina, Belgium, France, Israel, Italy, Japan, and the United States participated. Mothers in the different countries were recruited from hospital birth notifications, patient lists of medical groups, newspaper birth announcements, and mass mailings, and they were selected to be homogeneous with respect to the following criteria: being primiparous, being at least 20 years of age, and living with their husbands in the same household. Table 1 shows the number of mothers participating in each country, their socioeconomic status (SES), their age and education,

TABLE 1
Demographic Characteristics of the Samples by Country

Country	N	SES[a]		Mother's age		Mother's education[b]		Child's age
		M	SD	M	SD	M	SD	M (months)
Argentina	35	50.8	9.7	28.7	3.5	6.3	1.1	20.6
Belgium	23	46.4	12.1	30.1	3.6	5.1	0.9	20.2
France	32	53.0	11.8	32.1	5.0	5.4	1.5	20.3
Israel	20	53.1	6.0	29.4	3.0	5.7	0.6	20.4
Italy	38	44.9	9.7	31.3	3.0	4.6	1.4	20.1
Japan	30	46.5	12.9	30.2	3.6	5.0	1.1	20.5
United States	36	51.8	7.8	32.6	4.0	6.0	0.8	20.1

Note: SES = socioeconomic status.
[a] Hollingshead (1975) Four Factor Index of Social Status.
[b] Hollingshead (1975) 7-point scale.

and the ages of their children. Although the seven samples were middle class on average, they represented a range from low to upper-middle SES as measured by the Hollingshead (1975; see also Gottfried, 1985; Pascual, Galperín, & Bornstein, 1993) Four Factor Index of Social Status (grand $M = 49.3$, $SD = 10.6$), $F(6, 207) = 3.41$, $p < .01$. The average age of the mothers was 30 years 10 months ($SD = 3$ years 8 months), $F(6, 207) = 5.03$, $p < .001$; their average educational level (measured on the 7-point Hollingshead scale) was 5.4 ($SD = 1.2$), $F(6, 207) = 9.85$, $p < .001$; and their average hours of work per week was 17.1 ($SD = 17.7$), $F(6, 205) = 3.11$, $p < .01$. All children were term at birth and healthy at the time of the study. The samples were balanced for sex of child, $\chi^2(6) = 1.71$, ns, and children averaged 20.3 months of age at the time of the study ($SD = 0.4$ months), $F(6, 207) = 11.28$, $p < .001$. Statistical differences in SES, mothers' age, education, and hours worked, and children's age may not be practicably meaningful; as a precaution, these variables, with the exception of child age in which the range of country means is 2 weeks, were examined as covariates in preliminary analyses (see below).

All of the data in this study were collected from mothers of normally developing children in intact families. Research on parenting beliefs and behaviors has concentrated almost exclusively on mothers in recognition of the fact that mothers have traditionally and across cultures assumed primary—if not exclusive—responsibility for early child care (see Barnard & Martell, 1995; Hill & Stafford, 1980; Leiderman, Tulkin, & Rosenfeld, 1977; Parke, 1995). We studied ideas about parenting near the end of the child's 2nd year. That is, we wanted information from mothers who were settled in the maternal role, whose parenting views had presumably stabilized, and whose experience was equivalent. Finally, the samples studied here were balanced with respect to sex of the child so that we could examine potential differences in parenting self-evaluations and in attributions between mothers of girls and mothers of boys (see Fagot, 1995; Maccoby & Jacklin, 1974).

Measurement Instruments and Procedures

All mothers completed three self-report questionnaires in their homes. Two questionnaires were designed to assess specific domains in the parental role, and one was designed to examine socially desirable response tendencies. To assure equivalence across countries, we arranged to have these instruments, originally constructed and written in English, translated into Spanish, Dutch, French, Hebrew, Italian, and Japanese and then back-translated by bilingual Argentine, Belgian, French, Israeli, Italian, and Japanese natives. In addition, the present authors (experienced professionals in psychology and each a native of one of the countries in the study) reviewed the instruments for cultural appropriateness.

Self-evaluations of parenting. The Self-Perceptions of the Parental Role instrument (SPPR; MacPhee, Benson, & Bullock, 1986) contains 22 items representing four scales that assess different aspects of the mother's parental role: Competence, Satisfaction, Investment, and Role Balance (as parent, spouse, worker, and friend). The SPPR draws on social psychological theories of self-esteem (Harter, 1983) and coercion (Patterson, 1980). Each item has a pair of statements that describe contrasting end points of the dimension in question, thereby minimizing socially desirable responses. For example, one of the items states "some parents do a lot of reading about how to be a good parent" but "other parents don't spend much time reading about parenting." The respondent chooses the statement that better describes her and then checks "sort of true for me" or "really true for me." Scores for each scale were the unweighted mean of responses to the items comprising the scale. Possible scores range from 1 (*low perceived*) competence (etc.) to 5 (*high perceived*) competence (etc.). There are four response items, weighted 1, 2, 4, and 5 to accord with the absence of a response indicating that the item was equally like and unlike the respondent. In a sample of 309 mothers of 12- to 48-month-old children who were used to develop the scales, each scale of the SPPR formed a distinct factor with crossloadings of only 3 of the 22 items; the factors accounted for 53.7% of the total item variance (MacPhee et al., 1986). Each scale (5 or 6 items) had high alpha coefficients (range $= .72$ to $.80$). Scale scores for self-perceived parental competence, satisfaction, investment, and role balance shared between 0.4% and 29.2% of the variance. Self-Perceptions of the Parental Role test-retest reliabilities (r) across a 21-day interval for 53 mothers of 18-month-olds ranged from .82 to .92 for the four scales (Seybold, Fritz, & MacPhee, 1991). In terms of predictive validity, MacPhee et al. (1986) reported that SPPR Competence and Satisfaction scales correlated with What I Am Like scale scores for nurturance and adequacy as a provider. Moreover, a structural equation model of the antecedents of 105 mothers' perceived parental competence fit several predicted relations: Mothers with less intrapsychic dissonance between how they actually parent and how they would ideally like to parent reported more comptence in their parenting (Bornstein, Haynes, Painter, Tamis-LeMonda, & Pascual, 1997).

In the present data set, a four-factor solution of the 22 items with oblique rotation also yielded factors that corresponded well, although not perfectly, with the scales: Two items from the Competence scale loaded nearly equally on the Competence, Satisfaction, and Role Balance factors and one item from the Role Balance scale (indexing perceived interference of parenting on the marriage bond) failed to load on any factor. The four factors accounted for 35% of the variance among the items. Across the seven countries, alpha coefficients were .72, .68, .64, and .59 for Competence, Satisfaction, Investment, and Role Balance, respectively; excluding the item indexing perceived interference of parenting on the marriage bond improved the alpha coefficient for Role Balance to .67. Scale scores for self-perceived parental competence, satisfaction, and role balance shared 14% to 26% of variance, but scores on parental investment were unrelated to scores on the other scales (0.4% to 3%). Self-Perceptions of the Parental Role scale scores behaved very similarly across the seven countries compared to the way they behaved in MacPhee et al.'s (1986) sample in the United States, supporting their use in this cross-cultural study. To assure that the Role Balance item that failed to load on any factor did not unduly influence any findings, we repeated all analyses involving Role Balance with that item removed from the scale and, in the one case in which a difference in findings emerged, that difference is reported.

Attributions of parenting. The Parent Attributions Questionnaire (PAQ; MacPhee, Seybold, & Fritz, n.d.; Sirignano & Lachman, 1985) contains five causal attributions to explain successes and failures in seven parenting tasks. The causes were (a) the mother's ability, (b) the mother's effort, (c) the mother's mood, (d) the difficulty of the task, and (e) the child's behavior (see Weiner et al., 1972). The seven parenting tasks were (a) dressing,

(b) bathing, (c) comforting, (d) teaching, (e) disciplining, (f) communicating, and (g) playing. For example, one of the items for a successful outcome asks "When I am able to comfort my child when he or she cries or is upset, it is because (a) I am good at this, (b) this is easy to do, (c) my child makes this easy to do, (d) I have tried hard, and (e) I am in a good mood." The five causal attributions for each parenting task were ranked in terms of mothers' endorsements of each explanation, and the average rank for each cause across the seven parenting tasks was determined separately for successful and unsuccessful outcomes. The mean aggregated rankings were empirically distributed as continuous variables and, under the assumption that they index a tendency to attribute success or failure in parenting to a particular cause, lend themselves to parametric analysis. In a study of 80 married men and women, Sirignano and Lachman (1985) reported that alpha coefficients of the five explanations (average ratings for a–e) for success were .77, .74, .78, .81, and .86, respectively; coefficients of the five explanations for failure were .87, .76, .87, .88, and .86, respectively. Scale scores for the five attributions for success shared between 0.8% and 21.6% of variance, and those for the five attributions for failure shared between 0.9% and 52.8% of variance (MacPhee et al., n.d.).

In the present data set, 10 common factor analyses for the seven items belonging to the 10 scales each yielded a single factor that accounted on the average for 45% of the variance among the items (range = 31% to 67%). Alpha coefficients for the five explanations (a–e) for success were .83, .74, .87, .80, and .83, respectively; coefficients for the five explanations for failure were .93, .77, .85, .83, and .88, respectively. Attributions of success to various causes tended to correlated negatively with each other (mean $r = -.34$, range $= -.19$ to $-.43$); exceptions were a slight positive correlation between attributions of success to effort and to task difficulty ($r = .16$), and virtually no correlation between attributions of success to mood and to effort or to child behavior. Attributions of failures to various causes also tended to correlate negatively with each other (mean $r = -.43$, range $= -.11$ to $-.65$); exceptions were a moderate positive correlation between attributions of failure to effort and to task difficulty ($r = .43$), a slight positive correlation between attributions of failure to mood and to child behavior ($r = .19$), and virtually no correlation between attributions of failure to mood and to effort. These patterns of relations among the scales and the indices of the internal consistency of the scale items support the applicability of the PAQ of this cross-cultural sample.

The SPPR and PAQ shared little variance—on average, less than 1%: Across the seven countries, the mean absolute correlation of the four SPPR scale scores with the five PAQ attributions of success was .07 (range $= -.16$ to .23). The mean absolute correlation of the four SPPR scale scores with the five attributions of failure was .09 (range $= -.18$ to .23).

Social desirability. In the Social Desirability Scale (SDS; Crowne & Marlowe, 1960), 33 items are used to assess a person's tendency to respond to questions in a socially desirable fashion. For example, one of the items states "I never hesitate to go out of my way to help someone in trouble." Once the mother decides whether each statement item describes her, she then checks "True" or "False." This scale was used to control the SPPR and PAQ for potential cross-cultural differences in self-serving bias (see Chandler, Shama, Wolf, & Planchard, 1981; Markus & Kitayama, 1991). Crowne and Marlowe (1960) reported that test–retest reliability (r) for the SDS is .89.

Preliminary Analyses

Univariate and bivariate distributions of the dependent variables were examined for normalcy, homogeneity of variance, and outliers (Tukey, 1977). To resolve problems of non-normalcy and heterogeneity of variance, several transformations were required (see Winer, Brown, & Michels, 1991): The SPPR Satisfaction scale and the PAQ subscale attributing success to child behavior were raised to the fourth power; the PAQ subscales attributing failure to ability and failure to child behavior were raised to the third power; the SPPR Investment scale, the PAQ subscale attributing success to task difficulty, and the PAQ subscale attributing failure to effort were raised to the one-half power; and the PAQ subscale attributing failure to mood was transformed to its natural log. These transformations resolved kurtosis and heterogeneity of variance in the data, but some variables remained skewed, with likely negligible effects on nominal significance levels in the main analyses (see Glass, Peckham, & Sanders, 1972). Transformed variables were used in analyses; for clarity, untransformed means are presented in the figures. In all the analyses, the maximum available N was used; therefore, Ns in analyses differ.

Across all countries, the tendency of mothers to respond in a socially desirable fashion ($M = 17.2$, $SD = 4.9$) was comparable to that reported for other adult female samples in the United States (Bornstein, Haynes, O'Reilly, & Painter, 1996: $M = 16.3$, $SD = 4.9$, $N = 132$; O'Grady, 1988: $M = 15.2$, $SD = 4.8$, $N = 189$). As noted above, small but statistically significant cross-national differences emerged in SES and in mothers' age, education, and hours of employment. These variables as well as the SDS results were evaluated as covariates by examining their correlations with all dependent variables, collapsing across countries. Mothers' education correlated with the SPPR Competence and Satisfaction scales, and SDS correlated with the SPPR Role Balance scale (rs ranged from .16 to .20, ps < .01, one-tailed). Mothers' education also correlated with the SDS score ($r = -.23$, $p < .001$, one-tailed).

RESULTS

Effects on three sets of dependent variables—mothers' self-evaluations of their parenting, mothers' attributions of successes in parenting, and mothers' attributions of failures in parenting—were tested in separate multivariate analyses of covariance (MANCOVAs), using a 2 (child gender) × 7 (country) factorial design. Following identification of significant univariate effects within the MANCOVA, analyses of covariance (ANCOVAs), in which the effects for each dependent variable were controlled by the other dependent variables and a covariate if necessary, were conducted to test the uniqueness of univariate effects. Significant main effects for country were examined with simple contrasts: in these tests, the significance criterion for the 21 pairwise comparisons was adjusted to .014 with a modified Bonferroni inequality (Keppel, 1982).

Self-Evaluations of the Parental Role

Figure 1 displays means and 95% confidence intervals of the four scales of self-evaluations by country. In a preliminary MANCOVA of the effects of gender and country on

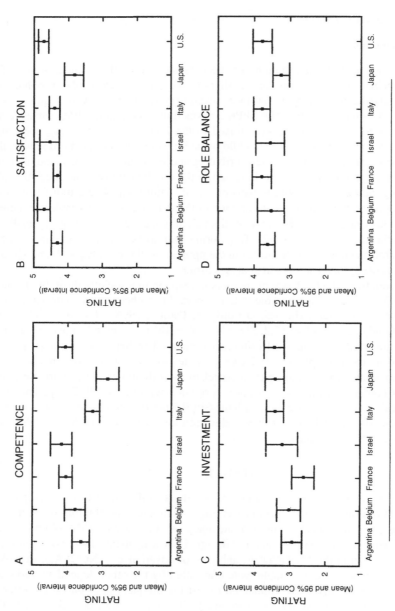

Figure 1. Maternal self-evaluations in four parenting domains (A, Competence: B, Satisfaction: C, Investment: D, Role Balance) in seven countries. (Plotted are mean values and 95% confidence intervals, untransformed and unadjusted for covariates.)

these scales, with mothers' education and SDS as covariates, mothers' education was not a significant multivariate covariate. To simplify the presentation and to maximize power, therefore, we conducted all analyses of effects on the four scales with SDS as the single covariate. (In this and all other analyses, the covariate had equal regression slopes in the cells of the design.) Controlling for SDS, $F(4, 181) = 3.09$, $p < .02$, the MANCOVA yielded a significant main effect for country on the four scales considered simultaneously, $F(24, 736) = 6.43$, $p < .001$; no gender effect for children or interactions of country with gender emerged.

Competence. Controlling for SDS, $F(1, 184) = 7.30$, $p < .01$, the univariate effect for country was significant, $F(6, 184) = 15.28$, $p < .001$. An ANCOVA, controlling by Satisfaction, Investment, Role Balance, and SDS, showed the same effect, $F(6, 188) = 9.14$, $p < .001$. Simple contrasts showed that Israeli and U.S. mothers rated themselves as more competent than did Argentine mothers and that Argentine, Belgian, French, Israeli, and U. S. mothers rated themselves as more competent than did Italian and Japanese mothers (see Figure 1A).

Satisfaction. Controlling for SDS, $F(1, 184) = 4.13$, $p < .04$, the univariate effect for country was significant, $F(6, 184) = 13.20$, $p < .001$. An ANCOVA, controlling by Competence, Investment, Role Balance, and SDS, showed the same effect, $F(6, 188) = 8.16$, $p < .001$. Simple contrasts showed that Belgian and U.S. mothers rated themselves as more satisfied in their parenting than did Argentine, French, and Italian mothers. Japanese mothers rated themselves as less satisfied in their parenting than did mothers from all other countries (see Figure 1B).

Investment. The univariate effect for country was significant, $F(6, 184) = 4.70$, $p < .001$. The univariate effect of SDS as a covariate was not significant, $F(1, 184) = 1.44$, *ns*. An ANCOVA, controlling by Competence, Satisfaction, and Role Balance, showed the same main effect for country, $F(6, 188) = 3.13$, $p < .01$. Simple contrasts showed that Italian and Japanese mothers reported more willingness to invest time and energy in parenting than did Argentine mothers and that Italian, Japanese, and U.S. mothers reported more willingness to invest time and energy in parenting than did French mothers (see Figure 1C).

Role balance. Controlling for SDS, $F(1, 184) = 8.12$, $p < .005$, the univariate effect for country was significant, $F(6, 184) = 2.61$, $p < .02$. In an ANCOVA, controlling by Competence, Satisfaction, Investment, and SDS, the same effect was only marginally significant, $F(6, 188) = 2.09$, $p < .06$. However, in an identical ANCOVA in which the revised Role Balance scale was used (in which the item that failed to load on any SPPR factor was excluded), the effect of country was significant, $F(6, 188) = 3.65$, $p < .01$; this is the one instance in which exclusion of the item from the scale for Role Balance influenced statistical decisions. Simple contrasts showed that French, Italian, and U.S. mothers reported more balance in their multiple roles than did Japanese mothers (see Figure 1D).

Attributions for Success in Parenting

Figure 2 shows means and 95% confidence intervals of the five causes to which mothers attributed success in parenting in the seven countries. The SDS was correlated with the attribution of success to effort ($r = .17$, $p < .05$, two-tailed), and mothers' education was

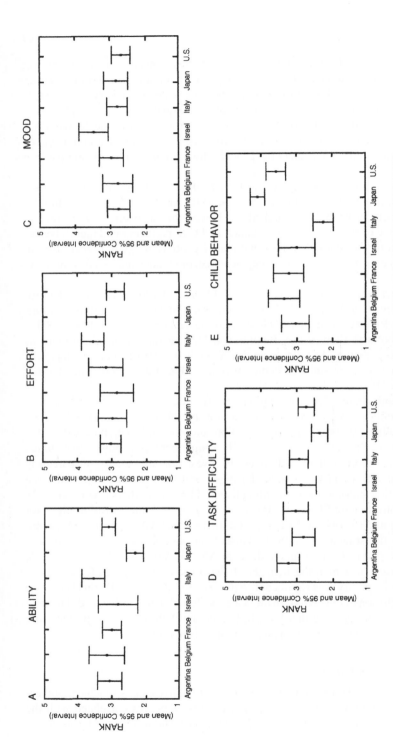

Figure 2. Maternal attributions for success in parenting to five causes (A, Ability; B, Effort; C, Mood; D, Task Difficulty; E, Child Behavior) in seven countries. (Plotted are mean values and 95% confidence intervals, untransformed and unadjusted for covariates.)

not correlated with any attribution of success; therefore, all analyses of effects on attributions of success were conducted with SDS as the single covariate. A MANCOVA yielded a significant main effect for country, $F(30, 865) = 3.74$, $p < .001$; no gender effect for children or for interaction of country with gender emerged. The SDS was not a significant multivariate covariate, $F(5, 169) = 1.41$, ns.

Ability. The univariate effect for country was significant, $F(6, 173) = 5.46$, $p < .001$. An ANCOVA, controlling by effort, mood, task difficulty, and child behavior, showed the same effect, $F(6, 170) = 4.37$, $p < .001$. Simple contrasts showed that Italian mothers attributed success in parenting to their own ability more than did French and Israeli mothers and that Argentine, Belgian, French, Italian, and U.S. mothers attributed success in parenting to their own ability more than did Japanese mothers (see Figure 2A).

Effort. The univariate effect for country was significant, $F(6, 173) = 2.19$, $p < .05$. An ANCOVA, controlling by ability, mood, task difficulty, and child behavior, showed the same effect, $F(6, 170) = 4.54$, $p < .001$. Simple contrasts showed that Italian mothers attributed success in parenting to their own effort more than did French mothers (see Figure 2B).

Mood. The univariate effect for country was not significant, $F(6, 173) = 1.76$, ns. Mothers did not differ across countries in attributing successes in their own parenting to mood (see Figure 2C).

Task difficulty. The univariate effect for country was significant, $F(6, 173) = 3.44$, $p < .01$. An ANCOVA, controlling by ability, effort, mood, and child behavior, showed the same effect, $F(6, 170) = 5.33$, $p < .001$. Simple contrasts showed that Argentine, French, and Italian mothers attributed success in parenting to relative difficulty of the parenting task more than did Japanese mothers (see Figure 2D).

Child behavior. The univariate effect for country was significant, $F(6, 173) = 8.36$, $p < .001$. Simple contrasts showed that Japanese mothers attributed success in parenting to their child's behavior more than did mothers from all other countries and that Belgian, French, and U.S. mothers attributed success in parenting to their child's behavior more than did Italian mothers (see Figure 2E). However, when the country effect was controlled by ability, effort, mood, and task difficulty, it attenuated to nonsignificance, $F(6, 170) = 1.59$, ns: There were no differences among countries in mothers' attributions of success in parenting that were unique to their child's behavior.

Attributions for Failure in Parenting

Figure 3 presents means and 95% confidence intervals of mothers' attributions of failure by country. Mothers' education correlated with attributions of failure to ability and to child behavior ($r = -.16$, $p < .05$ and $r = .20$, $p < .01$, two-tailed, respectively), and SDS was not correlated with any attribution of failure; therefore, mothers' education was used as the single covariate in analyses of effects on attributions of failure. A MANCOVA yielded significant main effects for country, $F(30, 905) = 4.34$, $p < .001$; no child gender main effect or interaction of country with child gender emerged. Mothers' education was not a significant multivariate covariate. $F(5, 177) = .77$, ns.

Ability. The univariate effect for country was significant, $F(6, 181) = 11.65$, $p < .001$. Simple contrasts showed that Argentine, French, and Italian mothers attributed failure in

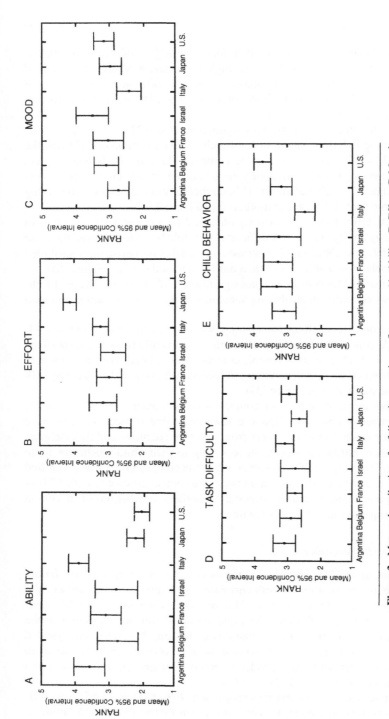

Figure 3. Maternal attributions for failure in parenting to five causes (A, Ability; B, Effort; C, Mood; D, Task Difficulty; E, Child Behavior) in seven countries. (Plotted are mean values and 95% confidence intervals, untransformed and unadjusted for covariates.)

parenting to their own ability more than did Japanese and U.S. mothers and that Argentine and Italian mothers attributed failure in parenting to their own ability more than did Belgian and Israeli mothers. However, when the country effect was controlled by effort, mood, task difficulty, and child behavior, it attenuated to nonsignificance, $F(6, 178) = 1.35$, ns, and there were no differences among countries in mothers' attributions of failure in parenting that were unique to their own ability (see Figure 3A).

Effort. The univariate effect for country was significant, $F(6, 181) = 9.75$, $p < .001$. An ANCOVA, controlling by ability, mood, task difficulty, and child behavior, showed the same effect, $F(6, 178) = 3.91$, $p < .001$. Simple contrasts showed that Japanese mothers attributed failure in parenting more to their own lack of effort than did mothers from all other countries. Italian and U.S. mothers attributed failure in parenting to lack of effort more than did Argentine mothers (see Figure 3B).

Mood. The univariate effect for country was significant, $F(6, 181) = 3.25$, $p < .01$. An ANCOVA, controlling by ability, effort, task difficulty, and child behavior, showed the same effect, $F(6, 178) = 2.73$, $p < .01$. Simple contrasts showed that Belgian, Israeli, Japanese, and U.S. mothers attributed failure in parenting to their own mood more than did Italian mothers (see Figure 3C).

Task difficulty. The univariate effect for country was not significant, $F(6, 181) = 1.56$, ns. Mothers did not differ across countries in attributing failures in their own parenting to task difficulty (see Figure 3D).

Child behavior. The univariate effect for country was significant, $F(6, 181) = 4.03$, $p < .001$. Simple contrasts showed that U.S. mothers attributed failure in parenting to their child's behavior more than did Argentine mothers and that Belgian, French, Israeli, and U.S. mothers attributed failure in parenting to their child's behavior more than did Italian mothers. However, when the country effect was controlled by ability, effort, mood, and task difficulty, it attenuated to nonsignificance, $F(6, 178) = 1.91$, ns; there were no differences among countries in mothers' attributions of failure in parenting that were unique to their child's behavior (see Figure 3E).

DISCUSSION

This study assessed cultural variation in primiparous mothers' self-evaluations of their competence, satisfaction, investment, and role balance in parenting and in their attributions for parenting successes and failures to their own abilities, efforts, and moods as well as to task difficulties and to child behaviors. We sought to investigate mothers' self-perceptions in these two domains of caregiving ideas on the grounds that researchers' greater insight into each will contribute to their understanding parenting more fully and that these ideas help define the climate of child growth, play a direct role in child development, and contribute to the transmission of aspects of culture concerned with parenting. It is important to note that, from a social cognition viewpoint, self-evaluations and attributions constitute key ways that "people make sense of other people and themselves" (Fiske & Taylor, 1984, p. 12), and they appear to possess the significant characteristic of "accessibility"—beliefs that are more accessible can be expected to reflect norms or widely held agreements within a culture and relate to, influence, or rationalize behavior quickly or effectively.

Before proceeding to discuss the main findings, one needs to note that these date derive from self-reports of mothers about specific parenting ideas and that the respondents were mothers of children of one specific age. Furthermore, the sample sizes are limited, educational levels of mothers are relatively high, and participating families are from delimited, if majority, samples in different countries, some of which are known for their pluralistic populations. Our findings might apply uniquely to the self-evaluations and attributions in parenting that we assessed; studies of mothers with children at different ages or stages might yield different patterns of results; fathers' self-evaluations and attributions could differ from those of mothers; and variation in self-evaluations and attributions might be expected from different educational levels or subcultures in any of these nation states. These factors certainly limit the generalizability of the findings by parenting task, setting, and population, and the results reported should certainly not be taken to stand as stereotypical of all citizens in the countries observed. Nonetheless, verbal reports of thought processes are common in everyday life and constitute an essential form of data in cognitive science (Ericson & Simon, 1993), and some important psychological constructs, such as private parenting ideas, are open to study principally by self-report.

The present study contributes to a greater understanding of parenting by documenting some normative aspects of self-evaluations and attributions in child rearing and by providing evidence that cultural background is systematically associated with different parenting ideas. Even when samples are relatively similar with respect to a range of sociodemographic factors, parenting ideas appeared to vary with culture of origin. When systematic associations of maternal SES, age, education, and employment status; social desirability in responding; and child age and gender—all of which might influence parental ideas—were removed from consideration, self-evaluations and attributions of parenting still reflected cultural proclivities. Indeed, these as well as other sampling restrictions (e.g., parity and ecology) actually aid the cross-cultural comparisons undertaken here because the samples were similar on these variables. In the balance of this discussion, we first review similarities across cultures, then comment on cultural specifics in these domains of parenting, and finally reflect on their implications for parenting per se.

Cultural Similarity in Parenting Ideas

Mothers in these seven cultural groups shared remarkably few patterns of self-evaluation and attribution of parenting. Argentine, Belgian, French, Israeli, Italian, Japanese, and U.S. mothers gave equivalent weight to their child's behavior as a source of positive and negative outcomes of parenting (when other attributions were controlled), as they did their own ability as a source of parenting failures; notably, no country effects were unique to child behavior. Moreover, mothers of girls and mothers of boys did not differ in reported self-evaluations and attributions in parenting. If any generalization emerges from these limited similarities, it is that when they were directly responsive to children, mothers everywhere reported the most similarities (a child effect); otherwise, cultural differences reigned pervasively over self-evaluations and attributions.

Common responses observed in mothers' self-evaluations and attributions could reflect one or more sources. These include native panhuman tendencies in parenting; shared reactions to similarities in developmental experiences, intact nuclear families, or urbanized, industrialized, and developed societies, such as we studied; a historical convergence in parenting ideas; or an increasing prevalence of homogeneous beliefs about parenting, resulting from exposure to education or mass media (see Bornstein, 1995; Papoušek & Papoušek, 1995; Ryback et al., 1980). These are related and not necessarily mutually exclusive reasons. It will challenge future research in parenting to adjudicate how these various possibilities might help to explain similarities found in parenting ideas among individuals from different regions of the globe.

Cultural Variation in Parenting Ideas

Many more culture-specific patterns than cross-cultural similarities in maternal self-evaluations and attributions emerged. Although some country differences attenuated when associated scales were covaried, most maintained even after covariation, constituting conservative findings. Of course, child-rearing attitudes and activities can be expected to be adapted to specific societal settings and needs (Bornstein, 1995; Bronfenbrenner, 1979, 1989; Harkness & Super, 1996; Lerner, 1989; Okagaki & Divecha, 1993; Smetana, 1994; Valsiner, 1987). Some variation in beliefs that emerged in different parenting domains coincided with acknowledged cultural values and confirmed our expectations; a few did not. The following summarize country profiles, noting salient findings, but obviously only apply to the samples that we studied. Nonetheless, cultures are characterized by "dominant" and "recessive" messages (in Salzman's, 1981, phraseology), giving prominence to one view while keeping multiple views possible.

Argentine mothers rated themselves relatively low in competence and investment, thought they succeeded best when parenting tasks were not difficult, and blamed their lack of ability for parenting failures. This pattern accords with descriptions of the Argentine middle-class mother as fearful of making mistakes that could make her child unhappy in the future. She is reflective and hesitant, she is self-critical and self-questioning, and she hopes to improve herself as a mother. Argentine women appear to be insecure in their mothering and report that there are no clear answers about how to parent; according to one, "you never know for sure if you are doing a good job," especially with a firstborn. Society does not reinforce feelings of security: Contemporary Argentina lacks a public health care system to provide adequate help or advice in child rearing; instead, mothers seek and make do with ad hoc suggestions from relatives or friends. This situation tends to undermine mothers' beliefs in their own part in the parenting role.

Belgian mothers live in a society that offers good support and security, a circumstance that appears to articulate with reports of the way they feel as parents: Belgian mothers described high levels of satisfaction with their own parenting. An efficient national child-care support agency guides parents (providing demonstration sessions, periodicals, consultancies, home visits, and health care information workshops) and functions remedially as well as preventively. The Belgian school system is distinguished and compulsory to the age of 18 years. Finally, Belgian mothers expect that their children will behave well and ease their responsibilities as parents. These factors could generally contribute to making parents who feel informed, comfortable, and secure in themselves and in the parental role. With the exception of satisfaction, however, it was surprising that Belgian mothers were, relatively speaking, neither very high nor very low in their self-evaluations (see competence) or attributions (see ability); of course, these factors could equally contribute to a sensible realism about parenting.

French mothers rated their investment in parenting and the importance of effort to parenting successes as relatively low. This pattern of findings is congruent with the French view that it is important to be a spouse and a mother at the same time (good role balance) and not necessary to be available to a child at all times. French mothers are less invested in parental training but rather reputedly rely on intuitions and a very modern, highly touted, and widely used infant and child day-care system (Richardson & Marx, 1989). French mothers are more likely than mothers in most other nations to think that successes in parenting come because the tasks are easy. French mothers believe that parenting should come naturally and do not necessarily believe that their efforts change children: If they have to exert extra effort in child rearing, they do not consider themselves good or "genuine" mothers.

Israeli mothers rated themselves high in competence, saw successful parenting as being in the right frame of mind, and did not report failures in parenting as attributable to task difficulty. Israeli society places a high value on having children and appears to foster relatively positive self-perceptions in mothers. Israeli mothers believe that parenting is a social experience that involves others, like relatives and friends, and that mothers' perceptions of satisfaction in parenting in Israel are high. Given the general emphasis on child rearing, it is surprising that investment was not more highly rated, but these assessments may reflect the diffusion of child-rearing responsibilities that is common in Israel.

Italian mothers rated themselves relatively low in competence, as expected, a finding that agrees with the belief that parents play only a little role in children's growth. Unexpectedly, Italian mothers also attributed success to their own efforts and abilities and were least likely to attribute success to child behaviors and failures to the difficulty of the task. This pattern of findings only partially agrees with the belief, regarded as common in Italy, that growth in childhood is natural: Italian mothers reportedly think that the child's development unfolds spontaneously and partially reject effectiveness of adult intervention. According to our data, the principal factors underlying Italian maternal attributions of success are ability and effort: Mothers report that they can influence the development of their child and that the child's own behavior contributes less to parenting successes or failures. These data indicate that Italian mothers attribute the affective and emotional well-being of children to themselves. Clearly, more work is needed to reconcile these empirical results with discussions found in the research literature.

Japanese mothers reported themselves to be the least competent or satisfied in their parenting among mothers in seven cultures, although they are high in investment. It is not socially acceptable in Japan to make claims for one's ability (Japanese might believe in their ability but may not say it). In line with cultural predictions, Japanese mothers apparently think that good children and easy tasks are most important to parenting success and use the phrase *ease of care* (*te no kakaranai*) colloquially to describe a baby or a child. But Japanese mothers also maintained, not unexpectedly, that their own ability matters little next to their ascribing successes and failures in parenting to effort. If a child is not developed or an activity is not accomplished, the mother did not work hard enough. The modern mother in Japan cannot indulge her young children the way she would like (or is expected) to, this fact of life may be reflected in Japanese mothers' relative dissatisfaction with the role balance of parenting versus work. As a whole, however, the Japanese pattern of self-perceptions and attributions in parenting is consonant with cultural conventions of modesty and self-effacting attitudes.

As expected, *U.S.* mothers rated themselves as relatively competent and satisfied with their parenting, and they shied away from attributing parenting failures to their own abilities. Mothers in the United States generally tend to be optimistic and positive when evaluating their parenting: U.S. culture prizes individual effort, and American mothers see parenting as a personal achievement as well as an achievement of their children. Their investment in child rearing is high, and, as a consequence, they are confident in themselves. At the same time, U.S. mothers rank child behavior relatively high with respect to parenting successes.

Cross-cultural behavioral comparisons lend some credence to the psychological reality of these self-report data. Consider two of the cultures: Japan and the United States. Mothers in the United States rated their own ability and Japanese mothers their own effort as relatively responsible for parenting successes in accord with extant cross-cultural behavioral observations of U.S. and Japanese mothers' relative understanding and investment in parenting activities (e.g., Bornstein, 1994; Fogel et al., 1992; Stevenson & Lee, 1990). Caudill and Weinstein (1962, p. 15) contended the following:

> In Japan, the infant is seen more as a separate biological organism who from the beginning, in order to develop, needs to be drawn into increasingly interdependent relationships with others. In America, the infant is seen more as a dependent biological organism who, in order to develop, needs to be made increasingly independent of others.

It is not surprising that Japanese mothers attribute parenting successes to child behavior more than American mothers and attribute parenting failures to child behavior less than American mothers. However, some discordance between acknowledged characteristics of the culture and the nature of parental reports was prominent: As indicated above, Belgian mothers seem intermediate in their self-evaluations and attributions in spite of the fact that their society seems optimal in terms of its support of parenting; Israeli mothers do not appear to be highly invested in parenting in spite of the fact that their culture emphasizes child rearing so much, and the pattern of Italian mothers does not accord with the common belief in Italy that growth in childhood is natural.

Discerning the antecedents of cultural variation in parenting ideas will also challenge future research. Parents' self-evaluations and attributions presumably derive from many sources, which provide for the ongoing dynamic construction of parenting ideas based on the interplay of individual and group level influences. In part, parents in different cultures may inherit or may incorporate different "ready-made schema" or "culturally-packaged beliefs" about children and parenting (Goodnow, 1995; Papoušek & Papoušek, 1995). However, one can also expect parenting schema to be adapted by individuals on the basis of their own personological characteristics, idiosyncratic experiences with children, and external comparisons. Parental ideas could also be constructed on the basis of how parents themselves were parented or as co-constructions with children. Thus, parenting ideas are also affected by learning and experience (Holden, 1995; McGillicuddy-DeLisi & Sigel, 1995). The view that parenting ideas evolve from multiple individual and social factors (Bornstein, 1995; Luster & Okagaki, 1993) implies that these ideas can vary from one culture to another and exercise different effects over child development in different cultures (e.g., Lightfoot & Valsiner, 1992; Palacios, 1990; Palacios, Gonzalez & Moreno, 1992; Valsiner, 1989). To decompose the dynamics of the mutual influences of individual difference and cultural factors, researchers may undertake further studies of parenting ideas most advantageously in multiple cultural contexts.

Implications for Parenting

In this study, we directly assessed several ideas about parenting in mothers in seven cultures. The few similarities and significant differences across countries that emerged have general implications for parenting and also pose specific questions for additional research on self-evaluations and attributions of parenting and parents' roles as mediators and moderators of child development. First, these self-perception and attribution scales showed little conceptual or empirical overlap in an international sample, reinforcing the notion that parenting is characterized by a modularity of ideas as well as behaviors (see Bornstein, 1989, 1995; see also Joshi & MacLean, 1997). The culturally differentiated patterns of components of self-evaluations and attributions provide additional evidence for this modularity.

Second, mothers' ideas about effective and affective parenting perhaps qualify as "zero-order beliefs," or ideas that Bem (1970) argued are so culturally ingrained and widely shared that they unconsciously influence thought and action. On this argument, self-perceptions and attributions will have specific consequences for parenting. In terms of competence, for example, a parent who believes she or he can help determine a child's intelligence or personality may be more active in teaching or in guiding the child. Parental attitudes, such as perceived efficacy, may influence the amount of effort and engagement that a parent exerts. Satisfaction in parenting can lead to different levels of involvement with children, from financial contributions to the family to more immediate nurturance that, in turn, fosters mental development, emotional security, and behavioral adjustment in children. The attributions that parents make about the causes of their successes and failures may likewise foretell the quality of parent–child interactions and, perhaps, the child's development (e.g., Bugental, Blue, & Cruzcosa, 1989; Goodnow, 1995). Perceiving child development as outside parental control leads to greater affective and physiologically aroused responses and to holding the child responsible for her or his behavior. The lower the control the parent perceives she or he has compared to the child, the more likely the parent is to become irritated and to fall back on coercive child-rearing strategies. Along these lines, Bugental et al. (1989) distinguished mothers' attributions for parenting as "self-referent" or "child referent" and found that parents' affect toward their children related to the sources that they perceived as responsible for child development. In the same vein, parents are likely to attribute child achievements to child rearing and child deviations from the norm to child disposition or the environment (Himmelstein, Graham, & Weiner, 1991). Indeed, shared attributions may pervade family life (Fincham & Grych, 1991). Of course, one must keep in mind that the meanings and implications attached to "competence" and "satisfaction" in self-evaluations of parenting and to attributions for parenting "successes" and "failures" can vary by culture (Bornstein, 1995).

Cross-cultural information on child-rearing ideologies can help developmental psychology better explicate variations in child-rearing practices and their antecedents, child development, and its goals. Much previous research in the field of parenting has failed to control for confounds in social class and child age, for example, thereby obscuring interpretations of cultural differences. The present study addresses these problems and others, such as the use of over-generalized, blunt, or global instruments that assess personality rather than parenting per se; failure to control for self-serving bias; and reliance on a limited number of cultures studied. In this study, we used two conceptually targeted instruments to address specific questions about parenting beliefs, took account of social desirability of response bias, and recruited mothers from seven locales around the world. Some central tasks that face future multicultural research in parenting will be to examine how and why adults in different societies come to possess similar and different parental self-evaluations and attributions; to explicate more precisely the processes by which adults in different societies use self-evaluations and attributions about their parenting to set the social agenda that guide day-to-day child rearing; and to discern what the differentiated effects of parenting self-evaluations and attributions may be in child development.

REFERENCES

Aguinis, M. (1988). *Un pais de novela* [A fictional country].] Buenos Aires, Argentina: Editorial Planeta.

Azar, S. T., Robinson, D. R., Hekimian, E., & Twentyman, C. T. (1984). Unrealistic expectations and problem-solving ability in maltreating and comparison mothers. *Journal of Consulting and Clinical Psychology, 52,* 687–691.

Azuma, H. (1986). Why study child development in Japan? In H. W. Stevenson, H. Azuma, & K. Hakuta (Eds.), *Child development and education in Japan* (pp. 3–12). New York: Freeman.

Baldwin, A. L., Cole, R. E., & Baldwin, C. P. (Eds.). (1982). Parental pathology, family interaction, and the competence of the child in school. *Monographs of the Society for Research in Child Development, 47* (5, Serial No. 197).

Bandura, A. (1986). *Social foundations of thought and action.* Englewood Cliffs, NJ: Prentice-Hall.

Barnard, K. E., & Martell, L. K. (1995). Mothering. In M. H. Bornstein (Ed.), *Handbook of parenting* (Vol. 3, pp. 3–26). Mahwah, NJ: Erlbaum.

Bellah, R. N., Madsen, R., Sullivan, W. M., Swindler, A., & Tipton, S. M. (1985). *Habits of the heart: Individualism and commitment in American life.* New York: Harper & Row.

Bem, D. (1970). *Beliefs, behaviors, and human affairs,* Belmont, CA: Brooks/Cole.

Benedict, R. (1938). Continuities and discontinuities in cultural conditioning. *Psychiatry, 1,* 161–167.

Bornstein, M. H. (1989). Cross-cultural developmental comparisons: The case of Japanese–American infant and mother activities and interactions. What we know, what we need to know, and why we need to know. *Developmental Review, 9,* 171–204.

Bornstein, M. H. (1991). Approaches to parenting in culture. In M. H. Bornstein (Ed.), *Cultural approaches to parenting* (pp. 3–19). Hillsdale, NJ: Erlbaum.

Bornstein, M. H. (1994). Cross-cultural perspectives on parenting. In G. d'Ydewalle, P. Eelen, & P. Bertelson (Eds.), *International perspectives on psychological science: Volume 2. State of the art lectures presented at the XXVth International Congress of Psychology, Brussels, 1992* (pp. 359–369). Hove, England: Erlbaum.

Bornstein, M. H. (1995). Parenting infants. In M. H. Bornstein (Ed.), *Handbook of parenting* (Vol. 1, pp. 3–39). Mahwah, NJ: Erlbaum.

Bornstein, M. H., Haynes, O. M., O'Reilly, A. W., & Painter, K. (1996). Solitary and collaborative pretense play in early childhood: Sources of individual variation in the development of representational competence. *Child Development, 67*, 2910–2929.

Bornstein, M. H., Haynes, O. M., Painter, K. M., Tamis-LeMonda, C. S., & Pascual, L. (1997). *Determinants of maternal competence in parenting.* Unpublished manuscript, National Institute of Child Health and Human Development, Rockville, MD.

Bornstein, M. H., & Lamb, M. E. (1992). *Development in infancy: An introduction* (3rd ed.). New York: McGraw-Hill.

Bornstein, M. H., Maital, S., Tal, J., & Baras, R. (1995). Mother and infant activity and interaction in Israel and in the United States: A comparative study. *International Journal of Behavioral Development, 18*, 63–82.

Bornstein, M. H., Tal, J., Rahn, C., Galperin, C. Z., Pêcheux, M. G., Lamour, M., Azuma, H., Toda, S., Ogino, M., & Tamis-LeMonda, C. S. (1992). Functional analysis of the contents of maternal speech to infants of 5 and 13 months in four cultures: Argentina, France, Japan, and the United States. *Developmental Psychology, 28*, 593–603.

Bornstein, M. H., Tal, J., & Tamis-LeMonda, C. S. (1991) Parenting in cross-cultural perspective: The United States, France, and Japan. In M. H. Bornstein (Ed.), *Cultural approaches to parenting* (pp. 69–90). Hillsdale, NJ: Erlbaum.

Bronfenbrenner, U. (1979). *The ecology of human development.* Cambridge, MA: Harvard University Press.

Bronfenbrenner, U. (1989). Ecological systems theory. *Annals of Child Development, 6*, 187–249.

Bugental, D. B. (1992). Affective and cognitive processes within threat-oriented family systems. In I. E. Sigel, A. V. McGillicuddy-DeLisi, & J. J. Goodnow (Eds.), *Parental belief systems: The psychological consequences for children* (2nd ed., pp. 219–248). Hillsdale, NJ: Erlbaum.

Bugental, D., Blue, J., & Cruzcosa, M. (1989). Perceived control over caregiving outcomes: Implications for child abuse. *Developmental Psychology, 25*, 532–539.

Bugental, D. B., & Shennum. W. A. (1984). "Difficult" children as elicitors and targets of adult communication patterns: An attributional-behavioral transactional analysis. *Monographs of the Society for Research in Child Development, 49* (1, Serial No. 205).

Carugati, F., Emiliani, F., & Molinari, L. (1989). Being a mother is not enough: Theories and images in the social representations of childhood. *Revue Internationale de Psychologie Sociale, 3*, 289–306.

Caudill, W., & Weinstein, H. (1962). Maternal care and infant behavior in Japan and America. *Psychiatry, 32*, 12–43.

Chandler, T. A., Shama, D. D., Wolf, F. M., & Planchard, S. K. (1981). Multiattributional causality: A five cross-national samples study. *Journal of Cross-Cultural Psychology, 12*, 207–221.

Crowne, D. P., & Marlowe, D. (1960). A new scale of social desirability independent of psychopathology. *Journal of Consulting Psychology, 24*, 349–354.

Darling, N., & Steinberg, L. (1993). Parenting style as context: An integrative model, *Psychological Bulletin, 113*, 487–496.

Dix, T. (1991). The affective organization of parenting: Adaptive and maladaptive processes. *Psychological Bulletin, 110*, 3–25.

Doi, T. (1973). *The anatomy of dependence* (J. Bester, Trans.). Tokyo: Kodansha International.

Donati. P. (1985). Famiglia e politiche sociali [Family and social policy]. Milan: Angeli.

Donati, P. (Ed.). (1993). *Terzo rapporto sulla famiglia in Italia* [Third report on the Italian family]. Milan: San Paolo.

Edwards, C. P., Gandini, L., & Giovaninni, D. (1996). The contrasting developmental timetables of parents and preschool teachers in two cultural communities. In S. Harkness & C. M. Super (Eds.), *Parents' cultural belief systems: Their origins, expressions, and consequences* (pp. 270–288). New York: Guilford Press.

Emiliani, F., & Molinari, L. (1995). *Rappresentazioni ed affetti* [Affect and representation]. Milan: Raffaello Cortina Editore.

Ericson, K. A., & Simon, H. A. (1993). *Protocol analysis: Verbal reports as data*. Cambridge, MA: MIT Press.

Fagot, B. I. (1995). Parenting boys and girls. In M. H. Bornstein (Ed.), *Handbook of parenting* (Vol. 1, pp. 163–183). Mahwah, NJ: Erlbaum.

Fillol, T. R. (1991). *Social factors in economic development: The Argentine case*. Westport, CT: Greenwood Press.

Fincham, F. D., & Grych, J. H. (1991). Explaining family events in distressed and nondistressed couples: Is one type of explanation used consistently? *Journal of Family Psychology, 4*, 341–353.

Fiske, S. T., & Taylor, S. E. (1984). *Social cognition*. New York: Random House.

Fogel, A., Stevenson, M. B., & Messinger, D. (1992). A comparison of the parent–child relationship in Japan and the United States. In J. L. Roopnarine & D. B. Carter (Eds.), *Parent–child relations in diverse cultural settings* (pp. 35–49). Norwood, NJ: Ablex.

Glass, G. V., Peckham, P. D., & Sanders, J. R. (1972). Consequences to failure to meet assumptions underlying the fixed-effects analyses of variance and covariance. *Review of Educational Research, 42*, 237–288.

Goodnow, J. J. (1995). Parents' knowledge and expectations. In M. H. Bornstein (Ed.), *Handbook of parenting* (Vol. 3, pp. 305–332). Mahwah, NJ: Erlbaum.

Goodnow, J. J., & Collins, W. A. (1990). Development according to parents: *The nature, sources, and consequences of parents' ideas*. Hillsdale, NJ: Erlbaum.

Gottfried, A. W. (1985). Measures of socioeconomic status in child development research: Data and recommendations. *Merrill-Palmer Quarterly, 31*, 85–92.

Harkness, S., & Super, C. M. (Eds.). (1996). *Parents' cultural belief systems: Their origins, expressions, and consequences*. New York: Guilford Press.

Harter, S. (1983). Developmental perspectives on the self-system. In P. H. Mussen (Series Ed.) & E. M. Hetherington (Vol. Ed.), *Handbook of child psychology: Vol. 4. Socialization, personality, and social development* (pp. 275–385). New York: Wiley.

Hill, C. R., & Stafford, F. P. (1980). Parental care of children: Time diary estimate of quantity, predictability and variety. *Journal of Human Resources. 15*, 219–239.

Himmelstein, S., Graham, S., & Weiner, B. (1991). An attributional analysis of maternal beliefs about the importance of childrearing practices. *Child Development, 62*, 301–310.

Holden, G. W. (1995). Parental attitudes toward childrearing. In M. H. Bornstein (Ed.), *Handbook of parenting* (Vol. 3, pp, 359–392). Mahwah, NJ: Erlbaum.

Hollingshead, A. B. (1975). *Four factor index of social status.* New Haven, CT: Yale University, Department of Sociology.

Izraeli, D. N. (1992). Culture, policy, and women in dual earner families in Israel. In S. Lewis, D. N. Izraeli, & H. Hootmans (Eds.), *Dual earner families: International perspectives* (pp. 19–45). London: Sage.

Johnston, C., & Mash, E. J. (1989). A measure of parenting satisfaction and efficacy. *Journal of Clinical Child Psychology, 18,* 167–175.

Joshi, M. S., & MacLean, M. (1997). Maternal expectations of child development in India, Japan, and England. *Journal of Cross-Cultural Psychology, 28,* 219–234.

Keppel, G. (1982). *Design and analysis: A researcher's handbook.* Englewood Cliffs, NJ: Prentice-Hall.

Kojima, H. (1986). Child rearing concepts as a belief-value system of the society and the individual. In H. W. Stevenson, H. Azuma, & K. Hakuta (Eds.), *Child development and education in Japan* (pp. 39–54). New York: Freeman.

Leiderman, P. H., Tulkin, S. R., & Rosenfeld, A. (Eds.). (1977). Culture and infancy: Variations in the human experience. New York: Academic Press.

Lerner, R. M. (1989). Developmental contextualism and the life span view of person–context interaction. In M. H. Bornstein & J. S. Bruner (Eds.), *Interaction in human development* (pp. 217–239). Hillsdale, NJ: Erlbaum.

LeVine, R., Miller, P. M., & West, M. M. (Eds.) (1988). *Parental behavior in diverse societies.* San Francisco: Jossey-Bass.

Lightfoot, C., & Valsiner, J. (1992). Parental belief systems under the influence: Social guidance of the construct of personal cultures. In I. Sigel, A. McGillicuddy-DeLisi, & J. Goodnow (Eds.), *Parental belief systems: The psychological consequences for children* (2nd ed., pp. 393–414). Hillsdale, NJ: Erlbaum.

Luster, T., & Okagaki, L. (Eds.). (1993). *Parenting: An ecological perspective,* Hillsdale, NJ: Erlbaum.

Maccoby, E. E., & Jacklin, C. N. (1974). *The psychology of sex differences.* Stanford, CA: Stanford University Press.

Maccoby, E. E., & Martin, J. A. (1983). Socialization in the context of the family: Parent–child interaction. In P. H. Mussen (Series Ed.) & E. M. Hetherington (Vol. Ed.), *Handbook of child psychology. Socialization, personality, and social development* (Vol. 4, pp. 1–101). New York: Wiley.

MacPhee, D., Benson, J. B., & Bullock, D. (1986, April). *Influences on maternal self-perceptions.* Paper presented at the Fifth Biennial International Conference on Infant Studies, Los Angeles.

MacPhee, D., Seybold. J., & Fritz, J. (n.d.). *Parental attributions and self-esteem among mothers of delayed children.* Unpublished manuscript.

Maital, S. L. (1983). *Are mothers ready for preschool when their children are? The effects of mothers' separation ambivalence on the child's entry to preschool.* Unpublished doctoral dissertation, Temple University, Philadelphia.

Markus, H. R., & Kitayama, S. (1991). Culture and the self: Implications for cognition, emotion, and motivation. *Psychological Review, 98,* 224–253.

McGillicuddy-DeLisi, A. V., & Sigel, I. E. (1995). Parental beliefs. In M. H. Bornstein (Ed.), *Handbook of parenting* (Vol. 3, pp. 333–358). Mahwah, NJ: Erlbaum.

Miller, S. A. (1988). Parents' beliefs about children's cognitive development. *Child Development, 59,* 259–285.

Molinari, L. (1991). Identità sociale e conflitto di ruoli: Principi organizzatori di rappresentazioni sociali dello sviluppo infantile [Social identity and role conflicts: Principles organizing the social representation of child development]. *Giornale Italiano di Psicologia, XVIII*, 97–118.

Mouton, P. Y., & Tuma, J. M. (1988). Stress, locus of control, and role satisfaction in clinic and control mothers. *Journal of Clinical Child Psychology, 17*, 217–224.

Murphey, D. A. (1992). Constructing the child: Relations between parents' beliefs and child outcomes. *Developmental Review, 12*, 199–232.

New, R. S. (1988). Parental goals and Italian infant care. In R. A. Le-Vine, P. M. Miller, & M. M. West (Eds.), *New directions for child development: Vol. 40. Parental behavior in diverse societies* (pp. 51–63). San Francisco: Jossey Bass.

New, R. S. (1994). Child's play—una cosa naturale: An Italian perspective. In J. L. Roopnarine. J. E. Johnson, & F. H. Hooper (Eds.), *Children's play in diverse cultures* (pp. 123–147). Albany: State University of New York Press.

New, R. S., & Richman, A. L. (1996). Maternal beliefs and infant care practices in Italy and the United States. In S. Harkness & C. M. Super (Eds.), *Parents' cultural belief systems: Their origins, expressions, and consequences* (pp. 385–404). New York: Guilford Press.

Newberger, C. M., & Cook, S. J. (1983). Parental awareness and child abuse: A cognitive-developmental analysis of urban and rural samples. *American Journal of Orthopsychiatry, 53*, 512–514.

Okagaki, L., & Divecha, D. J. (1993). Development of parental beliefs. In T. Luster & L. Okagaki (Eds.), *Parenting: An ecological perspective* (pp. 35–67). Hillsdale, NJ: Erlbaum.

O'Grady, K. E. (1988). The Marlowe-Crowne and Edwards Social Desirability Scales: A psychometric perspective. *Multivariate Behavioral Research, 23*, 87–101.

Owen, M. T., & Cox, M. J. (1988). Maternal employment and the transition to parenthood. In A. E. Gottfried & A. W. Gottfried (Eds.), *Maternal employment and children's development: Longitudinal research* (pp. 85–119). New York: Plenum.

Palacios, J. (1990). Parents' ideas about the development and education of their children: Answers to some questions. *International Journal of Behavioral Development, 13*, 137–155.

Palacios, J., Gonzalez, M. M., & Moreno, M.-C. (1992). Stimulating the child in the zone of proximal development: The role of parents' ideas. In I. E. Sigel, A. V. McGillicuddy-DeLisi, & J. J. Goodnow (Eds.), *Parental belief systems: The psychological consequences for children* (2nd ed., pp. 71–94). Hillsdale, NJ: Erlbaum.

Papoušek, H., & Papoušek, M. (1995). Intuitive parenting. In M. H. Bornstein (Ed.), *Handbook of parenting* (Vol. 2, pp. 117–136). Mahwah, NJ: Erlbaum.

Parke, R. D. (1995). Fathers and families. In M. H. Bornstein (Ed.), *Handbook of parenting* (Vol. 3, pp. 27–63). Mahwah, NJ: Erlbaum.

Pascual, L. (1991). *Democracy and educational reforms in Argentina: Possibilities and limitations.* Paper presented at the Annual Conference of the Comparative and International Education Society, Pittsburgh, PA.

Pascual, L., Galperín, C., & Bornstein, M. H. (1993). La medición del nivel socioeconómico y la psicología evolutiva: El caso Argentino [The measurement of socioeconomic level and developmental psychology: The Argentine case]. *Revista Interamericanca de Psicologia/Interamerican Journal of Psychology, 27*, 59–74.

Pascual, L., Schulthess, L., de Galperín, C. Z., & Bornstein, M. H. (1995). Las ideas de las madres sobre la crianza de los hijos en Argentina [Ideas of mothers about child development in

Argentina]. *Revista Interamericana de Psicologia/Interamerican Journal of Psychology, 29*, 23–38.

Patterson, G. R. (1980). Mothers: The unacknowledged victims. *Monographs of the Society for Research in Child Development, 45* (5, Serial No. 186).

Pêcheux, M.-G., & Labrell, F. (1994). Parent – infant interaction and early cognitive development. In A. Vyt, H. Bloch, & M. H. Bornstein (Eds.), *Early childhood development in the French tradition* (pp. 255–267). Hillsdale, NJ: Erlbaum.

Peres, Y., & Katz, R. (1981). Stability and centrality: The nuclear family in modern Israel. *Social Forces, 59*, 687–704.

Peres, Y., & Katz, R. (1991). The family in Israel: Change and continuity. In L. Shamgar-Handelman & R. Bar-Yoseph (Eds.), *Families in Israel* (pp. 9–32). Jerusalem: Academon.

Peterson, C., & Seligman, M. E. P. (1984). Causal explanations as a risk factor for depression: Theory and evidence. *Psychological Review; 91*, 347–374.

Rabain-Jamin, J., & Sabeau-Jouannet, E. (1997). Maternal speech to 4-month-old infants in two cultures: Wolof and French. *International Journal of Behavioral Development, 20*, 425–451.

Richardson, G., & Marx, E. (1989). *A welcome for every child. How France achieves quality in child care: Practical ideas for the United States.* New York: French-American Foundation.

Rosenthal, M. K. (1992). Nonparental care in Israel: A cultural historical perspective. In M. Lamb, R. Sternberg, C. Hwang, & A. Broberg (Eds.), *Child care in context: Cultural perspectives* (pp. 305–330). Hillsdale, NJ: Erlbaum.

Rosenthal, M. K., & Zilkha, E. (1987). Mothers and caregivers as partners in socializing the young child. In L. Shamgar Handelman & R. Palomba (Eds.), *Alternative patterns of family life in modern societies* (pp. 119–131). Rome: Institue de Ricerche Sulla Popolazione.

Rubin, K. H., & Mills, R. S. L. (1992). Parents' thoughts about children's socially adaptive and maladaptive behaviors: Stability, change, and individual differences. In I. Sigel, A. McGillicuddy-DeLisi, & J. Goodnow (Eds.), *Parental belief systems* (2nd ed., pp. 41–68). Hillsdale, NJ: Erlbaum.

Ryback, D., Sanders, A. L., Lorentz, J., & Koestenblatt, M. (1980). Child-rearing practices reported by students in six cultures. *Journal of Social Psychology, 110*, 153–162.

Sabatier, C. (1994). Parental conceptions of early development and developmental stimulation. In A. Vyt. H. Bloch, & M. H. Bornstein (Eds.), *Early child development in the French tradition* (pp. 299–314). Hillsdale, NJ: Erlbaum.

Sagi, A., & Koren-Karie, N. (1993). Daycare centers in Israel: An overview. In M. Cochran (Ed.), *International handbook of daycare policies and progress* (pp. 269–290). Westport, CT: Greenwood.

Salzman, P. C. (1981). Culture as enhabilmentis. In L. Holey & M. Stuchilk (Eds.), *The structure of folk models* (pp. 223–256). London: Academic Press.

Seybold, J., Fritz, J., & MacPhee, D. (1991). Relation of social support to the self-perceptions of mothers with delayed children. *Journal of Community Psychology, 19*, 29–36.

Shamgar-Handelman, L. (1990). Childhood as a social phenomenon: National report, Israel. *Eurosocial Report, 36*, 7–67.

Shanan, J. (1975). Cross-cultural perspectives on the perception of motherhood by mothers. *The family: 4th International Congress of Psychosomatic Obstetrics and Gynecology* (pp. 50–65). Basel, Switzerland: Karger.

Shwalb, D. W., Shwalb, B. J., & Shoji, J. (1996). Japanese mothers' ideas about infants and temperament. In S. Harkness & C. M. Super (Eds.), *Parents' cultural belief systems: Their origins, expressions, and consequences* (pp. 169–191). New York: Guilford Press.

Shweder, R. A. (1991). *Thinking through cultures: Expeditions in cultural psychology*, Cambridge, MA: Harvard University Press.

Sirignano, S. W., & Lachman, M. E. (1985). Personality change during the transition to parenthood: The role of perceived infant temperament. *Child Development, 21,* 558–567.

Smetana, J. G. (Ed.), (1994). *Beliefs about parenting: Origins and developmental implications.* San Francisco: Jossey-Bass.

Stevenson, H. W., Azuma, H., & Hakuta, K. (Eds.). (1986). *Child development and education in Japan.* New York: Freeman.

Stevenson, H., & Lee, S. (1990). Contexts of achievement: A study of American, Chinese, and Japanese children, *Monographs of the Society for Research in Child Development, 55* (1–2, Serial No. 221).

Super, C. M., & Harkness, S. (1986). The developmental niche: A conceptualization of the interface of child and culture. *International Journal of Behavioral Development, 9,* 546–569.

Tukey, J. W. (1977). *Exploratory data analysis.* Menlo-Park, CA: Addison-Wesley.

Valsiner, J. (Ed.). (1987). *Cultural context and child development.* Norwood, NJ: Ablex.

Valsiner, J. (1989). *Human development and culture.* Cambridge, MA: Lexington Books.

Vonèche, J. J. (1987). The difficulty of being a child in French-speaking countries. In J. M. Broughton (Ed.), *Critical theories of psychological development* (pp. 61–86). New York: Plenum.

Weiner, B. (1985). An attributional theory of achievement motivation and emotion. *Psychological Review, 92,* 548–573.

Weiner, B., Frieze, I., Kukla, A., Reed, L., Rest, S., & Rosenbaum, R. M. (1972). Perceiving the causes of success and failure. In E. E. Jones et al. (Eds.), *Attribution: Perceiving the causes of behavior* (pp. 95–120). Morristown, NJ: General Learning Press.

Welles-Nyström, B., New, R., & Richman, A. (1994). The "good mother": A comparative study of Swedish, Italian and American maternal behavior and goals. *Scandinavian Journal of Caring Sciences, 8,* 81–86.

Whiting, J. W. M., & Child, I. L. (1953). *Child training and personality.* New Haven, CT: Yale University Press.

Whiting, B. B., & Whiting J. W. M. (1975). *Children in six cultures.* Cambridge, MA: Harvard University Press.

Winer, B. J., Brown, D. R., & Michels, K. M. (1991). *Statistical principles in experimental design* (3rd ed.). New York: McGraw-Hill.

Zeldin, T. (1983). *The French.* New York: Vintage Books.

8

Relationship Between Hunger and Psychosocial Functioning in Low-Income American Children

J. Michael Murphy, Ed.D., Cheryl A. Wehler, M.S., Maria E. Pagano, Ed.M.,
Michelle Little, B.A., Ronald E. Kleinman, M.D., and Michael S. Jellinek, M.D.

Objective: *Using large-scale surveys from nine states, the Community Child-*
hood Hunger Identification Project (CCHIP) estimates that 8% of Ameri-
can children under the age of 12 years experience hunger each year. CCHIP
operationalizes child hunger as multiple experiences of parent-reported food
insufficiency due to constrained resources. The current study examined the re-
lationship between food insufficiency and school-age, low-income children's
psychosocial functioning. The study also assessed the interinformant (parent
versus child) reliability and time-to-time reliability of the CCHIP measure.
Method: *Two hundred four school-age children and their parents from four*
inner-city public schools were interviewed using parent, teacher, and clinician
report measures of psychosocial functioning. Ninety-six children and their par-
ents were reinterviewed 4 months later. **Results:** *Hungry and at-risk for hunger*
children were twice as likely as not-hungry children to be classified as having
impaired functioning by parent and child report. Teachers reported higher lev-
els of hyperactivity, absenteeism, and tardiness among hungry/at-risk children
than not-hungry children. Parent and child reports of hunger were significantly
related to each other, and time-to-time reliability of the CCHIP measure was
acceptable. **Conclusions:** *Results of this study suggest that intermittent experi-*
ences of food insufficiency and hunger as measured by CCHIP are associated

Accepted August 15, 1997.

Dr. Murphy, Dr. Jellinek, Ms. Pagano, and Ms. Little are with the Child Psychiatry Service, Massachusetts
General Hospital, Boston, Drs. Murphy and Jellinek are also with the Department of Psychiatry, Harvard Med-
ical School, Boston. Ms. Wehler is with the Community Childhood Hunger Identification Project, C.A.W. and
Associates, Framingham, MA. Dr. Kleinman is with the Division of Pediatric Gastroenterology and Nutrition,
Massachusetts General Hospital and the Department of Pediatrics, Harvard Medical School.

This research was made possible by grants from the Kellogg Corporation and the Mid Atlantic Milk Marketing
Association and with the collaboration of the food service departments of the Baltimore and Philadelphia Public
Schools.

Reprint requests to Dr. Murphy, Massachusetts General Hospital, Child Psychiatric Service, 15 Parkman Street,
ACC 725, Boston, MA 02144.

0890-8567/98/3702–0163/$03.00/0©1998 by the American Academy of Child and Adolescent Psychiatry.

with poor behavioral and academic functioning in low-income children. The current study also supports the validity and reliability of the CCHIP measure for assessing hunger in children. J. Am. Acad. Child Adolesc. Psychiatry, 1998, 37(2): 163–170. **Key Words:** *hunger, low-income children, school breakfast, psychosocial functioning.*

Are food insufficiency and hunger a real problem for poor children in the United States, as some child advocates have claimed? Or, as skeptics have argued, are the experiences of food deprivation and poor-quality nutrition that children from low-income families sometimes experience merely mild exacerbators of other and far more devastating problems such as violence, drug addiction, and family breakdown? For the past decade, an academic and political debate over these questions has taken place in the fields of public health and public policy. Recent efforts to diminish or even eliminate the National School Breakfast and Lunch programs, as well as other programs that provide food for low-income children, have highlighted the issue of hunger for growing children and the potential relevance for clinicians who work with low-income children and their families.

Our understanding of the epidemiology of hunger among children in the United States advanced significantly in the early 1980s when several different groups of academic and policy researchers began to use the constructs of "food insufficiency" (Wehler et al., 1992) or "food insecurity" (Radimer et al., 1992) as a proxy for hunger. The most widely used measure of this sort was developed by the Community Childhood Hunger Identification Project (CCHIP), which conducted a series of studies using large, rigorously selected samples in 21 communities across the United States (Wehler et al., 1991, 1996a). CCHIP categorizes families and children as "hungry," "at risk for hunger," or "not hungry" on the basis of parent answers to eight standardized questions about child and family experiences of food insufficiency due to constrained resources.

The most recent summary of CCHIP's findings, based on the data from nine U.S. states, reports that 8% of children under the age of 12 experience hunger and that an additional 21% are at risk for hunger (Wehler et al., 1996a). According to CCHIP, hunger is most prevalent in children from the lowest-income families (e.g., recipients of Aid to Families With Dependent Children). In such samples, as many as 21% of children are found to be hungry and an additional 50% are classified as at risk for hunger on the CCHIP measure, suggesting that more than two thirds of all of the poor children in this country have had at least one experience of food insufficiency/hunger in the past year.

Studies from nonindustrialized countries have shown that *severe* undernutrition is associated with increased anxiety, attention deficits, school absence, and tardiness in school-age children (Barrett et al., 1982; Mora, 1979) and lower levels of social responsiveness in young children (Chavez and Martinez, 1979; Graves, 1976, 1978). Aggression has also been linked to undernutrition in both human and animal studies, although the human evidence has been largely anecdotal and/or poorly controlled (Gray, 1986; Halas et al., 1975). The only data currently available on the impact of intermittent episodes of food insufficiency and hunger comes from the CCHIP surveys (Wehler et al., 1991, 1996a), which have consistently shown that children who are classified as hungry are more likely to have mood and attention problems and more likely to be absent from school than poor children who are classified as not hungry. One limitation of these data has been that the information about child functioning, like the CCHIP measure itself, is based solely on parental report.

The fact that CCHIP data on the prevalence of food insufficiency and hunger are based on parent reports raises several issues. First, a parent report of multiple family experiences of food insufficiency does not necessarily mean that each child in the family has had the same experience. And even if the child has experienced food insufficiency, it does not follow that he or she has suffered from a clinically significant state of undernutrition. For now, however, short of inducing hunger in children in a laboratory setting to develop physiological measures, CCHIP appears to provide an acceptable way of estimating the prevalence of hunger and its relationship to other factors. One indicator of CCHIP's acceptability has been its wide use in the public policy arena and the adoption of its questions by a number of large-scale governmental surveys such as the National Health and Nutrition Examination Survey (NHANES) and by federal agencies such as the U.S. Department of Agriculture (Wehler et al., 1991, 1996a) and the U.S. Census Bureau (Bickel et al., 1996).

Since another study by the authors demonstrated a relationship between child hunger on CCHIP and a single measure of psychosocial impairment, the current study examined the relationship between child hunger as measured by parent reports on CCHIP and psychosocial problems assessed using standardized measures and multiple informants and academic functioning using school records of attendance and tardiness. Two secondary goals were to determine whether parental reports of food insufficiency were confirmed by a second informant and whether the CCHIP measure was stable over time. Toward these ends we examined the extent of agreement between parent and child answers to CCHIP questions and between parent answers to the CCHIP questions at two different administrations 4 months apart.

METHOD

Study Population and Sampling

Data for the current analyses came from a collaborative study of a free breakfast program in the Philadelphia and Baltimore Public Schools. Students and their parents in four schools (two in Philadelphia and two in Baltimore) were assessed on a battery of psychosocial, academic, and food sufficiency/hunger measures before the start of a free breakfast program in the schools. Teachers of all the students in the study were asked to complete a standardized behavior problem questionnaire before and after the free breakfast program began. The free breakfast program was made possible by Provision 2 of the U.S. Department of Agriculture school meal guidelines which permits free meals for all children in a given school under certain conditions in low-income areas. In Philadelphia more than 150 other schools had already implemented Universal Feeding, while in Baltimore only three other schools had tried the program at the time of this study.

In all four schools, the regular school breakfast was made available for free for all students at the beginning of the second semester. For the current study, students and their parents were interviewed in late January or early February prior to the start of Universal Feeding and then again in late May–early June after the program was implemented. In all four schools, children in grades 3 and higher were invited to participate in the study, although all children were eligible for a free breakfast. Two schools included kindergarten through grade 6, the third included kindergarten through grade 8, and the fourth included grades 5 through 8.

In Philadelphia, the parents of all 186 students in the fourth and fifth grades of an elementary school and 126 fifth- and eighth-grade students in four classrooms of a middle school were invited to participate in the study through letters that were sent home with students. After an additional invitation letter and follow-up phone calls, 125 (40%) of the 312 parents agreed to participate. When interviews were scheduled, 31 of the initially agreeing parents could not be scheduled, resulting in 94 complete parent/child interviews (75% of the agreeing sample and 30% of the total sample). In the two selected schools in Baltimore, the parents of all 367 students in the third through eighth grades were asked to participate in the study through invitation letter and follow-up phone calls, 41% (149/367) of the parents agreed to participate. When interviews were scheduled, 39 of the parents who initially agreed to participate could not be scheduled, leaving a sample of 110 children from the two Baltimore schools (74% of the agreeing sample and 30% of the total sample). Data on the 110 children from Baltimore and the 94 children from Philadelphia were combined, resulting in a sample of 204 children.

To save time and expense, the study design called for only half of the initial sample of 204 children to be reinterviewed at the end of the school year in late May, 4 months after the initial interviews. The parents of 106 children who had participated in the initial school breakfast interview were sent invitation letters for another interview. Students were randomly selected within three groups based on their pre–Universal Feeding school breakfast participation (rarely, sometimes, often) in order to yield a reinterview sample that had the same proportion of participants from the three breakfast groups at the time of the initial interviews (50% ate breakfast rarely, 25% sometimes, 15% often). After follow-up phone calls, 101 (96%) agreed to participate. When interviews were set up, five of the initially agreeing parents could not be scheduled, leaving a reinterview sample of 96 parents and children (91% of the agreeing sample and 95% of the parents who were recontacted).

The parent and child were interviewed separately, one by a master's-level research assistant and the other by a lay interviewer from the community. Lay interviewers were part-time or full-time employees of the school and had associates' or bachelors' degrees. They were trained in the administration of the simple measures prior to the start of the interviews, and their work was checked by the research assistant. All clinical coding was done by one of the authors. Parents and children were asked questions about food security and children's psychosocial, behavioral, and academic functioning; other questions about food and eating; and questions about the family's functioning and background. CCHIP hunger questions were asked at the end of the interviews after the other measures had been administered, and interviewers were blind to the family's CCHIP hunger status. The study was approved by the Human Studies Subcommittee at the Massachusetts General Hospital and by the research committees of the Philadelphia and Baltimore Public Schools. Participation of parents, children, and teachers was voluntary, and access to school records was made possible through a separate consent signed by parents.

TABLE 1

Community Childhood Hunger Identification Project Survey

Eight questions asked of the parent

Thinking about the past 12 months:

*1. Did your household ever run out of money to buy food to make a meal?
 2. Did you or adult members of your household ever eat less than you felt you should because there was not enough money to buy food?
*3. Did your child(ren) ever eat less than you felt they should because there was not enough money to buy food?
*4. Did your child(ren) ever say they were hungry because there was not enough food in the house?
*5. Did your child(ren) ever go to bed hungry because there was not enough money to buy food?
*6. Did you ever cut the size of your child(ren)'s meals or did they skip meals because there was not enough money to buy food?
 7. Did you or adult members of your household ever cut the size of your meals or skip meals because there was not enough money to buy food?
 8. Did you ever rely on a limited number of foods to feed members of your household because you were running out of money to buy food for a meal?

Five questions asked of the child constituting the Child Hunger Interview Child Report

Thinking about the past 12 months:

1. Did your household ever run out of money to buy food to make a meal?
2. Did you ever eat less than you felt you should because there was not enough money to buy food?
3. Did you ever tell your parent(s) that you were hungry because there was not enough food in the house?
4. Did you ever go to bed hungry because there was not enough money to buy food?
5. Did you ever cut the size of your meals or did you skip meals because there was not enough money to buy food?

*Questions comprising the Child Hunger Index Parent Report scale.

Measures

Background data. For the current study, the children's grade level, ethnicity, gender, and parental marital status were assessed from questions in the parent interview.

CCHIP hunger scale. The eight-item CCHIP hunger measure assesses experiences of food insufficiency in households in order to classify them as "hungry," "at risk for hunger," or "not hungry" (Table 1). Principal-component factor analyses have shown the content validity of the CCHIP measure to be excellent (Wehler et al., 1996b). Since there have been no published data on CCHIP's validity and time-to-time reliability, the current study addressed these issues.

Four of the eight questions on the CCHIP scale concern the children in the household, two concern hunger in adult members of the household, and two concern household food insufficiency. Children are classified as "hungry" if the parent responds positively to five or more of the eight questions concerning hunger in the past year. With a score of five, the parent must have responded positively to at least one question about the child's hunger, thus providing face validity that CCHIP is a measure of child hunger. Children are classified as at risk for hunger if the parent responds positively to one or as many as four of the eight food insufficiency questions. If the parent does not respond positively to any of the eight food insufficiency questions, the household and child are classified as not hungry. *Child hunger status.* The eight-item CCHIP scale was administered to parents at the time of the initial interviews and again after 4 months in the reinterview phase of the study to assess the time-to-time reliability of CCHIP. The full set of eight CCHIP questions was not administered to children because the investigators believed that the children would not have knowledge of three of the (parent/household hunger) questions. Instead, we asked children the five CCHIP questions that we thought that children as well as parents would have knowledge of, and then we assessed the interinformant agreement (convergent validity) of this modified CCHIP measure.

Solely for the purpose of this assessment, we created a five-item scale, the Child Hunger Index Parent (or Child) Report (CHI-P/CHI-C) (see Table 1). For parents and children, a total CHI-P or CHI-C score was computed by summing the yes answers to the five CCHIP questions. In an effort to match the relative distribution of hunger categories on the new measure with the distribution of categories on the standardized eight-item CCHIP measure, children who (or whose parents) responded positively to two or more of the above questions were classified as "hungry." When the child or parent responded positively to one of the questions, the child was classified as at risk for hunger on the CHI-P/CHI-C. Those who did not respond positively to any of the items were classified as not hungry. The degree of agreement between parent and child reports of the child's hunger (CHI-P versus CHI-C) could then be calculated. The degree of association between the child's report of hunger on the CHI-C and the parent's report of child hunger on the full eight-item CCHIP measure was also assessed.

For the assessment of time-to-time reliability, CCHIP hunger category based on parental response to the full eight-item CCHIP survey at time 1 and again at time 2 was used. *Parent report measures.* The Pediatric Symptom Checklist (PSC) is a brief, widely used, parent-completed questionnaire that has been validated as a screening measure to identify children with psychosocial problems (Jellinek and Murphy, 1988; Jellinek et al., 1986; Murphy and Jellinek, 1988; Murphy et al., 1992, 1996). The PSC consists of 35 items that are rated as "never," "sometimes," or "often" present and scored 0, 1, or 2, respectively. A total score is obtained by adding the scores for each of the items and impairment is defined as a total score of 28 or higher.

The Child Behavior Checklist (CBCL) is the most widely used parent report of children's symptoms and behaviors (Achenbach, 1991). It has been validated in normative samples for children aged 4 to 16 years (Achenbach, 1991). The CBCL consists of 118 items scored on a 3-point Likert scale. The parent indicates for each symptom whether it is "often," "sometimes," or "never" present. The individual symptoms are given scores of 2, 1, or 0 (often, sometimes, or never present), and a total score is obtained by adding the scores for each of the items. Following standard practices with the CBCL, cutoff scores based on the Total Behavior Problems item set were also used as a criterion of case/noncase rating (Achenbach, 1991).

Teacher report measure. The Conners Teacher Rating Scale-39 (CTRS-39) is one of the most frequently used teacher-reported symptom checklists. It consists of 39 items that assess hyperactivity and other behavioral problems in school-age children. Teachers check each item as not at all present, just a little present, pretty much present, or very much present, with numerical scoring weights of 0, 1, 2, and 3, respectively.

Although there are seven subscales on the CTRS-39, the most frequently used scale and the one that is recommended for behavior problem change studies is the Hyperactivity Index. The Hyperactivity Index is based on a subset of 10 items and has been demonstrated to be a valid and useful assessment tool (Boyle and Jones, 1985; Sandoval, 1981). Total scores on the CTRS-39 Hyperactivity Index have been shown to correlate reliably with the amount of observed motor activity in the classroom among normal school-age children (Kivlahan et al., 1982) as well as ratings of excessive talking (Minde, 1980). For all CTRS-39 subscales, a higher score indicates more symptomatology. The total symptom T score of the CTRS-39's Hyperactivity Index is the only one reported in the current study because the other subscales were not found to be significantly associated with hunger levels.

Interviewer-rated measure. After the interviews were completed, the researchers reviewed all parent and child questionnaire data for each case (excluding the hunger questions) and provided ratings of each child's overall functioning using the Children's Global Assessment Scale (CGAS). Using the cutoff defined by Shaffer and associates (1983), CGAS scores of 70 or below were considered indicative of a clinical range of impairment. The CGAS has been widely used for more than a decade, and the validity and reliability of the measure have been demonstrated (Green et al., 1994).

School records. Data on each child's absence and tardiness rates were collected from official school records for the fall term prior to the implementation of the free school breakfast program.

RESULTS

Background Characteristics and CCHIP Hunger

Of the 204 children in this sample, 82% (168) were from elementary grades (3 through 5) and 18% (36) were from middle school grades (grade 8). Eighty percent of children (164/204) were from African-American backgrounds. Approximately half of the children were male (47%; 96/204) and from single-parent families (47%; 95/204). According to the eight-item CCHIP scale, 65% (132/204) of children were classified as not hungry, 27% (56/204) were classified as at risk for hunger, and 8% of the children (16/204) were classified as hungry.

Children in the three CCHIP hunger groups did not differ significantly from each other with respect to grade, ethnicity, parental marital status, or city. Hunger category scores did differ significantly by gender, with female children somewhat more likely to be at risk for hunger than male children and somewhat less likely to be classified as hungry or not hungry ($\chi^2 = 15.4$, $df = 2$, $p < .001$).

Parent Report Measures and CCHIP Hunger

As shown in Table 2, CCHIP hunger group was significantly associated with both parent report measures of children's symptoms. Total CBCL score was significantly associated

TABLE 2

Child Adjustment Scores by Community Childhood Hunger Identification Project Categories

	Total		Hungry		At Risk		Not Hungry	
	n or Mean	(%)	n or Mean	(%)	n or Mean	(%)	n or Mean	(%)
	204	(100)	16	(8)	56	(28)	132	(65)
Parent report measures								
CBCL impaired*	31	(15)	3	(19)	15	(27)	13	(10)
CBCL mean score†	51.5		56.8		56.3		48.8	
PSC impaired	28	(14)	5	(31)	9	(16)	14	(11)
PSC mean score***	16.2		21.5		18.9		14.4	
Teacher report measure								
CTRS-39 HI mean score†	54.6		71.5		51.7		53.5	
Interviewer rating of child functioning								
CGAS impaired (<71)***	80	(40)	13	(81)	23	(41)	44	(34)
Mean CGAS score**	72.5		66.3		72.2		73.4	
School record measures[a]								
Days absent*	2.8		5.2		3.2		2.3	
Days tardy*	0.8		1.8		1.0		0.7	

Note: CBCL = Child Behavior Checklist; PSC = Psychosocial Screening Checklist; CTRS-39 HI = Conners Teacher Rating Scale/Hyperactivity Index; CGAS = Children's Global Assessment Scale.
[a] Absences/tardiness from school records for first semester.
* p < .05; ** p < .01; *** p < .001; † p < .0001.

with CCHIP hunger status ($F = 34.1$, $df = 2$, $p < .0001$), and impairment on the CBCL was also significantly associated with CCHIP hunger category, with rates of impairment that were twice as high in hungry and at-risk for hunger children as in not-hungry children ($\chi^2 = 8.5$, $df = 2$, $p < .05$). Total PSC score was significantly associated with CCHIP hunger status ($F = 22.3$, $df = 2$, $p < .001$). Although the PSC impairment rate was nearly three times higher for hungry children than for not-hungry children, this finding did not reach statistical significance.

Teacher Report Measures and CCHIP Hunger

The mean CTRS-39 Hyperactivity Index T score for children classified as hungry was significantly higher (71.5) than for children who were classified as at risk for hunger (51.7) or not hungry (53.5; $F = 37.5$, $df = 2$, $p < .0001$). Although the not-hungry children had slightly higher mean CTRS-39 Hyperactivity Index T scores than at-risk for hunger children, post hoc analysis (Duncan's multiple-range test) indicated that this difference was not statistically significant, whereas the differences between children classified as hungry versus at risk and hungry versus not hungry were statistically significant.

Interviewer Ratings and CCHIP Hunger

Interviewer-rated CGAS scores were significantly related to parent-reported CCHIP hunger status ($F = 4.1$, $df = 2$, $p < .01$). The mean total CGAS score was worst for hungry children, followed by at-risk for hunger children. Not-hungry children had the highest mean total CGAS score (indicative of the best functioning). Hungry and at-risk for hunger children were also more likely to be cases on the CGAS ($\chi^2 = 25.4$, $df = 2$, $p < .001$).

School Record Measures and CCHIP Hunger

Hungry and at-risk for hunger children were absent from school significantly more days than not-hungry children ($F = 4.2$, $df = 2$, $p < .05$) (Table 2). Hungry and at-risk for hunger children also had significantly higher rates of tardiness than not-hungry children ($F = 4.1$, $df = 2$, $p < .05$).

Time-to-Time Reliability of the CCHIP Hunger Scale

Table 3 shows the distribution of CCHIP hunger classifications at time 1 and time 2 based on the reports of the 96 parents in the reinterview sample. Comparison of CCHIP hunger status by parent report at initial interview and reinterview showed exact agreement for 73% of the subjects (70/96). Partial agreement was found for 22% of the subjects (21/96) and complete disagreement was found in only 5% of the subjects ($n = 5$), which was statistically significant ($\chi^2 = 39.4$, $df = 4$, $p < .0001$; $\kappa = .43$). The correlation between CCHIP total score at time 1 and time 2 was $r = .56$, indicating a rate of time-to-time reliability that would be considered acceptable.

TABLE 3

Time-to-Time Reliability of Parent Reports of Hunger on CCHIP Questions

Time 1 CCHIP Hunger Categories[†]	Total		Time 2 CCHIP Categories[a]					
			Not Hungry		At Risk		Hungry	
Total	96	(100)	73	(76)	19	(20)	4	(4)
Not hungry	59	(62)	55	(93)	3	(5)	1	(2)
At risk	26	(27)	14	(54)	12	(46)	0	(0)
Hungry	11	(11)	4	(36)	4	(36)	3	(27)

Note: Values represent *n* (%).
[a]Community Childhood Hunger Identification Project (CCHIP) Hunger Scale based on the full eight questions.
[†] $p < .0001$.

Agreement Between Parent and Child Reports of Hunger

Table 4 shows the agreement between the five-item CHI-P and the five-question CHI-C. Complete pre–Universal Feeding CHI-P and CHI-C data were available for 193 (95%) of the 204 subjects.

Hunger status by child report was significantly related to parent's report of child hunger at time 1 ($\chi^2 = 71.7, df = 4, p < .0001$). Exact agreement between parent and child report was found for 74% (142/193) of the sample, partial agreement was found for 23% (45/193), and full disagreement was found for 3% (6/193) of the subjects. Statistically, the degree of association ($\kappa = .36$) was in a range that is generally considered to indicate an acceptable level of agreement. As shown in Table 4, 85% (16/19) of the children whose parents reported hunger on the CHI-P measure were hungry (53%) or at risk for hunger (32%) on the CHI-C. Similarly, of the 14 children who were classified as hungry on the standard eight-item CCHIP measure, 93% (13/14) were classified as hungry (64%) or at risk (29%) by their own report on CHI-C ($\chi^2 = 80.9, df=4, p < .0001$; not shown).

TABLE 4

Parent and Child Reports of Hunger on Community Childhood Hunger Identification Project Questions

Parent Report (CHI-P)[†]	Total		Child Report (CHI-C)					
			Not Hungry		At Risk		Hungry	
Total	193	(100)	139	(72)	38	(20)	16	(8)
Not hungry	147	(76)	122	(83)	22	(15)	3	(2)
At risk	27	(14)	14	(52)	10	(37)	3	(11)
Hungry	19	(10)	3	(16)	6	(32)	10	(53)

Note: Values represent *n* (%). CHI-P = Child Hunger Index Parent Report; CHI-C = Child Hunger Index Child Report.
[†] $p < .0001$.

DISCUSSION

In the current study, the parent-reported CCHIP hunger score was significantly associated with psychosocial dysfunction as assessed by standardized measures filled out independently by parents, teachers, and clinicians, and with school records of absence and tardiness. These findings provide clear evidence of the association between parental report of food insufficiency due to constrained resources and children's behavioral and academic functioning.

In this study of low-income children, as in other samples, about one third of the children were found to have significant problems in psychosocial functioning as measured by the CGAS. Children from families coded as hungry on CCHIP were more than twice as likely to be rated as impaired as low-income children from the same communities whose parents did not report hunger. Hungry children were also two to three times more likely to receive scores in the impaired range on the other measures of emotional problems than not-hungry children. Behavioral and attention problems by teacher report were more prevalent in hungry than in at-risk for hunger or not-hungry children. Academic problems were also associated with hunger status; hungry children were absent and tardy twice as many days as not-hungry children. Since gender has never been related to hunger in other CCHIP studies and since it was not in our CCHIP study in Pittsburgh (Kleinman et al, in press) involving a larger number of cases, we concluded that the observed gender difference was artifactual.

The face validity of the CCHIP measure was shown by significant agreement between parent and child reports of hunger on the child-focused questions of the CCHIP measure, and the time-to-time reliability of the CCHIP measure was good. Descriptively, the fact that 85% of the children classified as hungry on the basis of parent report on the CHI-P measure and 93% of the children classified as hungry on the basis of the standard CCHIP measure gave answers that led them to be coded as hungry or at risk on the CHI-C—based on totally independent reports—provides strong evidence for the interinformant face validity of the CCHIP coding of child hunger.

A number of limitations of the study must be taken into account in interpreting its findings. Since only about one third of the parents of eligible students agreed to participate in the study, a sampling bias may have occurred. For example, it is possible that poorer families may have been less likely to participate. That the prevalence rates of hungry and at-risk for hunger children in the current study are lower than those reported in previous CCHIP studies with low-income families (Wehler et al., 1996a) suggests that this in fact may have been the case. However, even if low-income families or some other group were systematically less likely to participate, the relationship between CCHIP hunger and psychosocial impairment in the current sample would remain and would still be an important finding.

Another limitation is that there was a hunger-related feeding intervention between the first and second administrations of the CCHIP parent scale which may have influenced parents' rating of their children's hunger. However, since CCHIP assesses child/family food insufficiency over a 1-year period, it is unlikely, even if children had become markedly less hungry because of the school breakfast program, that their parent-reported CCHIP scores would have changed very much. Even if CCHIP scores had changed by time 2 for this reason, the result would have been an artifactually lower level of time-to-time reliability. Because time-to-time reliability was found to be acceptable even under the current circumstances, it is probable that time-to-time agreement would only be better under nonintervention (and shorter interval) test-retest conditions. Future studies could assess the stability and sensitivity of CCHIP by reinterviewing groups of parents who have lost benefits because of the recent welfare reforms to determine whether CCHIP scores increased.

These limitations notwithstanding, the results of this study suggest that the CCHIP hunger measure accurately documents the intermittent, subcatastrophic experiences of hunger that are common in some low-income families. The current study also shows that these experiences of hunger are associated with increased risk of psychosocial and academic impairment. Because the current study is cross-sectional rather than longitudinal, causality cannot be inferred and it is possible that hunger itself may not be the only or even the major cause of these children's problems. For example, if hunger is more likely to occur in multiproblem families and if these families are also more likely to experience violence, homelessness, or disorganization, then the latter experiences rather than the intermittent experiences of hunger may play a more important role in causing behavioral or academic problems. Whatever the causality, the current study does show that children in families classified as hungry by the CCHIP measure are two to three times more likely to have psychosocial and academic problems than children in low-income families classified as not hungry. These children are at exceptionally high risk, and further research designed to assess the causal links between hunger and psychosocial dysfunction is clearly warranted. Sadly, recent federal budget cuts are likely to increase the number of children who are hungry and in poverty.

Clinical Implications

Although the specific contribution of hunger is unknown, this study demonstrates that hunger is a risk factor associated with psychosocial dysfunction in poor children. During diagnostic evaluations, especially in poverty populations, child psychiatrists should ask about the availability of food and the presence of hunger. Clinicians should ensure that children and parents are fully aware of programs like Women, Infants, and Children (WIC), food stamps, and the National School Breakfast and Lunch programs for which many low-income children are eligible. Childhood hunger, a stress that should be remedied, may also be relevant to clinicians as a potential contributing factor to later aggressive behavior and school drop-out during adolescence.

REFERENCES

Achenbach TM (1991), *Manual for the Behavior Problem Checklist and Revised Behavior Profile.* Burlington: University of Vermont Department of Psychiatry

Barrett DE, Radke-Yarrow M, Klein RE (1982), Chronic malnutrition and child behavior: effects of early caloric supplementation on social and emotional functioning at school age. *Dev Psychol* 18:541–556

Bickel G, Andrews M, Klein B (1996), Measuring food security in the United States: a supplement to the CPS. In: *Nutrition and Food Security in the Food Stamp Program*, Hall D, Stavrianos M, eds, Alexandria, VA: United States Department of Agriculture, Food and Consumer Service

Boyle MH, Jones SC (1985), Selecting measures of emotional and behavioral disorders of childhood for use in general populations. *J Child Psychol Psychiatry* 26:137–159

Chavez A, Martinez M (1979), Consequences of insufficient nutrition on child characteristics and behavior. In: *Malnutrition, Environment and Behavior*, Levitsky DA, ed. New York: Cornell University Press

Graves PL (1976), Nutrition, infant behavior, and maternal characteristics: a pilot study in West Bengal, India. *Am J Clin Nutr* 29:305–319

Graves PL (1978), Nutrition and infant behavior: a replication study in the Katmandu Valley, Nepal. *Am J Clin Nutr* 31:541–551

Gray GE (1986), Diet, crime and delinquency: a critique. *Nutr Rev* May Suppl:89–94

Green B, Shirk S, Hanze D, Wanstrath J (1994), The Children's Global Assessment Scale in clinical practice: an empirical evaluation. *J Am Acad Child Adolesc Psychiatry* 33:1158–1164

Halas ES, Hanlon M, Sandstead H (1975), Intrauterine nutrition and aggression. *Nature* 257:221–222

Jellinek MS, Murphy JM (1988), Screening for psychosocial disorders in pediatric practice. *Am J Dis Child* 142:1153–1157

Jellinek MS, Murphy JM, Burns BJ (1986), Brief psychosocial screening in outpatient pediatric practice. *J Pediatr* 109:371–378

Kivlahan DR, Siegel IJ, Ullman DG (1982), Relationships among measures of activity in children. *J Pediatr Psychol* 7:331–344

Kleinman RE, Murphy JM, Little M et al. (in press), Hunger in children in the United States: potential behavioral and emotional correlates. *Pediatrics*

Minde KK (1980), Some thoughts on the social ecology of present day psychopharmacology. *Can J Psychiatry* 25:201–212

Mora JO (1979), Nutritional supplementation, early stimulation, and child development. In: *Behavioral Effects of Energy and Protein Deficits*, Brozek J, ed. Bethesda, MD: Department of Health, Education, and Welfare

Murphy JM, Ichinose C, Hicks RC et al. (1996), Utility of the Pediatric Symptom Checklist as a psychosocial screen in EPSDT. *J Pediatr* 129:862–869

Murphy JM, Jellinek MS (1988), Screening for psychosocial dysfunction in economically disadvantaged and minority group children: further validation of the Pediatric Symptom Checklist. *Am J Orthopsychiatry* 58:450–456

Murphy JM, Reede J, Jellinek MJ, Bishop SJ (1992), Screening for psychosocial dysfunction in inner-city children: further validation of the Pediatric Symptom Checklist. *J Am Acad Child Adolesc Psychiatry* 31:1105–1111

Radimer K, Olson CM, Greene CC, Campbell CC, Habitcht JP (1992), Understanding hunger and developing indicators to assess it in women and children. *J Nutr Educ* 24:36S–45S

Sandoval L (1981), Format effects in two teacher rating scales of hyperactivity. *J Abnorm Child Psychol* 9:203–218

Shaffer D, Gould MS, Brasic J et al. (1983), A children's global assessment scale (CGAS). *Arch Gen Psychiatry* 40:1228–1231

Wehler CA, Scott RI, Anderson JJ (1991), *The Community Childhood Hunger Identification Project: A Survey of Childhood Hunger in the United States*. Washington, DC: Food Research and Action Center

Wehler CA, Scott RI, Anderson JJ (1992), The Community Childhood Hunger Identification Project: a model of domestic hunger—Demonstration Project in Seattle, Washington. *J Nutr Educ* 24:29S–35S

Wehler CA, Scott RI, Anderson JJ (1996a), *The Community Childhood Hunger Identification Project: A Survey of Childhood Hunger in the United States.* Washington, DC: Food Research and Action Center

Wehler Ca, Scott RI, Anderson JJ (1996b), Development and testing process of the Community Childhood Hunger Identification Project Scaled Hunger Measure and its application for a general population survey. In: *Conference on Food Security Measurement and Research: Papers and Proceedings*, January 1994, Washington, DC, Technical Appendix A. Alexandria, VA: United States Department of Agriculture, Food and Consumer Service

9

What Matters? What Does Not? Five Perspectives on the Association Between Marital Transitions and Children's Adjustment

E. Mavis Hetherington, Margaret Bridges, and Glendessa M. Insabella
University of Virginia

This article presents an analysis of 5 views of factors that contribute to the adjustment of children in divorced families or stepfamilies. These perspectives are those that emphasize (a) individual vulnerability and risk; (b) family composition; (c) stress, including socioeconomic disadvantage; (d) parental distress; and (e) disrupted family process. It is concluded that all of these factors contribute to children's adjustment in divorced and remarried families and that a transactional model examining multiple trajectories of interacting risk and protective factors is the most fruitful in predicting the well-being of children.

In the past 30 years, there has been a significant decline in the proportion of two-parent families in first marriages and a complementary increase in the number of single-parent households and stepfamilies. These changes are the result of a rapid rise in the divorce rate that began during the 1960s (Simons, 1996) and also, to a lesser extent, of an increase in births to single mothers. Although there has been a modest decrease in the divorce rate since the late 1970s, almost one half of marriages end in divorce in the United States, and one million children experience their parents' divorce each year (U.S. Bureau of the Census, 1992). It is projected that between 50% and 60% of children born in the 1990s will live, at some point, in single-parent families, typically headed by mothers (Bumpass & Sweet, 1989; Furstenberg & Cherlin, 1991). Currently, stepfamilies make up approximately 17% of all two-parent families with children under 18 years of age (Glick, 1989).

Although the high divorce rate has been interpreted as a rejection of the institution of marriage, 75% of men and 66% of women eventually will remarry, suggesting that although people are rejecting specific marital partners, most are not rejecting marriage itself (Booth &

E. Mavis Hetherington, Margaret Bridges, and Glendessa M. Insabella, Department of Psychology, University of Virginia.

Correspondence concerning this article should be addressed to E. Mavis Hetherington, Department of Psychology, University of Virginia, 102 Gilmer Hall, Charlottesville, VA 22903-2477. Electronic mail may be sent to emh2f@virginia.edu

Edwards, 1992; Bumpass, Sweet, & Castro-Martin, 1990; Cherlin & Furstenberg, 1994; Ganong & Coleman, 1994). Since the 1960s, however, the annual rate of remarriage has actually declined as the divorce rate has increased. Moreover, divorces are more frequent in remarriages and occur at a rate 10% higher than that in first marriages (Bumpass et al., 1990; Cherlin & Furstenberg, 1994). Couples with remarried wives are almost twice as likely to divorce as are couples with remarried husbands. This association may be attributable to the 50% higher rate of dissolution in remarriages in which children from previous marriages are present (Tzeng & Mare, 1995), although the presence of children appears to be less relevant to the marital quality of African American couples (Orbuch, Veroff, & Hunter, in press). As a result of their parents' successive marital transitions, about half of all children whose parents divorce will have a stepfather within four years of parental separation, and 1 out of every 10 children will experience at least two divorces of their residential parent before turning 16 years of age (Furstenberg, 1988). These numbers underestimate the actual number of household reorganizations to which children are exposed because many couples cohabit before remarriage or cohabit as an alternative to remarriage (Bumpass & Raley, 1995; Bumpass, Sweet, & Cherlin, 1991; Cherlin & Furstenberg, 1994; Ganong & Coleman, 1994).

The national figures for marital transitions and family structure mask very different patterns among racial and ethnic groups because the social context of marriage varies across communities (Orbuch et al., in press). African American children are twice as likely as White children to experience at least one parental divorce (National Center for Health Statistics, 1988) and also are more likely to bear children out of wedlock in adolescence and adulthood (Demo & Acock, 1996; Tzeng & Mare, 1995; U.S. Bureau of the Census, 1992). In addition, African Americans and Hispanic Whites are less likely to divorce after separation and to remarry than are non-Hispanic Whites (Castro-Martin & Bumpass, 1989; Cherlin, 1992). Thus, in comparison with White children, more African American children spend longer periods of time in single-parent households, which often include kin and cohabiting partners.

As marriage has become a more optional, less permanent institution in contemporary American society, children in all ethnic groups are encountering stresses and adaptive challenges associated with their parents' marital transitions. Children from divorced and remarried families, in contrast to those from never-divorced families, exhibit more problem behaviors and lower psychological well-being. Little agreement exists, however, about the extent, severity, and duration of these problems because there is great diversity in children's responses to parental marital transitions (Amato & Keith, 1991a; Emery & Forehand, 1994; Hetherington, 1991b; McLanahan & Sandefur, 1994). Furthermore, although it is clear that marital dissension and dissolution, life in single-parent households, and remarriage present families and children with new experiences, risks, and resources, there is some disagreement on how these factors undermine or enhance the well-being of children.

THEORETICAL PERSPECTIVES ON MARITAL TRANSITIONS AND THE ADJUSTMENT OF CHILDREN

Five main theoretical perspectives have been proposed to explain the links between divorce and remarriage and children's adjustment. These perspectives are those emphasizing

(a) individual risk and vulnerability; (b) family composition; (c) stress, including socioeconomic disadvantage; (d) parental distress; and (e) family process.

Individual Risk and Vulnerability

It has been proposed that some characteristics of parents and children may influence their exposure and vulnerability to adversity. Some adults possess characteristics (e.g., antisocial behavior) that place them at increased risk for marital discord, multiple marital transitions, and other adverse life experiences (Capaldi & Patterson, 1991; Kitson & Morgan, 1990; Patterson & Dishion, 1988; Simons, Johnson, & Lorenz, 1996). Adults with psychological problems such as depression or antisocial behavior often select partners who also experience psychological difficulties (Merikangas, Prusoff, & Weissman, 1988), thereby increasing their risk for marital problems and dissolution. This is called the marital selectivity hypothesis. In addition, some children have attributes that increase their vulnerability or protect them from deleterious consequences of stresses associated with their parents' marital transitions (Amato & Keith, 1991a; Emery & Forehand, 1994; Hetherington, 1989, 1991b).

Family Composition

It is commonly assumed that two biological parents provide the optimal family environment for healthy child development and that any deviation from this family structure, such as single-parent families or stepfamilies, is problematic for children (Amato & Keith, 1991a; Kitson & Holmes, 1992; Simons, 1996). Much of the early theorizing about divorce and family structure focused on father absence.

Stress and Socioeconomic Disadvantage

This perspective emphasizes that marital transitions trigger a series of negative social and economic changes, stresses, and practical problems that can interfere with the well-being of parents and children. For custodial mothers and their children, divorce is related to a notable economic decline that is associated with living conditions that make raising children more difficult (McLanahan & Sandefur, 1994), whereas remarriage is associated with an increase in household income for single mothers. Although much of the research on stress has focused on economic stresses, both divorced and remarried families encounter other stresses related to changing family roles and relationships (Cherlin & Furstenberg, 1994; Hetherington & Stanley Hagan, 1995; Simons, 1996).

Parental Distress

This perspective suggests that stressful life experiences, including economic decline and adaptive challenges associated with divorce and remarriage, lead to parental strain, distress, and diminished well-being, which are reflected in psychological problems such as depression, anxiety, irritability, and antisocial behaviors, as well as stress-related health problems (Capaldi & Patterson, 1991; Forgatch, Patterson, & Ray, 1995; Hetherington,

1989, 1991b; Kiecolt-Glaser et al., 1987; Lorenz, Simons, & Chao, 1996; Simons & Johnson, 1996). There is great individual variability in response to negative life changes; some parents cope with such changes with apparent equanimity, whereas others exhibit marked affective disruption and distress.

Family Process

Finally, many researchers have emphasized that differences between nondivorced families and divorced and remarried families on process variables such as conflict, control, expression of positive and negative affect, and problem solving largely explain the effects of divorce and remarriage. It is argued that more proximal variables, such as discipline and child-rearing practices, are most important in affecting children's adjustment.

Although these perspectives often are presented as competing with each other, empirical support can be found for each, suggesting that they may best be considered as complementary hypotheses (Amato & Keith, 1991a; Simons, 1996). In this article, research on the five perspectives is reviewed, and the direct and indirect effects of the five factors on the adjustment of children and parents in divorced and remarried families are examined. Finally, a transactional model of marital transitions involving relationships among the factors is presented.

ADJUSTMENT OF CHILDREN IN DIVORCED
AND REMARRIED FAMILIES

There is general agreement among researchers that children, adolescents, and adults from divorced and remarried families, in comparison with those from two-parent, nondivorced families, are at increased risk for developing problems in adjustment (for meta-analyses, see Amato & Keith, 1991a, 1991b) and that those who have undergone multiple divorces are at a greater risk (Capaldi & Patterson, 1991; Kurdek, Fine, & Sinclair, 1995). For the most part, the adjustment of children from divorced and remarried families is similar (Amato & Keith, 1991a; Cherlin & Furstenberg, 1994). Children from divorced and remarried families are more likely than children from nondivorced families to have academic problems, to exhibit externalizing behaviors and internalizing disorders, to be less socially responsible and competent, and to have lower self-esteem (Amato & Keith, 1991a; Cherlin & Furstenberg, 1994; Hetherington, 1989). They have problems in their relationships with parents, siblings, and peers (Amato & Keith, 1991b; Hetherington, 1997).

Normative developmental tasks of adolescence and young adulthood, such as attaining intimate relationships and increasing social and economic autonomy, seem to be especially difficult for youths from divorced and remarried families. Adolescents from divorced and remarried families exhibit some of the same behavior problems found in childhood and, in addition, are more likely to drop out of school, to be unemployed, to become sexually active at an earlier age, to have children out of wedlock, to be involved in delinquent activities and substance abuse, and to associate with antisocial peers (Amato & Keith, 1991a; Conger & Chao, 1996; Demo & Acock, 1996; Elder & Russell, 1996; Hetherington & Clingempeel, 1992; McLanahan & Sandefur, 1994; Simons & Chao, 1996; Whitbeck,

Simons, & Goldberg, 1996). Increased rates of dropping out of high school and of low socioeconomic attainment in the offspring of divorced and remarried families extend across diverse ethnic groups (Amato & Keith, 1991b); however, the effect is stronger for females than for males (Hetherington, in press).

Adult offspring from divorced and remarried families continue to have more adjustment problems (Chase-Lansdale, Cherlin, & Kiernan, 1995; Hetherington, in press), are less satisfied with their lives, experience lower socioeconomic attainment, and are more likely to be on welfare (Amato & Keith, 1991b). Marital instability also is higher for adults from divorced and remarried families (Amato & Keith, 1991b; Glenn & Kramer, 1985; Hetherington, in press; McLanahan & Bumpass, 1988; Tzeng & Mare, 1995), in part because of the presence of a set of risk factors for divorce, including early sexual activity, adolescent childbearing and marriage, and cohabitation (Booth & Edwards, 1990; Hetherington, 1997). In addition, in comparison with young adults from nondivorced families, young adults from divorced and remarried families exhibit more reciprocated, escalating, negative exchanges, including denial, belligerence, criticism, and contempt, and less effective problem solving during their marital interactions (Hetherington, in press). This pattern is probably related to the intergenerational transmission of divorce, which is reported to be 70% higher in the first five years of marriage for adult women from divorced families than for those whose parents have remained married (Bumpass, Martin, & Sweet, 1991).

Although there is considerable consensus that, on average, offspring from divorced and remarried families exhibit more problems in adjustment than do those in nondivorced, two-parent families, there is less agreement on the size of these effects. Some researchers report that these effects are relatively modest, have become smaller as marital transitions have become more common (Amato & Keith, 1991a), and are considerably reduced when the adjustment of children preceding the marital transition is controlled (Block, Block, & Gjerde, 1986, 1988; Cherlin et al., 1991). However, others note that approximately 20%–25% of children in divorced and remarried families, in contrast to 10% of children in nondivorced families, have these problems, which is a notable twofold increase (Hetherington, 1989, 1991b; Hetherington & Clingempeel, 1992; Hetherington & Jodl, 1994; McLanahan & Sandefur, 1994; Simons & Associates, 1996; Zill, Morrison, & Coiro, 1993). Because these difficulties in adjustment tend to co-occur and appear as a single behavior-problem cluster (Jessor & Jessor, 1977; Mekos, Hetherington, & Reiss, 1996), the vast majority of children from divorced families and stepfamilies do not have these problems and eventually develop into reasonably competent individuals functioning within the normal range of adjustment (Emery & Forehand, 1994). This argument is not intended to minimize the importance of the increase in adjustment problems associated with divorce and remarriage nor to belittle the fact that children often report their parents' marital transitions to be their most painful life experience. It is intended to underscore the research evidence supporting the ability of most children to cope with their parents' divorce and remarriage and to counter the position that children are permanently blighted by their parents' marital transitions.

We turn now to an examination of some of the individual, social, economic, and family factors that contribute to the diversity in children's adjustment in divorced and remarried families. Each factor is discussed as it relates to the five perspectives on marital transitions.

INDIVIDUAL RISK AND VULNERABILITY OF PARENTS ASSOCIATED WITH DIVORCE AND REMARRIAGE

Some adults have attributes that increase their probability not only of having dysfunctional marital relationships but also for having other problematic social relationships within and outside of the family, displaying inept parenting behaviors, encountering stressful life events, and having decreased psychological well-being (Amato & Booth, 1996; Block et al., 1986). Longitudinal studies have found that, in adults as well as in children, many of the problems attributed to divorce and remarriage and their concomitant life changes were present before these transitions occurred.

Although psychological distress and disorders may increase after divorce, parents who later divorce are more likely preceding divorce to be neurotic, depressed, antisocial, or alcoholic; to have economic problems (Amato, 1993; Capaldi & Patterson, 1991; Forgatch et al., 1995; Gotlib & McCabe, 1990); and to have dysfunctional beliefs about relationships (Baucom & Epstein, 1990; Kelly & Conley, 1987; Kurdek, 1993). In their marital interactions, they exhibit poor problem-solving and conflict resolution skills, thus escalating reciprocation of negative affect, contempt, denial, withdrawal, and stable, negative attributions about their spouses' behavior, which in turn significantly increase their risk for marital dissolution and multiple divorces (Bradbury & Fincham, 1990; Fincham, Bradbury, & Scott, 1990; Gottman, 1993, 1994; Gottman & Levenson, 1992; Matthews, Wickrama, & Conger, 1996). Sometimes these patterns are later found in the marital relationships of their adult offspring (Hetherington, in press). In relationships with their children, parents whose marriages will later be disrupted are more irritable, erratic, and nonauthoritative as much as 8–12 years prior to divorce (Amato & Booth, 1996; Block et al., 1988). These factors contribute to problems in children's adjustment and family relations in nondivorced families, single-parent families, and stepfamilies.

CHILDREN'S INDIVIDUAL RISK, VULNERABILITY, AND RESILIENCY ASSOCIATED WITH ADJUSTMENT TO DIVORCE AND REMARRIAGE

In accord with the individual risk perspective, characteristics of children may make them vulnerable or protect them from the adverse consequences or risks associated with their parents' divorce or remarriage. Some of these attributes influence the experiences and adjustment of children long before marital transitions occur.

Children's Adjustment Preceding Divorce and Remarriage

Children whose parents later divorce exhibit poorer adjustment before the breakup (Amato & Booth, 1996; Amato & Keith, 1991a; Block et al., 1986; Cherlin et al., 1991). When antecedent levels of problem behaviors are controlled, differences in problem behaviors between children from divorced and nondivorced families are greatly reduced (Cherlin et al., 1991; Guidubaldi, Perry, & Nastasi, 1987). Several alternative interpretations of these findings can be made. First, it is likely that maladapted parents, dysfunctional family relationships, and inept parenting already have taken their toll on children's adjustment before a divorce occurs. Second, divorce may be, in part, a result of having to deal with a difficult child. Third, personality problems in a parent, such as emotionality and lack of self-regulation, that lead to both divorce and inept socialization practices also may be genetically linked to behavior problems in children (Jockin, McGue, & Lykken, 1996; McGue & Lykken, 1992).

Children in stepfamilies also exhibit more behavior problems before remarriage occurs, and some researchers have speculated that the adaptive difficulties of stepchildren may be largely the result of experiences in divorced families (Furstenberg, 1988). This seems unlikely, because there is an increase in adjustment problems immediately after a marital transition, and because children in newly remarried families show more problems than those in stabilized, divorced, one-parent households (Hetherington & Clingempeel, 1992) or than those in longer remarried, stabilized stepfamilies (Hetherington & Jodl, 1994).

Personality and Temperament

Children who have easy temperaments; who are intelligent, socially mature, and responsible; and who exhibit few behavior problems are better able to cope with their parents' marital transitions. Stresses associated with divorce and remarriage are likely to exacerbate existing problems in children (Block et al., 1986; Elder, Caspi, & Van Nguyen, 1992; Hetherington, 1989, 1991b). In particular, children with difficult temperaments or behavior problems may elicit negative responses from their parents who are stressed in coping with their marital transitions. These children also may be less able to adapt to parental negativity when it occurs and may be less adept at gaining the support of people around them (Hetherington, 1989, 1991b; Rutter, 1987). Competent, adaptable children with social skills and attractive personal characteristics, such as an easy temperament and a sense of humor, are more likely to evoke positive responses and support and to maximize the use of available resources that help them negotiate stressful experiences (Hetherington, 1989; Werner, 1988).

Developmental Status

Developmental status and gender are the child characteristics most extensively researched in relation to adaptation to divorce and remarriage; however, the results of these studies have been inconsistent. Investigations of children's age at divorce must consider both age at the time of the marital transition and age at the time of assessment. In most studies, these variables are confounded with the length of time since the divorce or remarriage occurred. Some researchers have found that preschool-age children whose parents divorce are at greater risk for long-term problems in social and emotional development than are older children (Allison & Furstenberg, 1989; Zill et al., 1993). It has been suggested that younger children may be less able to appraise realistically the causes and consequences of divorce, may be more anxious about the possibility of total abandonment, may be more likely to blame themselves for the divorce, and may be less able to utilize extrafamilial protective resources (Hetherington, 1989). This greater vulnerability of young children to divorce has not been reported by other investigators (Amato & Keith, 1991a).

In contrast, early adolescence seems to be an especially difficult time in which to have a remarriage occur. Early adolescents are less able to adapt to parental remarriage than are younger children or late adolescents (Hetherington, 1993; Hetherington & Clingempeel, 1992), perhaps because the presence of a stepparent exacerbates normal early adolescent concerns about autonomy and sexuality. In addition, adolescence and young adulthood are periods in which problems in adjustment may emerge or increase, even when divorce or remarriage has occurred much earlier (Amato & Keith, 1991a, 1991b; Bray & Berger, 1993; Hetherington, 1993, in press; Hetherington & Clingempeel, 1992; Hetherington & Jodl, 1994).

Gender

Although earlier studies frequently reported gender differences in response to divorce and remarriage, with divorce being more deleterious for boys and remarriage for girls (Hetherington, 1989), more recent studies have found that gender differences in response to divorce are less pronounced and consistent than was previously believed (Amato & Keith, 1991a). Some of the inconsistencies may be attributable to the fact that fathers' custody, joint custody, and the involvement of noncustodial fathers are increasing and that involvement of fathers may be more important for boys than for girls (Amato & Keith, 1991a; Clarke-Stewart & Hayward, 1996; Lindner-Gunnoe, 1993; Zill, 1988).

Some research has shown that boys respond to divorce with increases in conduct disorders and girls with increases in depression (Emery, 1982); however, both male and female adolescents from divorced and remarried families show higher rates of conduct disorders and depression than do those from nondivorced families (Amato & Keith, 1991a; Hetherington, 1993; Hetherington & Clingempeel, 1992; Hetherington & Jodl, 1994). Female adolescents and young adults from divorced and remarried families are more likely than their male counterparts to drop out of high school and college. Male and female adolescents are similarly affected in the likelihood of becoming teenage parents; however, single parenthood has more adverse effects on the lives of female adolescents (McLanahan & Sandefur, 1994). Female young adults from divorced and remarried families are vulnerable to declining socioeconomic status because of the sequelae of adolescent childbearing and school dropout. These sequelae are compounded in stepdaughters by early home leaving, which they attribute to family conflict (Cherlin & Furstenberg, 1994; Hetherington, 1997, in press).

Some girls in divorced, mother-headed families emerge as exceptionally resilient individuals, enhanced by confronting the increases in challenges and responsibilities that follow divorce (Hetherington, 1989, 1991b; Werner, 1993). Such enhancement is not found for boys following marital transitions or for girls in stepfamilies (Hetherington, 1989, 1991b). Boys, especially preadolescent boys, are more likely than girls to benefit from being in stepfather families (Amato & Keith, 1991a; Hetherington, 1993). Close relationships with supportive stepfathers are more likely to reduce antisocial behavior and to enhance the achievement of stepsons than of stepdaughters (Amato & Keith, 1991a; Hetherington, 1993; Lindner-Gunnoe, 1993; Zimiles & Lee, 1991). Girls are at greater increased risk than are boys for poor adjustment and low achievement when they are in either stepfather or stepmother families rather than in nondivorced families (Lee, Burkam, Zimiles, & Ladewski, 1994; Zimiles & Lee, 1991).

Some research suggests that living in stepfamilies is more beneficial to Black adolescents than to White adolescents, although these effects vary by gender. In contrast to the findings for White youths, young Black women in stepfamilies have the same rate of teenage parenthood as do those in two-parent, nondivorced families, and young Black men in stepfamilies are at no greater risk to drop out of high school than are those in two-parent families (McLanahan & Sandefur, 1994). McLanahan and Sandefur proposed that the income, supervision, and role models provided by stepfathers may be more advantageous for Black children because they are more likely than White children to live in more disorganized neighborhoods with fewer resources and social controls.

FAMILY COMPOSITION–PARENTAL ABSENCE AND THE ADJUSTMENT OF CHILDREN

The family composition or parental absence perspective proposes that a deviation in structure from a family with two first-married parents, biologically related to their children, is associated with increases in problem behavior in children. Two parents can provide support to each other, especially in their child rearing, as well as multiple role models and increased resources, supervision, and involvement for their children (Amato, 1995; Demo & Acock, 1996; Dornbusch et al., 1985; Furstenberg, Morgan, & Allison, 1987; Lamb, 1997). If father unavailability or absence is a critical factor in divorce, father custody or contact with a noncustodial parent, stepfather, or father surrogate should enhance children's adjustment. Furthermore, children who experience loss of their fathers through divorce or death should exhibit similar adjustment problems. Less theorizing has focused on mother absence, although similar hypotheses might be proposed for mothers.

Children and adults from homes with an absent parent due to either divorce or death have more problems in adjustment than do those in nondivorced families; however, significantly more problems are found in academic achievement, socioeconomic attainment, and conduct disorders for offspring from divorced families (Amato & Keith, 1991a; Felner, Ginter, Boike, & Cowen, 1981; Felner, Stolberg, & Cowen, 1975; Hetherington, 1972). Although children of both divorced and widowed women suffer the loss of their fathers and economic declines, the finding suggests that other factors moderate the differences in their outcomes. One of these factors may be greater support and involvement with the extended family, especially that of the lost parent's family, following death but not divorce (Hetherington, 1972). Another may be the greater conflict in families preceding divorce but not the death of a parent (Amato & Keith, 1991a).

The parental absence hypothesis also suggests that contact with noncustodial parents or joint custody should promote children's well-being; however, contact with both noncustodial mothers and fathers diminishes rapidly following divorce. More than 20% of children have no contact with their noncustodial fathers or see them only a few times a year, and only about one quarter of children have weekly visits with their divorced fathers (Seltzer, 1991). Black noncustodial fathers have higher rates of both regular contact and no contact with their children than do non-Hispanic White fathers (McLanahan & Sandefur, 1994).

Decreased paternal involvement is related to residential distance, low socioeconomic status, and parental remarriage (Seltzer, 1991). Seltzer and Brandreth (1994) noted that custodial mothers serve as "gatekeepers" (Ahrons, 1983), controlling noncustodial fathers' access to and the conditions of visits with their children. When conflict, resentment, and anger are high, the "gate" may be closed, and fathers may be discouraged or shut out. In contrast, when there is low conflict between divorced spouses, when mediation is used (Dillon & Emery, 1996), or when noncustodial fathers feel they have some control over decisions in their children's lives (Braver et al., 1993; Seltzer, 1991), paternal contact and child support payments are more likely to be maintained.

In contrast, noncustodial mothers are more likely than noncustodial fathers to sustain contact with their children and to rearrange their living situations to facilitate children's visits. They maintain approximately twice as much contact with their children as noncustodial fathers do and are less likely to completely drop out of their children's lives or to diminish contact when either parent remarries (Furstenberg & Nord, 1987; Furstenberg, Nord, Peterson, & Zill, 1983; Lindner-Gunnoe, 1993; Santrock, Sitterle, & Warshak, 1988; White, 1994; Zill, 1988). In addition, there is some evidence that noncustodial mothers, like noncustodial fathers, are more likely to maintain contact with sons than with daughters (Lindner-Gunnoe, 1993), although the preferential contact of fathers with sons is larger and more consistently obtained than that of mothers (Amato & Booth, 1991).

There is little support for the position that sheer frequency of contact facilitates positive adjustment in children (Amato & Keith, 1991a; King, 1994a, 1994b). However, as we discuss at greater length in the Family Process and the Adjustment to Divorce and Remarriage section, under conditions of low interparental conflict, contact with competent, supportive, authoritative noncustodial parents can have beneficial effects for children, and these effects are most marked for noncustodial parents and children of the same sex (Hetherington, 1989; Lindner-Gunnoe, 1993; Zill, 1988). Thus, it is the quality of contact, rather than the frequency, that is important (Amato, 1993; Emery, 1988; Furstenberg & Cherlin, 1991).

Research on custodial arrangements also has found few advantages of joint custody over sole residential custody. In a large study of custody in California, Maccoby and Mnookin (1992) found adolescents in the custody of their fathers had higher rates of delinquency, perhaps because of poorer monitoring by fathers. A meta-analysis of divorce by Amato and Keith (1991a), however, did not support the findings of poorer adjustment in children in families in which fathers have custody.

A corollary to the parental absence hypothesis would suggest that the addition of a stepparent might compensate for the loss of a parent. However, the family composition perspective implies that it is not only the presence of two parents but also biological relatedness to the parents that matter. Although divorce involves the exit of a family member, remarriage involves the restructuring of the family constellation with the entrance of a stepparent and sometimes stepsiblings. Predictions made about stepfamilies on the basis of the family composition hypothesis are unclear. On the one hand, the presence of a stepparent might compensate for the loss of the noncustodial parent by restoring a two-parent household. On the other hand, the child must confront an additional transition to another family with a nontraditional composition involving the addition of nonbiologically related family members to the household. In a family in which both divorced parents remarry, much more complex kin networks are created within and outside the household in a linked family system (Jacobson, 1982) or a binuclear family (Ahrons, 1979). A child's expanded kin networks may include stepsiblings, half siblings, and stepgrandparents, as well as stepparents and biologically related kin, and represent a marked deviation from the composition of the nondivorced nuclear family (Booth & Edwards, 1992; Bray, 1987, 1988; Bray, Berger, & Boethel, 1994; Burrell, 1995; Cherlin & Furstenberg, 1994; Giles-Sims, 1987).

STRESS, SOCIOECONOMIC DISADVANTAGE, AND THE ADJUSTMENT TO DIVORCE AND REMARRIAGE

The stress perspective attributes problems in the adjustment of children from divorced and remarried families to the increased stresses experienced in these families. Parents and children living in divorced families encounter a diverse array of stressful life events (Hetherington, Cox, & Cox, 1985; Simons et al., 1996). Both custodial mothers and fathers complain of task overload and social isolation as they juggle household, child-care, and financial responsibilities that are usually dealt with by two parents (Hetherington & Stanley Hagan, 1997). Noncustodial parents express concerns associated with the establishment of new residences, social networks, and intimate relationships; loss of children; problems with visitation arrangements; and continued difficulties in relations with their ex-spouses (Hetherington, 1989, 1991b; Hetherington & Stanley Hagan, 1997; Hoffman, 1995; Minton & Pasley, 1996).

In spite of the diversity in stresses associated with divorce, most attention by sociologists and economists has focused on the marked decrement in the income of custodial mothers following marital dissolution and its accompanying risk factors. Those investigators who support a socioeconomic disadvantage perspective suggest that controlling for income will eliminate or greatly diminish the association between family structure and children's well-being (McLanahan & Sandefur, 1994). In addition, because custodial fathers do not encounter the financial decrements experienced by custodial mothers and because remarriage is the fastest way out of poverty for single mothers, it might be expected that children in father-custody families and stepfamilies will exhibit fewer behavior problems than those in divorced mother-custody households.

Because of increased enforcement of noncustodial fathers' child support payments and changes in the labor force for women, it has been speculated that custodial mothers and their children may no longer experience such drastic economic declines following divorce. A recent review (Bianchi, Subaiya, & Kahn, 1997) suggests, however, that custodial mothers still experience the loss of approximately one quarter to one half of their predivorce income in comparison to only 10% by custodial fathers following divorce (Arendell, 1986; Cherlin, 1992; Emery, 1994; McLanahan & Booth, 1989). For custodial mothers, this loss in income is accompanied by increased workloads; high rates of job instability; and residential moves to less desirable neighborhoods with poor schools, inadequate services, often high crime rates, and deviant peer populations (McLanahan & Booth, 1989; McLanahan & Sandefur, 1994).

Although father-only families have substantially higher incomes than do families with divorced custodial mothers, a significant number of father-only families (18%) live in poverty, and fathers rarely receive child support (Meyer & Garasky, 1993). However, most father-custody families have financial, housing, child-care, and educational resources not available to divorced custodial mothers. Custodial fathers report less child-rearing stress than do custodial mothers, and their children show fewer problems (Amato & Keith, 1991a; Clarke-Stewart & Hayward, 1996). This could be attributed to economic advantages in father-custody families; however, even with income controlled, children in father-custody families—especially boys—show greater well-being than those in mother-custody families (Clarke-Stewart & Hayward, 1996).

Newly repartnered parents and their children report higher levels of both positive and negative life changes than do those in never-divorced families (Forgatch et al., 1995; Hetherington et al., 1985). Although there is a marked increase in income for divorced mothers following remarriage, conflicts over finances, child rearing, and family relations remain potent problems in stepfamilies (Bray & Berger, 1993; Hetherington, 1993; Hetherington & Jodl, 1994). The economic improvement conferred by remarriage is not reflected in the improved adjustment of children in stepfamilies, and the new stresses associated with remarriage often counter the benefits associated with increased income (Amato & Booth, 1991; Bray & Berger, 1993; Cherlin & Furstenberg, 1994; Demo & Acock, 1996; Forgatch et al., 1995; Hetherington & Clingempeel, 1992; Hetherington & Jodl, 1994).

PARENTAL DISTRESS AND THE ADJUSTMENT
TO DIVORCE AND REMARRIAGE

Investigators taking the parental distress perspective propose that stressors affect children's adjustment through parental distress and diminished well-being (Bank, Duncan, Patterson, & Reid, 1993; Forgatch et al., 1995; Lorenz et al., 1996; Simons & Beaman, 1996; Simons, Beaman, Conger, & Chao, 1992; Simons & Johnson, 1996). In this view, it is the parents' response to stress, rather than the stress itself, that is most salient for children's adjustment.

Signs of diminished parental well-being and distress, including anger, anxiety, depression, loneliness, impulsivity, feelings of being externally controlled, and emotional lability, may emerge or increase in the immediate aftermath of divorce (Hetherington, 1989, 1993; Pearlin & Johnson, 1977). In addition, newly remarried parents are often depressed or preoccupied as they cope with the challenges of their new family life (Hetherington & Clingempeel, 1992; Hetherington & Jodl, 1994). The mental health of parents in divorced and remarried families is related to children's adjustment through diminished competence in their parenting (Clarke-Stewart & Hayward, 1996; Forgatch et al., 1995; Hetherington, 1993; Lorenz et al., 1996; Simons, 1996).

The stresses associated with marital transitions place both residential and nonresidential parents at risk not only for psychological disorders (Hetherington, 1989, 1991b; Kitson & Morgan, 1990; Stack, 1989; Travato & Lauris, 1989) but also for disruption in immune system functioning (Kiecolt-Glaser et al., 1988) and concomitant increased rates of illness and morbidity, which are notable in divorced adults, especially in men (Burman & Margolin, 1992; Hu & Goldman, 1990; Riessman & Gerstel, 1985). Nonresidential fathers engage in more health-compromising and impulsive behaviors, such as alcohol consumption, than do fathers in any other family type (Umberson, 1987; Umberson & Williams, 1993) and are overrepresented among suicides and homicides (Bloom, Asher, & White, 1978).

Although depression remains higher in divorced women than in nondivorced women, by two years after divorce, women show less depression and more psychological well-being than do those who remain in conflict-ridden marriages with husbands who undermine their discipline and feelings of competence. The well-being of both men and women increases after the formation of a mutually caring, intimate relationship, such as a remarriage (Hetherington, 1993). Most parents do adapt to their new marital situation, with concomitant decreases in psychological and physical problems. In support of the parental distress perspective, even temporary disruptions in parents' health, social, and psychological functioning may make it difficult to be competent in parenting children who may be confused, angry, and apprehensive about a divorce or remarriage, and this inept parenting adversely affects children's adjustment (Chase-Lansdale & Hetherington, 1990; Emery, 1988; Emery & Dillon, 1994; Hetherington, 1989; Hetherington & Stanley Hagan, 1995; Maccoby & Mnookin, 1992).

FAMILY PROCESS AND THE ADJUSTMENT TO DIVORCE AND REMARRIAGE

Divorce and remarriage confront families with changes and challenges associated with pervasive alterations in family roles and functioning. The changes in family relationships can support or undermine the efforts of children to adapt to their new family situations. Proponents of the family process perspective argue that the impact of parental attributes, changes in family structure, socioeconomic disadvantage, and parental distress on children's adjustment is largely mediated by disruptions in family relationships and interactions, such as those involved in discipline and child-rearing practices (Demo & Acock, 1996; Forgatch et al., 1995; Hetherington, 1993; Simons & Beaman, 1996; Simons & Johnson, 1996). Without disruptions in family functioning, the former risk factors are less likely to compromise children's adjustment.

Relationships Between Divorced Couples

Marital conflict is associated with a wide range of deleterious outcomes for children, including depression, poor social competence and academic performance, and conduct disorders (Amato & Keith, 1991a; Cowan & Cowan, 1990; Davies & Cummings, 1994; Forehand, Brody, Long, Slotkin, & Fauber, 1986; Gottman & Katz, 1989; Peterson & Zill, 1986). Conflict, contempt, anger, and acrimony often antecede divorce, and in the immediate aftermath of marital disruption, conflict may escalate. Consequently, one of the most frequently asked questions about divorce is whether parents should stay together in an unhappy, conflict-ridden marriage for the sake of the children.

The hypothesis that conflict is a major contributor to problems in divorced families is substantiated by evidence that children in high-conflict, nondivorced families have more problems in psychological adjustment and self-esteem than do those in divorced families or in low-conflict, nondivorced families (Amato & Keith, 1991a; Amato, Loomis, & Booth, 1995). In addition, longitudinal prospective studies of divorce indicate that divorce improves the adjustment of children removed from contentious marriages but is deleterious for children whose parents had less overtly conflictual relationships preceding divorce (Amato et al., 1995). When measures of marital dissatisfaction rather than conflict are used, the advantages of divorce over unhappy marital situations are less marked (Simons, 1996) because many couples in unsatisfying marriages may not exhibit overt conflict (Gottman, 1994).

Although contact and conflict between divorced couples diminish over time, they remain higher for couples with children as they attempt to negotiate coparenting relationships and economic responsibilities (Masheter, 1991). Despite the fact that cooperative, mutually supportive, and nonconfrontational coparenting relationships are advantageous to parents and children, only about one quarter of divorced parents attain such relationships and an approximately equal number maintain acrimonious relationships (Maccoby & Mnookin, 1992). Most coparenting relationships after divorce evolve into parallel coparenting relationships not only with little communication or coordination of parenting but also with lessened conflict because of the disengaged relationships. Cooperative coparenting is most likely to occur when family size is small and when there was little conflict at the time of divorce (Maccoby, Buchanan, Mnookin, & Dornbusch, 1993). With little conflict and cooperative coparenting, children adapt better not only to their parents' divorce but also to their parents' remarriages, and they tend to have more positive relations with their stepparents (Bray & Berger, 1993; Crosbie-Burnett, 1991).

The sheer frequency of conflict may not be as detrimental as the type of conflict. Conflicts in which children are caught in the middle while parents denigrate each other, precipitate loyalty conflicts, communicate through the children, or fight about the children are most destructive to children's well-being (Buchanan, Maccoby, & Dornbusch, 1991; Maccoby et al., 1993; Maccoby & Mnookin, 1992). Children in highly conflicted families not only are more distressed but also may learn to exploit and mislead their parents and to escape monitoring of their activities when they are older (Hetherington, Law, & O'Connor, 1992). Even when children are not directly involved in their parents' conflicts, the adverse effects of conflicts may be experienced through increased parental irritability and diminished monitoring, support, and involvement (Patterson, 1991).

Relationships of Custodial Mothers and Children

Children in both mother- and father-custody families show more problems than do children in nondivorced families; however, most offspring in both types of divorced families eventually are reasonably well-adjusted. Because approximately 84% of children reside with their mothers following divorce (Seltzer, 1994), most studies of parent–child relations following marital dissolution have involved custodial mothers. Close relationships with supportive, authoritative mothers who are warm but exert firm, consistent control and supervision are generally associated with positive adjustment in children and adolescents (Bray & Berger, 1993; Forehand, Thomas, Wierson, Brody, & Fauber, 1990; Hetherington, 1989, 1993; Hetherington & Clingempeel, 1992; Maccoby et al., 1993; Simons & Johnson, 1996). In the immediate aftermath of divorce, there is a period of disrupted parenting characterized by irritability and coercion and diminished communication, affection, consistency, control, and monitoring (Hetherington, 1991a, 1991b, 1993; Simons & Johnson, 1996).

The parenting of divorced mothers improves over the course of the two years following divorce but remains less authoritative than that of nondivorced mothers, and problems in control and coercive exchanges between divorced mothers and sons may remain high (Hetherington, 1991a). Even in adulthood, relationships between sons and divorced mothers are less close than those in nondivorced families, whereas differences in closeness are not found for daughters (Booth & Amato, 1994). Preadolescent girls and their divorced mothers often have close, companionate, confiding relationships; however, in adolescence, there is a notable increase in conflict in these relationships (Hetherington, 1991a; Hetherington & Clingempeel, 1992). In comparison with adolescents in nondivorced, two-parent families, adolescents in divorced families and in stepfamilies experience the highest levels of mother-adolescent disagreements and the lowest levels of parental supervision (Demo & Acock, 1996). Both conflictive, negative parent–adolescent relationships and lack of monitoring are associated with involvement with antisocial peers—one of the most potent pathways to the development of delinquency, alcoholism, substance abuse, and teenage sexual activity and childbearing (Conger & Reuter, 1996; Hetherington, 1993; Simons & Chao, 1996; Whitbeck et al., 1996).

About one quarter to one third of adolescents in divorced and remarried families, in comparison with 10% of adolescents in nondivorced families, become disengaged from their families, spending as little time at home as possible and avoiding interactions, activities, and communication with family members (Hetherington, 1993; Hetherington & Jodl, 1994). This incidence is greater for boys in divorced families and for girls in stepfamilies. If disengagement is associated with lack of adult support and supervision and with involvement in a delinquent peer group, it leads to both antisocial behavior and academic problems in adolescents (Hetherington, 1993; Patterson, DeBaryshe, & Ramsey, 1989). However, if there is a caring adult involved with the adolescent outside of the home, such as the parent of a friend, a teacher, a neighbor, or a coach, disengagement may be a positive solution to a disrupted, conflictual family situation (Hetherington, 1993).

It has been noted that children in divorced families grow up faster, in part, because of early assignment of responsibilities (Weiss, 1979), more autonomous decision making (Dornbusch et al., 1985), and lack of adult supervision (Hetherington, 1991a; Thomson, McLanahan, & Curtin, 1992). Assignment of responsibility may be associated with resilience and unusual social competence in girls from divorced families; yet, if the task demands are beyond the children's capabilities, they also may be associated with low self-esteem, anxiety, and depression (Hetherington, 1989, in press). Furthermore, if adolescents perceive themselves as being unfairly burdened with responsibilities that interfere with their other activities, they may respond with resentment, rebellion, and noncompliance.

The restabilizing of family relations following a remarriage takes considerably longer than that following a divorce (Cherlin & Furstenberg, 1994). Whereas a new homeostasis is established in about two to three years following divorce, it has been estimated that the adjustment to remarriage may take as long as five to seven years (Cherlin & Furstenberg, 1994; Papernow, 1988; Visher & Visher, 1990). Because more than one quarter of remarriages are terminated within five years, with higher rates for families with children, restabilization never occurs in many stepfamilies.

In the first year following a remarriage, custodial mothers engage in less affective involvement, less behavior control and monitoring, and more negativity than nondivorced mothers (Bray & Berger, 1993; Hetherington, 1993; Hetherington & Clingempeel, 1992). Negative mother–child interactions are related to more disengagement, dysfunctional family roles, poorer communication, and less cohesion in stepfamilies (Bray, 1990). However, in long-established remarriages, the parenting of custodial mothers with their biological offspring becomes increasingly similar to that in nondivorced families (Bray & Berger, 1993; Hetherington, 1993; Hetherington & Clingempeel, 1992; Hetherington & Jodl, 1994).

Relationships of Custodial Fathers and Children

Although children usually live with their mothers following the dissolution of their parents' marriage, father-headed families have tripled since 1974, making them the fastest growing family type in the United States (Meyer & Garasky, 1993). Arrangements about physical custody are often made on the basis of personal decisions by parents and not on judicial decree, and the preponderance of maternal physical custody, even when joint legal custody has been granted, may reflect concerns fathers have about assuming full-time parenting (Maccoby et al., 1993; Maccoby & Mnookin, 1992). Boys and older children are more likely to be placed in father-only custody, but some girls and young children do live with their fathers. In contrast to custodial mothers, custodial fathers are a very select group of fathers who may be more child-oriented than most fathers. Fathers who seek custody of their children are more involved and capable than those fathers who have custody thrust on them because the mothers were unwilling or incompetent to parent (Hanson, 1988; Mendes, 1976a, 1976b). Once their families have restabilized, custodial fathers report less child-rearing stress, better parent–child relations, and fewer behavior problems in their children than do custodial mothers (Amato & Keith, 1991a; Clarke-Stewart & Hayward, 1996; Furstenberg, 1988).

There are different strengths and weaknesses in the parenting of custodial mothers and fathers. Although custodial mothers and custodial fathers are perceived to be similarly warm and nurturing with younger children (Warshak, 1986), mothers have more problems with control and with assignment of household tasks, whereas fathers have more problems with communication, self-disclosure, and monitoring of their children's activities (Chase-Lansdale & Hetherington, 1990; Furstenberg, 1988; Warshak, 1986). Moreover, fathers have special difficulties with monitoring adolescents' behavior, especially that of daughters (Buchanan, Maccoby, & Dornbusch, 1992; Maccoby et al., 1993).

Recent evidence indicates that adolescent adjustment is more predictable from the parenting of a custodial parent of the same sex than one of the opposite sex (Lindner-Gunnoe, 1993). This evidence parallels findings of the greater salience of same-sex parents in the adjustment of adolescents in nondivorced families (Furman & Buhrmester, 1992; Kurdek & Fine, 1993). In spite of this greater influence of same-sex custodial parents, both sons and daughters report feeling closer to their custodial parent than their noncustodial parent, regardless of whether the parent is a mother or a father (Hetherington & Clingempeel, 1992; Maccoby et al., 1993; White, Brinkerhoff, & Booth, 1985).

As has been found with mothers, when custodial fathers remarry, there are disruptions in father–child relationships, especially with daughters (Clingempeel, Brand, & Ievoli, 1984). Fathers may alter their caretaking relationships more radically than mothers do because fathers are more likely to expect a stepmother to play a major role in household tasks and parenting (Hetherington & Stanley Hagan, 1995). However, in long-established stepfamilies, there are few differences in parent–child relations between remarried fathers and their residential biological children and those fathers and children in nondivorced families (Hetherington & Jodl, 1994).

Relationships of Noncustodial Mothers and Children

Although less is known about noncustodial mothers than noncustodial fathers, nonresidential mothers maintain more contact with their children than do nonresidential fathers. It is not only in the quantity but also in the quality of parent–child relationships that these mothers and fathers differ. Noncustodial mothers are less adept than custodial mothers in controlling and monitoring their children's behavior, but they are more effective in these parenting behaviors than are noncustodial fathers (Furstenberg & Nord, 1987; Lindner-Gunnoe, 1993). Children report that noncustodial mothers are more interested in and informed about their activities; are more supportive, sensitive, and responsive to their needs; and are more communicative than noncustodial fathers (Furstenberg & Nord, 1987; Lindner-Gunnoe, 1993; Santrock & Sitterle, 1987). Therefore, it is not surprising that children report talking more about their problems and activities and feeling closer to noncustodial mothers than to noncustodial fathers (Lindner-Gunnoe, 1993), nor that noncustodial mothers have more influence over their children's development, especially their daughters' adjustment, than do noncustodial fathers (Brand, Clingempeel, & Bowen-Woodward, 1988; Lindner-Gunnoe, 1993; Zill, 1988). Noncustodial mothers' warmth, support, and monitoring enhance their children's scholastic achievement and diminish antisocial, externalizing problems (Lindner-Gunnoe, 1993). In appraising some research findings that children have fewer problems in the custody of fathers than in the custody of mothers (Amato & Keith, 1991a; Clarke-Stewart & Hayward, 1996), it must be considered that part of this effect may be attributable to the more active involvement of noncustodial mothers.

When a custodial father remarries, closeness to the noncustodial mother can have some disadvantages because it is related to children's lack of acceptance of a stepmother. In contrast, there is no association between the relationship with a noncustodial father and building a close relationship with a stepfather (Hetherington, 1993; Hetherington & Jodl, 1994; White, 1994).

Relationships of Noncustodial Fathers and Children

In contrast to mothers' behaviour, the postdivorce parenting behavior of fathers is less predictable from their predivorce behavior (Hetherington et al., 1985). Some previously attached and involved fathers find the enforced marginality and intermittent contact in being noncustodial fathers to be painful, and they drift away from their children. Other fathers, especially custodial fathers, rise to the occasion and increase their involvement and parenting competence. However, most nonresidential fathers have a friendly, egalitarian, companionate relationship rather than a traditional parental relationship with their children (Arendell, 1986; Furstenberg & Nord, 1987; Hetherington, Cox, & Cox, 1979; Munsch, Woodward, & Darling, 1995). They want their visits to be pleasant and entertaining and are hesitant to assume the role of disciplinarian or teacher. They are less likely than nondivorced fathers to criticize, control, and monitor their children's behavior or to help them with tasks such as homework (Bray & Berger, 1993; Furstenberg & Nord, 1987; Hetherington, 1991b).

Frequency of contact with noncustodial fathers and the adjustment of children are usually found to be unrelated (Amato & Keith, 1991a). Although obviously some degree of contact is essential, it seems to be the quality of the relationship and the circumstances of contact rather than frequency of visits that are most important (Amato, 1993; Emery, 1988; Furstenberg & Cherlin, 1991; Simons & Beaman, 1996). When noncustodial fathers are not just "tour guide" fathers but maintain more parentlike contact, participate in a variety of activities with their children, and spend holidays together, the well-being of children is promoted (Clarke-Stewart & Hayward, 1996). Under conditions of low conflict, the involvement of authoritative noncustodial fathers can enhance children's adjustment (Hetherington, 1989), especially that of boys (Lindner-Gunnoe, 1993). It can even, to some extent, protect the children from the adverse consequences of rejecting or incompetent noncustodial mothers (Hetherington, 1989). In contrast, under conditions of high conflict, frequent contact with noncustodial parents may exacerbate children's problems (Kline, Johnston, & Tschann, 1991).

Relationships Between Stepparents and Stepchildren

Papernow (1988) commented that the typical starting point for a stepfamily involving "a weak couple subsystem, a tightly bonded parent–child alliance, and potential interference in family functioning from an outsider" (p. 56) would be considered problematic in a traditional nondivorced family. Clinicians have remarked that any stepfamily that uses a traditional nuclear family as its ideal is bound for disappointment (Visher & Visher, 1990). Similar patterns of relationships in traditional families and stepfamilies may lead to different outcomes. Patterns of functioning and family processes that undermine or promote positive adjustment may differ in the two types of families (Bray & Berger, 1993). The complex relationships between families following remarriage may require less rigid family boundaries and more open, less integrated relations among the family subsystems.

Although both stepfathers and stepmothers feel less close to stepchildren than do non-divorced parents to their children, they, if not the stepchildren, want the new marriage to be successful (Brand et al., 1988; Bray & Berger, 1993; Hetherington, 1993; Kurdek & Fine, 1993). In the early stages of a remarriage, stepfathers have been reported to be like polite strangers, trying to ingratiate themselves with their stepchildren by showing less negativity but also less control, monitoring, and affection than do fathers in nondivorced families (Bray & Berger, 1992; Hetherington & Clingempeel, 1992). In longer established stepfamilies, a distant, disengaged parenting style remains the predominant one for stepfathers, but conflict and negativity, especially between stepparents and stepdaughters, can remain high or increase, especially with adolescents (Brand et al., 1988; Bray & Berger, 1993; Hetherington, 1993; Hetherington & Jodl, 1994). Some of the conflict in stepfamilies is due to the negative rejecting behavior of stepchildren toward stepparents (Bray & Berger, 1993; Hetherington & Clingempeel, 1992; Hetherington & Jodl, 1994). Even stepparents with the best intentions may give up in the face of persistent hostile behavior by stepchildren.

Conflict between stepfathers and stepchildren is not necessarily precipitated by the children. In fact, rates of physical abuse perpetrated by stepfathers on their stepchildren are 7 times higher than those by fathers on their biological children, and homicide rates for stepfathers are 100 times higher than those for biological fathers (Daly & Wilson, 1996; Wilson, Daly, & Weghorst, 1980). These differential rates are most marked with infants and preschool-age children (Daly & Wilson, 1996).

Stepmothers have a more difficult time integrating themselves into stepfamilies than do stepfathers. Remarried fathers often expect that the stepmothers will participate in child rearing, forcing the stepmothers into more active, less distant, and more confrontational roles than those required of stepfathers (Brand et al., 1988). Support by the fathers for the stepmothers' parenting and parental agreement on child rearing are especially important in promoting effective parenting in stepmothers (Brand et al., 1988). The assumption of the dominant disciplinarian role is fraught with problems for stepparents (Brand et al., 1988; Bray & Berger, 1993; Hetherington, 1991a), and although authoritative parenting can have salutary effects on stepchildren's adjustment, especially with stepfathers and stepsons, authoritative parenting is not always a feasible option in stepfamilies (Bray & Berger, 1993). When custodial parents are authoritative and when stepparents are warm and involved and support the custodial parents' discipline rather than making independent control attempts, children can be responsive and adjust well (Bray & Berger, 1993; Hetherington, 1989).

It is not only parent–child relationships but also relationships between siblings that are more conflictual and less supportive in divorced families and stepfamilies than in non-divorced families (Hetherington, 1991a). These effects are more marked for biologically related siblings than for stepsiblings (Hetherington & Jodl, 1994). Less involved, harsher parenting is associated with rivalrous, aggressive, and unsupportive sibling relationships in divorced and remarried families (Conger & Conger, 1996; Hetherington, 1991a, 1993; Hetherington & Clingempeel, 1992), and, in turn, these negative sibling relations lead to low social competence and responsibility and to more behavior problems in children (Hetherington & Clingempeel, 1992).

CONCLUSION: WHAT MATTERS? WHAT DOESN'T?

In reviewing the five perspectives, it is clear that each may influence children's adjustment. The first perspective, the individual risk and vulnerability hypothesis, is supported by evidence suggesting that children and their parents have attributes that directly contribute to their experiencing marital transitions and to having more difficulties in adjusting to them. These problems may be transmitted genetically from parents to children, or the effect on children's adjustment may be indirect, due to parents' ineffective child-rearing strategies. However, individual vulnerability to the adverse outcomes of divorce and remarriage seems to involve a complex interaction among an array of individual attributes, including personality, age, gender, and ethnicity, and the effects of these interactions have been difficult to differentiate.

The family composition–parental absence hypothesis is not as well supported by the evidence. Generally, children in never-divorced families with two parents are more competent than children whose parents have divorced. However, this theory would suggest that children's adjustment should benefit from the addition of a stepparent, yet there are few indications of lower levels of problems in children in stepfamilies as compared with children in divorced families. Furthermore, some studies indicate that especially in the early stages of a remarriage, stepchildren exhibit more difficulties than do children in stabilized, divorced, single-parent families (Amato & Keith, 1991a; Hetherington, 1993; Hetherington & Clingempeel, 1992; Hetherington & Jodl, 1994).

These comments must be qualified by findings indicating that the presence of a stepfather, especially with preadolescent boys, can attenuate problems in adjustment for stepsons, whereas the presence of either a stepmother or a stepfather may be associated with higher levels of problem behaviors for girls (Amato & Keith, 1991a; Hetherington, 1989; Hetherington & Jodl, 1994; Lee et al., 1994). These results, in conjunction with the somewhat inconsistent evidence that boys may also fare better in a father-custody family than in a mother-custody family (Amato & Keith, 1991a; Clarke-Stewart & Hayward, 1996; Zill, 1988), indicate that the presence of a father may have positive effects on the well-being of boys. Rather than rejecting the family composition–parental absence perspective, it should be concluded that there is not a simple main effect of family composition or parental absence but that it is modified by the reason for parental unavailability, the quality of family relationships, and the child's gender.

The findings thus far yield only modest support for marked direct effects of life stress and economic deprivation on children's adjustment. Even when income is controlled, children in divorced families show more problems than do those in nondivorced families (Amato & Keith, 1991a; Clarke-Stewart & Hayward, 1996; Demo & Acock, 1996; Guidubaldi et al., 1987; Hetherington, 1997, in press; Simons & Associates, 1996). In addition, although the income in stepfamilies is only slightly lower than that in nondivorced families, children in these families show a similar level of problem behavior to that in divorced mother-custody families (Amato & Keith, 1991a; Demo & Acock, 1996; Forgatch et al., 1995; Henderson, Hetherington, Mekos, & Reiss, 1996; Simons & Johnson, 1996). Thus, the effects of income do not seem to be primary and are largely indirect.

Some investigators using large-scale survey data report that as much as half of the effects of divorce on children's adjustment is attributable to economic factors (McLanahan & Sandefur, 1994); others find no direct effects of income but a major effect of the quality of family relationships that may alter children's adjustment (Demo & Acock, 1996). Furthermore, in studies in which income has been controlled, differences between offspring in divorced and nondivorced families remain (Amato & Keith, 1991a; Clarke-Stewart & Hayward, 1996; Demo & Acock, 1996; Guidubaldi et al., 1987; Hetherington, in press; Simons & Associates, 1996). Some of the inconsistencies in findings are due to methodological differences in studies. Surveys often have large representative samples but inadequate measures, sometimes involving only two or three items and single informants, to assess parental and family characteristics and family process variables. Studies using smaller, less representative samples but more reliable multimethod, multi-informant assessment, including observations, have found that much of the effects of family structure and economic stress are mediated by inept parenting (Forgatch et al., 1995; Simons & Johnson, 1996). Furthermore, there is some support in the research on stress, economic deprivation, and marital transitions for the individual risk position. As stated earlier, antisocial individuals are at greater risk not only for job instability, economic problems (Simons et al., 1992), and stressful life events but also for divorce (Capaldi & Patterson, 1991; Kitson & Holmes, 1992; Lahey et al., 1988), problems in successive marital relationships (Capaldi & Patterson, 1991), and incompetent parenting (Forgatch et al., 1995; Simons & Johnson, 1996).

Although it is true that parental distress increases in the aftermath of a divorce, research indicates that the effect of parents' well-being is largely mediated through their parenting. Even temporary disruptions in parents' physical and psychological functioning due to a marital transition interfere with their ability to offer support and supervision at a time when children need them most.

Although attributes of parents and children, family composition, stress and socioeconomic disadvantage, and parental distress impact children's adjustment, their effects may be mediated through the more proximal mechanism of family process. Dysfunctional family relationships, such as conflict, negativity, lack of support, and nonauthoritative parenting, exacerbate the effects of divorce and remarriage on children's adjustment. Certainly if divorced or remarried parents are authoritative and their families are harmonious, warm, and cohesive, the differences between the adjustment of children in these families and those in nondivorced families reduced. However, marital transitions increase the probability that children will not find themselves in families with such functioning. Research on the relationships between family members in nondivorced families and stepfamilies supports the family process hypothesis, suggesting that, in large part, it is negative, conflictual, dysfunctional family relationships between parents, parents and children, and siblings that account for differences in children's adjustment.

It has become fashionable to attempt to estimate the relative contributions of individual attributes, family structure, stresses, parental distress, and family process to the adjustment of children in divorced and remarried families. These attempts have led to conflicting results, futile controversies, and misleading conclusions because the amount of variance explained by the factors differs from sample to sample and varies with the methods and the data analytic strategies used. Moreover, different risk and vulnerability factors are likely to come into play and to vary in salience at different points in the transitions from an unhappy marriage to divorce, to life in a single-parent household, through remarriage, and into subsequent marital transitions. These risk factors will be modified by shifting protective factors and resources.

A transactional model of risks associated with marital transitions is perhaps most appropriate (see Figure 1). Divorce and remarriage increase the probability of parents and children encountering a set of interrelated risks. These risks are linked, interact, and are mediated and moderated in complex ways. These effects are illustrated in the model in different ways. For example, parental distress (e.g., maternal depression) does not have a direct effect on children's adjustment, which is not to say it does not have an impact. Instead, its influence is

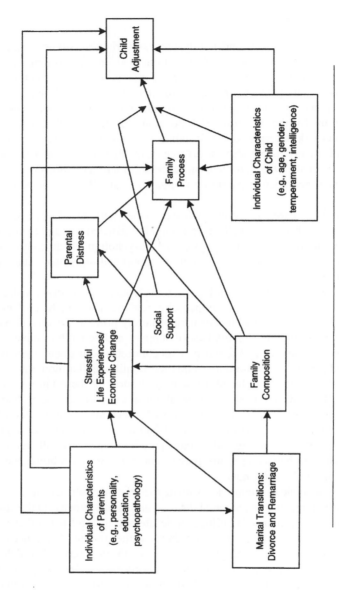

Figure 1. A transactional model of the predictors of children's adjustment following divorce and remarriage.

mediated through its link to family process, specifically the depressed mothers' diminished ability to effectively parent. In contrast, some variables moderate the relationship between other variables, such that the relationship depends on the level of the moderator. For example, children with difficult temperaments are expected to be more adversely affected by disruptions in family functioning than are children with easy temperaments. Thus, individual variables such as temperament can moderate the effect of family process on children's adjustment.

All family members encounter stresses associated with marital transitions, and it may be the balance between risks and resources that determines the impact of stresses on divorced and remarried parents and their children. All five of the factors described at the beginning of this article are associated with divorce and remarriage and with adverse outcomes for children. Studies using path analyses (e.g., Conger & Conger, 1996; Forgatch et al., 1995; Simons & Associates, 1996) have helped illuminate the patterns of linkages among these risks and have suggested that many of the risk factors are mediated by proximal experiences such as disruptions in parent–child or sibling relationships. However, the fact that a path is indirect does not reduce its importance. Figure 1 presents the theoretical model describing the linkages among these factors. A set of individual attributes, such as antisocial behavior, is associated with an increased risk of divorce and an unsuccessful remarriage; problems in social relationships, including parent–child relationships; and stressful life events. All family members encounter stresses as they deal with the changes, challenges, and restructuring of the family associated with marital transitions, but these vary for different family members and for divorce and remarriage. Divorce usually leads to the loss or the diminished availability of a father and the economic, social, and emotional resources he can provide, which increases the probability of poverty and its concomitant environmental and experiential adversities for divorced custodial mothers and their children. Although some of the effects of stresses, such as living in neighborhoods with high crime rates, poor schools, antisocial peers, and few job opportunities or resources, may impact directly on children's adjustment and attainment, other effects of stress in divorced families may be indirect and mediated through parental psychological distress, inept or altered parenting, and disrupted family processes. Stresses asociated with the changes and complexities in stepfamilies may also lead to distress and dysfunctional family functioning. Children, because of individual characteristics such as gender, temperament, personality, age, and intelligence, vary in their influence on family process and their vulnerability or resilience in dealing with their parents' divorce and remarriage and concomitant changes in family roles, relationships, and process. Thus, effects of the earlier risk factors on children's adjustment are mediated or moderated by associated transactional risk factors and often eventually by disruptions in family functioning. These indirect or mediated effects do not negate the importance of the earlier risk factors as a link in the transactional path of adversity leading to problems in child adjustment.

Static, cross-sectional slices out of the lives of parents and children in divorced or remarried families give a misleading picture of how risk and protective factors combine to influence the adjustment of children. An examination of the dynamic trajectories of interacting risk and protective factors associated with divorce and remarriage will yield a more valid and fruitful view of the multiple pathways associated with resiliency or adverse outcomes for children who have experienced their parents' marital transitions.

REFERENCES

Ahrons, C. R. (1979). The binuclear family: Two households, one family. *Alternative Lifestyles, 2,* 499–515.

Ahrons, C. R. (1983). Predictors of paternal involvement postdivorce: Mothers' and fathers' perceptions. *Journal of Divorce, 6,* 55–69.

Allison, P. D., & Furstenberg, F. F., Jr. (1989). How marital dissolution affects children: Variations by age and sex. *Developmental Psychology, 25,* 540–549.

Amato, P. R. (1993). Children's adjustment to divorce: Theories, hypotheses, and empirical support. *Journal of Marriage and the Family, 55,* 23–38.

Amato, P. R. (1995). Single-parent households as settings for children's development, well-being, and attainment: A social network/resources perspective. *Sociological Studies of Children, 7,* 19–47.

Amato, P. R., & Booth, A. (1991). Consequences of parental divorce and marital happiness for adult well-being. *Social Forces, 69,* 895–914.

Amato, P. R., & Booth, A. (1996). A prospective study of divorce and parent–child relationships. *Journal of Marriage and the Family, 58,* 356–365.

Amato, P. R., & Keith, B. (1991a). Parental divorce and adult well-being: A meta-analysis. *Journal of Marriage and the Family, 53,* 43–58.

Amato, P. R., & Keith, B. (1991b). Parental divorce and the well-being of children: A meta-analysis. *Psychological Bulletin, 110,* 26–46.

Amato, P. R., Loomis, L. S., & Booth, A. (1995). Parental divorce, marital conflict, and offspring well-being during early adulthood. *Social Forces, 73,* 895–915.

Arendell, T. (1986). *Mothers and divorce: Legal, economic, and social dilemmas.* Berkeley: University of California Press.

Bank, L., Duncan, T., Patterson, G. R., & Reid, J. (1993). Parent and teacher ratings in the assessment and prediction of antisocial and delinquent behaviors. *Journal of Personality, 61,* 693–709.

Baucom, D. H., & Epstein, N. (1990). *Cognitive–behavioral marital therapy.* New York: Brunner/Mazel.

Bianchi, S. M., Subaiya, L., & Kahn, J. (1997, March). *Economic well-being of husbands and wives after marital disruption.* Paper presented at the annual meeting of the Population Association of America, Washington, DC.

Block, J. H., Block, J., & Gjerde, P. F. (1986). The personality of children prior to divorce: A prospective study. *Child Development, 57,* 827–840.

Block, J. H., Block, J., & Gjerde, P. F. (1988). Parental functioning and the home environment in families of divorce: Prospective and concurrent analyses. *Journal of the American Academy of Child and Adolescent Psychiatry, 27,* 207–213.

Bloom, B. L., Asher, S. J., & White, S. W. (1978). Marital disruption as a stressor: A review and analysis. *Psychological Bulletin, 85,* 867–894.

Booth, A., & Amato, P. R. (1994). Parental marital quality, parental divorce, and relations with parents. *Journal of Marriage and the Family, 56,* 21–34.

Booth, A., & Edwards, J. N. (1990). Transmission of marital and family quality over the generations: The effects of parental divorce and unhappiness. *Journal of Divorce, 13,* 41–58.

Booth, A., & Edwards, J. N. (1992). Starting over: Why remarriages are more unstable. *Journal of Family Issues, 13,* 179–194.

Bradbury, T. N., & Fincham, F. D. (1990). Attributions in marriage: Review and critique. *Psychological Bulletin, 107,* 3–33.

Brand, E., Clingempeel, W. G., & Bowen-Woodward, K. (1988). Family relationships and children's psychosocial adjustment in stepmother and stepfather families. In E. M. Hetherington & J. D. Arasteh (Eds.), *Impact of divorce, single parenting, and stepparenting on children* (pp. 299–324). Hillsdale, NJ: Erlbaum.

Braver, S. L., Wolchik, S. A., Sandler, I. N., Sheets, V. L., Fogas, B., & Bay, R. C. (1993). A longitudinal study of noncustodial parents: Parents without children. *Journal of Family Psychology, 7,* 9–23.

Bray, J. H. (1987, August–September). *Becoming a stepfamily: Overview of The Developmental Issues in Stepfamilies Research Project.* Paper presented at the 95th Annual Convention of the American Psychological Association, New York.

Bray, J. H. (1988). Children's development during early remarriage. In E. M. Hetherington & J. D. Arasteh (Eds.), *Impact of divorce, single parenting, and stepparenting on children* (pp. 279–288). Hillsdale, NJ: Erlbaum.

Bray, J. H. (1990, August). *The developing stepfamily II: Overview and previous findings.* Paper presented at the 98th Annual Convention of the American Psychological Association, Boston.

Bray, J. H., & Berger, S. H. (1992). Nonresidential family–child relationships following divorce and remarriage. In C. E. Depner & J. H. Bray (Eds.), *Nonresidential parenting: New vistas in family living* (pp. 156–181). Newbury Park, CA: Sage.

Bray, J. H., & Berger, S. H. (1993). Developmental Issues in Stepfamilies Research Project: Family relationships and parent–child interactions. *Journal of Family Psychology, 7,* 76–90.

Bray, J. H., Berger, S. H., & Boethel, C. L. (1994). Role integration and marital adjustment in stepfather families. In K. Pasley & M. Ihinger-Tallman (Eds.), *Stepparenting: Issues in theory, research, and practice* (pp. 69–86). Westport, CT: Greenwood Press.

Buchanan, C. M., Maccoby, E. E., & Dornbusch, S. M. (1991). Caught between parents: Adolescents' experience in divorced homes. *Child Development, 62,* 1008–1029.

Buchanan, C. M., Maccoby, E. E., & Dornbusch, S. M. (1992). Adolescents and their families after divorce: Three residential arrangements compared. *Journal of Research on Adolescence, 2,* 261–291.

Bumpass, L. L., Martin, T. C., & Sweet, J. A. (1991). The impact of family background and early marital factors on marital disruption. *Journal of Family Issues, 12,* 22–42.

Bumpass, L. L., & Raley, R. K. (1995). Redefining single-parent families: Cohabitation and changing family reality. *Demography, 32,* 97–109.

Bumpass, L. L., & Sweet, J. A. (1989). *Children's experience in single-parent families: Implications of cohabitation and marital transitions* (National Study of Families and Households Working Paper No. 3). Madison: University of Wisconsin, Center for Demography and Ecology.

Bumpass, L. L., Sweet, J. A., & Castro-Martin, T. (1990). Changing patterns of remarriage. *Journal of Marriage and the Family, 52,* 747–756.

Bumpass, L. L., Sweet, J. A., & Cherlin, A. (1991). The role of cohabitation in declining rates of marriage. *Journal of Marriage and the Family, 53,* 913–927.

Burman, B., & Margolin, G. (1992). Analysis of the association between marital relationships and health problems: An interactional perspective. *Psychological Bulletin, 112,* 39–63.

Burrell, N. A. (1995). Communication patterns in stepfamilies: Redefining family roles, themes, and conflict styles. In M. A. Fitzpatrick & A. L. Vangelisti (Eds.), *Explaining family interactions* (pp. 290–309). Thousand Oaks, CA: Sage.

Capaldi, D. M., & Patterson, G. R. (1991). Relation of parental transitions to boys' adjustment problems: I. A linear hypothesis. II. Mothers at risk for transitions and unskilled parenting. *Developmental Psychology, 27,* 489–504.

Castro-Martin, T., & Bumpass, L. (1989). Recent trends and differentials in marital disruption. *Demography, 26,* 37–51.

Chase-Lansdale, P. L., Cherlin, A. J., & Kiernan, K. E. (1995). The long-term effects of parental divorce on the mental health of young adults: A developmental perspective. *Child Development, 66,* 1614–1634.

Chase-Lansdale, P. L., & Hetherington, E. M. (1990). The impact of divorce on life-span development: Short and long term effects. In P. B. Baltes, D. L. Featherman, & R. M. Lerner (Eds.), *Life-span development and behavior* (Vol. 10, pp. 105–150). Hillsdale, NJ: Erlbaum.

Cherlin, A. (1992). *Marriage, divorce, remarriage: Social trends in the U. S.* Cambridge, MA: Harvard University Press.

Cherlin, A. J., & Furstenberg, F. F. (1994). Stepfamilies in the United States: A reconsideration. In J. Blake & J. Hagen (Eds.), *Annual review of sociology* (pp. 359–381). Palo Alto, CA: Annual Reviews.

Cherlin, A. J., Furstenberg, F. F., Chase-Lansdale, P. L., Kiernan, K. E., Robins, P. K., Morrison, D. R., & Teitler, J. O. (1991). Longitudinal studies of effects of divorce in children in Great Britain and the United States. *Science, 252,* 1386–1389.

Clarke-Stewart, K. A., & Hayward, C. (1996). Advantages of father custody and contact for the psychological well-being of school-age children. *Journal of Applied Developmental Psychology, 17,* 239–270.

Clingempeel, W. G., Brand, E., & Ievoli, R. (1984). Stepparent–step-child relationships in stepmother and stepfather families: A multimethod study. *Family Relations, 33,* 465–473.

Conger, R. D., & Chao, W. (1996). Adolescent depressed mood. In R. L. Simons & Associates (Eds.), *Understanding differences between divorced and intact families: Stress, interaction, and child outcome* (pp. 157–175). Thousand Oaks, CA: Sage.

Conger, R. D., & Conger, K. J. (1996). Sibling relationships. In R. L. Simons & Associates (Eds.), *Understanding differences between divorced and intact families: Stress, interaction, and child outcome* (pp. 104–124). Thousand Oaks, CA: Sage.

Conger, R. D., & Reuter, M. A. (1996). Siblings, parents, and peers: A longitudinal study of social influences in adolescent risk for alcohol use and abuse. In G. H. Brody (Ed.), *Sibling relationships: Their causes and consequences* (pp. 1–30). Norwood, NJ: Ablex.

Cowan, P. A., & Cowan, C. P. (1990). Becoming a family: Research and intervention. In I. Sigel & G. A. Brody (Eds.), *Family research* (pp. 246–279). Hillsdale, NJ: Erlbaum.

Crosbie-Burnett, M. (1991). Impact of joint versus sole custody and quality of the co-parental relationship on adjustment of adolescents in remarried families. *Behavioral Sciences and the Law, 9,* 439–449.

Daly, M., & Wilson, M. I. (1996). Violence against stepchildren. *Current Directions in Psychological Science, 5,* 77–81.

Davies, P. T., & Cummings, E. M. (1994). Marital conflict and child adjustment: An emotional security hypothesis. *Psychological Bulletin, 116,* 387–411.

Demo, D. H., & Acock, A. C. (1996). Family structure, family process, and adolescent well-being. *Journal of Research on Adolescence, 6,* 457–488.

Dillon, P. A., & Emery, R. E. (1996). Divorce mediation and resolution of child custody disputes: Long-term effects. *American Journal of Orthopsychiatry, 66,* 131–140.

Dornbusch, S. M., Carlsmith, J. M., Bushwall, S. J., Ritter, P. L., Liederman, H., Hastrof, A. H., & Gross, R. T. (1985). Single parents, extended households, and the control of adolescents. *Child Development, 56,* 326–341.

Elder, G., Caspi, A., & Van Nguyen, R. (1992). Resourceful and vulnerable children: Family influences in stressful times. In R. K. Silbereisen & K. Eyferth (Eds.), *Development in context: Integrative perspectives on youth development* (pp. 165–194). New York: Springer.

Elder, G. H., Jr., & Russell, S. T. (1996). Academic performance and future aspirations. In R. L. Simons & Associates (Eds.), *Understanding differences between divorced and intact families: Stress, interaction, and child outcome* (pp. 176–192). Thousand Oaks, CA: Sage.

Emery, R. E. (1982). Interpersonal conflict and the children of discord and divorce. *Psychological Bulletin, 92,* 310–330.

Emery, R. E. (1988). *Marriage, divorce, and children's adjustment.* Newbury Park, CA: Sage.

Emery, R. E. (1994). *Renegotiating family relationships.* New York: Guilford Press.

Emery, R. E., & Dillon, P. A. (1994). Conceptualizing the divorce process: Renegotiating boundaries of intimacy and power in the divorced family system. *Family Relations, 43,* 374–379.

Emery, R. E., & Forehand, R. (1994). Parental divorce and children's well-being: A focus on resilience. In R. J. Haggerty, L. R. Sherrod, N. Garmezy, & M. Rutter (Eds.), *Stress, risk, and resilience in children and adolescents* (pp. 64–99). Cambridge, England: Cambridge University Press.

Felner, R. D., Ginter, M. A., Boike, M. F., & Cowen, E. L. (1981). Parental death of divorce and the school adjustment of young children. *American Journal of Community Psychology, 9,* 181–191.

Felner, R. D., Stolberg, A., & Cowen, E. L. (1975). Crisis events and school mental health referral patterns of young children. *Journal of Consulting and Clinical Psychology, 43,* 305–310.

Fincham, F. D., Bradbury, T. N., & Scott, C. K. (1990). Cognition in marriage. In F. D. Fincham & T. N. Bradbury (Eds.), *The psychology of marriage* (pp. 118–149). New York: Guilford Press.

Forehand, R., Brody, G., Long, N., Slotkin, J., & Fauber, R. (1986). Divorce/divorce potential and interparental conflict: The relationship to early adolescent social and cognitive functioning. *Journal of Adolescent Research, 1,* 389–397.

Forehand, R., Thomas, A. M., Wierson, M., Brody, G., & Fauber, R. (1990). Role of maternal functioning and parenting skills in adolescent functioning following divorce. *Journal of Abnormal Psychology, 99,* 278–283.

Forgatch, M. S., Patterson, G. R., & Ray, J. A. (1995). Divorce and boys' adjustment problems: Two paths with a single model. In E. M. Hetherington & E. A. Blechman (Eds.), *Stress, coping, and resiliency in children and families* (pp. 67–105). Mahwah, NJ: Erlbaum.

Furman, W., & Buhrmester, D. (1992). Age and sex differences in perceptions of networks of personal relationships. *Child Development, 63,* 103–115.

Furstenberg, F. F., Jr. (1988). Child care after divorce and remarriage. In E. M. Hetherington & J. D. Arasteh (Eds.), *Impact of divorce, single parenting, and stepparenting on children* (pp. 245–261). Hillsdale, NJ: Erlbaum.

Furstenberg, F. F., Jr., & Cherlin, A. J. (1991). *Divided families: What happens to children when parents part.* Cambridge, MA: Harvard University Press.

Furstenberg, F. F., Jr., Morgan, S. P., & Allison, P. D. (1987). Paternal participation and children's well-being after marital dissolution. *American Sociological Review, 52*, 695–701.

Furstenberg, F. F., Jr., & Nord, C. W. (1987). Parenting apart: Patterns of childrearing after marital disruption. *Journal of Marriage and the Family, 47*, 893–904.

Furstenberg, F. F., Jr., Nord, C. W., Peterson, J. L., & Zill, N. (1983). The life course of children of divorce: Marital disruption and parental contact. *American Sociological Review, 48*, 656–668.

Ganong, L. H., & Coleman, M. (1994). *Remarried family relationships*. Thousand Oaks, CA: Sage.

Giles-Sims, J. (1987). Social exchange in remarried families. In K. Pasley & M. Ihinger-Tallman (Eds.), *Remarriage and stepparenting: Current research and theory* (pp. 141–163). New York: Guilford Press.

Glenn, N. D., & Kramer, K. B. (1985). The psychological well-being of adult children of divorce. *Journal of Marriage and the Family, 47*, 905–912.

Glick, P. C. (1989). Remarried families, stepfamilies, and stepchildren: A brief demographic profile. *Family Relations, 38*, 24–27.

Gotlib, I., & McCabe, S. B. (1990). Marriage and psychopathology. In F. D. Fincham & T. N. Bradbury (Eds.), *The psychology of marriage* (pp. 226–257). New York: Guilford Press.

Gottman, J. M. (1993). A theory of marital dissolution and stability. *Journal of Family Psychology, 7*, 57–75.

Gottman, J. M. (1994). *What predicts divorce?* Hillsdale, NJ: Erlbaum.

Gottman, J. M., & Katz, L. F. (1989). Effects of marital discord on young children's peer interaction and health. *Developmental Psychology, 25*, 373–381.

Gottman, J. M., & Levenson, R. W. (1992). Marital processes predictive of later dissolution: Behavior, physiology, and health. *Journal of Personality and Social Psychology, 63*, 221–233.

Guidubaldi, J., Perry, J. D., & Nastasi, B. K. (1987). Growing up in a divorced family: Initial and long-term perspectives on children's adjustment. In S. Oskamp (Ed.), *Applied social psychology annual: Vol. 7. Family processes and problems* (pp. 202–237). Newbury Park, CA: Sage.

Hanson, S. M. H. (1988). Single custodial fathers and the parent–child relationship. *Nursing Research, 30*, 202–204.

Henderson, S. H., Hetherington, E. M., Mekos, D., & Reiss, D. (1996). Stress, parenting, and adolescent psychopathology in nondivorced and stepfamilies: A within-family perspective. In E. M. Hetherington & E. H. Blechman (Eds.), *Stress, coping, and resiliency in children and families* (pp. 39–66). Mahwah, NJ: Erlbaum.

Hetherington, E. M. (1972). Effects of father absence on personality development in adolescent daughters. *Developmental Psychology, 7*, 313–326.

Hetherington, E. M. (1989). Coping with family transitions: Winners, losers, and survivors. *Child Development, 60*, 1–14.

Hetherington, E. M. (1991a). Families, lies, and videotapes. *Journal of Research on Adolescence, 1*, 323–348.

Hetherington, E. M. (1991b). The role of individual differences in family relations in coping with divorce and remarriage. In P. Cowan & E. M. Hetherington (Eds.), *Advances in family research: Vol. 2. Family transitions* (pp. 165–194). Hillsdale, NJ: Erlbaum.

Hetherington, E. M. (1993). An overview of the Virginia Longitudinal Study of Divorce and Remarriage with a focus on early adolescence. *Journal of Family Psychology, 7*, 39–56.

Hetherington, E. M. (1997). Teenaged childbearing and divorce. In S. Luthar, J. A. Burack, D. Cicchetti, & J. Weisz (Eds.), *Developmental psychopathology: Perspectives on adjustment, risk, and disorders* (pp. 350–373). Cambridge, England: Cambridge University Press.

Hetherington, E. M. (in press). Social capital and the development of youth from nondivorced, divorced, and remarried families. In A. Collins (Ed.), *Relationships as developmental contexts: The 29th Minnesota Symposium on Child Psychology.* Hillsdale, NJ: Erlbaum.

Hetherington, E. M., & Clingempeel, W. G. (1992). Coping with marital transitions: A family systems perspective. *Monographs of the Society for Research in Child Development, 57*(2–3, Serial No. 227).

Hetherington, E. M., Cox, M., & Cox, R. (1979). Family interaction and the social, emotional, and cognitive development of children following divorce. In V. Vaughn & T. Brazelton (Eds.), *The family: Setting priorities* (pp. 89–128). New York: Science and Medicine.

Hetherington, E. M., Cox, M., & Cox, R. (1985). Long-term effects of divorce and remarriage on the adjustment of children. *Journal of the American Academy of Child Psychiatry, 24*, 518–539.

Hetherington, E. M., & Jodl, K. M. (1994). Stepfamilies as settings for child development. In A. Booth & J. Dunn (Eds.), *Stepfamilies: Who benefits? Who does not?* (pp. 55–79). Hillsdale, NJ: Erlbaum.

Hetherington, E. M., Law, T. C., & O'Connor, T. G. (1992). Divorce: Challenges, changes, and new chances. In F. Walsh (Ed.), *Normal family processes* (2nd ed., pp. 219–246). New York: Guilford Press.

Hetherington, E. M., & Stanley Hagan, M. S. (1995). Parenting in divorced and remarried families. In M. Bornstein (Ed.), *Handbook of parenting* (pp. 233–255). Hillsdale, NJ: Erlbaum.

Hetherington, E. M., & Stanley Hagan, M. S. (1997). The effects of divorce on fathers and their children. In M. Bornstein (Ed.), *The role of the father in child development* (pp. 191–211). New York: Wiley.

Hoffman, C. D. (1995). Pre- and post-divorce father–child relationships and child adjustment: Noncustodial fathers' perspectives. *Journal of Divorce and Remarriage, 23*, 3–20.

Hu, Y., & Goldman, N. (1990). Mortality differentials by marital status: An international comparison. *Demography, 27*, 233–250.

Jacobson, D. S. (1982, August). *Family structure in the age of divorce.* Paper presented at the 90th Annual Convention of the American Psychological Association, Washington, DC.

Jessor, R., & Jessor, S. L. (1977). *Problem behavior and psycho-social development.* New York: Academic Press.

Jockin, V., McGue, M., & Lykken, D. T. (1996). Personality and divorce: A genetic analysis. *Journal of Personality and Social Psychology, 71*, 288–299.

Kelly, E. L., & Conley, J. J. (1987). Personality and compatibility: A prospective analysis of marital stability and marital satisfaction. *Journal of Personality and Social Psychology, 52*, 27–40.

Kiecolt-Glaser, J. K., Fisher, L. D., Ogrocki, P., Stout, J. C., Speicher, C. E., & Glaser, R. (1987). Marital quality, marital disruption, and immune function. *Psychosomatic Medicine, 49*, 13–34.

Kiecolt-Glaser, J. K., Kennedy, S., Malkoff, S., Fisher, L. D., Speicher, C. E., & Glaser, R. (1988). Marital discord and immunity in males. *Psychosomatic Medicine, 50*, 213–229.

King, V. (1994a). Nonresidential father involvement and child well-being: Can dads make a difference? *Journal of Family Issues, 15*, 78–96.

King, V. (1994b). Variation in the consequences of nonresidential father involvement for children's well-being. *Journal of Marriage and the Family, 56*, 964–972.

Kitson, G. C., & Holmes, W. M. (1992). *Portrait of divorce: Adjustment to marital breakdown*. New York: Guilford Press.

Kitson, G. C., & Morgan, L. A. (1990). The multiple consequences of divorce. *Journal of Marriage and the Family, 52*, 913–924.

Kline, M., Johnson, J. R., & Tschann, J. M. (1991). The long shadow of marital conflict: A model of children's post-divorce adjustment. *Journal of Marriage and the Family, 53*, 297–309.

Kurdek, L. A. (1993). Predicting marital dissolution: A 5-year prospective longitudinal study of newlywed couples. *Journal of Personality and Social Psychology, 64*, 221–242.

Kurdek, L. A., & Fine, M. A. (1993). Parent and nonparent residential family members as providers of warmth, support, and supervision to young adolescents. *Journal of Family Psychology, 7*, 245–249.

Kurdek, L. A., Fine, M. A., & Sinclair, R. J. (1995). School adjustment in sixth graders: Parenting transitions, family climate, and peer norm effects. *Child Development, 66*, 430–445.

Lahey, B. B., Hartdagen, S. E., Frick, P. J., McBurnett, K., Connor, R., & Hynd, G. W. (1988). Conduct disorder: Parsing the confounded relation to parental divorce and antisocial personality. *Journal of Abnormal Psychology, 97*, 334–337.

Lamb, M. E. (1997). Fathers and child development: An introductory overview and guide. In M. E. Lamb (Ed.), *The role of the father in child development* (pp. 1–18). New York: Wiley.

Lee, V. E., Burkam, D. T., Zimiles, H., & Ladewski, B. (1994). Family structure and its effect on behavioral and emotional problems in young adolescents. *Journal of Research on Adolescence, 4*, 405–437.

Lindner-Gunnoe, M. (1993). *Noncustodial mothers' and fathers' contributions to the adjustment of adolescent stepchildren*. Unpublished doctoral dissertation, University of Virginia.

Lorenz, F. O., Simons, R. L., & Chao, W. (1996). Family structure and mother's depression. In R. L. Simons & Associates (Eds.), *Understanding differences between divorced and intact families: Stress, interaction, and child outcome* (pp. 65–77). Thousand Oaks, CA: Sage.

Maccoby, E. E., Buchanan, C. M., Mnookin, R. H., & Dornbusch, S. M. (1993). Post-divorce roles of mothers and fathers in the lives of their children. *Journal of Family Psychology, 7*, 24–38.

Maccoby, E. E., & Mnookin, R. H. (1992). *Dividing the child: Social and legal dilemmas of custody*. Cambridge, MA: Harvard University Press.

Masheter, C. (1991). Post-divorce relationships between ex-spouses: The roles of attachment and interpersonal conflict. *Journal of Marriage and the Family, 53*, 101–110.

Matthews, L. S., Wickrama, K. A. S., & Conger, R. D. (1996). Predicting marital instability from spouse and observer reports of marital interaction. *Journal of Marriage and the Family, 58*, 641–655.

McGue, M., & Lykken, D. T. (1992). Genetic influence on risk of divorce. *Psychological Science, 6*, 368–373.

McLanahan, S. S., & Booth, K. (1989). Mother-only families: Problems, prospects, and politics. *Journal of Marriage and the Family, 51*, 557–580.

McLanahan, S. S., & Bumpass, L. (1988). Intergenerational consequences of family disruption. *American Journal of Sociology, 94*, 130–152.

McLanahan, S., & Sandefur, G. (1994). *Growing up with a single parent: What hurts, what helps?* Cambridge, MA: Harvard University Press.

Mekos, D., Hetherington, E. M., & Reiss, D. (1996). Sibling differences in problem behavior and parental treatment in nondivorced and remarried families. *Child Development, 67,* 2148–2165.

Mendes, H. A. (1976a). Single fatherhood. *Social Work, 21,* 308–312.

Mendes, H. A. (1976b). Single fathers. *Family Coordinator, 25,* 439–444.

Merikangas, K. R., Prusoff, B. A., & Weissman, M. M. (1988). Parental concordance for affective disorders: Psychopathology in offspring. *Journal of Affective Disorders, 15,* 279–290.

Meyer, D. R., & Garasky, S. (1993). Custodial fathers: Myths, realities, and child support policy. *Journal of Marriage and the Family, 55,* 73–89.

Minton, C., & Pasley, K. (1996). Fathers' parenting role identity and father involvement: A comparison of nondivorced and divorced, nonresident fathers. *Journal of Family Issues, 17,* 26–45.

Munsch, J., Woodward, J., & Darling, N. (1995). Children's perceptions of their relationships with coresiding and non-custodial fathers. *Journal of Divorce and Remarriage, 23,* 39–54.

National Center for Health Statistics. (1988). *Current estimates from the National Health Interview Survey: United States. 1987* (DHHS Publication No. 88–1594). Washington, DC: U. S. Government Printing Office.

Orbuch, T. L., Veroff, J., & Hunter, A. G. (in press). Black couples, White couples: The early years of marriage. In E. M. Hetherington (Ed.), *Coping with divorce, single-parenting, and remarriage: A risk and resiliency perspective.* Mahwah, NJ: Erlbaum.

Papernow, P. L. (1988). Stepparent role development: From outsider to intimate. In W. R. Beer (Ed.), *Relative strangers: Studies of stepfamily processes* (pp. 54–82). Totowa, NJ: Rowman & Littlefield.

Patterson, G. (1991, March). *Interaction of stress and family structure and their relation to child adjustment.* Paper presented at the biennial meetings of the Society for Research on Child Development, Seattle, WA.

Patterson, G., DeBaryshe, B., & Ramsey, E. (1989). A developmental perspective on antisocial behavior. *American Psychologist, 44,* 329–335.

Patterson, G., & Dishion, T. J. (1988). Multilevel family process models: Traits, interactions, and relationships. In R. Hinde & J. Stevenson-Hinde (Eds.), *Relationships within families: Mutual influences* (pp. 283–310). Oxford, England: Clarendon Press.

Pearlin, L. I., & Johnson, J. S. (1977). Marital status, life-stresses and depression. *American Sociological Review, 42,* 704–715.

Peterson, J. L., & Zill, N. (1986). Marital disruption, parent–child relationships, and behavior problems in children. *Journal of Marriage and the Family, 48,* 295–307.

Riessman, C. K., & Gerstel, N. (1985). Marital dissolution and health: Do males or females have greater risk? *Social Science and Medicine, 20,* 627–635.

Rutter, M. (1987). Psychosocial resilience and protective mechanisms. *American Journal of Orthopsychiatry, 57,* 316–331.

Santrock, J. W., & Sitterle, K. A. (1987). Parent–child relationships in stepmother families. In K. Pasley & M. Ihinger-Tallman (Eds.), *Remarriage and stepparenting: Current research and theory* (pp. 273–299). New York: Guilford Press.

Santrock, J. W., Sitterle, K. A., & Warshak, R. A. (1988). Parent–child relationships in stepfather families. In P. Bronstein & C. P. Cowan (Eds.), *Fatherhood today: Men's changing roles in the family* (pp. 144–165). New York: Wiley.

Seltzer, J. A. (1991). Relationships between fathers and children who live apart: The father's role after separation. *Journal of Marriage and the Family, 53,* 79–101.

Seltzer, J. A. (1994). Consequences of marital dissolution for children. *Annual Review of Sociology, 20*, 235–266.

Seltzer, J. A., & Brandreth, Y. (1994). What fathers say about involvement with children after separation. *Journal of Family Issues, 15*, 49–77.

Simons, R. L. (1996). The effect of divorce on adult and child adjustment. In R. L. Simons & Associates (Eds.), *Understanding differences between divorced and intact families: Stress, interaction, and child outcome* (pp. 3–20). Thousand Oaks, CA: Sage.

Simons, R. L., & Associates. (Eds.). (1996). *Understanding differences between divorced and intact families: Stress, interaction, and child outcome.* Thousand Oaks, CA: Sage.

Simons, R. L., & Beaman, J. (1996). Father's parenting. In R. L. Simons & Associates (Eds.), *Understanding differences between divorced and intact families: Stress, interaction, and child outcome* (pp. 94–103). Thousand Oaks, CA: Sage.

Simons, R. L., Beaman, J., Conger, R. D., & Chao, W. (1992). Childhood experience, conceptions of parenting, and attitudes of spouse as determinants of parental behavior. *Journal of Marriage and the Family, 55*, 91–106.

Simons, R. L., & Chao, W. (1996). Conduct problems. In R. L. Simons & Associates (Eds.), *Understanding differences between divorced and intact families: Stress, interaction, and child outcome* (pp. 125–143). Thousand Oaks, CA: Sage.

Simons, R. L., & Johnson, C. (1996). Mother's parenting. In R. L. Simons & Associates (Eds.), *Understanding differences between divorced and intact families: Stress, interaction, and child outcome* (pp. 81–93). Thousand Oaks, CA: Sage.

Simons, R. L., Johnson, C., & Lorenz, F. O. (1996). Family structure differences in stress and behavioral predispositions. In R. L. Simons & Associates (Eds.), *Understanding differences between divorced and intact families: Stress, interaction, and child outcome* (pp. 45–63). Thousand Oaks, CA: Sage.

Stack, S. (1989). The impact of divorce on suicide in Norway, 1951–1980. *Journal of Marriage and the Family, 51*, 229–238.

Thomson, E., McLanahan, S. S., & Curtin, R. B. (1992). Family structure, gender, and parental separation. *Journal of Marriage and the Family, 54*, 368–378.

Travato, F., & Lauris, G. (1989). Marital status and mortality in Canada: 1951–81. *Journal of Marriage and the Family, 51*, 907–922.

Tzeng, J. M., & Mare, R. D. (1995). Labor market and socioeconomic effects on marital stability. *Social Science Research, 24*, 329–351.

Umberson, D. (1987). Family status and health behaviors: Social control as a dimension of social integration. *Journal of Health and Social Behavior, 28*, 306–319.

Umberson, D., & Williams, C. L. (1993). Divorced fathers: Parental role strain and psychological distress. *Journal of Family Issues, 14*, 378–400.

U. S. Bureau of the Census. (1992). *Marital status and living arrangements: March, 1992* (No. 468, Tables G & 5, Current Population Reports, Series P-20). Washington, DC: U. S. Government Printing Office.

Visher, E. B., & Visher, J. S. (1990). Dynamics of successful stepfamilies. *Journal of Divorce and Remarriage, 14*, 3–11.

Warshak, R. A. (1986). Father custody and child development: A review and analysis of psychological research. *Behavioral Sciences and the Law, 4*, 185–202.

Weiss, R. S. (1979). Growing up a little faster: The experience of growing up in a single-parent household. *Journal of Social Issues, 35*, 97–111.

Werner, E. E. (1988). Individual differences, universal needs: A 30-year study of resilient high-risk infants. *Zero to Three: Bulletin of National Center for Clinical Infant Programs, 8*, 1–15.

Werner, E. E. (1993). Risk, resilience, and recovery: Perspectives from the Kauaii Longitudinal Study. *Development and Psychopathology, 54*, 503–515.

Whitbeck, L. B., Simons, R. L., & Goldberg, E. (1996). Adolescent sexual intercourse. In R. L. Simons & Associates (Eds.), *Understanding differences between divorced and intact families: Stress, interaction, and child outcome* (pp. 144–156). Thousand Oaks, CA: Sage.

White, L. (1994). Stepfamilies over the life course: Social support. In A. Booth & J. Dunn (Eds.), *Stepfamilies: Who benefits? Who does not?* (pp. 109–137). Hillsdale, NJ: Erlbaum.

White, L. K., Brinkerhoff, D. B., & Booth, A. (1985). The effect of marital disruption on children's attachment to parents. *Journal of Family Issues, 6*, 5–22.

Wilson, M. I., Daly, M., & Weghorst, S. J. (1980). Household composition and the risk of child abuse and neglect. *Journal of Biosocial Science, 12*, 333–340.

Zill, N. (1988). Behavior, achievement, and health problems among children in stepfamilies. In E. M. Hetherington & J. D. Arasteh (Eds.), *Impact of divorce, single parenting, and stepparenting on children* (pp. 324–368). Hillsdale, NJ: Erlbaum.

Zill, N., Morrison, D. R., & Coiro, M. J. (1993). Long-term effects of parental divorce on parent–child relationships, adjustment, and achievement in young adulthood. *Journal of Family Psychology, 7*, 91–103.

Zimiles, H., & Lee, V. E. (1991). Adolescent family structure and educational progress. *Development Psychology, 27*, 314–320.

Part III

PEDIATRICS AND CHILD PSYCHIATRY

The three papers in this section address issues at the interface of child psychiatry and pediatrics: nonorganic failure to thrive; diabetic ketoacidosis; and headaches. Growth deficiency in the absence of organic causes, or nonorganic failure to thrive (NOFTT) has long been attributed to fundamental difficulties within the parent-child relationship. Collectively, studies of the attachment relationships of infants with NOFTT have suggested that children with this condition are at elevated risk for developing insecure attachment relationships in general, and disorganized relationships in particular. However, as Chatoor, Ganiban, Colin, Plummer and Harmon note in the critical introduction to their study of the relationship between attachment patterns and feeding problems in children of toddler age, interpretation of these findings is not as straightforward as earlier reports might suggest. As NOFTT is often confounded with other variables associated with disorganized attachments (type D) including child maltreatment, parental psychopathology, poverty and malnutrition, the association with type D attachments may not be generalizable to all populations of children with NOFTT. Moreover, prior research has not clearly always distinguished between subtypes of feeding problems that may lead to NOFTT. Thus an increased rate of type D attachments might well reflect the characteristics of a specific feeding disorder, rather than all feeding disorders.

In contrast, Chatoor and colleagues have confined their study to three clearly defined groups of children; toddlers with infantile anorexia, picky eaters, and healthy eaters. Children with eating disorders met diagnostic criteria previously established by Chatoor (Chatoor et al., 1998) for these conditions. Children with infantile anorexia had at least a one month history of food refusal, and were acutely and/or chronically malnourished (NOFTT). Their parents were anxious and concerned and parent-infant feeding interactions were conflictual. Picky eaters, conceptualized as exhibiting a subclinical form of infantile anorexia, had exhibited food selectivity for at least 1 month, and were not malnourished. Participants in each group, who ranged in age from 12–37 months, were matched for age, gender, ethnicity and socioeconomic status. Moreover, most subjects were drawn from highly educated, two-parent families in the upper to upper-middle socioeconomic classes. Children who exhibited signs and symptoms of a feeding disorder of attachment, (i.e. delays in cognitive, motor, and socioemotional development and/or maternal psychopathology associated with a lack of consistent care of the infant) were excluded.

Although insecure relationships were more frequent within the infantile anorexia group than with the picky eater or healthy eater groups, the majority of infants in each group displayed secure, organized attachments to their mothers as assessed with the Ainsworth Strange Situation. Nevertheless, the infantile anorexia group displayed the least security when degree of security was rated on a continuous scale. Moreover, percent ideal weight was positively correlated with attachment security, suggesting that an insecure infant–mother relationship is associated with a more severe expression of infantile anorexia. Contrary to the results of previous research, elevated rates of type D attachments were not present within the infantile anorexia group. These findings indicate that infantile anorexia can develop within a secure toddler–mother relationship. The results underscore the importance of distinguishing between the various subtypes of NOFTT and their different socioemotional correlates in designing interventions to address this very serious problem affecting infants and young children.

Although the importance of maintaining adequate metabolic control of insulin-dependent diabetes (IDDM) is unquestioned, the results of studies of the impact of psychiatric illness and family functioning have yielded inconsistent results. The investigation of psychiatric illness and family support in children and adolescents with diabetic ketoacidosis (DKA), reported in the second paper in this section, extends our understanding of how these factors may relate to noncompliance and poor control. Liss, Waller, Kennard, McIntire, Capra, and Stephens, compare compliance, psychiatric disorders, and family support in children with IDDM hospitalized with DKA and clinic patients who had no hospitalizations for DKA during the preceding 12 months. The 25 children and adolescents in each group were between 9 and 17 years, and were matched for sex, age, ethnicity, duration of diabetes, and socioeconomic class. Cross-sectional assessment measures included the Diagnostic Interview Schedule for Children, measures of general and diabetes-specific family functioning, and measures of self-esteem and social competence. Levels of glycosylated hemoglobin and information about compliance with treatment were also obtained.

Children with DKA were found to have a significantly higher number of psychiatric disorders, with 88% meeting criteria for at least one disorder as compared with 28% of the clinic patients. Diagnoses of anxiety, affective, and disruptive behavior disorders were most common. Subjects with DKA reported less insulin injection compliance, less compliance with diabetes diet and less compliance with urine testing than did the outpatients. Overall children with DKA reported more non-compliance with aspects of treatment than did their parents. Children with DKA also had significantly lower self-esteem scores and tended to be lower in intellectual and school status. Although neither children or parents in the two groups reported differences in overall family functioning, both parents of and children with DKA reported less diabetes-specific support, and less support in the area of diabetes-related empathy.

The authors suggest that the association between psychiatric illness and diabetes may be specific to diabetic children and adolescents with poor metabolic control. A thoughtful discussion delineates the ways in which the relationship between behavior and emotional disorder and DKA may be reciprocal and interactive. On a more practical note, Liss et al. recommend systematic psychiatric assessment of children and adolescents with DKA, most particularly because symptoms of anxiety and depression in this population may be confused with symptoms related to abnormal glycemia. Diagnosis and treatment of specific psychiatric disorders in children hospitalized with DKA need also to be combined with efforts to facilitate diabetes-specific family support which may facilitate compliance and metabolic control over the course of the illness, thereby contributing to a reduction in the frequency and severity of later complications.

Although the prevalence of headaches increases with age, headaches are a very common childhood complaint. The association between headaches and depression and anxiety has been clearly demonstrated in adults. However, the findings of epidemiologic studies of the association between headaches and psychiatric disorder in children have been difficult to interpret because of methodologic difficulties involving the definitions of the two central variables: headaches and psychopathology. The third paper in this section, by Egger, Angold, and Costello, which examines the association between chronic headaches and DSM-III-R defined psychiatric disorders, including depression, anxiety disorders, conduct disorder, oppositional defiant disorder and attention deficit hyperactivity disorder in a population-based sample of children and adolescents is designed to minimize these concerns.

Subjects, including 1,013 children aged 9–15 years, enrolled in the Great Smoky Mountain longitudinal study of the development of psychiatric disorders and need for mental health services in rural and urban youths, were evaluated annually over a 3 year period. Headaches that lasted at least 1 hour and occurred at least once a week during the 3 months prior to the interview were studied. Children and parents were separately interviewed about the child's psychiatric status and service use with the Child and Adolescent Psychiatric Assessment (CAPA), an instrument that enables interviewers to determine whether symptoms are present or absent, and to code their frequency, duration, and onset, with diagnoses generated by computerized algorithms.

Headaches that lasted at least 1 hour and occurred at least once a week during the previous 3 months were reported by 10% of this general population based sample. Older children reported more headaches than younger children and the prevalence rates were similar for boys and girls. Of children with a psychiatric diagnosis 20.5% reported headaches, compared with 9.2% of children without a major psychiatric diagnosis. A distinct gender difference was found between boys and girls in the associations between headaches and psychopathology. Girls with depression and anxiety disorders had a significantly greater prevalence of headaches than girls without an internalizing disorder, while among boys, headaches were significantly associated with conduct disorder.

The results of this study are consistent with the suggestion that CNS serotonergic dysregulation may be a common point of neurotransmitter abnormality in depression, anxiety, and headaches. Linking headaches with externalizing psychiatric symptoms, as well as internalizing symptoms suggests that CNS serotonergic dysfunction may be a common pathway for multiple interrelated somatic, psychosocial, and behavioral symptoms that may be expressed differently in boys and girls. Further exploration of the distinct gender differences found in this study is clearly warranted. Moreover, the findings suggest that children who present with complaints of recurrent, frequent headaches should be assessed for psychiatric disorders, particularly depression and anxiety in girls and conduct disorder in boys.

REFERENCE

Chatoor, I., Egan, J., Getson Menvielle, E., O'Donnell, R. (1998). Mother-infant interactions in infantile anorexa nervosa. *J Am Acad Child Adolesc Psychiatry* 27:535–540

10

Attachment and Feeding Problems: A Reexamination of Nonorganic Failure to Thrive and Attachment Insecurity

Irene Chatoor, M.D., Jody Ganiban, Ph.D., Virginia Colin, Ph.D., Nancy Plummer, B.A., and Robert J. Harmon, M.D.

Objective: *To examine the relationship between attachment patterns, degree of security, and feeding problems.* **Method:** *Three groups of toddlers (age range = 12–37 months) were included: toddlers with infantile anorexia (n = 33), picky eaters (n = 34), and healthy eaters (n = 34). Participants in each group were matched for age, socioeconomic status, gender, and ethnicity. Attachment patterns and degree of attachment security were assessed through the Ainsworth Strange Situation.* **Results:** *The infantile anorexia group exhibited a higher rate of insecure attachment relationships than the picky eater and healthy eater groups. When measured on a continuous scale, the infantile anorexia group also displayed a higher degree of insecurity than the other groups. Contrary to previous research, elevated rates of type D attachments were not present within the infantile anorexia group.* **Conclusions:** *Feeding problems and growth deficiencies can occur within the context of organized and secure attachment child–parent relationships. However, insecure attachment relationships may intensify feeding problems and may lead to more severe malnutrition. Implications for the treatment of specific feeding problems are discussed.* J. Am. Acad. Child Adolesc. Psychiatry, *1998, 37(11):1217–1224.*

Accepted June 22, 1998.

Dr. Chatoor is Professor of Psychiatry, George Washington University (GWU), and Vice Chair, Department of Psychiatry, Children's National Medical Center (CNMC), Washington, DC; Dr. Ganiban is Assistant Professor of Psychology, GWU; Dr. Colin is a research associate at CNMC; Ms. Plummer is a research associate in the Department of Psychiatry, University of Colorado School of Medicine, Denver; Dr. Harmon is Professor of Psychiatry and Pediatrics and Head, Division of Child Psychiatry, and Director of Infant Psychiatry and the Kempe Therapeutic Preschool, Denver.

This research was supported by grants to Dr. Chatoor from the NIMH (IK07 MH00791-01A1) and the Children's Hospital Research Foundation.

Reprint requests to Dr. Chatoor, Children's National Medical Center, 111 Michigan Avenue, N. W., Washington, DC 20010.

Key Words: *nonorganic failure to thrive, attachment, infantile anorexia, food refusal, feeding problems.*

Historically, feeding problems have been attributed to fundamental difficulties within the parent–child relationship. This perspective originated with Spitz's (1946) observation that lack of maternal care during infancy was associated with physiological symptoms, including poor food intake, growth retardation, disturbed sleep patterns, and poor immunological functioning. Such children also failed to thrive cognitively and emotionally, and they often displayed mental retardation, extreme passivity, and flattened affect. In later years, growth deficiency in the absence of organic causes became known as *nonorganic failure to thrive* (NOFTT) and was described as *reactive attachment disorder* in *DSM-III* (American Psychiatric Association, 1980). In general, it was assumed that these growth problems were caused by maternal deprivation, parental neglect, or physical abuse (Call, 1984; Kotelchuck, 1980). In this article we review recent research on the attachment relationships of infants with NOFTT and feeding problems. In addition, we report on our study that examined the attachment relationships of three groups of toddlers with and without feeding problems.

Current research has supported the link between care-giving environments and NOFTT. Children's quality of attachment with their caregivers is thought to reflect the history of their interactions with their caregivers (Ainsworth et al., 1978). Secure attachments result if children have had caregivers who are consistently sensitive and responsive to their needs. Conversely, insecure attachments result if children have had insensitive or nonresponsive caregivers. Several studies have found that 49% to 92% of children with NOFTT display insecure attachment patterns (Brinich et al., 1989; Crittenden, 1987; Gordon and Jameson, 1979; Ward et al., 1993). This rate is higher than that found within demographically matched control samples. The most recent studies further suggest that approximately 45% of infants with NOFTT display inconsistent or contradictory strategies for managing the stress of separations and reunions with caregivers (i.e., type D or disorganized attachment classifications: Crittenden, 1987; Ward et al., 1993). Similar rates of disorganized attachments have been found in a population of malnourished, impoverished Chilean infants (Valenzuela, 1990). Collectively, these studies suggest that children with NOFTT are at elevated risk for developing insecure attachment relationships in general, and disorganized relationships in particular.

However, in some studies the NOFTT was confounded with variables that have been previously associated with disorganized attachments (e.g., child maltreatment and parent psychopathology: Carlson et al., 1989; Main and Solomon, 1990). In addition, Valenzuela (1990) proposed that the interaction between poverty and malnutrition may place infants at risk for disorganized relationships. Specifically, she argued that malnourishment makes a child more irritable and difficult to manage. In turn, difficult temperament coupled with the stressors of poverty place such children at risk for disorganized attachments. In this view, disorganized attachments are the result of problematic interactions that arise from malnutrition and poverty, rather than the cause of malnutrition.

Regardless of the direction of effect, however, these data suggest that elevated rates of type D attachment could be symptomatic of maltreatment and parent psychopathology, or they may reflect the interaction between malnutrition with other variables. In either case, disorganized attachments cannot be solely attributed to feeding problems or to NOFTT. The importance of this point is underscored by Kotelchuck's (1980) contention that only 20% to 31% of cases of NOFTT are associated with gross neglect or maltreatment. Thus, the association between type D attachments and NOFTT found in previous studies may not be generalizable to all populations of children with NOFTT.

Another related difficulty is that previous research has not distinguished between subtypes of feeding problems that lead to NOFTT. Thus, the heightened rate of type D attachments may reflect the characteristics of a specific feeding disorder, rather than all feeding disorders. In recent years Chatoor (1997) has described several feeding disorders that present during infancy and early childhood and are associated with NOFTT. Two of these disorders are *feeding disorders of attachment* and *infantile anorexia*. A third feeding problem, *picky eating*, represents a subclinical form of infantile anorexia and is not associated with NOFTT. The diagnostic criteria for each of these feeding problems are presented in Table 1.

Although feeding disorder of attachment and infantile anorexia are associated with NOFTT (i.e., acute or chronic malnutrition without an identifiable organic cause), they exhibit different origins and sequelae. These disorders are also distinguishable by their age at onset and the presence of dyadic conflict during feeding situations versus overall neglect or maltreatment. Thus, within this framework, the children with NOFTT who have experienced maltreatment or neglect are best described as having a feeding disorder of attachment. For

TABLE 1
Diagnostic Criteria for Feeding Problems

Feeding disorder of attachment
  1. Onset between 2 and 8 months
  2. Infant demonstrates acute and/or chronic malnutrition
  3. Infant displays delays in cognitive, motor, and socioemotional development
  4. History of maternal psychopathology that is associated with lack of consistent care of the infant
  5. Poor parent–infant reciprocity during feeding

Infantile anorexia
  1. Onset between 6 months and 3 years (peak between 9 and 18 months), as infants make the transition to self-feeding
  2. Food refusal for at least 1 month
  3. Acute and/or chronic malnutrition
  4. Parental concern and anxiety over toddler's food refusal
  5. Conflictual parent–infant feeding interactions

Picky eating (subclinical form of infantile anorexia)
  1. Food selectivity for at least 1 month that involves all foods or only certain types
  2. No malnutrition
  3. Variable parental concern

Note: Criteria are further described by Chatoor et al. (1998).

these children, feeding problems and NOFTT are secondary to maternal deprivation or an extremely inconsistent caregiving environment. Chatoor (1997) has hypothesized that such environments ultimately lead to disinterest in food and overall physiological dysregulation similar to that described by Spitz (1946) in his seminal papers on hospitalism and anaclytic depression. Thus, the observed relationship between NOFTT and type D attachments may pertain to feeding disorder of attachment only.

Other children with NOFTT, however, display different feeding disorders, and thus different symptoms and implications for attachment relationships. In particular, infants with infantile anorexia do not display the passivity and lethargy apparent in infants with a feeding disorder of attachment (Chatoor, 1998). Their caregivers are also extremely involved with their children and express great anxiety over their children's failure to eat and to grow. Therefore, the children's feeding problems cannot be attributed to abuse, neglect, or deprivation. However, toddlers with infantile anorexia do experience a high level of conflict with their caregivers during feedings. Furthermore, Chatoor and colleagues (1988) have found that mothers of toddlers with infantile anorexia displayed less contingent responsiveness to their infants' cues and less positive engagement and reciprocity than mothers of thriving infants. Over time, such interactions may lead to insecure attachments (e.g., Fish and Stifter, 1995; Isabella, 1993; Isabella et al., 1989).

Furthermore, if problems persist during feedings, the children's food refusal will intensify and result in poor nutrition and growth. Thus, even in the absence of maltreatment, children with infantile anorexia are at greater risk for insecure attachment relationships than other children. Furthermore, attachment insecurity is expected to be highest among children who exhibit the highest degrees of malnutrition.

Infants with infantile anorexia may also be more likely to display type C-resistant attachments than other types of insecurity. Infants with type C attachments tend to become very distressed by brief separations from their caregivers and often seek comfort from their caregivers. However, these infants also resist their parents' attempts to soothe them. Thompson and Lamb (1984) found that "high emotionality" infants with insecure attachment relationships are more prone to display type C attachments than attachments that center on avoidance of the caregiver during stressful situations (i.e., type A-avoidant attachments) (see also Belsky and Rovine, 1987; Frodi and Thompson, 1985). This pattern of results has been replicated in additional studies with full-term and preterm infants. A recent study by Chatoor (1998) suggests that toddlers with infantile anorexia are more reactive, display more negative mood, and are more willful and generally more difficult to manage than typical infants. Therefore, given these temperament characteristics, toddlers with infantile anorexia may be at heightened risk for displaying type C attachment relationships.

Hypotheses

In the current study we examined the attachment patterns displayed by toddlers with infantile anorexia. We compared their attachment patterns with those of children who exhibit a subclinical form of infantile anorexia (picky eaters) and children who are healthy eaters. We hypothesized that (1) higher rates of insecure attachment patterns are present within the infantile anorexia group than within the picky eater and healthy eater groups, and the degree of malnutrition is related to the degree of insecurity displayed by infants; (2) within the infantile anorexia group, type C attachments are the most frequently observed insecure attachment type; and (3) the infantile anorexia group does not have a higher rate of type D attachments than the picky eater or healthy eater groups.

METHOD

Subject Recruitment

All toddlers with infantile anorexia and six toddlers in the picky eater group were referred to the study by pediatricians and gastroenterologists. Prior to inclusion in this study, organic causes for their feeding difficulties had been ruled out. Toddlers in the healthy eater group and 28 picky eaters were recruited from a large university pediatric clinic that serves a racially mixed population from diverse socio-economic strata. Within the clinic, potential participants were initially identified by parents' responses to a questionnaire that asked them to rate their children's feeding habits. The diagnostic status of each toddler was further confirmed by an extensive diagnostic evaluation that consisted of (1) obtaining the toddler's feeding, medical, and developmental histories; (2) observations of toddler–parent feeding situations; and (3) anthropometric assessments. After the diagnostic evaluation, toddlers were excluded from this study if (1) food refusal followed a traumatic event and met criteria for a posttraumatic feeding disorder; (2) the toddler suffered from a medical condition that compromised growth or caused discomfort or pain during feeding (e.g., cystic fibrosis, gastroesophageal reflux); (3) the toddler's gestational age was less than 36 weeks; (4) the toddler had a psychiatric illness (e.g., pervasive developmental disorder); (5) the mother suffered from an acute medical or mental illness that compromised her ability to care for her child and to participate in the study; or (6) the mother could not communicate in English. The remaining toddlers were classified as infantile anorexia, picky eater, or healthy eater by two psychiatrists ($\kappa = 0.89$). Disagreements over a child's diagnosis were resolved through discussion. Each of the children that met criteria for infantile anorexia, picky eater, or healthy eater were invited to participate in the study. During the recruitment of picky and healthy eaters, attempts were also made to identify children who matched the toddlers with infantile anorexia on the following dimensions: age, gender, socioeconomic status, and ethnicity.

Very few parents declined to participate in this study. Two parents of toddlers with infantile anorexia chose not to participate. One parent disagreed with the diagnosis of infantile anorexia, and one child was fearful of hospitals and could not complete the laboratory evaluations. The parents of a third child with infantile anorexia initially participated in the study. However, the child's mother became too ill to participate in the Strange Situation. Nine parents of healthy eaters and picky eaters who were contacted declined to participate in this study because of work schedules ($n = 6$) or distance from the laboratory site ($n = 3$).

The final sample consisted of three groups of toddlers (age range: 12–37 months) and their mothers: (1) toddlers with infantile anorexia ($n = 33$); (2) picky eaters ($n = 34$); and

TABLE 2
Demographic Characteristics by Diagnostic Group

	Diagnostic Group		
	Infantile Anorexia	Picky Eaters	Healthy Eaters
Age (months)	21.4	23.7	22.5
Age range	12–37	13–37	13–36
Female[a]	61	42	56
White (%)	58	58	59
African-American (%)	27	27	29
Latino (%)	3	6	6
Asian (%)	15	12	6
SES[b]	II	II	II
I[c]	41	35	32
II	29	32	44
III	9	26	9
IV	9	3	12
V	12	3	3

[a]Percentage of females in each group.
[b]Mean Hollingshead Four Factor Index rating of socioeconomic status (Hollingshead, 1975).
[c]Percentage of toddlers in each Hollingshead category.

(3) healthy eaters ($n = 34$). As indicated in Table 2, this study included toddlers from a wide range of economic classes and ethnic groups. However, most infants were white and from the two highest socioeconomic classes. In addition, although most mothers in this study had obtained college or professional degrees, they did not work outside of the home.

Measures

Assessment of Attachment: The Strange Situation. After the diagnostic evaluation was completed, the toddlers and their mothers returned to the laboratory for the Strange Situation. The Strange Situation consisted of a brief introduction, followed by seven 3-minute episodes (Ainsworth et al., 1978). During the Strange Situation, toddlers experienced two separations. During separation I, the toddlers were left with a female stranger for 3 minutes. During separation II, the toddlers were first left alone for 3 minutes, followed by 3 minutes with a female stranger. Each separation was followed by a 3-minute reunion with the caregiver.

Assessment of Nutrition. Nutritional status was assessed by calculating the toddlers' percent ideal weight. This number is the ratio between the child's current weight and the reference norm for the child's height (i.e., the 50th percentile of weight for the child's height). The normal range for percent ideal body weight is 90% to 110%.

Assessment of Attachment Classifications. Attachment classifications were based on the children's tendency to seek proximity, contact, or interactions with their caregivers or to avoid or resist their caregivers during reunions. Attachment organization was assessed by Ainsworth's attachment classification for infants (12–18-month-olds) (Ainsworth et al.,

1978) and by Cassidy and Marvin's (1989) coding scheme for 3- and 4-year-olds. Both scoring systems yield avoidant (type A), secure (type B), and ambivalent (type C) classifications. For participants who were between 18 and 36 months of age, attachment classifications were determined by using the guidelines devised by Schneider-Rosen (1990) in addition to the infant and preschool attachment systems. These guidelines use the same classifications (type A, B, and C) as the infant and preschool systems and provide behavioral and emotional indices that are age-appropriate for each classification.

Infants rated as type B tend to approach, seek, and maintain contact with their mothers when they are distressed. They also greet their mothers during reunions. Preschool children who are rated as type B typically explore and play actively with toys, are less wary of strangers, require minimal negotiation upon separations, and show little or no distress upon separation from their mothers. Infants rated as type A avoid proximity and contact with their mothers and limit interactions with their mothers. They generally display little distress during separations. Type A preschool children seem "disconnected" from their mothers, limit interactions and physical or eye contact with their mothers, and react neutrally during reunions. Infants rated as type C strongly seek contact with their mothers, but they also show angry resistance to contact and interactions with their mothers. Type C preschool children strongly resist separation from their mothers and are unlikely to play with toys during separations. They may show anger, resistance, and avoidance in addition to exaggerated dependency.

In recent years, a fourth attachment classification, type D, has been included in the infant and preschool coding systems (Cassidy and Marvin, 1989; Main and Solomon, 1990). Many infants with type D attachments display contradictory behaviors simultaneously or in quick succession. Their reactions to their parents may also vary greatly from the first reunion to the second reunion, or they may appear to be depressed and apprehensive throughout the Strange Situation. Such children may also display a number of atypical behaviors or "D signs," including behavioral stereotypies, dazing and stilling, and asymmetric movements. Preschool children who are classified as type D may interact with their mothers in a controlling-punitive and/or caregiving manner. In such cases, the relationship is characterized by role reversal. In addition to the criteria described by Cassidy and Marvin (1989) and Main and Solomon (1990), the children were rated on a 9-point scale that assessed the amount of D behavior they exhibited (Main and Solomon, 1990). Within the D behavior scale, a rating of 1 indicated that D behaviors were not demonstrated, a rating of 5 represented a moderate amount of D behaviors, and a rating of 9 represented a high occurrence of D-type behaviors. In the current study, a score of 5 or greater was used to classify children as having disorganized-type D relationships.

One of the authors (R.J.H.) has established reliability for scoring attachment behavior in both infants and preschool children. Another coder (N.P.) was trained in the attachment classification systems. Both coders were naive to the participants' group assignment and to their nutritional and economic status. Interrater agreement for 20 participants was $\kappa = 0.84$. All disagreements were discussed jointly and final attachment classifications were determined by consensus.

Security Scale. In addition to the attachment classification system, a 9-point Likert scale was also used to assess the children's degree of attachment security during the Strange

Situation (Security Scale: Cassidy and Marvin, 1989). The Security Scale differentiates between levels of security within and across the attachment categories. Thus, this continuous scale provides one with more precise information regarding the degree of security or insecurity a child displays than does the child's attachment classification. High scores (7–9) were assigned if secure behaviors predominated (e.g., child initiates interactions, responsive to parent), moderate scores (5) were assigned if equal amounts of insecure and secure behaviors were present, and low scores (1–3) were given if insecure behaviors predominated (e.g., avoidance, ambivalence, disorganization, or controlling behavior). Ratings were based on children's behavior during the Strange Situation and on the child's attachment classification. For example, if a child was rated as securely attached, he or she received a Security Scale rating of 7 to 9. Children who were classified as insecurely attached received scores less than 7. Interrater reliability was established for 20 participants ($r = 0.90$). All disagreements were resolved by assigning a final rating after discussion.

RESULTS

Hypothesis 1: Higher rates of insecure attachment patterns are present within the infantile anorexia group than within the picky eater and healthy eater groups. Furthermore, degree of malnutrition is negatively correlated with attachment security.

Attachment Classifications. The majority of toddlers in each group were securely attached to their caregivers (Table 3). However, diagnostic group was significantly related to frequency of insecure attachments (types A, C, and D) ($\chi^2_{2, N=101} = 8.0$, $p < .05$). Insecure relationships were more frequent within the infantile anorexia group than within the picky eater ($\chi^2_{1, N=67} = 6.7$, $p < .01$) or healthy eater groups ($\chi^2_{1, N=67} = 3.9$, $p < .05$). The picky eater and healthy eater groups did not differ in their rates of insecure attachments ($\chi^2_{1, N=68} = 0.5$, not significant [NS]).

Attachment Security Scale. The infantile anorexia group displayed the least security (Table 3). An analysis of variance detected a significant main effect for group ($F_{2, 98} = 5.8$, $p < .01$). A post hoc analysis (Duncan multiple range test, $\alpha = .05$) indicated that healthy eaters and picky eaters did not differ significantly. However, the children with

TABLE 3
Distribution of Attachment Classifications Across Diagnostic Groups

	Attachment Classification					
	Secure Attachment	Avoidant Attachment	Resistant Attachment	Disorganized Attachment	Security Scale Ratings	
Diagnostic Group	(Type B)	(Type A)	(Type C)	(Type D)	Mean	SD
Infantile anorexia						
($n = 33$)	20	4	7	2	4.9	2.1
Picky eaters						
($n = 34$)	30	3	1	0	6.1	1.3
Healthy eaters						
($n = 34$)	28	3	3	0	6.0	1.5

infantile anorexia displayed less security than the healthy and picky eater groups. In terms of malnutrition and attachment security, percent ideal weight was positively correlated with attachment security ($r_{101} = 0.31$, $p < .01$). This correlation suggests that the closer the toddlers were to their ideal weight for height, the more securely attached they seemed.

Hypothesis 2: Within the infantile anorexia group, type C attachments are the most frequently observed insecure attachment type.

Across the three diagnostic groups, 23 toddlers displayed insecure attachment relationships. Overall, more infants within the infantile anorexia group displayed type C attachments than the remaining groups. However, this difference failed to reach statistical significance ($\chi^2_{2,N=23} = 0.70$, NS).

Hypothesis 3: The infantile anorexia group does not have a higher rate of type D attachments than the picky eater or healthy eater groups.

Nine infants, three in each diagnostic group, exhibited D signs to various degrees. Of these nine infants, only two infants from the infantile anorexia group received a rating of 5 or higher on the D classification scale. Both infants were assigned type D attachment classifications. The remaining seven infants did not exhibit strong and/or frequent D behaviors and were assigned D ratings less than 5 (range = 2.0–3.5). Thus, these infants were given non-D attachment classifications. Two infants from the healthy eater group and three infants from the picky eater group were classified as type B-secure. One infant from the healthy eater group was classified as type A-avoidant. One infant from the infantile anorexia group was classified as type C-resistant.

To determine whether type D attachments were associated with infantile anorexia, we compared the frequency of this classification across the diagnostic groups. This analysis indicated that type D attachments were not significantly associated with diagnostic group ($\chi^2_{2,N=101} = 4.2$, NS).

DISCUSSION

Overall, the majority of infants in each group displayed secure, organized attachments to their mothers. In fact, the healthy eater and picky eater groups displayed higher rates of security than typically observed in previous studies with normative populations (e.g., van IJzendoorn et al., 1992). The highest rate of security was noted within the picky eater group (88%); however, their rate of security did not differ significantly from that of the healthy eaters (82%). The elevated rate of attachment security within these groups may reflect the demographics of the study sample. Specifically, most children in this study were drawn from highly educated, two-parent families in the upper to upper-middle socioeconomic classes. In a previous study with upper to upper-middle class families, Owen and colleagues (1984) reported security rates of 85% and 86% among infants aged 12 and 20 months, respectively. Similarly, Donovan and Leavitt (1989) reported security rates of 82% within a similar population of middle class families. Within that study the rate of security was even higher (90%) within a subsample of infants with mothers who had realistic perceptions of control over their own lives. Thus, this study demonstrated that security rates may even vary within populations. Conversely, the lowest rates of attachment security have been noted in some low socioeconomic populations (Easterbrooks et al., 1993; Egeland and Sroufe, 1981).

Thus, previous research suggests that the relatively high rates of secure attachments within each diagnostic group can be reasonably attributed to the demographic characteristics of the sample.

The heightened rate of security among infants who were picky eaters may also reflect compensatory mechanisms within the family. For example, Frankel and Harmon (1996) reported high rates of security (92%) among infants whose mothers experienced episodic bouts of depression. They hypothesized that when they recover, these mothers may compensate for their interactive difficulties during their depressive states. Thus, within the picky eater group, mothers might recognize feeding difficulties, but they may contain conflict to feeding situations or counteract problematic feeding interactions with positive play interactions.

Alternatively, a high rate of secure attachments within the picky eater group may also explain why these toddlers have not progressed to a more severe form of food refusal such as infantile anorexia. As discussed previously, secure attachments reflect a history of interactions in which parents have been consistently sensitive and responsive to their infants' cues. Thus, in the case of securely attached picky eaters, their parents may have been able to adapt to their problematic feeding behavior and minimize conflict during feeding. As a result, the picky eaters were able to form a secure attachment, and their food refusal did not intensify. This interpretation is supported by a significant positive correlation between the toddlers' percent ideal weight and attachment security: those toddlers with the highest nutritional status also tended to display higher levels of attachment security.

Contrary to previous research with children with NOFTT, type B-secure attachment was the most frequent attachment pattern within the infantile anorexia group. However, consistent with our hypothesis, insecure attachments were more frequent within the infantile anorexia group than within the other groups. In addition, when degree of security was rated on a continuous scale, the healthy and picky eater groups still displayed higher levels of security than the infantile anorexia group. These findings suggest that infantile anorexia is associated with more problematic child–parent relationships than is picky eating.

Consistent with our hypothesis, the rate of type C attachments was higher within the infantile anorexia group than in the other diagnostic groups. However, this difference did not reach statistical significance. This null finding may reflect the overall low rate of attachment insecurity displayed by the infantile anorexia group. Thus, the hypothesis could not be adequately tested. Alternatively, the toddlers with infantile anorexia may have learned to cope with their separation distress by seeking and accepting help from others, rather than by resisting help (cf., Braungart and Stifter, 1991).

Contrary to previous research with infants with NOFTT, type D attachments were not associated with infantile anorexia, which is a specific form of NOFTT. Only two toddlers in the infantile anorexia group displayed type D attachments. The discrepancy between the current study and past research may reflect several factors, including (1) our focus on a specific subtype of feeding disorder; (2) the absence of children who had experienced maltreatment; and (3) the upper to upper-middle class status of the families of most of the toddlers.

If the first explanation is correct, then the association between type D attachments and feeding problems may be relevant to only a subset of children with feeding problems.

Infantile anorexia is associated with intense conflict during feeding and with a high level of parental involvement and concern over the children's food refusal (Chatoor et al., 1985, 1997). In contrast, feeding disorder of attachment is typically associated with parental neglect, psychopathology, and extreme psychosocial stress. Consequently, feeding disorder of attachment subsumes a more pervasive disturbance in the infant–parent relationship than infantile anorexia or picky eating. Thus, in accordance with Chatoor's (1997) classification system, the observed association between type D attachments and NOFTT in previous research may reflect the inclusion of infants with feeding disorders of attachment.

If the second and third explanations are correct, then feeding problems and NOFTT may be associated with type D attachments only within the context of maltreating or impoverished environments. Previous studies that have detected the highest rates of type D attachments among children with NOFTT focused on young infants with histories of abuse (e.g., Crittenden, 1987) or infants in extreme poverty (Valenzuela, 1990). The link between type D attachments and maltreatment and neglect has been documented in earlier research (Carlson et al., 1989; Cicchetti and Barnett, 1991). In these studies, disorganization was attributed to the infants' fear of their caregivers. The link between poverty and disorganization has been elaborated upon by Valenzuela (1990), who proposed that chronic malnutrition may change infants' temperament characteristics by making them more irritable, clingy, and demanding than they would otherwise be. In turn, she hypothesized that when these difficult temperament characteristics are compounded with the stressors of extreme poverty, attachment disorganization may result.

However, it is notable that a Swedish study that eliminated the potential confounds of maltreatment and poverty and focused on middle class children found that children who exhibited food refusal and control groups did not differ in their rates of attachment security (Lindberg et al., 1996). Thus, type D attachments may be most prevalent when feeding problems are compounded by the stressors of abuse or poverty, or perhaps, these conditions reflect separate paths toward NOFTT.

Clinical Implications

Although this study demonstrated that infantile anorexia is associated with more insecure toddler–mother relationships than is observed in healthy or picky eaters, the majority of infantile anorexics displayed secure attachments to their mothers. These findings indicate that infantile anorexia can develop within a secure toddler–mother relationship. However, the significant correlation between the severity of malnutrition and the degree of attachment insecurity indicates that an insecure infant–mother relationship is associated with a more severe expression of infantile anorexia.

Our results also emphasize the importance of differentiating between various feeding disorders that possess different socioemotional correlates and in turn may require qualitatively different forms of interventions. For example, treatment for infantile anorexia does not need to focus on altering the toddler–mother relationship in general, but it should specifically address toddler–mother conflict during feeding. In contrast, feeding problems such as observed in feeding disorder of attachment may require exploration and remediation of the disturbed infant–mother relationship.

REFERENCES

Ainsworth MD, Blehar M, Waters E, Wall S (1978), *Patterns of Attachment: A Psychological Study of the Strange Situation*. Hillsdale, NJ: Erlbaum

American Psychiatric Association (1980), *Diagnostic and Statistical Manual of Mental Disorders, 3rd edition (DSM-III)*. Washington, DC: American Psychiatric Association

Belsky J, Rovine M (1987), Temperament and attachment security in the Strange Situation: an empirical rapprochement. *Child Dev* 58:787–795

Braungart J, Stifter C (1991), Regulation of negative reactivity during the Strange Situation: temperament and attachment in 12-month-old infants. *Infant Behav Dev* 14:349–364

Brinich E, Drotar D, Brinich P (1989), Security of attachment and outcome of preschoolers with histories of nonorganic failure to thrive. *J Clin Psychol* 18:142–152

Call JD (1984), Child abuse and neglect in infancy: sources of hostility within the parent–infant dyad and disorders of attachment in infancy. *Child Abuse Negl* 8:185–202

Carlson V, Cicchetti D, Barnett D, Braunwald K (1989), Disorganized/disoriented attachment relationships in maltreated infants. *Dev Psychol* 25:525–531

Cassidy J, Marvin RS (1989), Attachment organization in three- and four-year-olds: coding guidelines. Charlottesville, VA: Kluge Children's Rehabilitation Center

Chatoor I (1997), Feeding and other disorders of infancy. In: *Psychiatry*, Tasman A, Kay J, Lieberman J, eds. Philadelphia: Saunders, pp 683–701

Chatoor I (1998), Diagnosis and treatment of infantile anorexia. Paper presented at the Bien Meeting of the International Society of Infancy Studies, Atlanta

Chatoor I, Dickson L, Schaefer S, Egan J (1985), A developmental classification of feeding disorder associated with failure to thrive: diagnosis and treatment. In: *New Directions in Failure to Thrive: Research and Clinical Practice*, Drotar D, ed. New York: Plenum, pp 235–238

Chatoor I, Egan J, Getson P, Menvielle E, O'Donnell R (1988), Mother–infant interactions in infantile anorexia nervosa. *J Am Acad Child Adolesc Psychiatry* 27:535–540

Chatoor I, Hirsch R, Ganiban J, Persinger M, Hamburger E (1998), Diagnosing infantile anorexia: the observation of mother–infant interactions. *J Am Acad Child Adolesc Psychiatry* 37:959–967

Chatoor I, Hirsch R, Persinger M (1997), Facilitating internal regulation of eating: a treatment model for infantile anorexia. *Infants Young Child* 9:12–22

Cicchetti D, Barnett D (1991), Attachment organization in maltreated preschoolers. *Dev Psychopathol* 3:397–411

Crittenden PM (1987), Non-organic failure-to-thrive: deprivation or distortion? *Infant Ment Health J* 8:51–64

Donovan WL, Leavitt LA (1989), Maternal self-efficacy and infant attachment: integrating physiology, perceptions, and behavior. *Child Dev* 60:460–472

Easterbrooks A, Davidson CE, Chazan, R (1993), Psychosocial risk, attachment, and behavior problems among school-aged children. *Dev Psychopathol* 5:389–402

Egeland B, Sroufe LA (1981), Attachment and early maltreatment. *Child Dev* 52:44–52

Fish M, Stifter CA (1995), Patterns of mother–infant interaction and attachment: a cluster-analytic approach. *Infant Behav Dev* 18:435–446

Frankel KA, Harmon RJ (1996), Depressed mothers: they don't always look as bad as they feel. *J Am Acad Child Adolesc Psychiatry* 35:289–298

Frodi A, Thompson RA (1985), Infants' affective responses in the Strange Situation: effects of prematurity and quality of attachment. *Child Dev* 56:1280–1290

Gordon AH, Jameson JC (1979), Infant–mother attachment in patients with nonorganic failure to thrive. *J Am Acad Child Psychiatry* 18:251–259

Hollingshead AB (1975), *Four Factor Index of Social Status*. New Haven, CT: Yale University Department of Sociology

Isabella R (1993), Origins of attachment: maternal interactive behavior across the first year. *Child Dev* 64:605–621

Isabella R, Belsky J, von Eye A (1989), Origins of infant–mother attachment: an examination of interactional synchrony during the infant's first year. *Dev Psychol* 25:12–21

Kotelchuck M (1980), Nonorganic failure to thrive: the status of interactional and environmental etiologic theories. *Adv Behav Pediatr* 1:29–51

Lindberg L, Bohlin G, Hagekull B, Palmerus K (1996), Interactions between mothers and infants showing food refusal. *Infant Ment Health J* 17:334–347

Main M, Solomon J (1990), Procedures for identifying infants as disorganized/disoriented during the Ainsworth Strange Situation. In: *Attachment in the Preschool Years: Theory, Research, and Intervention*, Greenberg MT, Cicchetti D, Cummings EM, eds. Chicago: University of Chicago Press, pp 121–160

Owen MT, Easterbrooks MA, Chase-Lansdale L, Goldberg W (1984), The relation between maternal employment status and the stability of attachments to mother and to father. *Child Dev* 55:1894–1901

Schneider-Rosen K (1990), The developmental reorganization of attachment relationships. In: *Attachment in the Preschool Years: Theory, Research, and Intervention*, Greenberg MT, Cicchetti D, Cummings EM, eds. Chicago: University of Chicago Press, pp 185–220

Spitz R (1946), Anaclitic depression. *Psychoanal Study Child* 2:313–342

Thompson RA, Lamb M (1984), Assessing qualitative dimensions of emotional reponsiveness in infants' separation reactions in the Strange Situation. *Infant Behav Dev* 7:423–445

Valenzuela M (1990), Attachment in chronically underweight young children. *Child Dev* 61:1984–1996

van IJzendoorn MH, Goldberg S, Kroonenberg PM, Frenkel J (1992), The relative effects of maternal child problems on the quality of attachment: a meta-analysis of attachment in clinical samples. *Child Dev* 63:840–858

Ward MJ, Kessler DB, Altman SC (1993), Infant–mother attachment in children with failure to thrive. *Infant Ment Health J* 14:208–220

11

Psychiatric Illness and Family Support in Children and Adolescents With Diabetic Ketoacidosis: A Controlled Study

Deanna S. Liss, Ph.D., David A. Waller, M.D., Betsy D. Kennard, Psy.D., Donald McIntire, Ph.D., Patricia Capra, Ph.D., and Jacqualene Stephens, Ph.D.

Objective: *To compare compliance, psychiatric disorders, and family support in children with insulin-dependent diabetes mellitus (IDDM) hospitalized with diabetic ketoacidosis (DKA) and clinic controls.* **Method:** *Twenty-five youths hospitalized with DKA and 25 matched outpatient subjects with IDDM with no history of DKA during the preceding year were assessed cross-sectionally, using the Diagnostic Interview Schedule for Children, measures of general and diabetes-specific family functioning, and measures of self-esteem and social competence. Levels of glycosylated hemoglobin and information about compliance with the treatment regimen were obtained.* **Results:** *A significantly higher number of psychiatric disorders was observed in the hospitalized children, with 88% meeting criteria for at least one disorder (versus 28% of controls). Self-esteem and social competence were lower in the hospitalized group, and their families scored lower on problem-solving and diabetes-specific "warmth-caring."* **Conclusions:** *Children with recurrent DKA may be at greater risk of associated psychopathology than diabetic controls with no such history. DKA children's reports of noncompliance may be more sensitive than their parents' reports, and their families may lack warm, caring parent-child relationships.* J. Am. Acad. Child Adolesc. Psychiatry, *1998,*

Accepted December 12, 1997.

Drs. Liss, Kennard, and Capra are with the Division of Psychology, Dr. Waller is Director of the Division of Child and Adolescent Psychiatry, in the Department of Psychiatry; and Dr. McIntire is with Academic Computing Services, University of Texas Southwestern Medical Center, Dallas. Dr. Stephens is with Parkland Memorial Hospital's Health and Hospital System, Dallas. This article is based on the first author's doctoral dissertation.

The authors gratefully acknowledge Marilyn Borgersen, R.N., Bryan Dixon, M.D., Jose Gonzales, M.D., James Marks, M.D., Jane McKelvey, M.S.S.W., Pamela Okada, M.D., Perrin White, M.D., Robert Wiebe, M.D., and support from the Sarah M. and Charles E. Seay Chair in Child Psychiatry (Dr. Waller).

Reprint requests to Dr. Liss, 4016 McKinney Avenue # 304, Dallas, TX 75204.

0890-8567/98/3705–0536/$03.00/0©1998 by the American Academy of Child and Adolescent Psychiatry.

37(5):536–544. **Key Words:** *diabetic ketoacidosis, family, psychopathology, youths.*

Physiological consequences related to poor metabolic control of insulin-dependent diabetes mellitus (IDDM) (Diabetes Control and Complications Trial Research Group, 1994) require identification and management of factors related to noncompliance and poor control. Investigations of the impact of psychiatric illness and family functioning have produced inconsistent results. Diabetic individuals have been found to have a higher rate of psychiatric disorders than individuals without diabetes (Blanz et al., 1993). Diabetic individuals with poor metabolic control have been found to have a higher rate of psychiatric disorders than diabetic subjects in adequate control (Wrigley and Mayou, 1991), and have been found to have lower self-esteem (Kager and Holden, 1992; Jacobsen et al, 1987) and less social competence (Daviss et al., 1995). A longitudinal study (Kovacs et al., 1996) found that half of the children with IDDM followed for an average of 9 years met criteria for one or more psychiatric disorders, the most common being depressive, anxiety, and disruptive behavior disorders, and that the interaction between nondepressive psychiatric disorders and IDDM duration contributed to worse metabolic control. Psychiatric illness, especially depressive disorders, may also be a risk factor for development of retinopathy (Cohen et al., 1997; Kovacs et al., 1995). Family dysfunction has been shown to negatively impact a child's compliance behaviors and metabolic control (Anderson et al., 1981; Hauser et al., 1990). Several studies, however, found no significant pathology (psychiatric illness or family dysfunction) in children with diabetes or their families (Fairburn et al., 1991; Kovacs et al., 1989; Wilkinson, 1987).

This study, using a controlled study design, sought to delineate the relationship between psychiatric illness, family support, and diabetic control. The aims were (1) to compare the prevalence of psychiatric disorders in children and adolescents hospitalized with diabetic ketoacidosis (DKA) to matched outpatient control subjects with IDDM with no history of DKA during the preceding year, (2) to compare the self-esteem and social competence of subjects in these two groups, (3) to compare their family functioning from both a general perspective and specifically in relation to diabetes, and (4) to determine which variables can best predict assignment to each group.

METHOD

Subjects

Subjects were diabetic children and adolescents, male and female, aged 9 to 17 years. Age guidelines were chosen to match those of the Diagnostic Interview Schedule for Children (DISC) (Shaffer et al., 1996), with the lower limit of age 9 selected as an age at which children could reliably report their own symptoms. IDDM had been diagnosed at least 1 year previously. At the time of the study, subjects with DKA presented to Children's Medical Center of Dallas with DKA defined by (1) pH 7.25 or less, (2) carbon dioxide level less than 12 mEq/L, and (3) β-hydroxybuterate level greater than 4 mmol/L. During a 15-month period, the principal investigator made regular daily visits to the emergency room and medical units in an attempt to identify consecutive patients admitted with DKA.

However, an undetermined number of patients were admitted for 23-hour observation and discharged before being evaluated for this study. Therefore, the actual sample may represent patients with more severe DKA.

The child with DKA and his or her parent were given a verbal and written description of the study and invited to sign informed consent. Of 26 families recruited, only one parent–child pair declined, and they did not differ demographically from the sample as a whole. Potential subjects were identified by nurses and/or by an investigator (D.S.L.). During the child's hospital stay, after his or her medical condition had been stabilized, a battery of instruments was administered to the parent and child, and a blood sample was obtained from the child to measure glycosylated hemoglobin. First, the Passage Comprehension subtest of the Woodcock-Johnson Psycho-Educational Battery-Revised (Woodcock and Johnson, 1989, 1990) was administered to the child, to exclude children who did not have at least a third-grade reading level. No subject was excluded for this reason. Once parent and child had completed the evaluation instruments, a matched control subject was obtained from the Children's Endocrinology Center.

Control subjects selected from the Children's Endocrinology Center had no hospitalizations for DKA during the preceding 12 months. They were matched to DKA subjects exactly for sex, and as closely as possible for age, ethnicity, duration of diabetes, and socioeconomic class. Using demographic information provided by DKA subjects, an endocrine clinical nurse specialist reviewed a list of active patients in the Endocrinology Center to identify possible matches. She first identified several potential subjects of the same sex and ethnicity, and then looked for similar ages, durations of diagnosis, and socioeconomic status, an approach designed to diminish the introduction of additional bias into the study. Although it was not possible to match each subject on all variables, all subjects were matched exactly for sex, within 3 years of chronological age, within 3 years of duration of diagnosis, and within two socioeconomic categories. Parents of potential control subjects were contacted by phone to offer them the opportunity to participate. After providing informed consent, parents and children completed the same battery of instruments completed by the DKA subjects and parents. A blood specimen was also obtained from each control subject. A total of 50 subjects were evaluated, 25 with DKA and 25 outpatient controls. The demographic characteristics of these two groups are presented in Table 1, and analyses showed no significant differences.

Metabolic Control and Compliance

Glycosylated hemoglobin level is the most accurate indicator of overall glycemic control for the preceding 2 to 3 months (Gonen et al., 1977; Nathan et al., 1984). Higher glycosylated hemoglobin levels indicate poorer diabetic control. Blood samples were analyzed by the Bayer DCA 2000 Analyzer. The range of HbA1c for nondiabetics is 4% to 6%, whereas for older children and adolescents with diabetes the best range is 6% to 8%; values exceeding 9% indicate poorer glycemic control. This machine registers 14% as its highest value, although actual HbA1c levels may be higher. Eight of the DKA subjects had glycosylated hemoglobin levels which registered at "14% or above." Compliance with the diabetes treatment regimen was reported by subjects and their parents using an abbreviated version of the

TABLE 1
Demographic Characteristics by Group

Demographic Characteristic	DKA Group		Control Group		Test Statistic	p Values
Age (yr): mean (SD)	13	(1.94)	13	(2.31)	$t = 0.37$	.714
Duration of Dx (yr): mean (SD)	4.88	(2.57)	4.52	(2.16)	$t = 1.20$	.241
Gender: no.						
Males	11		11		$\chi^2 = 0.0$	1.00
Females	14		14			
SES: no. (%)						
Category 1	1	(4)	1	(4)		
Category 2	7	(28)	11	(44)	$\chi^2 = 1.56$	
Category 3	8	(32)	7	(28)		.82
Category 4	6	(24)	4	(16)		
Category 5	3	(12)	2	(8)		
Ethnicity: no. (%)						
Caucasian	11	(44)	14	(56)		
African-American	10	(40)	9	(36)	$\chi^2 = 1.41$	
Hispanic	3	(12)	1	(4)		.70
Asian	1	(4)	1	(4)		

Note: DKA = diabetic ketoacidosis; SES = socioeconomic status; Dx = diagnosis.

Diabetes Management Information Sheet, an instrument with adequate interrater reliability (Kovacs et al., 1985), although validity has not been assessed. The present version asks the respondent to use a Likert-like scale to rate the frequency of the child's compliance with insulin injections, diet, blood glucose monitoring, and urine testing. Parents were also asked to provide additional information about the child's diabetes management, including the number of hospitalizations for DKA since diagnosis and within the preceding year and the number of visits to the emergency room for DKA in the preceding year.

Psychiatric Disorders and Psychological Adjustment

Psychiatric disorders were assessed using the DISC (Version 2.3) (Shaffer et al., 1996), with data obtained from subjects and their parents. The DISC operationalizes DSM-III-R criteria for most Axis I diagnoses applied to children and adolescents and has been described as "the most highly structured of all instruments" and "the only instrument designed specifically and solely for epidemiological studies" (Costello, 1996, p. 462). It has demonstrated excellent sensitivity and specificity (Fisher et al., 1993) and satisfactory test-retest reliability (Jensen et al., 1995). A similar structured diagnostic interview for adults (the Diagnostic Interview Schedule) was found to be useful in detecting psychiatric illness in a diabetic population (Lustman et al., 1986). The DISC was administered by a doctoral graduate student in clinical psychology (D.S.L.), who was trained in its use by a clinician whose training included 2½ days of group instruction by professionals involved in the DISC's development at the New York State Psychiatric Institute. Instruction included item-by-item discussion, observation of videotaped DISC interviews, performing a DISC interview, and critique of performance. Training for the principal investigator in this project included detailed instructions on administration and scoring procedures, as well as critiques of videotaped practice interviews. Formal reliability data on the administration of the DISC between the clinician/trainer and the interviewer were not obtained. The Piers-Harris Children's Self-Concept Scale (Piers and Harris, 1967), a self-report measure demonstrated to have satisfactory psychometric properties (Cosden, 1984; Piers, 1984), was administered to provide a global measure of self-esteem. Parents of subjects completed the Social Competence scales of the Child Behavior Checklist (Achenbach and Edelbrock, 1981), an instrument with good reliability and validity (Mooney, 1984), to assess global functioning in daily childhood situations and activities.

Measures of Family Functioning and Psychiatric Symptoms of Parents

The Family Assessment Measure-III (Skinner et al., 1983), a self-report measure with adequate psychometric properties that assesses family strengths and problems (Halvorsen, 1991), was completed by children and parents. They also completed the Diabetes Family Behavior Scale (Waller et al., 1986), a self-report measure of diabetes-specific family functioning that has displayed satisfactory reliability (McKelvey et al., 1993).

Parental psychiatric symptoms, which could influence assessment of children on the DISC (Canning et al., 1993), were assessed using the Brief Symptom Inventory (Derogatis, 1975), a self-report measure demonstrating good psychometric properties (Broday and Mason, 1991).

Data Collection and Analysis

Data collection occurred October 1995 to January 1997. Subjects were recruited until 25 DKA subjects and 25 controls had been evaluated. Evaluations were performed by the principal investigator (D.S.L.), who was not blind to group assignment. Analysis involved comparison of descriptors of the two samples, using χ^2 analysis and Student *t* tests; individual comparisons between the paired groups on each of the variables, using Student *t* tests; and a stepwise multiple logistic regression to select variables for a statistical model used for group assignment. When multiple *t* tests were used, the significance level remained at .05, in keeping with recent theories of multiple univariate analysis (Aickin and Gensler, 1996; Cohen, 1994).

RESULTS

Metabolic Control and Compliance

Subjects with DKA had significantly higher HbA1c levels (mean = 12.4, SD = 1.7) than controls (mean = 9.3, SD = 1.5) ($t[23] = 6.08$, $p \leq .001$), and the actual difference was probably greater because eight of the DKA subjects had HbA1c levels of 14% or greater. Subjects with DKA also reported significantly more hospital admissions since their diabetes was diagnosed (mean = 7.0, SD = 8.1) than controls (mean = 0.6, SD = 1.4) ($t[24] = 4.09$,

$p \leq .001$) and significantly more presentations to the emergency room within the preceding year (mean $= 2.7$, SD $= 3.1$) than controls (mean $= 0.2$, SD $= 0.4$) ($t[24] = 4.05$, $p \leq .001$).

Subjects with DKA reported less insulin injection compliance (mean $= 8.0$, SD $= 5.8$) than controls (mean $= 12.4$, SD $= 7.9$) ($t[24] = 2.56$, $p = .02$); less compliance with the diabetes diet (mean $= 2.6$, SD $= 1.2$) than controls (mean $= 3.7$, SD $= 0.7$) ($t[24] = 4.30$, $p \leq .001$); and less compliance with urine testing (mean $= 2.3$, SD $= 1.1$) than controls (mean $= 3.9$, SD $= 3.9$) ($t[24] = 2.06$, $p = .05$). There was no difference in reported compliance with blood glucose testing. The only significant difference in the reports of parents was less compliance with the diabetes diet reported by parents of DKA subjects (mean $= 2.7$, SD $= 0.9$) compared with parents of controls (mean $= 3.4$, SD $= 0.8$) ($t[24] = 2.37$, $p = .03$).

Psychiatric Diagnoses and Psychological Adjustment

A significantly larger number of psychiatric diagnoses was reported by DKA children (mean $= 1.9$, SD $= 1.9$) compared with controls (mean $= 0.2$, SD $= 0.4$) ($t[24] = 4.74$, $p \leq .001$). A significantly larger number of diagnoses was also reported (for their children) by parents of DKA subjects (mean $= 1.7$, SD $= 1.6$) compared with parents of controls (mean $= 0.2$, SD $= 0.4$) ($t[24] = 4.65$, $p \leq .001$). Numbers of individual diagnoses reported by children and parents are presented in Table 2, the majority including anxiety, affective, and disruptive behavior disorders. Twenty-two DKA subjects (88%) met criteria for at least one psychiatric disorder, compared with 7 (28%) of the controls ($\chi^2[1, N = 50] = 18.47$, $p \leq .001$).

Children with DKA had significantly lower total self-esteem scores compared with controls (Table 3), reported lower self-esteem in behavioral functioning, and tended to be lower in intellectual and school status. Differences between DKA children and controls on the Anxiety subscale approached significance: DKA subjects reported relatively less self-esteem, a finding that indicates more anxiety. Children with DKA were described by their parents as having less overall social competence compared with controls, specifically as having less competence in activities and in school. There was no difference between reports of parents on the Social subscale.

Family Functioning and Psychiatric Symptoms of Parents

Responses of children and of parents in the DKA and control groups did not differ on overall family functioning measured by the Family Assessment Measure-III (Table 4). Subjects with DKA reported more family problems in the area of Task Accomplishment, whereas DKA parents reported more Role Performance problems. On the Diabetes Family Behavior Scale, DKA children reported less overall diabetes-specific family support than did controls. Although there was no difference between children's responses on the Guidance-Control subscale, DKA children reported less support on the Warmth-Caring subscale. DKA parents also reported less overall diabetes-specific family support than control parents. There was no difference between their responses on the Guidance-Control subscale, but DKA parents reported less support in the area of Warmth-Caring.

TABLE 2
DISC Diagnoses: Frequency Counts

| | No. Meeting Diagnosis | | | |
| | DKA Subjects | | Control Subjects | |
DISC Diagnosis	Child	Parent	Child	Parent
Anxiety disorders				
Simple phobia	11	5	0	1
Social phobia	6	5	0	0
Agoraphobia	0	0	0	0
Panic disorder	0	0	0	0
SAD	7	2	1	0
Avoidant disorder	3	0	0	0
Overanxious disorder	5	8	2	0
GAD	3	5	0	0
OCD	1	0	0	0
Affective disorders				
Major depression	6	3	0	0
Dysthymia	0	2	0	0
Mania/hypomania	0	0	1	0
Disruptive behavior disorders				
ADHD	4	4	0	0
ODD	0	4	0	1
Conduct disorder	1	0	0	0
Miscellaneous disorders				
Bulimia/anorexia	0	0	0	0
Elimination disorders	2	4	2	2
Tic disorders	0	0	0	0
Substance use disorders				
Alcohol abuse/dependence	0	0	0	0
Marijuana abuse/dependence	0	0	0	0

Note: DISC = Diagnostic Interview Schedule for Children; DKA = diabetic ketoacidosis; SAD = separation anxiety disorder; GAD = generalized anxiety disorder; OCD = obsessive-compulsive disorder; ADHD = attention-deficit hyperactivity disorder; ODD = oppositional defiant disorder.

The Brief Symptom Inventory indicated no differences in the overall indices. Parents' responses differed on the Somatization subscale, with DKA parents scoring higher (mean = 54.7, SD = 9.5) than control parents (mean = 49.5, SD = 9.0) ($t[24] = 2.08$, $p = .05$).

Stepwise Multiple Logistic Regression Analysis

Stepwise multiple logistic regression was used to determine which factors provided the statistical model of greatest predictive ability for group assignment. Every variable on which data were obtained was included in the analysis, allowing for examination of the predictive ability and interrelationships of groups of variables which may or may

TABLE 3
Comparison of Psychological Adjustment Variables by Group: Piers-Harris and CBCL

Psychological Adjustment Scales	DKA Child: Mean (SD)	Control Child: Mean (SD)	t Test Values	p Values
Piers-Harris scales				
Behavior	53.1 (7.8)	59.0 (8.7)	2.79*	.01
Intellectual & School Status	52.8 (9.5)	58.4 (11.4)	1.97	.06
Physical Appearance & Attributes	55.6 (11.1)	56.9 (11.5)	0.59	.563
Anxiety	52.8 (13.5)	58.6 (11.0)	1.93	.067
Popularity	52.3 (12.3)	55.5 (10.8)	1.04	.31
Happiness & Satisfaction	54.5 (9.7)	55.6 (9.2)	0.61	.548
Total	55.9 (9.6)	61.9 (11.2)	2.64*	.014
CBCL scales				
Activity	43.5 (9.6)	48.4 (7.1)	2.07*	.049
Social	41.7 (6.7)	45.2 (8.2)	1.72	.098
School	40.4 (8.8)	48.1 (8.2)	2.62*	.016
Total	40.3 (9.6)	48.5 (9.4)	3.19*	.004

Note: DKA = diabetic ketoacidosis; CBCL = Child Behavior Checklist.

TABLE 4
Comparison of Family Functioning Variables (Child-Related): FAM and DFBS

Family Functioning Variables	DKA Child: Mean (SD)	Control Child: Mean (SD)	t Test Values	p Values
FAM scales				
Task-Accomplishment	53.9 (8.4)	49.4 (8.2)	2.08*	.048
Role Performance	55.2 (9.4)	52.7 (9.7)	1.02	.318
Communication	52.7 (8.2)	51.1 (8.8)	0.84	.412
Affective Expression	52.9 (9.1)	52.5 (9.5)	0.17	.869
Involvement	54.3 (9.1)	51.2 (10.2)	1.12	.272
Control	54.3 (7.9)	50.4 (7.6)	1.86	.075
Values & Norms	51.7 (7.5)	50.7 (8.2)	0.45	.66
Social Desirability	45.5 (6.6)	50.2 (8.8)	2.37*	.026
Defensiveness	49.8 (8.4)	53.1 (10.9)	1.14	.266
Overall Family Functioning	53.7 (6.3)	51.2 (6.8)	1.43	.166
DFBS scales				
Warmth-Caring	50.2 (8.6)	55.3 (8.0)	2.75*	.011
Guidance-Control	40.4 (7.4)	42.5 (8.6)	1.23	.230
Total	141.5 (17.8)	152.9 (20.8)	2.75*	.011

Note: DKA = diabetic ketoacidosis; FAM = Family Assessment Measure; DFBS = Diabetes Family Behavior Scale.
*p < .05.

not have been significant at the univariate level of analysis. Significance levels of .10 were applied as a requirement for entry, as well as for maintaining a variable in the model (Draper and Smith, 1981; Hosmer and Lemeshow, 1989), since the error of omission was viewed as more serious than adding possibly spurious variables. The variable of greatest predictive ability for group assignment was compliance with diet reported by children ($\chi^2[1, N = 49] = 4.99$, $p = .03$), with higher scores (more compliant behaviors) predicting assignment to the control group. The complete model produced by the regression analysis included three factors: (1) compliance with diet reported by children; (2) number of DISC separation anxiety disorder symptoms endorsed by parents ($\chi^2[1, N = 49] = 4.27$, $p = .04$), with greater numbers of symptoms predicting assignment to the DKA group; and (3) overall number of DISC psychiatric diagnoses reported by parents ($\chi^2[1, N = 49] = 3.15$, $p = .08$), with greater numbers of diagnoses predicting assignment to the DKA group. Model R square ($R^2{}_L$) calculations using log likelihoods from the regression analysis, performed to provide an indication of the strength of this model, indicated that 50.9% of the variance between groups is accounted for by the three variables included in this model.

DISCUSSION

This study documents an association in diabetic children and adolescents between higher rates of psychopathology and hospitalization for DKA. Whereas others have reported a higher prevalence of psychiatric disorders in individuals with diabetes compared with a nonclinical population (e.g., Blanz et al., 1993), our results suggest that psychiatric disorders may be related specifically to diabetic children and adolescents with poor metabolic control, similar to findings of Mayou and colleagues (1991) in young diabetic adults. The number of hospitalizations and emergency room visits reported by parents in our study indicates that DKA subjects were in poorer control not only at the time of this study, but since the diagnosis of diabetes.

The relationship between psychiatric disorders and poorly controlled diabetes may be reciprocal and interactive. Psychopathology could be a consequence of poorly controlled diabetes. Repeated episodes of severe DKA would be stressful. Moreover, in a study in which patients' plasma glucose level was fixed by overnight insulin infusion at hyperglycemic and normoglycemic levels, Lustman and colleagues (1983) found that sustained high plasma glucose values induced physiological changes characteristic of a stress-like CNS arousal pattern, which could increase susceptibility to environmental stress and result in a variety of psychiatric symptoms. The relationship between psychopathology and hospitalization for DKA could also be attributable to the negative impact of psychopathology on the child or adolescent's diabetes. Psychiatric illness can influence blood glucose control indirectly by reducing adherence to the medical regimen, and directly by emotional arousal contributing to ketoacidosis by way of sympathochromaffin system activation and attendant catecholamine and corticosteroid release (Lustman et al., 1986). Similar reciprocal mechanisms could account for the recently described relationship between psychiatric illness (especially affective disorders) and the diabetic complication of retinopathy (Cohen et al., 1997; Kovacs et al., 1995).

The specific psychiatric disorders associated with DKA were anxiety, depressive, and attention/disruptive behavior disorders. The large number of anxiety disorders, especially simple phobia, social phobia, and separation anxiety disorder, is especially important to note because of their possible mutually influencing relationship with episodes of repeated illness and subsequent hospitalizations. Such anxiety symptoms may have developed over time across multiple hospitalizations, in which the child comes to fear illness and the many medical procedures associated with being hospitalized. Alternatively, a child who is typically overanxious may be too preoccupied to adequately follow the diabetes treatment regimen.

Families of DKA subjects were less effective at problem-solving and had less-defined family rules and roles. The absence of further significant findings using general family measures was not wholly unexpected, given previous studies which have also not found a significant relationship between metabolic control and general family functioning (Kovacs et al., 1989; Schafer et al., 1983). Using our measure of diabetes-specific family functioning, we found that both children and parents in the DKA group reported less diabetes-specific family support, and less support specifically in the area of diabetes-related "warmth/caring," or empathy. Empathy may have a mutually influenced relationship with repeated illness episodes. Parker (1983) noted that "a parental style of affectionless control may be a consequence of chronic disorder in a child" (p. 279), a finding that may be exaggerated in this study because the assessment was done when the parent may have been reacting strongly to the current DKA episode. Repeated illness may also be a consequence of parenting style. That DKA subjects in our study reported lower self-esteem, were described by their parents as having less social competence, and reported more noncompliance may reflect difficulties with a parenting style that emphasizes behavioral control at the expense of empathic responses (Buri, 1991; Daviss et al., 1995).

Subjects with DKA reported more noncompliance with diabetes treatment than did controls in three of four areas assessed; this finding suggests that noncompliance may have been a path by which psychiatric disorders and family dysfunction affected metabolic control. Diet compliance was found to be the most highly associated variable with assignment to the control group. For children, "the diet component of the diabetes regimen is perhaps the most complex and has been rated by youngsters as one of the most difficult aspects of diabetes treatment" (Reid et al., 1994, p. 333). Because the DKA children required hospitalization, it seems likely that their reports, which described more areas of noncompliance, were closer to the truth than those of their parents, which differed only on diet compliance. This suggests that parents of children with poorer metabolic control were not sufficiently aware of how much their children were failing to comply with the insulin injection and testing components of the medical regimen.

Parents in the DKA group differed from control parents only in having more somatization symptoms; this finding suggests that parental psychopathology was not a significant confounding factor for parental DISC assessments of their children. The lack of significant differences for parents of the more severely ill diabetic children may be explained by the fact that all parents in this study had children with a chronic illness, whereas previous research on the psychological functioning of parents of children with a chronic illness have typically included comparisons with parents of healthy children (Breslau et al., 1982; Canning et al.,

1993; Kovacs et al., 1985). Although parents of children who have psychiatric disorders tend to have higher rates of psychiatric disorders (Offord and Fleming, 1996), it may be that psychiatric disorders in DKA children in this study are more directly related to the course of their diabetes than to parental, hereditary, or environmental influences.

The regression analysis model included three variables (compliance with diet, separation anxiety disorder symptoms, and overall number of psychiatric disorders), which all relate to individual functioning. This may reflect the greater importance of individual (compared with family) variables, or it may indicate that not even our diabetes-specific measure was sensitive enough to capture the specific pattern of family behaviors and interactions that are most related to metabolic control (Anderson et al., 1997; Golden et al., 1985; Skyler, 1981). The failure of psychological adjustment factors (low self-esteem and social competence) to be identified in the regression analysis may indicate that it is the severity of psychiatric symptoms above a certain "disorder" threshold that determines impact on metabolic control. Lack of inclusion of a possible predictive factor in the regression model does not imply lack of association with outcome but indicates that the factor does not contribute significantly to accuracy of prediction, given knowledge of variables already included in the model. Total self-esteem scores, for example, are significantly associated with group assignment at the univariate level (Table 3) but do not enter the multivariate model, indicating no additional predictive capability over factors already describing group assignment.

This study has several limitations. The size of the two groups examined was relatively small. Few conclusions can be drawn regarding the psychological and family functioning of the few diabetic children in this study who are of Asian-American or Hispanic descent. An additional source of bias is the use of a single interviewer not blind to group assignment. Although the highly structured format of the DISC and detailed training in its administration help reduce such bias, self-report questionnaires addressing psychopathology in the subjects might have offset the lack of blinded DISC interviews. The interpretation of causality in this study is limited by its cross-sectional design. Future investigations using longitudinal studies that include assessment of children's perceptions of parenting with Parker's Parental Bonding Instrument (Parker, 1983), as well as more complete assessment of parental psychiatric status, may help define the complex interrelationships between these variables and metabolic control.

Conclusions and Clinical Implications

Children hospitalized for DKA have higher rates of psychopathology than children with diabetes who have no history of DKA during the preceding year. Since symptoms of anxiety and depression in this population may be confused with symptoms related to abnormal glycemia (Jacobson, 1996), systematic psychiatric diagnostic interviews may be critical. Attention should also be focused on DKA children's reports of noncompliance, as they may be more sensitive than their parents' reports. Families of children with poor metabolic control appear less organized and less efficient at problem-solving, have less well-defined family roles and rules, and demonstrate a diabetes-related parenting style that emphasizes control, but at the expense of empathy. Diagnosis and treatment of specific psychiatric disorders in children hospitalized with DKA, combined with attempts to optimize warm, caring, diabetes-specific family support, may improve compliance and metabolic control, thereby helping reduce later complications.

REFERENCES

Achenbach TM, Edelbrock C (1981), Behavioral problems and competencies reported by parents of normal and disturbed children aged four through sixteen. *Monogr Soc Res Child Dev* 46:188

Aickin M, Gensler H (1996), Adjusting for multiple testing when reporting research results: the Bonferroni vs Holm methods. *Am J Public Health* 86:726–728

Anderson BJ, Ho J, Brackett J, Finkelstein D, Laffel L (1997), Parental involvement in diabetes management tasks: relationships to blood glucose monitoring adherence and metabolic control in young adolescents with insulin-dependent diabetes mellitus. *J Pediatr* 130:257–265

Anderson BJ, Miller JP, Auslander WF, Santiago JV (1981), Family characteristics of diabetic adolescents: relationship to metabolic control. *Diabetes Care* 4:586–594

Blanz BJ, Rensch-Riemann BS, Fritz-Sigmund DI, Schmidt MH (1993), IDDM is a risk factor for adolescent psychiatric disorders. *Diabetes Care* 16:1579–1587

Breslau N, Stuch K, Mortimer E (1982), Psychological distress in mothers of disabled children. *Am J Dis Child* 136:682–686

Broday SF, Mason JL (1991), Internal consistency of the Brief Symptom Inventory for counseling center clients. *Psychol Rep* 68:94

Buri JR (1991), Parental authority questionnaire. *J Pers Assess* 57:110–119

Canning EH, Hanser SB, Shade KA, Boyce WT (1993), Maternal distress and discrepancy in reports of psychopathology in chronically ill children. *Psychosomatics* 34:506–511

Cohen J (1994), The earth is round (p < .05). *Am Psychol* 49:997–1003

Cohen ST, Welch G, Jacobson AM, De Groot M, Samson J (1997), The association of lifetime psychiatric illness and increased retinopathy in patients with type I diabetes mellitus. *Psychosomatics* 38:98–108

Cosden M (1984), Piers-Harris Children's Self-Concept Scale. In: *Test Critiques*, Vol 1, Keyser D, Sweetland R, eds. Kansas City, MO: Test Corporation of America, pp 511–521

Costello AJ (1996), Structured interviewing. In: *Child and Adolescent Psychiatry*, 2nd ed, Lewis M, ed. Baltimore: Williams & Wilkins, pp 457–464

Daviss WB, Coon H, Whitehead P, Ryan K, Burkley M, McMahon W (1995), Predicting diabetic control from competence, adherence, adjustment, and psychopathology. *J Am Acad Child Adolesc Psychiatry* 34:1629–1636

Derogatis LR (1975), *Brief Symptom Inventory*. Baltimore: Clinical Psychometric Research

Diabetes Control and Complications Trial Research Group (1994), Effect of intensive diabetes treatment on the development and progression of long-term complications in adolescents with insulin-dependent diabetes mellitus: Diabetes Control and Complications Trial. *J Pediatr* 125:177–188

Draper NR, Smith H (1981), *Applied Regression Analysis*. New York: Wiley Fairburn CG, Peveler RC, Davies B, Mann JI, Mayou RA (1991), Eating disorders in young adults with insulin dependent diabetes mellitus: a controlled study. *BMJ* 303:17–20

Fisher P, Shaffer D, Piacentini J et al. (1993), Sensitivity of the Diagnostic Interview Schedule for Children, 2nd edition (DISC-2.1) for specific diagnoses of children and adolescents. *J Am Acad Child Adolesc Psychiatry* 32:666–673

Golden MP, Herrold AJ, Orr DP (1985), An approach to prevention of recurrent diabetic ketoacidosis in the pediatric population. *J Pediatr* 107:195–200

Gonen B, Rubenstein AH, Rochman H, Tanega SP, Horwitz DL (1977), Haemoglobin Al: an indicator of the metabolic control of diabetic patients. *Lancet* 2:734–736

Halvorsen JG (1991), Self-report family assessment instruments: an evaluative review. *Fam Pract Res J* 11:21–55

Hauser ST, Jacobson AM, Lavori P et al. (1990), Adherence among children and adolescents with insulin-dependent diabetes mellitus over a four year longitudinal follow-up, II: immediate and long-term linkages with the family milieu. *J Pediatr Psychol* 15:527–542

Hosmer DW, Lemeshow S (1989), *Applied Logistic Regression.* New York: Wiley

Jacobson AM (1996), The psychological care of patients with insulin-dependent diabetes mellitus. *N Engl J Med* 334:1249–1253

Jacobson AM, Hauser ST, Wolfsdorf JI et al. (1987), Psychologic predictors of compliance in children with recent onset of diabetes mellitus. *J Pediatr* 110:805–811

Jensen P, Roper M, Fisher P et al. (1995), Test-retest reliability of the Diagnostic Interview Schedule for Children (DISC 2.1). *Arch Gen Psychiatry* 52:61–71

Kager AA, Holden EW (1992), Preliminary investigation of the direct and moderating effects of family and individual variables on the adjustment of children and adolescents with diabetes. *J Pediatr Psychol* 17:491–502

Kovacs M, Finkelstein R, Feinberg TL, Crouse-Novak M, Paulauskas S, Pollock M (1985), Initial psychologic responses of parents to the diagnosis of insulin-dependent diabetes mellitus in their children. *Diabetes Care* 8:568–575

Kovacs M, Kass RE, Schnell TM, Goldston D, Marsh J (1989), Family functioning and metabolic control of school-aged children with IDDM. *Diabetes Care* 12:409–414

Kovacs M, Mukerji P, Drash A, Iyengar S (1995), Biomedical and psychiatric risk factors for retinopathy among children with IDDM. *Diabetes Care* 18:1592–1599

Kovacs M, Mukerji P, Iyengar S, Drash A (1996), Psychiatric disorder and metabolic control among youths with IDDM. *Diabetes Care* 19:318–323

Lustman PJ, Harper GW, Griffith LS, Clouse RE (1986), Use of the Diagnostic Interview Schedule in patients with diabetes mellitus. *J Nerv Ment Dis* 174:743–746

Lustman PJ, Skor DA, Carney RM, Santiago JV, Cryer PE (1983), Stress and diabetic control. *Lancet* 1:588

Mayou R, Peveler R, Davies B, Mann J, Fairburn C (1991), Psychiatric morbidity in young adults with insulin-dependent diabetes mellitus. *Psychol Med* 21:639–645

McKelvey J, Waller D, North A et al. (1993), Reliability and validity of the Diabetes Family Behavior Scale (DFBS). *Diabetes Educ* 19:125–132

Mooney KC (1984), Child Behavior Checklist. In: *Test Critiques*, Vol 1, Keyser D, Sweetland R, eds. Kansas City, MO: Test Corporation of America, pp 511–521

Nathan DM, Singer DE, Hurxthal K, Goodson JD (1984), The clinical information value of the glycosylated hemoglobin assay. *N Engl J Med* 310:341–346

Offord DR, Fleming JE (1996), Epidemiology. In: *Child and Adolescent Psychiatry: A Comprehensive Textbook*, Lewis M, ed. Baltimore: Williams & Wilkins, pp 1166–1178

Parker G (1983), *Parental Overprotection: A Risk Factor in Psychosocial Development.* New York: Grune & Stratton

Piers EV (1984), *Revised Manual for the Piers-Harris Children's Self-Concept Scale*. Los Angeles: Western Psychological Services

Piers E, Harris D (1967), *Piers-Harris Children's Self-Concept Scale*. Nashville, TN: Counselor Recordings and Tests

Reid GJ, Dubow EF, Carey TC, Dura JR (1994), Contribution of coping to medical adjustment and treatment responsibility among children and adolescents with diabetes. *J Dev Behav Pediatr* 15:327–335

Schafer LC, Glasgow RE, McCaul KD, Dreher M (1983), Adherence to IDDM regimens: relationship to psychosocial variables and metabolic control. *Diabetes Care* 6:493–498

Shaffer D, Fisher P, Dulcan M et al. (1996), The NIMH Diagnostic Interview Schedule for Children (DISC Version 2.3): description, acceptability, prevalence rates, and performance in the MECA study. *J Am Acad Child Adolesc Psychiatry* 35:865–877

Skinner HA, Steinhauser PD, Santa-Barbara J (1983), The Family Assessment Measure. *Can J Community Ment Health* 2:91–105

Skyler JS (1981), Psychological issues in diabetes. *Diabetes Care* 4:656–657

Waller D, Chipman J, Hardy B et al. (1986), Measuring diabetes-specific family support and its relation to metabolic control: a preliminary report. *J Am Acad Child Psychiatry* 25:415–418

Wilkinson G (1987), The influence of psychiatric, psychological, and social factors on the control of insulin-dependent diabetes mellitus. *J Psychosom Res* 31:277–286

Woodcock RW, Johnson MB (1989, 1990), *Woodcock-Johnson Psycho Educational Battery-Revised*. Allen, TX: DLM Teaching Resources

Wrigley M, Mayou R (1991), Psychosocial factors and admission for poor glycaemic control: a study of psychological and social factors in poorly controlled insulin dependent diabetic patients. *J Psychosom Res* 35:335–343

12

Headaches and Psychopathology in Children and Adolescents

Helen Link Egger, M.D., Adrian Angold, M.R.C.Psych., and
E. Jane Costello, Ph.D.

Objective: *To examine the association between chronic headaches and DSM-III-R–defined psychiatric disorders, including depression, anxiety disorders, conduct disorder, oppositional defiant disorder, and attention-deficit hyperactivity disorder, in a population-based sample of children and adolescents.* **Method:** *1,013 children aged 9 to 15 years in the Great Smoky Mountains Study were evaluated annually over a 3-year period using the Child and Adolescent Psychiatric Assessment, a child and parent diagnostic psychiatric interview. Headaches that lasted at least 1 hour and occurred at least once a week during the 3 months prior to the interview were studied.* **Results:** *Girls with depression and anxiety disorders had a significantly greater prevalence of headaches than girls without an internalizing disorder. This association was not found for boys. Conduct disorder was significantly associated with headaches in boys. Each of these associations was constant with age.* **Conclusions:** *This study suggests that a distinct gender difference exists between boys and girls in the associations between headaches and psychopathology. Carroll's theory of dysfunction in central pain regulation as an underlying cause of depression is discussed in relation to the proposed serotonergic dysregulation common to headaches, depression, anxiety, aggression, and pain.* J. Am. Acad. Child Adolesc. Psychiatry, *1998, 37(9):951–958.* **Key Words:** *headaches, depression, anxiety, conduct disorder, epidemiology.*

In 1937, Wolff compiled migraine patients' recollections of their childhood personalities and concluded that they had been "delicate, shy, . . . [and] withdrawn" children, who also displayed "unusual stubbornness or inflexibility" (Wolff, 1937, p. 897). From this early portrait of the personality characteristics of migraine sufferers, researchers began to explore

Accepted April 13, 1998.
From the Department of Psychiatry and Behavioral Sciences, Duke University Medical Center, Durham, NC.
Reprint requests to Dr. Egger, Developmental Epidemiology Program, DUMC Box 3454, Durham, NC 27710.
0890-8567/98/3709–0951/$03.00/0©1998 by the American Academy of Child and Adolescent Psychiatry.

the association of headaches, first with broad personality traits and then with distinct psychiatric symptoms and syndromes, particularly depression and anxiety. Recent well-designed epidemiological studies of adults have demonstrated a strong association between headaches and depression and anxiety (Breslau and Davis, 1992; Merikangas et al., 1990, 1993; Stewart et al., 1994). Although there have been a number of clinical studies and a few epidemiological studies of headaches and psychopathology in children and adolescents, methodological difficulties have resulted in equivocal conclusions.

Headache Prevalence in Children

Epidemiological studies have shown that headaches are a very common childhood complaint. Migraines occur in 3% to 15% of children (Abu-Arefeh and Russell, 1995; Bille, 1962; Dalsgaard-Nielsen et al., 1970; Deubner, 1977; Egermark-Eriksson, 1982; Linet et al., 1989; Mortimer et al., 1992; Oster, 1972; Sillanpaa, 1983; Stang and Osterhaus, 1993; Vahlquist, 1955), while nonmigrainous headaches occurring at least monthly are seen in between 9% and 33% of children (Egermark-Eriksson, 1982; Oster, 1972; Sillanpaa, 1983; Vahlquist, 1955). Fifty percent to 80% of children report some type of headache in the past year (Barea et al., 1996; Deubner, 1977; Mortimer et al., 1992; Sillanpaa, 1983). The prevalence of headaches increases with age (Bille, 1962; Vahlquist, 1955).

Women report more headaches than men, and a number of researchers have found a similar gender difference in adolescents (Abu-Arefeh and Russell, 1995; Bille, 1962; Deubner, 1977; Egermark-Eriksson, 1982; Linet et al., 1989; Oster, 1972; Sillanpaa, 1983; Stang and Osterhaus, 1993), although three studies have reported no significant gender differences (Dalsgaard-Nielsen et al., 1970; Mortimer et al., 1992; Vahlquist, 1955).

Epidemiological Studies of Young Adults

Epidemiological studies of young adults have found significant associations between headaches and depression and anxiety disorders (Breslau et al., 1991; Breslau and Davis, 1992; Crisp et al., 1977; Linet et al., 1989; Merikangas et al., 1990, 1993; Moldin et al., 1993; Paulin et al., 1985). However, differing hypotheses regarding the etiology and nature of the association of headaches with depression and anxiety have been proposed. In a population-based study of 27- and 28-year-olds in Switzerland, Merikangas et al. (1990) were the first to use standardized *DSM-III* psychiatric diagnoses and clearly defined headache criteria to demonstrate that migraines were strongly associated with both depression and generalized anxiety disorder. On the basis of these young adults' recollections of the onset of childhood symptoms, Merikangas hypothesized that childhood anxiety disorders preceded the advent of migraines and that depressive disorders developed as later sequelae of these chronic headaches.

On the other hand, in a prospective, longitudinal study of 1,007 young adults (aged 21 through 30), Breslau et al. (1991) found a bidirectional influence between affective disorders and migraines, where each disorder increased the risk of the other disorder threefold.

Epidemiological Studies of Children

Three epidemiological studies (Bille, 1962; Passchier and Orlebeke, 1985; Vahlquist, 1955) have examined the associations between personality traits and psychiatric symptoms and headaches in children, yet were limited by their use of nonvalidated criteria of psychopathology.

Only one epidemiological study (Pine et al., 1996) has used validated diagnostic criteria to demonstrate an association between headaches and depression in children. Pine et al. concluded that headaches were twice as common in depressed adolescents as in nondepressed adolescents. Neither anxiety nor mixed anxiety and depression was found to be significantly associated with headaches.

These few epidemiological studies have been hampered by their definitions of the two central variables: headaches and psychopathology.

Definition of Headaches in Children

Although modified criteria (Prensky and Sommer, 1979; Vahlquist, 1955) for children's migraines have been defined, criteria specifically designed to describe the full range of children's headaches have not been delineated (Gladstein et al., 1993; Mortimer et al., 1992; Wober-Bingol et al., 1996). Headaches can be categorized in different ways. A distinction is commonly made between migrainous and nonmigrainous headaches (Headache Classification Committee of the International Headache Society, 1988), but headaches can also be categorized by their frequency (daily, weekly, or monthly), duration, and severity (Kristjansdottir and Wahlberg, 1993; Rothner, 1995) rather than the location and symptom complex of the headaches alone.

While the literature on migraines is vast, studies have also shown that significant psychiatric morbidity can be associated with nonmigrainous headaches (Holden et al., 1994; Kaiser, 1992; Solomon et al., 1992). A focus on migraines alone may narrow our understanding of the variables associated with the spectrum of childhood headaches. On the other hand, broad headache variables that do not specify duration, frequency, or date of onset of headache may result in nonspecific conclusions (e.g., Pine et al., 1996).

Definitions of Psychopathology

In both the clinical and epidemiological literature, nonvalidated measures of psychiatric symptoms dominate. Pine and colleagues' (1996) work is the only epidemiological population-based study of headaches in adolescents to define and measure psychopathology using *DSM-III* and *DSM-III-R* criteria.

Most clinical studies have focused on the association of headaches with internalizing disorders (Andrasik et al., 1988; Burke and Peters, 1956; Cooper et al., 1987; Cunningham et al., 1987; Guidetti et al., 1987; Kowal and Pritchard, 1990; Larsson, 1988; Ling et al., 1970; Maratos and Wilkinson, 1982; Prensky and Sommer, 1979). No clinical or population-based study of children or adolescents has examined the associations between headaches and each of the common Axis I psychiatric disorders. Bille (1962) described children with headaches as having decreased frustration tolerance, more temper tantrums, and more night terrors, but there have been no other studies examining the relationships between headaches in children and distinct externalizing disorders.

A broader study of the association between psychopathology and headaches in a longitudinal population sample of children, using rigorous *DSM* criteria for psychopathology as well as clearly delineated headache criteria, may provide a clearer understanding of the nature of the headache symptoms in relationship to psychopathology. The purposes of this study are to examine (1) the relationships between headaches and a broader range of common psychiatric diagnostic categories; (2) the possibility that there exists a different relationship between headaches and internalizing and externalizing disorders; and (3) whether there might be gender differences in the association between headaches and internalizing and externalizing disorders.

METHOD

Subjects and Procedures

The Great Smoky Mountains Study is a longitudinal study of the development of psychiatric disorders and need for mental health services in rural and urban youths. The details of the study design and instruments used can be found in Costello et al. (1996). Briefly, a representative sample of 4,500 children, aged 9, 11, and 13 years, identified through the Student Information Management System of the public school systems of 11 counties in western North Carolina, was selected using a household equal probability design. A screening questionnaire was administered to a parent (usually the mother), by telephone or in person. This consisted of 55 questions from the Child Behavior Checklist about the child's behavioral problems, together with some basic demographic and service use questions. All children scoring above a predetermined cutoff score of 20 (designed to include about 25% of the population) on the behavioral questions, and a 1-in-10 random sample of those scoring below the cutoff, were recruited for the longitudinal study. The data presented here are from the initial interview (wave 1) and 1-year (wave 2) and 2-year (wave 3) follow-ups. The sample consisted of 1,013 subjects.

Measures

A child and primary caretaker were separately interviewed about the child's psychiatric status and service use with the third edition of the Child and Adolescent Psychiatric Assessment (CAPA) (Angold et al., 1995), which generated *DSM-III-R* diagnoses. The reference period for this instrument was the 3 months prior to the interview.

Child and Adolescent Psychiatric Assessment

The CAPA is an interviewer-based interview which provides a structured questioning scheme that enables interviewers to determine whether symptoms, as defined in an extensive glossary, are present or absent, and to code their frequency, duration, and onset (Angold et al., 1995). Diagnostic 1-week test-retest reliabilities for child self-reports range from

0.55 for conduct disorder (CD) to 1.0 for substance abuse/dependence (κ or intraclass correlation) (Angold and Costello, 1995). Diagnoses and symptom scores are generated by computerized algorithms. As is currently the most usual practice in child and adolescent psychiatric research, a symptom was counted as being present if it was reported by either the parent or child.

Measurement of Headaches

The somatization section of the CAPA includes a number of items relating to headaches. Headaches were coded as present only if they lasted for at least 1 hour and occurred at least once a week during the preceding 3 months. No distinction was made between migrainous and nonmigrainous headaches. For those children who met this criterion, the following parameters were also assessed: (1) headache frequency; (2) headache duration; (3) headache onset; and (4) the impact of headaches on four factors: missing school, consulting a doctor, taking medication, and impairment of functioning at home and school.

Data Analysis

Mixed-effects hierarchical linear modeling served as the basic analytic technique. These models included a random effects component to correct for the covariance of the outcome variable within individuals over repeated observations. We also used "sandwich" variance estimate corrections with population weights to take into account the effects of two-stage sample procedure on both the parameter and variance estimates. The resulting parameters and significance values relating predictor (independent) and outcome (dependent) variables, therefore, represent unbiased general population estimates. For continuous data, such as frequency of headaches, Poisson regression was used, because in all such cases the outcomes were nonnormally distributed with heavy left tails. For binomial outcomes, hierarchical logistic regression was used.

To determine whether there were specific psychiatric diagnoses that were significantly associated with headaches, a mixed-effects hierarchical linear model was developed as follows: "Headaches" was the outcome variable, and predictor variables included depression, anxiety disorders, oppositional defiant disorder (ODD), CD, attention-deficit hyperactivity disorder (ADHD), age, and gender. The depression outcome variable included subjects who met criteria for *DSM-III-R*–defined major depression, dysthymia, or depression not otherwise specified. Anxiety disorders included separation anxiety, avoidant disorder, overanxious disorder, generalized anxiety, simple phobia, social phobia, panic disorder, and agoraphobia, All combinations of the variables, main effects and their multiple interactions, were included. Nonsignificant higher-order interactions were removed first, and terms with the largest, nonsignificant p values were removed from the model serially. Main effects that had been removed earlier were then reentered singly to ensure that they did not belong in the final model. If they remained nonsignificant, they were again removed. The final model contained the variables that were statistically significant (a p value $< .05$). All percentages reported were weighted. Where significant effects of gender were observed, separate models were constructed for girls and boys.

RESULTS

Prevalence of Headaches

The overall prevalence of headaches was 10.3%. Of 2,913 observations, 318 contained reports of headaches that lasted at least 1 hour and occurred at least weekly during the preceding 3 months. One hundred fifty-nine were in boys (10.4% of boys) and 159 were in girls (10.2% of girls). The prevalence of headaches increased substantially with age, with no significant difference between boys and girls (age odds ratio [OR] = 1.3, $p = .0002$).

Headaches and Psychopathology

Of children with a psychiatric diagnosis, 20.5% reported headaches, compared with 9.2% of children without a major psychiatric diagnosis (OR = 2.25, $p = .0004$). When the association of headaches with psychiatric diagnoses was assessed by gender, there was a striking difference between boys and girls. Of girls with at least one psychiatric diagnosis, 30.6% reported headaches ($F_{1,814} = 9.22$, $p = .003$), compared with 9.3% of girls without a psychiatric diagnosis. On the other hand, 13.1% of boys who met criteria for at least one psychiatric diagnosis complained of headaches ($F_{1,1016} = 2.76$, $p = .1$), compared with 9.2% of boys without a psychiatric diagnosis who reported headaches.

Because of this gender difference, separate models of the relationship between headaches and psychopathology were fit for boys and girls. Although age was strongly related to the presence of headaches, the associations between psychiatric diagnoses and headaches were constant across the age range in both genders.

Table 1 shows the prevalence of headaches in boys and girls with and without specific *DSM-III-R*–defined psychiatric diagnoses.

Internalizing Disorders and Headaches in Girls

Depression. Girls who were depressed had nearly a fourfold greater prevalence of headaches than girls who were not depressed (40.8% of depressed girls versus 10.5%

TABLE 1
Prevalence of Headaches in Children With and Without Psychiatric Disorders, by Gender

	Girls				Boys			
Dx	With Dx (%)	Without Dx (%)	OR	*p*	With Dx (%)	Without Dx (%)	OR	*p*
Depression	40.8	10.5	3.71	.02	9.0	9.6	NS	.29
Anxiety disorders	34.1	10.0	2.64	.04	14.4	9.4	NS	.23
CD	21.3	11.1	NS	.29	19.2	9.4	2.15	.03
ODD	30.3	10.7	NS	.13	10.0	9.6	NS	.63
ADHD	20.2	11.0	NS	.41	8.2	9.6	NS	.92

Note: Dx = psychiatric diagnosis; OR = odds ratio; CD = conduct disorder; ODD = oppositional defiant disorder; ADHD = attention-deficit hyperactivity disorder; NS = not significant.

of nondepressed girls had headaches). Depressed girls with headaches had more frequent headaches than did nondepressed girls with headaches (OR = 2.4, p = .0001; mean frequency 7 times/week versus 3 times/week). Seventy-five percent of depressed girls with headaches reported that their headaches occurred more than three times a week, compared with 30% of nondepressed girls with headaches. Depression did not affect the duration of headaches in girls.

Depressed girls with headaches missed school because of their headaches and took medication for their headaches significantly more often than nondepressed girls with headaches. Seventy percent of depressed girls with headaches reported missing school because of their headaches, compared with 13.7% of nondepressed girls with headaches (OR = 19.8, p = .002). Sixty-seven percent of depressed girls with headaches reported taking medication for their headaches, compared with 22.7% of nondepressed girls with headaches (OR = 11.7, p = .01).

Anxiety Disorders. Girls who met criteria for an anxiety disorder had a three times greater rate of headaches than girls who were not anxious (34.1% of girls with an anxiety disorder had headaches, whereas 10% of girls without anxiety disorders had headaches). Neither frequency nor duration of headaches was significantly different for girls with and without anxiety disorders who reported headaches. Moreover, girls with headaches who met criteria for anxiety disorders missed less school (OR = 0.08, p = .02; 4.9% versus 19.3%) and took less medication (OR = 0.18, p = .006; 10% versus 27.9%) than girls with headaches who did not meet criteria for an anxiety disorder.

Despite the significant comorbidity of depression and anxiety disorders in the population and their similar overall association with headaches, these two disorders had very different associations with the effects of headaches. Girls with depression reported more frequent headaches and more severe effects of headaches on their lives than girls with anxiety disorders, suggesting that the association of headaches with depression and anxiety may be distinct phenomena.

Externalizing Disorders and Headaches in Girls

For girls, neither CD, nor ODD, nor ADHD was significantly associated with the presence of headaches. When the three disorders were combined into an overall externalizing disorders variable, they still made no significant contribution to the prevalence of headaches in girls.

Nonetheless, while ODD was not found to be significantly associated with the overall prevalence of headaches in girls, it was associated with the quality and effects of headaches on girls' lives. For example, the headaches of girls with ODD lasted significantly longer than the headaches of girls without ODD (OR 2.3, p = .0004; mean without ODD = 3.5 hours; mean with ODD = 9.1 hours).

Table 2 details the effect of headaches on school attendance and use of medical intervention in girls with and without ODD.

Internalizing Disorders and Headaches in Boys

No aspect of headaches was associated with depression or anxiety in boys.

TABLE 2
Effects of Headaches for Girls With and Without Oppositional
Defiant Disorder

	Headaches With ODD (%)	Headaches Without ODD (%)	OR	p
Missed school because of headaches	52.2	15.5	8.1	.01
Consulted physician about headaches	65.0	19.9	5.0	.001
Took medication for headaches	66.1	23.4	4.1	.003

Note: OR = odds ratio; ODD = oppositional defiant disorder.

Externalizing Disorders and Headaches in Boys

Boys with CD had an increased prevalence of headaches (Table 1). Neither ODD nor ADHD was significantly associated with headaches in boys. If the three disorders are combined into an overall externalizing disorders variable, this summed variable does not have a significant association with the prevalence of headaches in boys.

Boys with headaches and CD were more than twice as likely to have headaches as boys who did not meet criteria for CD (Table 1). Of boys with headaches and CD, 68.8% reported that their headaches significantly interfered with their lives, compared with 31.5% of boys who reported headaches but not CD (OR 9.5, $p = .03$).

No statistically significant relationship between frequency or duration of headaches and any externalizing disorder (CD, ODD, ADHD) was found for boys. Boys with headaches and CD did not miss more school, consult a physician more often, or take more medicine for their headaches than boys with headaches who did not meet criteria for CD.

DISCUSSION

In this general population-based study of children in the rural southeastern United States, we found that 10% of children had headaches that lasted at least 1 hour and occurred at least once a week during the last 3 months. Older children reported more headaches than younger children. Both of these findings are consistent with previous epidemiological studies of migraines in children. A minority of epidemiological studies (Dalsgaard-Nielsen et al., 1970; Mortimer et al., 1992; Vahlquist, 1955) support our finding that gender does not affect headache rates in boys and girls aged 9 to 15 years. Since a clear 3:1 difference in rates of migraines between women and men has been shown, further exploration of the genesis of gender differences in rates of headaches, from a developmental perspective, would be valuable.

Depression and Anxiety Disorders

Although the prevalence rates of headaches were similar for boys and girls, the association between internalizing disorders and headaches was specific to girls. Thus, the interplay of affective disorders and headaches, both of which are twice to three times as common in adult women, appears to begin in childhood.

Girls who met criteria for a depressive disorder had a four times higher prevalence of headaches than did girls who were not depressed. This strong association between severe, recurrent headaches and depressive disorders is consistent with studies in adults (Breslau and Davis, 1992; Merikangas et al., 1990; Moldin et al., 1993) and in adolescents (Pine et al., 1996). Nonetheless, the distinct gender difference found in our sample of children and adolescents has not been previously reported.

Girls with an anxiety disorder had three times as many headaches as girls who did not have an anxiety disorder. This association was not simply the result of comorbidity or mixed depression/anxiety states, as Pine et al. (1996) found. While an association between anxiety disorders and headaches has been shown in the adult literature and suggested in the child and adolescent literature, Bille's (1962) finding that *girls* with migraines were anxious is one of the only studies that hinted at the gender specificity of the association. Our study is the first population-based study of children and adolescents to demonstrate an independent association between *DSM-III-R*–defined anxiety disorders and headaches.

Not only was the association between depressive and anxiety disorders independent, but the duration, frequency, and effect of headaches were very different for depressed girls compared with anxious girls. Depressed girls had more frequent headaches, missed more school, and took more medication for their headaches than girls with headaches who were not depressed. On the other hand, anxious girls missed fewer days of school and took less medication for their headaches than girls with headaches but without an anxiety disorder. Hypotheses about this difference between the headaches of depressed and anxious girls include (1) that frequency and duration of headaches may be shaped by the association with a specific affective disorder and thus may be one determinant of the effect of the headache on functioning; (2) that the experience of both headache pain and the psychic pain of depression intensifies the morbidity of the headaches (Carroll, 1983); and (3) anxious children's temperamental inhibition may interfere with their complaining about their headache pain. The nature of the relationship between affective disorders, quality of headaches, and effects on functioning is an area for future study.

Our findings tend to contradict Merikangas and coworkers' (1990) hypothesis that childhood anxiety leads to headaches which, in turn, trigger the onset of depression. Instead of a linear causality, our findings are more suggestive of a spectrum of associations between headaches and depression and anxiety, with variations in the characteristics of headaches linked with different affective and anxiety symptoms in the two sexes.

Conduct Disorder and Oppositional Disorder

While the child and adolescent literature has examined how headaches affect behavior at home and school, no previous studies have used *DSM* criteria to assess the association of specific externalizing disorders with headaches. Again, we found a distinct gender difference. Boys who met criteria for CD had twice as many headaches as boys without CD.

Girls with externalizing disorders did not have a greater prevalence of headaches. However, oppositional girls reported greater morbidity resulting from headaches than girls without ODD. The lack of an association between CD and headaches in girls may be due to a real gender difference or may be related to the very small number of girls in the sample who met criteria for CD.

Limitations

Most of the psychiatric literature on headaches has focused on the association of migraine headaches with psychopathology, but our headache criteria were not tailored to subcategorize types of headaches. Despite the lack of diagnostic precision, our criteria required sufficiently severe and frequent headaches to encompass the upper end of the spectrum of headache pain, which would include both migrainous and nonmigrainous headaches. By specifying that the headaches needed to occur at least once a week and last for at least 1 hour, we excluded headaches that occurred monthly with menstruation.

Despite the large cohort used in this study, the prevalence of certain disorders, for example CD in girls, was small, reflecting prevalence rates in the population. The sample was also too small to discern differences in children who endorsed headaches at one, two, or all three interviews. Another limitation of design was that "effect on quality of life" was assessed only for children who met criteria for headaches, thus limiting comparison of children with and without headaches on these functional variables. These questions merit further study using more waves of data and/or a larger initial population sample, as well as different variable comparisons from the Great Smoky Mountains database.

Clinical Implications

Many clinicians and some researchers have observed that depressed and anxious children have headaches and other somatic complaints (McCauley et al., 1991). Although the findings of this study are a preliminary exploration of this association, they do raise interesting questions about the role of headaches in the expression of specific psychiatric disorders in children and suggest that further consideration of the inclusion of headache criteria in select psychiatric criteria for children is warranted (Carlson and Kashani, 1988; Ryan et al., 1987). Although clear recommendations cannot be made from this study, our findings suggest that children who present with complaints of recurrent, frequent headaches should be assessed for psychiatric disorders, particularly depression and anxiety in girls and CD in boys. Further clinical studies assessing the effects of treatment for psychiatric disorders on children's headaches are also merited.

Research Implications

The distinct gender differences found in this study are striking. An exploration of the interaction of physiological differences between boys and girls, including hormonal and neurobiological differences, genetic differences, and differing effects of environmental factors including stress, trauma, family disruption, and familial psychopathology, could lead to a more comprehensive understanding of how and why the association of psychopathology with headaches differs for girls and boys.

Several researchers, including Pine et al. (1996), have suggested that CNS serotonergic dysregulation may be a common point of neurotransmitter abnormality in depression, anxiety, and migraines. Evidence for some commonality in their causal pathways includes the following: (1) decreased 5-hydroxyindoleacetic acid (5-HIAA), a market for low CNS serotonin functioning, is found in the CSF of subjects with depression and those with migraines (Mann et al., 1992); and (2) antidepressants that regulate serotonin are used to treat depression, anxiety disorders, headaches, and chronic pain. Our finding that an association exists between headaches and CD in boys and ODD in girls takes this model a step further. Studies have shown that aggression and hostility are associated with decreased levels of 5-HIAA in the CSF and that pharmacological regulation of serotonin can affect hostile and aggressive behavior (Brown et al., 1982; Lidberg et al., 1984; Virkkunen et al., 1987). Linking headaches with externalizing psychiatric symptoms, as well as internalizing symptoms, suggests that CNS serotonergic dysfunction (1) may be a common pathway for multiple interrelated somatic, psychosocial, and behavioral symptoms; and (2) may be expressed differently in boys and girls.

Finally, this study raises broader questions about the association between headaches and other types of somatic pain (Holroyd et al., 1993). Carroll (1983) has provided an integrative model for exploring this association in relation to psychopathology. He postulated that disturbance of the central pain is one of the three main dimensions that results in depression and mania. Disinhibition of central pain regulation underlies the psychic pain of depression and shapes the form of internal thoughts and behavior. This model links functional disturbances back to anatomic sites in the brain and a spectrum of neurotransmitter abnormalities. Common neurotransmitter mediation, as described above with serotonin playing a role in the regulation of headaches, depression, anxiety, aggression, and hostility, may lead not only to an understanding of the anatomical connections between these disorders but also to the development of clinical assessments to measure central pain regulation as it shapes experience and behavior. Carroll (1983) also suggested that one objective of clinical studies could be to develop assessments that specifically define and measure central pain regulation.

This is an important area for future exploration. An understanding of children's experience and perception of pain, the association of pain with children's internal states and external behaviors, as defined both by specific symptom clusters and *DSM*-defined psychopathology, and the effect of environmental factors on this association can inform both the definition and treatment of children's somatic and psychic pain.

REFERENCES

Abu-Arefeh I, Russell G (1995), Prevalence of headache and migraine in schoolchildren. *BMJ* 309:765–769

Andrasik F, Kabela E, Quinn S, Attanasio V, Blanchard EB, Rosenblum EL (1988), Psychological functioning of children who have recurrent migraine. *Pain* 34:43–52.

Angold A, Costello EJ (1995), A test-retest reliability study of child-reported psychiatric symptoms and diagnoses using the Child and Adolescent Psychiatric Assessment (CAPA-C). *Psychol Med* 25:755–762

Angold A, Prendergast M, Cox A, Harrington R, Simonoff E, Rutter M (1995), The Child and Adolescent Psychiatric Assessment (CAPA). *Psychol Med* 25:739–753

Barea LM, Tannhauser M, Rotta NT (1996), An epidemiologic study of headache among children and adolescents of southern Brazil. *Cephalalgia* 16:545–549

Bille B (1962), Migraine in school children: a study of the incidence and short-term prognosis and a clinical, psychological and encephalographic comparison between children with migraine and matched controls. *Acta Paediatr Scand* 51:15

Breslau N, Davis GC (1992), Migraine, major depression and panic disorder: a prospective epidemiologic study of young adults. *Cephalalgia* 12:85–90

Breslau N, Davis GC, Andreski P (1991), Migraine, psychiatric disorders, and suicide attempts: an epidemiologic study of young adults. *Psychiatry Res* 37:11–23

Brown GL, Ebert MH, Goyer PF et al. (1982), Aggression, suicide, and serotonin: relationships to CSF amine metabolites. *Am J Psychiatry* 139:741–746

Burke EC, Peters GA (1956), Migraine in childhood. *Am J Dis Child* 330–336

Carlson GA, Kashani JH (1988), Phenomenology of major depression from childhood through adulthood: analysis of three studies. *Am J Psychiatry* 145:1222–1225

Carroll BJ (1983), Neurobiologic dimensions of depression and mania. In: *The Origins of Depression: Current Concepts and Approaches*, Angst J, ed. Berlin: Springer-Verlag, pp 163–186

Cooper PJ, Bawden HN, Camfield PR, Camfield CS (1987), Anxiety and life events in childhood migraine. *Pediatrics* 79:999–1004

Costello EJ, Angold A, Burns BJ et al. (1996), The Great Smoky Mountains Study of Youth: goals, designs, methods, and the prevalence of *DSM-III-R* disorders. *Arch Gen Psychiatry* 53:1129–1136

Crips AH, Kalucy RS, McGuinness B, Ralph PC, Harris G (1977), Some clinical, social and psychological characteristics of migraine subjects in the general population. *Postgrad Med J* 53:691–697

Cunningham SJ, McGrath PJ, Ferguson HB et al. (1987), Personality and behavioural characteristics in pediatric migraine. *Headache* 21:16–20

Dalsgaard-Nielsen T, Engberg-Pedersen H, Holm HE (1970), Clinical and statistical investigations of the epidemiology of migraine. *Dan Med Bull* 17:138–147

Deubner DC (1977), An epidemiologic study of migraine and headache in 10–20 year olds. *Headache* 17:173–180

Egermark-Eriksson I (1982), Prevalence of headache in Swedish school-children. *Acta Paediatr Scand* 71:135–140

Gladstein J, Holden EW, Peralta L, Raven M (1993), Diagnoses and symptom patterns in children presenting to a pediatric headache clinic. *Headache* 33:497–500

Guidetti V, Fornara R, Ottaviano S, Petrilli A, Seri S, Cortesi F (1987), Personality inventory for children and childhood migraine: a case-controlled study. *Cephalalgia* 7:225–230

Headache Classification Committee of the International Headache Society (1988), Classification and diagnostic criteria for headache disorders, cranial neuralgias and facial pain. *Cephalalgia* 8 (suppl 7):9–28

Holden EW, Gladstein J, Trulsen M, Wall B (1994), Chronic daily headache in children and adolescents. *Headache* 34:508–514

Holroyd KA, France JL, Nash JM, Hursey KG (1993), Pain state as artifact in the psychological assessment of recurrent headache sufferers. *Pain* 53:229–235

Kaiser RS (1992), Depression in adolescent headache patients. *Headache* 32:340–344

Kowal A, Pritchard D (1990), Psychological characteristics of children who suffer from headache: a research note. *J Child Psychol Psychiatry* 31:637–649

Kristjansdottir RN, Wahlberg V (1993), Sociodemographic differences in the prevalence of self-reported headache in Icelandic school-children. *Headache* 33:376–380

Larsson B (1988), The role of psychological, health, behaviour and medical factors in adolescent headache. *Dev Med Child Neurol* 30:616–625

Lidberg L, Asberg M, Sundqvist-Stensman UB (1984), 5-Hydroxyindoleacetic acid levels in attempted suicides who have killed their children. *Lancet* 2:928

Linet MS, Stewart WF, Celentano DD, Ziegler D, Sprecher M (1989), An epidemiologic study of headache among adolescents and young adults. *J Am Acad Child Adolesc Psychiatry* 261:2211–2216

Ling W, Oftedal G, Weinberg N (1970), Depressive illness in children presenting as severe headache. *Am J Dis Child* 120:122–124

Mann JJ, McBridge PA, Brown RP (1992), Relationship between central and peripheral serotonin indexes in depressed and suicidal psychiatric inpatients. *Arch Gen Psychiatry* 49:442–446

Maratos J, Wilkinson M (1982), Migraine in children: a medical and psychiatric study. *Cephalalgia* 2:179–187

McCauley E, Carlson GA, Calderon R (1991), The role of somatic complaints in the diagnosis of depression in children and adolescents. *J Am Acad Child Adolesc Psychiatry* 30:631–635

Merikangas KR, Angst J, Isler H (1990), Migraine and psychopathology: result of the Zurich cohort study of young adults. *Arch Gen Psychiatry* 47:849–853

Merikangas KR, Merikangas JR, Angst J (1993), Headache syndromes and psychiatric disorders: association and familial transmission. *J Psychiatr Res* 27:197–210

Moldin SO, Scheftner WA, Rice JP, Nelson E, Knesevich MA, Akiskal H (1993), Association between major depressive disorder and physical illness. *Psychol Med* 23:755–761

Mortimer MJ, Kay J, Jaron A (1992), Epidemiology of headache and childhood migraine in an urban general practice using ad hoc, Vahlquist and IHS criteria. *Dev Med Child Neurol* 34:1095–1101

Oster J (1972), Recurrent abdominal pain, headache and limb pains in children and adolescents. *Pediatrics* 50:429–436

Passchier J, Orlebeke JF (1985), Headaches and stress in schoolchildren: an epidemiological study. *Cephalalgia* 5:167–177

Paulin JM, Waal-Manning J, Simpson FO, Knight RG (1985), The prevalence of headache in a small New Zealand town. *Headache* 25:147–151

Pine DS, Cohen P, Brook J (1996), The association between major depression and headache: results of a longitudinal epidemiologic study in youth. *J Child Adolesc Psychopharmacol* 6:153–164

Prensky AL, Sommer D (1979), Diagnosis and treatment of migraine in children. *Neurology* 29:506–510

Rothner AD (1995), Pathophysiology of recurrent headaches in children and adolescents. *Pediatr Ann* 24:458

Ryan N, Puig-Antich J, Ambrosini PJ et al. (1987), The clinical picture of major depression in children and adolescents. *Arch Gen Psychiatry* 44:854–861

Sillanpaa M (1983), Prevalence of headache in prepuberty. *Headache* 23:10–14

Solomon S, Lipton RB, Newman LC (1992), Clinical features of chronic daily headache. *Headache* 32:325–329

Stang PE, Osterhaus JT (1993), Impact of migraine in the United States: data from the National Health Interview Survey. *Headache* 33:29–35

Stewart W, Breslau N, Keck JPE (1994), Comorbidity of migraine and panic disorder. *Neurology* 44:S23–S27

Vahlquist B (1955), Migraine in children. *Int Arch Allergy Immunol* 7:348–355

Virkkunen M, Nuutila A, Goodwin FK, Linnoila M (1987), Cerebrospinal fluid monoamine metabolite levels in male arsonists. *Arch Gen Psychiatry* 44:241–247

Wober-Bingol C, Wober C, Wagner-Ennsgraber C et al. (1996), IHS criteria for migraine and tension-type headache in children and adolescents. *Headache* 36:231–238

Wolff H (1937), Personality features and reactions of subjects with migraines. *Arch Neurol Psychiatr* 37:895–921

Part IV

CLINICAL ISSUES

The papers selected for inclusion in this section direct attention to a range of issues that expand our understanding of aspects of the symptomatology and course of psychiatric illness in children. The first paper by Leckman, Zhang, Vitale, Lahnin, Lynch, Kim, and Peterson describes the course of tic severity in Tourette syndrome over the first two decades. Epidemiologic studies have documented a higher prevalence rate of Tourette syndrome (TS) among children as compared with adults. Although a rough time course of tic severity has been described, natural history studies have tended to include patients across a wide age range with widely different follow-up intervals.

Leckman and colleagues have addressed these issues by using data from a single birth-year cohort. Forty-two patients with TS, followed at the Yale Child Study Center, were recontacted an average of 7.3 years after their initial clinical evaluation. A birth cohort made it possible to make developmentally uniform cross-patient comparisons. Thirty-six parents and children participated in a series of semistructured interviews. A range of statistical procedures were used to model these data to provide estimates of the age of tic onset, the age when tics were at their worst, and their relation to the onset of puberty.

In this sample mean tic onset was 5.6+/-2.3 years, followed by a progressive pattern of tic worsening. The most severe period of tic severity occurred at a mean of 10.0+/-2.4 years. In almost 25% of the sample the frequency and forcefulness were sufficiently severe, during the worst ever period that school functioning was significantly compromised. However, in almost all cases, this period was followed by steady improvement. By 18 years of age almost 50% of the cohort was almost completely tic free. Neither the timing or severity of tics was associated with the onset of puberty.

The authors suggest that the explicit model of the time course of tic severity over the first 2 decades of life may well reflect normal biological events that become overtly expressed only because of the patient's TS vulnerability. Although the results of this study extend only through the second decade, they may be relevant to clinical practice. The authors note that many families find comfort in the realization that tic severity will likely decline during adolescence which may increase their ability to "live with tics," thus avoiding the potential adverse side effects of currently available psychotropic medications.

The second paper in this section, which addresses the question of whether multidimensionally impaired disorder is a variant of very early-onset schizophrenia, is one of a series of reports that have emerged from the National Institute of Mental Health (NIMH) clinical and biological studies of very early-onset schizophrenia (VEOS). In the course of screening cases for inclusion in these studies, some 30% of those initially reviewed were found to have complex developmental disorders and brief psychotic symptoms which did not meet DSM-III-R criteria for schizophrenia. This report describes the clinical characteristics of

19 children with atypical psychosis, in this article designated as "multidimensionally impaired" (MDI) and compares them with 29 children with DSM-III-R schizophrenia and 19 children with attention deficit hyperactivity disorder (ADHD).

The clinical characteristics of children with MDI include the following: 1) poor ability to distinguish fantasy from reality as evidenced by ideas of reference and brief perceptual disturbances during stressful periods or while falling asleep; 2) nearly daily periods of emotional lability disproportionate to precipitants; 3) impaired interpersonal skills despite desire to interact socially with peers; 4) multiple deficits in information processing, 5) occurring in the absence of formal thought disorder. Unlike children with ADHD, patients with MDI and patients with VEOS shared a similar pattern of early transient autistic features, post psychotic cognitive decline, and an elevated risk of schizophrenic-spectrum disorders among first-degree relatives. In contrast, the MDI group had significantly poorer scores on the Freedom From Distractibility factor on the WISC-R, a less deviant pattern of autonomic reactivity, and no progression to schizophrenia. The findings are interpreted as supporting the distinction of MDI as separate from other psychiatric disorders, and suggesting that the disorder lies within the schizophrenic spectrum.

Of particular interest is that transient features of pervasive developmental disorder (PDD) were significantly more prevalent in the MDI group than in the VEOS group. Although at the time of initial assessment, only one MDI child still met criteria for PDD, two other children had more than eight autistic symptoms in early childhood which had remitted by school age. This study contributes to the growing awareness that a considerable number of children who display complex developmental disorders and transient psychotic symptoms fall between the cracks of currently defined syndrome boundaries. The systematic description of the developmental, clinical, family history, and biological profile of this subgroup of atypically psychotic children provides a sound basis for further study of prognosis and optimal treatment strategies.

The characterizations of attachment patterns as secure, anxious avoidant, and anxious resistant have long been familiar to researchers and clinicians alike. In 1990, Main and Solomon directed attention to children who exhibited a diverse array of inexplicably disorganized, disorientated, and seemingly undirected or conflicting behavioral responses to the presence of the caregiver in the laboratory assessment of attachment, the Strange Situation. In the third paper in this section Elizabeth Carlson reports the results of a prospective longitudinal study of attachment disorganization/disorientation from a prospective longitudinal perspective. The report is based on data derived from the ongoing investigation of 157 participants in a larger longitudinal study of children and families whose mothers were recruited while receiving prenatal care at public health clinics in Minneapolis in 1975. In this study, attachment assessments were conducted using Ainsworth's Situation procedure (Ainsworth et al., 1978) at 12 and at 18 months. Videotaped Strange Situation assessments were reliably coded for attachment disorganization/disorientation using the classification scheme developed by Main and Solomon (1990). Disorganization/disorientation in infant-parent attachment was rated on a 9 point scale, and a disorganized/disoriented classification assigned to infant-mother dyads receiving a rating of 5 or higher. Other available data permitted the examination of relations between attachment disorganization/disorientation to endogenous (e.g., maternal medical history, infant temperament) and environmental (e.g., maternal caregiving quality, infant history of abuse) antecedents and to behavioral consequences from 24 months to 19 years.

With respect to antecedents, attachment disorganization was associated with single parenthood and with maternal risk for parenting difficulties. Infants with high ratings of disorganization were more likely to have experienced insensitive/intrusive caregiving as well as a variety of forms of maltreatment in the first year of life. Attachment disorganization was not associated with maternal history of serious medical or psychological problems, complications of pregnancy or delivery, reported maternal history of drug or alcohol use or infant anomalies, Brazelton scores at birth, or infant temperament at 3 months. Consequent variables included mother-child relationship quality at 24 and 42 months, child behavior problems in preschool, elementary school and high school and psychopathology and dissociation in adolescence. Structural equation models suggest that disorganization may mediate the relations between early experience and later psychopathology.

The data of the present study provide support for the validity of the rating of attachment disorganization/disorientation. However, as the authors point out, the relations reported in this study are relatively modest. Correlations from .20 to .40 between attachment disorganization/disorientation account for between 4% and 16% of the variance in the expression of outcome variables. Nevertheless, these results are consistent with the growing conviction, expressed by both clinicians and researchers alike, that disorganization is an attachment domain with potential implications for social behavior and psychopathology.

In the final paper in this section Bates, Dodge, Pettit, and Ridge explore the interaction of temperamental resistance to control and restrictive parenting in the development of externalizing behavior. The authors take as the starting point for the two investigations summarized in this report, Thomas and Chess' (1977) conceptualization of goodness of fit between a child's temperament and the expectations and resources of the child's home and schools. Theoretically, temperament does not lead to behavior problems by itself; it does so only in conjunction with particular environmental conditions. Consequently, in this report, child temperament and parental control were studied as interacting predictors of behavior outcomes.

The importance of replication in specifying interaction effects is underscored. Consequently, in the present report data deriving from two longitudinal studies were examined. In sample 1, which consisted of a core group of 90 children, data were ratings of resistant temperament and observed restrictive control during the first two years of life and ratings of externalizing behavior by parents and teachers at ages 7 to 10 years. In Sample 2 data included retrospective ratings of temperament during infancy and toddlerhood made in 156 children, observed parental restrictive control at age 5 years, and ratings of externalizing behavior at ages 7 to 11 years.

In both studies, the temperamental construct of impulsivity–unmanageability was operationalized as parental reports on a scale of resistance to control, As with any operational measure of temperament, parental reports of resistance to control reflect more than a purely biological definition of temperament. Nevertheless, contaminating factors are not so large as to eclipse the components of both stable and developmentally unfolding biologically rooted temperament and associated fundamental neural systems. The construct, maternal restrictive control, was derived from multivariate analyses of home observation data. This measure captures behaviors intended to stop or to punish the child, such as giving negative commands, removing objects from the child, scolding or spanking. However, elements of harsh punishment were not strongly indexed as observations of angry scolding or actual spanking were seldom directly observed.

In both samples, the temperamental resistance to control was more strongly related to externalizing behavior in children whose mother's were observed to be relatively low in control actions than when she had been high in control actions. The pattern was evident whether child outcome was measured at home or at school, and appeared not to be attributable to chance, distributional confounds, gender or SES. The authors provide a thoughtful discussion of two related questions: 1) how does the mother–child interaction affect the linkage of temperament and externalizing behavior; and 2) how does child temperament moderate linkage between parenting and child behavior? The report provides a timely update of many of the salient issues in temperament research as well as expanding understanding of the circumstances in which particular temperamental constellations may result in increased risk of psychiatric disorder in children and adolescents.

REFERENCES

Ainsworth, MDS., Blehar, M., Waters, E., Wall, S. (1978). *Patterns of Attachment.* Hillsdale, NJ: Erlbaum

Main, M., & Solomon, J. (1990) Procedures for identifying infants as disorganized/disoriented during the Ainsworth Strange Situation. In M. T. Greenberg, D. Chichetti, & E. M. Cummings (Eds.) *Attachment in the preschool years.* (pp. 121–160) Chicago: University of Chicago Press.

Thomas, A., & Chers, S. (1977). *Temperament and development.* New York: Brunner/Mazel.

PART IV: CLINICAL ISSUES

13

Course of Tic Severity in Tourette Syndrome: The First Two Decades

**James F. Leckman, MD*; Heping Zhang, PhD‡; Amy Vitale, BA*;
Fatima Lahnin, BA*; Kimberly Lynch, MSN*; Colin Bondi, MA*;
Young-Shin Kim, MD*; and Bradley S. Peterson, MD***

Objective: *Prevalence studies indicate a 10-fold higher rate of Tourette syndrome (TS) among children compared with adults. The purpose of this investigation was to examine the course of tic severity during the first 2 decades of life.* **Method:** *A birth-year cohort of 42 TS patients followed at the Yale Child Study Center was recontacted an average of 7.3 years after their initial clinical evaluation. Data concerning the onset and course of tic severity until 18 years of age were available on 36 TS patients. A variety of statistical techniques were used to model aspects of the temporal patterning of tic severity.* **Results:** *Mean (SD) tic onset at 5.6 (2.3) years of age was followed by a progressive pattern of tic worsening. On average, the most severe period of tic severity occurred at 10.0 (2.4) years of age. In eight cases (22%), the frequency and forcefulness of the tics reached a severe level during the worst-ever period such that functioning in school was impossible or in serious jeopardy. In almost every case this period was followed by a steady decline in tic severity. By 18 years of age nearly half of the cohort was virtually tic-free. The onset of puberty was not associated with either the timing or severity of tics.* **Conclusions:** *A majority*

ABBREVIATIONS. TS, Tourette syndrome; YCSC, Yale Child Study Center Tic Disorders Clinic; ADHD, attention deficit-hyperactivity disorder; OCD, obsessive-compulsive disorder; CGI, Clinical Global Impression (scale); SES, socioeconomic status; YGTSS, Yale Global Tic Severity Scale; ARRTS, annual rating of relative tic severity; STOBS-R, Schedule for Tourette and Other Behavioral Syndromes, Adult-on-Child Version, Revised; MSRPF, Modified Schedule for Risk and Protective Factors.

From the *Child Study Center, the Children's Clinical Research Center, and the Departments of Pediatrics and Psychiatry; and the ‡Division of Biostatistics, the Department of Epidemiology and Public Health, Yale University School of Medicine, New Haven, Connecticut.

Received for publication Jul 22, 1997; accepted Dec 9, 1997.

Reprint requests to (J.F.L.) Child Study Center, Yale University School of Medicine, PO Box 207900, New Haven, CT 06520-7900.

Address correspondence to: James F. Leckman, MD, Neison Harris Professor of Child Psychiatry and Pediatrics, Rm I-269 SHM, Child Study Center, Yale University School of Medicine, PO Box 207900, New Haven, CT 06520-7900.

of TS patients displayed a consistent time course of tic severity. This consistency can be accurately modeled mathematically and may reflect normal neurobiological processes. Determination of the model parameters that describe each patient's course of tic severity may be of prognostic value and assist in the identification of factors that differentially influence the course of tic severity. Pediatrics *1998;102:14–19;* **Key Words** Tourette syndrome, natural history, growth curve analysis, puberty.

Epidemiologic studies have indicated a higher prevalence rate of Tourette syndrome (TS) among children compared with adults. In children, prevalence rates as high as 50 per 10,000 have been reported.[1,2] Studies of adolescents and young adults have reported lower rates in the range 0.5 to 4.3 per 10,000.[3–5] In the one study that ascertained rates for both children and adults, using identical methods, a 10-fold difference was observed.[4,6] The reasons underlying this change in prevalence are not well-understood but likely reflect age-related variations in the natural history of the disorder that directly affect case ascertainment.[7,8]

By early adulthood, follow-up studies have consistently reported improvement in tic severity for a majority of TS patients.[9–11] Although a rough time course of tic severity has emerged, age-specific estimates of tic severity have not been reported. Typically, natural history studies of TS have included patients across a broad age range with widely varying follow-up intervals.[12] This cross-sectional, observational approach combined with the failure of most studies to identify key time points in the course of tic severity has made cross-patient comparisons difficult.

Gender- and stress-related hormonal factors have been implicated in the pathogenesis of TS.[13–16] Although speculation has focused on the role of gonadal androgens during the earliest stages of central nervous system (CNS) development in utero,[16,17] anecdotal case reports and evidence from clinical trials with antiandrogens support the view that alterations in the hormonal milieu during adolescence and adulthood can modulate tic severity.[18–20]

The present study was undertaken to document the time course of tic severity during the first 2 decades of life using data from a single birth-year cohort of TS patients. A birth cohort was selected to maximize our ability to make developmentally uniform cross-patient comparisons. In our analytic approach, we used a variety of statistical procedures to model these data to estimate the age of tic onset, the age when the tics were at their worst, as well as other model parameters. This model was then used to evaluate the a priori hypothesis that pubertal onset is associated with either the timing or degree of worst-ever tic severity.

METHOD

Subjects

Subjects in this study consisted of 36 patients with TS who had been diagnosed and evaluated at the Yale Child Study Center (YCSC) Tic Disorders Clinic. Subjects were selected on the basis of their participation in a case-control study of TS in which extensive data were collected concerning the time course of tic severity. This study identified all TS patients born in 1975 who had ever been evaluated at this YCSC clinic. All patients were initially diagnosed with the *Diagnostic and Statistical Manual of Mental Disorders*, 3rd ed (DSM-III) or 3rd ed, revised criteria for TS using previously described methods.[21] A total of 42 TS cases were ascertained. Of this number, 36 cases (86%) had sufficient information to be included in these analyses (32 males and 4 females).

Procedures and Measures

Demographic and clinical information was collected from four sources: the clinic chart, a preliminary telephone interview with a parent, two in-person interviews with a parent, and an in-person interview of the TS patient.

Chart review. A clinician with extensive experience with TS families (K.L.) abstracted information from the clinical record using a precoded form. Data recorded included demographic information; diagnostic status with regard to TS, attention deficit-hyperactivity disorder (ADHD), obsessive-compulsive disorder (OCD), and other comorbid conditions; and age of onset and severity at presentation of TS, ADHD, and OCD. Severity ratings were made using eight point ordinal Clinical Global Impression (CGI) scales previously developed at the YCSC for each of these disorders.[21] Relevant points on the TS-CGI scale include: *mild severity*, where the tic symptoms are judged not to interfere and not to be noticeable to most people; *moderate severity*, where the tics cause some problems in some areas of functioning (self-esteem, home life, peers relations, and/or school performance) and are noticeable to some people outside the family some of the time; *marked severity*, where the tic symptoms cause clear problems in more than one area of functioning and are frequent and quite noticeable in most situations most of the time; and *severe*, where the tic symptoms because of their frequency and forcefulness cause significant impairment in one or more area, such that functioning in usual settings is impossible or in serious jeopardy.

One clinic chart could not be located, but the case was clearly identified in the clinic roster permitting the case to be recontacted. In 10 randomly selected cases, another member of the research team (J.F.L.) independently reviewed the same record. Comparisons of age at evaluation, diagnostic status, age of onset, and scores on the respective CGI scales revealed a high level of agreement (Pearson correlations for age of tic onset and age at evaluation were $r = 0.98$ and $r = 0.83$, respectively). The interrater agreement for a diagnosis of TS was perfect, and the κ statistic values for the *Diagnostic and Statistical Manual of Mental Disorders*, 4th ed (DSM-IV) diagnoses of OCD and ADHD were excellent (0.83 and 0.77, respectively). The Spearman rank order correlations for the CGI scores were also excellent (ranging from $\rho = 0.79$ to $\rho = 1.00$). A comparison of data abstracted from the initial clinic evaluations of the 36 cases included in this analysis and the 6 remaining cases revealed no statistically significant differences with regard to age at evaluation, sex, socioeconomic status (SES), age of tic onset, or tic severity at initial evaluation.

Initial follow-up interview. After an initial letter describing the study and requesting consent, parents were contacted by telephone and inquiries were made concerning current demographic information; the history of the family's contact with the YCSC Tic Disorders Clinic; data concerning their child's tic disorder (age of onset, age when tics were at their most severe, medication history, and a rating of current tic severity using the Yale Global Tic Severity Scale [YGTSS][22]; comparable data concerning ADHD and OCD; and data concerning the onset and duration of puberty). The YGTSS is a standard clinical rating instrument for TS with excellent interrater agreement and other favorable psychometric properties including a high correlation with the TS-CGI scale.[22] A slightly modified and expanded form of the YGTSS was used in the telephone interview portion of the study.[23] This version has previously been shown to have a high level of agreement with YGTSS ratings independently made by experienced clinicians.[23] At the conclusion of the interview, families were invited to participate in a more in-depth in-person interview to take place in the family's home. Interviewers were blinded to the information abstracted from the chart record.

Parent interviews. After signed informed consent, parents participated in four semistructured in-person interviews. In the first interview, parents again reported on the course of their child's tic disorder (ratings of current and worst-ever tic severity using the YGTSS, annual rating of relative tic severity (ARRTS) using a 6-point ordinal scale (absent, least severe, mild, moderate, severe, and most severe) from which age of tic onset, and age of most severe tic symptoms were transcribed, and a current medication history). During the second interview, parents reported on comorbid conditions using a semistructured interview, the Schedule for Tourette and Other Behavioral Syndromes, Adult-on-Child Version, Revised (STOBS-R) that has been extensively used in family-genetic studies.[24,25] The STOBS-R also contains information concerning the onset of puberty. The third interview focused on putative risk factors, a main focus of the formal case control study, and used the Modified Schedule for Risk and Protective Factors (MSRPF) developed by John T. Walkup, J. F. L., and B. S. P.[26] In the final interview, parents were asked about their own tic histories as well as other psychopathology using the STOBS-R, child version. Because of the requirements of the case control study, different interviewers conducted the MSRPF and remained blinded to the information concerning tic severity. The results of the case-control aspects of this study will be reported elsewhere.

Patient interview. The TS patient was interviewed in-person using the STOBS-R. This information was supplemented by current and worst-ever ratings of tic severity based on the YGTSS.

Best estimate diagnoses. All available diagnostic information on TS patients and their parents were blindly and independently evaluated by two investigators (J.F.L. and B.S.P.). The resulting DSM-IV diagnostic ratings were compared and discrepancies were resolved using a previously described consensus procedure.[27]

Data Analysis

Data analysis was conducted in several stages. An initial aim was to describe the sample and compare ratings across the three time points (clinical evaluation, initial follow-up interview, and in-person interviews with parents and patients). The test-retest reliability of key ratings of tic onset, timing of worst-ever tic severity, current and worst-ever tic severity (using the YGTSS) were then evaluated in an effort to validate the ARRTS.

Examination of the time course of the tic severity curves derived from the ARRTS ratings for individual TS patients led to the development of a mathematical model of tic severity characterized by the identification of an initial point of tic onset, followed by a period of increasing tic severity, followed by an inflection point (corresponding to the period of worst-ever tic severity), after which the tic severity steadily declined. A statistical bootstrapping technique was then used to assess the variability of the estimates for each model parameter.[28]

Once this model was established, the hypothesis that the course of tic severity is related to the timing of puberty onset was evaluated by including the main effect of the age of puberty onset and its interaction terms in the model. This computation was carried out in SAS using PROC MIXED (SAS, Cary, NC).

RESULTS

On average, the 36 members of the YCSC 1975 birth cohort were evaluated at age 11.0 years (range: 5.9–16.9; SD: 2.9). The initial telephone follow-up interview occurred when the TS patients were, on average, 17.7 years of age (range: 17–20; SD: 0.7); and the in-person interviews with the parents and the TS patients took place when the patients were, on average, 18.4 years of age (range: 17–20; SD: 1.0). The average interval between the initial YCSC evaluation and the in-person interviews was 7.5 years (range: 1.2–12.1; SD: 2.7). All 36 patients met DSM-IV criteria for Tourette disorder. Of this number, 25 (69%) met lifetime DSM-IV criteria for ADHD (combined type–16 (44%), inattentive type–8 (22%), and hyperactive/impulsive type–1 (3%)). Another 13 (36%) cases met lifetime DSM-IV criteria for OCD. Most of the families were middle-class. The mean SES status of the families was 47.9 (range: 27–64; SD: 10.6).

Current Tic Status

At the time of the in-person interviews, when the TS patients were 18 years of age, tic symptoms for a majority of the 36 cases were minimal or absent. On average, the total tic score of the YGTSS assessed at the time of the in-person interviews with the parents and patients was 7.92 (actual range: 0–30 [possible range: 0–50]; SD: 9.53). Seventeen patients (47.2%) were entirely tic-free during the week before the in-person interviews. Another 4 patients (11.1%) had minimal tic symptoms (YGTSS total tic score of <10). Ten patients (27.7%) had mild symptoms (YGTSS total tic score of ≥10 but <20), and only 4 patients (11.1%) were judged to have a moderate or marked level of tic severity (YGTSS total tic score of ≥20 but <40).

Severity and Timing of Tics During the Worst Period

On average, the worst-ever total tic score on the YGTSS estimated at the time of the in-person interview was 29.8 (range: 4–49; SD: 10.9). Based on the frequency and forcefulness of their tics, 8 patients (22.2%) were judged during their worst period to have severe tics (YGTSS total tic scores ≥40 but <50) that were associated with a significant impairment in their primary social role such that functioning in usual settings was impossible or placed in serious jeopardy. Ten patients (27.8%) were judged during their worst period to have marked tic severity (tics frequent and quite noticeable in most situations most of the time; YGTSS total tic scores ≥30 but <40). Fourteen patients (38.9%) were judged during their

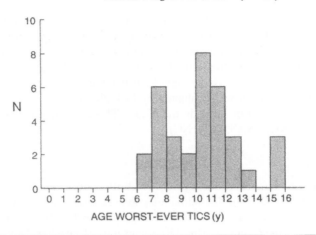

Figure 1. Age distribution of when tic symptoms were at their worst. This histogram presents the age at worst-ever tics as reported by parents during in-person interview.

worst period to have moderate tic severity (tics cause some problems and are noticeable to some people some of the time; YGTSS total tic scores ≥ 20 but <30). Only 4 patients (4.0%) were judged to have a mild level of tic severity during their worst period (YGTSS total tic score of <20).

Based on data collected during the initial telephone follow-up and the in-person interviews, the worst tics occurred between the ages of 6 and 15 years (mean: 10.0; SD: 2.4). Figure 1 presents a histogram of these data by year. The level of tic severity during the worst period was positively associated with the patient's age during the worst-ever period (Fig 2; Pearson $r = 0.58$, $N = 34$, $P < .0001$).

Predictive Value of Earlier Estimates of Tic Severity

Nine cases were judged to have mild tics during their initial clinic evaluation. Among this group, 3 cases continued to have only mild symptoms during their worst period. In each of these cases, no tics were evident at the time in-person interviews. In another 4 of the initially mild cases, their worst-ever tic severity was rated as moderate, and at the time of the in-person interviews tics were either absent ($N = 2$), minimal ($N = 1$), or mild ($N = 1$). Surprisingly, 2 cases judged to have mild tic severity at their YCSC evaluation were judged to have severe tic severity during their worst period, but fortunately in both cases at the time of the in-person interviews, their tic symptoms were either mild ($N = 1$) or moderate ($N = 1$) in severity.

Sixteen cases were judged to have moderate tic severity at the time of their initial YCSC evaluation. Among this group, 7 cases were judged to have either moderate ($N = 6$) or mild ($N = 1$) tic severity at the time of their worst symptoms. At the time of the in-person interviews, 5 of these cases were tic-free, 1 case had mild symptoms, and only 1 case continued with a moderate level of tic severity.

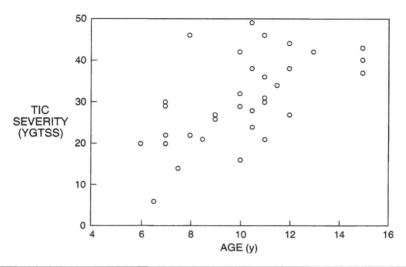

Figure 2. Association of age and level of worst-ever tic severity. This scattergram plots worst-ever tic severity versus age at worst-ever tic severity and suggests a positive association between these variables (Pearson r: 0.58, $N = 34$, $P < .0001$).

Of the 9 initially moderate cases remaining, 6 were judged to have marked tic severity during their worst period and 3 were judged to have severe tics. In this subgroup at the time of the in-person interviews, 1 case showed no tic symptoms, 3 had minimal symptoms, 4 had mild, and only 1 case continued with a moderate level of tic severity.

Ten cases presented at the time of their initial YCSC evaluation with a marked level of tics. Seven of these cases were judged to have either moderate ($N = 3$) or marked ($N = 4$) tic severity at the time of their worst symptoms. In this subgroup, 3 cases were tic-free at the time of the in-person interviews, three cases were rated as having mild tic severity, and in only 1 case did the tic severity remain at a marked level. The 3 remaining cases with marked severity at the time of their initial evaluation all had severe tic symptoms during their worst period. Remarkably, 2 of these cases showed no tic symptoms during their in-person interviews, and the remaining case had a mild level of tic severity at follow-up.

Tic severity at initial YCSC evaluation was not related to worst or current tic severity (worst: $F = 2.66$, $df = 2$, NS; current: $F = 0.05$, $df = 2$, NS). However, current tic severity was significantly correlated with both tic severity at the time of the initial telephone follow-up interview (Pearson $r = 0.66$, $P < .0001$) and with worst tic severity (Pearson $r = 0.37$, $N = 36$, $P < .03$).

Time Course of Tic Severity Ratings

A majority of TS patients displayed a consistent time course of tic severity. This consistency can be accurately modeled mathematically and may reflect normal biological processes that occur during the course of brain development. Using the ARRTS data collected at

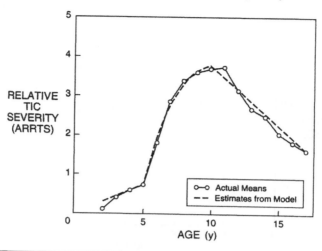

Figure 3. Plot of mean tic severity, ages 2 to 18 years. The solid line connecting the small circles plots the means of the annual rating of relative tic severity scores (ARRTS) recorded by the parents. The dashed line was generated using the modeling equations (Table 1) and the mean values for each of the coefficients and intercepts as determined by a statistical bootstrapping technique. Two inflection points are evident that correspond to the age of tic onset and the age at worst-ever tic severity, respectively.

the time of the in-person interviews, individual growth curves of tic severity were generated. Figure 3 presents the mean and SDs of these curves.

In an effort to validate key points along this composite curve, test-retest comparisons were made between the age of onset estimates made at the time of the initial YCSC evaluation, at the initial telephone follow-up interview, and the onset point derived from the ARRTS curves. The mean values for each of these estimates showed a high level of agreement (mean [SD] age of tic onset; estimated from the chart review: 5.8 years (1.7); from the initial telephone follow-up interview: 5.8 years (2.8); and from the ARRTS curves: 6.0 (2.7)). The test-retest reliability of these estimates was reasonably good (ARRTS estimate vs initial telephone follow-up: Pearson $r = 0.67$, $N = 31$, $P < .0001$; and ARRTS estimate vs chart review data: Pearson $r = 0.58$, $N = 32$, $P < .0001$). Fewer estimates were available to judge the test-retest reliability of the age of worst tic symptoms. The mean values for each of these estimates showed a good level of agreement (mean [SD] age of worst tic severity estimated from the initial telephone follow-up interview: 10.0 years (2.4); and from the ARRTS curves: 10.8 (3.1)). However, the test-retest reliability of these estimates, was only fair (ARRTS estimate vs initial telephone follow-up: Pearson $r = 0.48$, $N = 31$, $P < .007$).

Descriptively in 2 of the TS cases, the ARRTS curves had 2 points of maximal severity (relative tic severity = 5) separated by a period of 1 year or longer when the symptoms were not as severe. In both cases, rather than taking a mean value of these 2 points (and by doing so identifying a point in time when their tics were not as bad as either of the worst-ever points) a convention was established so that a worst-ever time point was selected on the

TABLE 1

Parameters for the Time Course of Tic Severity Function

Parameters	Mean (SD)
Age at onset (τ_1)	4.8 (0.50)
Age when tics were at their worst (τ_2)	9.9 (0.85)
Onset slope (α)	0.15 (0.05)
Intercept for quadratic function (β_0)	−11.9 (8.6)
Ascending slope (β_1)	3.5 (2.4)
Ascending quadratic coefficient (β_2)	−0.19 (0.16)
Intercept for linear decline (γ_0)	6.5 (1.1)
Slope for linear decline (γ_1)	0.29 (0.07)

basis of which period was of the longer duration. In another 5 cases, parents identified relative maximums in tic severity (relative tic severity <5) indicating a fluctuating course.

Mathematical Model of the Time Course of Tic Severity

Given the consistent time course of tic severity across patients, we formulated a mathematical model to describe precisely this pattern. This process is akin to comparing a patient's growth curve for height or weight to a composite curve for a larger number of patients. Based on an examination of the individual and composite ARRTS plots, the ARRTS data were partitioned into three segments. Let t denote age in years. The tic time course, $f(t)$ is characterized by:

$$f(t) = \begin{cases} \alpha t & \text{if } t \leq \tau_1 \\ \beta_0 + \beta_1 t + \beta_2 t^2 & \text{if } \tau_1 < t \leq \tau_2 \\ \gamma_0 + \gamma_1 t & \text{if } t > \tau_2 \end{cases} \tag{1}$$

where τ_1 refers to the age-at-onset and τ_2 is closely related, but not necessarily equal, to the age at which their tics were at their worst. Table 1 displays the parameter distributions of the tic time course function obtained from the bootstrap procedure.[28] A plot of this function is included in Fig 3. Individual growth curves were also generated. Mean values for each of the parameters obtained from individual curves were in close agreement with estimates obtained by bootstrap methods.

Timing of the Onset of Puberty and the Course of Tic Severity

The present study was undertaken, in part, to evaluate the a priori hypothesis that pubertal onset is associated with the period of worst-ever tic severity. This hypothesis was not supported in this group of patients. Age at pubertal onset was not associated with the age when the tics were at their worst ($r = 0.02$, NS) or degree of worst-ever tic severity ($r = 0.08$, NS). Similarly, when the timing of puberty onset was included in the time course model (Fig. 3), neither its main effect nor its interactions with any of the other parameters were significant.

In an effort to validate the age of pubertal onset, test-retest comparisons were made between the age of pubertal onset estimates made at the time of the initial telephone follow-up interview and during the in-person parental interview. The mean values for each of these estimates showed a high level of agreement (mean [SD] age of puberty onset: estimated from the initial telephone follow-up interview: 13.0 years (1.3); and the direct parental interview: 13.7 (1.7)). The test-retest reliability of these estimates was also reasonably good (direct parental interview estimate vs initial telephone follow-up: Pearson $r = 0.67$, $N = 31$, $P < .0001$).

DISCUSSION

The natural history of TS and other chronic tic disorders is not well-understood. In this report we present an explicit model of the time course of tic severity over the first 2 decades of life. This model extends the findings of previous follow-up studies by offering age-specific tic severity estimates and by defining a period of maximal tic severity that usually occurs between the ages of 8 and 12.[7-11] If confirmed, this pattern of ascending severity followed by a near linear decline may also clarify the differences in TS prevalence that are found when adult versus child populations are studied using similar methods.[4,6] By early adulthood, tic severity may have declined sufficiently that a TS diagnosis may no longer be warranted.

Before discussing the clinical implications of this study and its potential value, we should take note of its limitations. Recall bias may have influenced the parents' and the patients' reporting. Our use of test-retest procedures to determine the reliability of key informants and the use of blinded interviews of multiple informants (parents vs patients) support the accuracy of our findings. The documented decline in the YGTSS ratings from the initial telephone follow-up to the time of the in-person interviews directly supports the validity of the ARRTS ratings. Likewise, the consistency of the parental reports (in only 3 cases was there an inconsistency between the level of tic severity observed at evaluation and the family's estimate of tic severity during the worst period) lends support to validity of the time course of tic severity that emerges from this report.

A limitation concerning the mathematical modeling approach is that in a small number of cases ($N = 2$) more than one worst-ever time point was reported. In 5 other cases, relative maximums in tic severity were reported. Rather than seeing these as exceptional cases, it is probably better to consider the unimodal distributions of relative tic severity (seen in all the remaining cases) as being composed of multiple relative maximums in tic severity that are undetectable at this level of temporal scaling. This view is supported by the well-known waxing and waning pattern of tics that occur over weeks to months. This discussion raises the potentially important point that the temporal occurrence of tics may be determined by nonlinear dynamical processes.[29] One of the characteristic features of these nonlinear, chaotic, systems is that they are fractal in nature—that regardless of the temporal scaling (seconds, hours, weeks, months, years) a similar bursting intermittency is evident.[30] The tics occur in bouts, the bouts of tics occur in larger superbouts, and so forth. Viewed from this perspective, the unimodal tic severity curves seen in this study may be a reflection of the same processes that underlie both the occurrence of tics in bouts (temporal scaling at the level of seconds and milliseconds) and their waxing and waning pattern (temporal scaling at the level of weeks to months).

The processes that underlie tic onset and the usual time course of tic severity are largely unknown. Hormonal and neurochemical factors active early in CNS development have been the subject of speculation.[16,17,31] For example, exposure of the developing CNS to gonadal steroids has been implicated.[17–19] Although indirect evidence from this study may argue against increasing levels of gonadal androgens during male pubescence as a major risk factor for tic exacerbation, the complexity of hormonally mediated events in the brain surrounding adrenarche and puberty urge caution.[32] The consistency of the pattern observed across patients strongly suggests the presence of an underlying process. It is intriguing to speculate that this time course may reflect neurobiological events that normally occur during the course of brain development and that are overtly expressed only because of the patient's TS vulnerability.

Caution is warranted in the interpretation of the data concerning puberty onset because these data were not ascertained directly by physical examination or Tanner staging. If confirmed in subsequent studies, the data presented in this report may influence clinical practice. In our experience, families find comfort in the realization that tic severity will likely decline through adolescence. Such knowledge is likely to help families and pediatricians live with the tics and to delay the decision to begin psychotropic medications. Ages 8 through 12 are likely to be critical. If medications can be avoided through this period, the patient may have a good chance of never needing them. Although anti-tic medications are available, none are ideal. Over the longer term, starting medications may do more harm than good, given their potential adverse effects and the difficulties associated with medication withdrawal. This is particularly true of the standard neuroleptic agents such as haloperidol and pimozide.[33]

As discussed by Goetz and co-workers,[8] it is important to be mindful that tic severity early on is not necessarily a good predictor of later tic severity. For example, 20% of the mild cases at clinic evaluation went on to have severe tics. More importantly, 90% of the patients with marked tic severity at evaluation had mild or no tics by 18 years of age. The finding of an association between age of the patient when their tics were at their worst and the level of tic severity during that same period may have limited predictive value except when older adolescents present with severe tic symptoms—heralding a relatively poor prognosis.

The results of this study only extend to the end of the second decade. A minority of TS patients go on to have catastrophic outcomes in adulthood. Whether any of the parameters examined in this study have predictive value for the early identification of these individuals awaits further investigation.

ACKNOWLEDGMENTS

This research was supported by a grant from the March of Dimes (to B.S.P) and National Institutes of Health Grants MH-01232, MH-49351, MH-44843, MH-30929, HD-03008, HD-30712, and RR-06022.

We thank Drs Christopher R. Canny, Priscilla F. Canny, Donald J. Cohen, Diane Findley, Robert A. King, Robert A. Makuch, David L. Pauls, and Lawrence Scahill, and Sharon Ort for their assistance and comments on an earlier draft of this report.

REFERENCES

1. Comings DE, Hames JA, Comings BG. An epidemiological study of Tourette's syndrome in a single school district. *J Clin Psychiatry*. 1990;51:463–469

2. Nomoto F, Machiyama Y. An epidemiological study of tics. *Japan J Psychiatry Neurol*. 1990;44:649–655

3. Apter A, Pauls D, Bleich A, et al. An epidemiological study of Gilles de la Tourette's syndrome in Israel. *Arch Gen Psychiatry*. 1993;50:734–738

4. Burd L, Kerbeshian L, Wikenheiser M, et al. A prevalence study of Gilles de la Tourette's syndrome in North Dakota school-age children. *J Am Acad Child Psychiatry*. 1986;25:552–553

5. Robertson MM, Verrill M, Mercer M, Pauls DL. Tourette's syndrome in New Zealand: a postal survey. *Br J Psychiatry*. 1994;164:263–266

6. Burd L, Kerbeshian L, Wikenheiser M, et al. Prevalence of Gilles de la Tourette's syndromes in North Dakota adults. *Am J Psychiatry*. 1986;143:787–788

7. Erenberg G, Cruse RP, Rothner AD. The natural history of Tourette's syndrome: a follow-up study. *Ann Neurol*. 1987;22:383–385

8. Goetz CG, Tanner CM, Stebbins GT, Leipiz G, Carr WC. Adult tics in Gilles de la Tourette's syndrome: description and risk factors. *Neurology*. 1992;42:784–788

9. Bruun RD. The natural history of Tourette's syndrome. In: Cohen DJ, Bruun R, Leckman JF, eds. *Tourette's Syndrome and Tic Disorders: Clinical Understanding and Treatment*. New York, NY: John Wiley & Sons; 1988:21–39

10. Sandor P, Musisi S, Moldofsky H. Lang A. Tourette's syndrome: a follow-up study. *J Clin Psychopharmacol*. 1990;10:197–199

11. Torup E. A follow-up study of children with tics. *Acta Paediatr*. 1962;51:261–268

12. Kim YS, Leckman JF. Tics and Tourette's syndrome. In: Steinhausen H-C, Verhulst F, eds. *Risks and Outcomes in Developmental Psychopathology*. New York, NY: Oxford University Press. In press

13. Chappell PB, Riddle MA, Anderson GM, et al. Enhanced stress responsivity of Tourette's syndrome patients undergoing lumbar puncture. *Biol Psychiatry*. 1994;36:35–43

14. Leckman JF, Goodman WK, Anderson GM, et al. CSF biogenic amines in obsessive compulsive disorder and Tourette's syndrome. *Neuropsychopharmacology*. 1995;12:73–86

15. Chappell PB, Leckman JF, Goodman WK, et al. CSF corticotropin releasing factor is elevated in Tourette's syndrome. *Biol Psychiatry*. 1996;39:776–783

16. Peterson BS, Leckman JF, Scahill L, et al. Hypothesis. Steroid hormones and sexual dimorphisms modulate symptom expression in Tourette's syndrome. *Psychoneuroendocrinology*. 1992;17:553–563

17. Leckman JF, Peterson BS. The pathogenesis of Tourette's syndrome: role of epigenetic factors active in early CNS development. *Biol Psychiatry*. 1993;34:425–427

18. Leckman JF, Scahill L. Possible exacerbation of tics by androgenic steroids. *N Engl J Med*. 1990;322:1674

19. Peterson BS, Leckman JF, Scahill L, et al. Steroid hormones and Tourette's syndrome: early experience with antiandrogen therapy. *J Clin Psychopharmacol*. 1994;14:131–135

20. Peterson BS, Zhang H, Bondi C, Anderson GM, Leckman JF. A doubleblind, placebo-controlled, crossover trial of an antiandrogen in the treatment of Tourette's syndrome. *J Clin Psychopharmacol*. In press

21. Leckman JF, Ort SI, Towbin KE, Cohen DJ. Assessment of clinical severity of tic disorders. In: Cohen DJ, Bruun R, Leckman JF, eds. *Tourette's Syndrome and Tic Disorders: Clinical Understanding and Treatment*. New York, NY: John Wiley & Sons; 1988:55–78

22. Leckman JF, Riddle MA, Hardin MT, et al. The Yale Global Tic Severity Scale (YGTSS): initial testing of a clinician-rated scale of tic severity. *J Am Acad Child Adolesc Psychiatry*. 1989;28:566–573

23. Leckman JF, Walker WK, Goodman WK, Pauls DL, Cohen DJ. "Just right" perceptions associated with compulsive behaviors in Tourette's syndrome. *Am J Psychiatry*. 1994;151:675–680

24. Pauls DL, Hurst C. *Schedule for Tourette and Other Behavioral Disorders, Revised*. New Haven, CT: Child Study Center, Yale University; 1993

25. Pauls DL, Raymond CL, Stevenson JM, Leckman JF. A family study of Gilles de la Tourette's syndrome. *Am J Hum Genet*. 1991;48:154–163

26. Leckman JF, Hardin MT, Dolansky ES, et al. Perinatal factors in the expression of Tourette's syndrome. *J Am Acad Child Adolesc Psychiatry*. 1990;29:220–226

27. Leckman JF, Sholomskas D, Thompson WD, Belanger A, Weissman MM. Best estimate of lifetime psychiatric diagnosis: a methodologic study. *Arch Gen Psychiatry*. 1982;39:879–883

28. Efron B. Bootstrap methods: another look at the jackknife. *Ann Stat*. 1979;7:1–26

29. Peterson BS, Leckman JF. The temporal dynamics of tics in Gilles de la Tourette syndrome. *Biol Psychiatry*. In press

30. Selz KA, Mandell AJ. Critical coherence and characteristic times in brain stem neuronal discharge patterns. In: Davis J, McKenna J, Zornetzer S, eds. *Single Neuron Computation*. New York, NY: Academic Press; 1992:525–560

31. Leckman JF, Peterson BS, Anderson GM, Arnsten AFT, Pauls DL, Cohen DJ. Pathogenesis of Tourette's syndrome. *J Child Psychol Psychiatry*. 1997;38:119–142

32. Lephart ED. A review of brain aromatase cytochrome P450. *Brain Res Brain Res Rev*. 1996;22:1–26

33. Chappell PB, Scahill LD, Leckman JF. Future therapies of Tourette's syndrome. In: Janvokic J, ed. *Tourette's Syndrome—Neurologic Clinics of North America*. Philadelphia, PA: WB Saunders and Company: 1997:429–450

14

"Multidimensionally Impaired Disorder": Is It a Variant of Very Early-Onset Schizophrenia?

Sanjiv Kumra, M.D., Leslie K. Jacobsen, M.D., Marge Lenane, M.S.W., Theodore P. Zahn, Ph.D., Edythe Wiggs, Ph.D., Javad Alaghband-Rad, M.D., F. Xavier Castellanos, M.D., Jean A. Frazier, M.D., Kathleen McKenna, M.D., Charles T. Gordon, M.D., Amy Smith, B.A., Susan Hamburger, M.A., M.S., and Judith L. Rapoport, M.D.

Objective: *To examine the validity of diagnostic criteria for a subgroup of children with atypical psychosis (n = 19), designated here as "multidimensionally impaired." These children are characterized by poor attention and impulse control, psychotic symptoms, and poor affective control.* **Method:** *Children and adolescents (n = 19) meeting our criteria for multidimensionally impaired syndrome with onset of psychotic symptoms at or before age 12 years were identified from a total of 150 in-person screenings for very early-onset schizophrenia between 1990 and 1996. We compared the premorbid adjustment, family history, follow-up status, and laboratory measures for a subgroup of these children with those of (1) a rigorously defined group of 29 children with DSM-III-R schizophrenia and (2) 19 children with attention-deficit hyperactivity disorder.* **Results:** *Patients with multidimensionally impaired syndrome and patients with very early-onset schizophrenia shared a similar pattern of early transient autistic features, postpsychotic cognitive decline, and an elevated risk of schizophrenic-spectrum disorders among their first-degree relatives. This pattern was not seen in the attention-deficit hyperactivity disorder group. In*

Accepted February 21, 1997. All authors are with the Child Psychiatry Branch, National Institute of Mental Health, Bethesda, MD, except for Dr. Zahn (Laboratory of Psychology and Psychopathology, NIMH), Dr. Frazier (Harvard University School of Medicine, Boston), Dr. Gordon (University of Maryland School of Medicine, Baltimore), and Dr. McKenna (Northwestern University School of Medicine, Chicago).

The authors acknowledge the assistance of the NIMH Clinical Center staff members who cared for the patients in this study: K. Albus, D. Kaysen, W. Sharp, M.S.W., J. Liu, W. Marsh, J. Koeppel, D. Leichtner, and P. Lee. The authors thank Drs. L. Ingraham, J. Rumsey, F. Velkmar, D. Cohen, and R. Asarnow for their suggestions.

Reprint requests to Dr. Kumra, Child Psychiatry Branch, NIMH, Building 10, Room 6N240, 10 Center Drive MSC1600, Bethesda, MD 20892–1600.

contrast to very early-onset schizophrenia, the multidimensionally impaired group had significantly poorer scores on the Freedom From Distractibility factor on the WISC-R, a less deviant pattern of autonomic reactivity, and no progression to schizophrenia. **Conclusions:** *The findings support the distinction of the multidimensionally impaired cases as separate from those with other psychiatric disorders, and there is somewhat greater evidence to suggest that this disorder belongs in the schizophrenia spectrum.* J. Am. Acad. Child Adolesc. Psychiatry, 1998, 37(1):91–99. **Key Words:** *children, atypical psychosis, multidimensionally impaired, very early-onset schizophrenia.*

A clinical and neurobiological study of very early-onset schizophrenia (VEOS) has been ongoing at the National Institute of Mental Health (NIMH) since 1990. Approximately 30% of cases screened for childhood-onset schizophrenia had complex developmental disorders and brief psychotic symptoms which did not meet *DSM-III-R* criteria for schizophrenia (McKenna et al., 1994a). All patients reported brief hallucinations and delusions typically under stress which occurred a few times a month but showed no evidence of thought disorder. Although their psychotic symptoms were ego-dystonic and impaired functioning, these problems were intermittent and were less the focus of concern than their dramatic mood outbursts and periodic aggression, which had necessitated frequent psychiatric hospitalizations. The children in this cohort were socially deficient, but they eagerly sought social interactions and were distressed by their frequent peer rejection. The interviews, histories reported by parents, and extensive past test results of this group did not conform to any *DSM-III-R* disorder.

Our impression of a consistent clinical picture led to the proposal of a subgroup of children with atypical psychosis, which we provisionally labeled "multidimensionally impaired" (MDI), that shared the following characteristics:

1. Poor ability to distinguish fantasy from reality as evidenced by ideas of reference and brief perceptual disturbances during stressful periods or while falling asleep

2. Nearly daily periods of emotional lability disproportionate to precipitants

3. Impaired interpersonal skills despite desire to initiate social interactions with peers

4. Cognitive deficits indicated by multiple deficits in information processing

5. Absence of formal thought disorder

The interrater reliability was excellent for both the MDI disorder ($\kappa = .81$) and schizophrenia diagnoses ($\kappa = .77$) (McKenna et al., 1994a). Preliminary clinical comparisons of the two disorders (McKenna et al., 1994a,b) showed the MDI cohort to be predominantly male with more prominent comorbid attentional and impulse control difficulties and an earlier onset of behavioral problems, linguistic impairments, and psychotic symptoms than the childhood schizophrenics. They lacked the striking and pervasive disturbances in cognition, defective emotional rapport, bizarre hallucinations, and delusions which characterized the childhood schizophrenics. Although these data provided face validity for the

MDI construct, we did not know whether MDI and VEOS were etiologically heterogeneous or a single disorder that had variable expression due to moderating factors.

The present analysis is a comparison of 19 children with psychotic disorder not otherwise specified (labeled by us multidimensionally impaired) with children with (1) VEOS (onset of psychotic symptoms before age 12) ($n = 29$) and (2) attention-deficit hyperactivity disorder (ADHD) ($n = 19$). In this study, the groups are compared in a nonblind fashion with respect to premorbid adjustment, psychological testing, family history, preliminary follow-up, and autonomic activity. The considerable morbidity and substantial use of resources by the MDI group make even an exploratory analysis useful. Although the MDI group exhibited both inattentive, impulsive behaviors as well as psychotic symptoms, we hypothesized that the MDI group would have a distinctive profile more closely resembling VEOS.

METHOD

Subjects

Male and female patients aged 6 to 18 years with schizophrenia diagnosed according to *DSM-III-R* criteria with onset of psychotic symptoms by age 12 years were sought via national recruitment through professional and patient advocacy organizations. A premorbid IQ of less than 70 and the presence of medical or neurological disorders with psychiatric manifestations were exclusionary. A primary diagnosis of pervasive developmental disorder, dissociative disorder, mood disorder, conduct disorder, and/or personality disorder was exclusionary (McKenna et al., 1994a). Because early bipolar disorders may present with psychotic symptoms, we were careful to exclude patients who showed psychotic symptoms that were congruent and/or temporally concurrent with mood symptoms. During the period from May 1990 to June 1996, more than 750 charts were reviewed and 150 patients were screened in person.

To date, from 150 in-person screenings of patients referred for VEOS, 30 children (approximately 20%) not meeting *DSM-III-R* criteria for schizophrenia were given the label "multidimensionally impaired" (MDI). The current report is of the first 19 MDI children to complete an in-depth diagnostic evaluation and laboratory tests to better characterize this group. These children represented all those who were willing to participate in the 2- to 6-week inpatient evaluation. Eleven patients were not included in this study (five refused participation for clinical reasons such as potential loss of their residential placement, four patients who had been screened before the start of this inpatient study sought treatment elsewhere, and two patients were seen after June 1996). No significant demographic or clinical differences were found between the 19 patients included in this study and the 11 patients who were not included.

Clinical information for 10 MDI subjects and 23 VEOS subjects was reported previously (Alaghband-Rad et al., 1995, 1997; McKenna et al., 1994a,b).

Identical structured interviews, inpatient evaluation, and methods for analyses of adverse obstetrical events, premorbid difficulties, familial psychopathology, and autonomic activity were used for the MDI and VEOS groups. However, compared with the VEOS group, fewer MDI subjects (10/19) were observed off neuroleptic medication *during their stay at* the NIMH. Moreover, all clinical comparisons contained in this report were made by child psychiatrists who were aware of the patient's diagnosis.

Informed consent/assent was obtained from parents and children under protocols approved by the institutional review board at the NIMH. Interviews were conducted (VEOS, MDI) with two child psychiatrists present and videotaped.

For comparison, we used data from children ($n = 19$) with diagnosed ADHD who were matched to the MDI cohort by age, gender, socioeconomic status, and, where possible, intellectual ability. These children participated in studies conducted at the NIMH during the same time period (Castellanos et al., 1996; Elia et al., 1991). For the children with ADHD, *DSM-III-R* diagnoses were made using the Diagnostic Interview for Children and Adolescents-Parent Version (DICA-R-P) and Child Version (DICA-R-C) in a nonblind fashion (Reich and Welner, 1988). We did not have comparable data using structured instruments to assess for the presence of autistic symptoms, adverse obstetrical events, and personality disorders in the first-degree relatives of ADHD patients.

Procedure

Nineteen MDI patients were admitted for an extended inpatient evaluation lasting up to 6 weeks. Ten patients were not taking neuroleptic medication during their stay at the NIMH (four patients completed a 4-week diagnostic washout, four patients were medication-free at the time of admission, and two patients were taking mood stabilizers only).

Obstetrical and Premorbid History

The obstetrical records and premorbid histories of the MDI and ADHD children were reviewed in a fashion similar to that used for their schizophrenic counterparts by two psychiatrists (J.A., S.K.) as described elsewhere (Alaghband-Rad et al., 1995, 1997). Structured instruments or other reliable methods were used to assess obstetrical complications (Zax et al., 1977), pervasive developmental disorder symptoms (Rutter and Lord, 1991), pubertal development (Tanner, 1962), socioeconomic class (Hollingshead and Redlich, 1958), and learning disabilities (Schuerholz et al., 1995). We independently assessed 10 patients' charts (S.K., J.A.) and obtained excellent interrater reliability for the Rochester total obstetrical score (intraclass correlation coefficient $= .97$) and number of pervasive developmental disorder symptoms (intraclass correlation coefficient $= .86$). Only responses on the Autism Diagnostic Interview (Rutter and Lord, 1991) that were clearly abnormal were counted (i.e., scores of 2).

Fourteen (73%) of 19 MDI patients had IQ testing before coming to the NIMH (3 WWPSI, 9 WISC-R, 2 WISC-III); 7 were obtained prior to onset of psychosis and 7 soon after. If more than one IQ score existed, the highest was chosen as the most valid estimate of the child's performance.

At the NIMH, all subjects were administered the WISC-R (Wechsler, 1974), the Woodcock Johnson Psychoeducational Battery (ADHD) (Woodcock and Johnson, 1977), the Kaufman Test of Educational Achievement (MDI, VEOS) (Kaufman and Kaufman, 1985), and selected subtests of the Clinical Evaluation of Language Fundamentals-Revised (CELF-R) (MDI) to assess expressive (formulated sentences, sentence assembly) and receptive language (word classes, semantic relationships) (Semel et al., 1987). A neuropsychologist (E.W.) reviewed the test results for each patient. For this report, we used only the data of children who were motivated, attentive, and cooperative with the testing process. Therefore, the numbers of children completing each test vary.

Factor scores for each of the three WISC-R factors were computed for subjects (15 VEOS, 14 MDI, 19 ADHD) with Full Scale IQs greater than 70 at the NIMH (Kaufman, 1979).

For the Kaufman Test of Educational Achievement, 33 patients (12 MDI, 21 VEOS) were able to complete both reading subtests. An expressive or receptive language deficit (Baltaxe and Simmons, 1995) was diagnosed when a subtest score on the CELF-R was at least one standard deviation below the norm for the child's age level.

To date, 11 MDI patients have returned to the NIMH 2 years after initial evaluation and were clinically assessed by at least two psychiatrists (L.K.J., J.A., S.K.).

Family Data

In-person interviews were available for 78 (95%) of 82 first-degree relatives of 28 patients with VEOS, 38 (86%) of 44 first-degree relatives of 16 patients with MDI, and 28 (88%) of 32 parents of 16 patients participating in studies of ADHD (Castellanos et al., 1996; Elia et al., 1991). Relatives of adopted probands were excluded from this portion of the study. Eleven biological fathers were unavailable for interview (four MDI, three VEOS, four ADHD) and two biological fathers (both MDI) were deceased. All biological mothers of probands were interviewed in person. For the three adopted MDI patients, information about the psychiatric status of the biological mother was obtained from adoption records.

The VEOS, MDI, and ADHD samples underwent similar structured interview assessments: all relatives aged 18 years and older (25 MDI, 28 VEOS, 28 ADHD) were evaluated using the Schedule for Affective Disorders and Schizophrenia (Endicott and Spitzer, 1978). The diagnosis of personality disorders was made either using the Structured Interview for *DSM-III/DSM-IV* Personality (MDI, VEOS) (Pfohl et al., 1983) or by detailed clinical interview (ADHD). All full siblings aged between 6 and 18 years (15 MDI, 26 VEOS, 16 ADHD) were evaluated using the Diagnostic Interview for Children and Adolescents-Revised Version for Children (aged 6 through 12) or Adolescents (aged 13 through 17) (MDI, VEOS) (Reich and Welner, 1988) or by detailed clinical interview (ADHD).

Relatives were evaluated by trained interviewers, and their evaluations were reviewed by a board-certified child and adolescent psychiatrist (S.K.).

Autonomic Physiology

Sixteen MDI patients (14 male, 2 female) had been tested for this portion of the study; however, data for only 8 were usable, making these data very preliminary. Because neuroleptic drugs with high anticholinergic properties greatly affect psychophysiological measures (Zahn et al., 1991a), data for patients who were taking such medications (eight MDI) were discarded from the analyses. Thus, the data for 8 MDI cases were compared with those of 69 normal controls, 22 unmedicated patients with VEOS, and 26 unmedicated patients with ADHD (Zahn and Kruesi, 1993; Zahn et al., 1997).

Electrodermal activity (as indexed by skin conductance and heart rate) was assessed in a protocol which included a 3-minute rest period, a series of 10 nonsignal tones to elicit orienting responses, and a simple warned reaction time task. Details of this protocol have been described elsewhere (Zahn and Kruesi, 1993; Zahn et al., 1997). Heart rate and heart rate variability were age-corrected because these variables were correlated with age.

Data Analysis

Data are expressed as means ± standard deviations. Nominal variables were tested with the χ^2 and continuous measures with the Student's t test or repeated-measures analysis of variance. All analyses were two-tailed, with .05 as the threshold of statistical significance.

Statistical comparisons were made between groups only when identical assessment procedures were available.

RESULTS

Demographic and Clinical Characteristics

The clinical and demographic data for MDI, VEOS, and ADHD subjects are given in Table 1. Both groups of psychotic children had been ill for several years and all had received considerable prior treatment. Before coming to the NIMH, the MDI group had been treated with various psychotropic agents including neuroleptics (100%), mood stablizers (79%), antidepressants (63%), and stimulants (68%). Fewer adverse obstetrical events were reported for the children in this study than for adult schizophrenic patients, whose mean Rochester Obstetrical Scale total score was reported to be 4.72 (Zax et al., 1977).

Premorbid Course

The pattern of cognitive deterioration, depression in the Freedom From Distractibility factor, premorbid developmental delay, linguistic impairments, and learning disabilities that was seen in the MDI group was similar to that reported for VEOS (Alaghband-Rad et al., 1995, 1997; Asarnow et al., 1995).

Intellectual Performance

Prepsychotic IQ test results were available for 14 MDI patients. These patients were tested on average 10.2 ± 29.5 months (range, −60 to +42) before the onset of overt psychosis; their mean baseline Full Scale IQ was 98.5 (SD = 12.7).

Postpsychotic IQ testing for these 14 patients at NIMH was found to be more than one standard deviation below the population average (mean = 81.9, SD = 13.1). A significant decline from earlier scores was seen ($t = 5.09$, $p = .002$); both Performance IQ ($t = 4.09$, $p = .001$) and Verbal IQ ($t = 3.38$, $p < .05$) dropped.

The scores on the three WISC-R factors (Kaufman, 1979) were compared using a three-groups (between) by three-factor scores (within) repeated-measures analysis of variance. Because the group by factor interaction ($F[4,90] = 4.14$, $p < .004$) was statistically significant, post hoc testing between diagnostic groups was carried out. This analysis revealed that the Freedom From Distractibility factor was significantly lower in the MDI than in both

TABLE 1

Demographic and Clinical Characteristics of the Multidimensionally Impaired ($n = 19$), Very Early-Onset Schizophrenia ($n = 29$), and Attention-Deficit Hyperactivity Disorder ($n = 19$) Groups

	MDI	VEOS	ADHD		
Gender					
Male	16	14	16		
Female	3	15	3		
Race					
Caucasian	18	14	12		
African-American	0	9	5		
Other	1	6	2		
	Mean (SD)	Mean (SD)	Mean (SD)	F	p
Tanner stage	2.63 (1.71)	4.08 (1.36)	2.80 (1.82)	1.70	.20
Family socioeconomic status	3.00 (0.94)	2.83 (1.28)	2.63 (1.21)	0.47	.63
Rochester Obstetrical Scale					
(total score)	2.84 (2.71)	2.08 (2.18)	2.31 (2.21)	0.56	.57
Age (yr) of					
Onset of difficulties in					
development or behavior	1.50 (2.00)[a,b]	4.65 (3.44)	3.36 (2.39)	7.06	<.01
Onset of psychosis	7.89 (2.08)[a]	10.31 (2.00)	NA	16.22	<.01
Range	4–12	5–12			
First hospitalization	8.18 (1.51)[a]	11.64 (2.33)	NA	29.21	<.01
Seen at NIMH for screening	11.37 (2.69)	14.03 (2.16)	10.42 (1.43)	18.33	<.01
Range	6–16	9–18	6–12		
Full Scale IQ at NIMH					
All subjects	80.47 (11.81)[b]	74.83 (20.11)	96.11 (9.07)	11.06	<.01
Subjects with IQ > 70	85.29 (7.71)[b]	84.60 (16.58)	96.11 (9.07)	5.30	<.01
WISC-R factor scores					
Verbal Comprehension	93.91 (9.82)	89.19 (15.68)	98.69 (12.31)		
Perceptual Organization	90.86 (11.88)	85.28 (16.80)	99.58 (9.80)	7.26	<.01
Freedom From					
Distractibility	69.51 (11.60)[a,b]	80.49 (18.48)	91.78 (12.87)		

Note: MDI = multidimensionally impaired; VEOS = very early-onset schizophrenia; ADHD = attention-deficit hyperactivity disorder; NIMH = National Institute of Mental Health; NA = not applicable.
[a]MDI different from VEOS, $p < .05$ using a one-way analysis of variance.
[b]MDI different from ADHD, $p < .05$ using a one-way analysis of variance.

the ADHD and VEOS groups ($p < .05$) (Table 1). In the MDI group, the Freedom From Distractibility factor score was significantly lower than both the Verbal Comprehension and Perceptual Organization factors ($p < .05$). A similar pattern of intellectual performance was observed in the VEOS and ADHD groups, but it did not reach statistical significance.

As expected, both the MDI and VEOS children had considerable difficulty understanding what they read despite adequate word recognition skills. Reading decoding skills were significantly better than reading comprehension skills for both MDI and VEOS children ($p < .05$) (Table 2). The standard score for reading decoding was higher than Full Scale IQ (88.8 ± 14.4 versus 81.2 ± 12.0) in the MDI group ($n = 12$).

TABLE 2

Developmental Disorders and Lifetime Comorbidity for Other Psychiatric
Disorders in Patients With Multidimensionally Impaired Syndrome and Very
Early-Onset Schizophrenia

Diagnosis	MDI (n = 19)		VEOS (n = 29)	
	No.	(%)	No.	(%)
Mood disorders				
Major depressive episode	4	(21)	5	(17)
Any other mood disorder	2	(11)	2	(7)
Anxiety disorders				
Obsessive-compulsive disorder	0		2	(7)
Overanxious disorder	3	(16)	0	
Posttraumatic stress disorder	2	(11)	0	
Tourette's or chronic motor tic disorder	2	(11)	2	(7)
Any other anxiety disorder	2	(10)	2	(6)
Pervasive developmental disorder				
Met full criteria	3	(16)	3	(10)
Met two criteria	11	(58)[a,b]	1	(3)
Met one criterion	1	(5)	4	(14)
Disruptive behaviors				
ADHD	16	(84)[a]	8	(28)
Oppositional defiant disorder	4	(21)	1	(3)
Conduct disorder	1	(5)	2	(7)
Specific learning disability				
Reading	5	(26)	4	(14)
Arithmetic	8	(42)	9	(32)

Kaufman Test of Educational Achievement Subtest Scores[c]	MDI (n = 12)		VEOS (n = 20)	
	Mean	(SD)	Mean	(SD)
Reading Decoding	88.83	(14.39)	87.65	(18.89)[d]
Spelling	80.08	(15.86)	85.15	(17.84)
Reading Comprehension	78.50	(12.83)	65.25	(15.38)
Mathematic Applications	77.75	(10.93)	65.15	(22.23)
Mathematic Computation	66.00	(14.24)	70.40	(18.00)

Note: MDI = multidimensionally impaired; VEOS = very early-onset schizophrenia;
ADHD = attention-deficit hyperactivity disorder.
[a]MDI different from VEOS, $p < .05$.
[b]MDI different from ADHD, $p < .05$ by χ^2 analysis. All others nonsignificant.
[c] Subjects with IQ > 70.
[d] ADHD subjects were given the Woodcock-Johnson Psychoeducational Battery (Woodcock and Johnson, 1977).

Comorbid Psychiatric Disorders

Transient features of pervasive developmental disorder were significantly more prevalent in the MDI group than in the VEOS group (Table 2). At the time of initial evaluation, only one MDI child still met *DSM-III-R* criteria for pervasive developmental disorder. However, two other children had greater than eight autistic symptoms in early childhood which had remitted by school age. The following symptoms were reported by more than 25% of probands' mothers: solitariness, gross impairment in ability to make peer friendships, obsessive preoccupations, marked abnormalities in the form or content of speech, and marked impairment or inability to initiate or sustain a conversation.

On NIMH testing, expressive and receptive deficits were found in 13 (68%) of 19 MDI children and pure expressive deficits in an additional 11%. Z scores for the MDI children on these language measures are between 1.16 and 1.64 below those of 9-year-old normal children and comparable with scores for 9-year-old children identified as having language learning disabilities using the CELF-R (Semel et al., 1987).

Familial Psychopathology

The proportion of families with at least one member affected with schizotypal and/or paranoid personality disorder was similar in both the MDI and VEOS groups (8/16 versus 8/28, respectively; $\chi^2 = 0.2$, $p = .15$). Although there were no definite cases of schizophrenia in the first-degree relatives of the MDI group, adoption records of one of the MDI probands supported the diagnosis of schizophrenia (onset of psychotic symptoms, age 15) in the biological mother. Other conditions such as autism and mental retardation were not seen in the families of the MDI cohort; affective illness, anxiety disorders, and substance abuse were equally prevalent across the three groups.

Preliminary Follow-up Status

Preliminary analysis suggests that our criteria for MDI syndrome generally identified children with stable symptomatology, that is without progression to schizophrenia: 8 (72%) of 11 MDI patients have remained stable or improved over time; however, 3 (27%) of 11 have developed more severe chronic disorders since entry into the study. The three patients who deteriorated clinically were found at follow-up to have schizoaffective disorder (bipolar type) chiefly because the duration, severity, and overlap of their psychotic and affective symptoms had progressed over the 2-year interval.

Autonomic Physiology

In VEOS, a striking hyporesponsivity in skin conductance responses to both novel and significant stimuli has been observed, and this appears to be related to the severity of both positive and negative symptoms of schizophrenia (Zahn et al., 1997). In spite of small numbers, some significant differences in autonomic activity were seen between the eight MDI subjects (all taking medications with low anticholinergic properties) and the VEOS cohort, whereas the MDI subgroup more closely resembled the ADHD subjects on these measures.

The increase in skin conductance activity during the instructions for the reaction time task as indicated by skin conductance response magnitude (4.0 ± 3.1 versus 1.2 ± 2.0 microseconds; $p < .05$) and skin conductance level (5.6 ± 3.0 versus 2.6 ± 1.9 microseconds; $p < .01$) was much greater in MDI than in VEOS subjects, respectively.

During the reaction time task, the frequency (7.1 ± 1.3 versus 4.4 ± 2.1; $p < .01$) and magnitude of elicited skin conductance responses (0.50 ± 1.7 versus 0.16 ± 0.18 microseconds; $p < .05$) were greater in MDI than in VEOS subjects, respectively.

No significant differences in autonomic activity were found between MDI and ADHD subjects, with the exception that resting heart rate (beats per minute) was significantly lower in MDI than in ADHD subjects (71 ± 11 versus 82 ± 12; $p < .04$).

DISCUSSION

Exploratory analyses of clinical and test data for the MDI cohort indicate some consistent differences from their schizophrenic counterparts in that they had earlier cognitive and behavior difficulties, earlier age at onset of psychotic symptoms, a more striking depression in the Freedom From Distractibility scores, and a less deviant pattern of autonomic activity. These data along with the face validity and the overrepresentation of male subjects in the MDI group lend further support for the initial distinction of these two groups (McKenna et al., 1994a,b). Contrary to what one might expect, the earlier and more severe attentional impairments observed in the MDI group appear to be associated with a more benign outcome and less social impairment.

On the other hand, the MDI cohort share with the VEOS patients a pattern of premorbid developmental difficulties, a diminution in cognitive ability from a higher premorbid level, a discrepancy between word-reading ability and IQ, and increased rates of schizophrenic-spectrum disorders in first-degree relatives (Alaghband-Rad et al., 1995, 1997; Asarnow et al., 1987, 1995). These findings, along with the considerable psychiatric morbidity and the continued presence of brief psychotic episodes at 2-year follow-up, distinguish the MDI group from individuals with even severe forms of ADHD (Biederman et al., 1992, 1996; Cantwell and Baker, 1992; Wozniak et al., 1996), Asperger's disorder, and schizotypal personality disorder (Nagy and Szatmari, 1986; Wolff, 1991).

The striking pattern of transient features of pervasive developmental disorder, attention deficit, linguistic impairment, and cognitive decline seen very early in the MDI group is consistent with descriptions in the literature of VEOS (Alaghband-Rad et al., 1995; Asarnow et al., 1995; Baltaxe and Simmons, 1995; Cantor et al., 1982; Kolvin, 1971; Kolvin et al, 1971) and schizophrenic-spectrum disorders (Nagy and Szatmari, 1986; Wolff, 1991), and in part it has also been observed in children considered at high risk for schizophrenia (Fish, 1977; Fish et al., 1992; Parnas et al., 1982). This "neurointegrative defect" could reflect shared etiological factors with other developmental disorders that result in a disruption of brain development.

Clinical studies and genetic data support the distinction between autism and schizophrenia (Kolvin, 1971; Kolvin et al., 1971; Rutter et al., 1995; Volkmar and Cohen, 1991). In fact, language-delayed children presenting to a psychiatric clinic are most likely to have a final diagnosis of infantile autism or mental retardation (Cantwell and Baker, 1987). In addition, while schizophrenia may develop in some autistic children (Petty et al., 1984), these cases occur only at a chance rate (Volkmar and Cohen, 1991). However, autistic-like symptoms have been reported in subgroups of VEOS patients (Asarnow et al., 1995; Cantor et al., 1982), and the Yale Child Study Center has described a behavioral syndrome within the autistic spectrum somewhat similar to MDI, labeled multiplex developmental disorder. This early-onset disorder has been characterized by severe and persistent deficits in affect regulation, relatedness, and thought processes; treatment refractoriness; and increased rates of parental psychopathology (Cohen et al., 1986, 1994; Towbin et al., 1993; Van Der Gaag et al., 1995). These data provide additional support for the existence of a distinct subgroup of children (predominantly male) with autistic-like features and psychotic symptoms when *DSM-III-R* criteria are rigorously applied.

Although the MDI children showed some of the clinical features seen in autistic-spectrum disorders, they lacked the severe impairments in social interaction, stereotyped behaviors and interests, inability to engage in make-believe play, characteristic profile of intellectual performance, and deviant language development commonly seen in pervasive developmental disorders (Asarnow et al., 1987; Rutter et al., 1995). These differences along with the family history data would argue that MDI should be seen as a variant of VEOS rather than of pervasive developmental disorder.

The classification of children with psychotic conditions is fraught with complications (Werry et al., 1991; Werry and McClellan, 1992), and the nosological status and future diagnostic stability of the MDI group at this point remain unclear. The preliminary follow-up data, the pattern of intellectual performance on the WISC-R, and the autonomic reactivity data seen for the MDI group provide further justification for the separation of the MDI cases from the VEOS cohort. The lack of deterioration of progression seen for the majority of MDI patients at 2-year follow-up argues tentatively against the MDI syndrome as a prodrome for schizophrenia.

Alternatively, the MDI group may represent a variant of VEOS, since in the adult literature nonacute brief psychoses are considered to be milder forms of non affective psychoses (Susser et al., 1995). Consistent with this hypothesis, schizoaffective disorder has developed in 3 (27%) of 11 MDI patients. In addition, our preliminary data indicate that the pattern of brain morphology for MDI resembles VEOS rather than ADHD (S. Kumra, unpublished). Furthermore, 2 of 19 MDI patients included in this study were found to have sex chromosome aneuploidies, which has also been observed in cytogenetic studies of adult schizophrenics (DeLisi et al., 1994; Kumra et al., in press).

On the other hand, the MDI syndrome may represent an artificial grouping of severely impaired children who have strong comorbidity with behavioral and cognitive disorders that were highly selected by our national recruiting effort for VEOS.

Each of the patient groups showed deficits in attention and information processing. On reaction time studies, marked deficits in performance were seen in all three groups, with the MDI group most impaired (T. Zahn, unpublished; Zahn et al., 1991b). As reported for VEOS, the scores of the MDI children on the Freedom From Distractibility factor were below the range of normal children and significantly lower than the scores they obtained on the Verbal

Comprehension and Perceptual Organization factors (Asarnow et al., 1987); moreover, these scores were significantly lower than those of either patient group. The subtests that load on this factor make extensive demands on momentary processing because of their requirements for working memory, attention, and speed of responding (Asarnow et al., 1987). In contrast, achievement in word-reading ability (a putative measure of premorbid intellect) was relatively well-preserved in the MDI cohort and higher than IQ scores, a finding consistent with studies of adult schizophrenia (Goldberg et al., 1993).

With respect to autonomic reactivity, the MDI group did not show striking impairments in their ability to modulate arousal with environmental pressures as seen in VEOS. While the profile of the MDI patients more closely resembled that of the ADHD group on these measures, these findings are only suggestive because of the possible selection bias of MDI patients tested and because milder forms of schizophrenia have not been well-studied by these methods. In summary, neurobiological differences between VEOS, MDI, and ADHD provide conflicting data requiring further exploration.

Methodological Limitations

The methodological limitations for this overview must be kept in mind. As with many studies of childhood psychiatric disorders, our sample size for this study is small and many of the MDI patients were not studied drug-free during their stay at the NIMH, which may have masked the full extent of clinical symptomatology. However, our diagnostic assessments incorporated clinical data from the patients past drug-free periods and because these cases were nonresponders to typical neuroleptics referred for an inpatient clozapine trial, only more severe cases would have been referred.

Second, the data contained in this report were not ascertained in a blinded fashion, reports of premorbid delays were retrospective, and identical measures were not available across groups, which may well have biased these results. Other studies, however, support the present findings. While speech and language disorders are common in ADHD, features of pervasive developmental disorders and schizotypal personality disorder in first-degree relatives of children with ADHD appear rare (Biederman et al., 1992; Wozniak et al., 1995).

Despite these limitations, the paucity of comparative data on these groups of children and the considerable morbidity associated with childhood psychoses make this preliminary analysis worth sharing.

Clinical Implications

There is growing awareness of a sizable group of children with complex developmental disorders and transient psychotic symptoms who fall outside current syndrome boundaries (Dahl et al., 1986; Towbin et al., 1993; Van Der Gaag et al., 1995). While many of the symptoms of MDI can be seen in other psychiatric disorders, none of the children included in this study met full criteria for any other *DSM-IV* diagnosis with the exception of ADHD (McKenna et al., 1994a). The present report represents the first systematic study to address the developmental, clinical, family history, and biological profile of a subgroup of these children (Pincus et al., 1992; Robins and Guze, 1970).

For children who suffer from early and severe persistent disturbances such as those seen in MDI, their illness derails the processes that underlie socialization and the emergence of personal autonomy resulting in severe social disability (Cohen et al., 1994). The provision of a set of criteria for which there is some preliminary validation makes it more likely that this diagnostic area will capture the attention of clinical researchers and that paradigms will be used to provide consensus on diagnosis across programs (Pincus et al., 1992). The absence of this disorder from the current nomenclature has resulted in an inadequate knowledge base to guide clinicians about the prognosis and optimal treatment of children with atypical psychoses. We believe that because there is not a better descriptive category for these intermittently psychotic children with developmental impairments, many of the MDI children were inappropriately labeled as schizophrenic and received chronic neuroleptic treatment.

To further resolve whether the distinction between MDI and other disorders is useful for clinical practice, a more comprehensive clinical follow-up as well as treatment trials with atypical neuroleptics are currently under way.

REFERENCES

Alaghband-Rad J, Hamburger S, Giedd J, Frazier J, Rapoport J (1997), Childhood-onset schizophrenia; biological markers in relation to clinical characteristics, *Am J Psychiatry* 154:64–68

Alaghband-Rad J, McKenna K, Gordon CT et al. (1995), Childhood-onset schizophrenia: the severity of premorbid course. *J Am Acad Child Adolesc Psychiatry* 34:1273–1283

Asarnow R, Brown W, Strandburg R (1995), Children with a schizophrenic disorder: neurobehavioral studies. *Eur Arch Psychiatry Clin Neurosci* 245:70–79

Asarnow R, Tanguay P, Bott L, Freeman B (1987), Patterns of intellectual functioning in non-retarded autistic and schizophrenic children. *J Child Psychol Psychiatry* 28:273–280

Baltaxe C, Simmons J (1995), Speech and language disorders in children and adolescents with schizophrenia. *Schizophr Bull* 21:677–692

Biederman J, Faraone S, Mick E et al. (1996), Attention-deficit hyperactivity disorder and juvenile mania: an overlooked comorbidity? *J Am Acad Child Adolesc Psychiatry* 35:997–1008

Biederman J, Faraone SV, Keenan K et al. (1992), Further evidence for family-genetic risk factors in attention deficit hyperactivity disorder: patterns of comorbidity in probands and relatives in psychiatrically and pediatrically referred samples. *Arch Gen Psychiatry* 49:728–738

Cantor S, Evans J, Pearce J, Pezzot-Pearce T (1982), Childhood schizophrenia: present but not accounted for. *Am J Psychiatry* 139:758–762

Cantwell DP, Baker L (1987), Psychiatric symptomatology in language-impaired children: a comparison. *J Child Neurol* 2:128–133

Cantwell DP, Baker L (1992), Attention deficit disorder with and without hyperactivity: a review and comparison of matched groups. *J Am Acad Child Adolesc Psychiatry* 31:432–438

Castellanos FX, Giedd JN, Marsh WL et al. (1996), Quantitative brain magnetic resonance imaging in attention-deficit hyperactivity disorder. *Arch Gen Psychiatry* 53:607–616

Cohen D, Towbin K, Mayes L, Volkmar F (1994), Developmental psychopathology of multiplex developmental disorder. In: *Developmental Followup: Concepts, Genres, Domain and Methods*. Friedman SL, Haywood HC, eds. Orlando, FL: Academic Press, pp 155–179

Cohen DJ, Paul R, Volkmar FR (1986), Issues in the classification of pervasive and other developmental disorders: toward *DSM-IV. J Am Acad Child Psychiatry* 25:213–220

Dahl EK, Cohen DJ, Provence S (1986), Clinical and multivariate approaches to the nosology of pervasive developmental disorders. *J Am Acad Child Psychiatry* 25:170–180

DeLisi LE, Friedrich U, Wahlstrom J et al. (1994), Schizophrenia and sex chromosome anomalies. *Schizophr Bull* 20:495–505

Elia J, Borcherding BG, Rapoport JL, Keysor CS (1991), Methylphenidate and dextroamphetamine treatments of hyperactivity: are there true non-responders? *Psychiatry Res* 36:141–155

Endicott J, Spitzer RI (1978), A diagnostic interview: the Schedule for Affective Disorders and Schizophrenia. *Arch Gen Psychiatry* 35:857–862

Fish B (1977), Neurobiologic antecedents of schizophrenia in children: evidence for an inherited congenital neurointegrative defect. *Arch Gen Psychiatry* 34:1297–1313

Fish B, Marcus J, Hans S, Auerbach J, Perdue S (1992), Infants at risk for schizophrenia: sequelae of a genetic neurointegrative defect. *Arch Gen Psychiatry* 29:221–235

Goldberg T, Gold JM, Greenberg R et al. (1993), Contrasts between patients with affective disorders and patients with schizophrenia on a neuro-psychological test battery. *Am J Psychiatry* 150:1355–1362

Hollingshead AB, Redlich FC (1958), *Social Class and Mental Illness.* New York: Wiley

Kaufman A (1979), *Intelligent Testing With the WISC-R.* New York: Wiley

Kaufman AS, Kaufman NL (1985), *Kaufman Test of Educational Achievement.* Circle Pines, MN: American Guidance Service

Kolvin I (1971), Studies in the childhood psychoses, I: diagnostic criteria and classification. *Br J Psychiatry* 118:381–384

Kolvin I, Ounsted C, Humphrey M, McNay A (1971), Studies in the childhood psychoses, II: the phenomenology of childhood psychoses. *Br J Psychiatry* 118:385–395

Kumra S, Wiggs E, Krasnewich D et al. (in press), Association of sex chromosome anomalies with childhood-onset psychotic disorders. *J Am Acad Child Adolesc Psychiatry*

McKenna K, Gordon C, Lenane M, Kaysen D, Fahey K, Rapoport J (1994a), Looking for childhood-onset schizophrenia: the first 71 cases screened. *J Am Acad Child Adolesc Psychiatry* 33: 636–644

McKenna K, Gordon C, Rapoport J (1994b), Childhood-onset schizophrenia: timely neurobiological research. *J Am Acad Child Adolesc Psychiatry* 33:771–781

Nagy J, Szatmari P (1986), A chart review of schizotypal personality disorders in children. *J Autism Dev Disord* 16:351–367

Parnas J, Schulsinger F, Schulsinger H, Mednick S, Teasdale T (1982), Behavioral precursors of schizophrenia spectrum: a prospective study. *Arch Gen Psychiatry* 39:658–664

Petty L, Ornitz E, Michelman J, Zimmerman E (1984), Autistic children who become schizophrenic. *Arch Gen Psychiatry* 41:129–135

Pfohl B, Stangl D, Zimmerman E (1983), *Structured Interview for* DSM-III *Personality* (SIDP). University of Iowa Department of Psychiatry

Pincus H, Frances A, Davis W, First M, Widiger T (1992), *DSM-IV* and new diagnostic categories: holding the line on proliferation. *Am J Psychol* 149:112–117

Reich W, Welner Z (1988), *Diagnostic Interview for Children and Adolescents RC (*DSM-III-R *Version), Revised Version V-R.* St Louis: Washington University

Robins E, Guze S (1970), Establishment of diagnostic validity in psychiatric illness: its application to schizophrenia. *Am J Psychiatry* 126:107–111

Rutter M, Lord C (1991), *Autism Diagnostic Interview-Research*. London: MRC Child Psychiatry Unit

Rutter M, Taylor E, Hersov L (1995), *Child and Adolescent Psychiatry: Modern Approaches*. Oxford, England: Blackwell

Schuerholz LJ, Harris EL, Baumgardner TL et al. (1995), An analysis of two discrepancy-based models and a processing-deficit approach in identifying learning disabilities. *J Learn Disabil* 28:18–29

Semel E, Wiig EH, Second W (1987), *Clinical Evaluation of Language Fundamentals-Revised (CELF-R)*. San Antonio, TX: Psychological Corporation

Susser E, Fennig S, Jandorf L, Amador X, Bromer E (1995), Epidemiology, diagnosis, and course of brief psychoses. *Am J Psychiatry* 152:1743–1748

Tanner JM (1962), *Growth at Adolescence*. Oxford, England: Blackwell Scientific Publications

Towbin K, Dykens E, Pearson G, Cohen D (1993), Conceptualizing "borderline syndrome of childhood" and "childhood schizophrenia" as a developmental disorder. *J Am Acad Child Adolesc Psychiatry* 32:775–782

Van Der Gaag RJ, Buitelaar J, Ban EVD, Bezemer M, Njio L, Engeland HV (1995), A controlled multivariate chart review of multiple complex developmental disorder. *J Am Acad Child Adolesc Psychiatry* 34:1096–1106

Volkmar FR, Cohen DJ (1991), Comorbid association of autism and schizophrenia. *Am J Psychiatry* 148:1705–1707

Werry JS, McClellan JM (1992), Predicting outcome in child and adolescent (early onset) schizophrenia and bipolar disorder. *J Am Acad Child Adolesc Psychiatry* 31:147–150

Werry JS, McClellan JM, Chard L (1991), Childhood and adolescent schizophrenic, bipolar and schizoaffective disorders: a clinical and outcome study. *J Am Acad Child Adolesc Psychiatry* 30:457–465

Wechsler D (1974), *Wechsler Intelligence Scale for Children-Revised*. New York: Psychological Corporation

Wolff S (1991), "Schizoid" personality in childhood and adult life: the childhood picture. *Br J Psychiatry* 159:629–635

Woodcock RW, Johnson MB (1977), *Woodcock Johnson Psychoeducational Battery*. Allen, TX: DLM Teaching Resources

Wozniak J, Biederman J, Kiely K et al. (1995), Mania-like symptoms suggestive of childhood-onset bipolar disorder in clinically referred children. *J Am-Acad Child Adolesc Psychiatry* 34:867–876

Wozniak J, Biederman J, Mundy E, Mennin D, Faraone SV (1996), A pilot family study of childhood-onset mania. *J Am Acad Child Adolesc Psychiatry* 34:1577–1583

Zahn TP, Frith C, Steinhauer S (1991a), *Autonomic Functioning in Schizophrenia: Electrodermal Activity, Heart Rate, Pupillography*. Amsterdam: Elsevier Science Publishers

Zahn TP, Jacobsen LK, Gordon CT, McKenna K, Frazier JA, Rapoport JL (1997), Autonomic nervous system markers of psychopathology in childhood-onset schizophrenia. *Arch Gen Psychiatry* 54:904–912

Zahn TP, Kruesi M (1993), Autonomic activity in boys with disruptive behavior disorders. *Psychophysiology* 30:605–614

Zahn TP, Kruesi M, Rapoport J (1991b), Reaction time indices of attention deficits in boys with disruptive behavior disorders. *J Abnorm Child Psychol* 19:233–252

Zax M, Sameroff A, Babigian H (1977), Birth outcomes in the offspring of mentally disordered women. *Am J Orthopsychiatry* 47:218–230

15

A Prospective Longitudinal Study of Attachment Disorganization/Disorientation

Elizabeth A. Carlson

The research explores the antecedents and consequences of attachment dis-organization from a prospective longitudinal perspective. The relations of attachment disorganization/disorientation to endogenous (e.g., maternal medical history, infant temperament) and environmental (e.g., maternal caregiving quality, infant history of abuse) antecedents and to behavioral consequences from 24 months to 19 years are examined. For the 157 participants in the longitudinal study, attachment disorganization was correlated significantly with environmental antecedents (e.g., maternal relationship and risk status, caregiving quality, and infant history of maltreatment), but not with available endogenous antecedents. Infant history of attachment disorganization was correlated with consequent variables related to mother-child relationship quality at 24 and 42 months, child behavior problems in preschool, elementary school and high school, and psychopathology and dissociation in adolescence. Structural models suggest that disorganization may mediate the relations between early experience and later psychopathology and dissociation. The findings are considered within a developmental view of psychopathology, that is, pathology defined in terms of process, as a pattern of adaptation constructed by individuals in their environments.

INTRODUCTION

During the first year of life infants exhibit a repertoire of preadapted behaviors that become organized around an available adult caregiving figure. The behaviors (e.g., orienting, crying, clinging, signaling, and proximity-seeking) are directed toward the caregiver under conditions of fatigue, illness, threat, or stress, promoting the infant's survival (Bowlby, 1969/1982; Tracy, Lamb, & Ainsworth, 1976). This emerging organization or regulation of infant behavior with respect to the caregiver is attachment. At the core of attachment for human infants is the regulation of emotional experience, including the experience of fear.

Three major patterns of attachment in infancy (secure, anxious avoidant, and anxious resistant) are thought to represent organized dyadic strategies, regulating arousal or maintaining organization when the infant is alarmed and providing a secure base for exploration

(Main & Hesse, 1990; Sroufe & Waters, 1977). For infants classified as secure, the caregiver is experienced as available and responsive when the infant is overly aroused, and emotions are thought to operate in an integrated smoothly regulated fashion to serve the inner organization and felt security of the child (Sroufe, 1990). In contrast, anxious avoidant and anxious resistant organizational patterns reflect coherent means of maintaining proximity (in case of extreme threat) in the context of unavailable or intermittently available and unresponsive caregiving.

For some infants, however, no coherent organization of attachment behavior may evolve from the infant caregiver relationship. These infants may exhibit a diverse array of inexplicably disorganized, disoriented, and seemingly undirected or conflicting behavioral responses to the caregiver presence in the laboratory assessment of attachment, the Strange Situation (Main & Solomon, 1990). The responses include inconsistencies in usual sequences of behavior (e.g., approaching the door upon hearing the caregiver and running to the opposite side of the room upon the caregiver's entrance) and unusual behaviors (e.g., freezing, stilling) and stereotypies in the presence of the caregiver. Such cases are classified as anxiously attached, disorganized/disoriented. Whereas it is not uncommon for an infant to show stress-related behaviors at low levels of intensity when the caregiver is absent, when behaviors of this type are seen at higher levels of intensity in the caregiver's presence the behavior becomes difficult to explain.

It is believed that for these infants incomprehensible frightening or frightened caregiver behavior has disrupted or interfered with the formation of a coherent pattern of attachment (Main & Hesse, 1990). Whereas infants frightened or alarmed by an external environmental source inevitably seek proximity with the caregiver, caregiver behavior that frightens the attached infant places the infant in an irresolvable paradox in which the infant can neither approach the caregiver nor flee or shift attention to the environment. The caregiver serves as a source of fear as well as the biologically based, expectable source of reassurance.

In contrast to moderate levels of anger or anxiety that may serve to maintain closeness in anxious avoidant and anxious resistant attachment relationships, the concurrent activation of fear and attachment behavioral systems produces strong conflicting motivations for the child exhibiting disorganized behaviors. The infant is challenged to manage extreme arousal at a time when infant capabilities are insufficient to ensure self-regulation (when organization depends upon dyadic regulation). Proximity-seeking mixed with avoidance may result as infants attempt to balance conflicting tendencies. Freezing, dazing, and stilling may be the result of their mutual inhibition. Such extreme conflict and the premature reliance upon individual coping mechanisms are thought to interfere with the development and stability of effective relational strategies of emotional communication and ability to maintain internal organization.

Although validation by systemic home observations is just beginning (Jacobvitz, Hazen, & Riggs, 1997; Schuengel, van IJzendoorn, Bakermans-Kranenburg, & Blom, 1997), disorganized/disoriented attachment patterns are thought to be the direct effect of frightening behavior or trauma, or the second generation effect of frightened caregivers who have not resolved their own experiences of trauma or loss (Main & Hesse, 1990). In the latter case, the caregiver may withdraw from the infant as though the infant were the source of alarm or the caregiver may lapse into dissociated or trance-like states, greatly taxing the infant's organizing capacities. Research findings provide some support for these hypotheses. High levels of attachment disorganization/disorientation in infancy have been related to parental experiences of unresolved mourning (Main & Hesse, 1990) and to maternal histories of loss due to divorce, separation, and death (Lyons-Ruth, Repacholi, McLeod, & Silva, 1991). Attachment disorganization/disorientation (including the unclassifiable A/C pattern) has been related to infant histories of maltreatment (Carlson, Cicchetti, Barnett, & Braunwald, 1989), hostile and intrusive caregiving (Lyons-Ruth et al., 1991), maternal depression (Radke-Yarrow, Cummings, Kuczynski, & Chapman, 1985), and prenatal alcohol (O'Connor, Sigman, & Brill, 1987) and drug exposure (Rodning, Beckwith, & Howard, 1991). In studies of prenatal alcohol and drug exposure, researchers suggest that caregiver relationships were compromised by the ongoing drug or alcohol use and patterns of use interfering with parenting interaction and the parenting role.

Disorganized/disoriented behaviors such as stereotypies may be expected in neurologically impaired infants; however, there is no evidence that attachment disorganization reflects stable constitutional deficiencies in infants in normal samples (Main & Hesse, 1990). For example, no relation has been found between disorganized attachment status of infants with mother and a second parent (Main & Solomon, 1990; Steele, Steele, & Fonagy, in press) or infants with mother and a day-care provider (Krentz, 1982).

For the three major attachment relationship patterns, internalized regulatory patterns and expectations derived from a history of caregiver-infant interactions form the basis for rules that govern the child's interpretation and expression of emotions and behavior. Well-functioning regulatory patterns or distortions in early dyadic regulation serve as prototypes for later individual styles of maintaining emotional security (Kobak & Shaver, 1987; Main & Hesse, 1990; Sroufe, 1996; Sroufe & Waters, 1977). From this perspective, disturbed attachment relationships are linked to later psychopathology, not as early disorders of the infant, but as markers of a beginning pathological process, risk factors for later pathology in the context of a complex model of interactive biological and environmental variables (Cicchetti, Toth, & Bush, 1988; Sameroff & Emde, 1989; Sroufe, 1997).

Consistent with this probabilistic view, anxious avoidant and anxious resistant attachment organizational patterns are thought to represent working defensive strategies developed in response to insensitive (rejecting or unpredictable but not frightening) caregiving behavior. These patterns are likely to lead to classic disorders only in the context of continued caregiving difficulties and in combination with stressful or traumatic experience where defensive strategies are likely to break down. In contrast with the coherent behavioral strategies of avoidant and resistant attachment, attachment disorganization is identified *only* through lapses or slippages in control, orientation and/or organization when the caregiver, the only source of safety, is at the same time the source of alarm (Main, in press). The collapse of relational behavioral and attentional strategies in infancy may place infants at heightened risk for later pathology.

Attachment disorganization/disorientation has been found to be related to child behavior problems (characterized by aggression) although only a minority of children classified as disorganized in infancy were highly aggressive in preschool (Lyons-Ruth, Alpern, & Repacholi, 1993). In this prospective study, psychosocial problems contributed to the child's outcome for one subgroup of children classified as disorganized in infancy who later developed behavior problems. The effects of attachment status and maternal psychosocial problems (documented history of child maltreatment, inpatient psychiatric hospitalization, or reported depressive symptoms) were independent and additive rather than interactive; however, the authors note that previous analyses had indicated that mothers with psychosocial problems were more likely to develop insecure attachment relationships.

Liotti (1992) has suggested a link between early disorganization and later dissociative disorders based on a phenotypic resemblance between trance-like states and some forms of disorganized/disoriented behavior. Some infants receiving high ratings of disorganization/disorientation may enter hypnotic or trance-like states as a defense against frightening or frightened caregiver behavior (Liotti, 1992). Whereas not all disorganized behaviors relate clearly to dissociative phenomena, infant postures and sequences of behavior such as stilling resemble the lapses or slippages in orientation and control associated with dissociative disorders as described by Putnam (1985, 1989, 1993) and Hilgard (1986). Putnam (1993) notes that frequent trance-like states are the single best predictor of dissociative disorders in children. Such disorganized infants may be vulnerable to the development of dissociative disorders (e.g., fugue states, multiple personality disorder) should traumatic circumstances continue or intervene in later life (Liotti, 1992). Interactions with a caregiver who periodically becomes unpredictably frightening or frightened may leave the disorganized infant more vulnerable than others to developing anomalous ideation regarding space-time relations and physical causality (Liotti, 1992). Moreover, experiences that occur while the child is in a trance-like state may be processed differently or encoded in an altered form and, as a result, be difficult to retrieve or revise later.

Based on the idea that the brain changes in a use dependent manner and organizes in response to experience during development, Perry and his colleagues (Perry, Pollard, Blakley, Baker, & Vigilante, 1995) suggest that the internalization of specific patterns of neuronal activity associated with acute responses may account for vulnerability to dissociative disorders. Thus, "if in the midst of traumatic experience, a child dissociates and stays in a dissociative state for a long period of time (e.g., by re-exposure to evocative stimuli), the child will internalize a sensitized neurobiology related to dissociation predisposing to the development of dissociative disorders" (Perry et al., 1995, p. 283). On the other hand, if the child utilizes a hyperarousal response to trauma, prolonged or repeated reactivation of this "fight or flight" response pattern may sensitize neurobiological systems to an alternate form of dysregulation. Traumatic events or reminders of traumatic events may lead to abnormal persistence of fear or hyperaroused behavioral states (e.g., hypervigilance, hyperactivity, impulsivity). In either case, neurological components of an adaptive response to traumatic experience may become sensitized and more pervasive, resulting in maladaptive regulatory symptomatology.

In the present study, prospective longitudinal data are utilized to validate the rating of attachment disorganization and examine hypotheses related to antecedents and consequences of patterns of attachment disorganization/disorientation. First, the relations of attachment disorganization to endogenous (e.g., maternal medical history, infant temperament) and environmental (e.g., maternal caregiving quality, infant history of abuse) antecedent variables are explored. The goal of these analyses was to determine whether attachment disorganization results from relationship experience as hypothesized by Main and Hesse (1990) and/or endogenous factors as suggested by the nature of disorganized behaviors. Second, behavioral consequences of attachment disorganization/disorientation from 24 months to 19 years are examined. Attachment disorganization was expected to be related to subsequent mother-infant relationship quality and to individual psychopathology, in particular, dissociative symptomatology. Third, the contributions of attachment disorganization/disorientation to predictions of psychopathology and dissociation in adolescence are examined in relation to intervening measures of socioemotional functioning. Finally, the role of attachment disorganization as mediator of the effects of caregiving quality on later psychopathology and dissociation is examined. The study focuses on the correlational relations between continuous ratings of attachment disorganization/disorientation and antecedent and consequent measures to maximize the use of existing codable attachment assessment data.

METHOD

Participants

Participants were 157 infants (92 males, 65 females) and mothers drawn from a longitudinal study of children and families (Egeland & Brunnquell, 1979). Mothers were recruited while receiving prenatal care at public health clinics in Minneapolis in 1975. Children with sensory handicaps were excluded from the study. At the time of delivery, the mothers ranged in age from 12 to 34 years ($M = 20.66$, $SD = 3.87$); 68% of the mothers were single. Thirty-nine percent of the mothers had not completed high school. Eighty percent of the mothers were European American, 13% were African American, and the remaining 7% were American Indian, Latino, or Asian. Based on U.S. census occupational categories, 40% of heads of households were employed as either clerical, service workers, operatives, or craftsmen, 5% were employed in technical, managerial, or sales positions, 36% were unemployed when the infants were born, and 14% were students. This sample was found to be representative of the larger original sample ($N = 267$); the current participants and the attrition sample did not differ significantly with respect to demographic variables.

Procedure

Because longitudinal multivariate data afford the opportunity for multiple analyses regarding a particular phenomenon, it becomes critical to define a clear rationale or strategy for variable selection. The goal of the current study was to examine specific hypotheses concerning the antecedents and sequelae of disorganized attachment relations: the relations between early biological and environmental factors and attachment disorganization and links between attachment disorganization and later psychopathology. With this aim in mind, variables were chosen for inclusion in the study based on two criteria: whether they were (1) representative of constructs of interest (e.g., infant temperament, quality of caregiver infant regulation, child behavior problems, psychopathology) and (2) had proven to be powerful indicators in previous studies. All variables examined in the statistical analyses were explicitly chosen for this study based on these criteria, and all results of these analyses are reported here.

When possible throughout the study, data were combined to minimize subject loss, to utilize all information available, to minimize some sources of error, to keep the number of variables in the analyses as small as possible, and to insure high-quality data. In some cases, this involved averaging multiple assessments. Thus, measures of behavior problems were averaged across grades 1 through 6. The procedure not only counteracts idiosyncracies of individual teachers but also maintains an adequate sample size (if data were not available for a participant in a given year, the average from the other 3 years would be adequate).

Descriptive statistics for antecedent and consequent variables are presented in Tables 1 and 2, respectively. Descriptive statistics for the participant sample and the remaining sample (cases for whom no attachment assessments were available for rating of disorganization) were compared. Significant differences were found with respect to two consequent variables:

TABLE 1

Descriptive Statistics for Antecedent Variables of Disorganized/Disoriented Attachment in Infancy

Variables	M	SD	Range	Frequency 0	1	n
Endogenous:						
Maternal medical problems	.59	.80	0–3	· · ·	· · ·	150
Pregnancy complications	.45	.65	0–4	· · ·	· · ·	151
Drug/alcohol use	.17	.41	0–2	· · ·	· · ·	157
Premature birth	· · ·	· · ·	· · ·	138	19	157
Delivery complications	.73	.92	0–6	· · ·	· · ·	150
Infant anomalies	.38	.58	0–3	· · ·	· · ·	149
Brazelton (7, 10 days)	4.03	2.95	0–15	· · ·	· · ·	151
Carey temperament (3 months):						
Adaptability	.00	1.00	−2.59 to 3.24	· · ·	· · ·	151
Intensity	.00	1.00	−2.48 to 7.49	· · ·	· · ·	151
Low threshold	.00	1.00	−4.06 to 3.15	· · ·	· · ·	151
Infant social behavior (3 months)	.00	.85	−1.75 to 2.53	· · ·	· · ·	146
Environmental:						
Relationship status	· · ·	· · ·	· · ·	49	107	157
Maternal abuse history	· · ·	· · ·	· · ·	43	38	81
Psychological problems	· · ·	· · ·	· · ·	149	8	157
Maternal risk status (at infant's birth)	1.93	.69	1–3	· · ·	· · ·	80
Maternal caretaking skill	.00	1.00	−2.81 to 1.86	· · ·	· · ·	146
Maternal affective quality (3 months)	.00	1.00	−2.08 to 1.92	· · ·	· · ·	146
Maternal cooperation/sensitivity (6 months)	5.53	1.50	1–9	· · ·	· · ·	129
Infant abuse						
Overall abuse	.40	.90	0–4	· · ·	· · ·	157
Physical abuse	· · ·	· · ·	· · ·	139	18	157
Verbal abuse	· · ·	· · ·	· · ·	144	13	157
Psychological unavailability	· · ·	· · ·	· · ·	142	15	157
Neglect	· · ·	· · ·	· · ·	140	17	157

TABLE 2

Descriptive Statistics for Consequent Variables of Disorganized/Disoriented Attachment in Infancy

Variables	M	SD	Range	Sample Size
Quality of mother-child relationship (24 months)	3.06	1.06	1–5	135
Quality of mother-child relationship (42 months)	4.16	1.57	1–7	141
Preschool behavior problems (4½–5 years)	88.22	19.07	45–143	78
Teacher's Report Form (1, 2, 3, 6 grade):				
Total score	56.18	8.32	37–76	143
Externalizing	55.96	8.23	39–75	143
Internalizing	54.06	7.21	38–75	143
Dissociation	1.21	1.17	0–7	143
Emotional health rank (1, 2, 3, 6 grade)	47.13	22.21	7.59–96.66	144
Boundary dissolution (13 years)	2.80	1.60	1–7	128
Teacher's Report Form (high school):				
Total score	54.88	8.60	33–85	133
Externalizing	55.30	8.85	40–76	133
Internalizing	53.66	7.98	38–76	131
Dissociation	.86	1.36	0–9	144
Emotional health rank (high school)	51.00	25.00	3–100	134
K-SADS (17½ years):				
Psychopathology rating	3.17	1.85	1–7	129
Dissociation	.03	.21	0–2	129
DES dissociation (19 years)	33.82	36.96	0–185	128

Teacher's Report Form (TRF) rating of dissociation, grades 1–6, $t(189) = 2.32$, $p < .05$, current sample $m = 1.26$, $SD = 1.32$, $n = 143$; remaining sample $m = .77$, $SD = 1.01$, $n = 48$, TRF rating of dissociation, high school, $t(189) = 2.32$, $p < .05$, current sample $m = 1.22$, $SD = 1.19$, $n = 143$, remaining sample $m = .77$, $SD = .98$, $n = 48$. Gender differences within the participant sample were found with respect to the composite emotional health outcome variable only (see below).

Measures

Antecedent endogenous variables. Measures of endogenous infant characteristics (i.e., medical history, infant anomalies at birth, Brazelton assessments, Carey ratings) were included despite the fact that they may be considered weak or outdated indicators of temperament or biological factors. Given the nature of disorganized behaviors, it was considered important to examine hypotheses regarding biological/neurological contributions to attachment disorganization to the degree possible within the constraints of the longitudinal data set.

Medical history. Variables representing the mother's history of medical problems and complications during pregnancy and birth were derived from hospital records. These included (1) number of mother's serious medical problems prior to pregnancy, (2) number of medical complications during the mother's pregnancy, (3) drug/alcohol use prior to and/or during pregnancy (coded 0, 1, 2), (4) presence (coded 1) or absence (coded 0) of premature birth, and (5) number of medical complications at the time of delivery.

Infant anomalies. A variable representing frequency and severity of infant anomalies at birth was derived from hospital records. Infant conditions were rated on a 3 point scale taking into account number and severity of conditions reported. At the high end of the scale (rating $= 3$), multiple severe conditions (e.g., multiple infections at birth) were reported. At the low end of the scale (rating $= 0$), no anomalous conditions were reported.

Neonatal Behavioral Assessment Scale. The Neonatal Behavioral Assessment Scale (Brazelton, 1973) was administered for each infant at home on the infant's seventh and tenth days of life. The NBAS consists of 27 behavioral items (e.g., habituation to visual, auditory, and tactile stimulation, muscle tone, alertness) rated on 9 point scales and 17 reflex items (e.g., Babinski, moro, rooting, and sucking reflexes) rated as low, medium, or high. A nonoptimal score defined as the number of items on which the infant was judged to be functioning in the nonoptimal range indicates the infant's overall level of functioning. The average of the nonoptimal scores from the two assessments was used in the analyses.

Five examiners administered the NBAS. Two had been trained by Brazelton's associates, and three established reliability with the original trainees using the criteria of no more than one disagreement on the reflex items and/or no more than one scale score disagreement of more than one point. The two primary testers examined 67% of the infants. Interrater agreements averaged .93 for the entire sample.

Carey Infant Temperament Questionnaire (3 months). The Carey Infant Temperament Questionnaire (Carey, 1970) was completed by mothers at 3 months. The questionnaire assesses nine dimensions of temperament, including mood, approachability, adaptability, intensity, activity, persistence, threshold, rhythmicity, and distractibility. For each dimension, three responses are possible (e.g., low, medium, or high). (See Vaughn, Deinard, & Egeland, 1980, for comparison of Carey results from this sample and the standardization sample.)

A principal components analysis with VARIMAX rotation of the nine items yielded three factors labeled: adaptability/demandingness (items related to adaptability, mood, and approachability), intensity/activity (items related to intensity, activity, and persistence), and low threshold (items related to low threshold, rhythmicity, and distractibility). The three factor scores were used as variables in this study.

Infant social behavior during feeding (3 months). At 3 months postpartum, infant-mother pairs were observed in their homes during a feeding. Observers rated a range of maternal behaviors, infant behaviors, and interactions between the mother and infant (e.g., frequency of looking at the infant, cuddling by the infant, responsiveness of the caregiver to infant initiatives). A total of 33 maternal and child behaviors were rated by independent observers. The mean range of scores was 7 for the 15 9-point scales, 6 for the 10 7-point scales, 4 for 2 6-point scales, 4 for 4 5-point scales, and 2 for 1 3-point scale.

Prior to making home visits and collecting data, the observers were trained using video-taped feedings and established a median reliability of .85 using the Lawlis and Lu index (1972). Reliability checks throughout the course of the study maintained the overall level of agreement at 85%. The Lawlis and Lu measure of interrater reliability is defined as the proportion of ratees on whom the raters agree within the limits set, corrected for number of agreements expected by chance.

The data derived from the feeding observations were factor analyzed using a principal components analysis with VARIMAX rotation. A three factor solution was identified that accounted for 54.8% of the total variance. The first two factors were identified primarily by variables assessing the mother's care-giving skills (e.g., sensitivity, response to crying) and the quality of her affective interactions with the infant (e.g., expressiveness, verbalization). These two factors accounted for 41% and 37% of the common variance, respectively. The third factor was identified primarily by infant variables (e.g., infant social behavior, infant disposition). Descriptions of the items and the factor structure of the variables have been presented by Vaughn, Taraldson, Crichton, and Egeland (1980) and are not reproduced here. The three factors were used in the analyses presented here.

Antecedent environmental variables. Maternal histories of abuse and psychological problems. The presence (coded 1) or absence (coded 0) of maternal history of abuse and presence or absence of maternal history of psychological problems, including suicide attempts, were derived from hospital medical records (Egeland, Jacobvitz, & Sroufe, 1988).

Maternal relationship status (infant's birth). The status of the mother's marital or primary social relationships at the time of her infant's birth was recorded. The status was coded 1 (single, divorced, or long-term separation) or 0 (married or involved in a long-term relationship).

Maternal risk status (infant's birth). Mother's risk status for parenting difficulties was rated at the time of the infant's birth on a 3 point scale by public health clinic staff. Ratings were based on interview responses concerning maternal knowledge of development, expectations and preparation for the baby, and motivation to care for the baby. Mothers were rated 3 for high risk, 2 if expected to do well with support, and 1 for low risk (i.e., mother considered mature, competent, and motivated to care for the baby). Reliability coefficients were not available for this variable.

Maternal caretaking skill and affective quality during feeding (3 months). Factors related to maternal caretaking skill and affective quality during infant feeding were derived from home observations when infants were 3 months old. See "Infant Social Behavior during Feeding," above, for descriptions of the feeding observation and factor analysis.

Maternal Cooperation/Interference and Sensitivity/Insensitivity scales (6 months). Mother-infant interactions were rated on Ainsworth's Cooperation/Interference (intrusiveness) and Sensitivity/Insensitivity scales (Ainsworth, Blehar, Waters, & Wall, 1978) from feeding and play situations in the home when infants were 6 months old. Mothers and infants were observed for approximately 30 min during each of two feeding situations and for 20 min in a standardized play situation. In the first component of the play situation, mothers were asked to engage the infant in physical play, not mediated with toys; next, mothers were given a toy truck attached to a string and asked to "teach" the baby to retrieve the toy by pulling on the string. In the final component, the mothers were given several toys and asked to play with the baby in any way they chose.

The overall ratings of cooperation/interference and sensitivity/insensitivity across the feeding and play observations were used in these analyses. The central issue of the 9 point Cooperation/Interference scale is the extent to which the mother adapts the timing and quality of her interactions and initiations to the baby's state, mood, and current interests rather than disrupting the baby's ongoing activity. Maternal cooperation/interference has been found to be correlated negatively with subsequent behavior problems (Egeland, Pianta, & O'Brien, 1993). The focus of the 9 point Sensitivity/Insensitivity scale is the extent to which the mother reads and responds to her infant's cues and demonstrates an awareness of the infant's subjective state by adjusting her own behavior. This measure was shown to be a highly significant predictor of quality of attachment in this sample (Egeland & Farber, 1984).

Observers were graduate students and interviewers experienced with the families and measures and trained to reliability in the laboratory prior to home assessments. The Tinsley-Weiss index (Tinsley & Weiss, 1975) of interrater agreement for ordinal scales was calculated for each scale. The index is based on the Lawlis and Lu (1972) measure of interrater reliability, the proportion of ratees on whom the raters agree within the limits set, corrected for number of agreements expected by chance. The Tinsley and Weiss T value, patterned after Cohen's (1960) kappa, is concerned with the *degree* to which agreement is better than chance. The index ranges from 0 to 1.00, with 0 indicating expected chance agreement and 1 indicating perfect agreement (which in this case was defined as a 2 point or less discrepancy). The T values were .80 for the Cooperation/Interference scale and .66 for the Sensitivity/Insensitivity scale based on 24 cases. The Cooperation/Interference and Sensitivity/Insensitivity ratings were aggregated for purposes of this study ($r = .81$, $N = 195$).

Infant abuse history. Infant maltreatment was identified on the basis of information regarding child-rearing practices and maternal attitudes toward the child derived from (1) home observations of mother and infant when the infants were 7 and 10 days old and at 3, 6, 9, and 12 months; (2) home interviews with mothers including the Child Care Rating Scale (Egeland & Deinard, 1975) and questions regarding caregiving skills, feelings toward the infant, and disciplinary practices; (3) observations of the dyads and interviews with mothers conducted during mother-child visits to the public health clinic; and (4) laboratory observations of the dyads when the infants were 9, 12, and 18 months old.

Behaviors considered to be physically abusive ranged from frequent and intense spanking to unprovoked angry outbursts resulting in serious injuries, such as severe cigarette burns. In all instances, the abuse was seen as potentially physically damaging to the child.

Mothers identified as hostile/verbally abusive chronically found fault with their children and criticized them in an extremely harsh fashion. Whereas many physically abusive mothers were not constantly hostile or rejecting (but rather prone to violent, unprovoked outbursts), verbally abusive mothers engaged in constant berating and harassment of their children. At 24 months, children of hostile/verbally abusive mothers with or without physical abuse exhibited more frustration and anger compared with the control group, and toddlers with experiences of hostile but not physical abuse demonstrated more frustration oriented toward their mothers (Egeland & Sroufe, 1981).

Mothers considered to be psychologically unavailable were unresponsive to their children and, in many cases, passively rejecting of them. These mothers appeared detached and uninvolved with their children, interacting with them only when necessary. In general, they were withdrawn, displayed flat affect, and seemed depressed. At 24 months, frequency of frustration, whining and negative affect was greatest for children who had experienced psychologically unavailable care without physical abuse (Egeland & Sroufe, 1981).

Mothers rated as neglectful were irresponsible or incompetent in managing day-to-day child-care activities. They failed to provide for the necessary health or physical care of the children and did little to protect them from possible dangers in the home. Whereas these mothers sometimes expressed interest in their children's well-being, they lacked the skill, knowledge, or understanding to provide consistent, adequate care.

The validity of group placement was supported by a variety of information. All mothers in the physical abuse group had been under the care of child protection or had been referred to child protection by someone outside of the longitudinal project. Independent raters' observations of mothers and infants in limit-setting tasks at 12 and 18 months and a problem solving task at 24 months supported the identification of hostile/verbally abusive mothers and psychologically unavailable mothers. Mothers rated as neglectful were or had been under the care of the public health nurse or child protection.

For purposes of the present study, dyads were coded 1 for presence or 0 for absence of each of the four conditions: physical abuse, verbal abuse, psychological unavailability, and neglect (Egeland & Sroufe, 1981; Egeland, Sroufe, & Erickson, 1983). Dyads also were assigned a composite rating of abuse (0–4).

Quality of attachment (12, 18 months). Attachment assessments were conducted using Ainsworth's Strange Situation procedure (Ainsworth et al., 1978). The standardized laboratory procedure consists of eight brief episodes designed to activate infant attachment behavior through an increasingly stressful series of infant-mother separations and reunions. Individual differences in attachment relationships are coded with respect to the infant's gaining comfort in the mother's presence when stressed and using the mother as a secure base from which to explore. Based on the patterning of the infant's behavior across all episodes, infant-mother dyads are assigned to one of three major classifications: secure, anxious avoidant, or anxious resistant.

Strange Situation assessments were videotaped, and scoring was based on these records. Assessments at 12 and 18 months were coded by independent experienced coders. Two additional scorers were used to establish scoring agreement. Agreement with independent rescoring of the entire 12 month sample was 89% for the A, B, and C classifications. Agreement with independent rescoring of 25 randomly selected 18 month assessments was 92%. Disagreements were resolved by the more experienced coder after reviewing the videotape.

Videotaped Strange Situation assessments were available for disorganization/disorientation coding for 157 of the original participants in the longitudinal study.[1] Both 12 and 18 month assessments were available for 48 participants. Assessments at either 12 or 18 months were available for 74 and 35 participants, respectively.

Strange Situation assessments were coded for attachment disorganization/disorientation using the classification scheme developed by Main and Solomon (1990). Indices of disorganization/disorientation include (1) sequential display of contradictory behavior patterns; (2) simultaneous display of contradictory behavior patterns; (3) undirected, misdirected, incomplete, and interrupted movements and expressions; (4) stereotypies, asymmetrical movements, mistimed movements, and anomalous postures; (5) freezing, stilling, and

---

[1] All Strange Situation assessments were recorded originally on reel-to-reel tapes. Some assessments were lost initially because tapes were recycled and used for multiple assessments. Other assessments were lost due to the deterioration of reel-to-reel tape quality.

TABLE 3
Mean Disorganization Ratings by Major Attachment Classification at 12 and 18 Months

Assessment and Major Classification	Mean Rating	SD	n	Disorganized Classification Frequency	(%)
12 month:					
Anxious, avoidant	4.24	1.92	37	19	
Secure	2.31	1.62	55	8	
Anxious, resistant	4.33	2.23	30	16	
Total			122	43	(35%)
18 month:					
Anxious, avoidant	4.54	2.11	24	15	
Secure	3.26	2.30	39	12	
Anxious, resistant	4.10	2.43	20	9	
Total			83	36	(43%)

slowed movements and expressions; (6) direct indices of apprehension regarding the parent; (7) direct indices of disorganization or disorientation (see Appendix A for brief description). Disorganization/disorientation in infant-parent attachment was rated on a 9 point scale, and a disorganized/disoriented classification assigned to infant-mother dyads receiving a rating of 5 or higher (see Appendix B for rating criteria). Coders were trained by Mary Main, and interrater agreement was 86% based on 35 cases (selected at random with the restriction that half, or 17 cases, were classified as disorganized by the primary coder). Kappa was calculated to be .72.

Attachment disorganization ratings ranged from 1 to 9 with a mean rating of 3.75 ($SD = 2.29, N = 157$). See Table 3 for mean ratings of disorganization by major attachment classification. For purposes of analyses presented here, the overall rating of disorganization/disorientation (the highest rating assigned across the 12 and 18 month assessments) was used (Main, personal communication, 1995).

For the subsample of 48 for whom both 12 and 18 month assessments were available, disorganization ratings were positively correlated, $r(46) = .38$, $p < .01$. Of this subsample, 17 were classified disorganized/disoriented at both time periods, and 21 were stably classified as not disorganized. Seven participants moved from not disorganized to disorganized status. (Two of these participants simultaneously changed from resistant to avoidant attachment, two changed from secure to avoidant, and three were stably secure.) Three participants changed from disorganized to not disorganized status. (Two of these participants changed from resistant to secure attachment, and one moved from avoidant to resistant.) *Consequent variables: Early childhood. Quality of mother-child relationship (24 months).* The quality of the mother-child relationship at 24 months was assessed in a laboratory problem-solving procedure described by Matas, Arend, and Sroufe (1978). In this situation, the child is challenged to solve a series of problems of graded difficulty with mother available to help. The child's overall experience in this laboratory assessment was rated on a 5 point Likert-type scale. A high rating (rating = 5) is assigned when it is judged that the child has had a positive experience and would be even more confident in facing problems in subsequent experiences. A low rating (rating = 1) is assigned when it is judged that the child has had a very poor experience either due to belittling taunting, or abuse from the mother, or breaking down (losing control or having to leave the scene) with the mother failing to come to the rescue. This variable has been validated extensively as an index of the overall quality and effectiveness of the mother-child pair at this developmental period (Egeland et al., 1983; Erickson, Sroufe, & Egeland, 1985). Assessments were coded by two independent coders. Interrater reliability (Pearson product-moment correlation) was .87.

Quality of mother-child relationship (42 months). The quality of the mother-child relationship at 42 months was observed in a series of teaching tasks: (1) building block towers of specific proportions, (2) naming things with wheels, (3) matching colors and shapes on a form board, and (4) tracing a preset pattern through an etch-a-sketch maze. The tasks are just beyond the ability of most children, requiring the parent/caregiver to help the child complete the task and capturing the coping skills of the child and his or her capacity to use the mother as a supportive resource (see Erickson et al., 1985).

The quality of the mother-child interaction is reflected in a variety of variables derived from the teaching task. One of the most powerful variables related to regulation in the mother-child relationship, child's experience in the session, was selected for this study as an early indicator of dyadic functioning. The scale reflects the degree to which the child's experience in the session would result in feelings of success and competence on the tasks and of confidence in having a good relationship with his or her mother. At the high end of the 7 point scale, there are very positive interactions between mother and child, and through appropriate maternal assistance the child is able to complete the tasks with some sense of autonomy or problem-solving success. At the low end of the scale, the child is judged to have a negative experience in the session. There may be many mother-child conflicts or the mother may dominate or reject the child in ways that contribute to lower expectations of his or her own competence.

This relationship regulation variable discriminates children with and without a history of abuse in early childhood (Egeland et al., 1983) and children with and without behavior problems in preschool (Erickson et al., 1985). Assessments were coded by two independent coders. Average interrater reliability (Pearson product-moment correlation) was .78 for 87 participants.

Preschool behavior problems (4½ years). At 4½–5 years, the children participated in preschool or daycare. For each child, the Preschool Behavior Questionnaire (Behar & Stringfield, 1974) was completed by a teacher or child-care provider. This measure consists of 30 items associated with socioemotional problems in young children. The teacher was asked to check for each item: "Certainly applies" (scored 3 points), "Applies sometimes" (2 points), "Does not apply" (1 point). The Preschool Behavior Questionnaire was standardized on a sample of 496 children enrolled in normal preschools and 102 children enrolled in special education programs for emotionally disturbed children. The measure significantly discriminated normal and deviant groups of children. Interrater reliability (mean $r = .84$) and test-retest reliability (mean $r = .87$) were moderate.

Teachers also completed the 31 item Behavior Problem Scale (Erickson & Egeland, 1981), using the same format as the Preschool Behavior Questionnaire. The scale was devised to assess more severe behavior disturbances than those represented in the Preschool Behavior Questionnaire. Items are similar to those included in the Child Behavior Checklist (Achenbach & Edelbrock, 1986).

Scores from the two scales were positively correlated ($r = .82$, $N = 98$). The combined total score from the two measures (Erickson et al., 1985) was used in this study.

Consequent variables: Middle childhood and adolescence. Teacher's Report Form (grades 1, 2, 3, 6, high school). The Teacher's Report Form (TRF), the teacher version of the Child Behavior Checklist (CBCL; Achenbach & Edelbrock, 1986) was completed by the child's teacher toward the end of first, second, third, and sixth grades along with other measures of classroom adjustment. In high school, the measure was completed by the student's English teacher in grade 10. The Teacher's Report Form consists of 113 items describing behavioral problems associated with middle childhood (e.g., "Disobedient at school," "Gets in many fights," "Likes to be alone"). Each item is scored by the teacher to reflect occurrence, frequency, and severity of the problem ("Often and very true" = 2, "Sometimes or somewhat true" = 1, "Not true" = 1). The measure yields a total score, broad-band scores representing externalizing and internalizing dimensions of behavior problems, and a set of empirically derived factor scores representing syndromes of maladaptive behavior. For this study, elementary and high school data were analyzed separately. For the elementary years, composite Total, Externalizing, and Internalizing scores were derived by averaging T scores across grades 1, 2, 3, and 6. For the high school years, Total, Externalizing, and Internalizing T scores represent a single assessment.

The TRF has been normed on a large, representative national sample. Two-week test-retest reliabilities for the TRF Externalizing, Internalizing, and sub-scales ranged from .70 to .89 for girls (ages 6–11) and .82 to .92 for boys (ages 6–11). For adolescents, reliabilities ranges from .64 to .98 for girls (ages 12–16) and .74 to .92 for boys (ages 12–16). The authors report good convergent validity for the subscales (.62–.90 with corresponding scales of the Conner's Teacher Rating Scale) and good criterion-related validity in the form of significant differences between demographically similar referred and nonreferred children on all the TRF scales for all sex/age groups. Cronbach's alpha was calculated for each of the elementary school composite variables used in the present study (Total, alpha = .79; Externalizing, alpha = .82; Internalizing, alpha = .63). The TRF Total score stability coefficients ranged from .44 to .60 for grades 1 to 6 and .17 to .30 for elementary years to high school; Externalizing coefficients ranged from .50 to .61 for grades 1 to 6 and .24 to .38 for elementary to high school; and Internalizing coefficients ranged from .27 to .44 for grades 1 to 6 and −.02 to .18 for elementary to high school.

From the TRF, a scale representing dissociative symptoms was derived for each assessment period (grades 1, 2, 3, 6, and high school). Items were selected based on criteria for diagnoses of dissociative disorders (American Psychiatric Association, 1994; Putnam, 1989) and moderate to high item-total score correlations. The dissociative scales include five items: "Confused or seems to be in a fog"; "Gets hurt a lot, accident-prone"; "Explosive and unpredictable behavior"; "Stares blankly"; "Strange behavior." For the high school period, the dissociative scale includes the item "Deliberately harms self or attempts suicide" in place of the item "Gets hurt a lot, accident-prone" used in middle childhood. Cronbach's alpha was calculated for each of the dissociative scales (grade 1, alpha = .68; grade 2, alpha = .53; grade 3, alpha = .68; grade 6, alpha = .53; grades 1 through 6 combined, alpha = .68; high school, alpha = .63). Stability coefficients ranged from .20 to .46 for grades 1 to 6 and .08 to .15 for the elementary grades to high school.

Teacher rankings of emotional health/self-esteem (grades 1, 2, 3, 6, high school). The rank order measure of emotional health/self-esteem employs a teacher nomination procedure developed by staff of the longitudinal study. Rankings rather than ratings were used as a way of calibrating the hundreds of teachers involved in assessing the children. At grades 1, 2, 3, 6, and in high school, teachers were asked to rank order the students in their classes based on a written description of emotional health/self-esteem with the child most closely resembling the description to be ranked at the top. The emotional health/self-esteem measure refers to the degree to which the child is confident, curious, self-assured, and enjoys new experiences and challenges, becoming involved in whatever she or he does.

The child's score on this measure was recorded as the ratio of the inverse of the child's rank divided by the number of students in the class (i.e., if the child were ranked eleventh in a class of 30, she or he received a score of $.66 = (30 - 11 + 1)/30$). The reliability and validity of this procedure was supported by the findings of Connolly and Doyle (1981). Because a single teacher completed the rank orders, reliability figures are not available for the scales with this sample. In a separate study, however, multiple counselors independently rank ordered children participating in a 4 week summer-camp. Interrater reliability coefficients ranged from .63 to .81 on the emotional health rank orders. The rankings by teachers show significant stability from year to year: grades 1–2, $r(171) = .62$, $p < .001$, grades 2–3, $r(178) = .60$, $p < .001$, grades 3–6, $r(178) = .44$, $p < .001$, grade 6 to high school, $r(172) = .34$, $p < .001$. The rankings are significantly correlated with ratings of behavior problems: TRF Total score in grades 1–6, $r(189) = -.71$, $p < .001$, and with observed peer competence, $r(190) = .82$, $p < .001$ (Hiester, Carlson, & Sroufe, 1993). For this study, emotional health rankings for grades 1, 2, 3, and 6 were averaged and the composite was used in the analyses. Mean composited emotional health rankings for males and females differed significantly in elementary school, $t(142)$ value = 2.28, $p < .05$, males $m = 43.56$, $SD = 22$, $n = 83$; females $m = 51.98$, $SD = 21$, $n = 61$.

Parent-child relationship quality (13 years). At 13 years, adolescents and their mothers were videotaped in a laboratory situation. (Because only 44 "fathers" were living with the children at age 13, triadic data are not reported here.) The dyads were asked to complete four structured interaction tasks (based on Block & Block, 1980): (1) plan an antismoking campaign, (2) assemble a series of puzzles while the parent was blindfolded (the child was asked to guide the assembly), (3) discuss the effects of two imaginary/hypothetical happenings, and (4) complete a Q-sort of an ideal person. The dyadic interactions were assessed using a series of 7 point rating scales (J. Sroufe, 1991).

For the current analyses, the scale measuring boundary dissolution between parent and child was used as an indicator of dysfunction in the relationship. The scale captures the extent to which generational boundaries in the parent-child relationship are violated in one or more of the following ways: (1) spousification: the child is placed in the role of meeting the parent's needs for nurturance or assumes a leadership role in relation to the parent, (2) role diffusion characterized by peer-like behavior. These are viewed as problems in the developmental context of early adolescent emancipation. At the high end of the scale, indicators of generational boundary dissolution are frequent and pervasive, occurring consistently throughout the session. Examples include: (1) numerous or explicit examples of spousification with both parent and child initiating the behaviors, (2) high child caregiving or child control, coupled with disrespect of the parent by the child, and (3) high level of peer-like behavior and peer-like bickering. At the midpoint in the scale, appropriate parent-child roles are maintained during much of the session; however, indicators are prevalent, and appropriate boundaries are not fully reinstated when needed. Examples include: (1) a pervasive quality of sweetness or preciousness of the child to the parent, mild physical signs of spousification, or high playfulness with sexually provocative quality, (2) signs that the parent is avoiding parenting responsibiliities with the child assuming the caregiving or executive functions, and (3) peer-like behavior or lack of parental leadership with the introduction of negative interaction when the situation requires leadership. At the low end of the scale, clear and appropriate parent-child boundaries are maintained.

Ratings for this sample ranged from 1 to 7 ($M = 2.75$, $SD = 1.60$). Interrater reliability for this scale was $r = .62$ ($n = 129$). Percent agreement within 1 point was .79. Because the majority of assessments were rated by two coders, the final conferenced data are likely to be somewhat more reliable than indicated by the correlation coefficient.

Kiddie Schedule for Affective Disorders and Schizophrenia Rating (17½ years). At age 17½, adolescents were administered the Kiddie Schedule for Affective Disorders and Schizophrenia (K-SADS). The K-SADS provides both comprehensive assessment of symptoms relevant for a range of major psychiatric disorders and flexibility for interviewers to clarify questions and pursue inconsistencies that emerge during the interview. The K-SADS used in the present study integrates elements of two versions of the instrument. The present state edition (K-SADS-P) was employed to make graduated ratings of the severity of present symptoms and disorders on 6 and 4 point scales. The K-SADS-P was originally developed by Puig-Antich and Chambers (1978) and modified for DSM-III-R by Ambrosini and colleagues (e.g., KSADS-III-R; Ambrosini, Metz, Prabucki, & Lee, 1989). The epidemiological version of the instrument (K-SADS-E; Orvaschel, Puig-Antich, Chambers, Tabrizi, & Johnson, 1982) was used to rate past symptoms and disorders dichotomously (i.e., yes = present, no = absent). Modifications in questions were based upon provisional diagnostic criteria for DSM-IV (American Psychiatric Association, 1994).

The validity of the K-SADS-E was demonstrated by the finding that virtually all former patients reassessed obtained the same diagnosis as in their earlier assessment. The validity of the K-SADS-P has been shown in studies of sensitivity to changes during treatment and of biological correlates of diagnoses (e.g., reviewed by Costello, 1991).

Research on test-retest reliability within a 72 hr period (Chambers et al., 1985) found varied but generally moderate levels of agreement for major diagnoses, with low concordance for a heterogeneous group of anxiety disorders. Work by Ambrosini and colleagues (Ambrosini et al., 1989) on the interrater reliability of K-SADS-III-R found the mean kappa to be .79 for child-derived diagnoses and .84 for all mother-derived and child-derived diagnoses based on symptom information during the previous 12 months. Mean kappas for individual diagnoses: major depression, kappa = .83; overanxious disorder, kappa = .85;

separation anxiety, kappa = .85, simple phobia disorder, kappa = .64, oppositional disorder, kappa = .89, and attention deficit disorder, kappa = .88.

For purposes of the longitudinal study, the adolescent's overall history of psychopathology was rated on a 7 point Likert-type scale. Number and severity of past and present diagnoses are considered in assigning ratings. At the high end of the scale (rating = 7), the individual qualifies for multiple diagnoses of pathology, both past and present. At the low end of the scale, the individual qualifies for a single diagnosis that is less serious, such as simple phobia (rating = 2), or neither past nor present diagnoses (rating = 1). The adolescent's overall history of dissociative experiences was represented by the total number of past and present diagnoses of brief dissociative episodes, depersonalization episodes, and dissociative episodes derived from the K-SADS.

Dissociative Experiences Scale (DES) (19 years). The Dissociative Experiences Scale (DES) is a self-report form of the frequency of dissociative experiences in an individual's daily life, intended to be used as a screening device for dissociative disorders. Individuals quantify experiences by marking a response scale (0%–100%) for each of 28 items. The scale items cover experiences of memory disturbances, identity, awareness, and cognition (e.g., frequent day-dreaming, lack of memory for significant past events). The DES discriminates clinical and nonclinical samples and demonstrates good construct and criterion validity (Carlson & Putnam, 1993). Internal reliability ($r = .80$) and test-retest reliability ($r = .83$) are high.

RESULTS

Results of the study are presented in four sections. First, the relations of attachment disorganization to early endogenous and environmental factors are examined. Second, consequences of attachment disorganization are explored. Third, results of hierarchical multiple regression analyses are presented. These analyses examine the relative contribution of attachment disorganization to later psychopathology and dissociation. Finally, results of structural equation modeling are presented. The models test hypotheses that attachment disorganization may mediate the effect of early caregiving on later psychopathology and dissociation.

Antecedents of Attachment Disorganization

Zero order correlations were calculated to examine the relations between early endogenous and environmental variables and overall ratings of attachment disorganization (see Table 4). Attachment disorganization was associated with single parent-hood and with maternal risk for parenting difficulties. Infants with high ratings of disorganization were more likely to have experienced insensitive/intrusive caregiving as well as a variety of forms of maltreatment in the first year of life. Attachment disorganization was not associated with maternal history of serious medical problems or psychological problems, medical complications during pregnancy or delivery, or reported maternal history of abuse or drug/alcohol use. Also, disorganization was not associated with infant anomalies, Brazelton scores at birth, or infant temperament and behavior ratings at 3 months.

TABLE 4

Correlations between Antecedent Endogenous and Environmental Factors and
Disorganized/Disoriented Attachment

Antecedent Variables	Disorganized/Disoriented Attachment	n
Endogenous variables:		
Maternal medical history[a]	.07	(150)
Pregnancy complications[a]	.02	(151)
Maternal drug/alcohol use[b]	−.02	(157)
Premature birth[b]	−.07	(157)
Delivery complications[a]	−.05	(150)
Infant anomalies[b]	.04	(149)
Infant Brazelton (7, 10 days)[a]	.11	(151)
Carey questionnaire (3 months):		
Infant adaptability[a]	.03	(151)
Infant intensity[a]	−.05	(151)
Infant low threshold[a]	−.05	(151)
Infant social behavior (3 months)[a]	−.03	(146)
Environmental variables:		
Maternal relationship status[b]	.25***	(156)
Maternal history of abuse[b]	.12	(81)
Maternal psychological problems[b]	.10	(157)
Maternal risk status[b] (at infant's birth)	.27**	(79)
Maternal caretaking skill[a]	−.29***	(146)
Maternal affective quality[a] (3 months)	−.03	(146)
Maternal cooperation/sensitivity[a] (6 months)	−.38***	(129)
Infant abuse:		
Overall abuse[b]	.29***	(157)
Physical abuse[b]	.20**	(157)
Verbal abuse[b]	.09	(157)
Psychological unavailability[b]	.23***	(157)
Neglect[b]	.20**	(157)

[a]Two-tailed Pearson product-moment correlation coefficients.
[b]Kendall tau correlation coefficients.
*$p < .05$, **$p < .01$; ***$p < .001$.

Consequences of Attachment Disorganization

Zero order correlations were calculated to examine the relations between attachment disorganization in infancy and indices of socioemotional difficulties or pathology from 24 months through adolescence (see Table 5). Overall ratings of disorganization were correlated in expected directions with measures of mother-child relationship quality at 24 and 42 months, behavior problems in elementary school (TRF Internalizing scores and emotional health rankings), behavior problems in high school (TRF Total and Internalizing scores) and ratings of psychopathology at age 17½. Attachment disorganization was correlated with TRF-derived dissociative scores in middle childhood and adolescence. In particular,

TABLE 5

Correlations between Disorganized/Disoriented Attachment and Consequent Measures of Relationship Quality and Individual Psychopathology from 24 Months to 19 Years

Outcome Variables	Disorganized/Disoriented Attachment	n
Mother-child relationship quality:		
Confidence with mother (24 months)	−.24*	(135)
Experience with mother (42 months)	−.25**	(141)
Preschool behavior problem index (4½–5 years)	.40***	(78)
Teacher Report Form (grades 1, 2, 3, 6):		
Total Score	.17	(143)
Externalizing	.03	(143)
Internalizing	.19*	(143)
Dissociation	.26**	(143)
Emotional health rank (grades 1, 2, 3, 6)	−17*	(144)
Parent-child boundary dissolution (13 years)	−.11	(128)
Teacher Report Form (high school):		
Total Score	.21*	(133)
Externalizing	.11	(133)
Internalizing	.18*	(131)
Dissociation	.22**	(133)
Emotional health rank (high school)	−.14	(134)
K-SADS (17½ years):		
Psychopathology rating	.34***	(129)
Dissociation[a]	.19*	(129)
DES (19 years):		
Dissociation	.36***	(128)

Note: Coefficients are two-tailed Pearson product-moment correlations unless otherwise indicated.
[a]Kendall tau correlation coefficient.
$*p < .05; **p < .01; ***p < .001$.

disorganization was associated with the items "confused, seems to be in a fog," $r(141) = .31$, $p < .001$, and "gets hurt alot, accident prone," $r(141) = .26$, $p < .01$, in elementary school, and the items "confused, seems to be in a fog," $r(130) = .18$, $p < .05$, "strange behavior," $r(131) = .24$, $p < .01$, and "deliberately harms self or attempts suicide," $r(130) = .20$, $p < .02$, in high school. Disorganization also was related to overall history and concurrent self-report of dissociative episodes as measured by the K-SADS at age 17½ and DES at age 19, $r(127) = .34$ and $r(126) = .36$, $p < .001$, respectively.

Hierarchical Regression Analyses Predicting Psychopathology and Dissociation from Attachment Disorganization

Prediction of psychopathology. Hierarchical multiple regression procedures were used to examine the prediction of psychopathology in adolescence (rating of psychopathology derived from the K-SADS) from attachment organization and disorganization and intervening individual and relationship indices of socioemotional functioning (combined index of child behavior problems in grades 1–6 and parent-child relationship quality at 13 years). For purposes of regression analyses, avoidant, resistant, and overall insecure (avoidant or resistant) attachment data were recoded assigning scores of 0, 1, 2 for the number of times (at 12 and 18 months) infants were classified avoidant, resistant, and insecure, respectively. Attachment organization (avoidant score) was entered first in the regression equation to examine the hypothesis that disorganization may explain psychopathology in adolescence beyond that predicted by insecure attachment alone. Because resistant and overall insecure attachment scores were found not to be related significantly to psychopathology ratings in adolescence, these variables were not included in regression analyses.

Zero order correlations of the independent variables included in the regression equation with the outcome ratings of adolescent psychopathology were as follows: avoidant attachment score, $r(127) = .26$, $p < .01$, attachment disorganization rating, $r(127) = .34$, $p < .001$, composite TRF behavior problem Total score for grades 1 to 6, $r(127) = .45$, $p < .001$, parent-child relationship quality rating at 13 years, $r(119) = .19$, $p < .05$.

In regression analyses, avoidant attachment scores, attachment disorganization ratings, elementary school behavior problem scores, and ratings of parent-child relationship quality at 13 years each contributed significantly to the prediction of psychopathology in adolescence. The combined set of variables produced a multiple correlation of .55, accounting for 31% of the overall variance (see Table 6). Attachment disorganization ratings also significantly predicted psychopathology ratings controlling for avoidant attachment, behavior problems, and parent-child relationship quality, R^2 change $= .05$, F change $(4, 116) = 7.49$, $p < .05$.

Prediction of dissociation. Hierarchical multiple regression procedures were used to examine the prediction of dissociation in adolescence (DES scores) from attachment disorganization and intervening individual and relationship socioemotional variables (combined index of child behavior problems in grades 1–6, parent-child relationship quality at 13 years). Avoidant, resistant, and overall insecure attachment scores (coded 0, 1, 2) were not correlated with DES scores and were not included in regression analyses.

Zero order correlations of the independent variables included in the regression equation with the outcome DES scores were as follows: attachment disorganization rating, $r(126) = .36$, $p < .001$, composite TRF behavior problem Total score for grades 1–6, $r(126) = .22$, $p < .05$, parent-child relationship quality rating at 13 years, $r(117) = .05$, *ns*.

In regression analyses, attachment disorganization ratings and elementary school behavior problem scores contributed significantly to the prediction of dissociation in adolescence. The combined set of variables produced a multiple correlation of .42, accounting for 17% of the overall variance (see Table 7). Also, attachment disorganization ratings significantly predicted dissociation scores controlling for elementary school behavior problems and parent-child relationship quality, R^2 change $= .10$, F change $(2, 116) = 13.49$, $p < .001$.

Structural Models Examining Attachment Disorganization as Mediator of Early Caregiving Experience

Structural equation modeling (Browne & Cudeck, 1993; Browne & Mels, 1992) was employed to test hypotheses that attachment disorganization may mediate the relations

TABLE 6

Hierarchical Regression Predicting Ratings of Psychopathology (K-SADS) at 17½ Years from Disorganized Attachment in Infancy, Behavior Problem Index (TRF) in Middle Childhood, and Family Relationship Quality in Early Adolescence ($N = 120$)

Step and Independent Variables	R^2 Change	Beta	B	T	R^2	Overall F	df
I. Prediction from disorganized attachment controlling for avoidant attachment:							
1. Avoidant attachment score (12–18 months)	.07	.27	.74	3.00**	.07	8.99**	1,119
2. Avoidant attachment score	...	.18	.51	2.02*	...	...	...
Disorganization rating (12–18 months)	.06	.25	.20	2.71**	.13	8.41***	2,118
3. Avoidant attachment score	...	.14	.38	1.63	...	...	...
Disorganization rating	...	.21	.17	2.49*	...	...	...
TRF total score (grades 1, 2, 3, 6)	.16	.40	.09	5.01***	.28	15.13***	3,117
4. Avoidant attachment score	...	.14	.38	1.65	...	...	...
Disorganization rating	...	.23	.19	2.76**	...	...	...
TRF total score	...	.38	.08	4.73***	...	...	...
Relationship rating (13 years)	.03	.17	.19	2.11*	.31	12.79***	4,116

Note: Index of psychopathology in adolescence is 7 point rating of number and severity of K-SADS diagnoses.
* $p < .05$; ** $p < .01$; *** $p < .001$.

TABLE 7

Hierarchical Regression Predicting Dissociation Scores (DES) at 19 Years from Disorganized Attachment in Infancy, Behavior Problem Index (TRF) in Middle Childhood, and Family Relationship Quality in Early Adolescence ($N = 118$)

Step and Independent Variables	R^2 Change	Beta	B	T	R^2	Overall F	df
I. Prediction from disorganized attachment:							
1. Disorganization rating (12–18 months)	.12	.34	.36	3.93***	.12	15.44***	1,117
2. Disorganization rating	...	.31	.33	3.64***	...	...	...
TRF total score (grades 1, 2, 3, 6)	.05	.23	.24	2.72**	.17	11.85***	2,116
3. Disorganization rating	...	.32	.33	3.67***	...	...	...
TRF total score	...	.23	.23	2.61**	...	...	...
Relationship rating (13 years)	.01	.05	.01	.57	.17	7.96***	3,115

Note: Index of psychopathology in adolescence is 7 point rating of number and severity of K-SADS diagnoses.

*p < .05; **p < .01; ***p < .001.

364

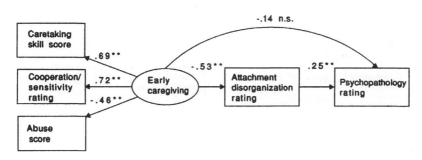

Figure 1. Structural model, M_1: Attachment disorganization as mediator of relations between early caregiving environment and psychopathology ratings (K-SADS) in adolescence. Error variances for measured indicators are not shown. The model accounts for 12% of the variance of the psychopathology rating. ** $p < .01$.

between (1) early caregiving and psychopathology at age 17½ and (2) early caregiving and dissociative experiences at age 19.

The first hypothesized model (Model M_1), shown in Figure 1, examined the relations between early caregiving, attachment disorganization, and psychopathology. The model includes pathos linking (1) early caregiving and attachment disorganization ratings, (2) early caregiving and psychopathology ratings, and (3) attachment disorganization ratings and psychopathology ratings. Three measured indicators of early caregiving included ratings of maternal caretaking skill at 3 months, ratings of maternal cooperation/sensitivity at 6 months, and infant history of abuse. Listwise Pearson correlations among the indicators of early caregiving and manifest variables (attachment disorganization ratings in infancy and K-SADS psychopathology ratings in adolescence) are presented in Appendix C. All factor loadings and path coefficients from early caregiving to attachment disorganization and attachment disorganization to psychopathology were significant at or beyond the .01 level. Results of the chi-square test of the model suggest an adequate fit to the data.

The second structural model (Model M_2, shown in Figure 2) tested the hypothesis that attachment disorganization may mediate the effects of early caregiving on dissociation (DES) scores at age 19. The model includes paths linking (1) early caregiving and attachment disorganization ratings, (2) early caregiving and DES scores, and (3) attachment disorganization ratings and DES scores. Three measured indicators of early caregiving were ratings of caretaking skill, ratings of maternal cooperation/sensitivity, and infant abuse history. Listwise Pearson correlations among manifest variables are presented in Appendix D. All factor loadings and path coefficients from early caregiving to attachment disorganization and attachment disorganization to dissociation as well as the indirect path from early caregiving to dissociation were significant at or beyond the .01 level. These results suggest that the effects of caregiving on dissociation may be direct as well as mediated by

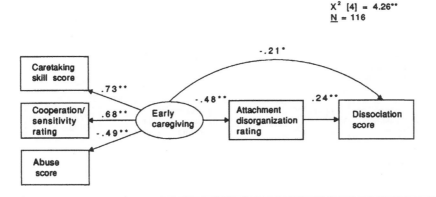

Figure 2. Structural model, M_1: Attachment disorganization as mediator of relations between early caregiving environment and dissociation score (DES) in adolescence. Error variances for measured indicators are not shown. The model accounts for 15% of the variance of the dissociation score. $^*p < .05; ^{**}p < .01$.

attachment disorganization. Results of the chi-square test of the mediation model suggest an adequate fit to the data.

DISCUSSION

In the present study, the etiology and consequences of attachment disorganization were examined using a prospective longitudinal design. Two central issues related to the validity of attachment disorganization/disorientation were tested: (1) the origins of disorganization in patterns of care (rather than in endogenous neuropathology) and (2) the consequences of disorganization for psychopathology and dissociative symptoms. Other critical propositions, such as the link between disorganization and infant experiences of abuse, were replicated. Structural equation models were employed to extend the understanding of relations between early caregiving experience and later symptomatic behavior and the mediating role of attachment disorganization.

With respect to the first hypothesis, results from analyses of disorganization etiology suggest that environmental factors (i.e., caregiving) influence the development of attachment disorganization. Attachment disorganization was related significantly to early environmental risk variables including maternal relationship status (i.e., living alone with an infant), maternal overall risk status, maternal caregiving style (intrusive versus cooperative, insensitive versus sensitive) as well as specific forms of maltreatment (e.g., physical abuse, psychological unavailability, and neglect). In this study, no evidence was found to support relations between endogenous factors and attachment disorganization. Disorganization ratings were not related to maternal medical history, pregnancy and delivery complications, infant anomalies, or infant temperament or behavior at birth and 3 months. These null findings are noteworthy given the nature of behaviors used to judge disorganization and disorientation.

Analyses of disorganization outcome data suggest that the quality of caregiving difficulties reflected in attachment disorganization may have significant consequences for the mother-child relationship and individual socioemotional functioning. In this study, attachment disorganization was related to the quality of the mother-child relationship at 24 and 42 months, individual behavior problems in preschool, elementary school, and high school, and diagnostic ratings of psychopathology at age 17½. Such simple predictability from infant behavior to disturbance at age 17 is unprecedented. Results of regression analyses and structural modeling begin to elucidate the contribution and relation of disorganization to later psychopathology. The findings suggest that (1) attachment disorganization may mediate the effects of caregiving quality on later psychopathology, (2) a history of attachment disorganization may contribute to or increase a child's risk for psychopathology even with anxious avoidant attachment quality, early behavior problems, and family relationship quality taken into account, and (3) whereas attachment disorganization, behavior problems, and parent child boundary problems independently predict psychopathology, the combination of these experiences best accounts for the occurrence of psychopathology in adolescence.

Based on data from this study, attachment disorganization may have particular long-term implications for the development of dissociative symptoms in childhood and adolescence. Attachment disorganization in infancy was related to dissociative symptoms as measured by rationally derived scales in elementary and high school, a semistructured diagnostic interview at age 17½, and a standardized self-report measure at age 19. Because one source of disorganized behaviors may be the second-generation effect of unresolved loss (Main & Hesse, 1990) or trauma (Carlson, 1990) and because many disorganized behaviors are thought to represent micro-dissociative experiences (Liotti, 1992), these initial relations are important.

Similar to patterns of relations between disorganization and psychopathology, results of regression analyses and structural modeling predicting dissociation suggest that (1) attachment disorganization may mediate some effects of early caregiving quality on later dissociative experiences, (2) disorganization may increase a child's risk for the development of dissociative symptomatology even with middle childhood behavior problems taken into account, and (3) the combination of disorganization and middle childhood behavior problems best predicts later dissociative symptomatology.

In general, the findings support a view of attachment as a relationship construct, a pattern of regulation or dysregulation that evolves from a dyadic history of interaction (Carlson & Sroufe, 1995; Sroufe, 1996). Variations in infant characteristics may be mediated by caregiver sensitivity to become part of dyadic organization (Susman-Stillman, Kalkoske, Egeland, & Waldman, 1996). Because environment makes possible the steady progress of maturational processes, disorganization of caregiving assistance in infant regulation during early months of rapid growth and maturation may have long-term effects on infant biological organization (Cicchetti, Ganiban, & Barnett, 1991; Collins & Depue, 1992; Greenough & Black, 1992; Kraemer, 1992). In particular, early exposure to trauma may have detrimental effects on neurological organization (Perry et al., 1995). Early distortions in relationship experience, in the regulation of behavior and emotion, place infants on pathways that probabilistically lead to later disturbance. From a developmental perspective, maladaptation evolves from the successive adaptations of individuals in their environments (Sroufe, 1997). The preliminary analyses of the contribution of disorganization to later psychopathology and dissociation in this study highlight the complex nature of relations among factors and processes interacting over time.

Although results of categorical (disorganized/not disorganized) analyses not reported here paralleled the correlational analyses, relations reported in this study were relatively modest (correlations from .20 to .40), and replication of the findings using the disorganization classification will be important. Researchers can be more confident of the patterns of findings if confirmed using categorical data based on a clinical criterion. For example, the stability of the disorganized attachment classification itself remains uncertain. For the original longitudinal sample, changes in major attachment classification (ABC) over time were found to be related in expectable ways to changes in the participants' lives (e.g., increase/decrease in life stress) (Egeland & Farber, 1984). Whereas changes in disorganization (as well as secure/insecure status) from 12 to 18 months in the subsample of this study tended toward insecurity, contributing factors are unclear. With a larger sample, it may be possible to examine the effects of intervening life events such as caregiver and infant experiences of separation, loss, and trauma.

There is also need for a careful etiological study of attachment disorganization, one that includes systematic home observations and measures of caregiver histories of unresolved loss/trauma and dissociative episodes and assessments of infant biological vulnerabilities and experiences of trauma. In the present study, an attempt was made to explore the antecedent relations of variations in patterns of disorganization (e.g., relations between history of abuse and apprehensive behaviors, caregiver history of loss and infant stilling, freezing behaviors, and so forth). The lack of sufficient background information and sample size in the current data set precluded such specific examination. Home observations and documentation of parent-infant interaction (i.e., frightening or frightened caregiver behavior) would provide important validation of disorganzied attachment patterns. Two such studies are under way (Jacobvitz et al., 1997; Schuengel et al., 1997).

The delineation of relations between caregiver history or infant experience and disorganized behavior patterns may help clarify whether the behaviors represent the lack of dyadic organization, the disorganization and reorganization of coherent patterns of regulation, or distinct attachment patterns. Because infants exhibiting high levels of disorganization appear to be particularly vulnerable to stress (Hertsgaard, Gunnar, Erickson, & Nachmias, 1995; Spangler & Grossmann, 1993), and the vulnerability appears to have significant long-term effects on social and emotional development, understanding the many aspects of the phenomenon is important and may prove fruitful for early prevention efforts and the development of intervention strategies. The contribution of the current study lies in the support provided for the validity of the rating of attachment disorganization/disorientation. Future investigators may be more confident that in assessing disorganization they are tapping into the attachment domain, with potential implications for social behavior and pathology.

ACKNOWLEDGMENTS

Preparation of this work and the research described here were supported by a National Institute of Mental Health postdoctoral training grant (MH 09744) to the author and a National Institute of Mental Health grant (MH 0864–08) to L. Alan Sroufe and Byron Egeland. I thank Alan Sroufe and Byron Egeland for their contributions to and support during this project.

ADDRESS AND AFFILIATION

Corresponding author: Elizabeth A. Carlson, Institute of Child Development, University of Minnesota, 51 East River Road, Minneapolis, MN 55455; e-mail: carls032@maroon.tc. umn.edu

APPENDIX A

Indices of Disorganized/Disoriented Attachment (Main & Solomon, 1990)

For Infants 12–18 Months Observed with Parent Present

I. Sequential display of contradictory behavior patterns

    A. Very strong displays of attachment behavior or angry behavior suddenly followed by avoidance, freezing, or dazed behavior

    B. Calm, contented play suddenly succeeded by distressed, angry behavior

II. Simultaneous display of contradictory behavior patterns

    A. The infant displays avoidant behavior simultaneously with proximity-seeking, contact-maintaining, or contact resisting

    B. Simultaneous display of other opposing behavioral propensities

III. Undirected, incomplete, and interrupted movements and expressions

    A. Seemingly undirected movements and expressions (many could also be considered misdirected or redirected)

    B. Incomplete movements

    C. Interrupted expressions or movements

IV. Stereotypies, asymmetrical and mistimed movements, and anomalous postures

    A. Asymmetries of expression or movement

    B. Stereotypies

    C. Assumption of anomalous postures

    D. Mistimed movements

V. Freezing, stilling, and slowed movements and expressions

"Freezing" is identified as the holding of movements, gestures, or positions in a posture that involves active resistance to gravity. For example, the infant sits or stands with arms held out waist high and to sides. "Stilling" is distinguished from freezing in that the infant is in a comfortable, resting posture that requires no active resistance to gravity. Freezing is considered a stronger marker of disorientation than stilling.

A. Freezing and stilling suggestive of more than momentary interruption of activity

B. Slowed movements and expressions suggesting lack of orientation to the present environment

VI. Direct indices of apprehension regarding parent

A. Expression of strong fear or apprehension directly upon return of parent, or when parent calls or approaches

B. Other indices of apprehension regarding the parent

VII. Direct indices of disorganization or disorientation

A. Any clear indices of confusion and disorganization in first moment of reunion with the parent

B. Direct indices of confusion or disorientation beyond the first moments of reunion with the parent

APPENDIX B

Rating Scale of Disorganization/Disorientation (Main & Solomon, 1990)

1. No signs of disorganization/disorientation.

3. Slight signs of disorganization/disorientation.

5. Moderate indices of disorganization/disorientation that are not clearly sufficient for a disorganized/disoriented category placement. No very strong indicators are present, and the indices that are present are not frequent enough, intense enough, or clear enough for the coder to be certain of a disorganized category placement. The coder will need to "force" a decision regarding whether the infant should be assigned to a D category based on (1) whether the infant's behavior seems inexplicable, indicative of momentary absence of a behavioral strategy, can be explained only by presuming that the infant is fearful of the parent, and/or is unable to shift attention away from the parent while simultaneously being inhibited in approaching the parent, (2) the timing of the appearance of disorganized behavior, (3) whether episodes of apparent disorganization are immediately succeeded by an approach to the parent.

7. Definite qualification for disorganized/disoriented attachment status, but disorganized behavior is not extreme.

9. Definite qualification for disorganized/disoriented attachment status: in addition, the indices of disorganization and disorientation are strong, frequent, or extreme.

APPENDIX C

TABLE C1
Correlation Matrix for Structural Model, M_1

Variables	1	2	3	4	5
Construct/indicators:					
Early caregiving:					
1. Caretaking skill factor score (3 months)					
2. Cooperation/sensitivity rating (6 months)	.489***				
3. Infant abuse rating (reversed)					
(birth to 18 months)	.370***	.309***			
Measured variables:					
4. Disorganized attachment rating					
(12–18 months)	−.349***	−.422***	−.190*		
5. Psychopathology rating					
(K-SADS) (17½ years)	−.181*	−.192*	−.150	.326***	

Note: $N = 117$ based on listwise exclusion of cases.
* $p < .05;$ *** $p < .001.$

APPENDIX D

TABLE D1
Correlation Matrix for Structural Model, M_2

Variables	1	2	3	4	5
Construct/indicators:					
Early caregiving:					
1. Caretaking skill factor score (3 months)					
2. Cooperation/sensitivity rating (6 months)	.496***				
3. Infant abuse rating (reversed)					
(birth to 18 months)	.377***	.307***			
Measured variables:					
4. Disorganized attachment rating					
(12–18 months)	−.333***	−.373***	−.190*		
5. Dissociation score (DES)					
(17½ years)	−.231*	−.179	−.260**	.340***	

Note: $N = 116$ based on listwise exclusion of cases.
* $p < .05;$ *** $p < .01;$ *** $p < .001.$

REFERENCES

Achenbach, T., & Edelbrock, C. (1986). *Manual for the teacher's report form and teacher version of the child behavior profile.* Burlington: University of Vermont, Department of Psychiatry.

Ainsworth, M. D. S., Blehar, M., Waters, E., & Wall, S. (1978). *Patterns of attachment.* Hillsdale, NJ: Erlbaum.

Ambrosini, P. J., Metz, C., Prabucki, K., & Lee, J. (1989). Videotape reliability of the third revised edition of the K-SADS. *Journal of the American Academy of Child and Adolescent Psychiatry*, *28*, 723–728.

American Psychiatric Association (APA). (1994). *Diagnostic and statistical manual of developmental disorders* (4th ed.). Washington, DC: American Psychiatric Association.

Behar, L., & Stringfield, S. (1974). A behavior rating scale for the pre-school child. *Developmental Psychology*, *10*, 601–610.

Block, J., & Block, J. H. (1980). The role of ego-control and ego-resiliency in the organization of behavior. In W. A. Collins (Ed.), *The Minnesota symposia on child psychology: Vol. 13. Development of cognition, affect, and social relations*. Hillsdale, NJ: Erlbaum.

Bowlby, J. (1982). *Attachment and loss: Vol. 1. Attachment* (2d ed.). New York: Basic Books. (Original work published 1969).

Brazelton, T. B. (1973). *A Neonatal Assessment Scale*. Phildelphia: Lippincott.

Browne, M. W., & Cudeck, R. (1993). Alternative ways of assessing model-fit. In K. A. Bollen & J. S. Long (Eds.), *Testing structural equation models* (pp. 136–162). Newbury Park, CA: Sage.

Browne, M. W., & Mels, G. (1992). *RAMONA user's guide*. Ohio State University, Columbus.

Carey, W. B. (1970). A simplified method for measuring infant temperament. *Journal of Pediatrics*, *77*, 188–194.

Carlson, E. A. (1990). *Individual differences in quality of attachment organization of high risk adolescent mothers*. Unpublished doctoral dissertation, Columbia University.

Carlson, E. A., & Sroufe, L. A. (1995). Contribution of attachment theory to developmental psychopathology. In D. Cicchetti & D. Cohen (Eds.), *Developmental psychopathology: Theory and methods* (Vol. *1*, pp. 581–617). New York: Wiley.

Carlson, E. B., & Putnam, F. W. (1993). An update on the Dissociative Experiences Scale. *Dissociation*, *7*, 16–27.

Carlson, V., Cicchetti, D., Barnett, D., & Braunwald, K. (1989). Disorganized/disoriented attachment relationships in maltreated infants. *Developmental Psychology*, *25*, 525–531.

Chambers, W., Puig-Antich, J., Hirsch, M., Paez, P., Ambrosini, P., Tabrizi, M. A., & Johnson, R. (1985). The assessment of affective disorders in children and adolescents by semi-structured interview: Test-retest reliability of the K-SADS-P. *Archives of General Psychiatry*, *42*, 606–702.

Cicchetti, D., Ganiban, J., & Barnett, D. (1991). Contributions from the study of high-risk populations to understanding the development of emotion regulation. In K. Dodge & J. Garber (Eds.), *The development of emotion regulation and dysregulation* (pp. 15–48). New York: Cambridge University Press.

Cicchetti, D., Toth, S., & Bush, M. (1988). Developmental psychopathology and incompetence in childhood: Suggestions for intervention. In B. Lahey & A. Kazdin (Eds.), *Advances in clinical child psychology* (Vol. *11*, pp. 1–71). New York: Plenum.

Cohen, J. (1960). A coefficient of agreement for nominal scales. *Educational and Psychological Measurement*, *20*, 37–46.

Collins, P., & Depue, R. (1992). A neurobehavioral systems approach to developmental psychopathology: Implications for disorders of affect. In D. Cicchetti & S. Toth (Eds.), *Developmental Perspectives on Depression: Rochester Symposium on Developmental Psychopathology* (Vol. *4*, pp. 29–101). Hillsdale, NJ: Erlbaum.

Connolly, J., & Doyle, A. (1981). Assessment of social competence in preschoolers: Teachers versus peers. *Developmental Psychology, 17,* 454–462.

Costello, A. (1991). Structured interviewing. In M. Lewis (Ed.), *Child and adolescent psychiatry: A comprehensive textbook* (pp. 463–472). Baltimore: Williams & Wilkins.

Egeland, B., & Brunnquell, D. (1979). An at-risk approach to the study of child abuse: Some preliminary findings. *Journal of the American Academy of Child Psychiatry, 18,* 219–235.

Egeland, B., & Deinard, A. (1975). *The Child Care Rating Scale.* Unpublished manuscript, University of Minnesota.

Egeland, B., & Farber, E. (1984). Infant-mother attachment: Factors related to its development and changes over time. *Child Development, 55,* 753–771.

Egeland, B., Jacobvitz, D., & Sroufe, L. A. (1988). Breaking the cycle of abuse: Relationship predictors. *Child Development, 59,* 1080–1088.

Egeland, B., Pianta, R., & O'Brien M. (1993). Maternal intrusiveness in infancy and child maladaptation in early school years. *Development and Psychopathology, 81,* 359–370.

Egeland, B., & Sroufe, L. A., (1981). Attachment and early maltreatment. *Child Development, 52,* 44–52.

Egeland, B., Sroufe, L. A., & Erickson, M. (1983). The developmental consequences of different patterns of maltreatment. *International Journal of Child Abuse and Neglect, 54,* 1168–1175.

Erickson, M., & Egeland, B. (1981). *Behavior problem scale technical manual.* Unpublished manuscript, University of Minnesota.

Erickson, M., Sroufe, L. A., & Egeland, B. (1985). The relationship between quality of attachment and behavior problems in preschool in a high risk sample. In I. Bretherton & E. Waters (Eds.), Growing points in attachment theory and research (pp. 147–186). *Monographs of the Society for Research in Child Development, 50*(1–2, Serial No. 209).

Greenough, W., & Black, J. (1992). Induction of brain structure by experience: Substrates for cognitive development. In M. R. Gunnar & C. A. Nelson (Eds.), *Minnesota Symposia on Child Psychology* (Vol. *24,* pp. 155–200). Hillsdale, NJ: Erlbaum.

Hertsgaard, L., Gunnar, M., Erickson, M. F., & Nachmias, M. (1995). Adrenocortical responses to the strange situation in infants with disorganized/disoriented attachment relationships. *Child Development, 66,* 1100–1106.

Hiester, M., Carlson, E. A., & Sroufe L. A. (1993). *The evolution of friendship in preschool, middle childhood, and adolescence: Origins in attachment history.* Paper presented at the biennial meeting of the Society for Research in Child Development, New Orleans.

Hilgard, E. R. (1986). *Divided consciousness: Multiple controls in human thought and action.* New York: Wiley.

Jacobvitz, D. B., Hazen, N. L., & Riggs, S. (1997, April). *Disorganized mental processes in mothers, frightening/frightened caregiving, and disoriented, disorganized behavior in infancy.* Paper presented at the biennial meeting of the Society for Research in Child Development, Washington, DC.

Kobak, R. R., & Shaver, P. (1987, June) *Strategies for maintaining felt security: A theoretical analysis of continuity and change in styles of social adaptation.* Paper presented at the conference in honor of John Bowlby's 80th Birthday, London.

Kraemer, G. W. (1992). A psychobiological theory of attachment. *Behavioral and Brain Sciences, 15,* 493–541.

Krentz, M. S. (1982): *Qualitative differences between mother child and caregiver child attachments in family daycare.* Unpublished doctoral dissertation, California School of Professional Psychology, Berkeley.

Lawlis, E. H., & Lu, E. (1972). Judgment of counseling process: Reliability agreement and error. *Psychological Bulletin, 78,* 17–20.

Liotti, G. (1992). Disorganized/disoriented attachment in the etiology of the dissociative disorders. *Dissociation, 4,* 196–204.

Lyons-Ruth, K., Alpern, L., & Repacholi, B. (1993). Disorganized infant attachment classification and maternal psychosocial problems as predictors of hostile-aggressive behavior in the preschool classroom. *Child Development, 64,* 572–585.

Lyons-Ruth, K., Repacholi, B., McLeod, S., & Silva, E. (1991). Disorganized attachment behavior in infancy: Short-term stability, maternal and infant correlates and risk-related subtypes. *Development and Psychopathology, 3,* 377–396.

Main, M. (in press). Discourse, prediction, and studies in attachment. Implications for psychoanalysis. In T. Shapiro & R. Emde (Eds.), *Some Empirical issues in Psychoanalysis, Journal of the American Psychoanalytic Association* (Suppl.).

Main, M., & Hesse, E. (1990). Parents' unresolved traumatic experiences are related to infant disorganized attachment status: Is frightened and/or frightening parental behavior the linking mechanism? In M. T. Greenberg, D. Cicchetti, & E. M. Cummings (Eds.), *Attachment in the preschool years* (pp. 161–182). Chicago: University of Chicago Press.

Main, M., & Solomon, J. (1990). Procedures for identifying infants as disorganized/disoriented during the Ainsworth Strange Situation. In M. T. Greenberg, D. Cichetti, & E. M. Cummings (Eds.), *Attachment in the preschool years* (pp. 121–160). Chicago: University of Chicago Press.

Matas, L., Arend, R. A., & Sroufe, L. A. (1978). Continuity of adaptation in the second year: The relationship between quality of attachment and later competence. *Child Development, 49,* 547–556.

O'Connor, M. J., Sigman, M., & Brill, N. (1987). Disorganization of attachment in relation to maternal alcohol consumption. *Journal of Consulting and Clinical Psychology, 55,* 831–836.

Orvaschel, H., Puig-Antich, J., Chambers, W., Tabrizi, M. A., & Johnson, R. (1982). Retrospective assessment of prepubertal major depression with the Kiddie-SADSE. *Journal of the American Academy of Child Psychiatry, 21,* 695–707.

Perry, B. D., Pollard, R. A., Blakley, T. L., Baker, W. L., & Vigilante, D. (1995). Childhood trauma, the neurobiology of adaptation, and "use dependent" development of the brain: How "states" become "traits." *Infant Mental Health Journal, 16,* 271–291.

Puig-Antich, J., & Chambers, W. (1978). *The schedule for affective disorders and schizophrenia for school-aged children.* New York: New York Psychiatric Institute.

Putnam, F. W. (1985). Dissociation as a response to extreme trauma. In R. P. Kluft (Ed.), *The childhood antecedents of multiple personality.* Washington, DC: American Psychiatric Press.

Putnam, F. W. (1989). *Diagnosis and treatment of multiple personality disorder.* New York: Guilford.

Putnam, F. W. (1993). Dissociative disorders in children: Behavioral profiles and problems. *Child Abuse and Neglect, 17,* 39–45.

Radke-Yarrow, M., Cummings, E. M., Kuczynski, L., & Chapman, M. (1985). Patterns of attachment in two- and three-year-olds in normal families and families with parental depression. *Child Development, 56,* 884–893.

Rodning, C., Beckwith, L., & Howard, J. (1991). Quality of attachment and home environments in children prenatally exposed to PCP and cocaine. *Development and Psychopathology, 3*, 351–366.

Sameroff, A., & Emde, R. (1989). *Relationship disturbances in early childhood.* New York: Basic Books.

Schuengel, C., van IJzendoorn, M. H., Bakermans-Kranenburg, M. J., & Blom, M. (1997, April). *Frightening, frightened, and dissociated behavior, unresolved loss and infant disorganization.* Paper presented at the biennial meeting of the Society for Research in Child Development, Washington, DC.

Spangler, G., & Grossmann, K. E. (1993). Biobehavioral organization in securely and insecurely attached infants. *Child Development, 64*, 1439–1450.

Sroufe, J. (1991). Assessment of parent-adolescent relationships: Implication for adolescent development. *Journal of Family Psychology, 5*, 21–45.

Sroufe, L. A. (1988). The role of infant-caregiver attachment in development. In J. Belsky & T. Nezworski (Eds.), *Clinical implications of attachment.* Hillsdale, NJ: Erlbaum.

Sroufe, L. A. (1990). An organizational perspective on the self. In D. Cicchetti & M. Beeghly (Eds.), *The self in transition: Infancy to childhood* (pp. 281–307). Chicago: University of Chicago Press.

Sroufe, L. A. (1996). *Emotional development: The organization of emotional life in the early years.* New York: Cambridge University Press.

Sroufe, L. A. (1997). Psychopathology as an outcome of development. *Development and Psychopathology, 9*, 251–268.

Sroufe, L. A., & Waters, E. (1977). Attachment as an organizational construct. *Child Development, 48*, 1184–1199.

Steele, H., Steele, M., & Fonagy, P. (in press). Associations among attachment classifications of mothers, fathers, and infants: Evidence for a relationship-specific perspective. *Child Development.*

Susman-Stillman, A., Kalkoske, M., Egeland, B., & Waldman, I. (1996). Infant temperament and maternal sensitivity as predictors of attachment security. *Infant Behavior and Development, 19*, 33–47.

Tinsley, H. E. A., & Weiss, D. J. (1975). Interrater reliability and agreement of subjective judgments. *Journal of Counseling Psychology, 22*, 358–376.

Tracy, R., Lamb, M., & Ainsworth, M. D. S. (1976). Infant approach behavior as related to attachment. *Child Development, 47*, 571–578.

Vaughn, B., Deinard, M. D., & Egeland, B. (1980). Measuring temperament in pediatric practice. *Journal of Pediatrics, 96*, 510–514.

Vaughn, B., Taraldson, B., Crichton, L., & Egeland, B. (1980). Relationships between neonatal behavioral organization and infant behavior during the first year of life. *Infant Behavior and Development, 3*, 47–66.

16

Interaction of Temperamental Resistance to Control and Restrictive Parenting in the Development of Externalizing Behavior

John E. Bates
Indiana University Bloomington

Kenneth A. Dodge
Vanderbilt University

Gregory S. Pettit
Auburn University

Beth Ridge
Concordia University

Child temperament and parental control were studied as interacting predictors of behavior outcomes in 2 longitudinal samples. In Sample 1, data were ratings of resistant temperament and observed restrictive control in infancy–toddlerhood and ratings of externalizing behavior at ages 7 to 10 years; in Sample 2, data were retrospective ratings of temperament in infancy–toddlerhood, observed restrictive control at age 5 years, and ratings of externalizing behavior at ages 7 to 11 years. Resistance more strongly related to externalizing in low-restriction groups than in high-restriction groups. This was true in both samples and for both teacher- and mother-rated outcomes. Several Temperament × Environment interaction effects have been reported previously, but this is one of very few replicated effects.

John E. Bates, Department of Psychology, Indiana University Bloomington; Gregory S. Pettit, Department of Family and Child Development, Auburn University; Kenneth A. Dodge, Department of Psychology and Human Development, Vanderbilt University; Beth Ridge, Department of Psychology, Concordia University.

We gratefully acknowledge the important financial and other contributions of the following to this work: J. Reid, G. Patterson, and M. Stoolmiller of the Oregon Social Learning Center; R. Rose, R. Viken, and J. Ullman; National Institute of Mental Health Grants MH28018 and MH42498; National Institute of Child Health and Human Development Grant HD30572; Indiana University Research and Graduate Studies Office; M. DelaFlor, D. Alexander, M. Gingerich, K. Bayles, and the many individuals in the families and research teams of the Bloomington Longitudinal Study and the Child Development Project.

Correspondence concerning this article should be addressed to John E. Bates, Department of Psychology, Indiana University, Bloomington, Indiana 47405. Electronic mail may be sent to batesj@indiana.edu

Most theoretical explanations of the development of behavior problems include child temperament factors and their interactions with qualities of the socializing environment. Thomas and Chess (1977) summarized these interactive processes in terms of goodness of fit between a child's temperament and the expectations and resources of the child's home and schools. In theory, temperament does not lead to behavior problems by itself; it does so only in conjunction with particular environments. Beyond this seminal idea, there has been little progress in detailing models of developmental interplay between temperament and environment, despite large numbers of studies on temperament. Additional descriptions of such effects are needed. The present article reports an empirical demonstration of one particular temperament-environment interaction. The article focuses on children's temperamental unmanageability, parents' restrictive control efforts, and children's externalizing behavior problem outcomes.

Temperament as a general construct refers to a broad array of behavior traits considered to be biologically rooted and, to one degree or another, early appearing. Temperament traits can be characterized as various forms of reactivity and self-regulation (Rothbart & Bates, 1998). Specific temperament dimensions are associated with distinct combinations of psychobiological substrates. Research has found several temperament traits to have direct, main-effects-type relations with behavior problems in a nonperfect but replicated pattern of partially differential linkage: Temperamental predictors of behavior problems include (a) irritability–difficultness, preceding both internalizing (e.g., anxious) and externalizing (e.g., aggressive) kinds of behavior problems; (b) behavioral inhibition–fearfulness, typically preceding internalizing more so than externalizing problems (but not always); and (c) impulsivity–unmanageability, typically preceding externalizing problems more than internalizing problems (Bates, 1989; Guerin, Gottfried, & Thomas, 1997; Rothbart & Bates, 1998; Sanson, Smart, Prior, & Oberklaid, 1993; Slotboom, Elphick, van Riessen, van Mill, & Kohnstamm, 1996). Details of the process by which temperament predicts later behavior problems are not known, but the evidence so far provides modest support for models of direct (e.g., continuity of personality traits) and indirect (e.g., through child's impact on parents) linear effects (Rothbart & Bates, 1998).

The temperament construct we chose to focus on was impulsivity–unmanageability. This choice was based on our major interest in aggression and externalizing problems. The chosen temperament construct is the one with the most differentiated relevance to externalizing behavior (Bates, 1989; Caspi, Moffitt, Newman, & Silva, 1996; Rothbart & Bates, 1998). The impulsivity–unmanageability trait was operationalized in the present study as parental reports on a scale of resistance to control.[1] The resistance to control construct emerged empirically in previous research on the kinds of infant behaviors parents might find difficult (see Bates & Bayles, 1984). The core behaviors in this trait are the child's failure to comply with parental attempts to stop or to redirect the child's action—for example, ignoring a parent's directive not to touch a breakable object. As with any operational measure of temperament, our parent report measure of resistance to control reflects more than the purely biological definition of temperament. Such an index contains

---

[1] We are grateful to G. A. Kohnstamm for suggesting this term and its conceptual roots.

components of psychometric error (some parts of which may be ultimately explained by currently unmeasured factors), perceptual biases in the person providing the ratings, as well as environmentally conditioned experience in the child. Those factors are not so large, however, that they eclipse the components of both stable and developmentally unfolding, biologically rooted temperament. A chain of evidence and theory supports, with caution, the use of the construct in general (Rothbart & Bates, 1998) and this index in particular (Bates & Bayles, 1984).

Theoretically, the concept of resistance to control can be seen, as a temperament construct that reflects several more basic temperament dimensions and associated differences in fundamental neural systems. In terms of reactivity, the key elements of resistance to control may be two: First, there may be a relatively strong attraction to rewarding stimuli, accompanied by excitement (controlled by the coordinated actions of the behavioral activation system, involving especially the caudate motor system, the accumbens motor system, the septohippocampal system, and the prefrontal cortex; Gray, 1991; see also Rothbart & Bates, 1998). Second, there may be a relatively weak level of basic social agreeableness (Lanthier & Bates, 1995) or warm, trusting, helpful responses to people (controlled by ventromedial hypothalamic structures receiving opiate projections from higher limbic regions; see Rothbart & Bates, 1998, for a brief review). It is also theoretically possible that resistance to control could partly depend on a weak fear–inhibition response to threats of punishment (controlled by loci in the septohippocampal system [Gray, 1991], with lateral asymmetry patterns of the anterior portions of the brain playing a role in the dynamic balance of emotions associated with inhibition and approach; Calkins & Fox, 1994). However, although we think inhibition differences may moderate resistant tendencies, we think they are less likely to be central to resistance because we have noted that a conceptually relevant dimension of distress in the context of novelty tends to vary independently of both resistance to control (Bates & Bayles, 1984) and externalizing behavior problems (Bates, Bayles, Bennett, Ridge, & Brown, 1991). In terms of self-regulation, resistance to control may further reflect difficulties in the effortful control of attention (related to the functioning of the frontal lobe's anterior cingulate gyrus) as well as vigilance (related to the activity of the locus coeruleus inhibiting the cingulate; Rothbart & Bates, 1998). Theoretically related to the effortful control construct is Newman's construct of response modulation (e.g., C. M. Patterson & Newman, 1993). According to Newman, differences in impulsivity are due not only to differences in affective responses to reward and the threat of punishment or nonreward but also to differences in the processing of peripheral cues that provide information about the consequences of responses. This produces differences in the ability to inhibit actions. We would argue that very young children's differences in response to caregivers' attempts to regulate their actions represent one substrate of the kinds of self-regulatory abilities that are seen as important in the adaptations of older children and adolescents. Current theory on self-regulation strongly emphasizes temperamental concepts (Barkley, 1996; Eisenberg et al., 1997; Kochanska, Murray, & Coy, 1997; Kopp, 1982; Olson, 1996). Children with higher levels of resistance to control may tend to have strong attraction to rewards, weak inhibitory competencies, and weak connections to the feelings of others. These traits would make it difficult to learn rules for conduct and would raise the risk for behavior disorders.

However, even though there are conceptual and empirical links between temperamental resistance to control and behavioral adaptations, in theory, temperament must operate through transactions with the socializing environment. Parenting characteristics have been the most frequently considered environmental antecedents of child behavior problems. Like temperament variables, parenting variables have been found to show direct, main-effects links with child adjustment (Hetherington & Martin, 1986; G. R. Patterson, Reid, & Dishion, 1992; Rothbaum & Weisz, 1994). And also like temperament, the links are of a typically modest-to-moderate order, with correlations in the range of .2 to .4 (e.g., see Rothbaum & Weisz, 1994). Not only current systems theories but also empirical findings of limited main-effects relations call for the study of Temperament × Environment interactions.[2] What characteristics of the environment, then, would be most likely to interact with child temperamental resistance to control? The parenting construct most conceptually relevant as a possible moderator of temperamental resistance to control would be parental restrictive control, involving behaviors intended to stop or to punish the child, such as giving negative commands, removing objects from the child, scolding, and spanking.[3] The extent to which a parent uses such behaviors has been found to be correlated with externalizing behavior problems (Coie & Dodge, 1998). It must be noted that restrictive control, especially as seen through an observer from outside the family, does not necessarily involve elements of harsh discipline, such as spanking and other efforts to inflict physical or emotional discomfort. At a conceptual level, restrictive control could moderate the effects of child temperamental resistance to control in at least two ways: High-level control could either create opportunities for exacerbation of parent–child conflict, leading to pathological development, or actually modulate the effect of temperament. We are aware of no theory that would allow a choice between these alternatives.

If the linkage of temperament and later adjustment is, in fact, moderated by parenting characteristics, empirical discovery of such an interaction effect would advance description and ultimately, perhaps, understanding of the process of development. By *discovery*, we mean finding a replicated pattern. By *interaction effect*, we mean a nonlinear effect rather than simply the summed effects of two or more main effects (Baron & Kenny, 1986; Rutter, 1983). Interaction implies that relations between two variables are affected by the level of a third variable.

Reports of relevant interaction effects are relatively infrequent (Bates, 1989; Rothbart & Bates, 1998; Rutter, 1983); however, they have been emerging. In one recent example, Hagekull and Bohlin (1995) found that preschool-age children with higher levels of temperamental manageability were less aggressive when they had high-quality day care than when they had low-quality care. Less manageable preschoolers' aggressiveness was not associated with quality of day care. Other intriguing examples have been reported by Brody,

---

[2]There is the possibility, as suggested by G. R. Patterson et al. (1992), that the links between parenting and child outcomes could also be enhanced by the use of analyses that statistically control for error of measurement, but results of such analyses still leave room for possible temperament–environment interaction effects.

[3]Positive behaviors, including affectionate and educative parenting, are also related to child externalizing problems (e.g., Pettit & Bates, 1989; Pettit, Bates, & Dodge, 1997). We chose restrictive control for our focus in this set of analyses because of its more obvious conceptual relevance to temperamental resistance to control as well as because of results of previous analyses in one of the data sets, as is described later.

Stoneman, and Gauger (1996); Henry, Caspi, Moffitt, and Silva (1996); Lerner and Lerner (1994); and Shaw, Owens, Vondra, Keenan, and Winslow (1996). What is particularly crucial at this point in research on Temperament × Environment interactions is the replication of effects. Replications of relevant interaction effects are very rare, but there are a few.

One replicated Temperament × Environment interaction effect in the literature is the finding that the congnitive development of highly active children is less adversely affected by living in an understimulating environment than that of inactive children (Wachs, 1992). There have also been replicated findings in which difficult children's cognitive development is more adversely affected by noisy environments than that of easy children (Wachs, 1992). More directly in the area of child psychopathology, Kochanska (1995) found an interaction between preschoolers' temperamental fearfulness and the nature of their relations with their mothers in predicting signs of conscience. Highly fearful children's signs of conscience (i.e., internalized self-control) were predicted by mothers' use of gentle rather than harsh, power-oriented forms of discipline. Gentle discipline theoretically promotes the development of internalized control in fearful children by keeping their anxiety levels low. In contrast, nonfearful children's internalized self-control behaviors were predicted by security of the mother–child attachment, as indexed by mother report on a Q sort, and not by gentle discipline. Kochanska interpreted this as being due to the fearless child's having developed a positive partnership with the mother and thereby acquiring internal controls. Kochanska (1991) had previously shown, in a sample of 8- to 10-year-olds, that fearful children tended to show more signs of conscience when their mothers used gentle control than when they used power assertion; in contrast, for the relatively fearless children, gentle control did not make a difference. In addition, the full interaction effect (Kochanska, 1995) was replicated in the main study's sample at a later age (Kochanska, 1997). A converging finding comes from a recent cross-sectional study of a small group of fourth- and fifth-grade boys by Colder, Lochman, and Wells (1997). These researchers found that temperamentally fearful children with parents who used harsh discipline were higher on teacher-rated aggression than both low-fear children with harsh parents and high-fear children with gentle parents.

Arcus and Gardner (1993) and Park, Belsky, Putnam, and Crnic (1997) provided an additional Temperament × Environment effect. Both studies found that early child negative reactivity interacted with parenting in forecasting later child (fearful) inhibition. Arcus and Gardner (1993) found that extremely reactive infants were less likely to develop into inhibited toddlers if their mothers were high in limit setting (similar to this article's core construct of restrictive control) than if their mothers were low in limit setting; however, extremely nonreactive infants were later low on inhibition, no matter the nature of maternal control. Park et al. (1997) found that infants who were high in temperamental negativity at about 1 year of age were rated as less behaviorally inhibited in a laboratory task at 3 years of age to the extent that their mothers and fathers were rated as affectively negative during home observations in Years 2 and 3. However, the inhibitedness of low-negativity infants was essentially uncorrelated with parental negativity. The two studies differ on ages of assessments and measures, but nevertheless, they can be interpreted as demonstrating a replicated interaction effect.

The shortage of replicated Temperament × Environment interaction effects may be partly a general problem of insufficient interest in replication in social development research and partly a function of the fact that there are so many possible effects that could be examined. However, the difficulty may also involve statistical power and the effects of outliers in the relatively small samples that are characteristic of longitudinal studies. After a sample has been subdivided on some characteristic, as in the typical interaction analysis, the groups may be too small for detecting the ordinary effect of modest–moderate size. Alternatively, in such limited samples, a few outliers may produce statistically significant interaction effects that are not more generally evident in the sample, or they may preclude detecting an interaction effect that is in fact more generally present. Even if one could assume adequate scaling and measurement, in nonexperimental studies, the typical properties of the joint distributions of a predictor and a moderator variable cause exponential drop-offs in the efficiency with which studies will detect interaction effects (McClelland & Judd, 1993). Such considerations have led some statistical experts to recommend increased efforts to analyze data visually (M. Stoolmiller, personal communication, Oregon Social Learning Center statistics seminar, fall 1995; Cleveland, 1993). It may also be useful to use structural equation modeling methods in addition to the more conventional multiple regression statistics. Whatever the analytic approach, however, replication would seem to be particularly important for interaction effects—if an effect replicates, complex concerns about joint distributions are mitigated, and there is more hope that theoretical interpretation of that effect might eventually be fruitful. As Rutter (1983) said, statistical procedures can help avoid spurious conclusions, but "replication provides the most important test" (p. 315).

In searching for Temperament × Environment interactions, the present study used data from two separate longitudinal data sets, the Bloomington Longitudinal Study (BLS; e.g., Bates et al., 1991) and the Child Development Project (CDP; e.g., Bates et al., 1994; Dodge, Bates, & Pettit, 1990; Pettit et al., 1997). In both studies, we measured the child's early temperament in the earliest years through similar mother-report items, but the measures were prospective from infancy in the case of the BLS and retrospective from age 5 in the case of the CDP. The retrospective questionnaire used in the CDP was validated prospectively in the BLS. We assessed parent–child interaction through observations at age 1 to 2 years in the BLS and at age 5 years in the CDP. We measured externalizing outcomes through teacher and parent reports on Achenbach questionnaires (Achenbach, 1991a, 1991b; Achenbach & Edelbrock, 1983, 1986) in middle childhood in both samples. The outcome measure represented an average of scores across the largest number of middle-childhood years available (ages 7, 8, and 10 years for the BLS and 7–11 years for the CDP). The decision to average was based first on the moderately large cross-age correlations of externalizing (e.g., Olweus, 1979) and the fact that analyses of individual years' outcomes produced very similar results—despite the fact that individual growth curves also showed considerable shifting from year to year. The decision to average was based second on the tendency of a shifting array of participants in any given year and on our desire to maximize sample sizes. The analytic approach was to first create groups on the moderator variable by median split and then to examine correlations and scatter plots. This was followed by structural model fitting. Our primary interest was in the predictiveness of temperament, moderated by parenting, rather than in the predictiveness of parenting as moderated by the temperament of the child. However, we also summarize findings on the latter question because we recognize that this has been the most frequent perspective in the relevant prior research.

The present study builds on a foundation of preliminary analyses in one of the two samples: the BLS. Previous BLS searches for interaction patterns revealed some patterns that were reasonably well replicated across the preschool years (Bates & Marvinney, 1993) but not in middle childhood. These searches emphasized a three-way interaction between temperament and two observed parenting dimensions: restrictive control and positive involvement. Further preliminary analyses (Bates, 1994a) suggested that the most consistent parenting moderator of the temperament–behavior problem link was restrictive control rather than positive involvement, with higher levels of linkage found in children with low-controlling mothers than in children with highly controlling mothers. Although this pattern was not directly suggested by any major theory, its presence in successive years of development recommended further study.

METHOD

Samples

Bloomington Longitudinal Study. At inception, the BLS sample consisted of families of 6-month-old infants, recruited without any commitment to longitudinal participation. Just before their infants were 6 months old, parents of most babies born in the Bloomington, Indiana, area were sent a brief temperament questionnaire (Bates et al., 1979). From the 68% who returned the questionnaire, we invited 247 to participate in a more detailed study representing balances on child sex, first- versus later-born status, and difficultness of temperament; 168 agreed. The distribution on a temperamental difficultness scale completed several weeks after the screening questionnaire, during the detailed assessment, approximated normal. At the first follow-up at age 13 months, 142 participated; at the second, age 24 months, 121 participated. Subsequent follow-ups included a core of approximately 90 participants, with a rotating group of 1 to 30 additional, varying according to the procedure and year (for method details on the 6- to 24-month phase, see Bates, Olson, Pettit, & Bayles, 1982; Pettit & Bates, 1984; Olson, Bates, & Bayles, 1982, 1984; for details on the 3- to 10-year phase, see Bates, Maslin, & Frankel, 1985; Bates & Bayles, 1984, 1988; Bates et al., 1991; Ridge, 1992). Analyses comparing participating versus nonparticipating families have revealed no systematic biases on sex of child, temperament, socioeconomic status (SES), and early childhood adjustment (Bates & Bayles, 1988). In the core sample most relevant to the present analyses, parental occupations were largely middle class (64% of families), which included skilled trades, white collar, and student, but there were also working-class families (22%) and upper-middle-class families (15%). The children in this core were 56% boys and 44% girls.

Child Development Project. The CDP sample consisted of families with 5-year-old children in three cities (small: Bloomington, Indiana; medium: Knoxville, Tennessee; large: Nashville, Tennessee), recruited during spring enrollment for kindergarten, except for the 15% who were late enrollees, purposely recruited in late summer or early fall. Families were approached at random, and about 70% of those approached agreed to participate.

Schools were selected to achieve a fuller representation of lower SES families than typical in volunteer community samples. From a larger sample of 585, a subsample of 156 participated in a further assessment procedure of home observation (9 others were observed but, for various technical and other reasons, did not have the relevant measure). The families were selected for balanced numbers of low, average, and moderately to highly aggressive children, as described by their mothers—and, where possible, fathers—on the Aggression scale of the Achenbach Child Behavior Checklist (CBCL; Achenbach & Edelbrock, 1983). The observation subsample represented both a wide range of SES (*M* Hollingshead four-factor index of SES = 40.85, *SD* = 15.28, range = 8–66) and the ethnic makeup of the study sites (84% European American, 15% African American, and 1% other). It was also balanced on sex of child (49% boys, 51% girls). These figures are comparable to those for the sample as a whole. (See Pettit, Bates, and Dodge, 1993, for method details regarding the observation subsample.)

Procedure

Bloomington Longitudinal Study. At 6, 13, and 24 months, the relevant measures in the BLS were collected through maternal-report questionnaires and home observations performed by trained observers. There were two 3-hr visits at both 6 and 24 months and one 3-hr visit at 13 months. Observations were recorded in the form of molecular event codes and a variety of ratings. During middle childhood, at ages 7, 8, and 10 months (±approximately 6 months), the relevant measures were collected through maternal and teacher questionnaires sent in the mail.

Child Development Project. At age 5 years, the relevant measures were collected through maternal questionnaires and two 2-hr observations around the family dinner time. Both procedures occurred in the summer preceding kindergarten or early in autumn. The observations were recorded in narrative form, segmented into events, and then coded. During middle childhood, at ages 7, 8, 9, 10, and 11 years, the relevant measures were from maternal and teacher questionnaires.

Measures

Resistance to control. This construct, resistance to control, refers to very early unmanageability. Toddlers scoring high on it may be socially unresponsive, dominating, or impulsive in their explorations. In moderate amounts and for shorter periods of time, such traits are developmentally normal; however, higher and more continuous levels may mark a risk for externalizing problems. In the BLS, resistance to control was assessed through the 13- and 24-month versions of the Infant Characteristics Questionnaire (ICQ; Bates, Freeland, & Lounsbury, 1979; Bates & Bayles, 1984). Resistance to control items are listed in Table 1. In the CDP, resistance to control was assessed through the retrospective ICQ (RICQ), in which the mother was asked when her child was age 5 years to rate the child's traits as an infant. Items are listed in Table 1. Partial validation of the RICQ in the BLS sample provides support for the use of this method. Maternal retrospective reports completed when the child was age 10 on the RICQ scales were related to ICQ scales completed at 6 to 24

TABLE 1
Overview of Predictor Measures

Construct	Data Set and Items
Temperamental resistance to control	BLS and CDP
	Persist in playing with objects when told to leave them alone;
	Continue to go someplace even when told "stop," "come here," "no-no";
	Upset when removed from something she or he is interested in but should not be getting into;
	How much cuddle and snuggle when held (scaled from *a lot* to *very little, seldom snuggles*).
Observed maternal restrictive control	BLS
	Molecular code factor composites
	Management (13 months; prohibit/scold/warn, take away object, restrain baby);
	Negative Control (24 months; prohibit, scold, repeat prohibition, physical punishment, remove or restrain child, remove object).
	Observer ratings composites
	HOME Avoidance of Restriction and Punishment (13 months; lack of hostility, punishment, physical restraint directed toward child by mother);
	Post-Observation Questionnaire Mother Non-Punitive (24 months; infrequent scold or punish, mild punishment).
	CDP
	Restrictive control events (5 years; child acts immaturely or irresponsibly, which is followed by mother negative control (e.g., prohibit, demand, yell, warn, criticize/scold/shame).

Note: BLS = Bloomington Longitudinal Study; CDP = Child Development Project; HOME = Home Observation for Measurement of the Environment.

months ($n = 79 - 94$), depending on the variable. RICQ resistance to control was correlated with its prospective counterpart to a significant degree, but its discriminant validity was less impressive than that for the other two scales. The correlations follow: Infancy difficultness (6–24 months) significantly predicted retrospective difficultness ($r = .58$) and resistance (.44) but not unadaptability (.08); infancy unadaptability (6–24 months) significantly predicted retrospective unadaptability (.34) but not difficultness (.06) or resistance (.14); infancy resistance to control (13–24 months) significantly predicted retrospective resistance (.34) and, to a trend degree, difficultness (.20, $p = .053$) but not unadaptability (–.02). On the basis of the psychometric shortcomings of very brief scales and the long time interval, we primarily interpreted the findings as showing a degree of accuracy in mothers' retrospective reports. A plausible secondary interpretation is that the mother is describing continuity in child personality. The interpretation that the correlations are due to consistent, global bias in maternal perception does not seem as likely, on the basis of arguments detailed in Bates (1994b) and Rothbart and Bates (1998). Even if it is not accepted that the RICQ

TABLE 2
Descriptive Statistics

Data Set and Variable	M	SD
Bloomington Longitudinal Study		
Maternal restrictive control ($n = 121$)	0.00	0.73
Resistance to control ($n = 129$)	0.01	0.79
Teacher-rated externalizing ($n = 136$)	11.42	11.35
Mother-rated externalizing ($n = 139$)	13.21	8.46
Child Development Project		
Mother restrictive control ($n = 156$)	3.41	4.53
Resistance to control ($n = 153$)	3.73	1.12
Teacher externalizing ($n = 146$)	6.51	7.77
Mother externalizing ($n = 144$)	9.82	6.84

Note: Variables 1 and 2 of the Bloomington Longitudinal Study (BLS) are sums of Z scores from ages 13 and 24 months, whereas the corresponding scores of the Child Development Project (CDP) are raw scores from age 5. To facilitate comparison with the BLS, CDP temperament scores are expressed in Figure 2 as standard scores. Externalizing scores in the BLS were computed with the Achenbach and Edelbrock (1983, 1986) algorithms, whereas in the CDP, they were computed with the Achenbach (1991a, 1991b) algorithms.

provides information about the child's earliest characteristics, the temperament measures were antecedent to the externalizing outcome measures by 2 to 6 years. Descriptive statistics for the resistance variables are listed in Table 2. Coefficient alpha internal consistencies were adequate—.76 for the BLS index and .83 for the CDP one.

Maternal restrictive control. Maternal restrictive control emerged from within- and across-time multivariate analyses of home observation data in the BLS. This construct refers to reactive efforts, such as prohibitions, warnings, and scoldings, to manage inconvenient or potentially harmful child actions. Although this measure involves restriction, it does not strongly index harsh punishment, because observers seldom saw even threats of physical punishment, much less strongly angry scolding or actual spanking. In the BLS, the measure was based on the average of factors within molecular event codes at ages 6, 13, and 24 months plus more subjective observer ratings on the Post-Observation Questionnaire (Olson et al., 1982). Interobserver reliability was adequate: Observer reliability correlations on total scores of individual codes in the molecular measures averaged .73, and observers agreed on a minimum of two thirds of the subjective rating items. Internal consistencies of composites were .7 or higher. Constituents of the composite are listed in Table 1. In the CDP, the measure was a single, complex variable from the age 5 home observations, involving a count of events in which the child engaged in some misbehavior and the mother responded with a restrictive effort to control the child's behavior. We have in the past described it as coercive control (McFadyen-Ketchum, Bates, Dodge, & Pettit, 1996; Pettit et al., 1993); however, it is not necessarily coercive in the sense of involving highly aversive behaviors. Interobserver reliability was adequate whether computed at the level of the content of narrative events (at a .75 average level of concordance), at the level of the general class of event (control, teaching, social contact, or reflective listening, at a κ average $= .64$), and or at the level of event descriptors (e.g., whether the event was initiated by the parent, whether it was cued by child misbehavior, and the nature of the control, κ average $= .64$). Descriptive statistics are in Table 2.

Externalizing behavior problems. Externalizing was measured through the parallel teacher and mother forms of the Achenbach (Achenbach, 1991a, 1991b; Achenbach & Edelbrock, 1983, 1986) questionnaires: the Teacher Rating Form and the CBCL. The BLS used the 1983 or 1986 algorithms for designating the individual first-order scales, and the CDP used the 1991 algorithms. The different scoring procedures result in nonidentical but highly correlated scores (Achenbach, 1991a, 1991b). The scores from the 3 (BLS) or 5 (CDP) middle-childhood ages were averaged together within source. Children with no score during the follow-through period were excluded. In the BLS, 2 or all 3 years of outcome data were present for 73% of the sample for teacher outcome data and 78% of the sample for mother outcome data. Reflecting the often-reported, moderate-to-high year-to-year stability for externalizing behavior, the alpha internal consistencies were .60 for the teacher score and .91 for the mother score. In the CDP, the majority of years' data were present for 94% of the sample for teacher scores and 93% for mother scores. Alphas were .85 and .92 for the teacher and mother scores, respectively. Thus, the summary externalizing indexes were quite reliable. Teacher and mother scores were treated separately rather than being combined into a composite or latent indicator because they are only modestly to moderately correlated (as is detailed later), and they describe distinctly different settings for child adjustment.

RESULTS

Direct Effects

Temperament. As shown in Table 3, the direct main effects of temperamental resistance to control confirmed previous results: Maternal perceptions of early resistance to control were, to a modest degree, correlated with middle-childhood externalizing problems, whether perceived by the teacher or the mother and whether in the BLS or the CDP data set.

TABLE 3
Direct Predictions of Middle-Childhood Externalizing Problems

Mode of Prediction and Data Set	Teacher EXT	Mother EXT
Temperamental resistance		
Bloomington Longitudinal Study	.22**	.30***
Child Development Project	.14***	.32***
Mother control		
Bloomington Longitudinal Study	.04 (*ns*)	−.01 (*ns*)
Child Development Project	.28***	.14*

Note: For the Bloomington Longitudinal Study, $ns = 104$–116; for the Child Development Project temperament prediction, $ns = 509$–525; for the home observation prediction by mother control, $ns = 144$–146. EXT $=$ externalizing.
*$p < .092$. **$p < .021$. ***$p < .001$.

Maternal behavior. Table 3 also shows correlations between observed restrictive control variables and later externalizing problems. For the BLS, the correlations were essentially zero, whereas for the CDP, the correlations were significant and of modest magnitude. The difference between BLS and CDP results here may reflect the different meanings of similar maternal behaviors with children of different ages. The BLS measure was taken during the 2nd year of life, and the variables in this composite have never had consistent main-effects-type relations with child behavior problems in this study (Bates & Bayles, 1988; Bates et al., 1985, 1991). The CDP measure was taken at age 5 years, so it is possible that the mother behavior here was more in response to child deviance rather than to developmentally normative and transitory misbehaviors.

Moderated Correlations

Analytic approach. The study's central questions were whether and how maternal restrictive control actions moderate the link between temperamental resistance to control and later externalizing behavior. We began our main analyses, then, with visual inspection of the scatter plots and correlations of externalizing outcomes predicted by temperamental resistance to control, viewed in groups defined by low versus high levels of observed maternal control. This was followed by multiple-groups, structural equation modeling as a test of the robustness of the apparent interaction effect. In secondary analyses, correlations between maternal control and externalizing outcomes were examined in groups defined by low versus high levels of temperamental resistance to control. Other secondary analyses considered possible confounds of the focal moderator effect, including child sex and family SES. The latter analyses were not followed by structural equation modeling.

Temperament predicting behavior, moderated by parenting. Participants were divided at the median of observed maternal restrictive control into two groups in each sample. We first examined scatter plots and associated correlations. These are shown in Figures 1 (BLS data) and 2 (CDP data). Despite methodological differences between the studies, the pattern of results was the same in each sample: When mothers were relatively low in restrictive control, there was a stronger relation between early temperament and later externalizing problems than when mothers were relatively high in control. This was true for both teacher- and mother-reported outcomes and in both the BLS and the CDP samples. It can also be noted in passing that the moderator effects were not attributable to any correlation between temperamental resistance and maternal restrictive control: The correlations between these two variables were .07 ($p = .429$) and .02 ($p = .825$) in the BLS and CDP, respectively.

Examination of the plots suggested further description of the lower degree of relation in the high-control subgroups: The effect is a small one, involving probably only small numbers of cases, and it appears to operate at both ends of the temperament continuum. For each graph, one may take the regression line of the low-restriction group as the reference line for comparing individuals in the high-restriction group with those in the low-restriction group. This shows, in the bottom panel of the figure, that there were a few highly resistant children in the high-restrictiveness groups whose externalizing outcomes were lower than might have been predicted by the low maternal control groups' regression lines. However, by looking at the top panel of the figure, with the same reference line, it also may be seen

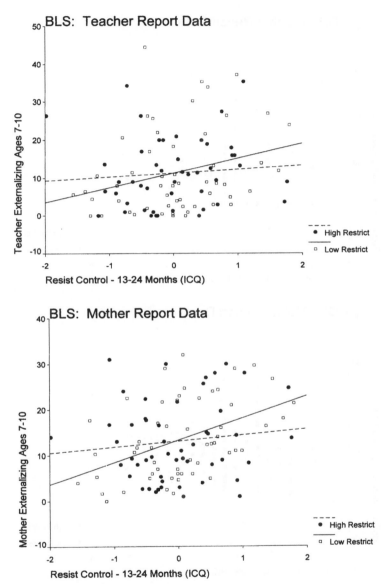

Figure 1. Scatter plots for the Bloomington Longitudinal Study (BLS) sample of temperamental resistance to control predicting externalizing outcomes as reported by teachers (top panel) and mothers (bottom panel). High Restrict = high restrictive control (for teachers, $r = .09, ns$; for mothers, $r = .11$, ns); Low Restrict = low restrictive control (for teachers, $r = .27$, $p = .05$; for mothers, $r = .44$, $p = .001$); Resist Control = child resistance to control; ICQ = Infant Characteristics Questionnaire.

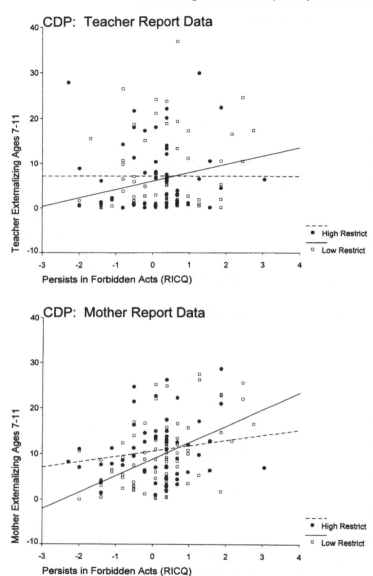

Figure 2. Scatter plots for the Child Development Project (CDP) sample of temperamental resistance to control predicting externalizing outcomes as reported by teachers (top panel) and mothers (bottom panel). High Restrict = high restrictive control (for teachers, $r = .01$, *ns*; for mothers, $r = .21$, $p = .13$); Low Restrict = low restrictive control (for teachers, $r = .22$, $p = .04$; for mothers, $r = .53$, $p = .000$); RICQ = Retrospective Infant Characteristics Questionnaire.

that there were, typically, a few low-resistant children in the high-control groups whose externalizing outcomes were higher than would have been predicted by the low group's regression line. This pattern suggests some interesting interpretations that are discussed later. For the moment, it is worth emphasizing that the main pattern is remarkably consistent: When the control of the mothers was observed to be relatively low, the resistant temperament of the child was more strongly predictive of levels of externalizing in middle childhood.

Parenting predicting behavior, moderated by temperament. We also considered the same interaction from the alternate perspective. We divided the samples at the median of child temperamental resistance to control and examined correlations between earlier maternal control and later child externalizing behavior. The resulting pattern of correlations was not quite as clear as the pattern obtained from the first perspective. It was symmetrical in the same way, but the correlations themselves were not as strong. The comparative patterns resembled the interaction as seen from the first perspective, but further research will need to confirm the apparent pattern, in which there were slightly stronger effects of restrictive parenting in the low-resistant children than in the high-resistant children. In the BLS, the correlations between maternal restrictive control and the externalizing outcomes in middle childhood in the low-resistant group were .17 and .12 (both *ns*) for teacher and mother outcomes, respectively, whereas in the high-resistant group, the corresponding correlations were .07 and −.11 (both *ns*). In the CDP, the corresponding two pairs of correlations were .39 ($p = .001$) and .18 ($p = .15$) in the low-resistant group and .19 ($p = .09$) and .10 (*ns*) in the high-resistant group. Statistics (*r* to *Z*) comparing the high- versus low-resistant groups' correlations did not reach significance, but three of four could be considered as approaching borderline significance: For the BLS comparisons, the *p*s were .12 and .13 for teacher and mother, respectively; for the CDP, they were .10 and .31 for teacher and mother, respectively. Further analyses on moderating effects of temperament on the maternal control-to-child externalizing link were not performed.

Structural Modeling

We chose to further evaluate the moderation of the temperament–behavior link by parenting in structural equation modeling using the EQS program (Bentler, 1995). The visual analysis did not provide a statistical test of the pattern's robustness. After deciding to do the structural equation modeling, and before actually doing it, however, we also performed a set of four conventional multiple regression tests, in which the product of the (centered) temperament and parenting variables was entered following the main effects. The results were inconclusive: For the respective studies and the teacher- and mother-report outcomes, betas (exact *p*s) were as follows: BLS: teacher outcome, −.17 (.085), mother outcome, −.15 (.122); CDP: teacher, −.11 (.182), mother, −.03 (.671).

To test in a more elegant way the hypothesis that the apparent differences between the low- versus high-restrictive control groups were due to chance, we compared the results of two structural models with contrasting assumptions about the groups' differences (Byrne, 1994; Hoyle, 1995, among others, provide a basic description of such models). The first model asks how well the data fit a simple path diagram in which the path coefficients between resistance and externalizing are expected to be nonzero but free to vary in any way with respect to one another. The second model asks how well the data fit the notion that the basic pattern of the data is one of equal paths in both the low- and the high-restrictive control groups. In other words, the second model assumes that maternal control does not moderate the relations of temperament and externalizing behavior. The comparison of the two models indicates the tenability of the interpretation that there is an interaction effect.

First, then, we tested a four-group model without constraints on the paths (i.e., allowing the relations between early resistance to control and the teacher and mother ratings of externalizing behavior to vary according to group). We did, however, include constraints on the error terms associated with the outcome variables. The error constraints amounted to assuming that controlling for their separate paths from child temperament, the mother and teacher ratings of externalizing behavior were correlated the same across high- and low-control groups. This was done to see whether the model could be simplified by the addition of constraints and to see if we needed to worry about possible complications in the interpretation of an interaction effect (e.g., possible nonequivalence of measurement of externalizing in the high- vs. low-maternal restriction groups). The relations between error terms were not assumed to be equal across samples, given that the teacher–mother Pearson correlation in the BLS was .20 ($p = .019$) and that in the CDP, it was .41 ($p < .001$; observation subsample only). Although we had used similar constructs, there were some measurement and scaling differences between samples. The basic model, illustrated in Figure 3, was repeated for all four groups (i.e., BLS and CDP, low and high control). Then, this four-group design was repeated in a model that constrained the temperament–externalizing behavior paths to be equivalent in the low- and high-control groups within each sample.

The first model, constraining only the residual correlations of the two dependent measures, provided an excellent fit to the data, $\chi^2(2, N = 239) = 0.705$, $p = .703$ (Bentler–Bonett normed fit index $= .990$; comparative fit index $= 1.000$). In addition, the Lagrange multiplier test showed that removing the requirement that the mother and teacher ratings'

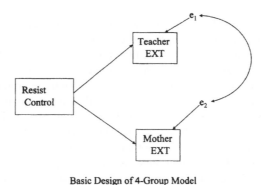

Basic Design of 4-Group Model

Figure 3. Basic design of multiple-group, structural model (repeated four times, for teacher- and mother-report outcomes and for Bloomington Longitudinal Study and Child Development Project data sets). EXT = externalizing behavior score.

TABLE 4
Structural Modeling Results

Group	Path Coefficient Resist → T Ext	Resist → M Ext	e_T	e_M	r_{eT-eM}
BLS low control	.27	.45	.96	.89	.05
BLS high control	.05	.10	.99	.99	.05
CDP low control	.32	.53	.95	.85	.40
CDP high control	−.03	.22	1.00	.98	.36

Note: Resist = temperamental resistance to control; T Ext = teacher-reported externalizing; M Ext = mother-reported externalizing; e_T = error associated with T Ext; e_M = error associated with M Ext; r_{eT-eM} = correlation between teacher and mother reports; BLS = Bloomington Longitudinal Study; CDP = Child Development Project. $\chi^2(2, N = 239) = 0.705$, $p = .703$; Bentler–Bonett normed fit index = .990; comparative fit index = 1.000.

correlations be equivalent across groups did not improve the fit. Thus, the model can be simpler, and it does not require us to evaluate nonequivalence across groups in the measurement of externalizing. The path coefficients are shown in Table 4.

The second model we tested, in addition to constraining the teacher–mother outcome correlations, also constrained the temperament–externalizing paths to be equal across groups within samples. This is, in essence, the no-interaction effect or null model. This model provided a worse fit to the data than the first, less constrained model, $\chi^2(6, N = 239) = 10.122$, $p = 120$. The probability of a fit this much worse (χ^2 difference = 9.317) occurring by chance is slightly greater than .05. Each of the four path constraints contributed to the multivariate Lagrange multiplier test (cumulative $\chi^2 = 9.347$, $p = .053$), indicating that the constraints of equal paths, within samples, worsened the model's fit. The probability estimate does not include information about the directional comparisons of coefficients so is analogous to a conservative two-tailed test. Because of our prediction of a particular direction of differences between the paths across the two levels of restrictive control, we estimated the probability of the effect's being spurious as something less than the nondirectional chi-square value. The statistical findings suggested that the orderly pattern observed in the correlations of the separate groups was relatively unlikely to be due to chance.

Additional Control Analyses

In addition to considering whether the effect was likely due to any relation between maternal control and the cross-situational meaning of the measure of externalizing, we also considered several other possible confounds. First, we asked whether there were artifactual distribution variations in temperament or behavior problems. Although the distributions were not perfectly equivalent across groups, they were rather similar. This can be seen impressionistically in the scatter plots (Figures 1 and 2). Within each source (mother or teacher) and study (BLS or CDP), the variances of externalizing scores in the low-restriction and high-restriction groups were quite similar, ranging from 8% difference at the most to less than 1% difference. None of the differences approached significance. Distributional properties probably do not account for the interaction effect. Second, we considered a possible confound with sex of child. The interaction did not depend on gender differences in the regressions as related to the maternal restrictive control group, as we saw by visually comparing the scatter plots for boys with the corresponding ones for girls. The pattern was one of similarity, with no consistent differences emerging in these comparisons. Third, we did the same kind of comparison for lower versus middle versus upper SES. No consistent pattern emerged, suggesting that the effect was not associated with SES.[4] Finally, using the same graphical analysis approach, we considered the possible further moderating role of observed maternal warmth. No evident pattern of moderation was found.

DISCUSSION

Children's early resistance to control predicted later externalizing behavior more accurately when the mother had been observed to be relatively low in control actions than when she had been high in control actions. This pattern was evident whether the child outcome was measured at home or at school in two separate longitudinal research projects and through both graphical and statistical analyses. This pattern does not seem to be attributable to chance, distributional confounds, gender, or SES. Efforts to explain the effect are justified by the present findings alone. However, in addition, the pattern resembles, in broad form, the effect found by Arcus and Gardner (1993) and Park et al. (1997) in which stern parenting reduced the likelihood of early child fearfulness being associated with later over-inhibition.

How Does the Mother–Child Interaction Affect the Linkage of Temperament and Externalizing Behavior?

The scatter plots show cases in which highly resistant children in the high-restriction group turned out better behaved than their counterparts in the low-restriction group, as well as cases of nonresistant children in the high-restriction group who turned out worse behaved than their less highly restricted counterparts. How might this pattern have occurred? First, considering the resistant child, if the parent's high level of control is consistent, over time it may reduce the impact of the child's early unmanageability, shaping higher levels of responsiveness to social limits. This assumes some degree of effectiveness in the parent's control. However, because the moderator effect was shown clearly in only handfuls of cases, some controlling parents may not have effectively altered the developmental process that links unmanageability and externalizing behavior. One can consider the hypothetical process from another angle, as in the case of a child high on resistance but observed to receive relatively

---

[4]These findings do not, of course, preclude direct main-effects-type relations between sex of child or SES and externalizing. Such effects are often found and were not relevant to the present study. The present findings also do not preclude the presence of direct main-effects-type correlations between SES and maternal restrictiveness, which have also been found frequently in past research, in which lower SES mothers are more restrictive. This is true in the present study, too, in both samples, with modest degrees of relations. Nevertheless, there are many lower SES mothers low in restrictive control and many higher SES mothers high in restrictive control, and visual comparisons do not suggest that the moderator effect of restrictive control is confounded with SES. In principle, these comparisons could be statistically tested through r-to-Z tests, structural modeling, or other techniques. However, we chose not to test them because the Ns would have been too small for adequate power.

little control: Perhaps the mother wished to avoid, at least during the observer's visit, the kind of conflict her temperament perceptions would have forecasted. Frequent occasions like this, especially if accompanied by episodically high irritability, such as in cases in which the mother is depressed or highly stressed (Campbell, Pierce, Moore, Marakovitz, & Newby, 1996), would facilitate the occurrence of coercive family process. Patterson et al. (1992) have demonstrated coercive process to be associated with the development of externalizing behavior problems. Speculatively, then, in at least some cases, highly controlling mothers prevent highly resistant children's temperamental resistance from leading to coercion training by bringing the child under control. Less controlling mothers, in contrast, perhaps because they feel more distress from the perceived uncontrollability of the child and tend to participate in coercive process, more often see their resistant children become behaviorally disruptive.

Second, considering the low-resistant cases, low parental control may be an optimal environment for the development of internalized self-control. When mothers were relatively light in their control of nonresistant children, the children typically showed few problem behaviors. Relatively low levels of control would provide ample opportunities for developing autonomous functioning (Kochanska, 1995) and thus would help the child to internalize social limits. Low-resistant children experiencing high control, however, may have fewer experiences of autonomy and thus less practice in cognitively and emotionally internalizing social limits. This might facilitate development of coercive, disruptive behavior patterns, especially when children are outside their highly controlling parents' reach. In addition, because they lack a high level of resistance to control, they suffer many interruptions without many "successes," which might lead to some level of frustration-based anger. Some child–mother dyads may even begin a coercive process—the training of increasing levels of defiance or other deviant behavior as an adaptive means of sometimes obtaining autonomy. Assuming that all children have some degree of autonomy-striving (White, 1959), even if they are highly responsive to external controls, a relatively nonresistant child could conceivably learn irritable, coercive responses in response to an interrupting environment.

We are partly modeling our interpretations on the elegant work of Kochanska (1995, 1997), who has found evidence that in developing signs of conscience, temperamentally fearless children respond to different aspects of mother–child interactions than do fearful children. Our temperament and outcome variables differ from Kochanska's, and we preferred to consider the interaction from the temperament–adjustment linkage perspective than from the parenting–adjustment linkage perspective. Nevertheless, our results do complement Kochanska's. We are, like Kochanska, suggesting that differences in maternal control interact with child temperamental differences in producing adjustment outcomes and that at its root, the interaction effect may involve the extent to which the child develops internalized self-control.[5]

As a supplement to the reported analyses, we also considered whether the effects of the interaction of resistant temperament and restrictive control would also extend to internalizing

---

[5]Preliminary analyses with temperamental unadaptability—partially akin to concepts of behavioral inhibition or fearfulness—as the moderator of the parental control variable in predicting externalizing did not provide a direct replication of the Kochanska effect. This could be due to many factors, especially because of differences in measurement and design.

behavior problems. The pattern of higher correlations between resistant temperament and externalizing scores in the low-restriction dyads versus the high-restriction dyads was partially repeated with the internalizing outcome. However, this was applied more clearly in the BLS than the CDP data, and when the effects of externalizing behavior were partialed out (because of the overlap between internalizing and externalizing scores), the pattern was further attenuated. Therefore, we conclude that the moderating effects of maternal control on the relation between early unmanageability and later adjustment are fairly specific to externalizing outcomes.

How Does Child Temperament Moderate Linkage Between Parenting and Child Behavior?

How child temperament moderates the effects of parenting on externalizing adjustment was not our central focus. However, findings from this perspective were consistent in pattern with our interpretations of the parenting-moderating-temperament effect. We tentatively interpreted the predictiveness of parenting measures as being slightly greater when the children were low in perceived resistance to control than when they were perceived to be high in resistance. With nonresistant children, high restriction forecasted more behavior problems, and low restriction forecasted fewer. However, among resistant children, two processes might cancel out part of the relation between parenting and behavior problems: Some resistant children's mothers are controlling, thereby reducing their chances of externalizing problems; some of their mothers are low in controlling, increasing their chances of behavior problems. This converges in form with the Hagekull and Bohlin (1995) finding that aggressiveness of temperamentally hard-to-manage children was less affected by day-care quality than that of manageable children.

Limitations

Although we consider the moderator effect robust and meaningful, we also remain aware of limitations. First, although the addition of an interaction term adds to the precision of the explanation, it adds only a small amount. We have tentatively ruled out several artifactual and substantive explanations of the effect. However, it remains possible that multivariate measurement models for the constructs of the study, more explicitly controlling for measurement error, would have allowed us to account for additional variance. Any measure of temperament, parenting, or adjustment has weaknesses, but sometimes combinations of measures from alternate perspectives can allow closer estimates of the theoretical construct. There are also possibilities of additional interacting factors. Some likely candidates are mentioned later. In addition, although the findings do conceptually converge with emerging theoretical–empirical models, they were not hypothesized on the basis of a clear a priori theory. The findings suggest that our observational measures of restrictive control reflect not only harsh, punitive parenting but also appropriate parenting, in some contexts. Before seeing these results, it would have been possible, especially for one who did not know the preliminary BLS findings, to predict that temperament's most adverse effects would be in the presence of restrictive parenting and conversely that the most adverse effects of restrictive parenting would be in the context of a resistant temperament, exactly opposite to the replicated pattern of findings. It would also have been possible, especially for one who knew the preliminary BLS findings, to predict what was, in fact, found. Further replications and extensions will be important.

Future Research

Assuming future replications of the effect, further specification of the developmental processes we have outlined should be sought. We will be particularly interested in how additional temperament elements may improve the model. Some interesting Temperament × Temperament interaction effects have been emerging (e.g., Eisenberg et al., 1996; Rothbart & Bates, 1998; Tremblay, 1992). One key question would be, What are the particular core temperament dimensions involved in the perceived resistance to control of a given child? One child may be high in resistance to control because of a very strong response to the potential rewards in stimuli, whereas another child is resistant because of low levels of executive control of attention and deficient verbal control of action. This distinction could change the socialization impact of both temperamental resistance and maternal restrictive control. Other theoretically independent temperament variables could also moderate effects of resistant temperament. For example, a resistant but fearful child's responses to parental or teacher control could produce developmentally different outcomes compared with the responses of a resistant, nonfearful child (Bates, Pettit, & Dodge, 1995). A second kind of additional moderator could be family structure or socializing efforts by other family members and friends. Another might be child physical attractiveness or intellectual development. A further moderator might be distinctions in the particular kinds of externalizing behavior problems. For example, perhaps resistant children in restrictive families show more covert symptoms, like stealing, and in nonrestrictive families, they might show more overt symptoms, like fighting. Ultimately, it will be useful to search for higher order interaction effects (i.e., controlling for levels of more than one moderator variable). However, as may be well illustrated in the present study, it is difficult to detect modest-sized but statistically robust effects, even with only one moderator variable in medium-sized longitudinal samples. Higher order tests will require larger samples either in single studies or pooled across studies.

REFERENCES

Achenbach, T. M. (1991a). *Manual for the Child Behavior Checklist/4–18 and 1991 Profile.* Burlington: University of Vermont, Department of Psychiatry.

Achenbach, T. M. (1991b). *Manual for the Teacher's Report Form and 1991 Profile.* Burlington: University of Vermont, Department of Psychiatry.

Achenbach, T. M., & Edelbrock, C. (1983). *Manual for the Child Behavior Checklist and Revised Child Behavior Profile.* Burlington: University of Vermont, Department of Psychiatry.

Achenbach, T. M., & Edelbrock, C. (1986). *Manual for the Teacher's Report Form and Teacher Version of the Child Behavior Profile.* Burlington: University of Vermont, Department of Psychiatry.

Arcus, D., & Gardner, S. (1993, March). *When biology is not destiny.* Paper presented at the biennial meeting of the Society for Research in Child Development, New Orleans, LA.

Barkley, R. A. (1996). Attention-deficit/hyperactivity disorder. In E. J. Mash & R. A. Barkley (Eds.), *Child psychopathology* (pp. 63–112). New York: Guilford.

Baron, R. M., & Kenny, D. A. (1986). The moderator–mediator variable distinction in social psychological research: Conceptual, strategic, and statistical considerations. *Journal of Personality and Social Psychology, 51,* 1173–1182.

Bates, J. E. (1989). Applications of temperament concepts. In G. A. Kohnstamm, J. E. Bates, & M. K. Rothbart (Eds.), *Temperament in childhood* (pp. 321–355). Chichester, England: Wiley.

Bates, J. E. (1994a, May). *Alternate pathways between temperament and adjustment in childhood.* Paper presented at the meeting of the Midwestern Psychological Association, Chicago.

Bates, J. E. (1994b). Parents as scientific observers of their children's development. In S. L. Friedman & H. C. Haywood (Eds.), *Developmental follow-up: Concepts, genres, domains, and methods* (pp. 197–216). San Diego, CA: Academic Press.

Bates, J. E., & Bayles, K. (1984). Objective and subjective components in mothers' perceptions of their children from age 6 months to 3 years. *Merrill-Palmer Quarterly, 30,* 111–130.

Bates, J. E., & Bayles, K. (1988). The role of attachment in the development of behavior problems. In J. Belsky & T. Nezworski (Eds.), *Clinical implications of attachment* (pp. 253–299). Hillsdale, NJ: Erlbaum.

Bates, J. E., Bayles, K., Bennett, D. S., Ridge, B., & Brown, M. M. (1991). Origins of externalizing behavior problems at eight years of age. In D. Pepler & K. Rubin (Eds.), *Development and treatment of childhood aggression* (pp. 93–120). Hillsdale, NJ: Erlbaum.

Bates, J. E., Freeland, C. B., & Lounsbury, M. L. (1979). Measurement of infant difficultness. *Child Development, 50,* 794–803.

Bates, J. E., & Marvinney, D. (1993, March). *Temperament, mother–child relations and marital harmony as predictors of child adjustment at 3–5 years.* Paper presented at the biennial meeting of the Society for Research in Child Development, New Orleans, LA.

Bates, J. E., Marvinney, D., Kelly, T., Dodge, K. A., Bennett, D. S., & Pettit, G. S. (1994). Child care history and kindergarten adjustment. *Developmental Psychology, 30,* 690–700.

Bates, J. E., Maslin, C. A., & Frankel, K. A. (1985). Attachment security, mother–child interaction, and temperament as predictors of behavior problem ratings at age three years [Special issue]. *Society for Research in Child Development Monographs: Growing Points in Attachment Theory and Research, 50* (1–2, Serial No. 209).

Bates, J. E., Olson, S. L., Pettit, G. S., & Bayles, K. (1982). Dimensions of individuality in the mother–infant relationship at six months of age. *Child Development, 53,* 446–461.

Bates, J. E., Pettit, G. S., & Dodge, K. A. (1995). Family and child factors in stability and change in children's aggressiveness in elementary school. In J. McCord (Ed.), *Coercion and punishment in long-term perspectives* (pp. 124–138). New York: Cambridge University Press.

Bentler, P. M. (1995). *EQS structural equations program manual.* Encino, CA: Multivariate Software.

Brody, G. H., Stoneman, Z., & Gauger, K. (1996). Parent–child relationships, family problem-solving behavior, and sibling relationship quality: The moderating role of sibling temperaments. *Child Development, 67,* 1289–1300.

Byrne, B. M. (1994). *Structural equation modeling with EQS and EQS/Windows: Basic concepts, applications, and programming.* Thousand Oaks, CA: Sage.

Calkins, S. D., & Fox, N. A. (1994). Individual differences in the biological aspects of temperament. In J. E. Bates & T. D. Wachs (Eds.), *Temperament: Individual differences at the interface of biology and behavior* (pp. 199–217). Washington, DC: American Psychological Association.

Campbell, S. B., Pierce, E. W., Moore, G., Marakovitz, S., & Newby, K. (1996). Boys' externalizing problems at elementary school age: Pathways from early behavior problems, maternal control, and family stress. *Development and Psychopathology*, *8*, 701–719.

Caspi, A., Moffitt, T. E., Newman, D. L., & Silva, P. A. (1996). Behavioral observations at age 3 predict adult psychiatric disorders: Longitudinal evidence from a birth cohort. *Archives of General Psychiatry*, *53*, 1033–1039.

Cleveland, W. S. (1993). *Visualizing data.* Summit, NJ: Hobart Press.

Colder, C. R., Lochman, J. E., & Wells, K. C. (1997). The moderating effects of children's fear and activity level on relations between parenting practices and childhood symptomatology. *Journal of Abnormal Child Psychology*, *25*, 251–263.

Dodge, K. A., Bates, J. E., & Pettit, G. S. (1990, December 21). Mechanisms in the cycle of violence. *Science*, *250*, 1678–1683.

Eisenberg, N., Fabes, R. A., Murphy, B., Karbon, M., Smith, M., & Maszk, P. (1996). The relations of children's dispositional empathy-related responding to their emotionality, regulation, and social functioning. *Developmental Psychology*, *32*, 195–209.

Eisenberg, N., Guthrie, I. K., Fabes, R. A., Reiser, M., Murphy, B. C., Holgren, R., Maszk, P., & Losoya, S. (1997). The relations of regulation and emotionality to resiliency and competent social functioning in elementary school children. *Child Development*, *68*, 295–311.

Gray, J. A. (1991). The neuropsychology of temperament. In J. Strelau & A. Angleitner (Eds.), *Explorations in temperament* (pp. 105–128). New York: Plenum.

Guerin, D. W., Gottfried, A. W., & Thomas, C. W. (1997). Difficult temperament and behaviour problems: A longitudinal study from 1.5 to 12 years. *International Journal of Behavioral Development*, *21*, 71–90.

Hagekull, B., & Bohlin, G. (1995). Day care quality, family and child characteristics, and socioemotional development. *Early Childhood Research Quarterly*, *10*, 505–526.

Henry, B., Caspi, A., Moffitt, T. E., & Silva, P. A. (1996). Temperamental and familial predictors of violent and nonviolent criminal convictions: Age 3 to age 18. *Developmental Psychology*, *32*, 614–623.

Hetherington, E. M., & Martin, B. (1986). Family factors and psychopathology in children. In H. C. Quay & J. S. Werry (Eds.), *Psychopathological disorders of childhood* (3rd ed., pp. 332–390). New York: Wiley.

Hoyle, R. H. (Ed.). (1995). *Structural equation modeling: Concepts, issues, and applications.* Thousand Oaks, CA: Sage.

Kochanska, G. (1991). Socialization and temperament in the development of guilt and conscience. *Child Development*, *62*, 1379–1392.

Kochanska, G. (1995). Children's temperament, mothers' discipline, and security of attachment: Multiple pathways to emerging internalization. *Child Development*, *66*, 597–615.

Kochanska, G. (1997). Multiple pathways to conscience for children with different temperaments: From toddlerhood to age 5. *Developmental Psychology*, *33*, 228–240.

Kochanska, G., Murray, K., & Coy, K. C. (1997). Inhibitory control as a contributor to conscience in childhood: From toddler to early school age. *Child Development*, *68*, 263–277.

Kopp, C. B., (1982). Antecedents of self-regulation: A developmental perspective. *Developmental Psychology*, *18*, 199–214.

Lanthier, R. P., & Bates, J. E. (1995, May). *Infancy era predictors of the Big Five personality dimensions in adolescence.* Paper presented at the meeting of the Midwestern Psychological Association, Chicago.

Lerner, J. V., & Lerner, R. M. (1994). Explorations of the goodness-of-fit model in early adolescence. In W. B. Carey & S. C. McDevitt (Eds.), *Prevention and early intervention: Individual differences as risk factors for the mental health of children: A festschrift for Stella Chess and Alexander Thomas* (pp. 161–169). New York: Brunner/Mazel.

McClelland, G. H., & Judd, C. M. (1993). Statistical difficulties of detecting interactions and moderator effects. *Psychological Bulletin, 114*, 376–390.

Olson, S. L. (1996). Developmental perspectives. In S. Sandberg (Ed.), *Hyperactivity disorders* (pp. 149–183). Cambridge, England: Cambridge University Press.

Olson, S. L., Bates, J. E., & Bayles, K. (1982). Maternal perceptions of infant and toddler behavior: A longitudinal, construct validation study. *Infant Behavior and Development, 5*, 397–410.

Olson, S. L., Bates, J. E., & Bayles, K. (1984). Mother–infant interaction and the development of individual differences in children's cognitive competence. *Developmental Psychology, 20*, 166–179.

Olweus, D. (1979). Stability of aggressive reaction patterns in males: A review. *Psychological Bulletin, 86*, 852–875.

Park, S.-Y., Belsky, J., Putnam, S., & Crnic, K. (1997). Infant emotionality, parenting, and 3-year inhibition: Exploring stability and lawful discontinuity in a male sample. *Developmental Psychology, 33*, 218–227.

Patterson, C. M., & Newman, J. P. (1993). Reflectivity and learning from aversive events: Toward a psychological mechanism for the syndromes of disinhibition. *Psychological Review, 100*, 716–736.

Patterson, G. R., Reid, J. B., & Dishion, T. J. (1992). *Antisocial boys*. Eugene, OR: Castalia.

Pettit, G. S., & Bates, J. E. (1984). Continuity of individual differences in the mother–infant relationship from 6 to 13 months. *Child Development, 55*, 729–739.

Pettit, G. S., & Bates, J. E. (1989). Family interaction patterns and children's behavior problems from infancy to age 4 years. *Developmental Psychology, 25*, 413–420.

Pettit, G. S., Bates, J. E., & Dodge, K. A. (1993). Family interaction patterns and children's conduct problems at home and school: A longitudinal perspective. *School Psychology Review, 22*, 403–420.

Pettit, G. S., Bates, J. E., & Dodge, K. A. (1997). Supportive parenting, ecological context, and children's adjustment: A seven-year longitudinal study. *Child Development, 68*, 908–923.

Ridge, B. A. (1992). *The role of self-esteem in adjustment in middle childhood and adolescence: A longitudinal investigation*. Unpublished doctoral dissertation, Indiana University, Bloomington.

Rothbart, M. K., & Bates, J. E. (1998). Temperament. In W. Damon (Series Ed.) & N. Eisenberg (Vol. Ed.), *Handbook of child psychology: Vol. 3. Social, emotional, and personality development* (5th ed., pp. 105–176). New York: Wiley.

Rothbaum, F., & Weisz, J. R. (1994). Parental caregiving and child externalizing behavior: A meta-analysis. *Psychological Bulletin, 116*, 55–74.

Rutter, M. (1983). Statistical and personal interactions: Facets and perspectives. In D. Magnusson & V. L. Allen (Eds.), *Human development: An international perspective* (pp. 295–319). New York: Academic Press.

Sanson, A., Smart, D., Prior, M., & Oberklaid, F. (1993). Precursors of hyperactivity and aggression. *Journal of the American Academy of Child and Adolescent Psychiatry, 32*, 1207–1216.

Shaw, D. S., Owens, E. B., Vondra, J. I., Keenan, K., & Winslow, E. B. (1996). Early risk factors and pathways in the development of early disruptive behavior. *Development and Psychopathology*, *8*, 679–699.

Slotboom, A.-M., Elphick, E., van Riessen, M., van Mill, I., & Kohnstamm, G. A. (1996, October). *Continuity in temperament/personality dimensions of children as perceived by parents: Relations between temperament and the Big Five*. Paper presented at the Occasional Temperament Conference, Eugene, OR.

Thomas, A., & Chess, S. (1977). *Temperament and development*. New York: Brunner/Mazel.

Tremblay, R. (1992). The prediction of delinquent behavior from childhood behavior: Personality theory revisited. In J. McCord (Ed.), *Advances in criminological theory: Vol. 3. Facts, frameworks, and forecasts* (pp. 193–230). New Brunswick, NJ: Transaction Publications.

Wachs, T. D. (1992). *The nature of nurture*. Newbury Park, CA: Sage.

White, R. W. (1959). Motivation reconsidered: The concept of competence. *Psychological Review*, *66*, 297–333.

Received February 26, 1997
Revision received January 14, 1998
Accepted January 14, 1998

Part V

CLINICAL ISSUES: FOLLOW-THROUGH STUDIES

This section includes three papers in which longitudinal data is used to clarify important clinical questions. Among these are the relationship between drug use/abuse and psychiatric disorders in adolescents and young adults. In the first paper Brook, Cohen and Brook present data derived from the study of a sample residing in two upstate New York counties and studied prospectively into adulthood. Three questions are addressed: 1) relation of psychiatric disorders and contemporaneous substance use; 2) relation of adolescent psychiatric disorder and young adult substance use; and 3) prediction of young adult psychiatric disorder from adolescent substance use.

Subjects were between 1 and 10 years of age at the time of initial recruitment. Mean age at the time of the adolescent and young adult assessments was $16.30 +/- 2.78$ years and $22.05 +/- 2.72$ years respectively. Psychiatric diagnoses were assessed by a supplemented version of the Diagnostic Interview schedule for Children Version 1 (DISC-1) using computer algorithms designed to match DSM-III-R criteria, to combine information from mothers and youths. Information regarding the use of tobacco, alcohol, marijuana, and other illicit drugs including cocaine, heroin, amphetamines, LSD, Quaaludes and barbiturates without a prescription, was obtained during interviews and from a paper-and pencil assessment of drug use.

Quantity/frequency measures of tobacco, alcohol, marijuana and illicit drug use were associated with an increased risk of contemporaneous psychiatric disorders, including depressive and conduct disorders in both adolescent and young adult males and females. The data provided no evidence that depressive disorders, anxiety disorders, or conduct disorders in late adolescence have an influence on later drug use, controlling for earlier drug use. Thus prior psychopathology has little effect on subsequent substance use, once the youngster is using drugs, prior psychopathology in adolescence is associated with young adult substance use, when prior adolescent substance use is controlled for. However, adolescent tobacco and illicit drug use levels predicted young adult antisocial, major depressive and anxiety disorders, and these relationships remained significant when the adolescent disorder included the prediction equation.

The findings have important public policy and clinical implications. Not only abuse but use of cigarettes, alcohol, marijuana, and illicit drugs is related to later psychiatric disorders. Although as the authors caution, this relationship may not be causal, as the possibility of a common diathesis cannot be eliminated, it is nevertheless important that attention be directed to the use of drugs and not focus only on abuse. Moreover, in clinical settings, substance use during early- and late-adolescence should signal a diligent search for signs and symptoms of incipient psychopathology.

The outcome of antisocial behavior in boys has been extensively studied. However, systematic information regarding the adult status of girls who exhibited symptoms of conduct disorder during childhood and adolescence is less well known. In the second paper in this section, Pajer addresses this deficit in the course of a critical review of the literature on the adult outcomes of antisocial girls. Five literature data bases, Dissertation Abstracts, 1984–1996; Sociological Abstracts, 1973–1996; Social Work Abstracts, 1977–1996: MEDLINE, 1966–1996; and PschLit, 1974–1996 were searched. Twenty studies that were 1) written in English; 2) presented data on girls with conduct disorder of delinquency, ages 13–18, or presented data on boys and girls in a format that permitted separate analyses of the girls; 3) reported adult follow-up data on the same subjects at age >19 years; or 4) presented cross-sectional data on adolescent antisocial behavior for any group of adult women were indentified.

Neither conduct disorder nor delinquency is rare among girls. In an epidemiologically defined sample of 15 year olds between 7.5%–9.5% of girls met criteria for conduct disorder, compared to 8.6%–12.2% of boys. Currently available information is clearly discrepant from the historical belief that the adult course of antisocial adolescent girls is relatively benign. Compared to their nonantisocial peers, these women have higher mortality rates, a 10- to 40-fold increase in criminal behavior, a range of psychiatric problems, dysfunctional and sometime violent relationships, poor educational achievement, less stable work histories, and higher rates of service utilization.

Similar to what has been described for boys, anecdotal and retrospective data suggest that there are at least two possible paths between antisocial deviance in girls and similar behavior in women. The first is a pattern of persistent aggressive antisocial behavior that begins in latency and continues through adolescence into adulthood, with a steady increase in the severity of offenses. The second path is characterized by adolescent onset of norm violating behavior, which escalates to more severe adult criminal activity in the context of substance abuse or continued association with deviant peers.

This review makes it amply clear that, similar to males, female adolescent antisocial behavior has important long-term individual and societal consequences. Programs designed to prevent and/or ameliorate antisocial behavior patterns in boys have achieved only limited success. Nevertheless, the focus of such studies needs to be expanded to include girls.

The final paper in this section, by Kremen, Buka, Seidman, Goldstein, Koren, and Tsaung examines the relation between IQ decline during childhood and adult psychotic symptoms in a 19-year longitudinal study. The study is an outgrowth of the hypothesis advanced by Barbara Fish, MD that an inherited neurointegrative deficit was specific for the schizophrenia phenotype and that "pandysmaturation" was an index of this defect in infancy. Although pandysmaturation, characterized by an abnormally uneven developmental profile, has been found in children of parents with schizophrenia, data on the adult outcomes of such children is limited. In the present study, the authors focused on IQ and IQ change over time as an indicator of developmental unevenness. They compared three hypotheses: that 1) low IQ, 2) large IQ fluctuations regardless of direction, or 3) large IQ declines would predict the presence of adult psychotic symptoms.

The subjects were 547 offspring from the National Collaborative Perinatal Project, a community sample that was unselected for psychiatric illness who underwent IQ testing at both ages 4 and 7 years. Adult psychiatric symptoms and lifetime DSM-III diagnoses were determined on the basis of version III of the National Institute of Mental Health Diagnostic Interview Schedule (DIS). After appropriate checks for reliability, a group of 18 subjects with probable or definite psychotic symptoms was identified. Deviant responder analyses were performed to divide the sample into the highest (largest IQ increase) and lowest (largest IQ decline) deciles, the next highest and lowest 15% and the middle 50%.

The 10% of individuals with substantial larger than expected IQ declines between the ages of 4 and 7 years had a rate of psychotic symptoms 16 years later that was nearly seven times as high as that for individuals without large childhood IQ declines, thus supporting the "directional IQ change" hypothesis. Parental socioeconomic status and IQ at age 7 also predicted adult psychotic symptoms. However, when IQ at age 7, IQ decline between ages 4 and 7, and socioeconomic status were all included in a logistic regression analysis, only IQ decline remained significant. Moreover the predictive value of childhood IQ decline was specific for psychotic symptoms. The group with large IQ declines was not more likely to manifest symptoms of mania, depression, anxiety disorders, antisocial personality disorders, or alcohol or drug abuse.

Although in this study, IQ decline is specific for psychotic symptoms, follow-up assessment when the study participants are further into the age of risk will be necessary to firmly establish specificity for schizophrenia. Nevertheless, the findings are consistent with the increasingly accepted idea that schizophrenia is a neurodevelopmental disorder.

17

Longitudinal Study of Co-occurring Psychiatric Disorders and Substance Use

Judith S. Brook, Ed.D., Patricia Cohen, Ph.D., and David W. Brook, M.D.

Objective: *To examine temporal priority in the relationship between psychiatric disorders and drug use.* **Method:** *Psychiatric assessments and drug use were completed at three different points in time, spanning 9 years. Structured interviews were administered to a cohort of youths and their mothers. Subjects were selected on the basis of their residence in either of two counties in upstate New York. The sample was predominantly white male and female youths, aged 1 through 10 years upon initial collection of data. Psychiatric diagnoses were assessed by a supplemented version of the Diagnostic Interview Schedule for Children Version 1, using computer algorithms designed to match DSM-III-R criteria to combine information from mothers and youths. Substance use information was obtained in the interviews.* **Results:** *A significant relationship was found to exist between earlier adolescent drug use and later depressive and disruptive disorders in young adulthood, controlling for earlier psychiatric disorders. Earlier psychiatric disorders did not predict changes in young adult drug use.* **Conclusions:** *Implications for policy, prevention, and treatment include (1) more medical attention needs to be given to the use of legal and illegal drugs; and (2) a decrease in drug use may result in a decrease in the incidence of later psychiatric disorders.* J. Am. Acad. Child Adolesc. Psychiatry, 1998, 37(3):322–330. **Key Words:** *psychiatric disorders, drug use, adolescence.*

Accepted October 9, 1997.

Drs. J. S. Brook and D. W. Brook are with the Department of Community Medicine, Mount Sinai School of Medicine, New York. Dr. Cohen is with the Department of Psychiatry, Columbia University, New York.

This research is supported by Research Scientist Award DA 00244 and research grant DA 03188, awarded to J.S.B. by NIDA, NIH. The authors thank Dr. Coryl Jones for her 15-year contribution to this program of research, Lisa Jaeger Czeisler for her research assistance, and Linda Capobianco for the preparation of this manuscript, as well as the editor of this Journal and two anonymous reviewers for their constructive suggestions.

Reprint requests to Dr. Judith S. Brook, Box 1044A, Mount Sinai School of Medicine, One Gustave L. Levy Place, New York, NY 10029.

During the past decade, attention has been increasingly focused on the relationship between drug use/abuse and psychiatric disorders. Several investigators have found a strong contemporaneous relationship between psychiatric disorders and drug use in both clinical samples and general population samples of adolescents (Boyle and Offord, 1991; Brook and Brook, 1990; Kessler et al., 1996) and adults (Breslau et al., 1993; Helzer and Pryzbeck, 1988; Kessler et al., 1996). For instance, Kessler et al. (1996) reported that mental disorders generally preceded the development of addictive disorders in people with both co-occurring disorders. Other researchers have reported a relationship between the diagnosis of conduct or emotional disorder and the frequency of alcohol and tobacco use (Boyle and Offord, 1991). The present study builds on previous research examining the origins of the relationship between psychiatric disorders and drug use in a sample of young adults studied since adolescence.

Three possible models may explain the relation between drug use and psychiatric disorders in adolescents and young adults. In the first model, psychiatric disorders lead to the use of drugs by at least one of several mechanisms. Psychiatric disorders may produce difficulties in parental monitoring and in the parent-child attachment relation, or in peer relationships, which may, in turn, facilitate substance use. However, it may be that adverse parental factors are risk factors for both psychiatric disorders and drug use. Since internalizing disorders can predict higher levels of later substance use, it may be that drug use is one way for adolescents and young adults to cope with intrapersonal distress (Glass, 1990; Khantzian, 1985; Neighbors et al., 1992). Several investigators (Christie et al., 1988; Deykin et al., 1987) reported that depression predicted drug abuse. In a recent article, earlier intrapsychic distress (depressive symptoms) was found to be associated with later illicit drug use (Brook et al., 1995). The authors concluded that legal and illegal drug use may reduce dysphoric mood at least temporarily.

Conduct disorders have also been found to increase the risk of drug use in both earlier and later adolescence. With several exceptions (Boyle et al., 1992; Bukstein et al., 1989; Deykin et al., 1987; Henry et al., 1993; Johnson and Kaplan, 1990), researchers have not controlled for earlier drug use when examining the effect of psychiatric symptoms on later drug use. Several other investigators have noted that child or adolescent psychiatric symptomatology is related to adolescent drug use (Rhode et al., 1996). Moreover, a number of earlier-onset mental disorders begin in adolescence, whereas subsequent addictive disorders do not emerge prior to young adulthood (Kessler et al., 1996). To our knowledge, there is little longitudinal empirical data on the effects of adolescent psychiatric disorders on young adult drug use.

The second possible model postulates that psychiatric disorders and drug use are correlated because both conditions share common etiological factors. Predisposing biological or genetic factors may include disorders of neurotransmitter functioning or metabolism. Psychosocial factors include risks from the broad sociocultural context or from peer, family, and personality domains. A number of sociocultural, peer, family, and personality attributes have been implicated in both psychiatric disorders (Angold, 1988; Fleming and Offord, 1990; Rutter et al., 1986) and drug use (Conrad et al., 1992; Miller and Slap, 1989). In a report based on these youngsters studied at earlier developmental stages, we found several childhood psychosocial risk factors (e.g., family) which were common to the following adolescent disorders: substance use and internalizing disorders, substance use and externalizing disorders, and internalizing and externalizing disorders. These findings were apparent even though there were a number of specific risk factors for each of the disorders (Cohen et al., 1990).

A third possible model would be that drug use leads to certain psychiatric disorders, perhaps as a result of the psychopharmacological or toxic effects of drugs of abuse on brain functioning or metabolism, or drug effects on psychological functioning. Although the evidence is sparse, there is the suggestion that drug use interferes with physiological, psychological, and emotional functioning. Findings of several other investigators also suggest that adolescent substance use precedes psychiatric disorders (Johnson and Kaplan, 1990; Kandel and Davies, 1986). Robins (1993) reported that substance abuse is strongly related to depression and crime, even with control on conduct disorder. To our knowledge there are no longitudinal studies that have examined these relations in adolescents who were followed into adulthood. In contrast, the use of a longitudinal approach in this study enables us to time-order the variables. When looking at the effects of earlier drug use on later psychiatric disorders, we examine their relationship controlling for earlier psychiatric conditions. Such control is critical if we are to conclude that psychiatric disorders represent a change resulting from drug use and do not merely reflect the earlier impact of psychiatric disorders on later drug use. These controls for temporal sequence and baseline measures enable us to make causal inferences with greater confidence.

The present research focuses on the relationship of drug use and psychiatric disorders in a sample of youths studied during childhood, adolescence, and young adulthood. This longitudinal study adds to the literature by elucidating the temporal order between psychiatric disorders and drug use. The aims of the study include the following: (1) to study the coexisting relationships between psychiatric disorders and drug use; (2) to examine the temporal relationships between earlier psychiatric disorders and the occurrence of later drug use (frequency of cigarette, alcohol, marijuana, and illicit substance use); and (3) to study the extent to which earlier drug use affects the development of later psychiatric disorders.

METHOD

Sample

The sample was based on a randomly selected cohort of families with children aged 1 through 10 years. These 975 subjects were selected on the basis of their residence in either of two counties in upstate New York in 1975. The children were studied prospectively into adulthood. At the time of the first follow-up in 1983 (Time 2, T_2), the sample consisted of 776 participants. The follow-up sample ($n = 745$) in 1986 (Time 3, T_3) retained 96% of the 1983 sample, and a third follow-up in 1992 (Time 4, T_4) included 94% of the 1986 sample ($n = 698$). The dropouts at T_1 were compared with those retained with regard to the measures used in this study. No significant differences emerged.

The 1986 family income distribution of the sample of 698 children studied longitudinally from mid-adolescence to young adulthood is shown in Table 1. The sample includes

TABLE 1
Sample Characteristics 1985–1986 ($N = 776$)

	n	%
Family income		
<$10, 000	62	8
$10,000–$17,999	194	25
$18,000–$29,999	372	48
$30,000–$59,999	78	10
≥$60, 000	70	9
On welfare	31	4
Residence		
Urban or suburban	590	76
Rural or small town	186	24
New York State	714	92
Homeowners	589	76
Demographics		
Intact families	512	66
White	706	91
Catholic	418	54

substantial numbers of adolescents and young adults living in poverty as well as middle and upper-middle class youths. It should be noted that a sample of children of these ages will show (1) a lower rate of poverty and (2) higher income than will a sample of younger children or a sample of children of all ages, because poverty and low income decrease with age. When these figures are compared with figures for the full sample of families seen in 1986, no group percentage of the total varies by more than one percentage point. Fifteen percent of the 1986 youths were living with a single parent, typically a divorced mother. Eight percent of the sample were nonwhite, predominantly African-American, with a small number of Native American youths. When studied in 1983, the children were 13.69 years old on the average (SD = 2.78). In the 1986 follow-up they were 16.30 years old on the average (SD = 2.78), and in the young adult follow-up in 1992 they were 22.05 years old (SD = 2.72). The percentage of drug users is presented below. The study design and the procedures used to obtain consent were approved by the institutional review boards at the Mount Sinai School of Medicine and Columbia University.

Measures

Psychiatric diagnoses were assessed by a supplemented version of the Diagnostic Interview Schedule for Children Version 1 (DISC-1) (Costello et al., 1982) using computer algorithms designed to match *DSM-III-R* criteria, to combine information from mothers and youths (Cohen et al., 1991). As noted in earlier publications, the most useful level of diagnoses has been reached when positive evidence that meets the formal diagnostic criteria has been supplemented with an elevation of at least one standard deviation on a syndrome-specific symptom and impairment measure. These diagnoses, which we consider to be moderate to severe, are used throughout this study. Evidence of the reliability and validity of these assessments comes from a comparison with clinical assessments of a portion of the sample, as well as more than 20 articles showing theoretically coherent relationships of diagnoses with risk factors, subsequent adverse outcome, and stability over time (Cohen et al., 1989, 1991). In the young adult assessments, the mothers were not used as informants, and interviews included additional criteria covering adult diagnoses (e.g., antisocial personality disorder, generalized anxiety disorder) not assessed during childhood.

Because of the high rates of comorbidity between diagnoses (Cohen et al., 1993), we examined diagnostic groups rather than individual diagnoses. As noted in our recent work (Cohen et al., 1993), there was diagnostic overlap consistent with the findings of others. For example, there was considerable comorbidity within the specific domains of psychopathology. Moreover, nearly half of the adolescents who received a disruptive behavior disorder diagnosis also received at least one other diagnosis. The disruptive behavior disorders in adolescence include conduct disorder, oppositional defiant disorder, and attention-deficit hyperactivity disorder. In adulthood, antisocial personality disorder was assessed. The anxiety disorders include separation anxiety, overanxious disorder of childhood, and social phobia. The depressive disorders include major depressive disorder and dysthymia; however, dysthymia was almost never diagnosable in adolescence in the absence of major depressive disorder. Substance dependence disorders and substance abuse disorders were very rare and were not separately examined in this study. For example, in 1986 fewer than 10% of the sample were alcohol abusers and fewer than 3% of the sample were marijuana or other illicit drug abusers. Tobacco was not assessed as a drug of abuse.

In addition to the assessment of substance abuse and dependence included in the DISC-1 interviews of mothers and youths, we included a paper-and-pencil assessment of drug use. At T_3 and T_4 the alcohol measures had 5-point rating scales from none (1) to more than three drinks a day (5). The T_3 and T_4 marijuana use measures each had 7-point rating scales ranging from none (0) to daily use (6); and T_3 and T_4 other illicit drug use measures had scales ranging from never (0) to daily use (6). Other illicit drug use measures included the use of illicit drugs other than marijuana (such as cocaine, heroin, amphetamines, and barbiturates without a prescription, LSD, and Quaaludes).

The percentages of adolescents and young adults who smoked cigarettes were as follows: never (54% and 33%, respectively); light, those who smoked a few times a year (17% and 16%, respectively); moderate, those who smoked half of a pack per day (20% and 37%, respectively); and heavy, those who smoked nearly every day (9% and 14%, respectively). The percentages of adolescents and young adults who drank alcohol were as follows: never (27% and 4%, respectively); light, those who drank three times a month or less (16% and 22%, respectively); moderate, those who drank once a week to several times a week (30% and 41%, respectively): and heavy, those who drank once daily or more than once daily (27% and 33%, respectively). The percentages of adolescents and young adults who used marijuana were as follows: never (56% and 29%, respectively); light, those who smoked only a few times a year but less than monthly (18% and 35%, respectively); moderate, those who smoked less than weekly but more than once a month (17% and 23%, respectively); and heavy, those who smoked once a week or more (9% and 13%, respectively). The percentages of adolescents and young adults who used other illicit drugs were as follows: never (56% and 72%, respectively); light, those who used drugs a few times a year but less than monthly (8% and 9%, respectively); moderate, those who used less than weekly but more than once a month (3% and 15%, respectively); and heavy, those who used once a week or more (4% and 4%, respectively). The levels of alcohol and illegal drug use are consistent with the definitions used by Johnston et al. (1995).

It has been shown that the additional privacy associated with this method of assessment may encourage a higher level of admission of participation in these activities. In all cases the written responses preceded the administration of the diagnostic interview. Many reports on this study have shown the relationship of these variables to theoretically relevant risks, correlates, and outcomes.

Statistical Analyses

Analyses of comorbidity between substance use and psychiatric disorders used χ^2 and Fisher's exact tests. Because of substantial skew, substance use measures were transformed to four levels prior to examination of relationships with diagnoses by means of graphical presentation and logistic regression analysis, as well as when predicted by earlier psychiatric diagnosis. Age and gender were statistically controlled in analyses, and change in substance use or psychiatric disorder was assessed by including earlier measures of the dependent variable in the equations.

RESULTS

Relation of Psychiatric Disorders and Contemporaneous Substance Use

We examined diagnostic rates for youths classified by level of substance use. Each substance was assessed at four levels of use: never, light, moderate, and heavy. Cross-sectional plots of psychiatric disorder rates were graphed by rate of substance use in adolescence and young adulthood. Although these analyses were carried out for males and females separately, all findings reported below were comparable for males and females within the limits of the small numbers of diagnoses in some groups; therefore, only data for the combined group are reported.

Rates of depressive disorder were roughly linearly and significantly related to level of use of tobacco, alcohol, marijuana, and other illicit drugs (Fig. 1). Although these relations were significant at all three points in time, data are presented only for T_3. However, in all cases, the largest relationship with depressive disorder was with contemporary tobacco use.

At no point in time was there a reliable correlation between level of substance use and rates of anxiety disorder (Fig. 2). Moreover, at all three time points, rates of substance use and disruptive behavior disorders (conduct disorder, oppositional defiant disorder, or attention-deficit hyperactivity disorder at T_2 and T_3; antisocial personality disorder at T_4) were elevated to a roughly similar extent in those who used more tobacco, alcohol, marijuana,

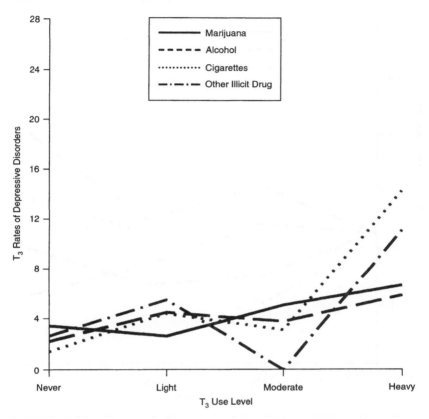

Figure 1. Relation of depressive disorders and drug use in adolescents.

and/or illicit drugs (Fig. 3). As noted earlier, disruptive behavior disorders refer to conduct disorder, oppositional defiant disorder, and attention-deficit hyperactivity disorder (T_2, T_3). At T_4, antisocial personality disorder was assessed.

In sum, these figures show that tobacco use had the strongest and most consistent of the cross-sectional drug use relationships with depression, while all kinds of drug use were similarly related to disruptive behavior disorders.

Relation of Adolescent Psychiatric Disorder and Young Adult Substance Use

We shifted to logistic regression analyses to examine the prospective relationships independent of age and gender, both with and without inclusion of prior substance use in the model. All analyses controlled for age and gender differences and also examined potential differences in findings by age and gender.

The odds ratio (OR) of daily adult tobacco use was elevated in those with adolescent depression, but the large confidence interval (CI) showed that this prediction was very

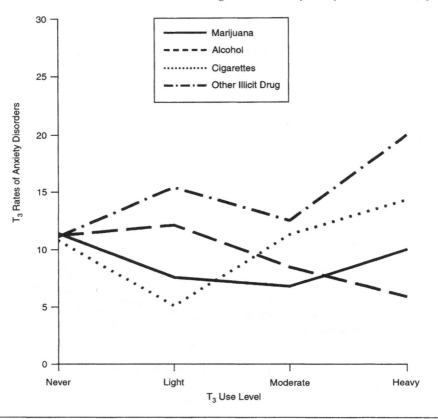

Figure 2. Relation of anxiety disorders and drug use in adolescents.

imprecise (OR = 2.33; 95% CI, 0.76 to 7.14). Furthermore, when adolescent tobacco use was added to the prediction equation, the OR for depression dropped to 1.12 (95% CI, 0.28 to 4.44), showing that this relationship was accounted for by tobacco use that may have preceded the depression. Conduct disorder similarly was not predictive of adult tobacco use in analyses controlling for adolescent tobacco use (OR = 0.80; 95% CI, 0.37 to 1.75). We also examined the level of adult tobacco use as a scaled variable in order to allow for the possibility that while daily use may not be related, the frequency of smoking may increase in those with prior disruptive behavior disorders. However disruptive behavior disorders were again not significantly related to adult-onset smoking, controlling for earlier smoking ($\beta = .36$, SE = .23). Parallel analyses demonstrated that alcohol and marijuana use were not related to earlier psychiatric disorders. In addition, adult illicit drug use was not related to earlier depressive or conduct disorder independent of earlier illicit drug use.

In sum, there was virtually no prospective evidence that prior psychopathology in adolescence is associated with young adult substance use, controlling for prior adolescent substance use.

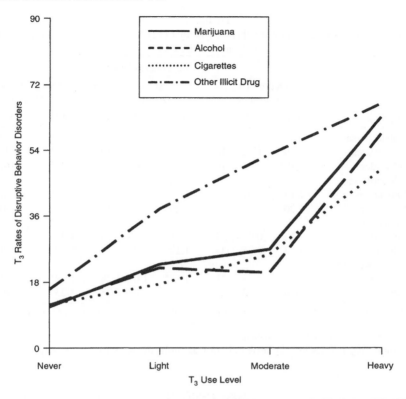

Figure 3. Relation of disruptive behavior disorders and drug use in adolescents.

Predicting Young Adult Psychiatric Disorder From Adolescent Substance Use

In these analyses we used the four-level scaled measure of substance use to predict young adult psychiatric disorder in logistic regression analyses. Again, we controlled for age and gender differences in disorder rates and examined the adolescent substance use predictor both by itself and in equations including adolescent psychiatric disorder (Table 2).

Adolescent tobacco and illicit drug use levels predicted young adult antisocial, major depressive, and anxiety disorders, and these relationships remained significant, and at most only slightly reduced, when the adolescent disorder was included in the prediction equation (Table 2). Alcohol use significantly predicted anxiety and antisocial personality disorders, net of (with control on) earlier psychiatric disorder. The magnitude of the odds for alcohol use indicated more than doubling of the rate of occurrence of each type of disorder for heavy users compared with nonusers. Marijuana use was related to later antisocial personality disorder, controlling for contemporaneous conduct disorder, again showing a substantial effect.

All of the previous analyses were repeated to determine whether there were differences in effects of age or gender. Although such effects might be found in a larger sample, none were statistically significant here.

TABLE 2

Increase in Odds of Young Adult Psychiatric Disorder (T_4) Associated With Adolescent (T_3) Substance Use Level

	Psychiatric Disorders					
	Depressive Disorders		Anxiety Disorders		Antisocial Personality Disorder	
Drug Use	OR	95% CI	OR	95% CI	OR	95% CI
Level of tobacco use						
Net of covariates[a]	1.19*	1.02–1.40	1.21*	1.05–1.39	1.37*	1.14–1.64
Net of disorder[b]	1.19*	1.01–1.40	1.20*	1.04–1.38	1.24*	1.02–1.51
Level of alcohol use						
Net of covariates[a]	1.14	0.91–1.42	1.30*	1.07–1.57	1.36*	1.08–1.71
Net of disorder[b]	1.30	0.88–1.90	1.29*	1.06–2.11	1.27*	1.01–1.63
Level of marijuana use						
Net of covariates[a]	1.13	0.95–1.34	1.15	0.99–1.34	1.44*	1.20–1.73
Net of disorder[b]	1.13	0.95–1.34	1.16	1.00–1.35	1.30*	1.06–1.59
Level of illicit drug use						
Net of covariates[a]	1.16*	1.03–1.31	1.14*	1.02–1.28	1.32*	1.16–1.52
Net of disorder[b]	1.16*	1.03–1.41	1.15*	1.02–1.28	1.23*	1.06–1.32

Note: Net of covariates (disorder) refers to control on the covariates (disorders). OR = odds ratio; CI = confidence interval.

[a]Covariates age and gender used in all equations.

[b]Partialing earlier major depression, any anxiety disorder, any disruptive behavior disorder, respectively.

*$p < .05$.

DISCUSSION

Before turning to a discussion of the various models of the relationship of psychiatric disorders and drug use over time, we will first discuss the comorbidity findings. As regards drug use, quantity/frequency measures of tobacco, alcohol, marijuana, and illicit drug use were associated with an increased risk of psychiatric disorders, including depressive and conduct disorders. This was true of both adolescent and young adult males and females, when examined cross-sectionally. Our findings extend those of Boyle and Offord (1991) by demonstrating that the relationships between psychiatric disorders and drug use obtained during adolescence are also apparent in young adulthood.

Given the evidence to indicate comorbidity between certain psychiatric disorders and drug use, causal hypotheses regarding the nature of the relation between psychiatric symptoms and drug use were tested. The first model tested the hypothesis that psychiatric disorders precede drug use. Several investigators have reported that psychiatric symptoms precede and/or contribute to drug use (Boyle et al., 1993; Bukstein et al., 1989; Christie et al., 1988; Deykin et al., 1987; Henry et al., 1993; Kandel and Davies, 1986; Russell et al., 1994), as well as substance use disorders (Kessler, 1995). There was no evidence that depressive disorders, anxiety disorders, or conduct disorders in late adolescence have an influence on later drug use, controlling for earlier drug use. Earlier psychopathology (e.g., childhood conduct disorder) may affect later drug use; however, once the adolescent starts to use drugs, depressive disorders, anxiety disorders, and conduct disorders do not have an additional impact on young adult drug use.

The results are not consistent with the findings of other investigations and suggest that prior psychopathology has no effect on subsequent substance use, once the youngster is using drugs. There are several differences between our study and those of other investigators. They include (1) the nature and age of the sample, (2) the omission of psychiatric diagnoses in other studies, and (3) lack of control on earlier drug use when examining the effect of psychiatric diagnoses on later drug use. Such differences in the design and analyses limit the comparability of the findings. One might add that since there is no relationship between earlier psychiatric diagnoses and later drug use (controlling for earlier drug use), the evidence suggests that whatever common factors contribute to both psychiatric disorders and substance use may conceivably be limited to their effects in childhood and early adolescence.

The third model suggests that earlier drug use is linked with later psychiatric disorders. For example, drug use (alcohol, tobacco, marijuana, and illicit drugs) was related to later depressive disorders, with control on earlier depressive disorders. The findings are in accord with Robins (1993), who reported that substance abuse predicts depression.

The findings that drug use continued to be a predictor of psychiatric disorders—independent of overlapping variance with the subjects' initial psychiatric disorders—adds considerable important information. First, it helps to rule out the possibility that the drug use was epiphenomenal, in the sense of being a reaction to or otherwise determined by the individual's psychiatric disorder. It is likely that the adverse effects of drug use on psychiatric disorders continue to accumulate during the individual's development. Several investigators have reported that earlier substance use may be associated with later psychiatric disorders during adolescence (Bukstein et al., 1989; Johnson and Kaplan, 1990; Kandel and Davies, 1986). What possible mechanisms could link earlier drug use and later depressive disorders? One mechanism may involve the drugs' effects on physiological disequilibrium or intrapersonal conflicts which accumulate over time and produce psychiatric disorders. In our earlier work, we hypothesized that drug use leads to certain psychiatric disorders, perhaps as a result of the psychopharmacological or toxic effects of drugs or certain of their metabolites on physiological disequilibrium or mental difficulties.

The second mechanism may involve the drug's effects on interpersonal and role functioning. Thus, drug use may interfere with parent-child relations (Newcomb and Bentler, 1988), which, in turn, are related to the development of depressive disorders. Drug use may also impair relations with such contemporaries as friends, siblings, and significant others, which may alternately be manifested in depressive disorders. A deviant peer group is a likely mediator for the association between drug use and antisocial personality disorders. Drug users may select friends who are deviant, which may then result in the drug users adopting the antisocial behavior of their deviant friends through imitation (Kandel and Davies, 1986). Newcomb and Bentler (1988) suggested that drug use may jeopardize normal adolescent development, which would also involve such interaction with peers. Intrapersonal stressors may interact with interpersonal factors and thus eventually lead to psychiatric disorders.

Our findings concur with Newcomb and Bentler's (1988) results on the destructive nature of cigarette use. Our study indicates that adolescent cigarette smoking was associated with later depressive, anxiety, and anti-social personality disorders. Since cigarettes are more frequently used than alcohol and illegal drugs, a decrease in cigarette use might possibly result in a reduction of adult depressive and antisocial personality disorders. This of course would have to be studied experimentally.

The study may be looked at in the context of having several limitations. First, although we discuss some possible mechanisms to explain the relationship between early drug use and later psychopathology, it is important to note that these relationships may not be causal. Since adolescent drug use may be a marker for subjects who will later develop psychiatric disorders, we must be extremely tentative in any statements we make regarding causality. For example, there may be a common diathesis which serves to increase the risk of both drug use and psychopathology. The risk diathesis model holds that genetic predispositions interact with a variety of psychosocial, behavioral, and contextual risk factors to cause both drug use and perhaps psychiatric disorders (Brook et al., 1990). Second, we used rigorous diagnostic criteria in making psychiatric diagnoses; nevertheless, it is important to note that impairment may occur even though full categorical criteria are not met. If this were the case, it could be that symptoms of the disorder and substance use actually have a reciprocal relation over time.

As noted earlier, because of the high rates of comorbidity between diagnoses, we examined diagnostic groups rather than individual diagnoses. This limits our ability to study relations between specific diagnoses and drug use. Related to this, the number of comorbid psychiatric disorders probably affects the level of substance use. Future research should shed light on these critical issues. In this study, we had modest levels of substance use. Had we had higher levels of substance use, the findings might have been even stronger. Finally, the magnitude of the earlier drug effects on later psychopathology, although statistically significant, was somewhat modest. This study did not examine the interaction of drug use with personality, attitudinal, behavioral, familial, and peer risk factors. It is possible that the risk for later psychopathology in adulthood among adolescents who use drugs and at the same time are vulnerable would be considerable. Furthermore, it is important to note that relationships emerged with control on earlier drug use.

Clinical Implications

Despite these caveats, the findings indicate that not only abuse but use of cigarettes, alcohol, marijuana, and illicit drugs is related to later psychiatric disorders. Given that the use of drugs precedes the onset of psychiatric disorders, such as major depression and antisocial personality disorder, it is critical that attention be given to the use of drugs and not focus only on abuse. Consequently, from a policy perspective, the results suggest that the greater availability of illegal drugs may be accompanied by an increase in psychiatric disorders. When one encounters drug use, one must consider that this may be a precursor not only for later drug abuse or dependence but also for later psychopathology. Diagnostically, therefore, one should look for signs or symptoms that demonstrate the beginnings of early psychopathology in early- and late-adolescent substance users.

The findings also have implications for interventions. Health professionals need to focus on both legal and illegal drug use as well as abuse, as drug use also has serious consequences. The powerful and consistent effects of adolescent drug use and abuse on young adult functioning imply that drug use during adolescence should represent an important target for intervention programs involving prevention and treatment. In terms of treatment, the findings suggest that adolescent drug use itself perhaps should be regarded in a number of cases as an early indicator for psychiatric intervention and should not be regarded solely as relatively benign or age-limited. Early treatment may serve to mitigate the later adverse psychopathological effects of substance use as well as to lessen the other, longer-term adverse effects of substance use. Furthermore, it may be that the impact of drug use on young adult psychiatric disorders has greater effects on adolescents who are vulnerable because of the existence of other risk factors (e.g., a weak parent–child attachment).

REFERENCES

Angold A (1988), Childhood and adolescent depression, I: epidemiological and aetiological aspects. *Br J Psychiatry* 152:601–617

Boyle MH, Offord DR (1991), Psychiatric disorders and substance use in adolescence. *Can J Psychiatry* 36:699–705

Boyle MH, Offord DR, Racine YA, Fleming JE, Szatmari P, Links PS (1993), Predicting substance use in early adolescence based on parent and teacher assessments of childhood psychiatric disorder: results from the Ontario Child Health Study follow-up. *J Child Psychol Psychiatry* 34:535–544

Boyle MH, Offord DR, Racine YA, Szatmari P, Fleming JE, Links PS (1992), Predicting substance use in late adolescence: results from the Ontario Child Health Study follow-up. *Am J Psychiatry* 149:761–767

Breslau M, Kilbey M, Andreski P (1993), Vulnerability to psychopathology in nicotine-dependent smokers: an epidemiologic study of young adults. *Am J Psychiatry* 150:941–946

Brook DW, Brook JS (1990), The etiology and consequences of adolescent drug use. In: *Prevention and Treatment of Drug and Alcohol Abuse: Alcohol and Drug Abuse Reviews*, Watson RR, ed. Clifton, NJ: Humana Press, pp 339–362

Brook JS, Brook DW, Whiteman M, Gordon AS, Cohen P (1990), The psychosocial etiology of adolescent drug use and abuse. *Genet Soc Gen Psychol Monogr* 116:111–267 (entire monograph)

Brook JS, Whiteman M, Finch S, Cohen P (1995), Aggression, intrapsychic distress and drug use: antecedent and intervening processes. *J Am Acad Child Adolesc Psychiatry* 34:1076–1083

Bukstein OG, Brent DA, Kaminer Y (1989), Comorbidity of substance abuse and other psychiatric disorders in adolescence. *Am J Psychiatry* 146:1131–1141

Christie KA, Burke JD, Regier DA, Rae DS, Boyd JH, Locke BZ (1988), Epidemiologic evidence for early onset of mental disorders and higher risk of drug abuse in young adults. *Am J Psychiatry* 145:971–975

Cohen P, Brook JS, Cohen J, Velez CN, Garcia M (1990), Common and uncommon pathways to adolescent psychopathology and problem behavior. In: *Straight and Devious Pathways From Childhood to Adulthood*, Robins L, Rutter M, eds. London: Cambridge University Press, pp 242–248

Cohen P, Cohen J, Kasen S et al. (1993), An epidemiological study of disorders in late childhood and adolescence, I: age-and gender-specific prevalence. *J Child Psychol Psychiatry* 34:851–867

Cohen P, Kasen S, Brook JS, Streuning EL (1991), Diagnostic predictors of treatment patterns in a cohort of adolescents. *J Am Acad Child Adolesc Psychiatry* 30:989–993

Cohen P, Velez CN, Brook JS, Smith J (1989), Mechanisms of the relationship between perinatal problems, early childhood illness, and psychopathology in late childhood and adolescence. *Child Dev* 60:701–709

Conrad KM, Flay BR, Hill D (1992), Why children start smoking cigarettes: predictors of onset. *Br J Addict* 87:1711–1724

Costello A, Edelbrock C, Kalas R, Kessler M, Klaric SA (1982), *Diagnostic Interview Schedule for Children (DISC)*. Bethesda, MD: National Institute of Mental Health

Deykin EY, Levy JC, Wells V (1987), Adolescent depression, alcohol and drug abuse. *Am J Public Health* 77:178–182

Fleming JE, Offord DR (1990), Epidemiology of childhood depressive disorders: a critical review. *J Am Acad Child Adolesc Psychiatry* 29:571–580

Glass RM (1990), Blue mood, blackened lungs. *JAMA* 264:1583–1584

Helzer JE, Pryzbeck TR (1988), The co-occurrence of alcoholism with other psychiatric disorders in the general population and its impact on treatment. *J Stud Alcohol* 49:219–224

Henry B, Feehan M, McGee R, Stanton W, Moffitt TE, Silva P (1993), The importance of conduct problems and depressive symptoms in predicting adolescent substance use. *J Abnorm Child Psychol* 21:469–480

Johnson RJ, Kaplan HB (1990), Stability of psychological symptoms: drug use consequences and intervening processes. *J Health Soc Behav* 31:277–291

Johnston LD, O'Malley PM, Bachman JG (1995), *National Survey Results on Drug Use From the Monitoring the Future Study, 1975–1994*, Vol 1: *Secondary Students* (NIH Publication 95–4026). Rockville, MD: National Institute on Drug Abuse

Kandel DB, Davies M (1986), Adult sequelae of adolescent depressive symptoms. *Arch Gen Psychiatry* 43:255–262

Kessler RC (1995), The national comorbidity survey: preliminary results and future directions. *Int J Methods Psychiatr Res* 5:139–151

Kessler RC, Nelson CB, McGonagle KA, Edlund MJ, Frank RG, Leaf PJ (1996), The epidemiology of co-occurring addictive and mental disorders: implications for prevention and service utilization. *Am J Orthopsychiatry* 50:36–43

Khantzian EJ (1985), The self-medication hypothesis of addictive disorders: focus on heroin and cocaine dependence. *Am J Psychiatry* 142:1259–1264

Miller SK, Slap G (1989), Adolescent smoking: a review of prevalence and prevention, *J Adolesc Health Care* 10:129–135

Neighbors B, Kempton T, Forehand R (1992), Co-occurrence of substance abuse with conduct, anxiety, and depression disorders in juvenile delinquents. *Addict Behav* 17:379–386

Newcomb MD, Bentler PM (1988), Impact of adolescent drug use and social support on problems of young adults: a longitudinal study. *J Abnorm Psychol* 97:64–75

Rhode P, Lewinsohn PM, Seeley JR (1996), Psychiatric comorbidity with problematic alcohol use in high school students. *J Am Acad Child Adolesec Psychiatry* 35:101–109

Robins LN (1993), Childhood conduct problems, adult psychopathology, and crime. In: *Mental Disorder and Crime*, Hodgins S, ed. London: Sage, pp 173–192

Russell JM, Newman SC, Bland RC (1994), Drug abuse and dependence. *Acta Psychiatr Scand* 89:54–62

Rutter M, Izard CE, Read PB (1986), *Depression in Young People: Developmental and Clinical Perspectives*. New York: Guilford

18

What Happens to "Bad" Girls? A Review of the Adult Outcomes of Antisocial Adolescent Girls

Kathleen A. Pajer, M.D., M.P.H.

Objective: *The purpose of this article is to review critically the data on the adult outcomes of adolescent girls with antisocial behavior.* **Method:** *Five literature databases were searched for studies on the adult outcomes of girls with either conduct disorder or delinquency.* **Results:** *Twenty studies met the inclusion criteria. As adults, antisocial girls manifested increased mortality rates, a 10- to 40-fold increase in the rate of criminality, substantial rates of psychiatric morbidity, dysfunctional and often violent relationships, and high rates of multiple service utilization. Possible explanations for these findings include a pervasive biological or psychological deficit or baseline heterogeneity in the population of antisocial girls.* **Conclusions:** *This review establishes that female adolescent antisocial behavior has important long-term individual and societal consequences. At present, there are insufficient data to enable us to prevent these outcomes or treat them if they occur. Future research should include cross-sectional studies detailing the phenomenology of female antisocial behavior and longitudinal investigations that not only track development into adulthood but also explore the role of potential modifying variables such as prefrontal lobe dysfunction and psychiatric comorbidity.*
(Am J Psychiatry 1998; 155:862–870)

Jennifer is a 16-year-old girl who was brought to the emergency room for suicidal ideation. During an argument with her mother about telephone privileges, Jennifer grabbed a knife and threatened to kill her mother and herself. In the emergency room, she reported depressed mood "when I'm grounded and stuck in the house." She denied true suicidality,

Received June 9, 1997; revision received Nov. 18, 1997; accepted Dec. 4, 1997. From the Department of Psychiatry, Allegheny University of the Health Sciences. Address reprint requests to Dr. Pajer, Allegheny University of the Health Sciences, Allegheny Campus, Four Allegheny Center, Suite 806, Pittsburgh, PA 15212; kpajer@aherf.edu (e-mail).

Supported by NIMH grant MH-01285.

The author thanks George Vaillant, M.D., Magda Stouthamer-Loeber, Ph.D., and Rolf Loeber, Ph.D., for discussions that provided the impetus for this review and William Gardner, Ph.D., for detailed comments on an earlier draft of the paper.

stating, "I just figured that would get her to let me use the phone." Jennifer also denied any homicidal intent, although on occasion she has hit her mother hard enough to leave bruises. She received an outpatient psychiatric evaluation a year ago but refused to return for treatment. Other problems include a history of truancy since age 13, running away, and several arrests for shoplifting and fighting. She is currently on house arrest for assaulting another girl.

What happens to girls like Jennifer as they mature into women? Do they continue their antisocial activities? Do they develop significant psychiatric morbidity? How do they behave as partners, parents, and workers? These questions have been extensively studied with respect to males (1–5) but not females. This curious omission is due to long-standing beliefs that female adolescent antisocial behavior is rare, primarily sexual in nature, and associated with a benign course in adulthood (6–11). For example, in 1968, J. Cowie (a leading researcher in the field of delinquency) wrote, "In the first place, the delinquent girl is much less frequent than her male counterpart, and ... she is less interesting. Her offenses take predominantly the form of sexual misbehavior, of a kind to call for care and protection rather than punishment. ... Delinquency in the male at an equivalent age is very much more varied, dangerous and dramatic" (12).

In the last decade, however, reports in both the scientific literature and the lay press have challenged these notions (13–18). In the first portion of this article, I briefly present evidence that antisocial behavior among adolescent girls is neither rare or restricted to premarital sexual activity. I then review all the studies that provide data on the adult outcomes of these girls. In the last section of the article, I offer interpretations of these data, concluding with suggestions for the focus of future research.

ISSUES IN THE STUDY OF FEMALE ANTISOCIAL BEHAVIOR

Conduct Disorder and Delinquency: Similarities and Differences

We find data on antisocial girls in the psychiatric literature on conduct disorder and the juvenile justice literature on delinquent girls. The diagnosis of conduct disorder, which was not formalized until 1978, specifies a clustering of antisocial behaviors that persists for at least 6 months (DSM-IV). Before 1978, adolescents with antisocial behavior were categorized as having a runaway reaction, group delinquency reaction, or unsocialized aggressive reaction (DSM-II).

A girl adjudicated as delinquent has committed either a status or a criminal offense, all of which are behaviors included in the conduct disorder criteria, although girls with conduct disorder are often not classified as delinquent because they have not been caught. Many delinquent girls are arrested for both types of offenses, but the behaviors result in different consequences. Status offenses (e.g., running away) are unique to juveniles and are regarded as indications for legal supervision. Criminal offenses (e.g., assault) are behaviors that are considered illegal in any age group, but the penalties for juveniles are less severe. A girl can be adjudicated as delinquent for just one act, but most incarcerated girls meet the criteria for conduct disorder (19). In the juvenile justice research literature, girls may also be classified as delinquent on the basis of their scores on delinquency self-report inventories.

Is Antisocial Behavior Among Girls Rare?

Neither conduct disorder nor delinquency is rare among girls. One review (20) reported that conduct disorder is the second most common diagnosis given to adolescent girls, and another investigation (21) revealed that 8% of 17-year-old girls met the criteria for the disorder. A large epidemiologic study of 15-year-olds (22) reported that 7.5%–9.5% of the girls met the criteria for conduct disorder, compared to 8.6%–12.2% of the boys.

Estimating the prevalence of female delinquency is more complicated. The validity of arrest data, which led to the conclusion that female delinquency was uncommon, has been questioned on the basis of gender bias in the justice system (23–26). This bias resulted in reluctance to arrest girls, coupled with a tendency toward psychiatric referrals (27). Paradoxically, this bias also resulted in harsher sentencing, with longer institutionalizations for girls who were actually convicted, in comparison with boys arrested for similar offenses (28–31). The self-report literature supports bias in the judicial system; girls report higher rates of antisocial behavior in this context than the official records indicate (32–38).

It is commonly believed that females in our society are less violent than males. However, if violent crimes against family members or same-sex peers are analyzed separately, the gender gap narrows considerably (39), and the rate of violent crimes among girls and women appears to be increasing (13–15, 40). There is also an interaction between race and gender, with black girls arrested for more aggressive acts than white girls (38, 41–44).

Is Antisocial Behavior Among Girls Predominantly Sexual?

Two lines of evidence suggest that this belief is also the result of bias in the judicial process. First, self-reports of delinquency indicate that girls report the same patterns of antisocial behavior as boys, with the exception of sexual assault (32–38). Second, although delinquency statistics demonstrate that girls are convicted of sexual crimes (e.g., prostitution) more frequently than boys, it is important to point out that until the 1970s, arrested girls were frequently subjected to gynecologic examinations (boys did not undergo analogous examinations). Evidence of sexual activity often led to a charge of sexual delinquency, regardless of the initial offense (26). This practice was based on the notion that delinquent girls were the primary vectors for venereal disease (11, 26).

Does Antisocial Behavior of Adolescent Girls Have a Benign Course?

Historically, the belief was that the adult course for these girls was relatively benign (6–11). The most common pathological adult outcome for antisocial boys was adult criminality (1–5); since the prevalence of criminality in women was so low, it was assumed that most antisocial girls "outgrew" their deviance. Furthermore, marriage and childbearing, long considered indications of healthy adult adjustment for any female, were outcomes frequently found among antisocial girls, lending further support to the perception that these girls did relatively well.

The robust relationship between delinquent behavior among boys and criminal behavior among men is an excellent example of what developmental psychopathologists call "homotypic continuity," i.e., a strong correlation between a disorder at one point in time and the same symptoms at a further point in time. In contrast, "heterotypic continuity" describes the relationship between a disorder at one point in the life cycle and continued dysfunction at another point in time, but with different signs and symptoms (45–47).

For males, the homotypic continuity between adolescent and adult antisocial behavior is stronger when one "looks backward" from adulthood to adolescence than it is in the data from prospective studies. This finding has been interpreted as evidence of desistance from pathological behavior. However, it may actually be an indication of undetected heterotypic continuity, since research has focused so heavily on studying the rate of criminality. Similarly, it is possible that the apparently benign adult course of antisocial girls may, in truth, be a reflection of heterotypic continuity, or continued dysfunction, but with different manifestations in adulthood. The purpose of this review is to summarize what is known about adult outcomes of antisocial adolescent girls, searching for evidence of homotypic continuity, heterotypic continuity, or both.

METHOD

I searched five literature databases for studies on the adult outcomes of antisocial girls: 1) Dissertation Abstracts, 1984–1996 (used to minimize the effect of publication bias); 2) Sociological Abstracts, 1973–1996; 3) Social Work Abstracts, 1977–1996; 4) MEDLINE, 1966–1996; and 5) PsycLit, 1974–1996. The search terms were "girl" and "female" combined individually with "conduct disorder," "delinquency," "antisocial," and "crime." The references from the search articles were then used to locate other studies.

Studies were used if they met the following criteria: 1) they were written in English; 2) they presented data on girls with conduct disorder or delinquency, ages 13–18, or presented such data on boys and girls in a format suitable for separate analyses of the girls; 3) they reported adult follow-up data on the same subjects, as defined by age ≥19 years (I would have included sequential cohort studies, but none were found); or 4) they presented cross-sectional data on adolescent antisocial behavior for any group of adult women.

RESULTS

General Features of the Studies

Twenty studies met the inclusion criteria. (Several studies presented relevant data but did not meet the inclusion criteria. A list of these articles is available on request.) The data on mortality, criminality, psychiatric morbidity, marriage, parenting, education, occupation, and service utilization are presented below. Table 1 and table 2 summarize the general features of the studies of girls with conduct disorder and delinquent girls, respectively. The investigations span most of this century. Since conduct disorder is a relatively recent diagnostic category, as discussed above, the earlier studies focused on delinquent girls. The most commonly used design was the uncontrolled follow-up study, and follow-up periods ranged from 1 to 41 years, with a median of 15 years. I found five cross-sectional investigations that presented data on the adolescent antisocial behavior of women who were

TABLE 1
Studies of Adult Outcomes of Girls With Conduct Disorder

Study	Design	Number of Subjects	Age (years)	Race	Location	Date(s) of Study	Follow-Up Period (years)	Comments
Bardone et al., 1996 (48)	Birth cohort (1971–1972)	405	15 at adolescent data collection	93% white	New Zealand	1986–1987	6	Conduct disorder: N = 37; depression: N = 27; no problem: N = 341
Robins, 1966 (49)	Historical prospective	172	Median = 13	100% white	USA	1924–1929	30	Antisocial: N = 99; other problems: N = 43; normal: N = 30
Zoccolillo et al., 1992 (50)	Historical prospective	118	9–15	100% white	UK	1964	12	Subjects were girls in group homes and normal girls; compared girls with conduct disorder (N = 26) and all those without (N = 92)
Storm-Mathisen and Vaglum, 1994 (51)	Uncontrolled follow-up	39	6–19	100% white	Norway	1961	18–21	"Pure" conduct disorder: N = 12
Zoccolillo and Rogers, 1991 (52)	Uncontrolled follow-up	55	13–16	89% white	USA	1987–1988	2–4	"Pure" conduct disorder: N = 23; delinquency: N = 13; depression: N = 17; phobia: N = 25
Rowe et al., 1996 (53)	Cross-sectional	53	16–48	—	—	—	—	Subjects with depression were interviewed about adolescent conduct disorder
Robins and Price, 1991 (54)	Cross-sectional	11,105	18–70	67%–86% white; 10%–26% black	USA (five sites)	1980	—	Subjects from the general population were interviewed about adolescent conduct disorder

TABLE 2
Studies of Adult Outcomes of Delinquent Girls

Study	Design	Number of Subjects	Age (years)	Race/Ethnicity	Location	Date(s) of Study	Follow-Up Period (years)	Comments
Werner and Smith, 1992 (55)	Birth cohort (1955)	276	13-18 for adolescent data collection	Hawaiian, Filipino, Japanese, other nonwhite	USA (Hawaii)	1977 (last adolescent data)	13-14	Delinquency only: N = 9; mental illness only: N = 21; delinquency and mental illness: N = 13; no problem: N = 233
Lewis et al., 1991 (56)	Uncontrolled follow-up	21	Mean = 15	81% white; 19% black	USA	—	7-12	48% (N = 10 of 21) referred for violent behavior
Rosenbaum, 1989 (57)	Uncontrolled follow-up	240	"Juvenile offenders"	51% white; 30% black; 19% other	USA	Early 1960s	17-19	Subjects were in experimental community program
Rydelius, 1988 (58)	Uncontrolled follow-up	224	Mean = 16	100% Swedish	Sweden	1967	18	Subjects were in reform schools
Gibbens, 1975 (59)	Uncontrolled follow-up	350	15-16	—	UK	1950s	15	Subjects were in "remand" homes
Cowie et al., 1968 (12)	Uncontrolled follow-up	318	14-17	—	UK	1958	4-5	Subjects were in "classifying" school
Gibbens, 1959 (60)	Uncontrolled follow-up	185	14-17	—	UK	1951-1953	2-4	Subjects were on probation
Otterström, 1946 (61)	Uncontrolled follow-up	687	8-16	100% Swedish	Sweden	1903-1940	4-41	Range of delinquency from "at risk" (N = 244) to "sentenced" (N = 53)
Ahnsjö, 1941 (62)	Uncontrolled follow-up	2,448	Mean = 15	100% Swedish	Sweden	1903-1937	1-15	Subjects were in detention homes and reformatories
Healy and Bronner, 1926 (63)	Uncontrolled follow-up	225	"Greater than 14"	100% white	USA	1909-1914	7-14	Subjects were repeat offenders
Smith, 1994 (64)	Cross-sectional	11	Mean = 34	36% white; 64% black	USA	1992-1993		Aggressive subjects were interviewed about delinquency
Sommers and Baskin, 1994 (65)	Cross-sectional	85	Mean = 29	12% white; 69% black; 19% Hispanic	USA	1990		Subjects incarcerated for nondomestic violent felonies were interviewed about delinquency
Cloninger and Guze, 1970 (66)	Cross-sectional	66	Median = 27	52% white; 45% black	USA	1969		Subjects were released felons interviewed about delinquency

depressed, incarcerated, or from the general population in the Epidemiologic Catchment Area (ECA) study. There is a striking paucity of black subjects across the studies of adolescents, although four of the five cross-sectional investigations included black women.

Mortality

Adult mortality rates were reported in 10 studies. Five of the 10 studies reported mortality rates of 6%–11% (49, 51, 52, 56, 58), and rates of 0%–2% were found in the other five (12, 55, 61–63). Investigations conducted after 1960 reported higher death rates, except for the Kauai Longitudinal Study (55), which reported a rate of 0%.

The highest mortality rates were found for girls with conduct disorder and delinquent girls who either were in reform schools or had comorbid neuropsychiatric impairment. The proportions were similar, in spite of follow-up intervals ranging from 2–4 years to 30 years, suggesting that most of the deaths occurred in early adulthood.

Three studies provided comparison data from the normal population. In one study (49), 7% of a conduct disorder sample had died 30 years later (all of the deaths were natural), compared to 5% of the nonantisocial patients and 10% of the control subjects. The population-based death rate for women at the time was 7%. The 18-year mortality rate in a study of the population of all Swedish girls committed to "state-run probationary schools" (58) was 10% (77% of the deaths were violent), compared to an expected rate of 1.1%–2.6% in the general population. In a 2- to 4-year uncontrolled follow-up of girls with conduct disorder from an inpatient unit (52), it was reported that 6% of the girls had died violently. The age-matched normal population rate for violent deaths was 0.034%.

Criminality

Sixteen studies reported data on adult crime. All used arrest data, except the Dunedin Multidisciplinary Health and Development Study (48), which used a self-report inventory of illegal activities. Four prospective studies of girls with conduct disorder reported adult crime rates ranging from 33% to 50% (48, 49, 51, 52). The crime rate in adulthood for delinquent girls ranged from 10% to 96%, although the rates clustered around 25%–46% in the majority of the studies (12, 55–57, 59–63). Adult crime rates were higher in all groups of antisocial girls than in any group of either normal control subjects or girls with other psychiatric problems.

The highest rates of adult criminality (71% and 96%) were found in two follow-up studies of delinquent girls (56, 57). These women were also unusual in that they committed crimes such as burglary and assault, rather than the usual "female" crimes of shoplifting, drug use, and prostitution. The lowest prevalence of adult criminality (10%–25%) was found in samples of girls on probation or institutionalized in less confining settings (12, 60–62). These girls probably were less severely antisocial at baseline. Girls with psychiatric comorbidity had the highest rates of adult criminality in two of three studies (55, 56), but the rates were similar in a third that compared criminal activity among conduct-disordered girls with and without depression (48).

In cross-sectional investigations of incarcerated women, one study (66) reported that 35% of them had been arrested as juveniles. Another study (64) found that 73% of a sample of convicted felons had histories of delinquency and that most had been charged with criminal offenses (in contrast to status offenses). However, this group was very aggressive, and all the women had histories of severe abuse. Violent female offenders in another study (65) reported that 56% of them had engaged in fights, 38% had carried weapons, and 74% had been truant.

Psychiatric Morbidity

Psychiatric morbidity, as defined by outcomes varying from commitment to an institution to formally diagnosed disorders, was investigated in 12 studies; three studies (48–50) compared girls with conduct disorder and normal girls. Fourteen percent to 60% of the girls with conduct disorder had adult psychiatric problems, compared to 0%–40% of the normal girls, depending on whether disorders or hospitalizations were counted. Another study (55) reported that 13% of a group of delinquent girls with comorbid psychiatric disorders had adult symptoms, but that *none* of the girls who were only delinquent developed psychiatric problems.

Six uncontrolled follow-up studies (12, 51, 52, 56, 59, 62) reported that 23%–38% of girls with conduct disorder and 3%–90% of delinquent girls demonstrated psychopathology as adults. Four studies provided data on the continuity between adolescent antisocial behavior and antisocial personality disorder. Robins's study (49) demonstrated that antisocial girls as women had higher rates of antisocial personality disorder than either normal control subjects or other types of former patients. This relationship was confirmed in a birth cohort-study (48), where mean scores on an antisocial personality disorder symptom scale were significantly higher for young women with baseline conduct disorder than for women who were normal or depressed as adolescents. In another study (50), 35% of the girls with conduct disorder met the criteria for antisocial personality disorder as adults, compared to 0% of the girls without conduct disorder. An uncontrolled follow-up (51) identified antisocial personality disorder in 23% of women with histories of conduct disorder. Examination of the ECA data (54) revealed strong continuity between conduct disorder and externalizing disorders.

Investigators have also studied the rates of adult hysteria, substance abuse, and depression in antisocial girls. Robins (49) reported that 21% of the referred antisocial girls became women with hysteria. Others (50) reported that 42% of girls with conduct disorder developed a "dramatic" personality disorder as young women; 55% of these also met the criteria for antisocial personality disorder. A cross-sectional study of female criminals (66) revealed that 65% of them met criteria for sociopathy and 40% met criteria for hysteria.

Four studies (49, 51, 52, 56) demonstrated that 40%–70% of girls with conduct disorder or delinquency develop substance abuse problems as women. Suicidal behavior was the most commonly used measure of depression, and rates were as high as 90% (52, 56). When depression was formally measured (48), rates were much lower. In light of these data, the suicidal behavior may have resulted from either antisocial personality disorder or substance abuse, rather than an affective disorder. In support of this interpretation, Rowe et al. (53)

reported that 62% of depressed women had no history of conduct disorder, 25% had one or two symptoms, and only 13% had three or more symptoms. A history of conduct disorder had no effect on the course of depression or response to treatment.

Parenting Behavior

Three studies presented data on parenting skills. In Robins's study (49), 36% of the offspring of mothers with histories of conduct disorder were placed outside the home, a rate higher than that for either normal women or other former patients. These mothers had sons with higher arrest rates than the sons of other women or the sons of men who had been antisocial adolescents.

Mothers in the Kauai Longitudinal Study (55) who had been delinquent had a higher rate of family court involvement than other women. Thirty-three percent of the women with delinquency plus psychiatric problems had a family court record, compared to 8% of the delinquency-only group and 4% of the control subjects. Similarly, in a sample of neuropsychiatrically impaired delinquent girls (56), 15 of 21 became pregnant, and 80% of them could not provide safe, stable environments for their children.

Marriage

The proportions of antisocial girls who married ranged from 19% to 100%, depending on the length of follow-up and the age of the subjects (12, 48–50, 55, 56, 66). There was a trend toward early marriage. In one sample (49), 21% of the antisocial girls married before the age of 17, compared to 9% of the normal control subjects and 8% of the nonantisocial former patients. Thirty-three percent of female criminals with past histories of delinquency reported that they had married before they were 18 years old (66). In another study (48), even those who were not married had a higher rate of early cohabitation.

Four studies presented data on the quality of these relationships. In one investigation (49), antisocial girls developed into women with higher rates of divorce and extramarital sexual activity than either normal control subjects or other types of patients. Sixty-five percent of the antisocial group had marital problems, including many women who were married to abusive or alcoholic men. This finding was replicated in a sample of neuropsychiatrically ill delinquent girls (56); 10% of these subjects were divorced by their early 20s, and 62% of those living with a partner were in violent relationships. Girls with conduct disorder at 21 years of age were 3.9 times more likely to have been involved in a mutually violent relationship than either normal or depressed control girls (48). None of the delinquent girls in the Kauai Longitudinal Study (55) were happy in their marriages; one-third of them ranked their marriage as their biggest concern, compared to 14% of the normal control subjects.

Education and Occupation

Academic achievement and occupational success were assessed by six studies each. In the Kauai Longitudinal Study (55), 40% of the delinquent subjects did not go beyond high school, compared to 9% of the group without problems. Similarly, in the Dunedin Multidisciplinary Health and Development Study (48), girls with conduct disorder were 3.8 times more likely to have no school certificate (similar to a high school diploma) than the healthy control subjects, although depressed girls were 5.8 times more likely to demonstrate this outcome. In two uncontrolled follow-ups of clinical samples (52, 56), only 10%–29% of the subjects had completed high school.

The data on occupational outcomes are conflicting. One study (49) reported that 15% of the women with antisocial histories were unemployed, compared to 7% of the other former patients and 0% of the normal control subjects. Eleven percent of the antisocial group reported 10 or more jobs in the previous 10 years, compared to 1% of the other former patients and 0% of the normal control subjects. In another follow-up of more impaired delinquent girls (56), only 29% had any job training, with histories of moving from one low-paying job to another. However, an uncontrolled follow-up of delinquent girls on probation (60) found that 48% of them had "good or very fair records" of work. Zoccolillo et al. (50) reported that only 7% of women with conduct disorder had a history of occupational problems, similar to the rate of 9% for women without conduct disorder. There were no differences in employment outcomes between women in the conduct disorder, depressed, and normal groups of the Dunedin Multidisciplinary Health and Development Study (48).

Service Utilization

Service utilization outcomes included welfare, involvement with social services agencies (e.g., child protection agencies), and medical care. Social services were required by 55% of women with antisocial histories, compared to 35% of nonantisocial patients and 10% of normal control subjects (49). The antisocial group also had the highest rate of physician utilization: 23% versus 0% for the nonantisocial group and 10% for the normal control subjects. Women with conduct disorder histories in the Dunedin Multidisciplinary Health and Development Study (48) were 3.7 times more likely to use multiple sources of welfare than healthy control subjects or depressed girls, a finding similar to results from two other studies (56, 61).

Global Adult Functioning

With a simple summary measure of adult functioning, Robins (49) found that nearly one-half of antisocial adolescent girls developed into adults with poor adjustment in multiple domains. Similarly, the girls with conduct disorder in the Dunedin Multidisciplinary Health and Development Study (48) averaged nearly three adult adjustment problems, compared to one for the normal control subjects and two for the depressed girls. The delinquent girls in the Kauai Longitudinal Study (55) had more problems coping with adult life. Women with histories of delinquency plus mental health problems had the worst outcome, 42% of them having two or more coping problems, compared to 12% of the normal women, 25% of the delinquency-only group, and 26% of the girls with only psychiatric problems.

Zoccolillo et al. (50) found that a past history of conduct disorder was not strongly associated with any one specific adverse outcome, but that 62% of the girls with conduct disorder had difficulties in two or more domains of adult functioning, compared to 9% of the girls without conduct disorder. Two uncontrolled follow-ups of girls with conduct disorder (51, 52) reported that nearly 20% of each sample adjusted poorly to adulthood.

DISCUSSION

These data indicate that the adult course for many adolescent girls with antisocial behavior is not benign. Compared to their nonantisocial peers, these women have higher mortality rates, a 10- to 40-fold increase in criminal behavior, a variety of psychiatric problems, dysfunctional and sometimes violent relationships, poor educational achievement, less stable work histories, and higher rates of service utilization.

Continuity Between Adolescent and Adult Pathology

The data clearly support a model of homotypic continuity. At least 25%–50% of antisocial girls engage in adult criminal behavior, and recent delinquency follow-up studies suggest that the rates may be even higher in contemporary cohorts. The cross-sectional studies report that 60%–80% of women with criminal records have histories of antisocial behavior as teenagers. Taken together, these findings imply that antisocial behavior in adolescence is the initial step in the predominant pathway to female adult crime.

Do these girls have an antisocial lifestyle that simply persists into adulthood? Do they start with minor infractions, progressing to more severe criminal behavior? Is there a pattern of misconduct followed by a quiescent period, then emergence of a different type of crime in adulthood? Anecdotal and retrospective data suggest that there are at least two paths between antisocial deviance in girls and such behavior in women (14, 64, 65, 67, 68). The first is a pattern of persistent, aggressive antisocial behavior beginning during latency and continuing throughout adolescence into adulthood, with a steady increase in the severity and aggressiveness of offenses. The second path is characterized by norm violations starting in the teen years, escalating to more severe adult criminal activity in the context of substance abuse or continued association with deviant peers. These paths are similar to some of those described in boys (4, 5, 69–71), although the findings need to be replicated in controlled prospective studies of girls.

Antisocial behavior among adolescent girls was not associated just with adult crime. Regardless of the outcome measure used, the studies reported that substantial percentages of antisocial girls did poorly in adulthood. This multiplicity of adverse outcomes may be a reflection of 1) latent heterogeneity in the population, with subgroups of girls who at baseline may have different prognoses (susceptibility bias) or 2) a large proportion of antisocial girls who display problems in multiple domains of adult life (heterotypic continuity). The data indicate that both conditions may be in operation.

It is quite probable that the population of antisocial girls contains subgroups defined by baseline characteristics that may have prognostic significance, for example, aggression, psychiatric comorbidity, history of abuse, or family dynamics. If a correction for this heterogeneity is not made in the sampling process or in the data analysis, adverse outcomes may show up in every domain. However, this would be a reflection of susceptibility bias, with each of the subgroups developing the outcomes unique to them, rather than a reflection of the majority of the girls having widespread pathology.

In support of this explanation, several studies examined the effects of baseline aggression or psychiatric comorbidity and reported that groups of girls with these characteristics each had sets of outcomes different from those of the girls without them (12, 48, 52, 55, 56, 62). Future cross-sectional studies of antisocial girls and women should be designed to identify subgroups with potentially different outcomes. Similarly, longitudinal studies should include measurements of the prognostic effects of aggression and baseline psychiatric comorbidity as well as explore the effects of variables such as history of abuse, family psychiatric history, and family functioning.

Although susceptibility bias could explain the variety of untoward outcomes, six studies (48–52, 55) reported that one-half of the girls had serious problems in multiple domains of their adult lives, data that clearly support a model of heterotypic continuity. There are two possible mechanisms for heterotypic continuity: 1) there may be a core biological or psychological deficit underlying symptoms in both stages of life, or 2) adolescent antisocial behavior may derail the normal developmental process so significantly in these girls that it seriously compromises their ability to cope with adulthood.

A core biological or psychological deficit would generate a picture of heterotypic continuity by producing maladaptive behavior across all adult domains. Several biological or psychological abnormalities have been associated with antisocial behavior (primarily in males) and could potentially be the mechanism(s) for heterotypic continuity, but I will discuss only the two most likely deficits—prefrontal lobe dysfunction and poor attachment.

Prefrontal lobe dysfunction has been suggested as a potential biological deficit in antisocial behavior (72, 73). Abnormalities in one or all of the three prefrontal lobe circuits responsible for executive functions, mood regulation, and motivation would result in women characterized by impulsivity, short attention span, difficulty planning or delaying gratification, inability to learn from experience, mood instability, and poor motivation, all of which would impair normal adult functioning. Research into the relationship between prefrontal lobe function and antisocial behavior has predominantly focused on executive functions in deviant males (73). Two studies that included antisocial girls (74, 75), however, reported that girls with inattention, distractibility, and impulsivity had higher rates of psychosocial impairment. We have no data on any other aspects of prefrontal lobe function and no research using more sophisticated diagnostic techniques such as imaging. Further research should be done on the role of prefrontal lobe dysfunction in antisocial females.

A core psychological deficit in attachment has long been postulated as an etiologic factor in antisocial behavior (76) but could also be the mechanism for the heterotypic continuity reported here. Poor attachment has been associated with the inability to form and maintain stable adult relationships with partners, children, peers, and coworkers. This could certainly explain the pervasive dysfunction in women with histories of adolescent antisocial behavior. Most of the studies on the effects of attachment are cross-sectional, use self-report delinquency measures, and have been done on males, but several (77–79) have studied female adolescents and reported that attachment difficulties are associated with antisocial behavior. We clearly need to investigate the developmental effect of poor attachment as a factor in adverse adult outcomes.

The second possible mechanism explaining heterotypic continuity is interference with normal adolescent development. This derailment may occur because antisocial behavior prevents girls from learning the social and psychological skills needed for adulthood, or because antisocial conduct may expose girls to situations in which each behavioral choice leads to further deviance. There are no data with which to test this hypothesis, but prospective studies of development in girls with other types of problems, such as early puberty, histories of institutionalization, or depression (80–83), indicate that such experiences can derail normal development and lead to multiple poor outcomes in adulthood. We need to collect detailed longitudinal data from antisocial females about the impact of their behaviors on their daily lives. To determine whether antisocial deviance has a uniquely deleterious effect on development, comparison data should also be collected from normal girls and girls with other psychiatric disorders.

Limitations of the Studies

Although the results of this review are provocative, it is important to point out limitations of the studies. The most significant is the absence of data on the nonwhite female population. This is particularly troubling given the higher arrest rate for black females. Few of the studies used control groups, many samples were small, and larger samples were often heterogeneous with regard to type of antisocial behavior. A variety of data collection methods were used, ranging from public registries to clinical interviewing. There was an assortment of outcome measures, and cohort effects were of particular concern in the definition of conduct disorder, changes in the definition of sexual deviance, and changes in institutionalization practices over the past century.

Directions for Future Research

In spite of these limitations, this review establishes that female antisocial behavior has important individual and societal consequences. The studies reviewed here suggest that if we do a 10-year follow-up on Jennifer, described at the beginning of this article, we are likely to find that she has not graduated from high school, has had multiple, unstable relationships, is using drugs and alcohol, uses aggression to solve conflicts, has received psychiatric and social services, has been in jail, and has had difficulties caring for her children. Our understanding of the developmental trajectories of antisocial girls and women is so limited, however, that as policy makers or clinicians, we do not know how to prevent or treat such outcomes.

Several lines of research should be developed to resolve these issues. In all types of studies, particular emphasis should be placed on including antisocial females from nonwhite populations, and comparison data should be collected not only from normal females but from psychiatric groups as well. The first type of further research needed is phenomenological studies of antisocial girls and women. This would allow us to assess the validity of our current diagnostic criteria for conduct disorder in girls (20) as well as identify variables in adolescence that may have long-term prognostic value, such as aggression, psychiatric comorbidity, and type of delinquent behavior. Second, we need cross-sectional studies of the rates of prefrontal lobe dysfunction and poor attachment in antisocial females to determine whether these are important factors in the trajectories to adult pathology. Third, the next generation of longitudinal studies on antisocial adolescent girls should be designed with multiple data collection points, should track subgroups of antisocial girls with potentially different prognoses, and should assess brain and psychological changes over time. Data from these three types of studies will give us the knowledge necessary to develop treatment and secondary prevention strategies for girls like Jennifer.

REFERENCES

1. Glueck S, Glueck E: Juvenile Delinquents Grown Up. New York, Commonwealth Fund, 1940
2. McCord W, McCord J: Psychopathy and Delinquency. New York, Grune & Stratton, 1956
3. West DJ, Farrington DP: The Delinquent Way of Life. London, Heinemann, 1977
4. Loeber R: The natural histories of juvenile conduct problems, substance use and delinquency: evidence for development progressions. Advances in Clin Psychol 1988; 2:73–124
5. Moffitt TE: Adolescent-limited and life-course-persistent antisocial behavior: a developmental taxonomy. Psychol Rev 1993; 100:674–701
6. Thomas WI: The Unadjusted Girl. Boston, Little, Brown, 1937
7. Cohen A: Delinquent Boys. Glencoe, Ill, Free Press, 1955
8. Cloward R, Ohlin LE: Delinquency and Opportunity. New York, Free Press, 1960
9. Morris RR: Female delinquency and relational problems. Social Forces 1964; 43:82–89
10. Smith LS: Sexist assumptions and female delinquency, in Women, Sexuality and Social Control. Edited by Smart C, Smart B. London, Routledge & Kegan Paul, 1978, pp 72–88
11. Kunzel RG: Fallen Women, Problem Girls: Unmarried Mothers and the Professionalization of Social Work, 1890–1945. New Haven, Conn, Yale University Press, 1993
12. Cowie J, Cowie V, Slater E: Delinquency in Girls. London, Heinemann, 1968
13. Loper AB, Cornell DG: Homicide by juvenile girls. J Child and Family Studies 1996; 5:323–336
14. Mann CR: When Women Kill. Albany, State University of New York Press, 1996
15. Molidor CE: Female gang members: a profile of aggression and victimization. Soc Work 1996; 41:251–257
16. Smith L: In suburbs, concern grows over girls' criminal activity. Washington Post, Oct 20, 1995, p A1
17. Mehren E: The throwaways. Los Angeles Times, April 12, 1996, p E1
18. Mehren E: As bad as they wanna be. Los Angeles Times, May 17, 1996, p E1
19. Myers WC, Burket RC, Lyles WB, Stone L, Kemph JP: DSM-III diagnoses and offenses in committed female juvenile delinquents. Bull Am Acad Psychiatry Law 1990; 18:47–54
20. Zoccolillo M: Gender and the development of conduct disorder. Developmental Psychopathology 1993; 5:65–78
21. Kashani JH, Orvaschel H, Rosenberg TK, Reid JC: Psychopathology in a community sample of children and adolescents: a developmental perspective. J Am Acad Child Adolesc Psychiatry 1989; 28:701–706
22. Fergusson DM, Horwood LJ, Lynskey MT: Prevalence and comorbidity of DSM-III-R diagnoses in a birth cohort of 15-year-olds. J Am Acad Child Adolesc Psychiatry 1993; 32:1127–1134

23. May D: Delinquent girls before the courts. Med Sci Law 1977; 17:203–212

24. Offord DR, Abrams N, Allen N, Poushinsky M: Broken homes, parental psychiatric illness, and female delinquency. Am J Orthopsychiatry 1979; 49:252–264

25. Chesney-Lind M: Girls and status offenses: is juvenile justice still sexist? Criminal Justice Abstracts 1988; 20:144–165

26. Odem ME: Delinquent Daughters: Protecting and Policing Adolescent Female Sexuality in the United States, 1885–1920. Chapel Hill, University of North Carolina Press, 1995

27. Westendorp F, Brink KL, Roberson MK, Ortiz IE: Variables which differentiate placement of adolescents into juvenile justice or mental health systems. Adolescence 1986; 21:23–37

28. Chesney-Lind M: Judicial enforcement of the female sex role: the family court and the female delinquent. Issues in Criminology 1973; 8:51–69

29. Datesman SK, Scarpitti FR: Female delinquency and broken homes: a reassessment. Criminology 1975; 13:33–55

30. Sarri R: Unequal protection under the law: women and the criminal justice system, in The Trapped Woman: Catch-22 in Deviance and Control. Edited by Figueira-McDonough J, Sarri R. Beverly Hills, Calif, Sage Publications, 1987, pp 394–426

31. Schwartz IM, Steketee MW, Schneider VW: Federal juvenile justice policy and the incarceration of girls. Crime and Delinquency 1990; 36:503–520

32. Vaz EW: Middle-Class Juvenile Delinquency. New York, Harper & Row, 1967

33. Williams JR, Gold M: From delinquent behavior to official delinquency. Social Problems 1972; 19:209–228

34. Hindelang MJ: Age, sex, and the versatility of delinquent involvements. Social Problems 1971; 18:522–534

35. Cernkovich SA, Giordano PC: A comparative analysis of male and female delinquency. Sociological Quarterly 1979; 20:131–145

36. Figueira-McDonough J, Barton WH, Sarri RC: Normal deviance: gender similarities in adolescent subcultures, in Comparing Female and Male Offenders. Edited by Warren MQ. Beverly Hills, Calif, Sage Publications, 1981, pp 17–45

37. Loy P, Norland S: Gender convergence and delinquency. Sociological Quarterly 1981; 22:275–283

38. Wolfgang M: Delinquency in two birth cohorts. Am Behavioral Scientist 1983; 27:75–80

39. Balthazar ML, Cook RJ: An analysis of the factors related to the rate of violent crimes committed by incarcerated female delinquents. J Offender Counseling, Services, and Rehabilitation 1984; 19:103–118

40. Durant RH, Getts AG, Cadenhead C, Woods ER: The association between weapon carrying and the use of violence among adolescents living in and around public housing. J Adolesc Health 1995; 17:376–380

41. Lewis DK: Black women offenders and criminal justice, in Comparing Female and Male Offenders. Edited by Warren MQ. Beverly Hills, Calif, Sage Publications, 1981, pp 89–105

42. Lewis DO, Shanok SS, Pincus JH: A comparison of the neuropsychiatric status of female and male incarcerated delinquents: some evidence of sex and race bias. J Am Acad Child Psychiatry 1982; 21:190–196

43. Farnworth M, McDermott J, Zimmerman SE: Aggregation effects on male-to-female arrest rate ratios in New York State, 1972–1984. J Quantitative Criminology 1988; 4:121–135

44. Sommers I, Baskin D: Sex, race, age, and violent offending. Violence Vict 1992; 7:191–201

45. Rutter M: Pathways from childhood to adult life. J Child Psychol Psychiatry 1989; 30:23–51

46. Rutter M: Adolescence as a transition period: continuities and discontinuities in conduct disorder. J Adolesc Health 1992; 13:451–460

47. Cicchetti D, Cohen DJ: Perspectives on developmental psychopathology, in Developmental Psychopathology, vol 1: Theory and Methods. Edited by Cicchetti D, Cohen DJ. New York, John Wiley & Sons, 1995, pp 3–20

48. Bardone AM, Moffitt TE, Caspi A, Dickson N, Silva PA: Adult mental health and social outcomes of adolescent girls with depression and conduct disorder. Developmental Psychopathology 1996; 8:811–829

49. Robins LN: Deviant Children Grown Up: A Sociological and Psychiatric Study of Sociopathic Personality. Baltimore, Williams & Wilkins, 1966

50. Zoccolillo M, Pickles A, Quinton D, Rutter M: The outcome of childhood conduct disorder: implications for defining adult personality disorder and conduct disorder. Psychol Med 1992; 22:971–986

51. Storm-Mathisen A, Vaglum P: Conduct disorder patients 20 years later: a personal follow-up study. Acta Psychiatr Scand 1994; 89:416–420

52. Zoccolillo M, Rogers K: Characteristics and outcome of hospitalized adolescent girls with conduct disorder. J Am Acad Child Adolesc Psychiatry 1991; 30:973–981

53. Rowe JB, Sullivan PF, Mulder RT, Joyce PR: The effect of a history of conduct disorder in adult major depression. J Affect Disord 1996; 37:51–63

54. Robins LN, Price RK: Adult disorders predicted by childhood conduct problems: results from the NIMH Epidemiologic Catchment Area Project. Psychiatry 1991; 54:116–132

55. Werner EE, Smith RS: Overcoming the Odds: High Risk Children From Birth to Adulthood. Ithaca, NY, Cornell University Press, 1992

56. Lewis DO, Yeager CA, Cobham-Portorreal CS, Klein N, Showalter C, Anthony A: A follow-up of female delinquents: maternal contributions to the perpetuation of deviance. J Am Acad Child Adolesc Psychiatry 1991; 30:197–201

57. Rosenbaum JL: Family dysfunction and female delinquency. Crime and Delinquency 1989; 35:31–44

58. Rydelius PA: The development of antisocial behavior and sudden death. Acta Psychiatr Scand 1988; 77:398–403

59. Gibbens TCN: Female offenders. Br J Psychiatry 1975; 9:326–333

60. Gibbens TCN: Supervision and probation of adolescent girls. Br J Delinquency 1959; 10: 84–103

61. Otterström E: Delinquency and children from bad homes: a study of their prognosis from a social point of view. Acta Paediatr 1946; 33(suppl 5):1–326

62. Ahnsjö S: Delinquency in girls and its prognosis. Acta Paediatr 1941; 28(suppl 3):1–327

63. Healy W, Bronner AF: Delinquents and Criminals: Their Making and Unmaking. New York, Macmillan, 1926

64. Smith V: The Experiences of Women Who Are Aggressive: An Analysis of Incarcerated Women From a Gestalt Therapy Theoretical Perspective (doctoral dissertation). Cincinnati, The Union Institute, 1994

65. Sommers I, Baskin DR: Factors related to female adolescent initiation into violent street crime. Youth and Society 1994; 25:468–489

66. Cloninger CR, Guze SB: Psychiatric illness and female criminality: the role of sociopathy and hysteria in the antisocial woman. Am J Psychiatry 1970; 127:303–311

67. Gilfus ME: From victims to survivors to offenders: women's routes of entry and immersion in street crime. Women and Criminal Justice 1992; 4:63–89

68. Dunlap E, Johnson BD, Manwar A: A successful female crack dealer: a case study of a deviant career. Deviant Behavior 1994; 15:1–25

69. Loeber R, LeBlanc M: Toward a developmental criminology, in Crime and Justice, vol 12. Edited by Tonry M, Morris N. Chicago, University of Chicago Press, 1990, pp 375–473

70. Sampson RJ, Laub JH: Crime in the Making: Pathways and Turning Points Through the Life Course. Cambridge, Mass, Harvard University Press, 1990

71. Nagin DS, Farrington DP: The onset and persistence of offending. Criminology 1992; 30:501–523

72. Pennington BF, Ozonoff S: Executive functions and developmental psychopathology. J Child Psychol Psychiatry 1996; 37:51–87

73. Scarpa A, Raine A: Biology of wickedness. Psychiatr Annals 1997; 27:624–629

74. Moffitt TE, Henry B: Neuropsychological assessment of executive functions in self-reported delinquents. Developmental Psychopathology 1989; 1:105–118

75. Aronowitz B, Liebowitz M, Hollander E, Fazziui E, Durlach-Misteli C, Frenkel M, Mosovich S, Garfinkel R, Saoud J, DelBene D, Cohen L, Jaeger A, Rubin AL: Neuropsychiatric and neuropsychological findings in conduct disorder and attention-deficit hyperactivity disorder. J Neuropsychiatry Clin Neurosci 1994; 6:245–249

76. Fonagy P, Target M, Steele M, Steele H: The development of violence and crimes as it relates to security of attachment, in Children in a Violent Society. Edited by Osofsky JD. New York, Guilford Press, 1997, pp 150–177

77. Gardner L, Shoemaker DJ: Social bonding and delinquency: a comparative analysis. Sociological Quarterly 1989; 30:481–500

78. Seydlitz R: The effects of age and gender on parental control and delinquency. Youth and Society 1991; 23:175–201

79. Torstensson M: Female delinquents in a birth cohort: tests of some aspects of control theory. J Quantitative Criminology 1990; 6:101–115

80. Brown GW: Causal paths, chains and strands, in Studies of Psychosocial Risk: The Power of Longitudinal Data. Edited by Rutter M. Cambridge, England, Cambridge University Press, 1988, pp 285–314

81. Caspi A, Elder GH: Emergent family patterns: the intergenerational construction of problem behaviors and relationships, in Relationships Within Families: Mutual Influences. Edited by Hinde A, Stevenson-Hinde J. Oxford, England, Clarendon Press, 1988, pp 218–240

82. Magnusson D: Individual Development From an Interactional Perspective: A Longitudinal Study. Hillsdale, NJ, Lawrence Erlbaum Associates, 1988

83. Quinton D, Rutter M: Parental Breakdown: The Making and Breaking of Intergenerational Links. Aldershot, England, Gower, 1988

19

IQ Decline During Childhood and Adult Psychotic Symptoms in a Community Sample: A 19-Year Longitudinal Study

William S. Kremen, Ph.D., Stephen L. Buka, Sc.D., Larry J. Seidman, Ph.D., Jill M. Goldstein, Ph.D., Danny Koren, Ph.D., and Ming T. Tsuang, M.D., Ph.D., D.Sc.

Objective: *The goal of this study was to examine cognitive antecedents of psychosis by determining whether variability in IQ during childhood was predictive of psychotic symptoms in adulthood.* **Method:** *Deviant responder analyses were used to examine prospectively the relationship of IQ at ages 4 and 7 to psychotic symptoms at age 23 in 547 offspring from a community sample (National Collaborative Perinatal Project) that was unselected for psychiatric illness. The authors compared three hypotheses: that 1) low IQ, 2) large IQ fluctuations regardless of direction, or 3) large IQ declines would predict the presence of adult psychotic symptoms.* **Results:** *The 10% of individuals with substantially larger than expected IQ declines from age 4 to 7 had a rate of psychotic, but not other psychiatric, symptoms at age 23 that was nearly seven times as high as the rate for other persons. Parental socioeconomic status and IQ at age 7 also predicted adult psychotic symptoms. However, when IQ at age 7, IQ decline between age 4 and 7, and socioeconomic status were all included in a logistic regression analysis, only IQ decline remained significant.* **Conclusions:** *There is an increased likelihood of developing psychotic symptoms in adulthood for a subgroup of*

Revised version of a paper presented at the 5th International Congress on Schizophrenia Research, Warm Springs, Va., April 8–12, 1995. Received July 7, 1997; revision received Dec. 24, 1997; accepted Jan. 5, 1998. From the Department of Psychiatry, University of California, Davis, School of Medicine, Sacramento; the Harvard Department of Psychiatry at Massachusetts Mental Health Center, Boston; the Harvard Department of Psychiatry at Brockton-West Roxbury VA Medical Center, Brockton, Mass.; the Harvard Institute of Psychiatric Epidemiology and Genetics, Boston; the Department of Epidemiology, Harvard School of Public Health, Boston; the Neuro-psychology Laboratory, Massachusetts Mental Health Center, Boston; and the Department of Psychology, Haifa University, Haifa, Israel. Address reprint requests to Dr. Kremen, Department of Psychiatry, University of California, Davis, School of Medicine, 4430 V St., Sacramento, CA 95817; wskremen@ucdavis.edu (e-mail).

Supported in part by grants from NIMH (grant MH-50647 to Dr. Tsuang), the Stanley Foundation (to Dr. Buka), and the National Alliance for Research on Schizophrenia and Depression (to Dr. Kremen).

The authors thank Gwen Zornberg, M.D., for evaluation of symptom criteria and Stephen V. Faraone, Ph.D., for statistical consultation.

individuals with substantially greater than expected IQ declines during child-hood. IQ decline is specific for psychotic symptoms, but follow-up assessment when the study participants are futher into the age of risk will be necessary to determine specificity for schizophrenia. The authors discuss the implications of this early cognitive downturn for a neurodevelopmental view of schizophrenia.
(Am J Psychiatry 1998; 155:672–677)

Longitudinal studies are critically important for identifying childhood abnormalities that predict schizophrenia and schizophrenia spectrum disorders. High-risk and follow-back studies have the advantage of being specifically targeted for schizophrenia, but they are also subject to the problem of lack of representativeness. For example, relatively few individuals with schizophrenia have a parent with schizophrenia. General population studies avoid some of the potential biases inherent in high-risk and follow-back studies. Prospective data about developmental antecedents of schizophrenia from general population samples provide a valuable complement to high-risk studies.

High-risk studies have shown that childhood attentional impairments predict adult schizophrenia spectrum disorders or associated symptoms (1–3). Childhood and adolescent affective deficits also appear to be important factors in schizophrenia spectrum outcomes in high-risk children (4, 5). Family instability and poor childhood social or school adjustment have been associated with adult schizophrenia-related outcomes in high-risk and follow-back studies (6–9). Psychophysiological, neurological, and motor abnormalities have been found to be predictive of adult schizophrenia in high-risk studies (9, 10). In community sample studies, impaired childhood social adjustment, delayed motor development, speech problems, poor educational test performance, and mothers rated as having less than average parenting skills were each a significant predictor of adult schizophrenia (11, 12).

Low childhood IQ (or other measures of general intellectual ability) was also a predictor of adult schizophrenia in studies using each of the preceding strategies (12–16). The focus of this article is on change in IQ during childhood as a predictor of adult psychotic symptoms in a community sample unselected for psychiatric illness.

Our thinking about IQ change was influenced by the ideas of Barbara Fish, M.D., although she did not specifically address this issue. In conducting assessments over time, investigators have usually looked for stability of deficits or abnormalities. In contrast, Fish, who began studying infants at risk for schizophrenia in the 1950s, focused more on change over time than on stability (10). She postulated that an inherited neurointegrative defect was specific for the schizophrenia phenotype. "Pandysmaturation" was later invoked as an index of this defect in infancy. It consisted of 1) transient retardation and accelerated return to normal of motor or visual-motor development, 2) an abnormal developmental profile whereby earlier items on a single developmental examination are failed and later items are passed, and 3) retardation in skeletal growth (10). Several high-risk studies have shown patterns of uneven development consistent with pandysmaturation in children of parents with schizophrenia, although there are few data on the relationship to adult outcomes (10).

In several instances, predictors from the studies just discussed were based on assessments at multiple points in time. Not only does this approach help to illuminate the developmental trajectory of schizophrenia-related disorders, but it is also likely to reduce false positive predictions (17, 18). Using the notion of variability in a broader fashion, Hanson et al. (19) examined intraindividual cognitive variability in children with an index of variability across measures and over time (ages 4 and 7). They standardized psychological test scores, including IQ measures, and calculated the variance of the scores for each individual. The proportion of children with high variance scores was significantly higher for the high-risk children than for the low-risk children.

These considerations suggest three alternative hypotheses regarding the relationship between childhood IQ and adult schizophrenia or psychotic symptoms. First, a "low IQ" hypothesis would be that low IQ in and of itself is a predictor of adult schizophrenia or psychotic symptoms. Second, a "nondirectional IQ change" hypothesis parallels the notion of uneven development or deviation from an expected trajectory; that is, large fluctuations in IQ during childhood, regardless of the direction of change, are a predictor. Third, a "directional IQ change" hypothesis would be that a large change in a specified direction is a predictor; the logical choice in this case would be IQ decline.

METHOD

Participants

The participants were a subset of the offspring at the Providence, R.I., site of the National Collaborative Perinatal Project. Details of the National Collaborative Perinatal Project, which was designed to evaluate factors associated with neurodevelopmental disorders of childhood, have been described previously (20). Pregnant women were recruited, usually at their first prenatal visit, at 12 locations in the United States from 1959 to 1966. The women were followed throughout pregnancy, and their children were followed to age 7. Extensive prenatal and maternal data were collected, along with results of repeated medical, neurological, and psychological examinations of the children. A total of 4,140 pregnancies were included in the Providence cohort (21).

Buka et al. (21) followed up a selected sample of 1,068 individuals comprising offspring with pregnancy and delivery complications and a matched group without complications. At follow-up, 140 were deceased, adopted, or otherwise ineligible. Of the remaining 928, 693 (75%) were interviewed at an average age of 23 years. There were no differences in interview rates for the individuals with and without complications. Face-to-face interviews were conducted with 85% of the offspring; 15% were interviewed by telephone. The present sample of individuals who underwent IQ testing at both ages 4 and 7 comprises 547 (79%) of the 693 interviewed offspring (59% of the total eligible cohort). Of the 547 participants, 316 (58%) were women and 381 (70%) were white; the mean parental socioeconomic rating at study entry (N = 528) was 45.2 (SD = 18.8) on a 0–99 scale based on a U.S. Census Bureau instrument (22). This group of 547 was similar to the entire sample of 693 in terms of sex distribution, age at assessment, and parental socioeconomic status, but it had fewer minority participants. Written informed consent was obtained from all participants after the research procedures were fully explained.

Measures

Diagnosis and symptom ratings. Adult psychiatric symptoms and lifetime DSM-III diagnoses were determined on the basis of version III of the National Institute of Mental Health Diagnostic Interview Schedule (DIS), a structured interview suitable for large community samples (23). The DIS was administered by trained interviewers. We placed particular emphasis on minimizing false positive ratings of psychotic symptoms. In accordance with standard DIS administration procedures, if the interviewee acknowledged any symptoms, he or she was further queried to determine symptom severity and any known precipitating conditions. Subthreshold symptoms and symptoms attributed to medications, substance use, and/or physical conditions did not qualify. In addition, the interviewers were instructed to ask for and record verbatim examples of potentially qualifying symptom. Two expert diagnosticians subsequently reviewed all available information and reevaluated the presence of psychotic symptoms to rule out those that were not clinically meaningful. For example, a person responded positively to a question about events having particular and unusual meaning specifically for him or her; on review it was determined that this individual was alluding to personal values rather than delusions of reference.

Of the 547 offspring, 25 experienced psychotic symptoms according to the DIS interview alone. The expert reevaluation, on which there was complete interrater agreement, resulted in far more conservative ratings; seven individuals originally rated as having psychotic symptoms were reclassified as nonpsychotic. On the basis of the reevaluation, eight (2%) of the 547 offspring were rated as having definite psychotic symptoms at age 23; 18 (3%) individuals were included when the threshold was probable or definite psychotic symptoms. Among these 18 individuals, there were five with persecutory delusions, five with hallucinations, one with bizarre delusions, one with delusions of reference, one with other delusions, two with hallucinations and persecutory delusions, and three with persecutory and bizarre delusions. In the analyses, the group of 18 offspring with probable or definite psychotic symptoms was compared with the remainder of the sample (without psychotic symptoms).

IQ measures. The Stanford-Binet IQ test (24) was administered at age 4. An abbreviated version of the Wechsler Intelligence Scale for Children (WISC) (25) including the information, vocabulary, digit span, comprehension, block design, picture arrangement, and coding subtests was administered at age 7. To provide a common metric, we standardized the IQ measures so that each had a mean of 100 and a standard deviation of 15 for the entire Providence sample of the National Collaborative Perinatal Project. These are the general population means and standard deviation values for the WISC, whereas the Stanford-Binet test has a mean of 100 and a standard deviation of 16. Mean IQs for the study sample are shown in table 1.

Indices of IQ change. We applied a regression approach to avoid the psychometric artifacts inherent in raw difference scores, i.e., the curvilinear relationship between difference scores and total score for any two tests (26). For the entire Providence sample, we regressed standardized age 7 IQs on age 4 IQs (N = 2,688). The residual (observed minus predicted) score tells how much higher or lower than expected an individual is from the predicted score; residual scores are comparable regardless of absolute level of performance. Thus,

TABLE 1
Childhood IQs of Offspring in a Community Sample Who Were
Interviewed at Age 23

Group and Measure	Age at Assessment (years)	IQ Mean	SD
All participants (N = 547)			
Stanford-Binet IQ test[a]	4	98.16	15.50
WISC[b]	7	96.94	13.16
Participants with adult psychotic symptoms (N = 18)			
Stanford-Binet IQ test[a]	4	93.67	20.78
WISC[b]	7	87.67	16.78

[a] Stanford-Binet Intelligence Test (24).
[b] Abbreviated version of the Wechsler Intelligence Scale for Children (25).

when we refer to IQ change, we are actually referring to increase or decline in comparison with expectation based on predicted score.

For this method to be valid, the pairs of tests being used should be fairly highly correlated (26). The correlation (r) between the Stanford-Binet test and the WISC was 0.65 (df = 2686) for the entire Providence sample and 0.60 (df = 545) in the present study (p < 0.001 in both cases).

Because only a small proportion of the general population would be expected to experience psychotic symptoms, we hypothesized that if IQ change were a meaningful predictor variable, then individuals at the extremes of the IQ change distribution would be most likely to develop psychotic symptoms. Consequently, we performed deviant responder analyses (17), dividing the 547 offspring into the highest (largest IQ increase) and lowest (largest IQ decline) deciles, the next highest and lowest 15%, and the middle 50%.

RESULTS

Figure 1 shows the proportion of participants with adult psychotic symptoms grouped by amount of IQ change from age 4 to 7. The subgroups other than that with the largest IQ decline did not differ in rates of later psychotic symptoms ($\chi^2 = 4.10$, df = 3, p = 0.25). Only individuals who had very large declines were more likely to experience later psychotic symptoms. Consequently, we compared the group with largest IQ decline (bottom decile; N = 54) with the other four groups combined (N = 493).

Individuals in the bottom decile (those with much larger than expected declines from age 4 to 7) were significantly more likely to have psychotic symptoms at age 23: 13% (seven of 54) versus 2% (11 of 493) ($\chi^2 = 17.61$, df = 1, p = 0.0001; odds ratio = 6.62, 95% confidence interval = 2.52 − 17.42). Table 2 shows characteristics of the seven participants who had both larger than expected childhood IQ declines and adult psychotic symptoms. Analyses based on raw differences, rather than residualized scores, between age 4 and 7 IQs did not significantly predict psychotic symptoms; the rates of psychotic symptoms at

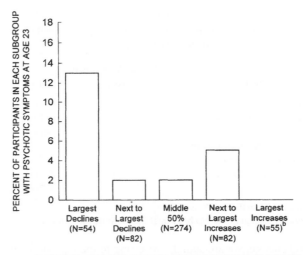

IQ CHANGE FROM AGE 4 TO 7 (BASED ON RESIDUALIZED SCORES)

Figure 1. Psychotic Symptoms at Age 23 as a Function of IQ Change From Age 4 to 7 in a Community Sample (N = 547)[a]
[a]Includes individuals with probable or definite psychotic symptoms. IQ change is the standardized difference between observed age 7 IQ and predicted age 7 IQ, given each individual's age 4 IQ.
[b]There were no participants with psychotic symptoms in this group.

age 23 were 7% for the participants with the largest raw childhood IQ decline (four of 54) and 3% for the remainder of the respondents (14 of 493) ($\chi^2 = 3.05$, df $= 1$, p $= 0.08$).

Age 7 IQ alone predicted psychotic symptoms at age 23 nearly as well as the residualized score did. As with the residualized scores, the bottom decile of age 7 IQs (IQ ≤ 80) was compared with all others combined. The participants with low age 7 IQs were significantly more likely to have psychotic symptoms at age 23: 11% (six of 54) versus 2% (12 of 493) ($\chi^2 = 10.80$, df $= 1$, p $= 0.0001$). In contrast, when the bottom decile for age 4 IQs was compared to the rest of the participants, there was no significant difference in the rates of later psychotic symptoms: 6% (three of 54) versus 3% (15 of 493) ($\chi^2 = 0.97$, df $= 1$, p $= 0.33$).

The question of whether the results could be accounted for simply by low age 7 IQ warranted further examination because a group with large IQ declines between ages 4 and 7 would also be more likely to have relatively low IQs at age 7. We divided the participants into four groups: 1) low age 7 IQ with large IQ decline between ages 4 and 7, 2) "normal" age 7 IQ with large IQ decline between ages 4 and 7, 3) low age 7 IQ with small IQ decline or increase between ages 4 and 7, 4) "normal" age 7 IQ with small IQ decline or increase between ages 4 and 7. "Low" age 7 IQ was defined as 80 or below (bottom decile). "Normal" IQ was used as a shorthand reference to IQs above 80. "Large" IQ decline between ages 4 and 7 refers to the bottom decile for decline (i.e., largest IQ declines). The results are illustrated in figure 2. There was a highly significant trend across these four groups such that the two groups with the largest IQ declines (two leftmost bars in figure 2) had the

TABLE 2
Characteristics of Offspring in a Community Sample (N = 547) Who Had Both Psychotic Symptoms at Age 23 and the Largest IQ Declines Between Ages 4 and 7 (N = 7)[a]

Participant	Sex	Type of Psychotic Symptoms	Raw IQ[b]		Standardized IQ[b,c]		Decline in Raw IQ
			Stanford-Binet IQ at Age 4	WISC IQ at Age 7	Stanford-Binet IQ at Age 4	WISC IQ at Age 7	
1	F	Persecutory delusions	100	72	100	75	25
2	F	Persecutory delusions; hallucinations	117	90	115	94	21
3	F	Hallucinations	109	79	108	83	25
4	F	Other delusions	42	46	49	48	1
5	M	Hallucinations	91	76	92	80	12
6	M	Bizarre delusions	90	78	91	82	9
7	F	Persecutory delusions	117	88	115	92	23
Mean for all participants			95.14	75.57	95.71	79.14	16.57
Mean excluding participant 4[d]			104.00	80.50	103.50	84.33	19.17

[a]The seven individuals from the 18 with psychotic symptoms who were also among the 10% of the sample with the largest IQ declines from age 4 to 7 based on residualized scores. However, the IQs in the table are not residualized scores.
[b]Stanford-Binet Intelligence Test (24) or abbreviated Wechsler Intelligence Scale for Children (25).
[c]Standardized scores were based on a mean of 100 and a standard deviation of 15 for both the WISC and the Stanford-Binet test.
[d]Because participant 4 had an extremely low IQ at age 4, her predicted IQ for age 7—based on the regression approach—was substantially higher than her age 4 IQ. Thus, the residualized value, comparing the large predicted increase with her minimal actual change, indicated a substantial decline from her predicted IQ. The study results held up when this participant was excluded from the analyses.

445

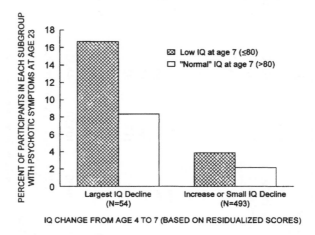

Figure 2. Psychotic Symptoms at Age 23 as a Function of Age 7 IQ and IQ Change From Age 4 to 7 in a Community Sample (N = 547)[a]
[a]Includes individuals with probable or definite psychotic symptoms. IQ change is the standardized difference between observed age 7 IQ and predicted age 7 IQ, given each individual's age 4 IQ. The "Largest IQ Decline" group is the 10% of the entire sample with the largest IQ declines; the "Increase or Small IQ Decline" group is the rest of the sample.

highest proportions of individuals with psychotic symptoms at age 23 (Mantel-Haenszel $\chi^2 = 20.75$, df = 3, p = 0.001).

We also considered the potential role of demographic factors in these results. The sex ratio did not differ between groups: 39% women and 61% men for the group with large IQ declines versus 43% women and 57% men for the rest of the sample ($\chi^2 = 0.27$, df = 1, p = 0.60). Socioeconomic status could also be an important factor in the prediction of psychotic symptoms because it is often associated with IQ (27). There were modest correlations between socioeconomic status and IQ at ages 4 and 7 (r = 0.30, df = 531, p < 0.001 in both cases). Socioeconomic status was significantly lower in the group with the largest IQ decline (mean = 40.09, SD = 21.18) than in the other study participants (mean = 46.42, SD = 29.40) (t = 2.25, df = 531, p = 0.02), but there was no significant difference between the mean scores of the participants with and without psychotic symptoms (mean = 48.22, SD = 19.08, versus mean = 45.69, SD = 19.69) (t = −0.054, df = 531, p = 0.59). Thus, socioeconomic status appeared to be associated with IQ decline but not with later psychotic symptoms.

As another way of examining the relationship among these factors, we performed a logistic regression analysis in which IQ change, age 7 IQ, and socioeconomic status were included as predictors of the presence or absence of psychotic symptoms at age 23. IQ change and age 7 IQ were each dichotomized at the bottom decile because theoretical considerations led us to focus on the extreme end of the distributions (i.e., the deviant responders). Socioeconomic status was dichotomized on the basis of a median split to maximize statistical power. The overall model was highly significant ($\chi^2 = 15.20$, df = 3, p < 0.002). When each predictor variable was tested after adjustment for the other predictors, the results were as follows—IQ change: $\chi^2 = 6.10$, df $= 1$, p < 0.02; age 7 IQ: $\chi^2 = 1.55$, df $= 1$, p $= 0.21$; socioeconomic status: $\chi^2 = 2.84$, df $= 1$, p < 0.10. Although low socioeconomic status may have some predictive value, these results are consistent with the notion that IQ change from age 4 to 7 is a more important predictor of psychotic symptoms at age 23 than either socioeconomic status or age 7 IQ alone.

Finally, we examined the ability of IQ decline between ages 4 and 7 to predict other types of psychiatric symptoms. Large IQ decline was not associated with nonpsychotic symptoms, whether we looked at the presence of any symptoms or the 10% of individuals with the most symptoms in a given DIS category. This relationship was assessed for symptoms in the following DIS modules: depression; mania; anxiety disorders (including phobias, panic disorder, and obsessive-compulsive disorder); antisocial personality disorder; childhood conduct disorder; alcohol abuse; drug abuse; and total number of any symptoms. The differences in rates of these symptoms between the group with large IQ declines and the other participants were trivial and in some cases were in the opposite direction of the results for psychotic symptoms.

DISCUSSION

We found that a substantially larger than expected IQ decline from age 4 to 7 was associated with a rate of psychotic symptoms 16 years later that was nearly seven times as high as that for individuals without large childhood IQ declines. This result supports the "directional IQ change" hypothesis; that is, a large decline, not simply a large fluctuation, predicted later psychotic symptoms. There was also support for the "low IQ" hypothesis in that low age 7 IQ alone also predicted psychotic symptoms at age 23. However, further analysis suggested that IQ decline was a more important factor. This distinction is perhaps most clearly seen by inspection of figure 2; individuals with low age 7 IQs who did not experience substantial IQ decline between ages 4 and 7 (second bar from right) still had a lower rate of psychotic symptoms at age 23 than individuals with "normal" age 7 IQs who did experience substantial IQ decline during childhood (second bar from left). Our data also indicated that IQ decline was a stronger predictor of psychotic symptoms than was parental socioeconomic status.

Given the small number of individuals with psychotic symptoms, we chose to include those with either probable or definite symptoms. Although inclusion of individuals with probable symptoms could have increased the false positive rate, at least two considerations argue against the possibility that false positives contributed to the observed results. First, it is likely that our review of the DIS interviews substantially reduced false positives; seven of the 25 individuals originally classified as positive for psychotic symptoms were reclassified as negative. Second, false positives would be most likely to reduce the chances of finding significant results. Indeed, there were slightly stronger significance levels for analyses comparing only the eight individuals with definite psychotic symptoms to the rest of the sample.

The predictive value of childhood IQ decline was specific for psychotic symptoms. The group with large IQ declines was not more likely to manifest symptoms of mania, depression, anxiety disorders, antisocial personality disorder, or alcohol or drug abuse. Despite the specificity of the findings, we cannot be certain about specificity for schizophrenia per se. Four individuals in this study were diagnosed with schizophrenia or schizophreniform disorder at the age 23 assessment. One of those was in the large-IQ-decline group (one of 54, or 1.85%); there was one in each of the next three groups and none in the large-increase group (three of 493, or 0.61%). Thus, the large-IQ-decline group had about double the roughly 1% population prevalence of schizophrenia and the rest of the participants had a somewhat lower than expected rate. This corresponds to an odds ratio of 2.83, which, however, was not significant. On the other hand, at age 23 the study participants were in the early part of the risk period for schizophrenia. Some nonschizophrenic participants, including those who have not yet experienced any psychotic symptoms, may still go on to develop schizophrenia.

Parallels between the present study and studies of schizophrenia further suggest that our findings are indeed likely to be relevant to schizophrenia. Studies of schizophrenia have examined and supported the "low childhood IQ" hypothesis (12–16). Other findings emphasize the value of looking at developmental changes or trajectories. Findings from one longitudinal study of a community sample (12) showed some consistency with the "IQ decline" hypothesis, showing a trend toward increasing overrepresentation of preschizophrenic individuals in the lower one-third of the distribution of intellectual functioning assessed at ages 8, 11, and 15. There is evidence that differences other than IQ between high-risk and control children are greater during adolescence than during earlier childhood (2, 28). In showing a meaningful difference between individuals with low IQs at age 7 whose IQs were always low and those whose low IQs represent substantial declines from age 4, our data suggest the importance of even earlier developmental trajectories, at least in regard to development of psychotic symptoms. Few studies have examined prospective data from this early in childhood (5, 10). Moreover, the present study was carried out with a community sample that was unselected for psychiatric illness, thus extending the generalizability of the findings beyond that of high-risk samples.

Although predictive of psychotic symptoms, childhood IQ decline may still not, strictly speaking, be an entirely causal factor. IQ decline would be more likely to be a truly causal factor if it were largely the result of extrinsic, socioenvironmental factors. However, if socioenvironmental influences were the primary cause, it seems unlikely that IQ decline would predict psychotic symptoms only. In addition, socioeconomic status, which might be considered an extrinsic factor, was less strongly predictive of psychotic symptoms than was IQ decline. IQ decline also remained significant as a predictor even after socioeconomic status was accounted for. Thus, a more parsimonious explanation may be that childhood IQ decline reflects neurobiological processes intrinsic to the specific development of psychotic symptoms. If childhood IQ decline is specific for schizophrenia and not just psychotic symptoms, this explanation would also be consistent with the increasingly accepted notion of schizophrenia as a neurodevelopmental disorder.

REFERENCES

1. Cornblatt BA, Lenzenweger MF, Dworkin RH, Erlenmeyer-Kimling L: Childhood attentional dysfunctions predict social deficits in unaffected adults at risk for schizophrenia. Br J Psychiatry 1992; 161:59–64

2. Mirsky AF: The Israeli High-Risk Study, in Relatives at Risk for Mental Disorder. Edited by Dunner DL, Gershon ES, Barrett JE. New York, Raven Press, 1988, pp 279–296

3. Mirsky A, Ingraham L, Kugelmass S: Neuropsychological assessment of attention and its pathology in the Israeli cohort. Schizophr Bull 1995; 21:193–217

4. Erlenmeyer-Kimling L, Cornblatt BA, Rock D, Roberts S, Bell M, West A: The New York High-Risk Project: anhedonia, attentional deviance, and psychopathology. Schizophr Bull 1993; 19:141–153

5. Walker EF, Grimes KE, Davis DM, Smith AJ: Childhood precursors of schizophrenia: facial expressions of emotion. Am J Psychiatry 1993; 150: 1654–1660

6. Watt NF: Patterns of childhood social development in adult schizophrenics. Arch Gen Psychiatry 1978; 36:160–165

7. Walker E, Hoppes E, Mednick S, Emory E, Schulsinger F: Environmental factors related to schizophrenia in psychophysiologically labile high-risk males. J Abnorm Psychol 1981; 49:313–320

8. Marcus J, Hans SL, Nagler S, Auerbach JG, Mirsky AF, Aubrey A: Review of the NIMH Israeli Kibbutz-city study and the Jerusalem infant development study. Schizophr Bull 1987; 13:426–438

9. Cannon TD, Mednick SA, Parnas J: Antecedents of predominantly negative- and predominantly positive-symptom schizophrenia in a high-risk population. Arch Gen Psychiatry 1990; 47:622–632

10. Fish B, Marcus J, Hans SL, Auerbach JG, Perdue S: Infants at risk for schizophrenia: sequelae of a genetic neurointegrative defect: a review and replication analysis of pandysmaturation in the Jerusalem Infant Development Study. Arch Gen Psychiatry 1992; 49:221–235

11. Done DJ, Crow TJ, Johnstone EC, Sacker A: Childhood antecedents of schizophrenia and affective illness; social adjustment at ages 7 and 11. BMJ 1994; 309:699–703

12. Jones P, Rodgers B, Murray RM: Child developmental risk factors for adult schizophrenia in the British 1946 birth cohort. Lancet 1994; 344:1398–1402

13. Aylward E, Walker E, Bettes B: Intelligence in schizophrenia: meta-analysis of the research. Schizophr Bull 1984; 10:430–459

14. Erlenmeyer-Kimling L, Rock D, Squires-Wheeler E, Roberts S, Yang J: Early life precursors of psychiatric outcomes in adulthood in subject at risk for schizophrenia or affective disorders. Psychiatry Res 1991; 39:239–256

15. Crow TJ, Done DJ, Sacker A: Childhood precursors of psychosis as clues to its evolutionary origins. Eur Arch Psychiatry Clin Neurosci 1995; 154:61–69

16. Russell AJ, Munro JC, Jones PB, Hemsley DR, Murray RM: Schizophrenia and the myth of intellectual decline. Am J Psychiatry 1997; 154:635–639

17. Kremen WS, Seidman LJ, Pepple JR, Lyons MJ, Tsuag MT, Faraone SV: Neuropsychological risk indicators for schizophrenia: a review of family studies. Schizophr Bull 1994; 20:103–119

18. Faraone SV, Kremen WS, Lyons MJ, Pepple JR, Seidman LJ, Tsuag MT: Diagnostic accuracy and linkage analysis: how useful are schizophrenia spectrum phenotypes? Am J Psychiatry 1995; 152:1286–1290

19. Hanson DR, Gottesman II, Heston LL: Some possible childhood indicators of adult schizophrenia inferred from children of schizophrenics. Br J Psychiatry 1976; 129:142–154

20. Niswander Kr, Gordon M: The Women and Their Pregnancies. Philadelphia, WB Saunders, 1972

21. Buka SL, Tsuang MT, Lipsitt LP: Pregnancy/delivery complications and psychiatric diagnosis: a prospective study. Arch Gen Psychiatry 1993; 50: 151–156

22. Myrianthopoulos NC, French KS: An application of the US Bureau of the Census socioeconomic index to a large, diversified patient population. Soc Sci Med 1968; 2:381–389

23. Robins LN, Helzer JE, Croughan J, Ratcliff KS: The National Institute of Mental Health Diagnostic Interview Schedule: Its history, characteristics, and validity. Arch Gen Psychiatry 1981; 38:381–389

24. Terman LM, Merrill MA: Stanford-Binet Intelligence Test: Manual for the 3rd Revision (Form LM). Boston, Houghton-Mifflin, 1960

25. Wechsler D: Manual for the Wechsler Intelligence Scale for Children. New York, Psychological Corp, 1949

26. Chapman LJ, Chapman JP: Strategies for resolving the heterogeneity of schizophrenics and their relatives using cognitive measures. J Abnorm Psychol 1989; 98:357–366

27. Matarazzo JD: Wechsler's Measurement and Appraisal of Adult Intelligence, 5th ed. New York, Oxford University Press, 1972

28. Dworkin R, Lewis J, Cornblatt B, Erlenmeyer-Kimling L: Social competence deficits in adolescents at risk for schizophrenia. J Nerv Ment Dis 1994; 182:103–108

Part VI

TREATMENT ISSUES

In the first paper in this section Howlin reviews psychological and educational treatments for autism. Autism, a pervasive developmental disorder, is characterized by profound deficits in communication and social understanding and by ritualistic and obsessional behaviors. Although the etiology or etiologies are unknown, genetic factors are most probably implicated in many cases. Parents often begin to have serious concerns about their child's development during the first year of life. Early worries tend to coalesce around abnormalities in communication, play or social responsiveness, or repetitive behaviors. As development proceeds, behavioral patterns are affected by the degree of cognitive impairment. Although autism can occur in individuals of all levels of ability, around 70–75% have some associated learning disabilities and around 50% have IQ's that are below 50. Those with severe to profound cognitive impairments are unlikely to develop useful speech, and will require specialized education and life-long care. Outcome is more variable among the 20% or so who have IQ's within the normal range. Many improve with age, and some may have successful careers, live more or less independently, and develop friendships. Others, however, remain highly dependent throughout their lives.

The fact that some children do show substantial improvements as they grow older has led to claims that particular treatments can significantly affect outcome, or even bring about a "cure." Howlin underscores the fact that to date there is no good evidence that any cures for autism exist. She emphasizes that while it is important not to appear unduly pessimistic or dismissive, it is equally important to try to help parents understand that there is no universal panacea. Nevertheless, it is now well established that early intervention, appropriately adapted to each individual child's pattern of strengths and weaknesses can have a significant impact on minimizing or avoiding behavioral problems and in helping to ensure that children are able to develop their existing skills to the fullest.

Howlin describes the principal diagnostic features of autism, linking each to specific behavioral problems as they may appear in both less able and more able children. Such considerations provide the basis for a functional analysis of problems that require specific intervention. In addition, effective treatment planning must also include information regarding cognitive and communicative capacity. The author summarizes well established interventions. In addition, helpful strategies for improving communication, ameliorating social difficulties, and coping with obsessional and ritualistic behaviors are described. The role of pharmacological treatments and educational placement is also discussed.

This paper provides the clinician with an excellent guide. Adherence to its recommendations will provide families with autistic children with "the information and support they need, in order to enable them to identify problems at an early stage, and to help them evolve management strategies that will minimize the impact of the child's social, communicative, and obsessional problems in later life." (p. 473)

The paper by Last, Hansen, and Franco is a report of a controlled study contrasting the efficacy of cognitive-behavioral treatment and educational-support therapy in the treatment of school refusal. School refusal is a relatively widespread psychiatric symptom that poses serious consequences, both in the short and long term. Clinically, behavioral treatments, most particularly exposure-based techniques have been used extensively to treat anxiety-based school refusal, but studies of effectiveness have been limited almost exclusively to single-case studies and uncontrolled case series.

The subjects of the present report included 56 children and adolescents who ranged in age from 6 to 17 years, who met the following criteria: 1) anxiety based school refusal; 2) current enrollment in elementary, middle or high school; 3) current DSM-III-R anxiety disorder diagnosis; 4) at least 10% absenteeism from classes for at least 1 month before intake; 5) no current diagnosis of major depression; and 6) no current use of psychiatric medication. Subjects were randomly assigned to either cognitive-behavioral therapy (CBT) or educational-support therapy (ES). Treatment was provided once/week with sessions lasting for 60 minutes. Detailed descriptions of each treatment modality are provided. The principal components of CBT included graduated in vivo exposure and coping self-statement training. ES therapy was a combination of educational presentations and supportive psychotherapy in which children were encouraged to talk about their fears and learn to distinguish between fear, anxiety, and phobias. In contrast to CBT, ES therapists refrained from providing specific encouragement for children to confront feared situations and children were not verbally reinforced for attending school, or taught how to modify maladaptive thoughts.

Both treatment groups had high and comparable expectations of therapeutic success. Contrary to the expectations of the investigators, however, the findings showed no differences between the cognitive-behavioral treatment and the educational-support treatment. Both treatments produced statistically and clinically meaningful improvements after 12 weeks as indicated by improved school attendance, and reduction in anxiety and depressive symptomatology. Treatment gains were maintained in both groups at a 4 week follow-up. Younger children and children with higher baseline school attendance levels showed the greatest improvement during therapy. Overall, the results underscore the effectiveness of psychosocial treatments for school refusal. However a more precise understanding of how factors such as age, duration, sociodemographic, and family attributes may relate to the differential effectiveness of alternative treatments requires further study.

20

Practitioner Review: Psychological and Educational Treatments for Autism

Patricia Howlin

St George's Hospital Medical School, London, U.K.

The review discusses various interventions that have been used in the treatment of children with autism. It concludes that no single mode of treatment is ever likely to be effective for all children and all families. Instead, intervention will need to be adapted to individual needs and the value of approaches that involve a functional analysis of problems is explored. It is suggested that many so called "challenging" behaviours result from the child's fundamental difficulties in communication and social understanding, or from the ritualistic and obsessional tendencies that are also characteristic of autism. Possible ways in which parents and teachers might deal with problems in these areas are discussed. The importance of early diagnosis, and with it early, practical advice for families is stressed.

Keywords: *Autism, intervention, prevention of problems.*

BACKGROUND

Autism is a pervasive developmental disorder that is usually apparent from early childhood (Volkmar, Stier, & Cohen, 1985). It is characterised by profound deficits in communication and social understanding and by ritualistic and obsessional behaviours. Although associated with a range of possible causes, genetic factors are probably implicated in the majority of cases (Bailey et al., 1995; Le Couteur et al., 1996).

The condition was first systematically described by Leo Kanner in the U.S.A. in 1943, but a remarkably similar account, written by Hans Asperger in Austria, appeared at much the same time (for an annotated translation of Asperger's initial paper, see Frith, 1991). Although there continues to be some debate about whether the two conditions described are quantitatively or qualitatively different (Lord & Rutter, 1994), current research suggests that there are few substantive differences, either in early history or outcome, between high-functioning children with autism and those with Asperger syndrome (Szatmari, Bartolucci, & Bremner,

Requests for reprints to: Dr Patricia Howlin, Department of Psychology, St George's Hospital Medical School, Cranmer Terrace, London SW17 0RE, U.K.

1989; Wing, 1981). ICD-10 and DSM-IV criteria for Asperger syndrome note the same obsessional and social-communication deficits as in autism; the distinguishing features are the presence of relatively normal cognitive skills and the lack of early language delays in individuals with Asperger syndrome.

Prevalence

Once considered to be a very rare condition, affecting only 3–4 individuals in every 10,000 (Lotter, 1996; Wing & Gould, 1979), recent studies have suggested much higher prevalence rates. Fombonne (1997), in a recent overview of epidemiological research, found estimates to vary from 0.7 to 15.5 per 10,000. His analysis indicates that although the average figure for children with "classic" autism is around 5 per 10,000, the rates are much higher if children within the wider "autistic spectrum" are included. This term includes individuals who "share a triad of impaired social interaction, communication, and imagination, associated with a rigid, repetitive pattern of behaviour . . . The triad can be recognised at all levels of intelligence and can occur alone or together with any other physical or psychological disorder" (Wing, 1996). On the basis of this definition, Wing concludes that the prevalence of individuals within the total autistic spectrum may be as high as 91 per 10,000.

Despite the wide variation in these figures, it is clear that children with autistic spectrum disorders are to be found much more frequently than was once thought. Moreover, because of their high rates of behavioural disturbance, such children may make considerable demands on Child Psychiatric or Learning Disability services.

The Course of the Disorder

It is now widely accepted that autism has an onset in infancy or early childhood (Volkman et al., 1985), and many parents have serious concerns about their child's development in the first year of life (Frith, Soares, & Wing, 1993; Gillberg et al., 1990; Howlin & Moore, 1997; Johnson, Siddons, Frith, & Morton, 1992; Smith, Chung, & Vostanis, 1994). These early anxieties tend to focus around abnormalities in communication, play, or social responsiveness, or on repetitive behaviours.

As children grow older, the pattern of their development is largely affected by their degree of cognitive impairment. Although the syndrome of autism can occur in individuals of all levels of ability, the majority (around 70–75%) have some associated learning disabilities and around 50% have an IQ below 50. In those with severe to profound cognitive impairments useful speech is unlikely to develop; this group also tends to develop more disturbed behaviours, such as self-injury, and will almost invariably require specialist education and life-long care. In the 20% or so of individuals who have an IQ within the normal range, outcome is much more variable. Most individuals tend to improve with age (Eaves & Ho, 1996; Gillberg & Steffenberg, 1987; Lockyer & Rutter, 1969, 1970; Piven, Harper, Palmer, & Arndt, 1995), but whereas for some, adolescence brings about an upsurge in problems, for others, notably those who become more aware of their difficulties, it can be a period of remarkable improvement and change (Kanner, 1973). Within this group, some individuals remain highly dependent throughout their lives; others make successful careers, they may live more or less independently, develop friendships or even (in a tiny minority of cases) get married (see Howlin, 1997a, in press for review). Nevertheless, even amongst those who make greatest progress, their communication and social problems continue to affect many aspects of their lives, as first-hand accounts by people such as Donna Williams (1992, 1994), Temple Grandin (1992), or Jim Sinclair (1992) clearly illustrate.

TREATMENTS FOR AUTISM

The fact that some children do show substantial improvements as they grow older has led to claims that particular treatments can significantly affect outcome, or even bring about a "cure." Among such interventions are "Holding" therapy (Richer & Zappella, 1989; Welch, 1988); music therapy (Trevarthen, Aitken, Papoudi, & Roberts, 1996); scotopic sensitivity training, which involves the wearing of specialist spectacles (Irlen, 1995); auditory integration, which focuses on desensitisation to sounds of particular frequencies (Rimland & Edelson, 1994, 1995; Stehli, 1992); as well as various drug and vitamin treatments (see Howlin, 1997b, for a detailed review of different therapies).

Few if any of these claims are supported by adequate experimental data. One such example, prominent in the early 1990s, was "Facilitated Communication." This involved physical support (to the hand, arm, or wrist) to help children use communication boards of various kinds. The technique was said to demonstrate that individuals with autism were actually of superior intellect, and was claimed to lead to "Communication Unbound" (Biklen, 1993). Subsequent controlled investigations have consistently indicated that responses are almost invariably under the control of the facilitator, not the client (Bebko, Perry, & Bryson, 1996; Green, 1994).

A variety of teaching approaches has also been promoted as having a significant impact on outcome. These include the Japanese-based "Daily Life Therapy," with its focus on highly structured, physically oriented programmes, practised in the Higashi schools (see Gould, Rigg, & Bignell, 1991, for details). The "Options" method of Kaufman (1981), which relies on therapists participating in the child's ritualistic and obsessional behaviours in order to foster social contacts, also claims "miraculous" results. Another approach, currently receiving much publicity, is the intensive early intervention programme of Lovaas and his colleagues (McEachin, Smith, & Lovaas, 1993; Lovaas, 1993; Perry, Cohen, & DeCarlo, 1995). It is said that 42% of children with autism "maintain normal functioning at follow-up" (average age of 11.5 years) if they are exposed to very intensive (40 hours per week), home-based behavioural programmes from around the ages of 2 to 4 years (Lovaas, 1996). Although the value of behavioural approaches has clearly been demonstrated in many studies, including those of Lovaas himself, these recent claims have aroused criticism concerning possible biases in subject selection, problems of research design, and, most importantly, in the definitions of "normality" used (Schopler, Short, & Mesibov, 1989). Thus, children are claimed to have "recovered" if they are of normal IQ and can be assimilated into mainstream education. Since around 20% of all autistic children are of normal intellectual ability, and many attend mainstream schools despite showing the characteristic triad of impairments, such criteria cannot be used as evidence of normal or even near normal functioning (Mesibov, 1993).

From a practical point of view, too, this approach poses many problems. The programme involves 40 hours of one-to-one intervention a week for at least 2 years and, whereas some families many be able to cope with such demands, the cost for others in emotional, financial, or practical terms is often far too high. Moreover, although programmes of this kind may enhance short-term progress there is little to show that the benefits last beyond childhood. Thus Howlin, Goode, and Rutter (unpublished data) found that, in adulthood, there were few if any significant differences, either in cognitive attainments or in measures of independent living, between individuals who had received home-based behavioural programmes when they were younger, and their matched controls who had not.

ADVISING PARENTS ABOUT DIFFERENT TREATMENTS

To date, there is no good evidence that any cures for autism exist. Many able children do well despite totally inadequate provision, and to a great extent eventual outcome is dependant on innate cognitive, linguistic, and social abilities. However, clinicians are frequently approached by parents who have heard or read about particular "miracle cures" and who, understandably, want to know whether the treatment will work for their own child. Although it is important not to appear unduly pessimistic or dismissive, it is equally important to try to help parents understand that there can be no universal panacea. After all, even within physical medicine, drugs that have brought widespread advantages to many, such as aspirin or antibiotics, may prove ineffective or even harmful for certain individuals. Before parents succumb to the temptation of parting from large amounts of money, or in some cases (as in specialist boarding school provision) from their own child, the clinician should help them to try to obtain as much information as possible, not only about the children for whom the treatment has worked, but also about the characteristics of those for whom it has been less successful. (Claims that the treatment works equally well for everyone need to be treated with particular caution.) They should ask whether treatment seems to work better with older or younger children; for those with or without language; or those who are more, or less, cognitively able. Parents should be encouraged to find out what sort of assessments are carried out prior to treatment and what methods (other than selective anecdotal reports) have been used to assess outcome. They also need accurate information about what happens to other children with autism as they grow older, so that reported outcomes following treatment can be judged in the light of what might be expected in the absence of any special treatments. Before jumping headlong into therapy, families should be helped, too, to weigh up the overall cost of treatment; the amount of time that will be involved; any foreseeable pressures or restrictions on other aspects of family life; or the possible impact on the child of having to cope with major change, or even separation from the family. Finally, detailed information should also be provided on *local* facilities, support groups, educational provision, and so forth. These are unlikely to have been widely advertised, nor to have featured in the national press, but may well be able to provide families and children with much-needed, and sometimes highly effective, help. If parents are better informed of what is available within their own area, they may find less need to seek solutions further afield.

The clinician needs to avoid encouraging unrealistic expectations about future progress whilst not giving parents too pessimistic a view of what the child is likely to achieve. Thus, it is now well established that early intervention, appropriately adapted to each individual child's pattern of strengths and weaknesses, can have a significant impact on minimising or avoiding behavioural problems and in helping to ensure that children are able to develop their existing skills to the full (Howlin & Rutter, 1987).

Understanding the Problems of Children with Autism

Articles on the association between autism and "challenging" behaviour appear throughout the child psychiatric literature. Similarly, behavioural journals abound with detailed accounts of the techniques that have been successful in modifying aggressive, destructive, and (although to a lesser extent) self-injurious behaviours. However, whereas the seriousness of such problems cannot be underrated, it is also important to recognise that, given the severity of their social and communication deficits and their need for ritual and routine, many children with autism perhaps show far *fewer* challenges than might be expected. Imagine for a moment how any "normal" person might react to a world in which they are able to understand almost nothing of what is happening around them; in which they are thrown daily into an everchanging and unpredictable environment; where they lack even the rudimentary verbal skills necessary to make their needs known; where they have no access to the internalised, imaginative facilities that are so crucial for dealing effectively with anxiety, uncertainty, and distress. Most such "normal" individuals would rapidly resort to a whole range of retaliatory behaviours, which if simply responded to by "time-out," or "extinction," or even rewards for "incompatible behaviour" would probably escalate dramatically. Of course, problem behaviours in autism, as in any other conditions, will be maintained or increased by the attention or reinforcement they elicit, and techniques such as time out, extinction, or differential reinforcement can serve an important role (see Emerson, 1995). However, they are not specific to the treatment of autism. The focus of this article, therefore, will be on the underlying causes of behavioural disturbances and the role that social, communication, and obsessional difficulties play in causing or maintaining these (see Table 1). Intervention strategies, too, will concentrate on the need to improve functioning in these areas, rather than on the direct elimination of problems.

DEVELOPING INTERVENTION PROGRAMMES

Pre-treatment Assessments

Before embarking on any treatment programme it is essential to obtain adequate information, not only on the behaviours to be modified, but on the child as well. This is because apparently similar problems can have very different causes in different children, or within the same child at different times. For example, "aggressive behaviour," may result from a child's inability to communicate; because he or she lacks more effective strategies to control the environment; because of the attention such behaviours receive; because of frustration, distress, anxiety, or because of disruption to rituals and routines. Moreover, in many instances, a combination of these variables may be operating. Pain or physical illness are other important factors to bear in mind. Certain stereotyped and self-injurious behaviours, for example, have been found to follow minor illnesses including dermatitis and otitis media

TABLE 1

The Principal Diagnostic Features of Autism and Their Association with Behaviour Problems

Area of Deficit	Associated Problems	
	Less Able Children	More Able Children
Impairments in communication and understanding		
Inadequate language	Frustration, aggression; unacceptable attempts to control environment	Inappropriate use of speech (echolalia, verbal routines, obsessional questions etc.)
Poor comprehension	Anxiety, distress, and disruptive behaviours	Apparent lack of co-operation
Lack of internal language	No ability to play or occupy self	Poor imaginative skills; limited self control
Impairments in social understanding		
Lack of social awareness	Withdrawal and isolation	Attempts to socialise often inappropriate; may offend or antagonise others
	Disturbed/disruptive and inappropriate behaviours in public	Inability to "read" others' feelings makes them appear insensitive, callous, even cruel
Obsessions and rituals		
Obsessional behaviour patterns	Can severely limit the acquisition of other more productive behaviours/skills	May involve other people in routines/rituals; can impose major limitations on other people's activities too
Disruption of routines	Can result in serious distress, disruption and aggression	
Dislike of change	Leads to very rigid and inflexible patterns of behaviour and great distress and anxiety if change is necessary	
Obsessional interests		May be pursued regardless of the consequences. Constant talk about these can antagonise others

458

(Hall, 1997; Oliver, 1995). As children with autism may suffer more frequently from ear infections (Konstantareas & Homatidis, 1987), it is clearly important for the clinician to rule these out as a possible cause of episodic behavioural changes, especially in nonverbal children. Gunsett, Mulick, Fernald, and Martin (1989) also stress the importance of carrying out medical screening *before* any psychological programmes are implemented in patients with profound learning disabilities. In a series of 13 cases, referred for self-injurious behaviours, 10 were found to have a physical basis for the behaviour. These included limb fractures, hernias, urinary tract infections, ear infections, bowel problems, incorrect medication, toxic levels of anticonvulsants, and progressive brain deterioration.

Individual Assessment

As noted earlier, autism is frequently referred to as a "spectrum" disorder (Wing, 1996), in that it can range from relatively mild to profoundly handicapping. Similarly, it can affect children across the entire cognitive continuum, and is found in those who are nonverbal as well as those whose spoken language is apparently unimpaired.

Dealing with the temper tantrums of a nonspeaking 4-year-old child with an IQ of 30 will require very different strategies to those appropriate for a highly verbal 14-year-old with an IQ of 130. Programmes that are pitched inappropriately high or low will be unlikely to succeed. Thus, standardised cognitive and linguistic assessments can be a crucial component of any intervention, since informal observations alone may give a misleading impression on intellectual ability. Children who appear alert and interested in their environment, or who have one or two isolated skills, may mistakenly be viewed as very intelligent; those who are able to follow simple instructions (often only with accompanying gesture or other cues) may be described, quite erroneously, as "understanding every word you say"; children who have an extensive expressive vocabulary may actually have very limited comprehension skills. Conversely, children whose speech is slow and halting, and who appear to show little interest in the activities around them, may be classified as having severe learning difficulties, when in fact many aspects of their cognitive development lie within the normal range.

Unfortunately, because of the social and communication difficulties associated with autism, it is often believed that traditional psychometric testing has little or no role to play in assessment. Many psychologists, especially within the educational system, still tend to rely on unstructured observations. Although these are undoubtedly important, a relatively brief testing session can reveal unsuspected areas of skill or deficit, which may be very relevant for intervention. Moreover, as long as the appropriate tests are used, cognitive assessments on autistic children are just as reliable as testing in other groups (Rutter, 1985). The Appendix provides information on standardised tests of language and cognition that have proved useful when working with this group of children (see also Marans, 1997).

Behavioural Assessment

Traditional behavioural therapy has long espoused the ABC approach to the analysis of behavioural problems. Thus, following precise delineation of the *Behaviour* to be modified, attempts are made to identify the Antecedents and the Consequences of that behaviour. However, in the case of many children with autism, a focus on the observed behaviour does not necessarily lead to the most appropriate form of treatment (Emerson & Bromley, 1995). It may also prove extremely difficult to establish, with any degree of certainty, either the antecedents or the consequences of the behaviour *as perceived by the child*. For example, a child might begin to self-injure in a particular setting, because he or she has been reminded of an earlier (but no longer existing) distressing occurrence that had previously ceased when self-injury commenced. In such a case, direct observations will be of little use in identifying the relevant variables.

Because the observed *form* of a challenging behaviour may give few clues as to its real role, recent intervention studies have focused instead on the *function* or "message" of that behaviour. The aim is to establish what it achieves for all the individuals concerned (carers as well as children) and to explore the alternative behaviours that might be encouraged to replace it (Sturney, 1996).

THE FUNCTIONAL ANALYSIS OF BEHAVIOUR

Highly sophisticated, experimental studies of the "challenging" behaviours shown by children with autism have consistently demonstrated that many such behaviours serve an important communicative function (Durand, 1990). Indeed, analyses of these behaviours suggest that they may sometimes be the only way in which a child with limited linguistic abilities can rapidly, effectively, and predictably control his or her environment.

Five main functions of aggressive, self-injurious, stereotyped, or other disruptive behaviours have been identified (Durand & Carr, 1991; Durand & Crimmins, 1988). These are:

1. To indicate the need for help or attention.

2. To escape from stressful situations or activities.

3. To obtain desired objects.

4. To protest against unwanted events/activities.

5. To obtain stimulation.

If the primary function of a behaviour can be identified it is then possible to provide the child with alternative means to obtain the same ends. The choice of strategy taught will depend on the child's cognitive and linguistic ability, but might range from teaching him to push a button, lever, or switch, or to use signs, symbols, pictures, or words and simple phrases (such as "Help me"). As long as the newly acquired behaviour has a rapid and predictable impact on the child's environment this can result in significant reductions in undesirable behaviours (Durand & Carr, 1991).

Despite the surge in publications emanating from this approach in recent years, it is important to be aware that the majority of studies has been conducted in highly staffed experimental settings. Detailed analyses of the possible functions of undesirable behaviours may require considerable time, expertise, and technology and are often impracticable within mainstream settings. As Owens and MacKinnon (1993) note, "Functional analysis isn't as easy as ABC." Emerson and Bromley (1995) also warn of the problems inherent in this approach. Human behaviour will always be determined by many factors, and by different factors at different times, and they found that often it was not possible to determine the function underlying a particular challenging behaviour. In around 25% of cases, no specific function could be identified, and a third of behaviours appeared to be influenced by multiple factors. Hall (1997), in a very sophisticated assessment of self-injurious and stereotyped behaviours in 16 children with severe to profound learning disabilities, was able to identify a consistent underlying function for self-injury in only 4 cases and for stereotyped behaviours in 6 cases. Moreover, knowledge of the function underlying one class of behaviours is not necessarily of any value in predicting the behavioural function underlying other forms of challenging behaviour shown by the same individual.

A further problem with studies employing this methodology is that they do not tend to use random control trials. Most are multiple baseline, single-case, or small group reports, and although those that have been published are certainly encouraging, there is no way of ascertaining how many unsuccessful studies may also have been conducted.

Despite these difficulties, it is apparent that this approach to assessment and treatment can play a major role in reducing challenging behaviours. A number of rating scales or questionnaires have now been produced to assist carers in identifying the possible functions of disruptive behaviours (see Sturmey, 1996). The most widely used of these is the "Motivation Assessment Scale" (Durand & Crimmins, 1988), which attempts to classify behaviour into four main categories: attention seeking; self stimulatory; escape or avoidance; or as indicating the need for help or assistance. However, there are doubts about the reliability and validity of this scale when used in naturalistic settings, and, more importantly, the four summary categories cannot encompass all the possible reasons for disruptive behaviours. In particular, they cannot identify idiosyncratic or multifunction causes (Sturmey, 1995).

A somewhat less complex questionnaire has been developed by Schuler, Peck, Willard, and Theimer (1989). This can be used by parents or teachers and, by systematically exploring how the child expresses his or her need to do something (sit by someone, get attention, obtain food or other object, protest if something is taken away, etc.), this process can again help to indicate how behaviours that are often viewed as "inappropriate" (screaming; self-injury; tantrums; aggression etc.) can have important communicative functions. This information can then be used to plan ways in which alternative and more acceptable responses might be established. Moreover, by helping carers to appreciate that such behaviours may be a function of poor *communication* skills, rather than being "deliberate" acts of aggression or provocation, this approach can also have a very positive effect on other people's attitudes and responses towards the child.

In the following sections, strategies for dealing with the problems that appear to underlie many challenging behaviours are described. However, again, although there are many single-case and small group studies, often using multiple baseline or ABA type designs, that testify to the success for these techniques, there are very few randomised treatment trials. Thus, information on overall success rates, or on the types of children or problems for which the treatments are most/least successful, remains very limited.

INCREASING COMMUNICATIVE SKILLS

Despite some intrinsic problems, the emphasis in "functional analysis" studies on the need to develop effective communication skills has had a significant impact on therapy. It is estimated that around half of all children with autism fail to develop functional speech (Lord & Rutter, 1994), and even amongst those with a good expressive vocabulary there are persisting and pervasive impairments in the communicative use of language, and in understanding complex or abstract concepts.

For younger children, who are able to use some words or sounds spontaneously, individualised language programmes are important for improving comprehension, increasing the complexity of speech, or correcting problems of intonation or articulation. However, it is essential that such programmes are aimed at a level that is appropriate to the child's cognitive and linguistic development and that the words or concepts involved are ones that are of direct relevance to the child. Language cannot be taught in brief, 1-hour speech therapy sessions, but language therapists can play a crucial role in ensuring that all those living and working with the child use effective and consistent strategies to encourage speech, develop imaginative skills, and improve understanding. Descriptive assessments of the way in which children use and understand language, such as the Derbyshire Language Scheme, the Pragmatics Profile of Early Communication Skills (which is based on a structured parental interview, Dewart & Summers, 1988), or the Social Use of Language Programme (Rinaldi, 1992) can also be used to provide guidelines for improving receptive and conversational skills. As long as the words taught are of practical value to the child, in that they allow him or her immediate access to desired objects or activities, then artificial rewards should not be needed. Indeed, there is evidence that the unnecessary introduction of extrinsic reinforcers may actually interfere with learning (Howlin & Rutter, 1987).

Follow-up studies indicate that most children with autism who have not developed useful speech by the age of 6 or 7 years remain very impaired in their ability to communicate verbally. For them, some form of alternative communication system will be required, and the appropriate choice of system will depend on the child's particular pattern of skills and disabilities. Layton and Watson (1995) provide a useful breakdown of the different skills required for using signs, pictures or written words (see Table 2).

Sign systems, especially those developed for use with children with learning disabilities, have been widely used to augment communication skills. The Makaton system, for example (Walker, 1980), is extensively used in schools in the U.K. This has several different levels of complexity, and now incorporates symbols as well as signs. However, in the case of children with autism, the evidence to show that communication can be significantly enhanced by the acquisition of sign is, in fact, somewhat limited. Thus, Kiernan (1983) found that although some children had acquired an extensive signing vocabulary (400 sign combinations) or had begun to use speech after 2 to 3 years, others had managed to learn only 1 or 2 signs. Other studies indicate that problems of generalisation and maintenance are similar to those experienced in verbal training programmes. Attwood, Frith, and Hermelin (1988) found that the signing of children with autism was very similar to their use of language—i.e. it was stereotyped, repetitive, and used mainly to achieve the child's immediate needs. Signing was rarely used to share experiences, to express feelings or emotions, or to communicate in a reciprocal and spontaneous fashion.

TABLE 2
Assessment for Communication Strategies (from Layton & Watson, 1995)

	Signing	Pictures/Pictographs	Writing
Characteristics			
Easily shaped	Yes	Yes	Fairly
Portability	High	Moderate	High
Permanence	No	Yes	Yes
Speed	Moderate/Low	Low	High/Moderate
Phrases possible	Moderate	Limited	Yes
Iconicity	Some	Yes	No
Reciprocity	Limited	Limited	High
Skills required			
Motor skills	Yes	No	Yes
High co-operation	Not initially	Not initially	Not initially
Demands on others' understanding	Yes	No	No

On the whole, a pictorially based system makes least demands on cognitive, linguistic, or memory skills, although again it is essential that the pictures or photographs used reflect the individual's particular interests or needs. It also seems to be important for the child to take an *active role* in using and handling such materials (e.g. using Velcro or stickers to indicate the activities completed, or to be done, rather than looking passively at charts constructed by others). The PECS (Picture Exchange Communication System) of Bondy and Frost (1996) is a good example of how this can be done.

Once the association between the activity/object and picture/symbol/chart is established, individualized sets of photographs or pictures can be used very effectively to increase both communication and understanding (Quill, 1995). Whatever system is used must be readily available to the child and his carers. Possible ways of ensuring easy access are to have the picture/symbol/word sets on cards in a simple "Filofax" system; attached to the child's belt; in a hip bag; or worn, like an identity badge, on a chain. Materials also need to be strongly bound, and quickly replaceable. Equipment that is forever getting lost, or dog-eared cards that no-one can read, are of little use.

Computerised communicative devices have become steadily more sophisticated in recent years. Some are now specially designed for children with autism, in that they have a specific focus on turn taking and reciprocal interaction. Interchangeable keyboards of increasing complexity make it possible for children to progress gradually from single-symbol boards (with for example a large red square or circle that will emit a sound to attract attention) to, eventually, the independent use of multisymbol displays, which are personally tailored to the individual's own environment, needs or interests. Computers can, of course, also be very valuable general teaching aids for more able children who may respond better to visually, rather than verbally, presented material. However, when using computers with this group, care needs to be taken to ensure that some social interaction is also required, otherwise an obsession with the technology may take over.

Some parents understandably express concerns that, by focusing on alternative forms of communication, this will minimise the chances of their child ever learning to speak.

However, developing competence in the use of signs or symbols may actually encourage some previously nonverbal children to use speech (Howlin, 1989). And, for those who do not, it is crucial to establish an effective and socially acceptable form of communication as early as possible.

It is also important to be aware that children with no *apparent* language difficulties may also require some augmentative communication systems from time to time. Almost all children with autism, no matter how able, have difficulties with abstract language or in dealing with complex sequences of instructions. Thus, although they may understand the *individual words* spoken, they may well misinterpret or fail to understand the underlying meaning of what is said. If told, "Go and ask your mum if she wants a cup of tea" they may well do so, but are unlikely to bring back any reply! In such circumstances it is essential that the speaker makes sure that the words used adequately convey what is wanted (i.e. "Go and ask your mum if she wants a cup of tea and then come straight back and tell me what she said"). In addition, especially when the task requirements are more complex, checklists of simple instructions, picture or cartoon sequences of the activities to be completed, or symbols designating the tasks to be done, can all help greatly to improve co-operation.

One example of a very successful, visually based instructional system is the TEACCH educational programme, initially developed in North Carolina (Schopler, Mesibov, & Hearsey, 1995). This relies heavily on visual cues or "jigs," so that throughout the child's school day, different coloured work areas or different coloured containers are used to indicate where the child should be; what he or she should be doing; where work should begin or be placed when finished; and even where to play. This combination of a highly structured and visually based programme can be very effective in improving work-related skills and reducing inappropriate behaviours. However, as with any treatment package, it is important that the basic components are adapted to suit the needs of the individual and his or her environment. It is also important to plan for the gradual reduction of such cues if the child is eventually to be able to function in less structured surroundings (Jordan & Powell, 1995).

Echolalic Speech

Echolalia, both immediate and delayed, is a common feature of autism. Although often considered as inappropriate and noncommunicative, as well as sometimes being extremely irritating, careful analysis indicates that much echoing serves identifiable, and important, communicative functions (Prizant & Schuler, 1987; Rydell & Prizant, 1995). As with any other "autistic" behaviour it is crucial to assess the role that the echolalia serves before attempts are made to modify it.

Echoing may be an indication of children's lack of understanding; it may be important in helping them to consolidate what others say, as well as providing them with the opportunity to practise new words or expressions. Moreover, in that echolalia is likely to increase when children are distressed or anxious, it may signify that they are experiencing undue pressure (Rydell & Mirenda, 1994). Repetition can also play a role in rehearsing potentially worrying situations, in dealing with feelings of anger, or in helping to allay anxiety. Greater understanding of *why* such behaviours may occur, and recognition of the potential importance of these, should lead to more appropriate intervention strategies, with a focus on altering the factors causing the echolalia, rather than on the symptom itself.

Ensuring that instructions or questions are fully understood, by simplifying the language used, or supplementing this with pictures, written instructions, or other cues, may significantly reduce stereotyped and echolalic speech (Rydell & Prizant, 1995). Repetitive questioning (which often tends to escalate the more adults respond to it), may also be reduced by directing the child to charts, pictures, calendars, or lists, which provide him or her with the required information in a more permanent form. Dealing with unnecessary stress, by supplying the child with adequate help in cognitively or socially demanding situations, may also have a considerable impact. Minimising disruption to daily routine, ensuring that daily life is as predictable and as consistent as possible, and that necessary changes are predicted well in advance, can all help to decrease the frequency of repetitive speech.

Stereotyped speech (bombarding visitors with questions about the make of their car; or lengthy monologues about the lighting systems on particular railway networks) may be an indication that although the child wishes to make social contact, he or she lacks the necessary conversational skills. Again, help to initiate and cope with basic conversational exchanges—perhaps by utilising role-play or drama techniques—is often the most effective way of addressing problems of this kind.

Of course, stereotyped speech may sometimes be used deliberately because of the attention it generates. Repetitive phrases, swearing, or other provocative utterances often provoke a rapid response from adults and other children, and are all too easily reinforced. In such cases, as well as increasing the child's repertoire of appropriate speech, strategies involving extinction (no reinforcement) or "time out" (removal of ongoing rewards) may be necessary. Such techniques, if used *consistently*, can have a rapid and positive effect on behaviour—the problem lies in being consistent. Thus, swearing or other abusive language may be relatively easy to ignore by parents who are relaxed and in control. After a sleepless night; when under stress; or in conditions where they have little control (e.g. in church, on the top of a bus, or in a supermarket queue) it can be almost impossible not to respond. Intermittent reinforcement of this kind can actually result in an increase in unwanted behaviour, and hence extinction programmes, although highly effective in principle, can prove much more difficult to implement in practice. Parents also need to be given support during the early stages of such programmes when the "extinction burst" (an initial increase in the behaviour when reinforcement is first withdrawn) is likely to occur.

Improving Others' Communication Skills

Although, with appropriate help and encouragement, children with autism may show improvements in both their use and understanding of language, the communication deficit is central to the disorder and no amount of therapy will overcome this entirely. Much can be achieved, however, by making the adults in the child's environment more attentive to the language that they themselves use. Instructions should be simple and concise, and every attempt made to ensure that the words used actually mean what they say. Metaphor, slang, and colloquialisms are all best avoided, whilst irony or threats such as "I'll kill you if you do that again" can cause untold distress. Even vague concepts such as "Perhaps"; "I'll think about it"; "We'll see" are liable to produce confusion and anxiety. If the child is required to do something, an unambiguous request such as "Please give me the bread" will be more productive than a phrase such as "Can you pass the bread?" (which might well be answered in the affirmative but without resulting in any action). Other apparently minor changes in wording can have surprising effects. One girl's severe distress at being told, prior to a trip to France, that she would be "going to sleep on the train" changed to pleasure and relief when this was altered to "going to bed in the train." A teenage boy who became rude and abusive if ever he was asked by teachers or doctors "What year is your birthday?" (the obvious answer, to him, was "Every year") answered politely if they asked instead, "What year were you born?"

Unfortunately, predicting in advance what particular turn of phrase is likely to give rise to problems is very much a matter of trial and error. However, whenever a request is not complied with, or if a statement meets with an upsurge in echolalia, irritation, or anxiety, the speaker should first assume that what he or she has said has been misunderstood or misinterpreted. Simplifying or changing the words that are used may have a much greater impact than attempts to modify the child's response. And again, the value of written or pictorial cues to augment the words used cannot be over-emphasised.

AMELIORATING SOCIAL DIFFICULTIES

The social impairment in autism affects almost every aspect of the child's functioning, whatever his or her intellectual ability. In children who are more severely handicapped, highly inappropriate behaviours such as screaming, undressing, or masturbating in public may be a major cause of disturbance. In the case of those who are more able, the problems tend to be much more subtle, and include impairments in empathy, social understanding, or reciprocity and synchronisation (i.e. saying or doing things that in themselves are not unacceptable, but at the wrong time, in the wrong place, or with the wrong person).

In many ways, the more obvious social problems are often easier to deal with. Firm and consistent guidance is needed from the outset about what behaviours are, or are not, acceptable. If, as a small child, there are clear and invariable rules—such as never undressing or masturbating in public, not touching strangers or their belongings—and if the child also learns that disruptive behaviour in response to such prohibitions results in the cessation of more pleasurable activities, then such behaviours are much less likely to give rise to problems in later childhood. Children with autism are, by definition, somewhat rigid in their behaviour patterns, and if acceptable behaviours are established when they are very young these will tend to persist. The converse, of course, is also true, so that once unacceptable behaviours take hold, they will be very difficult to shift in later years, especially as the child grows bigger. Parents, however, may need a great deal of help and support during these early years if they are to develop effective management strategies. Young children with autism are clearly often deeply disturbed and confused, and most parents, unwilling to increase their distress, will tend to give in to many of their demands. Helping parents to understand when it is acceptable or necessary to say "No," and to recognise when consistency is crucial, can help to avoid future problems. Removing a screaming 3-year-old from a shop because he cannot have what he wants may be embarrassing enough; attempts to remove a screaming 13-year-old will prove far more difficult.

It is also important that parents are made aware of behaviours that, although not necessarily inappropriate in a young child, may become progressively more unacceptable as he or she grows older. A young girl who warmly hugs and kisses everyone she meets, or a little boy who loves the feel of women's tights, may be treated with fond indulgence. The same behaviours in older teenagers or adults will provoke a very different response! Difficulties in social understanding and awareness mean that the child with autism will either be impervious to other peoples' changed reactions or that they will be totally confused by the fact that behaviours that were once tolerated, even encouraged, are suddenly deemed to be "wrong." On the whole, it is far preferable to introduce simple and invariable rules (you only kiss people in the family; you can only touch mummy's tights) that may be relaxed in later years if necessary, than to have initially very loose guidelines that suddenly have to be made more restrictive. A toddler who has been allowed to take off all his clothes whenever he wanted will find it very difficult to change this behaviour when he begins attending school. On the other hand, a child who has only ever been allowed to take her clothes off in the home can be taught, as she grows older, that it may be acceptable to remove her clothes in other *specified* situations, such as the family doctor's surgery.

The major problem, here, is that social behaviour is not governed by simple rules; if such rules do exist they are highly complex and constantly changing according to the social context. Nevertheless, as far as the child with autism is concerned it is preferable to have consistent (if sometimes inadequate) rules than no rules at all. It is dealing with more complex and subtle social deficits that presents much more of a challenge. Knowing how to make friends, recognising what other people are feeling or thinking, and reacting appropriately, are fundamental human aptitudes; they are not rule-based skills that are acquired through teaching. Thus, interventions designed to overcome such basic deficits are almost certain to be limited in their effectiveness. There is some evidence that social skills groups, specifically designed for children or adults with autism, can improve certain aspects of social functioning (Mesibov, 1984; T. I. Williams, 1989), but on the whole generalisation to untrained settings tends to be limited. Social skills training is best conducted in each and every situation to which the child is exposed, so that he or she learns how to respond appropriately at home, with relatives, in shops, at school, or with the peer group. Each of these situations will require different social strategies and teaching in situ is far more likely to be effective than teaching in the relative isolation of a "social skills group."

Learning how to interact appropriately with children of their own age is often one of the most difficult and demanding tasks for a child with austism. The "rules" of engagement; of knowing how to enter a group of children; how to join in with their activities; and how to talk to them, are all highly complex, unwritten, generally poorly understood (Dodge, Schlundt, Schocken, & Delugach, 1983), and hence almost impossible to teach. Because of this, some researchers have shifted the focus of attention onto nonautistic peers, systematically teaching them to play and interact more effectively with the child with autism (Lord, 1995a; Wolfberg & Schuler, 1993). Roeyers (1996) has also shown that simply providing nonhandicapped peers with information about children with autism and general instructions about ways to encourage them to play can improve the frequency and style of joint interactions. Programmes of this kind can result in important short-term gains, and are clearly important for improving opportunities for integration. Nevertheless, they do require skilled input from teachers if the interactions are to be effective, and it can prove difficult to maintain peers' co-operation over the longer term (Lord, 1984).

Other recent approaches to the treatment of social problems have focused on more fundamental deficits in "theory of mind." The inability of children with autism to "mind-read," i.e. to understand other people's beliefs, ideas, thoughts or feelings, has received much attention over recent years (see Baron-Cohen, 1995, for an excellent summary). Several studies have found that even after relatively brief intervention programmes involving computers, pictures, photographs, toys, or actors, children with autism do show improvements in their ability to understand beliefs and emotions (Swettenham, 1995; Ozonoff & Miller, 1995; Hadwin, Baron-Cohen, Howlin, & Hill, 1996). Not unexpectedly, given the brevity and limitations of such programmes, generalisation to other, untrained aspects of "theory of mind" is poor. Nevertheless, even this limited success suggests that training packages specifically designed to increase the ability to "mind-read" could be an important and valuable addition to the educational curricula for many children with autism (Howlin, Baron-Cohen, Hadwin, & Swettenham, in press).

COPING WITH OBSESSIONAL AND RITUALISTIC BEHAVIOURS

Ritualistic and obsessional behaviours are a further major cause of problems in autism. Many different ways of dealing with these problems have been reported in the literature, but generally it seems that a "graded change" approach to intervention is the most effective. For a child with autism, obsessional and ritualistic activities often play a crucial role in reducing anxiety or in providing them with some control over what is otherwise a very confusing and unpredictable world (see Jolliffe, Lansdown, & Robinson, 1992). If an attempt is suddenly made to restrict or prohibit such behaviours, this can lead to unacceptably high levels of anxiety and distress, and because of the resulting disturbance most parents quickly give in. Moreover, without careful planning, children may well develop replacement rituals or obsessions that prove even more disruptive.

In order to maintain parental co-operation and consistency, it is generally more effective to modify the behaviour *gradually*, until it no longer interferes with the child's, or the family's, other activities. Howlin and Rutter (1987) and Schopler (1995) describe a variety of strategies that can be used to reduce obsessional and ritualistic behaviours. However, the crucial goals are to minimise anxiety and distress (for both parents and child); to aim for gradual but achievable behavioural change, rather than dramatic improvements; to weigh up the potential advantages, as well as obvious disadvantages, of the obsession and wherever possible to capitalise on these.

The following guidelines seem to be particularly helpful.

1. *Establish clear and consistent rules* for: *Where and When* the activity is permitted; *Who* it can be carried out with; or *How long* it can go on for. This ensures that the child knows not only when the behaviour in *not* permitted, but also when it *is* allowed.

2. *Ensure that change is introduced one step at a time*, so that any distress to the child is kept to a minimum. Setting very small goals optimises the chance of long-term success.

3. *Explore possible underlying factors.* High levels of obsessional behaviour are often an indication of uncertainty, anxiety, or distress. Such problems can be reduced significantly by ensuring that the child's daily programme is predictable, and appropriately stimulating and structured.

4. *Consider possible environmental modifications.* Reducing unnecessary demands on the child, encouraging more flexible attitudes in adults, or making relatively simple modifications to the daily routine or environment can also help to reduce obsessional behaviours. In mainstream schools, for example, many children with autism become very distressed (and hence more ritualistic) if they are forced to take part in group games or "join in" at play times, or when they have to scramble to find somewhere to sit at the start of each lesson. Allowing children to avoid such socially demanding situations by letting them spend play/game times in the library or carrying out other tasks, or providing them with a set place in which to sit, may again have much greater impact than a complex behavioural programme.

5. *Help children to cope with change.* Although a structured and settled daily programme is essential for progress, it is neither possible, nor productive, to avoid change completely. Fortunately, in many cases it is *unpredictable* change that causes most difficulties. Thus, the solution is to ensure that the child is fully aware of what is going to happen at any time. Since verbal explanations are rarely adequate, visual representations (in the form of picture calendars, symbols, or written lists) of forthcoming activities, or of alterations to the regular routine, are most likely to be effective.

6. *Make use of obsessions.* Although it may sometimes be necessary to eliminate certain ritualistic activities entirely, on the whole, once an acceptable level of control is reached, obsessional behaviours and interests can have many positive features. They may serve as extremely powerful reinforcers for developing more productive activities (Howlin & Rutter, 1987); they may also be an essential source of comfort or self-occupation for a child with few other interests or abilities. Follow-up studies suggest, too, that if obsessional skills and interests are appropriately encouraged and developed they can play a crucial role in later social and educational integration (Kanner, 1973).

Table 3 presents an example of how one child's overwhelming obsession with Thomas the Tank Engine trains was gradually overcome by his parents' using several of the strategies described above. By the time he was 3 years old, they realised that the obsession was becoming so pervasive that they had to intervene in some way. At that age their son would wear only Thomas the Tank Engine clothes, spent all his time watching, or reenacting Thomas videos, and talked of almost nothing else.

PHARMACOLOGICAL TREATMENTS

Although behavioural approaches to intervention are usually the most desirable form of treatment for younger autistic children, there are times when, because of severe behavioural disturbance (especially self-injury or aggression), sleeping problems, overactivity, anxiety

TABLE 3
Stages in Setting Limits on a 3-year-old Boy's Obsession with Thomas the Tank Engine

---

1 Picture calendar, indicating when access to "Thomas" videos and train sets is allowed, produced by parents.
2 Videos made unavailable before school; "Thomas" book read over breakfast instead.
3 Videos restricted to one per evening after school; weekend access unrestricted; unlimited access to train sets.
4 Limits on "Thomas" clothing imposed; school agree that no "Thomas" clothes can be worn there. No restrictions at home.
5 Access to "Thomas" train sets gradually restricted by increasing alternative activities (including "Thomas" books, board games, etc.)
6 New electric train set provided at home; allowed in conjunction with some "Thomas" toys; but not train sets
7 "Thomas" trains moved to grandmother's house; access only available at weekends. Interests in trains, generally, encouraged.

---

or depression, or marked obsessional and compulsive behaviours, medication may be considered. In the U.S.A. pharmacological interventions are very common, and in a recent survey of 838 carers of children with autism, conducted by Aman, van Bourgondien, Wolford, and Sarphare (1995) it was found that over 50% were taking some form of drug or vitamin treatment. Although most medication was prescribed for specific behavioural reasons, or for physical problems such as epilepsy, some drugs, notably fenfluramine and more recently certain selective serotonin uptake inhibitors (fluoxetine and fluvoxamine; Lewis, 1996; McDougle et al., 1996), have been recommended as a means of reducing autistic symptomatology more generally.

However, evaluations of even the most commonly used drugs are frequently inadequate (Lewis, 1996). Campbell, Schopler, Cueva, and Hallin (1996) conclude that only haloperidol, fenfluramine, naltrexone, clomipramine, and clonidine have been appropriately investigated, and all of these have their drawbacks and unwanted side effects. As for the myriad of other pharmacological treatments that have been tried over the years, Campbell et al. (1996) warn "No conclusions can be made concerning the efficacy and safety of these agents because the findings are based on small sample sizes and open studies without placebo control." (For updates on the effects of other drug treatments see recent reviews by Lewis, 1996; Campbell & Cueva, 1995.)

EDUCATIONAL PLACEMENT

Although there may be no miracle cures for autism, it has long been recognised that the provision of appropriately structured educational programmes is one of the most important aspects of successful treatment (Rutter & Bartak, 1973; Schopler, Brehm, Kinsbourne, & Reichler 1971).

Effective teaching programmes (such as TEACCH; Schopler et al., 1995) stress the importance of appropriate environmental organisation and the use of clear visual cues to circumvent communication difficulties, as well as the need to develop individually based learning programmes. Within this framework, however, there are many different approaches to teaching, some of which involve integrated provision, some segregation, and some a mixture of the two. The essential component is that educational strategies and curricula should be adapted to the specific patterns of skills and disabilities shown by the child with autism (see Jordan & Powell, 1995; Powell & Jordan, 1997 for descriptions of a variety of imaginative and innovative techniques that can be used to enhance learning). It is also generally more productive—and certainly more rewarding for all concerned—to focus on developing the child's existing skills, rather than attempting to overcome fundamental deficits. Equal emphasis needs to be placed, too, on meeting children's social and emotional needs. For more able children in particular, this latter goal can prove difficult to achieve. In specialised schooling it is often not possible to provide them with sufficient intellectual stimulation; on the other hand, unless extra support is provided within mainstream school, teasing and bullying by other pupils, and lack of understanding from teachers, may often result in severe emotional stress.

There is good evidence (Rogers, 1996) to show that the most effective educational programmes are those that begin early (between the ages of 2 to 4), and once the right placement is found this can help greatly to reduce the pressure on families. And if parents, teachers, and other professionals work together, this will markedly improve the consistency of management techniques and help to ensure the generalisation and maintenance of newly acquired behaviours. Thus, for any clinician involved in the treatment of autism, good liaison with Educational services, to ensure that the child receives early and appropriate provision, is a vital component of any package of care.

OTHER APPROACHES TO INTERVENTION

The clinician may also need to ensure that the family's needs in other areas are appropriately addressed. Respite care, on a planned and regular basis, can offer parents the rest they often so badly need, provide them with the opportunity to spend time with their other children, and give the child with autism the chance to spend time away from home. Families may also need guidance to ensure that they receive all the benefits to which they are entitled. Money may not improve the child's behaviour, but worrying about the lack of it can certainly interfere with parents' ability to cope. Even apparently minor benefits, such as a Disabled Parking Badge, can make the difference between being able to take the child shopping or not.

Finally, of course, the child with autism may need help in his or her own right. Cognitive-behavioural strategies to help cope with anxiety, fears or anger may prove effective with older, more able children, although these rarely work in isolation and generally require the co-operation of both school and family. For some children with severe emotional problems, psychoanalytically based interventions may be considered (Maratos, 1996), although there is little good evidence that such approaches are helpful (Campbell et al., 1996). Nevertheless, for older, more able children with autism, individual psychotherapy or counselling may be useful in helping them to deal with anxiety or depression, and the pain that comes from recognising their difficulties and differences. However, experience suggests that this *must* be combined with direct practical advice on how to deal with problems, otherwise children tend to become obsessed with the past, or with other possible explanations for their difficulties, making it almost impossible for them to "move on" in a positive way.

HELP FOR CHILDREN WITH ASPERGER SYNDROME (OR WITH HIGH-FUNCTIONING AUTISM)

Although often described as a "mild" variant of autism, the symptoms of Asperger syndrome are, in many cases, just as pervasive and as devastating as those of less able children. However, because of their relatively high cognitive ability, and their *apparently* competent use of language, this group of children is often least well served or understood. In fact, many have extensive linguistic and comprehension difficulties (especially involving abstract or complex concepts); their understanding of the more subtle aspects of social interaction is often profoundly limited, and their obsessional interests and behaviours also prove a barrier to social integration. Many, too, are painfully aware of their deficits and differences. However, only a minority receive any specialist provision. Most have to cope in mainstream school with little or no help. Their parents may be dismissed as over-protective, or too lax, and can find it very difficult to get the support or advice that they need. Moreover, the children's good vocabulary, and even their well-developed obsessional interests, frequently give the impression that they are capable of far higher levels of achievement than is actually the case. Others' expectations of their social and academic potential tend to be unrealistically high, and when these expectations are not met the children are viewed as negative, unco-operative, unmotivated, or rude and manipulative. Seemingly so close to "normality," there is constant pressure for them to "fit in" in ways that would never be demanded of a less able autistic child. This can lead to enormous pressure, resulting in extreme levels of anxiety and stress, which in turn further impede social and educational progress.

Because of their very uneven profile of skills and deficits, these children may require even more highly specialised help than those with global learning difficulties. Unfortunately, such help is rarely available, and although provision for autistic children generally has improved markedly over the past few decades, our knowledge of how to help this particular group effectively lags far behind.

THE NEED FOR EARLY DIAGNOSIS

Despite growing awareness of the need for early intervention and support for children with autism and their families, diagnosis before the age of 3 years is still rare (Baron-Cohen et al., 1996). In a recent large-scale survey in the U.K. (Howlin & Moore, 1997), the average age of diagnosis for children with autism was 5.5 years; for children with Asperger syndrome the age of diagnosis was considerably later, at 11.3 years. It was also clear from this survey that parents continue to face many delays and frustrations in their attempts to obtain a diagnosis.

It is important, of course, to be aware that early diagnosis has problems as well as advantages. Accurate diagnosis in children aged 2 years or under is known to present difficulties. Judgements based on clinical diagnosis may not always agree with diagnosis based on formal diagnostic criteria, such as the ADI or CARS (Autism Diagnostic Interview-Revised; Lord, Rutter, & Le Couteur, 1994; Childhood Autism Rating Scale; Schopler, Reichler, & Renner, 1986), and there can be particular problems in distinguishing between children with autism and nonautistic, nonverbal children with severe cognitive impairments (Lord, 1995b; Lord, Storuschuk, Rutter, & Pickles, 1993). Nevertheless, even when children are as young as 2 years, diagnosis based on skilled clinical judgement is relatively stable, and by the age of 3 years children tend to meet criteria on a variety of diagnostic measures (Lord, 1995).

Unnecessary delays in diagnosis have important practical implications. There is evidence (Rogers, 1996) to show that the most effective intervention programmes are those that begin early—between the age of 2 to 4 years. It also seems that the establishment of appropriate management strategies in the early years can help to minimise, or even avoid, many subsequent behavioural problems (Howlin & Rutter, 1987).

First, it is apparent that the development of effective, if simple communication strategies from early childhood will almost certainly help to reduce or avoid disruptive behaviours, which may otherwise become the child's principal means of controlling his or her environment (Durand & Carr, 1991).

Second, as already noted, it is essential not to allow or encourage behaviours in young children that will be viewed as "challenging" or unacceptable as they grow older. All too frequently, when the behaviour of an older child or adolescent gives cause for concern, it becomes apparent that the behaviour itself has not changed, and may well have been in existence for many years previously. Problems arise not because the nature of the behaviour has changed, but because other people's attitudes to it have altered.

Third, behaviours may become unacceptable as individuals become more skilled or determined at carrying them out. For example, one young child had a relatively innocuous obsession with watching people's washing machines. Family friends and neighbours were happy to encourage this, but by the time he was 17 he was in constant trouble with the police for breaking into property in order to indulge his obsession.

Fourth, particularly in the case of rituals and obsessions, there is an inverse relationship with many appropriate behaviours (Koegel, Valdez-Menchaca, & Koegel, 1994). Thus there is real risk that if such behaviours are not brought under effective control when the child is young they may steadily escalate until they interfere with many other activities. Understandably, the bewildered parents of a young infant tend to give in to the screams or tantrums that can occur because they have taken the "wrong" route, or have tried to change the way in which a task is completed. Over the years, however, the child's demands may become increasingly Draconian, until parents find themselves trapped in a web of complex and elaborate routines.

Without appropriate help, parents are unlikely to be able to identify potential problems, or will lack the courage and consistency to respond firmly to these, because of fears that resistance will further distress or damage their child. It is the role of professionals to provide families with the information and support they need, in order to enable them to identify problems at an early stage, and to help them evolve management strategies that will minimise the impact of the child's social, communicative, and obsessional problems in later life.

REFERENCES

Aman, M. G., van Bourgondien, M. E., Wolford, P. L., & Sarphare, G. (1995). Psychotropic and anticonvulsant drugs in subjects with autism: Prevalence and patterns of use. *Journal of the American Academy of Child and Adolescent Psychiatry, 34,* 1672–1681.

Attwood, T., Frith, U., & Hermelin, B. (1988). The understanding and use of gestures by autistic and Down's syndrome children. *Journal of Autism and Developmental Disorders, 18,* 241–258.

Bailey, A., Le Couteur, A., Gottesman, I., Bolton, P., Simenoff, E., Yuzda, E., & Rutter, M. (1995). Autism as a strongly genetic disorder; evidence from a British twin study. *Psychological Medicine, 25,* 63–77.

Baron-Cohen, S. (1995). *Mindblindness: An essay on autism and theory of mind.* Cambridge, MA: MIT Press.

Baron-Cohen, S., Cox, A., Baird, G., Swettenham, J., Nightingale, N., Morgan, K., Drew, A., & Charman, T. (1996). Psychological markers in the detection of autism in infancy in a large population. *British Journal of Psychiatry, 168,* 158–163.

Bebko, J. M., Perry, A., & Bryson, S. (1996). Multiple method validation study of facilitated communication: II Individual differences and subgroup results. *Journal of Autism and Developmental Disorders, 26,* 19–42.

Biklen, D. (1993). *Communication unbound: How facilitated communication is challenging traditional views of autism and ability/disability.* New York: Teachers College Press.

Bondy, A., & Frost, L. (1996). Educational approaches in preschool: Behavior techniques in a public school setting. In E. Schopler & G. B. Mesibov (Eds.), *Learning and cognition in autism* (pp. 311–334). New York: Plenum Press.

Campbell, M., & Cueva, J. E. (1995). Psychopharmacology in child and adolescent psychiatry: A review of the past seven years. Part II. *Journal of the American Academy of Child and Adolescent Psychiatry, 34,* 1262–1272.

Campbell, M., Schopler, E., Cueva, J. E., & Hallin, A. (1996). Treatment of autistic disorder. *Journal of the American Academy of Child and Adolescent Psychiatry, 35,* 134–143.

Dewart, H., & Summers, S. (1988). *Pragmatics profile of early communication skills.* Windsor, U.K.: NFER.

Dodge, K., Schlundt, D., Schocken, I., & Delugach, J. (1983). Competence and children's sociometric status: The role of peer group entries. *Merrill-Palmer Quarterly, 29,* 306–309.

Durand, B. M. (1990). *Severe behavior problems: A functional communication approach.* New York: Guilford Press.

Durand, B. M., & Carr, E. G. (1991). Functional communication training to reduce challenging behaviour: Maintenance and application in new settings. *Journal of Applied Behavior Analysis, 24,* 251–254.

Durand, B. M., & Crimmins, D. B. (1988). Identifying the variables maintaining self-injurious behavior. *Journal of Autism and Developmental Disorders, 18,* 99–117.

Eaves, L. C., & Ho, H. H. (1996). Brief report: Stability and change in cognitive and behavioral characteristics of autism through childhood. *Journal of Autism and Developmental Disorders, 26,* 557–570.

Emerson, E. (1995). *Challenging behaviour: Analysis and intervention.* Cambridge: Cambridge University Press.

Emerson, E., & Bromley, J. (1995). The form and function of challenging behaviours. *Journal of Intellectual Disability Research, 39*, 388–398.

Fombonne, E. (1997). Epidemiological studies of autism. In F. Volkmar (Ed.), *Autism and developmental disorders.* New York: Cambridge University Press.

Frith, U. (1991). *Autism and Asperger syndrome.* Cambridge: Cambridge University Press.

Frith, U., Soares, I., & Wing, L. (1993). Research into the earliest detectable signs of autism: What parents say. *Communication, 27*, 17–18.

Gillberg, C., Ehlers, S., Schaumann, H., Jakobsson, G., Dahlgren, S. O., Lindblom, R., Bagenholm, A., Tjus, T., & Blidner, E. (1990). Autism under age 3 years: A clinical study of 28 cases referred for autistic symptoms in infancy. *Journal of Child Psychology and Psychiatry, 31*, 921–934.

Gillberg, C., & Steffenberg, S. (1987). Outcome and prognostic factors in infantile autism and similar conditions: A population-based study of 46 cases followed through puberty. *Journal of Autism and Developmental Disorders, 17*, 272–288.

Gould, G. A., Rigg, M., & Bignell, L. (1991). *The Higashi experience: The report of a visit to the Boston Higashi School.* London: National Autistic Society Publications.

Grandin, T. (1992). An inside view of autism. In E. Schopler & G. B. Mesibov (Eds.), *High functioning individuals with autism* (pp. 105–125). New York: Plenum Press.

Green, G. (1994). The quality of the evidence. In H. C. Shane (Ed.), *Facilitated communication: The clinical and social phenomenon* (pp. 156–226). San Diego, CA: Singular Press.

Gunsett, R. P., Mulick, J. A., Fernald, W. B., & Martin, J. L. (1989). Brief report: Indications for medical screening prior to behavioral programming for severely and profoundly mentally retarded clients. *Journal of Autism and Developmental Disorders, 19*, 167–172.

Hadwin, J., Baron-Cohen, S., Howlin, P., & Hill, K. (1996). Can we teach children with autism to understand emotions, belief or pretence? *Development and Psychopathology, 8*, 345–365.

Hall, S. (1997). *The early development of self-injurious behaviour in children with developmental disabilities.* Unpublished PhD thesis, University of London.

Howlin, P. (1989). Changing approaches to communication training with autistic children. *British Journal of Disorders of Communication, 24*, 151–168.

Howlin, P. (1997a). *Autism: Preparing for adulthood.* London: Routledge.

Howlin, P. (1997b). Prognosis in autism: Do specialist treatments affect outcome? *European Child and Adolescent Psychiatry, 6*, 55–72.

Howlin, P. (in press). Outcome in adult life for individuals with autism. In F. Volkmar (Ed.), *Autism and developmental disorders.* New York: Cambridge University Press.

Howlin, P., Baron-Cohen, S., Hadwin, J., & Swettenham, J. (in press). *Teaching children with autism to mindread. A practical manual for parents and teachers.* Chichester, U.K.: Wiley.

Howlin, P., & Moore, A. (1977). Diagnosis in autism: A survey of over 1200 parents. *Autism: The International Journal of Research and Practice, 1*, 135–162.

Howlin, P., & Rutter, M. (1987). *Treatment of autistic children.* Chichester, U.K.: Wiley.

Irlen, H. (1995). Viewing the world through rose tinted glasses. *Communication, 29*, 8–9.

Johnson, M. H., Siddons, F., Frith, U., & Morton, J. (1992). Can autism be predicted on the basis of infant screening tests? *Developmental Medicine and Child Neurology, 34*, 316–320.

Jolliffe, T., Lansdown, R., & Robinson, T. (1992). *Autism: A personal account.* London: The National Autistic Society.

Jordan, R., & Powell, S. (1995). *Understanding and teaching children with autism.* Chichester, U.K.: Wiley.

Kanner, L. (1943). Autistic disturbances of affective contact. *Nervous Child, 2,* 217–250.

Kanner, L. (1973). *Childhood psychosis: Initial studies and new insights.* New York: Winston/Wiley.

Kaufman, B. (1981). *A miracle to believe in.* New York: Doubleday.

Kiernan, C. (1983). The use of non-vocal communication systems with autistic individuals. *Journal of Child Psychology and Psychiatry, 24,* 339–376.

Koegel, L. K., Valdez-Menchaca, M. C., & Koegel, R. L. (1994). Autism: Social communication difficulties and related behaviors. In V. B. Van Hasselt & M. Hersen (Eds.). *Advanced abnormal psychology* (pp. 165–187). New York: Plenum.

Konstantareas, M. M., & Homatidis, S. (1987). Ear infections in autistic and normal children. *Journal of Autism and Developmental Disorders, 20,* 591–593.

Layton, T. L., & Watson, L. R. (1995). Enhancing communication in non-verbal children with autism. In K. Quill (Ed.), *Teaching children with autism: Strategies to enhance communication and socialization* (pp. 73–104). New York: Delmar.

Le Couteur, A., Bailey, A., Goode, S., Pickles, A., Robertson, S., Gottesman, I., & Rutter, M. (1996). A broader phenotype of autism: The clinical picture in twins. *Journal of Child Psychology and Psychiatry, 37,* 785–802.

Lewis, M. H. (1996). Brief report: Psychopharmacology of autism spectrum disorders. *Journal of Autism and Developmental Disorders, 26,* 231–236.

Lockyer, L., & Rutter, M. (1969). A five to fifteen year follow-up study of infantile psychosis: III Psychological aspects. *British Journal of Psychiatry, 115,* 865–882.

Lockyer, L., & Rutter, M. (1970). A five to fifteen year follow-up study of infantile psychosis: IV Patterns of cognitive abilities. *British Journal of Social and Clinical Psychology, 9,* 152–163.

Lord, C. (1984). The development of peer relations in children with autism. In F. J. Morrison, C. Lord, & D. P. Keating (Eds.), *Applied developmental psychology* (pp. 166–230). New York: Academic Press.

Lord, C. (1995a). Facilitating social inclusion: Examples from peer intervention programs. In E. Schopler & G. Mesibov (Eds.) *Learning and cognition in autism* (pp. 221–239). New York: Plenum Press.

Lord, C. (1995b). Follow-up of two-year-olds referred for possible autism. *Journal of Child Psychology and Psychiatry, 36,* 1365–1382.

Lord, C., & Rutter, M. (1994). Autism and pervasive developmental disorders. In M. Rutter, E. Taylor, & L. Hersov (Eds.), *Child and adolescent psychiatry: Modern approaches* (3rd Ed.) (pp. 569–593). Oxford: Blackwell.

Lord, C., Rutter, M., & Le Couteur, A. (1994). Autism Diagnostic Interview-Revised: A revised version of a diagnostic interview for caregivers of individuals with possible pervasive developmental disorders. *Journal of Autism and Developmental Disorders, 24,* 659–685.

Lord, C., Storuschuk, S., Rutter, M., & Pickles, A. (1993). Using the ADI-R to diagnose autism in preschool children. *Infant Mental Health Journal, 14,* 234–252.

Lotter, V. (1966). Epidemiology of autistic conditions in young children. I: Prevalence. *Social Psychiatry, 1,* 163–173.

Lovaas, O. I. (1993). The development of a treatment-research project for developmentally disabled and autistic children. *Journal of Applied Behavior Analysis, 26,* 617–630.

Lovaas, O. I. (1996). The UCLA young autism model of service delivery. In C. Maurice (Ed.), *Behavioral intervention for young children with autism* (pp. 241–250). Austin, TX: Pro-Ed.

Marans, W. D. (1997). Communication assessment. In D. J. Cohen & F. R. Volkmar (Eds.), *Handbook of autism and pervasive developmental disorders* (pp. 427–447). New York: John Wiley.

Maratos, O. (1996). Psychoanalysis and the management of pervasive developmental disorders, including autism. In C. Trevarthen, K. Aitken, D. Papoudi, & J. Robarts (Eds.), *Children with autism: Diagnosis and interventions to meet their needs* (pp. 161–171). London: Jessica Kingsley.

McDougle, C. J., Naylor, S. T., Cohen, D. J., Volkmar, F. R., Heninger, G. R., & Price, L. H. (1996). A double blind, placebo-controlled study of fluvoxamine in adults with autistic disorder. *Archives of General Psychiatry, 53,* 1001–1008.

McEachin, J. J., Smith, T., & Lovaas, O. I. (1993). Long-term outcome for children with autism who received early intensive behavioral treatment. *American Journal of Mental Retardation, 97,* 359–372.

Mesibov, G. B. (1984). Social skills training with verbal autistic adolescents and adults: A program model. *Journal of Autism and Developmental Disorders, 14,* 395–404.

Mesibov, G. B. (1993). Treatment outcome is encouraging: Comments on McEachin et al. *American Journal of Mental Retardation, 97,* 379–380.

Oliver, C. (1995). Self-injurious behaviour in children with learning disabilities: Recent advances in assessment and intervention. *Journal of Child Psychology and Psychiatry, 36,* 909–928.

Owens, R. G., & MacKinnon, S. (1993). The functional analysis of challenging behaviours: Some conceptual and theoretical problems. In R. S. P. Jones & C. B. Eayrs (Eds.), *Challenging behaviour and intellectual disability: A psychological perspective* (pp. 224–239). Avon, U.K.: BILD Publications.

Ozonoff, S., & Miller, J. (1995). Teaching theory of mind: A new approach to social skills training for individuals with autism. *Journal of Autism and Developmental Disorders, 25,* 415–434.

Perry, R., Cohen, I., & DeCarlo, R. (1995). Case study: Deterioration, autism and recovery in two siblings. *Journal of the American Academy of Child and Adolescent Psychiatry, 34,* 233–237.

Piven, J., Harper, J., Palmer, P., & Arndt, S. (1995). Course of behavioral change in autism: A retrospective study of high-IQ adolescents and adults. *Journal of the American Academy of Child and Adolescent Psychiatry, 35,* 523–529.

Powell, S., & Jordan, R. (Eds.) (1997). *Autism and learning: A guide to good practice.* London: David Fulton.

Prizant, B., & Schuler, A. (1987). Facilitating communication: Language approaches. In D. Cohen & A. Donnellan (Eds.), *Handbook of Autism and Pervasive Developmental Disorders* (pp. 316–332). New York: Wiley.

Quill, K. A. (1995). *Teaching children with autism: Strategies to enhance communication and socialization.* New York: Delmar.

Richer, J., & Zappella, M. (1989). Changing social behaviour: The place of Holding. *Communication, 23,* 35–39.

Rimland, B., & Edelson, S. M. (1994). The effects of Auditory Integration Training on autism. *American Journal of Speech-Language Pathology, 5,* 16–24.

Rimland, B., & Edelson, S. M. (1995). Brief report: A pilot study of Auditory Integration Training in autism. *Journal of Autism and Developmental Disorders, 25,* 61–70.

Rinaldi, W. (1992). *Social Use of Language Programme.* Windsor, U.K.: NFER.

Roeyers, H. (1996). The influence of nonhandicapped peers on the social interaction of children with a pervasive developmental disorder. *Journal of Autism and Developmental Disorders, 26,* 303–320.

Rogers, S. J. (1996). Brief report: Early intervention in autism. *Journal of Autism and Developmental Disorders, 26,* 243–246.

Rutter, M. (1985). Infantile autism and other pervasive developmental disorders. In M. Rutter & L. Hersov (Eds.), *Child and adolecent psychiatry: Modern approaches* (2nd Edn.) (pp. 545–566). Oxford: Blackwell.

Rutter, M., & Bartak, L. (1973). Special educational treatment of autistic children: A comparative study. II. Follow-up findings and implications for services. *Journal of Child Psychology and Psychiatry, 14,* 241–270.

Rydell, P. J., & Mirenda, P. (1994). The effects of high and low constraint utterances on the production of immediate and delayed echolalia in young children with autism. *Journal of Autism and Developmental Disorders, 24,* 719–730.

Rydell, P. J., & Prizant, B. (1995). Assessment and intervention strategies for children who use echolalia. In K. A. Quill (Ed.), *Teaching children with autism: Strategies to enhance communication and socialization* (pp. 105–132). New York: Delmar.

Schopler, E., Brehm, S. S, Kinsbourne, M., & Reichler, R. J. (1971). Effects of treatment structure on development in autistic children. *Archives of General Psychiatry, 20,* 174–181.

Schopler, E., Mesibov, G. B., & Hearsey, K. (1995). Structured teaching in the TEACCH system. In E. Schopler & G. B. Mesibov (Eds.), *Learning and cognition in autism* (pp. 243–267). New York: Plenum Press.

Schopler, E., Reichler, R. J., & Renner, B. R. (1986). *The Childhood Autism Rating Scale (CARS) for diagnostic screening and classification of autism.* New York: Irvington.

Schopler, E., Short, A., & Mesibov, G. (1989). Relation of behavioral treatment to "normal functioning": Comment on Lovaas. *Journal of Consulting and Clinical Psychology, 57,* 162–164.

Schuler, A. L., Peck, C. A., Willard, C., & Theimer, K. (1989). Assessment of communicative means and functions through interview: Assessing the communicative capabilities of individuals with limited language. *Seminars in Speech and Language, 10,* 51–61.

Sinclair, J. (1992). Bridging the gap: An inside out view of autism (Or, do you know what I don't know?). In E. Schopler & G. B. Mesibov (Eds.), *High functioning individuals with autism* (pp. 294–302). New York: Plenum Press.

Smith, B., Chung, M. C., & Vostanis, P. (1994). The path to care in autism: Is it better now? *Journal of Autism and Developmental Disorders, 24,* 551–564.

Stehli, A. (1992). *The sound of a miracle; a child's triumph over autism.* London: Fourth Estate Publications.

Sturmey, P. (1995). Analog baselines: A critical review of the methodology. *Research in Developmental Disabilities, 16,* 269–284.

Sturmey, P. (1996). *Functional analysis in clinical psychology.* Chichester, U.K.: Wiley.

Swettenham, J. (1995). Can children with autism be taught to understand false beliefs using computers? *Journal of Child Psychology and Psychiatry, 37,* 157–166.

Szatmari, P., Bartolucci, G., & Bremner, R. S. (1989). Asperger's syndrome and autism: A comparison of early history and outcome. *Developmental Medicine and Child Neurology, 31,* 709–720.

Trevarthen, C., Aitken, K., Papoudi, D., & Roberts, J. M. (1996). *Children with autism. Diagnosis and interventions to meet their needs.* London: Jessica Kingsley.

Volkmar, F., Stier, D., & Cohen, D. (1985). Age of recognition of pervasive developmental disorders. *American Journal of Psychiatry, 142,* 1450–1452.

Walker, M. (1980). *The Makaton vocabulary* (Revised Edn.). Camberley, U.K.: The Makaton Vocabulary Development Project.

Welch, M. (1988). *Holding time.* London: Century Hutchinson.

Williams, D. (1992). *Nobody nowhere.* London: Corgi Books.

Williams, D. (1994). *Somebody somewhere.* London: Corgi Books.

Williams, T. I. (1989). A social skills group for autistic children. *Journal of Autism and Developmental Disorders, 19,* 143–156.

Wing, L. (1981). Asperger's syndrome: A clinical account. *Psychological Medicine, 11,* 115–129.

Wing, L. (1996). Autistic spectrum disorders. *British Medical Journal, 312,* 327–328.

Wing, L., & Gould, J. (1979). Severe impairments of social interaction and associated abnormalities in children: epidemiology and classification. *Journal of Autism and Developmental Disorders, 9,* 11–29.

Wolfberg, P. J., & Schuler, A. L. (1993). Integrated play groups: A model for promoting the social and cognitive dimensions of play. *Journal of Autism and Developmental Disorders, 23,* 1–23.

APPENDIX

Cognitive and Language Tests for Use with Children with Autism

This is not meant as a comprehensive list, but includes tests that have been found useful in follow-up and research studies. The author and publisher of the tests are given in parentheses.

The tests listed (with the exception of the Play Test) provide standardised scores as well as age equivalents since these are necessary for any comparative studies. However, there are also many other scales available that can be used to inform clinicians about the child's functioning in different areas.

Tests of general cognitive ability. Bayley Scales of Infant Development (Bayley, 1993; The Psychological Corporation: Sidcup, U.K.)
Age range: 1–42 months
Normative sample: American
Type: Mainly nonverbal tests; useful for very young or very delayed children. Provides IQ and Mental Age scores.

Kaufman Assessment Battery for Children (Kaufman, 1983; NFER-Nelson: Windsor, U.K.)
Age range: 30 months–12.5 years
Normative sample: American
Type: Mixture of verbal and nonverbal tests. Assesses sequential processing, simultaneous processing, and achievement. Supplies helpful profile of skills and difficulties, which can then be used for designing educational programmes. Provides Percentile Ranks, Age Equivalent, and Standard scores.

Leiter International Performance Scale Battery (Leiter, 1948 & 1979; NFER-Nelson: Windsor, U.K.)

Age range: 2–18 years

Normative samples: European and American

Type: Nonverbal tests; largely involving matching and sequencing. Developed specifically for children with hearing/linguistic problems; however level of conceptual understanding required can present difficulties for young autistic children. Works best with older/more able group. Provides IQ and Mental Age scores.

Merrill-Palmer Pre-School Performance Scale (Stutsman, 1931; NFER-Nelson: Windsor. U.K.)

Age range: 18 months–6 years

Normative sample: American

Type: Verbal and nonverbal tests; credit can be given for omitted items. Despite having very old norms has been shown to have good predictive validity (as long as child is able to complete several different tasks). Requires little or no verbal understanding; materials tend to maintain children's interest and hence useful for nonverbal children. Provides IQ, Mental Age, and Percentile scores.

Ravens Progressive Matrices (Raven; NFER-Nelson: Windsor)

Age range: Child to older adults

Normative samples: American; British and many others

Type: Test of perceptual ability. Requires little or no verbal ability/explanation, but tasks themselves difficult for most very young and/or delayed children. Colour form usually best for young children and Board form (in which pieces attached with velcro) can be particularly useful in this group. Provides Age Equivalent scores.

Vineland Adaptive Behavior Scales (Sparrow, Balla, & Cicchetti, 1984; Circle Pines, MN: American Guidance Service).

Age range: 0–19 years

Normative sample: American

Type: Informant based scale; assesses motor, social, communication, and daily living skills. Also contains items on maladaptive behaviour. Useful if co-operation on other tests cannot be obtained. However, cultural differences can lead to some problems when used with non-American subjects. Correlations with other measures of IQ are only modest in Learning Disabled samples. Provides Standard Scores and Age Equivalents for functioning in the different domains.

Wechsler Intelligence Scale for Children–Third UK Edition (WISC-III UK) (Wechsler, 1992; The Psychological Corporation: Sidcup, U.K.)

Age range: 6–16 years

Normative samples: U.K. (but many other editions available)

Type: Verbal and nonverbal tests, almost all requiring some verbal comprehension. Supplies helpful profile of skills and difficulties. Assesses Performance, Verbal, and Full Scale IQ. Younger children tend to cope better with the Performance Scale, but older, more able subjects may do better on the Verbal Scale. Provides IQ, Age Equivalent, and Standard Scores.

Wechsler Pre-school and Primary Scale of Intelligence: Revised UK Edition (WPPSI-R UK) (Wechsler, 1990; The Psychological Corporation: Sidcup, U.K.)
Age range: 3–7 years
Normative samples: U.K. (but many other editions available)
Type: Verbal and nonverbal tests mostly requiring some verbal comprehension. Assesses Performance, Verbal, and Full Scale IQ. Experience suggests that only the most able autistic children in this age group can cope well with the materials. (Merrill Palmer is often more viable option). Provides IQ, Age Equivalent, and Standard scores.

Tests of language and play. British Picture Vocabulary Scale (Dunn, Dunn, Whetton, & Pintilie, 1982; NFER-Nelson: Windsor, U.K.)
Age range: 2.5–18 years
Normative sample: British (but based on American Peabody Picture Vocabulary Test)
Type: Assesses verbal comprehension. Child is required to identify one picture from a set of four. Not very useful/interesting for very young or very linguistically delayed children. In older, more verbal group, the wide age range is valuable and a short version is also very quick and easy to administer. However, because of very circumscribed nature of task, may not provide very accurate assessment of linguistic functioning within the wider social context. Provides Age Equivalent, Standard Scores, and Percentiles.

Expressive One Word Vocabulary Test (Gardner, 1982; Western Psychological Services: Los Angeles, CA)
Age range: 1.1–12 years. Upper extension: to 18 years
Normative sample: American
Type: Assesses expressive vocabulary. Child is required to name individual pictures. Again, not very useful/interesting for very young or very delayed children. Wide age range is useful, although some items very "American." Like BPVS, nature of task very circumscribed. Provides Age Equivalent, Standard Scores and Percentiles.

Reynell Developmental Language Scales: Second Revision (Reynell & Huntley, 1985; NFER-Nelson: Windsor, U.K.)
Age range: 1–7 years
Normative sample: British
Type: Scored from observations of child and structured tasks with toys and pictures. Even quite young children seem to enjoy the materials. Low age ceiling the main drawback. Provides Age Equivalent and Standard Scores for Comprehension and Expression.

Symbolic Play Test: Second Edition (Lowe & Costello, 1988; NFER-Nelson: Windsor, U.K.)
Age range: 1–3 years
Normative sample: British
Type: Scored from observations of child and structured tasks with toys. Enjoyed by quite young children but low age ceiling the main drawback. Provides only Age Equivalent scores.

Test of Reception of Grammar (TROG; Bishop, 1989; MRC Applied Psychology Unit: Cambridge)
Age range: 3–11 years
Normative sample: British
Type: Assesses grammatical understanding. Child selects one picture from set of three. Useful for more verbal children; one of few well standardised tests of grammatical ability, although again skills tested rather circumscribed. Provides Age Equivalent, Standard Scores, and Percentiles.

21

Cognitive-Behavioral Treatment of School Phobia

Cynthia G. Last, Ph.D., Cheri Hansen, M.S., and Nathalie Franco, Ph.D.

Objective: *To conduct a controlled group outcome investigation of the efficacy of cognitive-behavioral treatment for school phobia.* **Method:** *Fifty-six children with school phobia were randomly assigned to 12 weeks of cognitive-behavioral therapy or an attention-placebo control condition. Pre- and posttreatment school attendance, self-reported anxiety and depression, and diagnostic status were compared.* **Results:** *Both the experimental and control treatments were equally effective at returning children to school. Both treatments also were effective in reducing children's anxiety and depressive symptoms. Follow-up revealed no differences between groups when the children reentered school the next school year.* **Conclusions:** *Overall, results suggest that psychosocial treatments are effective at returning school-phobic children to school and that the highly structured cognitive-behavioral approach may not be superior to more traditional educational and supportive treatment methods.* J. Am. Acad. Child Adolesc. Psychiatry, *1998, 37(4):404–411.* **Key Words:** *anxiety disorders, school phobia, treatment outcome.*

School phobia is a relatively widespread psychiatric disturbance that poses serious short- and long-term consequences. Anxiety about attending school and resultant school avoidance can stem from a variety of anxiety disorders, but most typically separation anxiety or a phobic disorder (Last et al., 1987; Last and Strauss, 1990; Ollendick and Mayer, 1984). Historically, the label "school phobia" has been applied to both types of children; however, we prefer the more generic term "school refusal" and will use it throughout the remainder of this article to describe the population being studied.

Accepted November 12, 1997.

Dr. Last is Professor of Psychology and Director of the Anxiety Treatment Center at the Center for Psychological Studies, Nova Southeastern University, Coral Springs, FL. Ms. Hansen is a doctoral student at the Center for Psychological Studies, Nova Southeastern University. Dr. Franco was a postdoctoral fellow at Nova Southeastern University and currently is Assistant Professor at Barry University, Miami Shores, FL.

This study was supported by NIMH grant MH 49584.

Reprint requests to Dr. Last, 3111 University Drive, Suite 307, Coral Springs, FL 33065.

0890-8567/98/3704–0404/$03.00/0©1998 by the American Academy of Child and Adolescent Psychiatry.

Clinically, behavioral treatments, particularly exposure-based techniques, have been used extensively to treat anxiety-based school refusal. The basis for using this approach was derived, for the most part, from the treatment literature for adult anxiety disorders, particularly phobias. Numerous controlled studies of adult phobic patients have shown that exposure to feared objects or situations promotes fear reduction and increases approach behavior (Barlow and Beck, 1984). Utilization of these techniques has been extended to phobic child patients; however, for school refusers, published reports demonstrating the successful application of exposure-based techniques have been limited almost exclusively to single-case studies and uncontrolled case series (e.g., Ayllon et al., 1970; Kennedy, 1965; Patterson, 1965; Perkin et al., 1973; Smith and Sharpe, 1970).

In fact, to our knowledge, only one group comparison study has been conducted to date that has investigated the efficacy of exposure treatment for anxiety-based school refusal (Blagg and Yule, 1984). In this study, Blagg and Yule compared outcome for three treatment conditions: (1) prolonged in vivo exposure (flooding), (2) inpatient hospitalization, and (3) individual psychotherapy plus home tutoring. Results indicated that the exposure treatment was superior to the other two treatment conditions, with 83%, 31%, and 0% of each group, respectively, showing regular school attendance during the year after treatment. Interpretation of these findings, however, is limited by lack of random assignment to treatment condition, essentially rendering the study uncontrolled.

In light of the above, it is clear that the use of exposure-based techniques to treat school-refusing youngsters does not have an adequate scientific base in the empirical child literature. Specifically, *not one* controlled group outcome study has been conducted to date examining the efficacy of this intervention for anxiety-based school refusal.

In the current study, we investigate the efficacy of a cognitive-behavioral treatment for school refusers by comparing outcome to that of a credible attentionplacebo control condition, which adequately controls for the nonspecific effects of treatment (i.e., therapist contact, time, etc.), but does not overlap with the presumably active ingredients of the cognitive-behavioral treatment. While we had considered comparing our experimental treatment to a waiting-list control group as a first step in examining the efficacy, we opted not to do so primarily for feasibility reasons—that is, parents of school-refusing children will not agree to delay the onset of treatment. Including the attention-placebo condition assured parents that their child would be receiving immediate clinical attention.

METHOD

Subjects

Subjects included 56 children and adolescents who were referred to the School Phobia Program at the Anxiety Treatment Center of Nova Southeastern University from September 1993 through April 1995. On the basis of telephone screenings, youngsters who were suspected of having anxiety-based school refusal were scheduled for intake evaluations. Participation was offered to children/adolescents and their families if they met the following criteria: (1) anxiety-based school refusal; (2) current enrollment in elementary, middle, or high school; (3) current *DSM-III-R* anxiety disorder diagnosis; (4) at least 10% absenteeism from classes for at least 1 month before intake; (5) no current diagnosis of major depression; and (6) no current use of psychiatric medication. Those who agreed to participate were reevaluated immediately before the first treatment session, where they again were required to meet inclusion criteria in order to enter the study (see "Procedure").

During the 2-year period of the study, 105 children were evaluated for possible inclusion. Of the 105, 29% ($n = 30$) did not meet inclusion criteria at intake, 4% ($n = 4$) met criteria at intake but refused participation, and 13% ($n = 14$) met criteria at intake but no longer met criteria at the time of the first treatment session. One subject moved out of the country between the intake and first treatment session. Children who were excluded from or refused participation in the study were offered treatment services at the Anxiety Treatment Center or other appropriate facility.

Procedure

At the intake evaluation, the child and at least one parent were interviewed separately by a trained clinician with a modified version of the Schedule for Affective Disorders and Schizophrenia for School-Age Children-Present Episode version (K-SADS-P) (Last, unpublished). This modified version of the K-SADS-P includes comprehensive sections on all *DSM-III-R* disorders and allows evaluation of both current and past psychopathology. Information on sociodemographic variables (age, gender, race, marital status, and socioeconomic status [SES]) was also obtained at this time. The Hollingshead (1975) Four-Factor Index was used to assess SES.

An abbreviated version of the K-SADS-P was administered immediately before the first treatment session to screen out youngsters who no longer met inclusion criteria and to obtain accurate pretreatment baseline data. The abbreviated K-SADS-P evaluates current psychopathology and includes sections on *DSM-III-R* anxiety disorders, affective disorders, and oppositional defiant disorder.

Subjects were assigned randomly to either cognitive-behavioral therapy (CBT) or educational-support therapy (ES). Treatment was provided once a week for 12 consecutive weeks, with sessions lasting approximately 60 minutes each. Each of the two treatment conditions is described in detail below:

Cognitive-behavioral therapy. This treatment approach is similar to that used by Barlow et al. (1984) for adult agoraphobics, modified by Last (unpublished) for the treatment of anxiety-based school refusal (treatment manual available upon request). The treatment consists of two main components: graduated in vivo exposure and coping self-statement training.

Graduated in vivo exposure focuses on having the child return to school in a stepwise or gradual manner. During the first treatment session, an individualized Fear and Avoidance Hierarchy is constructed using information provided by the child and parents. The hierarchy contains 10 items covering the variety of school-related situations the child currently fears and avoids, including situations that elicit varying degrees of fear and avoidance (i.e., from minimal to maximal). At each treatment session, the parent and child rerate the hierarchy, and the child receives a homework assignment consisting of one item from the hierarchy to be practiced each school day until the next treatment session. Initial homework assignments are given from the lower end of the hierarchy; assignments increase in difficulty as treatment progresses. The therapist maintains telephone contact to monitor progress and provide reinforcement between session. The therapist also maintains contact with a "school contact person" (e.g., guidance counselor, teacher, etc.) who, in effect, serves as an on-site behavior therapist.

Cognitive self-statement training is used to assist the child in initiating and completing homework assignments (Meichenbaum, 1977). During session 2, children are taught to identify their maladaptive thoughts when anticipating or confronting anxiety-producing situations and, subsequently, to replace those thoughts with more adaptive, coping self-statements. Coping self-statements are used before and during exposure sessions to help reduce anticipatory anxiety and decrease anxiety during homework assignments.

Educational-support therapy. This treatment approach is a modification of that used by Silverman (1993) for simple phobic children and Heimberg et al. (1990) for social-phobic adults (treatment manual available upon request). Previous studies have demonstrated that this control condition produces evaluations of credibility and outcome expectations similar to those generated by experimental treatment conditions, such as behavior therapy (Heimberg et al., 1990; W.K. Silverman, W.M. Kurtines, G.S. Ginsburg, B. Rabian, and C. Fergurson, unpublished).

ES is a combination of educational presentations and supportive psychotherapy in which children are encouraged to talk about their fears and learn to distinguish between fear, anxiety, and phobias. Children are told that they will be provided with information they can use to help them overcome their difficulty attending school.

At each treatment session, children receive handouts that outline the next session and pose questions for the children to consider. Written responses are brought to the following session and form the basis for discussion. Children are asked to maintain a daily diary to keep track of things they are afraid of, what thoughts and feelings they associate with these fears, how often they occur, and how they handle these fears.

In the first portion of each session, the daily diary and handouts from the previous week are reviewed. Children are asked to share any specific fears or concerns that occurred during the previous week. Subsequently, topics relevant to school-refusing children such as fear, anxiety, phobias, and maladaptive thinking are presented. Unlike CBT, therapists refrain from providing specific encouragement or instructions for children to confront feared situations, and children are not verbally reinforced for attending school. Furthermore, no instruction is provided to teach them how to modify their maladaptive thoughts.

Measures

Treatment credibility. Treatment credibility and outcome expectations were assessed at the end of sessions 1, 4, and 7. Three items were administered separately to the child and parent. The items assessed the extent to which the treatment (1) was logical, (2) was expected to be successful, and (3) would be recommended to others. Each item was rated on a 0 to 8 scale (higher scores indicating greater credibility). A mean rating score based on the average of the three ratings was computed separately for the child and parent.

Outcome. School Attendance Record. During each treatment session, information about school attendance was obtained from the child and parent for each day of the school week and, subsequently, verified by school personnel. School attendance was defined as time spent in the classroom, not including time spent in school but outside the classroom (e.g., nurse's office, guidance counselor's office, principal's office, hallways, etc.) or time spent in school but in the presence of a family member. School attendance for each week was calculated as the number of hours the child attended school divided by the number of hours school was in session multiplied by 100 to yield a measure of percentage of attendance. Legitimate absences (e.g., illness not related to anxiety) were not included in calculations.

Global Improvement Scale. Mid- (session 7) and posttreatment (session 13); the child, parent, and therapist independently rated the subject's overall improvement since the beginning of the treatment program on a 7-point scale ranging from very much worse to completely well (Gittelman-Klein and Klein, 1971).

Fear Survey Schedule for Children-Revised. The Fear Survey Schedule for Children-Revised (FSSC-R) (Ollendick, 1983) contains 80 items and assesses level of fearfulness to stimuli that commonly elicit anxiety in children. Items are rated on a 3-point scale ("none," "some," or "a lot"). A total fear score is obtained by summing scores for all items. The FSSC-R has demonstrated high internal consistency and moderate test-retest reliability; it also correlates well with other anxiety measures (Ollendick, 1983; Ollendick et al., 1989). Children completed the FSSC-R at intake and the last treatment session.

Modified State-Trait Anxiety Inventory for Children. The Modified State-Trait Anxiety Inventory for Children (STAIC-M) (Fox and Houston, 1983) is a modification of the STAIC (Spielberger, 1973). Respondents indicate how frequently they experience anxiety symptoms ("hardly ever," "sometimes," or "often"); separate scores reflect levels of cognitive, somatic, and overall trait anxiety. The STAIC-M has shown moderate to high internal consistency and construct validity (Fox and Houston, 1983; Papay and Spielberger, 1986).

Children's Depression Inventory. The Children's Depression Inventory (CDI) (Kovacs, 1992) provides an indication of subjects' overall level of depressive symptomatology. Children are presented 27 groups of three statements; they respond by choosing the one that best describes their feelings over the past 2 weeks. A total score is obtained by summing the 27 responses. The CDI has demonstrated good internal consistency, adequate test-retest reliability, and good construct and predictive validity (Kovacs, 1992).

Posttreatment Diagnosis. At the final treatment session, the abbreviated K-SADS-P was again administered to the child and parent. The assessment was performed by a trained interviewer blind to the child's initial diagnosis.

Follow-up. Four weeks after the completion of the treatment program, phone interviews were conducted with the parent and child to obtain a report of school attendance during the preceding 4 weeks. These reports subsequently were verified by school personnel. Subjects also reported whether or not they sought additional treatment for school refusal during the 4 weeks after completion of the study.

Telephone interviews were again conducted with one of the child's parents 2 weeks into the school year after completion of the treatment program to assess school reentry after summer vacation. For subjects experiencing difficulty, parents were asked whether the child was (1) refusing to go to school, (2) leaving school early, (3) not staying in classes, (4) calling a parent, (5) anxious or upset before or during school, and (6) experiencing physical symptoms (e.g., headaches, stomachaches, etc.) before or during school. On the basis of the information provided, the clinician rated the overall severity of school refusal on a 4-point scale, ranging from mild to extreme.

Dropouts

Of the 56 subjects, 9 (16%) discontinued treatment in the study *before* midtreatment. All of these subjects had been assigned to the CBT group. Reasons for not completing the study included the following: treatment terminated because of excessive cancellations ($n = 3$), family sought additional treatment ($n = 3$), and family refused continued participation ($n = 3$). An additional 6 (11%) subjects (CBT = 3; ES = 3) discontinued participation *after* midtreatment but *before* the posttreatment assessment at session 13. Reasons included the following: family sought additional treatment ($n = 3$), treatment terminated because of excessive cancellations ($n = 1$), family refused continued participation ($n = 1$), and family moved away ($n = 1$).

Statistical analyses revealed no significant differences on any pretreatment sociodemographic or clinical variable between subjects who did not complete the entire treatment protocol ($n = 15$) and those who completed the study ($n = 41$). In addition, there were no differences between subjects who dropped out before midtreatment ($n = 9$) and those who completed at least half the sessions ($n = 47$) on any of the pretreatment variables examined.

Data Analyses

To assess possible differences between treatment conditions, t tests for continuous variables and χ^2 tests with the Yates correction for continuity for categorical variables were performed. Fisher's Exact Test was used for comparisons when expected cell frequencies were less than five. Analysis was conducted on sociodemographic (age, gender, race, marital status, and SES) and clinical pretreatment variables (school attendance, diagnosis associated with school refusal, and duration of current school refusal episode).

Midtreatment results are reported for those who completed at least half the sessions ($n = 47$; CBT = 23, ES = 24), and posttreatment results are reported for those who completed the study ($n = 41$; CBT = 20, ES = 21). Results revealed no differences in midtreatment findings when reanalyzing data using only the 41 treatment completers.

Separate repeated-measures analyses of variance (ANOVAs) (parent, child) were conducted to determine possible differences between the treatment conditions on the credibility ratings given by parent and child in sessions 1, 4, and 7. To determine the effects of treatment on outcome, a 2 (treatment group) × 3 (time) repeated-measures ANOVA was conducted, using session 13 attendance as the dependent measure. Separate 2 (treatment group) × 2 (time) repeated-measures ANOVAs were conducted to determine differences in questionnaire scores between pre- and posttreatment.

Because the standard repeated-measures multivariate ANOVA does not handle the missing data resulting from subjects who terminated treatment between the 7th and 13th sessions, the outcome analysis on school attendance also was conducted using two different procedures available in SAS (univariate repeated-measures analysis as split-plot design and mixed-model procedure) (Littell et al., 1991, 1996). Both procedures handle missing data in repeated-measures analysis. Findings from the three procedures were comparable, and results are reported for the mixed-model procedure.

Sociodemographic and clinical variables were also examined to determine possible effects on treatment outcome. Separate ANOVAs were conducted for gender, race, marital status, SES level, and primary diagnosis, using attendance at session 13 as the dependent vaiable. For two continuous variables (age and duration of school refusal), achievement of at least 95% attendance by session 13 (yes, no) was used as the outcome measure.

RESULTS

Sociodemographic and clinical characteristics. Children's ages ranged from 6 to 17 years (CBT mean = 11.67, SD = 3.00; ES mean = 12.40, SD = 2.79). Approximately two thirds of the sample were female (CBT 56% [n = 13]; ES 62% [n = 15]). Most of the children were white (CBT 92% [n = 21]; ES 88% [n = 21]), and the remainder were black (CBT 4% [n = 1]; ES 4% [n = 1]) or Hispanic (CBT 4% [n = 1]; ES 8% [n = 2]). Approximately two thirds were from two-parent households (CBT 78% [n = 18]; ES 58% [n = 14]) and from middle/upper SES (Hollingshead strata I, II, and III) (CBT 78% [n = 18]; ES 54% [n = 13]). Pretreatment school attendance varied from 0 to 90% (CBT mean = 26.43, SD = 36.97; ES mean = 30.12, SD = 33.26), and duration of school refusal ranged from 2 to 260 weeks (CBT mean = 51.35, SD = 71.86; ES mean = 60.46, SD = 58.80). Analyses revealed no significant differences between the two groups on any of these pretreatment variables.

The specific nature of anxiety related to school varied greatly between children and included being separated from parents, evaluated by peers, and concerned about competence. Based on K-SADS-P evaluations, the diagnosis associated with school refusal was considered the most impairing and, thus, the primary diagnosis. Primary diagnoses included phobic disorders (simple or social; 58%), separation anxiety disorder (32%), avoidant disorder (4%), overanxious disorder (4%), and panic disorder (2%). Fifty-three percent of children in our sample had more than one anxiety disorder. Comorbid diagnoses also included oppositional defiant disorder (9%) and trichotillomania (2%).

Interrater diagnostic agreement for session 1 abbreviated K-SADS-P interviews was obtained by having a second clinician independently review audiotapes of interviews and assign *DSM-III-R* diagnoses. Reliability was calculated for 41% (n = 23) of the interviews at session 1. The k coefficients for the specific anxiety disorders were as follows: any phobic disorder = .78, separation anxiety disorder = .73, avoidant disorder = .78, and overanxious disorder = .78.

Treatment credibility. Parents and children in both treatment conditions rated the treatment as highly credible. Treatments were rated on a scale from 0 to 8, with higher scores indicating greater credibility. Means and standard deviations of children's credibility ratings were as follows: session 1, CBT 6.00 (1.77), ES 5.81 (2.15); session 4, CBT 5.97 (1.91), ES 6.07 (1.83); session 7, CBT 5.86 (1.92), ES 5.78 (1.81). Parents rated the treatments as follows: session 1, CBT 6.84 (1.28), ES 6.46 (1.59); session 4, CBT 6.17 (1.63), ES 6.42 (1.83);

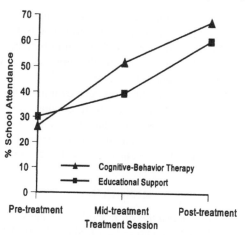

Figure 1. Percentage of school attendance pre-, mid-, and posttreatment for cognitive-behavioral therapy and educational-support therapy.

session 7, CBT 6.21 (1.75), ES 6.53 (1.77). No significant differences were found between the two treatment conditions or across time for either parent or child credibility ratings.

Outcome analyses. School Attendance. The extent to which change in school attendance over time differed by treatment group was explored in this analysis (Fig. 1). For CBT, the mean percentage of school attendance for pre-, mid-, and posttreatment was 26.43, 51.65, and 67.35, respectively. For ES, the mean percentage of school attendance for pre-, mid-, and posttreatment was 30.12, 39.47, and 59.98, respectively.

There was a significant main effect for time ($F[2, 129] = 20.64$, $p < .001$, effect size = .459), indicating that school attendance significantly improved over time for both conditions. Follow-up comparisons indicate that subjects improved significantly both from pre- (mean = 28.32, SD = 34.79) to midtreatment (mean = 45.43, SD = 42.69; $F[1, 45] = 11.20$, $p = .002$) and from mid-to posttreatment (mean = 63.57, SD = 44.95; $F[1, 39] = 11.78$, $p < .001$). Neither the treatment group × time interaction nor main effect of treatment group was significant (effect sizes = .088 and .008, respectively).

School attendance also was analyzed by examining the percentage of children in each of the two groups who reached 95% attendance by mid- or posttreatment. By midtreatment, 22% ($n = 5$) of CBT children and 21% ($n = 5$) of ES children had reached 95% attendance. By posttreatment, 65% ($n = 13$) of subjects in CBT had reached 95% attendance, compared with 48% ($n = 10$) of subjects in ES. The χ^2 tests revealed no significant differences between treatment groups on this outcome measure.

Global Improvement. Global improvement ratings were grouped into two categories: (1) *worse* (ratings of slightly/somewhat worse, much worse, and very much worse) *or no change;* and (2) *better* (rating of slightly/somewhat better, much better, or completely well). Separate χ^2 analyses were conducted for child, parent, and therapist ratings, both mid- and posttreatment.

Mid- and posttreatment, most subjects in both conditions received ratings of "better" by children, parents, and therapists. Midtreatment percentages of CBT subjects with ratings of "better" were as follows: 76% child ($n = 16$), 86% parent ($n = 18$), and 77% therapist ($n = 17$). For ES subjects, the percentages were 79% child ($n = 19$), 79% parent ($n = 19$), and 67% therapist ($n = 16$). Posttreatment ratings of "better" for CBT subjects were as follows: 95% child ($n = 18$), 90% parent ($n = 17$), and 84% therapist ($n = 16$); for ES subjects, the percentages were 100% child ($n = 21$), 95% parent ($n = 20$), and 81% therapist ($n = 17$). Analyses revealed no significant differences between the two treatment conditions for any of the ratings.

Global improvement ratings also were analyzed by examining children who showed marked improvement, i.e., ratings of "much better/completely well." Midtreatment, the percentage of subjects with global improvement ratings of "much better/completely well" for CBT for each of the raters was as follows: 57% child ($n = 12$), 48% parent ($n = 10$), and 50% therapist ($n = 11$). For ES subjects, the percentages were 50% child ($n = 12$), 38% parent ($n = 9$), and 33% therapist ($n = 8$). Posttreatment percentages for CBT were as follows: 74% child ($n = 14$), 53% parent ($n = 10$), and 74% therapist ($n = 14$). For ES subjects, the percentages were 76% child ($n = 16$), 71% parent ($n = 15$), and 62% therapist ($n = 13$). Analyses revealed no statistically significant differences.

Anxiety and Depressive Symptomatology. Improvement in children's levels of fear, anxiety, and depressive symptoms was assessed by comparing pre- and posttreatment scores on the FSSC-R, STAIC-M (total, cognitive, and somatic trait anxiety), and CDI (Table 1).

TABLE 1
Self-Report Questionnaires

Measure/Treatment Group	Pretreatment		Posttreatment		Pre vs. Post	CBT vs. ES
	Mean	SD	Mean	SD		
FSSC-R					$p < .01$	NS
CBT	128.16	32.79	110.11	24.21		
ES	134.80	27.40	121.45	22.12		
STAIC-M (total)					$p < .01$	NS
CBT	36.68	12.52	30.11	9.43		
ES	42.60	7.82	32.70	7.00		
STAIC-M (cognitive)					$p < .01$	NS
CBT	27.58	10.17	22.37	7.49		
ES	31.35	7.03	23.50	6.54		
STAIC-M (somatic)					$p < .01$	$p < .01$
CBT	15.16	4.95	12.95	3.26		
ES	19.35	5.18	15.45	5.23		
CDI					$p < .01$	$p < .05$
CBT	11.95	8.01	5.00	7.52		
ES	16.16	7.25	9.53	6.19		

Note: CBT = cognitive-behavioral therapy; ES = educational-support therapy; FSSC-R = Fear Survey Schedule for Children-Revised; STAIC-M = Modified State-Trait Anxiety Inventory for Children; CDI = Children's Depression Inventory.

Pretreatment scores on each of the measures were compared for the two groups. No significant differences emerged on any of the measures, with one exception: the ES group scored significantly higher than the CBT group in somatic anxiety before treatment ($F[1, 37] = 6.66$, $p < .05$).

A main effect of time was significant for each of the measures (all p values $< .01$), indicating that selfreported anxiety and depressive symptoms decreased significantly after treatment.

Significant pre- to posttreatment differences between groups were found for depression and somatic trait anxiety. Children in the CBT group experienced a greater reduction in CDI scores by posttreatment ($F[1, 36] = 4.76$, $p < .05$) than children in the ES group. Conversely, children in the ES treatment showed significantly greater decreases in somatic trait anxiety compared with those in CBT ($F[1, 37] = 7.66$, $p < .01$). No differences between groups were found for any of the other measures.

Posttreatment Diagnosis. Pre- and posttreatment diagnoses were compared to determine whether children who completed treatment continued to meet *DSM-III-R* criteria for their primary anxiety disorder. Sixty-five percent ($n = 13$) of the CBT completers and 50% ($n = 10$) of ES completers no longer met diagnostic criteria at posttreatment; this difference was not statistically significant. Overall, children who no longer met diagnostic criteria at posttreatment had significantly better school attendance at posttreatment than those who maintained their diagnosis ($F[1, 37] = 13.38$, $p = .001$).

Follow-up. Four-Week School Attendance. School attendance at the 4-week follow-up was available for 71% ($n = 29$) of subjects who completed treatment; attendance data could not be obtained for subjects who completed treatment at or near the end of the school year (CBT = 6; ES = 5). In addition, school attendance could not be obtained for one ES subject because the child was being home-schooled by the mother.

School attendance was analyzed by examining pretreatment, posttreatment, and follow-up attendance data. Responses were grouped into four categories: (1) maintained improvement (improvement in school attendance from pre- to posttreatment with no change in improvement at follow-up): CBT = 65% ($n = 9$), ES = 40% ($n = 6$); (2) showed further improvement (improvement in school attendance from pre- to posttreatment and further improvement at follow-up): CBT = 14% ($n = 2$), ES = 13% ($n = 2$); (3) relapsed (improvement in school attendance from pre- to posttreatment but decline in attendance at follow-up): CBT = 7% ($n = 1$), ES = 7% ($n = 1$); and (4) never improved (no improvement in attendance from pre- to posttreatment or at follow-up): CBT = 14% ($n = 2$), ES = 40% ($n = 6$). Thus, the majority of children who improved during therapy maintained treatment gains or continued to show improvement by the 4-week follow-up assessment, with no significant differences between the two groups.

New School Year Reentry. In the CBT group, 40% of treatment completers (8/20) reported having no difficulty returning to school the following school year, 30% (6/20) were rated as having "mild" difficulty, 10% (2/20) had "moderate" difficulty, and 20% (4/20) had "extreme" difficulty. For the ES group, 52% (11/21) of treatment completers reported no difficulty going back to school, 19% (4/21) were rated as having "mild" difficulty, 5% (1/21) as having "moderate" difficulty, and 24% (5/21) as "extreme." Thus, about 30% of each of the treatment groups reported significant ("moderate" or "extreme") difficulty returning to school. Neither the percentage of children reporting difficulty nor the severity of school refusal differed significantly between the two groups.

We also looked at the relationship between posttreatment attendance and return to school the following year. Level of school attendance at session 13 was inversely related to degree of difficulty returning to school; children who reached 95% attendance by posttreatment experienced significantly lower levels of difficulty reentering school the following year than children who had not attained at least 95% attendance ($F[1, 39] = 8.08$, $p < .01$). In fact, only 15% (2/13) of "successful" CBT completers and 10% (1/10) of "successful" ES completers showed significant difficulty returning to school the following school year.

Sociodemographic and Clinical Characteristics as Predictors of Outcome. To determine the possible effects of pretreatment variables on outcome, several sociodemographic (age, gender, parents' marital status, and SES), clinical (school attendance at session 1, duration of school refusal), and diagnostic (primary diagnosis at session 1) variables were examined for all subjects who completed the treatment program. Subjects with higher school attendance at session 1 were significantly more likely to have completely improved, as measured by 95% or greater school attendance at session 13 ($F[1, 39] = 11.85$, $p = .001$). In addition, younger children were more likely than older children to achieve 95% attendance by posttreatment ($F[1, 39] = 7.97$, $p < .01$). No significant effects were found for any of the other variables. Unfortunately, we were unable to examine whether pretreatment variables differentially affected the two treatments because of small numbers of subjects in the individual conditions.

DISCUSSION

Contrary to expectation, our findings showed no differences between the cognitive-behavioral, exposure-based treatment and the educational-support treatment. Both treatments produced statistically and clinically meaningful improvements after 12 weeks, as indicated by a variety of measures. Moreover, treatment gains were maintained (or increased) in both groups at a 4-week follow-up. Overall, younger children and children with higher baseline school attendance levels showed the greatest improvement during therapy.

The positive outcome for children in the educational-support group parallels reports of success using a similar treatment protocol with phobic adults (Heimberg et al., 1990) and phobic children (Silverman et al., unpublished). The educational-support treatment was used to control for the nonspecific effects of therapy (e.g., therapist contact, time, etc.) and contained no direct instructions to return to school. In practice it appears that children in that group began slowly going back to school after completing about half (6 weeks) of the treatment program.

By contrast, the cognitive-behavioral treatment included specific and direct instructions for children to gradually increase their exposure to the school environment, i.e., return to school. This approach may have heightened anxiety levels and, in turn, contributed to the 16% dropout rate observed for the CBT group prior to midtreatment.

Some of our treatment completers (in both groups) showed significant difficulty returning to school the following school year. This finding is consistent with our clincial experience— children being treated for school phobia often show increased levels of difficulty returning to school after a 3-day weekend or longer holiday break. The long summer vacation may represent a prolonged period of negative reinforcement, during which school-phobic children enjoy the absence of school-related anxiety achieved by total avoidance of the school setting. *Clinical implications.* On the basis of our results, one could hypothesize that the support and information provided in the educational-support treatment gave the students a "foundation" that was then used to approach school gradually. In addition, children in the educational-support condition were taught to identify, but not modify, maladaptive thinking. It could be that children were able to take the next step, i.e., modify their maladaptive cognitions, without specific instructions to do so. If this is the case, it may be that the specific, structured approach to school reentry used in the cognitive-behavioral treatment is not necessary for getting children with anxiety-based school refusal back into school. Moreover, the relatively high early dropout rate in the CBT group can be viewed as lending additional support for using an educational-support approach rather than a strictly behavioral one.

Alternatively, it may be that the effectiveness of both treatments was due to the role of nonspecific effects, including, but not limited to, perceived therapist and therapy effectiveness. As indicated by treatment credibility ratings, both treatment groups had high (and comparable) expectations of therapeutic success.

Our results suggest that strategies need to be implemented in order to maintain treatment gains into the following school year. Clinically, we have found that conducting "booster" treatment sessions before and during the beginning of the new school year is helpful in reducing difficulty with school reentry. Such issues need to be addressed by future research in this area.

Unfortunately, our sample sizes for the two treatments precluded us from examining whether sociodemographic and/or clinical characteristics were related to differential treatment effects. As suggested by Silverman and colleagues (Burke and Silverman, 1987; Kearney and Silverman, 1990), it may be that the treatment of school refusal is prescriptive, with different children responding differently to alternative types of treatment. For example, specific anxiety disorder diagnoses associated with school refusal, as well as the child's age, duration and degree of school absenteeism, and familial variables, may affect treatment response. Future research, using larger samples, should examine these possibilities.

REFERENCES

Ayllon T, Smith D, Rogers M (1970), Behavioral management of school phobia. *J Behav Ther Exp Psychiatry* 1:125–138

Barlow DH, Beck JG (1984), The psychosocial treatment of anxiety disorders: current status, future directions. In: *Psychotherapy Research: Where Are We and Where Should We Go?* Williams JBW, Spitzer RL, eds. New York: Guilford, pp 29–69

Barlow DH, O'Brien GT, Last CG (1984), Couples treatment of agoraphobia. *Behav Ther* 15:41–58

Blagg NR, Yule W (1984), The behavioral treatment of school refusal: a comparative study. *Behav Res Ther* 22:119–127

Burke AE, Silverman WK (1987), The prescriptive treatment of school refusal. *Clin Psychol Rev* 7:353–362

Fox JE, Houston BK (1983), Distinguishing between cognitive and somatic trait and state anxiety in children. *J Pers Soc Psychol* 45:862–870

Gittelman-Klein R, Klein DF (1971), Controlled imipramine treatment of school phobia. *Arch Gen Psychiatry* 25:199–215

Heimberg RG, Dodge CS, Hope DA, Kennedy CR, Zollo LJ, Becker RE (1990), Cognitive behavioral group treatment for social phobia: comparison with a credible placebo control. *Cognit Ther Res* 14:1–23

Hollingshead AB (1975), *Four-Factor Index of Social Status*. New Haven, CT: Yale University Department of Sociology

Kearney CA, Silverman WK (1990), A preliminary analysis of a functional model of assessment and treatment for school refusal behavior. *Behav Modif* 14:340–366

Kennedy WA (1965), School phobia: rapid treatment of fifty cases. *J Abnorm Psychol* 70:285–289

Kovacs M (1992), *Children's Depression Inventory Manual*. North Tonawanda, NY: Multi-Health Systems

Last CG, Francis G, Hersen M, Kazdin AE, Strauss CC (1987), Separation anxiety and school phobia: a comparison using *DSM-III* criteria. *Am J Psychiatry* 144:653–657

Last CG, Strauss CC (1990), School refusal in anxiety disordered children and adolescents. *J Am Acad Child Adolesc Psychiatry* 29:31–35

Littell RC, Freund RJ, Spector PC (1991), *SAS System for Linear Models*, 3rd ed. Cary, NC: SAS Institute, pp 272–274

Littell RC, Milliken GA, Stroup WW, Wolfinger RD (1996), *SAS System for Mixed Models*. Cary, NC: SAS Institute, pp 87–134

Meichenbaum DH (1977), *Cognitive Behavior Modification*. New York: Plenum

Ollendick TH (1983), Reliability and validity of the Revised Fear Survey Schedule for Children (FSSC-R). *Behav Res Ther* 21:685–692

Ollendick TH, King NJ, Frary RB (1989), Fears in children and adolescents: reliability and generalizability across gender, age and nationality. *Behav Res Ther* 27:19–26

Ollendick TH, Mayer JA (1984), School phobia. In: *Behavioral Treatment of Anxiety Disorders*, Turner SM, ed. New York: Plenum, pp 367–411

Papay JP, Spielberger CD (1986), Assessment of anxiety and achievement in kindergarten and first- and second-grade children. *J Abnorm Child Psychol* 14:279–286

Patterson GR (1965), A learning theory approach to the treatment of the school phobic child. In: *Case Studies in Behavior Modification*, Ullmann LP, Krasner K, eds. New York: Holt, Rinehart & Winston, pp 279–285

Perkin GJ, Rowe GP, Farmer RG (1973), Operant conditioning of emotional responsiveness as a prerequisite for behavioral analysis: a case study of an adolescent school phobic. *Aust N Z J Psychiatry* 7:180–183

Silverman WK (1993), Behavioral treatment of childhood phobias: an update and preliminary research findings. In: *Psychosocial and Combined Treatment for Childhood Disorders*: Development and Issues, Hibbs E, chair. Symposium conducted at the meeting of the New Clinical Drug Evaluation Unit Program, Boca Raton, FL, June

Smith RE, Sharpe TM (1970), Treatment of a school phobia with implosive therapy: *J Consult Clin Psychol* 35:239–243

Spielberger CD (1973), *Manual for the State-Trait Anxiety Inventory for Children (Form Y)*. Palo Alto, CA: Consulting Psychologists Press

For Product Safety Concerns and Information please contact our EU representative GPSR@taylorandfrancis.com Taylor & Francis Verlag GmbH, Kaufingerstraße 24, 80331 München, Germany

T - #0073 - 270225 - C0 - 229/152/27 - PB - 9780415645867 - Gloss Lamination